CW00918704

A DIGEST OF WTO JURISPRUDENCE ON PUBLIC INTERNATIONAL LAW CONCEPTS AND PRINCIPLES

In its first twenty years, the WTO dispute settlement system generated over 350 decisions totalling more than 60,000 pages. These decisions contain many statements by WTO adjudicators regarding the law of treaties, state responsibility, international dispute settlement and other topics of general public international law. This book is a collection of nearly one thousand statements by WTO adjudicators relating to admissibility and jurisdiction; attribution of conduct to a State; breach of an obligation; conflicts between treaties; countermeasures; due process; evidence before international tribunals; good faith; judicial economy; municipal law; non-retroactivity; reasonableness; sources of international law; sovereignty; treaty interpretation; and words and phrases commonly used in treaties and other international legal instruments. This comprehensive digest presents summaries and extracts organized systematically under issue-specific sub-headings, making this jurisprudence easily accessible to students and practitioners working in any field of international law.

GRAHAM COOK is Counsellor with the Legal Affairs Division of the WTO Secretariat in Geneva. In that capacity, he has served as a legal advisor to numerous WTO dispute settlement panels.

A DIGEST OF WTO JURISPRUDENCE ON PUBLIC INTERNATIONAL LAW CONCEPTS AND PRINCIPLES

Graham Cook

CAMBRIDGE
UNIVERSITY PRESS

CAMBRIDGE
UNIVERSITY PRESS

University Printing House, Cambridge CB2 8BS, United Kingdom

Cambridge University Press is part of the University of Cambridge.

It furthers the University's mission by disseminating knowledge in the pursuit of education, learning and research at the highest international levels of excellence.

www.cambridge.org
Information on this title: www.cambridge.org/9781107102767

© Graham Cook 2015

This publication is in copyright. Subject to statutory exception and to the provisions of relevant collective licensing agreements, no reproduction of any part may take place without the written permission of Cambridge University Press.

First published 2015

Printed in the United Kingdom by TJ International Ltd. Padstow Cornwall

A catalogue record for this publication is available from the British Library

Library of Congress Cataloging in Publication data
Cook, Graham, author.
A digest of WTO jurisprudence on public international law concepts and principles/Graham Cook.
pages cm
ISBN 978-1-107-10276-7 (Hardback : alk. paper)
1. World Trade Organization. 2. International law. 3. Treaties. I. Title.
K4610.C665 2015
343.08′7–dc23
2015003330

ISBN 978-1-107-10276-7 Hardback

Cambridge University Press has no responsibility for the persistence or accuracy of URLs for external or third-party internet websites referred to in this publication, and does not guarantee that any content on such websites is, or will remain, accurate or appropriate.

CONTENTS

FOREWORD
The panther is a cat! But is it a leopard or a lion?

Not too long ago, one could make waves by claiming that WTO rules are, after all, just treaty rules. They are, in biological terms, but a 'genus' of the broader 'family' of public international law, much like panthers are a genus of the broader cat family.

Many GATT negotiators thought differently. They portrayed their agreement as special, a self-contained economic contract setting out a balance of concessions, rather than legally binding rules part of international law. In many ways, this remains the approach today in, for example, most of international financial regulation: highly technical, detailed rules, but not considered by their drafters as 'binding' or 'international law'.

Reading this digest, one realizes just how fast and comprehensively perceptions have changed. Graham Cook's extraordinary work offers a structured overview of nearly one thousand statements by WTO panels and the WTO Appellate Body on topics of general public international law. To the extent they are still out there, this digest should silence those who continue to believe that WTO law is a self-contained regime, that WTO panels can only consider WTO covered agreements, or that one can be an effective WTO lawyer without knowing public international law.

Yet, Mr Cook's message goes beyond the idea that WTO law is part of public international law, i.e. that public international law plays a role also in WTO dispute settlement. His work demonstrates to specialists in other fields of international law (say, human rights or environmental lawyers) that they too can actually learn something about public international law by looking at WTO jurisprudence. It is, to come back to my biological metaphor above, not just that the panther, finally, realizes that it is part of the cat family; other cats (even domestic cats) can actually learn something about what it means to be a cat by observing the panther's features, habits and behaviour.

Changing metaphors, and contemplating this time the cover picture of this digest, within the four walls of the WTO building grew a surprisingly rich and vigorous tree of public international law; a tree that few insiders would have predicted when they constructed the WTO edifice in 1994. The tree has deep and long roots that reach way beyond the WTO covered agreements. It is nurtured by customary international law, general principles of law and even non-WTO treaties. Given its size and strength today the tree should also inspire other fields of international law. The tree may have been hidden from sight. With this work, everyone is on notice.

How can one summarize the WTO's approach to general international law? In the 1990s, many public international law commentators lamented the proliferation of specialized international tribunals. They feared that these tribunals would develop their own rules of international law in an unstoppable process of fragmentation. The reality, at least when looking at WTO jurisprudence twenty years later, turned out differently. If anything, the WTO has taken a rather traditional, conservative view of general international law, following as much as it could statements by the International Court of Justice or the UN's International Law Commission. No WTO-specific approach to general international law topics has really developed. Rather than distancing itself from general international law or giving general rules a trade-specific interpretation, WTO jurisprudence has used public international law as a centralizing or uniting factor, bringing (the panther of) WTO law closer to the broader (cat) family of public international law. If anything, what marks the WTO approach to, for example, treaty interpretation is an almost obsessive sticking to what the Vienna Convention provides for, not a liberal approach of adjusting rules of interpretation to the specifics of trade. As the author puts it (at paragraph 15.32), 'WTO adjudicators have been wary of certain forms of reasoning by reference to object and purpose, and have generally been cautious about attaching too much weight to the object and purpose of a treaty as a basis for its interpretation.'

More WTO-specific may be the heavy reliance on a *de facto* rule of precedent of especially WTO Appellate Body rulings and a complete neglect in panel and Appellate Body reports of academic scholarship or 'teachings of the most highly qualified publicists' for anything other than general international law.

General international law, as this digest demonstrates, fills the gaps left by treaties. It is the glue that binds the different sub-branches together. General international law ensures the existence of international law as a 'legal system'. The fact that the WTO applies it is not trivial or meaningless. It confirms that the WTO treaty is part of 'the family'.

At the same time, so far, only one of the two core lessons have been drawn from the fact that the WTO is part of public international law. Today, WTO jurisprudence clearly confirms that the WTO treaty must be applied and interpreted in the broader context of general international law. This centralizing or uniting theme has given us ample and rich references to rules on burden and standard of proof, evidence, good faith, due process, attribution, jurisdiction, countermeasures and treaty interpretation. Features and insights common to the broader cat family have played their role in our assessment and analysis of the panther. But there is a second lesson to be drawn from the fact that WTO law is part of the system of international law. That is, its unavoidable interaction not just with general international law but also with other, non-WTO treaties and other sub-branches of international law, including free trade agreements between a sub-set of WTO Members.

In other words, that the panther (genus *panthera*) is part of the cat family also unites it with other subfamilies or genera within the family such as the cougar, the cheetah or the domestic cat. What is more, also the panther is, in turn, but a genus that includes several species, *in casu*, the jaguar, leopard, lion and tiger, all four of which are *panthera* but after all quite distinct. The WTO may have found its place as part of the broader international law family; it is still struggling to learn from and find its place *vis-à-vis* other sub-branches of international law including sub-branches within its own field of international trade law, in particular free trade agreements.

This second lesson or consequence of being part of the international law 'system' is not a centralizing or uniting theme ('we are all cats'). It is a centrifugal or distinguishing force, calling for the recognition of the diversity between States and the contractual freedom of States to add to WTO rules or 'change their minds', waive or adapt pre-existing WTO rules and to decide for themselves to which treaty or norm they want to give preference. This second theme, still largely unresolved in the WTO today, is not a centralizing or uniting one, but a centrifugal one allowing for regional and State-to-State differences in legal relationships amongst WTO Members ('as panthers we may all be cats, but some of us are lions, others jaguars, leopards or tigers'). With 160 WTO Members, including more recently China, Saudi Arabia and Russia, such *inter se* diversity is unavoidable. For WTO dispute settlement to impose the same one-size fits all straitjacket on all WTO Members is unrealistic. It does not correspond to reality (WTO Members are party to a panoply of very diverse trade and non-trade agreements) and is normatively undesirable (it denies the sovereign right of countries to consent to other treaties in fulfilment of their own, diverse preferences).

At this juncture, the big question is how to combine the benefits of a multilateral treaty like the WTO with the undeniable existence of plurilateral, regional and bilateral agreements on trade and non-trade issues, in the WTO (e.g. bilateral settlement agreements or agreements to hold open hearings in deviation from the DSU) and outside the WTO (e.g. free trade agreements with WTO-plus and WTO-minus elements)? As the Appellate Body put it in one of its most recent statements on the issue (see paragraph 4.24 in this Digest): 'In a multilateral context such as the WTO, when recourse is had to a non-WTO rule for the purposes of interpreting provisions of the WTO agreements, a delicate balance must be struck between, on the one hand, taking due account of an individual WTO Member's international obligations and, on the other hand, ensuring a consistent and harmonious approach to the interpretation of WTO law among all WTO Members.' The Appellate Body left it at this, without providing its view on the issue of whether 'relevant rules of international law *applicable in the relations between the parties*' in Article 31.3(c) of the Vienna Convention allows WTO panels to refer only to non-WTO treaties binding on *all WTO Members* (in practice, almost impossible) or also to non-WTO agreements between a sub-set of WTO Members *party to the dispute* (in the case at hand, a bilateral EU–US agreement on aircraft subsidies).

Three guiding principles should be followed to solve this dilemma.

First, a WTO panel should normally refer to a non-WTO treaty only if both disputing parties have consented to this treaty (the principle of State consent). To interpret or apply the WTO treaty in a particular way with reference to a non-WTO treaty that one of the disputing parties never consented to can only be done with extreme caution (but see paragraphs 4.11, 4.17, 4.27–4.36 and 15.31 of this Digest, in each case giving meaning to the WTO treaty as it applies to *all WTO Members* with reference to a non-WTO treaty that is *not* binding on all WTO Members). Crucially, where the WTO treaty is interpreted or applied in a given way with reference to a non-WTO treaty binding on the disputing parties, this interpretation or application cannot affect other WTO Members, not party to the dispute, since they may not have consented to the non-WTO treaty nor were they party to the dispute. In other words, an EU–US bilateral agreement on aircraft, where it is relevant, may well influence the outcome of an EU–US dispute before the WTO; it cannot influence the outcome of a WTO dispute between any other pair of WTO Members. Not to give effect to the EU–US bilateral agreement, where it is relevant, would contravene the contractual freedom of States. As long as a WTO panel refers to the bilateral agreement for the purpose of deciding *claims under WTO covered agreements*, a WTO panel would then not 'add to or diminish the rights and obligations provided in the covered agreements' contrary to DSU Article 3.2; it was the EU and the US as sovereign States who did so. As Graham Cook points out (at paragraph 14.2, with reference in particular to the *China – Raw Materials* case), 'panels and the Appellate Body emphasized that States may exercise their sovereignty by negotiating and entering into treaties. In this regard, there is support in WTO jurisprudence for the proposition that the right of entering into international engagements is an attribute of State sovereignty, such that restrictions on the exercise of sovereign rights that a State voluntarily accepts through a treaty cannot be considered as an infringement of its sovereignty.'

Countries genuinely worried about the Appellate Body 'adding or diminishing' their WTO rights should be concerned not so much about reference to non-WTO treaties they explicitly consented to, and more about the WTO's *de facto* rule of precedent (where the Appellate Body, not WTO Members, is 'making law') or reference to non-WTO treaties as facts or to general principles (such as good faith or due process) they never explicitly consented to.

Second, a WTO panel should only refer to a non-WTO treaty if such treaty is both valid and legal. The treaty cannot violate *jus cogens* or be concluded by coercion, fraud or corruption or be based on error, nor can it be explicitly prohibited in the WTO treaty (such as voluntary export restraints prohibited in Article 11 of the Safeguards Agreement; in contrast, free trade agreements are explicitly permitted in GATT Article XXIV, GATS Article V and the Enabling Clause). The non-WTO treaty should also be legal in the sense that it does not affect the rights or obligations of third parties (the principle of *pacta tertiis nec nocent nec prosunt*): a bilateral agreement cannot exchange an exclusive concession in violation of the MFN rights of third parties unless it meets GATT Article XXIV; also a settlement agreement under the DSU must comply with MFN.

Third, a non-WTO treaty can only disapply or prevail over a WTO provision if such non-WTO treaty amounts to a valid waiver of WTO rights or takes precedence over the WTO provision pursuant to conflict rules of international law. That a State can waive its WTO rights or consent to something that would otherwise constitute WTO breach (e.g. waive the DSU right to confidential Appellate Body proceedings as in *US – Continued Suspension*) is explicitly permitted in the ILC Articles on State Responsibility (Article 20 on consent as a circumstance precluding wrongfulness and Article 45(a) on waiver as loss of the right to invoke State responsibility) as well as the Vienna Convention (Article 41 on *inter se* modification of multilateral treaties). In both cases, they are subject to the *pacta tertiis* rule stated earlier: the waiver or modification cannot affect third-party rights. As discussed in paragraphs 15.44 and 15.45 of this Digest, the Appellate Body (in *US – Clove Cigarettes* and *US – Tuna II (Mexico)*) recognized that Article IX:2 of the WTO Agreement on authoritative interpretations is not the only way for WTO Members to further interpret or clarify the WTO treaty. They can also do so pursuant to simple 'subsequent agreements between the parties' as provided for in Article 31.3(a) of the Vienna Convention (as memorialized, for example, in the Doha Ministerial Declaration or a TBT Committee decision, neither of which refers to Article IX:2). Similarly, the fact that the WTO Agreement has specific rules on waiver or treaty amendment does not prevent WTO Members from waiving their rights unilaterally or by agreement, or from modifying the WTO treaty *inter se* as long as they do so in line with the relevant rules of general international law, especially the *pacta tertiis* rule (such waiver or modification agreement could then also be referred to as 'subsequent agreement between the parties regarding the interpretation of the treaty or the application of its provisions' under Article 31.3(a)).

Conflict rules of international law, in turn, start from the assumption that all treaties are of the same hierarchical value but that the parties may explicitly agree on which treaty prevails (e.g. that an FTA prevails over the WTO or that an

FTA in violation of GATT Article XXIV remains subject to MFN in the WTO), in the absence of which principles such as *lex posterior* or *lex specialis* will decide on priority.

So far WTO Members have been reluctant to invoke non-WTO treaties as self-standing defences against allegations of WTO breach. They have preferred to invoke such treaties to influence the interpretation of, for example, general exceptions in the GATT itself. To date these exceptions (GATT Article XX), allowing for *unilateral* deviations from the GATT with reference to health, environmental or public morals concerns, have been interpreted so broadly as to arguably cover most issues that WTO Members may *mutually* agree on in non-WTO treaties. More pressing is the question of whether the Appellate Body would be willing to defer to, for example, a forum exclusion clause in a free trade agreement such as NAFTA or the EU treaty (treaties explicitly allowed for under GATT Article XXIV) that prevents a State from filing a particular dispute to the WTO (e.g. because it was filed previously under the FTA). The Appellate Body has not directly answered this question. Yet, its jurisprudence, as listed in this Digest, shows the way.

Firstly, WTO panels have exclusive subject-matter jurisdiction over WTO claims. This jurisdiction may be hard to contract-out from in another treaty. Yet, a WTO panel may have jurisdiction over a claim, but that claim may be inadmissible. As Graham Cook puts it (in footnote 4 of Chapter 1): 'jurisdiction refers to the scope of the subject-matter that a complaining party can bring before a particular adjudicative body (which is constant and does not change from case to case), whereas inadmissibility concerns an alleged action or omission by a particular complaining party in a particular set of circumstances that may or must lead that adjudicative body to decline to examine a particular claim that otherwise falls within its subject-matter jurisdiction'. A forum exclusion clause in an FTA may not take away a WTO panel's jurisdiction. However, it can still lead to the inadmissibility of a claim before the WTO.

Second, the Appellate Body has confirmed that a restriction to a WTO Member's 'right to a WTO panel' cannot be 'lightly inferred' and that 'there should be a clear and unambiguous basis in the relevant legal instruments for concluding that such a restriction exists' (paragraph 1.3 in this Digest, quoting *US – FSC*). At the same time, the Appellate Body acknowledged that there may be 'a legal impediment to the exercise of a panel's jurisdiction' and that mutual understandings between WTO Members could preclude 'complainants . . . from initiating Article 21.5 proceedings . . . if the parties to these Understandings had, either explicitly or by necessary implication, agreed to waive their right to have recourse to Article 21.5' (paragraph 1.5, quoting *Mexico – Taxes on Soft Drinks* and *EC – Bananas III (Article 21.5 – Ecuador II)*). Since settlement understandings are outside 'WTO covered agreements' as much as FTAs are, a forum exclusion clause in an FTA could, therefore, be a 'legal impediment' to the exercise of a panel's jurisdiction (i.e. can make a claim inadmissible) to the extent this clause expresses an agreement to waive specific WTO rights. In other words, the question is not whether an FTA clause can waive the right to a WTO panel (it can); the question is whether 'the language' in such clause 'reveal[s] clearly that the parties intended to relinquish their rights' (paragraph 1.5) and whether the waiver leaves third-party rights unaffected. As the Appellate Body found in *US – Continued Suspension* (Annex IV, paragraph 6), a WTO Member can waive its right to a closed Appellate Body hearing (even though DSU Article 17.10 mandates that Appellate Body proceedings 'shall be' confidential) for as long as 'the right to confidentiality of third participants *vis-à-vis* the Appellate Body is not implicated by the joint request'.

These are core issues that remain to be decided in WTO dispute settlement. After 20 years, there can be no doubt that the panther is a cat. In the years ahead, we will know whether the WTO offers the flexibility for panthers to be jaguars, leopards, lions or tigers.

Joost Pauwelyn
Geneva, 2 December 2014.

DISCLAIMER

Any opinions expressed or implied in what follows reflect the author's personal opinions and should not be attributed to the WTO Secretariat.

ACKNOWLEDGMENTS

Work on this digest was greatly facilitated by the WTO Secretariat's *Analytical Index* and *Appellate Body Repertory* (also published by Cambridge University Press), tradelawguide.com's Article Citator, Jurisprudence Citator and Terms and Phrases tools, and worldtradelaw.net's Case Law Index and Full Text Search function. I thank my colleagues in the Legal Affairs Division who found the time to make valuable comments on a draft, and Martin Goyette for conceiving and taking an inspired cover photo.

PREFACE

One would suspect that WTO jurisprudence contains at least a few useful statements relating to general public international law principles and concepts. But just how much useful material would one expect to find? After all, WTO adjudicators are tasked with examining alleged violations of the specific obligations contained in the WTO agreements. And, although Article 3.2 of the DSU expressly instructs adjudicators to clarify the WTO agreements 'in accordance with customary rules of interpretation of public international law', does that allow concepts and principles of public international law apart from those relating to treaty interpretation to be considered? And to what extent does any such consideration merely take the form of passing references,[1] as distinguished from more significant and substantial clarification and application of public international law concepts and principles? Moreover, to what extent are any statements by WTO adjudicators concerning those concepts and principles capable of wider application, as opposed to being inextricably linked to the context of the underlying textual provisions of the WTO agreements?

If WTO jurisprudence contained a very large number of statements relating to general public international law concepts and principles, one might expect to find numerous citations to WTO jurisprudence in public international law treatises, in the jurisprudence of other international courts and tribunals, and in the work of the International Law Commission (ILC). Instead, one finds scant reference to WTO jurisprudence in public international law treatises.[2] There is only one reference to GATT/WTO jurisprudence in all of the decisions

---

[1] It has been said that 'judgments by the ICJ received only nominal adoption into the GATT regime, simply referred to in the footnotes of decisions as opposed to being directly applied in the body of a ruling'. J. Cameron and K. Gray, 'Principles of International Law in The WTO Dispute Settlement Body' (2001) 50(2) *International and Comparative Law Quarterly* pp. 248–98, footnote 52.

[2] For example, I. Brownlie and J. Crawford, *Brownlie's Principles of Public International Law*, 8th edn (Oxford University Press, 2012), pp. 353, 368, 543, 544, 548, 563, 565 and 740. Shaw's *International Law*, 6th edn (Cambridge University Press, 2008), with a 58-page table of cases covering a wide range of international and domestic courts and tribunals, refers to just three Appellate Body decisions.

and advisory opinions of the International Court of Justice (ICJ) (and it is found in a dissenting opinion, and it criticizes the ICJ majority decision for not following WTO panel practice concerning the use of scientific experts).[3] There are not very many references to WTO jurisprudence in the commentaries of the ILC, and one ILC member has recently questioned whether WTO jurisprudence is looked at closely enough by public international lawyers.[4]

Work on this digest was prompted by the suspicion that WTO jurisprudence is an untapped goldmine of jurisprudence on public international law concepts and principles, and that a systematic review of the roughly 60,000 pages of WTO jurisprudence generated to date would unearth a large number of key statements by WTO adjudicators (i.e. the Appellate Body, panels, and arbitrators) relating to a wide range of general international law topics. The resulting mass of material collected in this digest speaks for itself. First, in the context of adjudicating claims of violation under the WTO agreements, WTO adjudicators have considered a wide range of ancillary concepts and principles of general international law, including but not limited to those regarding the law of treaties, State responsibility, and international dispute settlement. Statements by WTO adjudicators on general international law concepts and principles are by no means limited to the customary international law rules of treaty interpretation.[5] Second, many concepts and principles have been the subject of substantial clarification and application, as opposed to simply passing references. Third, many statements and lines of jurisprudence are not inextricably linked to particular provisions of the WTO agreements in a way that would reduce their value to public international lawyers working in different contexts. To quote from Lauterpacht and McNair's preface to an early volume of the *International Law Reports* (which at that time bore the title *Annual Digest and Reports of Public International Law Cases*):

---

[3] In their joint dissenting opinion in the *Pulp Mills* case, Judges Al-Khasawneh and Simma disagreed with the Court's decision not to appoint experts *proprio motu*, and observed that '[i]t is perhaps the World Trade Organization, however, which has most contributed to the development of a best practice of readily consulting outside sources in order better to evaluate the evidence submitted to it; in fact, it was devised as a response to the needs of the dispute resolution process in cases involving complex scientific questions.' The judges recalled several aspects of WTO panel practice and cited to several panel decisions. *Pulp Mills on the River Uruguay (Argentina v. Uruguay)*, Merits, 2010 ICJ Reports, p. 14 (20 April), Joint Dissenting Opinion of Judges Al-Khasawneh and Simma, para. 16.

[4] D. McRae, 'International Economic Law and Public International Law: The Past and The Future' (2014) 17(3) *Journal of International Economic Law* 627, at 632.

[5] With respect to the direction in Article 3.2 to apply customary international law 'rules of interpretation', the Panel in *Korea – Procurement* did not read this direction as implying that other rules of international law are necessarily inapplicable. The Panel stated that '[w]e should also note that we can see no basis here for an *a contrario* implication that rules of international law other than rules of interpretation do not apply. The language of [Article] 3.2 in this regard applies to a specific problem that had arisen under the GATT to the effect that, among other things, reliance on negotiating history was being utilized in a manner arguably inconsistent with the requirements of the rules of treaty interpretation of customary international law.' Panel Report, *Korea – Procurement*, footnote 753.

The work of which this book is the first-fruits was prompted by the suspicion that there is more international law already in existence and daily accumulating 'than this world dreams of' ... As the work has progressed that suspicion has ripened into a certainty ... [T]he resulting mass of raw material forms a body of authority which both in quality and in variety has exceeded our expectations.[6]

The purpose of this guide is to make the wealth of statements by WTO adjudicators on general international law concepts and principles more easily accessible, in particular for those working or studying in non-WTO fields of international law. It provides a comprehensive and systematically organized digest of nearly one thousand extracts from WTO jurisprudence covering the following general international law topics: (i) admissibility and jurisdiction; (ii) the attribution of conduct to a State; (iii) the breach of an obligation; (iv) conflicts between treaties; (v) countermeasures; (vi) due process; (vii) evidence before international tribunals; (viii) good faith; (ix) judicial economy; (x) municipal law; (xi) non-retroactivity; (xii) reasonableness; (xiii) the sources of international law; (xiv) sovereignty; (xv) treaty interpretation; and (xvi) words and phrases commonly used in treaties and other international legal instruments.

This work is inspired by several books that have examined the contributions of particular international courts and tribunals to the development of international law. The best-known book of this kind is *The Development of International Law by the International Court*,[7] in which Lauterpacht reviewed the jurisprudential contributions of the Permanent Court of International Justice and the International Court of Justice on a range of concepts and principles of general public international law, including treaty interpretation, the role of judicial precedent, principles of judicial caution and restraint, jurisdictional issues, State responsibility, and sovereignty. In *The Development of International Law by the European Court of Human Rights*,[8] Merrills reviewed that court's jurisprudential contributions to topics such as treaty interpretation, State responsibility, reservations, estoppel and waiver, due process, and the relationship between treaties and general international law. Brower and Brueschke devoted a significant part of their book on *The Iran–United States Claims Tribunal* to examining that tribunal's jurisprudential contributions to general international law, including the treatment of evidence before international

---

[6] A. D. McNair and H. Lauterpacht (eds.), *Annual Digest of Public International Law Cases, Volume 3, Years 1925–1926* (Cambridge University Press, 1929), at p. ix.
[7] H. Lauterpacht, *The Development of International Law by the International Court* (Stevens & Sons, 1958), which was a revised version of H. Lauterpacht, *The Development of International Law by the Permanent Court of International Justice* (Longmans, Green and Co., 1934). See also O. Spiermann, *International Legal Argument in the Permanent Court of International Justice: The Rise of the International Judiciary* (Cambridge University Press, 2005); and J. Sloan and C. J. Tams (eds.), *The Development of International Law by the International Court of Justice* (Oxford University Press, 2013).
[8] J. G. Merrills, *The Development of International Law by the European Court of Human Rights* (Manchester University Press, 1988).

tribunals, treaty interpretation, State responsibility and estoppel.[9] Other works have looked at the development of international law by the Permanent Court of Arbitration,[10] the International Criminal Tribunal for Rwanda[11] and the Special Court for Sierra Leone.[12]

There are two ways in which this digest differs from the above-mentioned works that inspired it. First, most of those works examined the particular court or tribunal's jurisprudential contributions not only on general international law, but also with respect to core concepts and principles in specialized fields of international law – international human rights law in the case of the ECHR, international investment law in the case of the Iran–United States Claims Tribunal, and international criminal law in the case of some of the others mentioned above. This digest focuses exclusively on those statements by WTO adjudicators concerning general public international law concepts and principles.[13] It does not, for example, cover the extensive body of WTO jurisprudence relating to national treatment and most-favoured-nation obligations found in the WTO agreements; although that body of WTO jurisprudence is perhaps relevant to the interpretation of national treatment and most-favoured-nation provisions typically found in bilateral investment treaties[14] and other international trade agreements, those are not general public international law concepts or principles. Second, as its title suggests, this work is a 'digest' of relevant WTO jurisprudence, as opposed to an

[9] C. N. Brower and J. Brueschke, *The Iran–United States Claims Tribunal* (Martinus Nijhoff, 1998), Part III, 'Contributions of the Iran–United States Claims Tribunal to Public International Law', pp. 263–368, and Chapter 19, 'The Tribunal's Jurisprudence as a Source of Public International Law', pp. 631–56.

[10] J. G. Merrills, 'The Contribution of the Permanent Court of Arbitration to International Law and to the Settlement of Disputes by Peaceful Means', in P. Hamilton, H. C. Requena, L. van Scheltinga and B. Shifman (eds.), *The Permanent Court of Arbitration: International Arbitration and Dispute Resolution, Summaries of Awards, Settlement Agreements and Reports* (Kluwer, 1999), pp. 3–31.

[11] L. J. van den Herik, *Contribution of the Rwanda Tribunal to the Development of International Law* (Martinus Nijhoff, 2005).

[12] C. C. Jalloh, 'The Contribution of the Special Court for Sierra Leone to the Development of International Law' (2007) 15(2) *African Journal of International and Comparative Law*, pp. 165–207.

[13] Consideration was given to inserting the word 'general' before 'public international law' in the title of this work. Sometimes brevity beats precision.

[14] In the context of international economic law, there are various works examining the potential relevance of WTO jurisprudence on national treatment (and other obligations) to the interpretation of similar obligations in other international trade and investment agreements. For example, see G. Cook, *Importing GATT/WTO Jurisprudence into NAFTA Chapter Eleven to Define the Standards of International Investment Law* (University of British Columbia, 2001, available at www.law.libary.ubc.ca); J. Kurtz, 'The Use and Abuse of WTO Law in Investor–State Arbitration: Competition and its Discontents' (2009) 20(3) *European Journal of International Law* 749; G. Tereposky and M. Maguire, 'Utilizing WTO Law in Investor–State Arbitration', in A. W. Rovine (ed.), *Contemporary Issues in International Arbitration and Mediation: The Fordham Papers* (Martinus Nijhoff, 2011), pp. 247–83; A. Mitchell, 'Variations on a Theme: Comparing the Concept of "Necessity" in International Investment Law and WTO Law' (2013) 14 *Chicago Journal of International Law* 93.

academic monograph – its added value comes from the identification and systematic organization of the relevant jurisprudence, in such a way as to help researchers quickly identify relevant cases. It is best left to others to critically evaluate that jurisprudence, or draw out the possible implications of that jurisprudence for future cases, or compare and contrast that jurisprudence with the jurisprudence of other international courts or tribunals, and/or engage with the substantial body of literature that exists on some of the topics covered.

Statements by WTO adjudicators on general public international law concepts and principles should be taken into account by lawyers working in other fields of public international law, for at least two reasons. First, as Schwarzenberger observed in *International Law as Applied by International Courts and Tribunals*, '[c]ompared with the dicta of textbooks and the practice of this or that State, the decisions of international courts have an authority and reality which cannot be surpassed'.[15] WTO panels, arbitrators and the Appellate Body function as international judicial tribunals. They are required to resolve the disputes that come before them exclusively on the basis of law and legal reasoning. It is true that the WTO agreements use a considerable amount of non-judicial terminology when describing the dispute settlement system,[16] but WTO adjudicators function in essentially the same way as any other international judicial tribunal. In the words of one panel, 'an inquiry of a peculiarly economic and political nature' is 'notably ill-suited' to WTO panels, 'whose function is fundamentally legal'.[17] In the words of the Appellate Body, WTO adjudicators are engaged in the exercise of 'the judicial function'.[18] A second reason why statements by WTO adjudicators on public international law concepts and principles should be taken into account is that WTO adjudicators have developed a body of jurisprudence that is remarkably consistent and coherent. The role and influence of the WTO Appellate Body has been important in this regard. As others have explained, '[t]he repeated quotation and citation of earlier decisions in standing tribunals will result in a *jurisprudence constante* which, precisely because it is repeated and *constante*, tends to acquire a certain natural authority and influence that even the most carefully crafted award of an *ad hoc* tribunal is unlikely to command.'[19]

---

[15] G. Schwarzenberger, *International Law. Volume I: International Law as Applied by International Courts and Tribunals* (Stevens & Sons, 1945), p. 2. See also *Barcelona Traction, Light and Power Company, Limited (Belgium v. Spain)*, Merits, Separate Opinion of Judge Sir Gerald Fitzmaurice, 1970 ICJ Reports, p. 64, para. 2 ('judicial pronouncements of one kind or another constitute the principal method by which the law can find some concrete measure of clarification and development').

[16] In the WTO dispute settlement system, 'panels' and the 'Appellate Body' issue 'reports' that contain 'recommendations' addressed to a plenary organ (i.e. the Dispute Settlement Body), which then adopts those recommendations (unless all WTO Members agree otherwise).

[17] Panel Report, *Brazil – Aircraft*, para. 7.89.

[18] Appellate Body Report, *Mexico – Corn Syrup (Article 21.5 – US)*, at para. 36.

[19] V. Lowe and A. Tzanakopoulos, 'The Development of the Law of the Sea by the International Court of Justice', in J. Sloan and C. Tams (eds.), *The Development of International Law by the International Court of Justice* (Oxford University Press, 2013), pp. 177–93, at p. 186.

This digest aims to be comprehensive, and is based on a review of all WTO decisions generated over the period 1995–2014. By my count,[20] a total of 352 decisions were issued during this period. These include: (i) 191 panel reports (including 162 panel reports in original proceedings, and 29 panel reports in compliance proceedings under Article 21.5 of the DSU to determine the existence and WTO-consistency of measures taken to comply with earlier rulings); (ii) 112 Appellate Body reports (including 94 Appellate Body reports reviewing original panel reports, and 18 Appellate Body reports in Article 21.5 proceedings); and (iii) 49 arbitral awards and decisions (including 27 arbitration awards under Article 21.3(c) of the DSU to determine the reasonable period of time for implementing rulings and recommendations, 19 arbitration decisions in proceedings under Article 22.6 of the DSU and Articles 4 and/or 7 of the SCM Agreement to determine the level of retaliation in the event of non-compliance, 1 arbitration award under Article 25 of the DSU, and 2 arbitration awards under special procedures). This digest also contains extracts from about a dozen panel reports from the GATT era.

Stating that this digest aims to be comprehensive does not amount to a representation that it presents all relevant statements by all WTO adjudicators on all of the topics covered herein. It does not. To the contrary, considerable care has been taken to identify and exclude from this digest those statements and lines of jurisprudence that are linked to specific provisions of the WTO agreements in a way that potentially reduces their relevance for those working in other fields of public international law. As a result, for some of the topics covered, the statements collected in this digest only represent a fraction, and in some instances a very small fraction (e.g. countermeasures), of what WTO adjudicators have had to say on the topic. In addition, care has been taken to keep this digest to a manageable length, keeping the extracts as short as possible, and avoiding duplication as far as possible. For all of the topics covered, it aims to highlight the cases and statements that are likely to be of the greatest interest and utility to lawyers working in other fields of public international law. In other words, this digest tries to present all the 'greatest hits' of WTO jurisprudence for public international lawyers working in other fields of international law.

---

[20] A note on the figures presented here: (i) when the parties to a WTO dispute reach a bilateral settlement during the course of a proceeding, the WTO adjudicator still issues a report/award, which simply notes that a bilateral agreement was reached and does not contain any findings or analysis by the adjudicator – such reports are not counted in these figures; and (ii) when there are multiple complainants challenging the same matter, the WTO adjudicator may issue its separate reports in the form of a single document – these are counted as only one report in these figures; and (iii) WTO panels sometimes issue preliminary rulings on jurisdiction (or other points) as separate documents, which are then deemed to be an integral part of their final report – such rulings are not counted separately in these figures.

EDITORIAL CONVENTIONS

This digest adheres to the following editorial conventions:

- The material is divided into multiple chapters and sub-sections, systematically broken down under issue-specific sub-headings.
- Each sub-section is introduced by a concise overview of relevant jurisprudence relating to the concept, principle or issue in question, followed by key extracts from WTO panel, Appellate Body and arbitration decisions.
- Where there are multiple cases addressing an issue under a particular sub-heading, they are generally presented in chronological order; in some instances cases are grouped together, out of strict chronological order, if they are closely linked to one another.
- All WTO cases and agreements are referred to by their standard short titles. The glossary that follows sets out the full title (and brief explanation) of the WTO agreements referenced most frequently in this work. The table of cases that follows sets out the full citation for all WTO cases cited.
- All extracts are introduced by short explanatory sentences, which present the context for the statements being quoted.
- Original footnotes within extracted passages are omitted, except where they contain substantial discussion; when retained, such footnotes are reproduced immediately below the extracted passage.
- No emphasis is added to any of the extracts. Thus, wherever there is any emphasis in an extract, it is found in the original.
- Within quoted material, ellipses (. . .) are used to indicate where text within a sentence, a paragraph or larger section has been omitted. Ellipses are not used at the beginning or ending of passages reproduced in quotations. Square brackets are used to indicate required editorial changes, which have been kept to a strict minimum.

GLOSSARY OF COMMONLY USED TERMS

Panel Report	WTO panels are comprised of three individuals, appointed on an *ad hoc* basis, to make findings on the consistency of the challenged measure(s) with one or more obligations contained in the WTO agreements. Panels make findings on disputed questions of law and fact. Panel decisions are referred to as 'reports'. Panels are the adjudicators of first instance, and their decisions are subject to review by the Appellate Body.
Appellate Body Report	The Appellate Body is a standing body of seven individuals with demonstrated expertise in law, three of whom serve on a particular appeal. Appeals are limited to issues of law covered in the panel report and legal interpretations developed by the panel. Decisions of the Appellate Body are referred to as 'reports'.
Article 21.3(c) Award	Where the measure(s) at issue are found to be inconsistent with one or more WTO obligations, the Member concerned is entitled to a reasonable period of time to bring the measure(s) into conformity with those obligations. In the absence of agreement between the disputing parties, the time-period is determined through arbitration pursuant to Article 21.3(c) of the DSU. The decision of the arbitrator (in all cases to date, a current or former member of the Appellate Body) is referred to as an 'award'.
Article 21.5 Panel Report	Where the parties disagree as to whether the Member concerned has brought the WTO-inconsistent measure(s) into conformity with its obligations within the reasonable period of time, the matter is referred to a 'compliance panel' pursuant to Article 21.5 of the DSU. The compliance panel is composed of the same individuals from the original panel where possible, and its report may be appealed to the Appellate Body in the same way as an original panel report.
Article 22.6 Decision	Where the Member concerned has not brought the measure(s) found to be WTO-inconsistent into compliance with its obligation(s) within the reasonable period of time for doing so, the complaining party may request authorization from the WTO to suspend concessions or other obligations. Where the Member concerned objects to the level of retaliation requested, the matter is referred to arbitration pursuant to Article 22.6 of the DSU (and Articles 4 and/or 7 of the SCM Agreement, where

	applicable). The Arbitrator, which is composed of the same individuals from the original panel where possible, issues a 'decision'.
GATT	The General Agreement on Tariffs and Trade, negotiated in 1947, contains thirty-eight provisions governing trade in goods. As a consequence of the GATT being superseded by the WTO in the 1990s, the GATT was formally terminated and these provisions were incorporated by reference into the new WTO Agreement, along with associated understandings, protocols and decisions, as the 'GATT 1994'. The other WTO agreements dealing with trade in goods (e.g. the SCM Agreement) elaborate and expand upon the provisions of the GATT.
GATT Panel	A panel that was established and issued its report under the dispute settlement system that existed under the GATT, i.e. prior to the establishment of the WTO.
WTO Agreement	The framework agreement, consisting of 16 articles, to which the other WTO agreements and associated legal instruments are annexed and made an integral part. Its full title is the Marrakesh Agreement Establishing the World Trade Organization.
WTO agreements	A common way of referring collectively to the nearly two dozen agreements that are annexed to and made an integral part of the WTO Agreement. Also referred to as the 'covered agreements', which is the more formal term to refer to the closed list of agreements that fall within the scope and coverage of the WTO dispute settlement mechanism.
DSU	The WTO agreement consisting of twenty-seven articles and four appendices that govern the resolution of disputes over the interpretation and application of the WTO agreements (subject to some special and additional rules and procedures on dispute settlement contained in the other covered agreements). Its full title is the Understanding on Rules and Procedures Governing the Settlement of Disputes.
Anti-Dumping Agreement	A WTO agreement consisting of eighteen provisions and two annexes that regulate Members' imposition of anti-dumping duties on dumped imports (i.e. goods sold at prices below their cost of production or the price at which they are sold in the producer's home country). Its detailed provisions on the conduct of domestic anti-dumping duty investigations parallel the provisions on domestic countervailing duty investigations contained in the SCM Agreement. It elaborates and expands on Article VI of the GATT, and its full title is the Agreement on Implementation of Article VI of the General Agreement on Tariffs and Trade 1994.
SCM Agreement	A WTO agreement consisting of thirty-two provisions and seven annexes that regulate the provision of subsidies, and that also regulate Members' imposition of countervailing duties on subsidized imports. It elaborates and expands on Articles VI and XVI of the GATT, and its full title is the Agreement on Subsidies and Countervailing Measures.
Agreement on Agriculture	The Agreement on Agriculture contains twenty-one articles and five annexes that establish special rules relating to agricultural

	products, including subsidies and safeguards for agricultural products.
Agreement on Safeguards	The Agreement on Safeguards contains fourteen provisions and one annex that elaborate and expand upon Article XIX of the GATT, which provides that countries can take emergency safeguard measures to protect a domestic industry from increased imports in certain circumstances.
SPS Agreement	The Agreement on the Application of Sanitary and Phytosanitary Measures contains fourteen articles and three annexes that regulate certain types of safety standards that affect imports, including measures to ensure food safety and to prevent the spread of pests.
TBT Agreement	The Agreement on Technical Barriers to Trade contains fifteen articles and three annexes that regulate certain types of product regulations and standards that are not covered by the SPS Agreement.
TRIMs Agreement	The Agreement on Trade-Related Investment Measures contains nine articles and one annex that clarify the applicability of Articles III and XI of the GATT to investment measures related to trade in goods.
TRIPS Agreement	The Agreement on Trade-Related Aspects of Intellectual Property Rights contains seventy-three provisions relating to the protection of intellectual property rights. Among other things, it incorporates by reference the obligations contained in certain other pre-existing international treaties on intellectual property rights.
GATS	The General Agreement on Trade in Services contains twenty-nine articles and eight annexes, which regulate measures affecting trade in services. Some of its provisions, including those on national treatment, most-favoured-nation treatment, and general exceptions, parallel the basic obligations and rights relating to trade in goods that are contained in the GATT.
Schedules	Detailed and lengthy schedules list the commitments made by each individual WTO Member specifying the tariff and/or other market access treatment granted to imported goods (GATT Schedules) or service-providers (GATS Schedules). Schedules, which collectively total tens of thousands of pages, are incorporated by reference into the WTO agreements.
ATC	The Agreement on Textiles and Clothing was an agreement containing nine articles and an annex that permitted Members to maintain certain GATT-inconsistent measures for a transitional period of several years following the entry into force of the WTO agreements. Among other things, it contained special rules on safeguard measures.
Tokyo Round Codes	The Tokyo Round negotiations of the 1970s led to the adoption of agreements, which were known as 'codes', by a subset of GATT parties on subsidies and countervailing duties, anti-dumping measures and other non-tariff measures. These codes were the precursors to the Anti-Dumping Agreement, the SCM Agreement and various other WTO agreements relating to trade in goods.

TABLE OF GATT/WTO CASES

1

ADMISSIBILITY AND JURISDICTION

1.1 Introduction

In international dispute settlement proceedings, respondents often argue, as a **1.1**
first line of defence, that one or more of the claims either are inadmissible, or fall
outside of the jurisdiction of the international court or tribunal. In contentious
proceedings before, for example, the International Court of Justice, a judgment
on the merits is frequently preceded by a separate judgment addressing the
respondent's objections on admissibility and/or jurisdiction; likewise, rulings on
admissibility and/or jurisdiction are a 'standard feature'[1] in the context of
investor–State disputes. The issues relating to admissibility and jurisdiction that
arise most frequently in the context of WTO dispute settlement are derived
from specific provisions of the DSU.[2] These provisions do not embody concepts
or principles of general international law, which makes WTO jurisprudence
related to those specific provisions of limited relevance or applicability in
other contexts. This chapter reviews statements of wider applicability by
WTO adjudicators relating to other issues of admissibility and jurisdiction.
International decisions 'are replete with fine distinctions between Jurisdiction

---

[1] C. Schreuer, *The ICSID Convention: A Commentary* (Cambridge University Press, 2001), p. 531.
[2] These issues are: (i) whether the complainant's *request for the establishment of a panel* impermissibly
broadens the scope of the dispute by including measures and/or claims under treaty provisions that
were not included in the complainant's *request for consultations*, as required by Article 4 of the
DSU; (ii) whether the complainant's *request for the establishment of a panel* is defective by virtue of a
failure to identify the measures at issue and the claims of violation with sufficient precision, as
required by Article 6.2 of the DSU; (iii) whether the complainant has, in the course of the
proceeding, challenged measures or claimed violations of treaty provisions that were not identified
in the *request for the establishment of a panel*, and which therefore fall outside of the panel's *terms of
reference* pursuant to Article 7 of the DSU; (iv) whether issues raised on appeal comply with the
rules governing *notices of appeal* contained in the Working Procedures for Appellate Review; and
(v) whether, in the context of compliance panel proceedings pursuant to Article 21.5 of the DSU,
the measures challenged by the complainant are measures '*taken to comply*' with the original
recommendations and rulings.

and admissibility'.[3] It is not clear that the distinction between admissibility and jurisdiction carries any legal implications in the context of WTO dispute settlement, and this may explain why it has not been discussed by panels and the Appellate Body (and why it would seem that the two terms have sometimes been used interchangeably by WTO adjudicators).[4] The first part of this chapter reviews, under the rubric of the 'admissibility of claims', statements by WTO adjudicators on: (i) restrictions on admissibility not being lightly inferred; (ii) acquiescence, estoppel and waiver; (iii) absence of legal interest/standing; (iv) failure to implead an 'essential party'; (v) failure to join cases; (vi) failure to exhaust local remedies; (vii) *forum non conveniens*; and (viii) *res judicata*. The second part of this chapter reviews, under the rubric of the 'jurisdiction over claims', statements by WTO adjudicators on: (i) the rule governing claims falling outside of a tribunal's subject-matter jurisdiction; (ii) implied restrictions arising from overlapping jurisdictional competencies among different bodies; (iii) a tribunal's duty to address jurisdictional issues on its own motion; (iv) the timeliness of jurisdictional objections and rulings; and (v) the distinction between jurisdictional issues and issues going to the merits of a case.

1.2   Admissibility of claims

1.2 There have been few, if any, cases in which WTO adjudicators have found that one or more claims were inadmissible on the basis of general international law concepts or principles (as distinguished from specific procedural requirements and limitations contained in the DSU). WTO adjudicators have consistently emphasized that restrictions on the right to bring claims may not be lightly

---

[3] *Waste Management Inc.* v. *United Mexican States*, ICSID Case No. ARB(AF)/98/2, Dissenting opinion of Keith Highet, 8 May 2000, para. 57.

[4] For commentary on several issues relating to admissibility and jurisdiction in the context of WTO dispute settlement, see I. Van Damme, 'Inherent Powers of and for the WTO Appellate Body', Working Paper Centre for Trade and Economic Integration, Graduate Institute of International and Development Studies, Geneva, 2008, available at www.graduateinstitute.ch/ctei/page2142. html, pp. 15–35. One understanding of the distinction between admissibility and jurisdiction, and that which is reflected in the organization of jurisprudence in this chapter, is that jurisdiction refers to the scope of the subject-matter that a complaining party can bring before a particular adjudicative body (which is constant and does not change from case to case), whereas inadmissibility concerns an alleged action or omission by a particular complaining party in a particular set of circumstances that may or must lead that adjudicative body to decline to examine a particular claim that otherwise falls within its subject-matter jurisdiction. In other words, a tribunal may find that a claimant's conduct in a particular case renders one or more of its claims, which fall within the tribunal's jurisdiction, inadmissible. The same would apply *mutatis mutandis* with respect to a respondent's defences. The distinction between issues of admissibility and issues of jurisdiction, and the characterization of a respondent's objection as falling into the one or the other category, carries considerable importance in the context of some international dispute settlement systems. Notably, in the field of international commercial arbitration and investor–State dispute settlement, errors by a tribunal relating to its jurisdiction (as distinguished from errors relating to its findings on admissibility) constitute a basis for setting aside or annulling a tribunal's award.

assumed or inferred. The interrelated concepts of acquiescence, estoppel and waiver have been raised in a number of GATT/WTO cases, often in connection with the respondent's argument that one or more claims of violation were inadmissible on the grounds that the challenged measure(s) had been in force for a long period of time. To date, adjudicators have rejected all arguments based on acquiescence, estoppel and waiver. To date, panels and the Appellate Body have also rejected all arguments that the complainant lacked a legal (or other) 'interest' in the dispute and/or 'standing' to invoke the responsibility of the responding Member, that a complainant's failure to join its case to an earlier one brought by another complainant rendered it inadmissible, that consideration of the claims should be dismissed or deferred until the complainant had attempted to resolve the issue in another international forum, or that the dispute would more appropriately be pursued before another international dispute settlement mechanism. In cases where the respondent argued that one or more claims was inadmissible on the basis of such general international law concepts or principles, WTO adjudicators have often proceeded on an *arguendo* approach and reasoned that, assuming for the sake of argument that the concept or principle in question is applicable in WTO dispute settlement, one or more of the conditions for the application of that concept or principle were not met on the facts of the case.[5]

1.2.1 Restrictions on admissibility not lightly inferred[*]

In *US – FSC*, the Panel examined a claim that certain US tax exemptions were **1.3** subsidies contingent upon export performance, and therefore prohibited by Article 3.1(a) of the SCM Agreement. Footnote 59 to item (e) of the Illustrative List of Export Subsidies in Annex 1 to the SCM Agreement provides, in respect of certain types of tax measures, that 'Members shall normally attempt to resolve their differences using the facilities of existing bilateral tax treaties or other specific international mechanisms, without prejudice to the rights and obligations of Members under GATT 1994'. The United States argued, on the basis of footnote 59, that the Panel should 'defer' or 'dismiss' all of the European Communities' claims relating to the tax measure at issue until the European Communities had attempted to resolve the issue at the OECD, or in the 'competent authority' process under the relevant bilateral tax treaties. The Panel rejected the United States' argument. In the course of its analysis, the Panel stated:

> In considering the preliminary objection raised by the United States, we take as
> a starting-point that, under Article XXIII of GATT 1994, the DSU and Article
> 4 of the SCM Agreement, a Member has the right to resort to WTO dispute

---

[5] For WTO jurisprudence on the use of *arguendo* reasoning, see Section 9.3.2.
[*] See also the cases in Section 4.2.1. ('The narrow definition of and presumption against 'conflict' in international law').

settlement at any time by making a request for consultations in a manner consistent with those provisions. This fundamental right to resort to dispute settlement is a core element of the WTO system. Accordingly, we believe that a panel should not lightly infer a restriction on this right into the WTO Agreement; rather, there should be a clear and unambiguous basis in the relevant legal instruments for concluding that such a restriction exists.[6]

1.4 In *Mexico – Taxes on Soft Drinks*, Mexico requested that the Panel decline to exercise its jurisdiction until a parallel NAFTA dispute settlement proceeding had been completed. The Panel declined Mexico's request. On appeal, the Appellate Body agreed with the Panel's statement that, in the absence of 'a legal impediment to the exercise of a panel's jurisdiction',[7] a WTO panel 'would seem ... not to be in a position to choose freely whether or not to exercise its jurisdiction'.[8] The Appellate Body did not consider it necessary, in the circumstances of that dispute, to elaborate on the types of situations that could give rise to a 'legal impediment to the exercise of a panel's jurisdiction'.

1.5 In *EC – Bananas III (Article 21.5 – Ecuador II) / EC – Bananas III (Article 21.5 – US)*, the Appellate Body stated that the relinquishment of rights granted by the DSU 'cannot be lightly assumed'. In that case, the Appellate Body examined whether certain understandings that the European Communities had concluded with the United States and Ecuador (following the original panel and Appellate Body proceeding in *EC – Bananas III*) prevented the complainants from subsequently initiating compliance proceedings pursuant to Article 21.5 of the DSU. In the course of its analysis, the Appellate Body stated:

> We consider that the complainants could be precluded from initiating Article 21.5 proceedings by means of these Understandings only if the parties to these Understandings had, either explicitly or by necessary implication, agreed to waive their right to have recourse to Article 21.5. In our view, the relinquishment of rights granted by the DSU cannot be lightly assumed. Rather, the language in the Understandings must reveal clearly that the parties intended to relinquish their rights.[276]

> ───────────
> [276] In this respect, we note the International Court of Justice, Preliminary Objections, *Case concerning the Temple of Preah Vihear (Cambodia* v. *Thailand)*, Judgment of 26 May 1961, ICJ Reports (1961) 32, addressing the interpretation of declarations of acceptance of the compulsory jurisdiction of the Court. In order to determine whether Thailand had recognized as compulsory the jurisdiction of the Court, the Court considered that the 'sole relevant question' was whether Thailand's declaration clearly revealed such intention.[9]

───────────

[6] Panel Report, *US – FSC*, para. 7.17.   [7] Appellate Body Report, *Mexico – Soft Drinks*, para. 54.
[8] Appellate Body Report, *Mexico – Taxes on Soft Drinks*, para. 53.
[9] Appellate Body Report, *EC – Bananas III (Article 21.5 – Ecuador II) / EC – Bananas III (Article 21.5 – US)*, para. 217.

1.2.2 Acquiescence, estoppel and waiver[10]

In the GATT dispute on *EEC – Import Restrictions*, the Panel recognized that **1.6**
the restrictions at issue had been in existence for many years, without being
challenged by any GATT contracting party. However, the Panel concluded that:

> [T]his did not alter the obligations which contracting parties had accepted under
> GATT provisions. Furthermore the Panel considered it would be erroneous to
> interpret the fact that a measure had not been subject to [dispute settlement
> under] Article XXIII over a number of years, as tantamount to its tacit accept-
> ance by contracting parties.[11]

In *EEC – Pasta Subsidies*, the GATT Panel observed that the European **1.7**
Communities had notified other GATT contracting parties of its subsidies on
pasta products in accordance with the notification requirements in Article XVI:1
of the GATT, and that such measures had remained unchallenged over a period
of years. However, the Panel found that:

> [T]he notifications under Article XVI:1 of certain export subsidies on processed
> agricultural products did neither require nor preclude contracting parties
> from challenging the legality of such practices. As contracting parties were
> under no legal obligation to challenge the legality of export subsidies of other
> contracting parties, the mere abstaining from such a legal challenge could
> not be relied upon as acquiescence to or construed as approval of the legality
> of such export subsidies. In this context the Panel noted that another Panel
> had concluded that the fact that certain practices had been in force for some
> time without being the subject of complaints was not, in itself, conclusive
> evidence that there was a consensus that they were compatible with the
> General Agreement.[12]

In another GATT case, *EEC (Member States) — Bananas I*, the measures at **1.8**
issue had been in place, and their existence notified to other GATT contracting parties, over a number of years. The GATT Panel addressed several
interrelated arguments under the heading 'Subsequent practice, acquiescence
and estoppel':

> The Panel noted the EEC's argument that subsequent practice of the CON-
> TRACTING PARTIES, or of the parties to the dispute, with respect to the
> banana import régimes of EEC member States, had resulted in a modification of
> the rights and obligations under Part II of the General Agreement, or in the
> complaining parties being estopped (i.e. legally prevented) from raising such
> rights. In examining this argument, the Panel considered that such modification
> or estoppel could only result from the express, or in exceptional cases implied,
> consent of such parties or of the CONTRACTING PARTIES.

---

[10] See also Chapter 8 generally (Good Faith), and Section 15.8 (Subsequent practice).
[11] GATT Panel Report, *EEC – Import Restrictions*, para. 28.
[12] GATT Panel Report, *EEC – Pasta Subsidies*, para. 4.10 (citing *EEC-Import Restrictions*, supra).

The Panel considered that the decision of a contracting party not to invoke a right under the General Agreement at a particular point in time could be due to circumstances that change over time. For instance, a contracting party may not wish to invoke a right under the General Agreement pending the outcome of a multilateral trade negotiation, such as the Uruguay Round, or pending an assessment of the trade effects of a measure. The decision of a contracting party not to invoke a right *vis-à-vis* another contracting party at a particular point in time can therefore, by itself, not reasonably be assumed to be a decision to release that other contracting party from its obligations under the General Agreement. The Panel noted in this context that previous panels had based their findings on measures which had remained unchallenged for long periods of time. The Panel therefore found that the mere fact that the complaining parties had not invoked their rights under the General Agreement in the past had not modified these rights and did not prevent them from invoking these rights now.

With respect to subsequent practice of the CONTRACTING PARTIES, the Panel considered that the mere fact that the EEC had notified these restrictions to the CONTRACTING PARTIES, and that such measures had not been acted upon by them until now had not changed the obligations of the EEC under the General Agreement. Any action of the CONTRACTING PARTIES on these notifications would normally have resulted from a request for such action by individual contracting parties. Since, for the reasons set out in the preceding paragraph, the mere failure to make such a request could not be interpreted as a decision to abandon the right to make such a request, the mere inaction of the CONTRACTING PARTIES could not in good faith be interpreted as the expression of their consent to release the EEC from its obligations under Part II of the General Agreement.[13]

1.9 In *EC – Bananas III (Article 21.5 – EC)*, the European Communities took certain measures to implement the DSB recommendations and rulings in *EC – Bananas III*, and then requested the establishment of a compliance panel under Article 21.5 of the DSU with the mandate 'to find that the above-mentioned implementing measures of the EC must be presumed to conform to WTO rules unless their conformity has been duly challenged under the appropriate DSU procedures' – which the complainants had not done. In the course of its analysis, the Panel observed that:

> [T]he failure, as of a given point in time, of one Member to challenge another Member's measures cannot be interpreted to create a presumption that the first Member accepts the measures of the other Member as consistent with the WTO Agreement. In this regard, we note the statement by a GATT panel that 'it would be erroneous to interpret the fact that a measure has not been subject to Article XXIII over a number of years, as tantamount to its tacit acceptance by contracting parties'.[14]

---

[13] GATT Panel Report, *EEC (member States) – Bananas I*, paras. 361–3.
[14] Panel Report, *EC – Bananas III (Article 21.5 – EC)*, para. 4.13 (citing GATT Panel Report, *EEC – Import Restrictions*, para. 28).

In *Guatemala – Cement II*, Argentina invoked the concepts of acquiescence and **1.10**
estoppel with respect to 'the lack of reaction' by Mexico, in the course of the
anti-dumping investigation at issue, to certain alleged violations of the Anti-
Dumping Agreement. The Panel found that Mexico was 'under no obligation to
object immediately' to the violations it subsequently alleged before the Panel,
and could not therefore be considered as having acquiesced to belated notification by Guatemala, to insufficiency in the public notice, or to delay in providing
the full text of the application, much less to have given 'assurances' to Guatemala
that it would not later challenge these actions in WTO dispute settlement.
In the course of its analysis, the Panel distinguished 'acquiescence' from 'estoppel', stating:

> We note that 'acquiescence' amounts to 'qualified silence', whereby silence in
> the face of events that call for a reaction of some sort may be interpreted as a
> presumed consent. The concept of estoppel, also relied on by Guatemala in
> support of its argument, is akin to that of acquiescence. Estoppel is premised on
> the view that where one party has been induced to act in reliance on the
> assurances of another party, in such a way that it would be prejudiced were
> the other party later to change its position, such a change in position is
> 'estopped', that is precluded.[15]

In *EC – Asbestos*, the parties disagreed on whether the measure at issue was a **1.11**
technical regulation falling within the scope and coverage of the TBT Agreement. In this regard, Canada argued that the European Communities had
recognized that the TBT Agreement applied to the measure at issue by notifying
the measure at issue (a Decree) to the WTO Committee on Technical Barriers
to Trade, and also by virtue of statements allegedly made during the confidential
consultations relating to this dispute. The Panel stated:

> From a legal point of view, the question seems to be whether there is *estoppel* on
> the part of the EC because they notified the Decree or because of their
> statements, including those during the consultations. This would be the case
> if it was determined that Canada had legitimately relied on the notification of
> the Decree and was now suffering the negative consequences resulting from a
> change in the EC's position. In this case, however, it does not appear that
> Canada was able legitimately to rely on a notification to the Committee on
> Technical Barriers to Trade or on a statement made during the consultations.
> We consider that notifications under the TBT Agreement are made for reasons
> of transparency. It has been recognized that such notifications do not have any
> recognized legal effects. Furthermore, notification under the TBT Agreement is
> one of the few ways of notifying this type of measure for a Member who wishes
> to show transparency in good faith. Lastly we consider that both the notification
> and the comments made by the EC during the consultations or in another

---

[15] Panel Report, *Guatemala – Cement II*, para. 8.23 (citing V. D. Degan, *Sources of International Law* (Martinus Nijhoff Publishers, 1997), pp. 348–9; I. Brownlie, *Principles of International Law* (Clarendon Press, pp. 640–2)).

context constitute observations on the legal characterization of the Decree. Claims regarding the legal characterization of a fact by the parties, however, cannot bind the Panel.[16]

1.12 In *India – Autos*, India argued that the European Communities' claims were inadmissible because they were already resolved through a bilateral settlement between the parties arising out of an earlier dispute. The Panel observed that 'there may be an argument that a general principle such as *estoppel* may apply' in such circumstances.[17] However, the Panel found that, even if the conclusion of a mutually agreed solution could in some cases preclude a panel from hearing a dispute, the agreement at issue here did not do so given its wording and scope.[18]

1.13 In *Argentina – Poultry Anti-Dumping Duties*, Brazil challenged an Argentine anti-dumping measure before a MERCOSUR Ad Hoc Tribunal and then, having lost that case, initiated WTO dispute settlement proceedings against the same measure. Argentina argued that Brazil was 'estopped' from pursuing its claims before the WTO panel (and/or that the Panel should treat the prior ruling as a 'relevant rule of international law' under Article 31(3)(c) of the Vienna Convention – see para. 4.16 below). Argentina argued that the essential elements of estoppel are '(i) a statement of fact which is clear and unambiguous; (ii) this statement must be voluntary, unconditional, and authorized; (iii) there must be reliance in good faith upon the statement . . . to the advantage of the party making the statement'.[19] The Panel found that the conditions identified by Argentina for the application of the principle of estoppel were not satisfied in that case (and therefore considered it unnecessary to determine whether the three conditions proposed by Argentina were sufficient for the application of that proposal). First, the Panel found that Brazil had made no clear statement that was inconsistent with its subsequent conduct:

> We do not consider Argentina's response sufficient to establish that the three conditions it identified for the application of the principle of estoppel are fulfilled in the present case. Regarding the first condition identified by Argentina, we do not consider that Brazil has made a clear and unambiguous statement to the effect that, having brought a case under the MERCOSUR dispute settlement framework, it would not subsequently resort to WTO dispute settlement proceedings. In this regard, we note that the panel in *EEC (Member States) – Bananas I* found that estoppel can only 'result from the express, or in exceptional cases implied consent of the complaining parties'. We agree. There is no evidence on the record that Brazil made an express

---

[16] Panel Report, *EC – Asbestos*, para. 8.60 (citing *North Sea Continental Shelf* case, 1969 ICJ Reports, p. 26, para. 30; P. Daillier and A. Pellet, *Droit international public*, 5th edn (1994), p. 834, citing Guggenheim, *Traité de droit international public*, Volume II, p. 158).
[17] Panel Report, *India – Autos*, footnote 364.   [18] *Ibid.*, paras. 7.105–7.135.
[19] Panel Report, *Argentina – Poultry Anti-Dumping Duties*, para. 7.20 and footnote 41 (citing I. Brownlie, *Principles of Public International Law* (Clarendon Press, 1990), p. 641).

statement that it would not bring WTO dispute settlement proceedings in respect of measures previously challenged through MERCOSUR. Nor does the record indicate exceptional circumstances requiring us to imply any such statement. In particular, the fact that Brazil chose not to invoke its WTO dispute settlement rights after previous MERCOSUR dispute settlement proceedings does not, in our view, mean that Brazil implicitly waived its rights under the *DSU*. This is especially because the Protocol of Brasilia, under which previous MERCOSUR cases had been brought by Brazil, imposes no restrictions on Brazil's right to bring subsequent WTO dispute settlement proceedings in respect of the same measure. We note that Brazil signed the Protocol of Olivos in February 2002. Article 1 of the Protocol of Olivos provides that once a party decides to bring a case under either the MERCOSUR or WTO dispute settlement forums, that party may not bring a subsequent case regarding the same subject-matter in the other forum. The Protocol of Olivos, however, does not change our assessment, since that Protocol has not yet entered into force, and in any event it does not apply in respect of disputes already decided in accordance with the MERCOSUR Protocol of Brasilia. Indeed, the fact that parties to MERCOSUR saw the need to introduce the Protocol of Olivos suggests to us that they recognized that (in the absence of such Protocol) a MERCOSUR dispute settlement proceeding could be followed by a WTO dispute settlement proceeding in respect of the same measure.[20]

In *Argentina – Poultry Anti-Dumping Duties*, the Panel also found that Argentina failed to demonstrate the existence of any detrimental reliance on statements allegedly made by Brazil:

Quoted in full, the third condition reads 'there must be reliance in good faith upon the statement either to the detriment of the party so relying on the statement or to the advantage of the party making the statement'. Citing the same author, another panel has asserted that '[e]stoppel is premised on the view that where one party has been induced to act in reliance on the assurances of another party, in such a way that it would be prejudiced were the other party later to change its position, such a change in position is "estopped", that is precluded'. In our view, merely being inconvenienced by alleged statements by Brazil is not sufficient for Argentina to demonstrate that it was induced to act in reliance of such alleged statements. There is nothing on the record to suggest to us that Argentina actively relied in good faith on any statement made by Brazil, either to the advantage of Brazil or to the disadvantage of Argentina. There is nothing on the record to suggest that Argentina would have acted any differently had Brazil not made the alleged statement that it would not bring the present WTO dispute settlement proceedings. In its abovementioned response to Question 66, which was specifically addressing this issue, Argentina simply stated that it 'is now suffering the negative impact of [Brazil's] change of position' (regarding its earlier practice of not pursuing WTO cases following MERCOSUR rulings in respect of the same subject-matter), without explaining

---

[20] Panel Report, *Argentina – Poultry Anti-Dumping Duties*, para. 7.38 (citing GATT Panel Report, *EEC (Member States) – Bananas I*, para. 361; Panel Report, *Guatemala – Cement II*, footnote 791).

further the nature of that 'negative impact'. Argentina's vague assertion regarding 'negative impact' is not sufficient to demonstrate that it was induced to act in reliance on the alleged statement by Brazil, and that it is now suffering the negative consequences of the alleged change in Brazil's position. For these reasons, we reject Argentina's claim that Brazil is estopped from pursuing the present WTO dispute settlement proceedings.[21]

1.14 In *EC – Export Subsidies on Sugar*, the European Communities argued that the complainants were estopped from bringing certain claims because the alleged violations would have been flagrant and immediately manifest upon the conclusion of the WTO agreements, yet the complainants remained silent on the issue for a number of years. At the outset of its analysis, the Panel set forth the following definition of the principle of estoppel:

> The Panel notes that parties and third-parties to this dispute do not seem to agree on the nature of the principle on estoppel and its exact parameters. Muller and Cottier define it as follows:
>
>> 'It is generally agreed that the party invoking estoppel "must have been induced to undertake legally relevant action or abstain from it by relying in good faith upon clear and unambiguous representations by the other State".'[22]

The Panel in *EC – Export Subsidies on Sugar* proceeded with its analysis by assuming *arguendo* that the principle of estoppel is applicable in WTO dispute settlement proceedings, and then found that there was no basis in the circumstances of that case for finding that the complaining parties were estopped from bringing their claims. In the course of its analysis, the Panel stated:

> In the Panel's view, Brazil's and Thailand's silence concerning the European Communities' base quantity levels as well as with respect to the ACP/India sugar Footnote does not amount to a clear and unambiguous representation upon which the European Communities could rely, especially considering that, in the Panel's view, there was no legal duty upon the Complainants to alert the European Communities to its alleged violations. Furthermore, it is not possible to identify any facts or statements made by the Complainants where they have admitted that the EC measure was WTO consistent or where they have promised that they would not take legal action against the European Communities. In the Panel's view the 'silence' of some of the Complainants cannot be equated with their consent to the European Communities' violations, if any. Moreover, the Complainants' silence cannot be held against other WTO Members who, today, could decide to initiate WTO dispute settlement proceedings against the European Communities. In other words, even if the three Complainants had remained completely silent on this issue, their silence could not be considered a commitment binding on other

---

[21] Panel Report, *Argentina – Poultry Anti-Dumping Duties*, para. 7.39 (citing Panel Report, *Guatemala – Cement II*, para. 8.23).

[22] Panel Report, *EC – Export Subsidies on Sugar (Australia)*, para. 7.61 (citing J. P. Müller and T. Cottier, in *Encyclopaedia of Public International Law*, ed. Max Planck Institute (North Holland, 1992), p. 116).

Members to the extent that it would contradict the provisions of the *Agreement on Agriculture* or which could remove the European Communities' alleged inconsistencies with its WTO obligations.[23]

In *EC – Export Subsidies on Sugar*, the Appellate Body upheld the Panel's **1.15** analysis and found that the complainants had 'acted in good faith, under Article 3.10 of the DSU, in the initiation and conduct of the present dispute settlement proceedings and have not been estopped, through their actions or silence', from bringing the claims of violation at issue.[24]

In *EC – Bananas III (Article 21.5 – Ecuador II) / EC – Bananas III (Article 21.5 –* **1.16** *US)*, the Appellate Body examined whether certain Understandings that the European Communities had concluded with the United States and with Ecuador, following the original panel and Appellate Body proceeding in *EC – Bananas III*, prevented the complainants from subsequently initiating compliance proceedings pursuant to Article 21.5 of the DSU. In the course of its analysis, the Appellate Body stated:

> Although not using the term, the European Communities, in the present cases, in fact advances an estoppel argument. The Appellate Body addressed this dimension of the principle of good faith in *EC – Export Subsidies on Sugar* . . . [I]f a WTO Member has not clearly stated that it would not take legal action with respect to a certain measure, it cannot be regarded as failing to act in good faith if it challenges that measure. In that vein, the Appellate Body found, in *EC – Export Subsidies on Sugar*, that it was not possible to identify any facts or statements made by the complainants admitting that the European Communities' measure was WTO-consistent or promising that they would not take legal action against the European Communities. In the present cases, if the complainants were to be regarded as being estopped from initiating these Article 21.5 proceedings, such estoppel would have to attach to a representation outside of the Understandings on Bananas. This, however, is not the case. Therefore, we consider that the United States and Ecuador have not failed to act in good faith in requesting compliance proceedings pursuant to Article 21.5.[25]

In *EC and certain member States – Large Civil Aircraft*, the European Commu- **1.17** nities argued that the terms of a bilateral agreement between itself and the United States gave rise to a waiver, and/or an estoppel, as regards the parties' right to bring a WTO challenge regarding subsidies granted prior to 1992. The Panel rejected the European Communities' argument. As regards the panel reports in *Guatemala – Cement II* and *Argentina – Poultry Anti-Dumping Duties*, the Panel clarified that 'these panels did *not* establish that the principle of estoppel applies in WTO dispute settlement proceedings; rather, the respective

---

[23] Panel Report, *EC – Export Subsidies on Sugar (Australia)*, para. 7.73.
[24] Appellate Body Report, *EC – Export Subsidies on Sugar*, para. 320.
[25] Appellate Body Report, *EC – Bananas III (Article 21.5 – Ecuador II) / EC – Bananas III (Article 21.5 – US)*, paras. 227–8.

panels proceeded on the basis that, even if *arguendo* a principle of estoppel in the terms contended for did exist, it was not established on the specific facts of the case.'[26] As regards the bilateral agreement at issue, the Panel concluded that the elements of the European Communities' own definition of the principle of estoppel were not met:

> [W]e do not consider that Article 2 of the 1992 Agreement can be interpreted as an agreement between the parties that pre-1992 support measures are deemed to be compatible with the GATT/WTO subsidies disciplines, or that the parties thereby waived their rights to challenge pre-1992 measures as being inconsistent with those disciplines. Even assuming *arguendo* that the Panel were to accept the European Communities' submissions as to the basis for applying the principle of estoppel in the context of WTO dispute settlement (on which we express no view), we would also reject the European Communities' request for preliminary rulings on this ground because we consider that Article 2 falls far short of being a 'clear and unambiguous statement' in the sense required by the first element of the European Communities' own definition of the principle of estoppel. We also note that, although the European Communities asserts that it has complied with its obligations under the 1992 Agreement concerning the level of support it has provided to its large civil aircraft industry, it has not identified any behaviour that would amount to detrimental reliance on the alleged representation made by the United States.[27]

1.18 In *China – GOES*, the Appellate Body indicated that a panel is entitled to rely on 'representations' made before it by a party, and that if a party then wished to advance a different position on appeal, that party would have to explain why its statements are no longer to be relied upon.[28]

1.19 In several cases, WTO adjudicators recognized that a disputing party may waive certain rights in the course of a dispute settlement proceeding. For example, in *Mexico – Corn Syrup (Article 21.5 – US)*, the Appellate Body stated that 'a Member that fails to raise its objections in a timely manner, notwithstanding one or more opportunities to do so, may be deemed to have waived its right to have a panel consider such objections.'[29]

1.2.3 Absence of legal interest/standing

1.20 In *EC – Bananas III*, the European Communities argued that a complaining party must have a 'legal interest' in bringing certain claims, and that the United States, which did not export bananas to the European Communities, had no such legal interest with respect to certain claims. In the context of rejecting the

---

[26] Panel Report, *EC and certain member States – Large Civil Aircraft*, footnote 1914.
[27] *Ibid.*, para. 7.104.   [28] Appellate Body Report, *China – GOES*, para. 195.
[29] Appellate Body Report, *Mexico – Corn Syrup (Article 21.5 – US)*, para. 50.

EC argument, the Panel considered that a number of ICJ decisions would support finding that the United States had a 'legal interest' in that case:

> [I]n our view a Member's potential interest in trade in goods or services and its interest in a determination of rights and obligations under the WTO Agreement are each sufficient to establish a right to pursue a WTO dispute settlement proceeding. Moreover, we note that this result is consistent with decisions of international tribunals.[361]

---

[361] The International Court of Justice has not defined the concept of legal interest in specific terms. However, a number of its cases would support finding a legal interest in this case. For example, in the *Wimbledon* case, the Permanent Court of International Justice found that a state could raise a claim with respect to the Kiel Canal even though its fleet did not want to use it, suggesting that a potential interest was sufficient for a legal interest. PCIJ (1923), Ser. A, no. 1, 20. In *Northern Cameroons (Preliminary Objections)*, the ICJ stated:

> The function of the Court is to state the law, but it may pronounce judgment only in connection with concrete cases where there exists at the time of adjudication an actual controversy involving a conflict of legal interest between the parties. The Court's judgment must have some practical consequence in the sense that it can affect existing legal rights or obligations of the parties, thus removing uncertainty from their legal relations.
>
> (ICJ Reports (1963), 33–34)

Here, our decision will have such an effect to the extent that the EC is obligated to revise the challenged measures. See also Part II of the Draft Articles on State Responsibility, art. 40.2(e)–(f), provisionally adopted by the Drafting Committee of the International Law Commission. A/CN.4/ L.524, 21 June 1996.[30]

In *EC – Bananas III*, the Appellate Body upheld the Panel's finding on this issue. **1.21** For its part, the Appellate Body reasoned that ICJ decisions relating to the concept of a 'legal interest' did not establish a general rule of international law that applies in all international litigation:

> The participants in this appeal have referred to certain judgments of the International Court of Justice and the Permanent Court of International Justice relating to whether there is a requirement, in international law, of a legal interest to bring a case.[66] We do not read any of these judgments as establishing a general rule that in all international litigation, a complaining party must have a 'legal interest' in order to bring a case. Nor do these judgments deny the need to consider the question of standing under the dispute settlement provisions of any multilateral treaty, by referring to the terms of that treaty.

---

[66] The EC's appellant's submission in paras. 9–10 refers to the ICJ and PCIJ Judgments in: the *South West Africa Cases*, (Second Phase), ICJ Reports

---

[30] Panel Report, *EC – Bananas III (US)*, para. 7.50.

1966, p. 4; the *Case Concerning the Barcelona Traction, Light and Power Company, Limited* (Second Phase), ICJ Reports 1970, p. 4; the *Mavrommatis Palestine Concessions Case*, PCIJ (1925) Series A, No. 2, p. 1; the *SS 'Wimbledon'* case, PCIJ (1923) Series A, No. 1, p. 1; and the *Case Concerning the Northern Cameroons*, ICJ Reports 1963, p. 4. The Complaining Parties' appellee's submission, in para. 364, also refers to the ICJ Judgment in the *South West Africa Cases*.[31]

1.22 In *EC – Bananas III (Article 21.5 – US)*, i.e. the subsequent compliance proceeding, the European Communities again raised an issue of whether the United States had standing to commence the proceedings. Having noted that the United States was a complaining party in the original proceedings in which the European Communities' bananas regime was found to be inconsistent with the WTO covered agreements, the Panel went on to state:

> [T]he United States, as an original complainant, holds a particular interest in ensuring that the measure in question is brought into conformity with the WTO agreements. The European Communities has failed to rebut the existence of that particular interest. Accordingly, the Panel does not need to conduct, under the current compliance proceedings, a separate analysis of whether, in the words of the European Communities, 'the alleged violation of a WTO rule sufficiently "touches" upon the interests of the [United States] so as to justify [that] party's "standing" to commence dispute settlement proceedings'.[32]

1.23 In *Korea – Dairy*, the Panel recalled prior WTO jurisprudence and rejected Korea's argument that there is a requirement for an 'economic interest' to bring a matter to the Panel:

> In *EC – Bananas*, the Appellate Body stated that the need for a 'legal interest' could not be implied in the DSU or in any other provisions of the WTO Agreement and that Members were expected to be largely self-regulating in deciding whether any DSU procedure would be 'fruitful'. We cannot read in the DSU any requirement for an 'economic interest'. We also note the provisions of Article 3.8 of the DSU, pursuant to which nullification and impairment is presumed once violation is established.[33]

1.2.4 Failure to implead an essential party

1.24 In *Turkey – Textiles*, Turkey argued that the Panel should dismiss India's claims because they were directed only against Turkey, while the measures at issue were taken pursuant to a regional trade agreement between Turkey and the European Communities and therefore, according to Turkey, the European Communities should also have been a party to the dispute. The Panel found that it did not have

---

[31] Appellate Body Report, *EC – Bananas III*, para. 133.
[32] Panel Report, *EC – Bananas III (Article 21.5 – US)*, para. 7.34.
[33] Panel Report, *Korea – Dairy*, para. 7.13.

the authority to direct that a WTO Member be made a third party or otherwise participate in a panel proceeding, and/or to find that a claim was inadmissible in the absence of such participation. In this context, the Panel stated:

> It is relevant to recall the case law of the International Court of Justice (ICJ). The ICJ has not declined to exercise jurisdiction in cases similar to this one. For example in the ICJ *Military and Paramilitary Activities In and Against Nicaragua* case, the US argued that the application brought by Nicaragua was inadmissible because Nicaragua had not also impleaded third countries whose participation was essential. The ICJ dismissed this argument, saying:

>> There is no doubt that in appropriate circumstances the Court will decline . . . to exercise the jurisdiction conferred upon it where the legal interests of a State not party to the proceedings 'would not only be affected by a decision, but would form the very subject-matter of the decision' . . . Where however claims of a legal nature are made by an Applicant against a Respondent in proceedings before the Court, and made the subject of submissions, the Court has in principle merely to decide upon those submissions, with binding force for the parties only, and no other State . . . Other States which consider that they may be affected are free to institute separate proceedings, or to employ the procedure of intervention. *There is no trace, either in the Statute or in the practice of international tribunals, of an 'indispensable parties' rule* of the kind argued for by the United States, which would only be conceivable in parallel to a power, which the Court does not possess, to direct that a third State be made a party to proceedings.

> The ICJ *Phosphate Lands in Nauru* case concerned a proceeding initiated by Nauru against Australia alone in respect of the administration of a fund in favour of Nauru. The case was based on an international treaty whereby Australia, New Zealand and the United Kingdom were co-administrators of the fund. The ICJ exercised jurisdiction despite the absence of the two other administering authorities since the legal interest of those third countries (which could be affected by the result of the dispute) did not form the subject-matter of the dispute which was the legal relationship between Australia and Nauru. The ICJ stated:

>> In the present case, a finding . . . regarding the existence or the content of responsibility attributed to Australia by Nauru might well have implications for the legal situation of the two other States concerned, but no finding in respect of that legal situation will be needed as a basis for the Court's decision on Nauru's claims against Australia. Accordingly, the Court cannot decline to exercise its jurisdiction.

> In its separate opinion, Judge Shahabuddeen added:

>> To return to the question under examination, as to whether Australia may be sued alone, I consider that an affirmative answer is required for three reasons. First, the obligations of the three Governments under the Trusteeship Agreement were joint and several. Second, assuming that the obligations were joint, this did not by itself prevent Australia from being sued alone. Third, a possible judgment against Australia will not

amount to a judicial determination of responsibility of New Zealand and the United Kingdom.

The practice of the ICJ indicates that if a decision between the parties to the case can be reached without an examination of the position of the third state (i.e. in the WTO context, a Member) the ICJ will exercise its jurisdiction as between the parties. In the present dispute, there are no claims against the European Communities before us that would need to be determined in order for the Panel to assess the compatibility of the Turkish measures with the WTO Agreement.[249]

---

[249] We are aware that the ICJ has declined to exercise its jurisdiction when it concluded that the real 'subject-matter of the dispute' is the legal position of a third country which is not before it. In the *Monetary Gold Removed from Rome in 1943* case, Italy brought a case against the United Kingdom claiming it had priority over both the British and Albanian claims to the gold in question. However, Albania took no part in the dispute. The ICJ declined to exercise its jurisdiction because it would have been necessary to decide upon the international responsibility of Albania – the very subject-matter of the dispute – without her consent. (See [1954] ICJ Reports, p. 32.) In the *Case of East Timor*, Portugal complained against Australia concerning a treaty between Australia and Indonesia for the delimitation of the continental shelf between Australia and Indonesian-occupied East Timor. Indonesia had not been impleaded by Portugal and had not applied for permission to intervene as a third party. The ICJ declined to exercise its jurisdiction because it would have had to rule, as a prerequisite, on the lawfulness of the possession of East Timor by Indonesia, which was not present in the case. (See [1995] ICJ Reports, pp. 90–106)[34]

1.2.5 Failure to join cases

1.25 In *India – Patents (EC)*, India requested that the Panel find the EC complaint inadmissible, on the grounds that, since it was feasible for the European Communities to have brought its complaint simultaneously with an earlier US complaint on the same matter, the European Communities was required to do so. India argued that the successive complaints amounted to unwarranted harassment, created a risk of contradictory decisions, and wasted resources. The Panel recognized that India's concerns were 'serious', but stated that it could not make a ruling *ex aequo et bono*:

> While we recognize that these are serious concerns, this Panel is not an appropriate forum to address these issues.

---

[34] Panel Report, *Turkey – Textiles*, paras. 9.8–9.10 (citing *Military and Paramilitary Activities In and Against Nicaragua* (1984), 431; *Certain Phosphate Lands in Nauru* ('*Nauru*'), 1992 ICJ Reports, p. 240 (26 June); pp. 261–2; *Nauru* case; Separate Opinion of Judge Shahabuddeen, at 271).

According to Article 11 of the DSU, the Panel's role is to 'make an objective assessment of the matter before it, including an objective assessment of the facts of the case and the applicability and conformity with the relevant covered agreements'. Furthermore, under Article 3.2 of the DSU, the purpose of the panel process is to 'clarify the existing provisions of [covered] agreements in accordance with customary rules of interpretation of public international law'. The same paragraph goes on to state that 'Recommendation and rulings of the DSB cannot add to or diminish the rights and obligations provided in the covered agreements', and Article 19.2 also states that '. . . in their findings and recommendations, the panel and the Appellate Body cannot add to or diminish the rights and obligations provided in the covered agreements'. Thus, the Panel is required to base its findings on the language of the DSU. We simply cannot make a ruling *ex aequo et bono* to address a systemic concern divorced from explicit language of the DSU.[35]

1.2.6 Failure to exhaust local remedies

In *US – Norwegian Salmon AD*, a GATT case, the United States argued that **1.26** the failure of Norway and/or Norwegian exporters to raise certain issues before the US investigating authority in the course of the underlying anti-dumping investigation precluded Norway from raising those issues before the Panel. In the course of the proceeding, the United States and Norway engaged in a detailed exchange of arguments regarding the scope of the general international law rule regarding exhaustion of local remedies, including whether it applied only in cases where a State was bringing a claim on behalf of one or more of its nationals.[36] However, the GATT Panel ultimately considered it unnecessary to rule on the applicability of the exhaustion of local remedies rule in that case, because the United States clarified that this was not the basis for its argument:

> The United States had argued that the rationale behind this concept of 'exhaustion of administrative remedies' was akin to the rationale behind the public international law doctrine of exhaustion of local remedies. However, when Norway argued against application of the legal doctrine of exhaustion of local remedies in this dispute, the United States had clarified that it had not sought application of this doctrine. Consequently, the issue of application of the doctrine of exhaustion of local remedies to dispute settlement under the Agreement was not before the Panel.[37]

In *Argentina – Textiles and Apparel*, the United States claimed that Argentina **1.27** violated Article II of the GATT by applying duties on certain products in excess of its bound rate on those products, which was 35 per cent. Argentina argued

---

[35] Panel Report, *India – Patents (EC)*, paras. 7.22–7.23.
[36] GATT Panel Report, *US – Norwegian Salmon AD*, paras. 33, 37–9, 45–7.
[37] *Ibid.*, para. 348.

that, if duties in excess of that rate had been paid, there was a domestic mechanism in place to challenge any such customs determination. The Panel rejected Argentina's defence. Without framing the issue in terms of the 'exhaustion of local remedies', the Panel stated:

> Article II of GATT imposes an unconditional obligation on a WTO Member to offer to other Members treatment not less favourable than that provided for in its Schedule. A Member violates this obligation, regardless of whether that Member provides a remedy for such violation in its domestic legal system. Notwithstanding how efficient such domestic court system may be, until the court system acts the Member is in violation of its WTO obligations. Moreover, it is not certain that the violation will ever be corrected since such correction is conditional on a decision by the Argentine importer or the holder of the clearance documents to initiate a domestic action.[38]

1.28 The Panel in *US – Section 211 Appropriations Act* referred to the exhaustion of local remedies rule in the context of interpreting Article 43 of the TRIPS Agreement. The first sentence of this provision requires that Members make civil judicial procedures available to intellectual property rights holders to enforce their rights. The Panel considered that such procedures must be 'effective' in terms of the enforcement of intellectual property rights. In the Panel's view, this interpretation was analogous to and consistent with the exhaustion of local remedies rule under general international law:

> Although the rule of exhaustion of local remedies is not applicable in this case, as the interpretation and application of a treaty between states is what is primarily at issue rather than the infringement of rights of individuals, it bears pointing out that in cases involving this rule it has been universally recognized that the remedies available under national law must be 'effective' in nature, i.e. they must open the possibility of a genuine remedy for the (private) complainant. See Jennings and Watts, eds., *Oppenheim's International Law*, 9th edn, Vol. I, pp. 522–566; and Ian Brownlie, *Principles of Public International Law*, 5th edn, p. 500–501.[39]

1.2.7 *Forum non conveniens*[*]

1.29 In *EC – Chicken Cuts*, the Panel examined an issue relating to tariff classification for customs purposes. In that case, the respondent had suggested to the complainants that the dispute be taken to the World Customs Organization to the extent that it concerned matters of classification. In responding to a request for information from the Panel, the WCO itself suggested that, prior to the WTO

---

[38] Panel Report, *Argentina – Textiles and Apparel*, para. 6.68.
[39] Panel Report, *US – Section 211 Appropriations Act*, footnote 131.
[*] See also the cases in Section 1.2.1. ('Restrictions on admissibility not lightly inferred') and Section 1.3.2 ('Implied restrictions arising from overlapping jurisdictional competencies among different bodies').

Panel making its decision, the parties should follow the WCO dispute settlement procedures. The Panel stated:

> We understand that, once seized of a matter, Article 11 prevents a panel from abdicating its responsibility to the DSB. In other words, in the context of the present case, we lack the authority to refer the dispute before us to the WCO or to any other body.
>
> . . .
>
> The Panel is mindful of the respective jurisdiction and competence of the WCO and the WTO and, in fact, we specifically raised this issue with the parties during the course of these proceedings. Nevertheless, we consider that we have been mandated by the DSB in this dispute to determine whether the European Communities has violated Article II of the GATT 1994 with respect to the products at issue.[40]

In *Mexico – Taxes on Soft Drinks*, Mexico requested that the Panel decline to **1.30** exercise its jurisdiction in favour of an Arbitral Panel under Chapter Twenty of the NAFTA. In this regard, Mexico argued that the US claims were linked to a broader dispute between the two countries related to trade in sweeteners under the NAFTA. In Mexico's view, under those circumstances, it would not be appropriate for the Panel to make findings on the United States' claims under the WTO agreements. In Mexico's opinion, only a panel established under the NAFTA would be in a position to 'address the dispute as a whole'. The Panel declined Mexico's request. In the course of its analysis, the Panel stated:

> Even assuming, for the sake of argument, that a panel might be entitled in some circumstances to find that a dispute would more appropriately be pursued before another tribunal, this Panel believes that the factors to be taken into account should be those that relate to the particular dispute. We understand Mexico's argument to be that the United States' claims in the present case should be pursued under the NAFTA, not because that would lead to a better treatment of this particular claim, but because it would allow Mexico to pursue another, albeit related, claim against the United States. The Panel fears that if such a matter were to be considered then there would be no practical limit to the factors which could legitimately be taken into account, and the decision to exercise jurisdiction would become political rather than legal in nature.[41]

1.2.8 *Res judicata*

See Section 13.5.3 for WTO jurisprudence relating to the concept of *res* **1.31** *judicata*.

---

[40] Panel Report, *EC – Chicken Cuts (Brazil)*, paras. 7.56, 7.59.
[41] Panel Report, *Mexico – Taxes on Soft Drinks*, para. 7.17.

1.3 Jurisdiction over claims

WTO adjudicators have equated a panel's 'terms of reference' with the concept of 'jurisdiction',[42] and have consistently applied the general rule that an adjudicator may not rule on claims falling outside of its subject-matter jurisdiction. In several cases, panels and the Appellate Body have rejected the view that implied limitations on their jurisdiction could be inferred from the coexistence of other bodies with overlapping jurisdictional competencies. Panels and the Appellate Body have articulated and acted on the principle that they are competent to rule on issues relating to their own jurisdiction, that they must address certain fundamental jurisdictional issues on their own initiative in the absence of any objection from a party, that issues of jurisdiction are of such a fundamental nature as to preclude an adjudicator from rejecting a jurisdictional objection on the grounds that it was not raised in a timely manner, and that issues going to the merits of a claim should be addressed on the merits and not as preliminary jurisdictional issues.

1.3.1 The general rule governing claims outside of a tribunal's subject-matter jurisdiction

1.32 In *Brazil – Desiccated Coconut*, the Appellate Body explained that a panel's terms of reference establish the 'jurisdiction' of the panel by defining the precise claims at issue in the dispute:

> A panel's terms of reference are important for two reasons. First, terms of reference fulfil an important due process objective – they give the parties and third parties sufficient information concerning the claims at issue in the dispute in order to allow them an opportunity to respond to the complainant's case. Second, they establish the jurisdiction of the panel by defining the precise claims at issue in the dispute.[43]

1.33 In *India – Patents (US)*, the Appellate Body found that the Panel exceeded its 'jurisdiction' by considering the United States' claim that India violated Article 63 of the TRIPS Agreement – a claim that had not been included in the US panel request, and which was hence outside of the Panel's terms of reference. The Appellate Body stated:

---

[42] In the context of WTO dispute settlement, Articles 6 and 7 of the DSU are the provisions that govern a panel's 'terms of reference': Article 6 provides that the complainant's request for the establishment of a panel shall, among other things, identify the specific measures at issue and the legal basis of the complaint sufficient to present the problem clearly; Article 7 then provides that a panel's 'terms of reference' are to examine, in light of the relevant provisions in the WTO 'covered agreement(s)' cited by the parties to the dispute, the matter referred to in the complainant's panel request. The DSU does not contain the term 'jurisdiction'. However, panels and the Appellate Body have equated a panel's resulting terms of reference with its 'jurisdiction'.

[43] Appellate Body Report, *Brazil – Desiccated Coconut*, p. 21.

The jurisdiction of a panel is established by that panel's terms of reference, which are governed by Article 7 of the DSU. A panel may consider only those claims that it has the authority to consider under its terms of reference. A panel cannot assume jurisdiction that it does not have. In this case, Article 63 was not within the Panel's jurisdiction, as defined by its terms of reference. Therefore, the Panel had no authority to consider the alternative claim by the United States under Article 63.[44]

In *EC and certain member States – Large Civil Aircraft*, the Panel ruled that it did **1.34** not have the 'jurisdiction' to make findings with respect to a bilateral agreement between the United States and the European Communities, as it was not a covered agreement:

> Article 7.2 of the DSU requires panels to 'address the relevant provisions in any covered Agreement or Agreements cited by the parties to the dispute.' The 'covered Agreements' cited by the United States in document WT/DS316/2 [the panel request] include the DSU, the GATT 1994 and the SCM Agreement. As the 1992 Agreement is not a covered Agreement cited by the United States in document WT/DS316/2, or contained in the list of covered Agreements in Appendix 1 to the DSU, or one of the instruments included in the GATT 1994, we do not have jurisdiction to determine the rights and obligations of the parties under the 1992 Agreement.[45]

In the *EC – Bananas* dispute, the parties had recourse to arbitration, outside of **1.35** the normal DSU rules and procedures, to resolve certain technical issues relating to the European Communities' implementation of the DSB rulings and recommendations in that dispute. The Arbitrator's limited mandate was defined in an Annex to the so-called Doha Waiver. The Arbitrator found that a particular claim fell outside of the scope of its mandate, and stated:

> [T]he jurisdiction of the Arbitrator is governed by the terms of the Annex. That mandate is limited, specifically, to determining whether the 'envisaged rebinding would result in at least maintaining total market access for MFN banana suppliers'. The Arbitrator is not free to expand its mandate. It must find its jurisdiction in the instrument establishing its authority. There is no indication that the Arbitrator may determine other matters … The Arbitrator finds, therefore, that this claim by Honduras, Panama and Nicaragua is beyond its jurisdiction.[46]

In *Mexico – Soft Drinks*, Mexico argued that the United States' alleged violation **1.36** of the NAFTA called into question the applicability of Mexico's WTO obligations towards the United States in the context of that dispute. Specifically, Mexico argued that the Panel should find the United States' claims inadmissible on the basis of the principle, articulated by the ICJ in the *Factory at Chorzów*

---

[44] Appellate Body Report, *India – Patents (US)*, para. 92.
[45] Panel Report, *EC and certain member States – Large Civil Aircraft*, para. 7.89.
[46] Award by the Arbitrator, *EC – The ACP–EC Partnership Agreement*, para. 46.

case, that a party cannot avail itself of the fact that the other has not fulfilled some obligation, or has not had recourse to some means of redress, if the former party has, by some illegal act, prevented the latter from fulfilling the obligation in question, or from having recourse to the tribunal which would have been open to it.[47] The Appellate Body rejected this argument on the grounds that it would lead to panels and the Appellate Body having to adjudicate non-WTO disputes:

> [T]his would entail a determination whether the United States has acted consistently or inconsistently with its NAFTA obligations. We see no basis in the DSU for panels and the Appellate Body to adjudicate non-WTO disputes. Article 3.2 of the DSU states that the WTO dispute settlement system 'serves to preserve the rights and obligations of Members under the *covered agreements*, and to clarify the existing provisions of *those agreements*' (emphasis added). Accepting Mexico's interpretation would imply that the WTO dispute settlement system could be used to determine rights and obligations outside the covered agreements.[48]

1.3.2 Implied restrictions arising from overlapping jurisdictional competencies among different bodies[*]

1.37 In *US – Shrimp*, the Appellate Body examined whether a US trade measure relating to the conservation of exhaustible natural resources was justified under Article XX(g) of the GATT. The Appellate Body noted that WTO Members had created the WTO Committee on Trade and Environment, whose terms of reference are to identify the relationship between trade measures and environmental measures, and to make appropriate recommendations on whether any modifications of WTO provisions are required, including with respect to the surveillance of trade measures for environmental purposes. None of the parties argued that the Appellate Body was precluded from considering issues pending elsewhere (*lis alibi pendens*), and the Appellate Body stated:

> Pending any specific recommendations by the CTE to WTO Members on the issues raised in its terms of reference, and in the absence up to now of any agreed amendments or modifications to the substantive provisions of the GATT 1994 and the *WTO Agreement* generally, we must fulfill our responsibility in this specific case, which is to interpret the existing language of the chapeau of Article XX by examining its ordinary meaning, in light of its context and object and purpose in order to determine whether the United States measure at issue qualifies for justification under Article XX.[49]

---

[47] Permanent Court of International Justice, *Factory at Chorzów (Germany* v. *Poland)*, Jurisdiction, 1927, PCIJ, Series A, No. 9, p. 31.
[48] Appellate Body Report, *Mexico – Soft Drinks*, para. 56.
[49] Appellate Body Report, *US – Shrimp*, para. 155.
[*] See also the cases in Section 1.2.1. ('Restrictions on admissibility not lightly inferred') and Section 1.2.7. ('*Forum non conveniens*').

In *Brazil – Aircraft*, the Panel was called upon to examine Article 27.4 of the **1.38** SCM Agreement, which provides in relevant part that a developing country Member shall eliminate its export subsidies within a period shorter than that provided for in that provision 'when the use of such export subsidies is inconsistent with its development needs'. The Panel considered that the WTO's SCM Committee would be 'far better equipped to perform this type of examination' as compared with a panel, but it was unable to conclude that this clause was not susceptible of application by a dispute settlement panel. The Panel stated:

> In considering this issue, we note that this element of Article 27.4 is troubling from the perspective of a panel . . . We recognize that as written this clause is mandatory, and a conclusion that this clause was not susceptible of application by a panel would be inconsistent with the principle of effective treaty interpretation. On the other hand, an examination as to whether export subsidies are inconsistent with a developing country Member's development needs is an inquiry of a peculiarly economic and political nature, and notably ill-suited to review by a panel whose function is fundamentally legal.[239] Further, the SCM Agreement provides panels with no guidance with respect to the criteria to be applied in performing this examination. We consider that it is the developing country Member itself which is best positioned to identify its development needs and to assess whether its export subsidies are consistent with those needs. Thus, in applying this provision we consider that panels should give substantial deference to the views of the developing country Member in question.

> ---
> [239] It may be noted that under Article 27.14, '[t]he Committee [on Subsidies and Countervailing Measures] shall, upon request by an interested Member, undertake a review of a specific export subsidy practice of a developing country Member to examine whether the practice is in conformity with its development needs.' In our view, a body such as the Committee is far better equipped to perform this type of examination than is a panel.[50]

In *India – Quantitative Restrictions*, India argued that, in view of the competence **1.39** of the WTO's Balance-of-Payments (BOP) Committee and the General Council with respect to BOP restrictions under Article XVIII:12 of the GATT and the BOP Understanding, the Panel erred in finding that it was competent to review India's justification for its BOP restrictions. The Appellate Body rejected India's argument. The Appellate Body considered that the competence of the Panel to review all aspects of BOP restrictions had to be determined in light of the wording of the relevant legal provisions in the WTO agreements. With respect to India's argument relating to 'institutional balance', the Appellate Body summarized India's position as follows:

---
[50] Panel Report, *Brazil – Aircraft*, para. 7.89.

In support of its claim of legal error, India argues that there is a principle of institutional balance which requires panels, in determining the scope of their competence, to take into account the competence conferred upon other organs of the WTO. According to India, the drafters of the *WTO Agreement* created a complex institutional structure under which various bodies are empowered to take binding decisions on related matters. These bodies must cooperate to achieve the objectives of the WTO, and can only do so if each exercises its competence with due regard to the competence of all other bodies. In order to preserve a proper institutional balance between the judicial and the political organs of the WTO with regard to matters relating to balance-of-payments restrictions, review of the justification of such measures must be left to the relevant political organs, i.e. the BOP Committee and the General Council. In light of the powers attributed to these organs under Article XVIII:12 of the GATT 1994 and the *BOP Understanding*, panels should, according to India, refrain from reviewing the justification of balance-of-payments measures under Article XVIII:B.

During the oral hearing, India conceded that the principle of institutional balance, as defined by it, does not flow from a general principle of international law. India argues, however, that, while there is no explicit textual basis for this principle in the *WTO Agreement*, it is nevertheless a principle of WTO law.[51]

The Appellate Body responded to India's argument regarding a 'principle of institutional balance' by emphasizing the absence of any conflict between the competence of panels, on the one hand, and that of the BOP Committee and the General Council on the other:

We are cognizant of the competence of the BOP Committee and the General Council with respect to balance-of-payments restrictions under Article XVIII:12 of the GATT 1994 and the *BOP Understanding*. However, we see no conflict between that competence and the competence of panels. Moreover, we are convinced that, in considering the justification of balance-of-payments restrictions, panels should take into account the deliberations and conclusions of the BOP Committee, as did the panel in *Korea – Beef*.

We agree with the Panel that the review by panels of the justification of balance-of-payments restrictions would not render redundant the competence of the BOP Committee and the General Council. The Panel correctly pointed out that the BOP Committee and panels have different functions, and that the BOP Committee procedures and the dispute settlement procedures differ in nature, scope, timing and type of outcome.[52]

1.40 In *Turkey – Textiles*, the Panel concluded that it could assess the WTO-consistency of any specific measure adopted in connection with the formation of a customs union, but not the WTO-consistency of a customs union as such. The Panel considered that the second issue would generally be a matter for the WTO's Committee on Regional Trade Agreements since it involves a broad

---

[51] Appellate Body Report, *India – Quantitative Restrictions*, paras. 98–9.   [52] *Ibid.*, paras. 103–4.

multilateral assessment of matters which concern the WTO Membership as a whole. On appeal, the Appellate Body noted that this finding had not been appealed, and was therefore not before it, but recalled its finding in *India – Quantitative Restrictions*:

> The Panel maintained that 'it is arguable' that panels do not have jurisdiction to assess the overall compatibility of a customs union with the requirements of Article XXIV. We are not called upon in this appeal to address this issue, but we note in this respect our ruling in *India – Quantitative Restrictions on Imports of Agricultural, Textile and Industrial Products* on the jurisdiction of panels to review the justification of balance-of-payments restrictions under Article XVIII:B of the GATT 1994.[53]

Also in *Turkey – Textiles*, the Panel considered its relationship to the WTO's **1.41** Textiles Monitoring Board, a body established pursuant to the WTO Agreement on Textiles and Clothing. The Panel rejected the respondent's argument 'that the [WTO's Textiles Monitoring Board] should have been seized of the matter under Article 8 of the Agreement on Textiles and Clothing (ATC) prior to its referral to the DSB',[54] and found that the matter before it was 'not a matter covered by the provisions of the ATC, and could not fall under the exclusive jurisdiction of the TMB'.[55]

1.3.3 Tribunal's duty to address jurisdictional issues *proprio motu*

In *US – 1916 Act*, the Appellate Body stated: **1.42**

> We note that it is a widely accepted rule that an international tribunal is entitled to consider the issue of its own jurisdiction on its own initiative, and to satisfy itself that it has jurisdiction in any case that comes before it. See, for example, *Case Concerning the Administration of the Prince von Pless (Preliminary Objection)* (1933) PCIJ Ser. A/B, No. 52, p. 15; Individual Opinion of President Sir A. McNair, *Anglo-Iranian Oil Co. Case (Preliminary Objection)* (1952) ICJ Rep., p. 116; Separate Opinion of Judge Sir H. Lauterpacht in *Case of Certain Norwegian Loans* (1957) ICJ Rep., p. 43; and Dissenting Opinion of Judge Sir H. Lauterpacht in the *Interhandel Case (Preliminary Objections)* (1959) ICJ Rep., p. 104. See also M. O. Hudson, *The Permanent Court of International Justice 1920–1942* (MacMillan, 1943), pp. 418–419; G. Fitzmaurice, *The Law and Procedure of the International Court of Justice*, Vol. 2 (Grotius Publications, 1986), pp. 530, 755–758; S. Rosenne, *The Law and Practice of the International Court* (Martinus Nijhoff, 1985), pp. 467–468; L. A. Podesta Costa and J. M. Ruda, *Derecho Internacional Público*, Vol. 2 (Tipográfica, 1985), p. 438; M. Diez de Velasco Vallejo, *Instituciones de Derecho International Público* (Tecnos, 1997), p. 759. See also the award of the Iran–United States Claims Tribunal in *Marks & Umman v. Iran*, 8 Iran–

---

[53] Appellate Body Report, *Turkey – Textiles*, para. 60.
[54] Panel Report, *Turkey – Textiles*, para. 9.15.   [55] *Ibid.*, para. 9.85.

United States CTR, pp. 296–97 (1985) (Award No. 53-458-3); J. J. van Hof, *Commentary on the UNCITRAL Arbitration Rules: The Application by the Iran–US Claims Tribunal* (Kluwer, 1991), pp. 149–150; and Rule 41(2) of the rules applicable to ICSID Arbitration Tribunals: International Centre for Settlement of Investment Disputes, Rules of Procedure for Arbitration Proceedings (Arbitration Rules).[56]

1.43 In *US – Section 110(5) Copyright Act (Article 25)*, the parties agreed to have recourse to arbitration under Article 25 of the DSU. The Arbitrators stated:

> As recalled by the Appellate Body in *United States – Anti-Dumping Act of 1916*, it is a widely accepted rule that an international tribunal is entitled to consider the issue of its own jurisdiction on its own initiative. The Arbitrators believe that this principle applies also to arbitration bodies.[24] In case there be any question as to the jurisdiction of the Arbitrators to deal with this dispute, we provide brief reasons for our conclusion that we do have the necessary jurisdiction.
>
> ───────────
> [24] This is evidenced by Article 21 of the Optional Rules of the Permanent Court of Arbitration for arbitrations involving international organizations and States. See, Permanent Court of Arbitration: Optional Rules for Arbitration involving International Organizations and States, effective 1 July 1996, International Bureau of the Permanent Court of Arbitration, The Hague, The Netherlands.[57]

1.44 In *Mexico – Corn Syrup (Article 21.5 – US)*, the Appellate Body indicated that panels must deal with issues of jurisdiction, if necessary on their own motion:

> We believe that a panel comes under a duty to address issues in at least two instances. First, as a matter of due process, and the proper exercise of the judicial function, panels are required to address issues that are put before them by the parties to a dispute. Second, panels have to address and dispose of certain issues of a fundamental nature, even if the parties to the dispute remain silent on those issues. In this regard, we have previously observed that '[t]he vesting of jurisdiction in a panel is a fundamental prerequisite for lawful panel proceedings.' For this reason, panels cannot simply ignore issues which go to the root of their jurisdiction – that is, to their authority to deal with and dispose of matters. Rather, panels must deal with such issues – if necessary, on their own motion – in order to satisfy themselves that they have authority to proceed.[58]

1.45 In *US – Anti-Dumping Measures on Oil Country Tubular Goods*, the Panel concluded that Mexico failed to set forth a claim regarding USDOC practice in sunset reviews in its request for establishment of a panel in this dispute, and therefore that this purported claim was beyond the scope of its terms of reference, and would make no findings on it. The Panel stated that 'while it is

[56] Appellate Body Report, *US – 1916 Act*, footnote 30.
[57] Award of the Arbitrators, *US – Section 110(5) Copyright Act (Article 25)*, para. 2.1.
[58] Appellate Body Report, *Mexico – Corn Syrup (Article 21.5 – US)*, para. 36 (citing Appellate Body Report, *US – 1916 Act*, para. 54).

true that the United States did not make a preliminary objection on this matter, we considered it appropriate, and indeed, necessary, to raise this issue on our own motion and resolve it'.[59]

Along the same lines, the Panel in *EC – IT Products* stated that panels **1.46** 'may choose to deal with issues on their own motion where it considers that they go to the heart of their jurisdiction, to satisfy themselves that they may proceed'.[60]

In *US – Clove Cigarettes*, both parties considered that the Panel would not be **1.47** exceeding its jurisdiction if it included regular cigarettes in the 'likeness' analysis under Article 2.1 of the TBT Agreement and Article III:4 of the GATT, notwithstanding that Indonesia's panel request specified that the imported and domestic 'like products' in this case were clove cigarettes and menthol cigarettes. The Panel stated:

> In spite of the parties' views, we consider that it is necessary for us to examine this issue as it touches upon our jurisdiction. In this respect, the Appellate Body has cautioned panels that there are certain inherent powers to their adjudicative function and that 'panels have the right to determine whether they have jurisdiction in a given case, as well as to determine the scope of their jurisdiction.' The Appellate Body has also clarified that 'it is a widely accepted rule that an international tribunal is entitled to consider the issue of its own jurisdiction on its own initiative' We shall therefore examine whether we would be exceeding our terms of reference if we include regular cigarettes in the likeness analysis.[61]

In *EC and certain member States – Large Civil Aircraft*, the United States **1.48** challenged not only individual instances of launch aid/member State financing (LA/MSF), but also what it termed the LA/MSF 'programme' as a whole. The Panel agreed with the European Communities that the United States failed to demonstrate the existence of an unwritten LA/MSF 'programme' On appeal, the Appellate Body found that the alleged measure was not actually identified in the panel request, and therefore fell outside of the Panel's terms of reference. The Appellate Body made this finding in the absence of the European Communities having raised this issue, and stated:

> Although the European Union did not raise procedural objections, under Article 6.2 of the DSU, against the United States' challenge to an unwritten LA/MSF Programme before the Panel or in its appellee's submission, 'certain issues going to the *jurisdiction* of a panel are so fundamental that they may be considered at

---

[59] Panel Report, *US – Anti-Dumping Measures on Oil Country Tubular Goods*, para. 7.20.
[60] Panel Report, *EC – IT Products*, para. 7.196.
[61] Panel Report, *US – Clove Cigarettes*, para. 134 (citing Appellate Body Report, *Mexico – Taxes on Soft Drinks*, para. 45; Appellate Body Report, *US – 1916 Act*, footnote 30 to para. 54).

any stage in a proceeding.' In this case, we have deemed it necessary to consider these issues on our own motion.[62]

1.49 In *China – Broiler Products*, the Panel recalled that 'a Panel must satisfy itself that the claims before it are properly within its terms of reference even in the absence of objections from the parties'.[63]

1.3.4 Timeliness of jurisdictional objections

1.50 In *US – 1916 Act*, the Appellate Body agreed with the Panel that it had still had to respond to certain jurisdictional objections, even if made at a late stage of the proceeding:

> We agree with the Panel that the interim review was not an appropriate stage in the Panel's proceedings to raise objections to the Panel's jurisdiction for the first time. An objection to jurisdiction should be raised as early as possible and panels must ensure that the requirements of due process are met. However, we also agree with the Panel's consideration that 'some issues of jurisdiction may be of such a nature that they have to be addressed by the Panel at any time.' We do not share the European Communities' view that objections to the jurisdiction of a panel are appropriately regarded as simply 'procedural objections'. The vesting of jurisdiction in a panel is a fundamental prerequisite for lawful panel proceedings. We, therefore, see no reason to accept the European Communities' argument that we must reject the United States' appeal because the United States did not raise its jurisdictional objection before the Panel in a timely manner.[64]

1.3.5 Jurisdictional issues versus issues going to the merits

1.51 In *Australia – Apples*, the Appellate Body found that the Panel erred by conflating the question of whether certain measures were identified in the panel request (and hence within its jurisdiction), with the question of the merits of any claim:

> The Panel, therefore, seems to have understood that the question of whether the 17 measures identified in the panel request *can violate*, or *cause the violation of*, the obligation in Annex C(1)(a) and Article 8 of the *SPS Agreement* was a jurisdictional question. We disagree with this approach by the Panel. For a matter to be within a panel's terms of reference – in the sense of Articles 6.2 and 7.1 of the DSU – a complainant must identify 'the specific measures at issue' and the 'legal basis of the complaint sufficient to present the problem clearly' ... Article 6.2 of the DSU does not impose any additional requirement, as the Panel's analysis implies, that a

---

[62] Appellate Body Report, *EC and certain member States – Large Civil Aircraft*, para. 791 (citing Appellate Body Report, *US – Carbon Steel*, para. 123).
[63] Panel Report, *China – Broiler Products*, para. 7.515.
[64] Appellate Body Report, *US – 1916 Act*, para. 54.

complainant must, in its request for establishment of a panel, demonstrate that the identified measure at issue *causes the violation of*, or *can violate*, the relevant obligation.

In this dispute, the Panel's analysis under Article 6.2 should have been confined to determining what New Zealand had identified as the specific measures at issue and, separately, what New Zealand had identified as the legal basis for its complaint (its claims). The Panel had already found in its preliminary ruling that New Zealand's panel request identified the 17 measures, and Annex C(1)(a) and Article 8 of the *SPS Agreement* as the basis for New Zealand's claims, and that, therefore, this matter was within the Panel's terms of reference.

By contrast, the question of whether the measures identified in the panel request can violate, or cause the violation of, the obligation in Annex C(1)(a) and Article 8 is a substantive issue to be addressed and resolved on the merits.[65]

Along the same lines, the Panel in *EC – Fasteners (China)* concluded that certain **1.52** objections went to the merits rather than jurisdiction, and 'must be resolved as part of the substance of the case, rather than a matter to be assumed in the context of resolving a preliminary objection'.[66] The Panel explained that '[w]hether the description of the claim makes legal sense is something to be scrutinized by the Panel in the course of the panel proceedings, on the basis of the arguments developed by the parties and the evidence presented'.[67]

In *China – Rare Earths*, China requested that the Panel issue a preliminary ruling **1.53** on whether certain obligations in its Accession Protocol were subject to the general exceptions contained in Article XX of the GATT. The Panel declined China's preliminary ruling request because, *inter alia*, it did not relate to an issue of procedure or jurisdiction:

> At the first substantive meeting with the parties, the Panel informed the parties that it would not issue a preliminary ruling on this matter. The Panel stated that the reasons were that the request concerned a complex issue of substance as opposed to an issue of procedure or jurisdiction and the Panel required sufficient time to carefully consider the extensive argumentation of the parties and third parties. The Panel indicated that it would address the issue in its Reports.[68]

---

[65] Appellate Body Report, *Australia – Apples*, paras. 423–5.
[66] Panel Report, *EC – Fasteners (China)*, para. 7.44.   [67] *Ibid.*, para. 7.45.
[68] Panel Report, *China – Rare Earths*, para. 1.14.

2

ATTRIBUTION OF CONDUCT

2.1 Introduction

This chapter reviews relevant WTO jurisprudence on the attribution of conduct **2.1**
to a State.[1] In *The Development of International Law by the European Court of
Human Rights*, Merrills noted that '[t]he Court is frequently faced with the
problem of deciding whether conduct of which the applicant complains can be
regarded as attributable to the respondent State. This issue, the scope of State
responsibility, is, of course, prominent in general international law.'[2] General
international law concepts and principles are codified in the International Law
Commission's Articles on the Responsibility of States for Internationally Wrongful Acts ('ILC Articles on State Responsibility'). The WTO agreements contain
several provisions relating to the attribution of conduct to the State.[3] Some of
those provisions contain concepts that are similar to those found in the ILC
Articles on State Responsibility, and for the most part the WTO agreements are
silent in respect of issues regarding the attribution of conduct to the State. It has
been said that 'there is no major *lex specialis* on attribution' in WTO law.[4] This
chapter reviews statements by WTO adjudicators of wider applicability on: (i) the
conduct of organs of a State (including the executive branch, the legislative

---

[1] For commentary, see S. M. Villalpando, 'Attribution of Conduct to the State: How the Rules of
State Responsibility may Be Applied Within the WTO Dispute Settlement System' (2002) 5(2)
Journal of International Economic Law 393; Y.N. Hodu, 'The Concept of Attribution and State
Responsibility in the WTO Treaty System' (2007) 4(3) *Manchester Journal of International
Economic Law* 62; and J. Bohanes and I. Sandford, 'The (Untapped) Potential of WTO Rules
to Discipline Private Trade-Restrictive Conduct' (2008) Social Science Research Network, at
papers.ssrn.com/sol3/papers.cfm?abstract_id=1166623.

[2] J. G. Merrills, *The Development of International Law by the European Court of Human Rights*
(Manchester University Press, 1988), p. 109.

[3] These provisions include, among others: (i) Article XXIV;12 of the GATT and paragraphs 13 and
14 of the Understanding on the Interpretation of Article XXIV of the GATT (measures taken by
regional or local governments); (ii) Article XVII of the GATT (State trading enterprises); and (iii)
Article 1.1(a)(1) of the SCM Agreement (financial contributions by governments, public bodies,
and any private bodies they entrust or direct).

[4] Villalpando, 'Attribution of Conduct to the State', p. 395.

branch, the judicial branch, government agencies, individual government officials, and sub-federal governments); (ii) the conduct of entities exercising elements of governmental authority; (iii) the conduct of private parties directed or controlled by a State; and (iv) conduct taken in the context of a customs union.

2.2 Conduct of organs of a State

2.2 Article 4 of the ILC Articles on State Responsibility, entitled 'Conduct of organs of a State', reads:

> 1. The conduct of any State organ shall be considered an act of that State under international law, whether the organ exercises legislative, executive, judicial or any other functions, whatever position it holds in the organization of the State, and whatever its character as an organ of the central Government or of a territorial unit of the State.
> 2. An organ includes any person or entity which has that status in accordance with the internal law of the State.

WTO panels and the Appellate Body have consistently affirmed that States are responsible for the acts or omissions of their executive branch, legislative branch, judicial branch, individual government officials, and sub-federal governments. In several cases, panels and the Appellate Body have found that the respondent was responsible for discriminatory treatment ensuing from decisions taken by the legislative or judicial organs of a State, notwithstanding that the executive branch and/or agencies thereof had made or were continuing to make efforts to remove or limit such discrimination.

2.2.1 Responsibility for all State organs and branches of government

2.3 The Panel in *US – 1916 Act* recalled that 'the responsibility of the Members under international law applies irrespective of the "branch of government" at the origin of the action having international repercussions'.[5]

2.4 In *US – Countervailing and Anti-Dumping Measures (China)* (DS449), the Panel examined a claim under Article X:3(b) of the GATT, which provides, *inter alia*, that each Member must maintain judicial or other tribunals for the review of certain actions taken by administrative agencies, and that their decisions must be implemented by such agencies. The parties disagreed on whether this obligation precludes the legislative branch from enacting legislation to supersede a decision reached by such a tribunal. In addressing this issue, the Panel stated:

> [W]e consider that formulating the issue so broadly, e.g. in terms of the applicability of Article X:3(b) to the 'legislative branch', may lead to confusion,

---

[5] Panel Report, *US – 1916 Act (Japan)*, para. 5.10.

insofar as it could be taken to suggest that what is legally relevant is the *source* of action – i.e. the legislature – rather than the *nature* of the action – i.e. the nature of the legislative action at issue. The United States is not arguing that it is not responsible for the actions of the legislature, and it is well established in WTO jurisprudence that, consistent with principles of general international law, a Member is responsible for the conduct of all State organs, including the legislature.[6]

2.2.2 Executive organs

In *US – Corrosion-Resistant Steel Sunset Review*, the Appellate Body indicated **2.5** that any act or omission attributable to a State can be a measure of that Member for purposes of dispute settlement proceedings, and observed that those 'acts or omissions that are so attributable are, in the usual case, the acts or omissions of the organs of the state, including those of the executive branch'.[7] The Appellate Body stated that '[b]oth specific determinations made by a Member's executive agencies and regulations issued by its executive branch can constitute acts attributable to that Member'.[8]

2.2.3 Legislative organs

In *US – Gasoline*, the Appellate Body found that the measure at issue was **2.6** applied in a manner that constituted arbitrary or unjustifiable discrimination within the meaning of Article XX of the GATT. In that case, the US Environmental Protection Agency (EPA) had previously made a proposal to change the measure in a way that would have removed or limited the discrimination at issue, but the US Congress subsequently enacted legislation denying the funding necessary to make that change. The Appellate Body stated:

> [The record of this case] does not reveal what, if any, efforts had been taken by the United States to enter into appropriate procedures in cooperation with the governments of Venezuela and Brazil so as to mitigate the administrative problems pleaded by the United States. The fact that the United States Congress might have intervened, as it did later intervene, in the process by denying funding, is beside the point: the United States, of course, carries responsibility for actions of both the executive and legislative departments of government.[9]

2.2.4 Judicial organs

In *US – Shrimp*, the Appellate Body examined a US ban on the importation of **2.7** shrimp that did not comply with certain US requirements relating to the method

---

[6] Panel Report, *US – Countervailing and Anti-Dumping Duties (China)*, para. 7.250 (citing Appellate Body Report, *US – Gasoline*, p. 28; Appellate Body Report, *US – Shrimp*, para. 173).
[7] Appellate Body Report, *US – Corrosion-Resistant Steel Sunset Review*, para. 81.
[8] *Ibid.*, footnote 79.   [9] Appellate Body Report, *US – Gasoline*, p. 28.

of harvesting. The measure initially applied only to fourteen countries, which were given a period of three years to adjust to the requirement. However, certain US court decisions subsequently directed the US Department of State to apply the ban on a worldwide basis, and as a consequence, all other countries were given significantly shorter 'phase-in' periods to adjust to those requirements. The Appellate Body found that the cumulative effect of this and other differences in treatment accorded under the measure was unjustifiable discrimination within the chapeau of Article XX of the GATT. In reaching that finding, the Appellate Body stated:

> We acknowledge that the greatly differing periods for putting into operation the requirement for use of TEDs resulted from decisions of the Court of International Trade. Even so, this does not relieve the United States of the legal consequences of the discriminatory impact of the decisions of that Court. The United States, like all other Members of the WTO and of the general community of states, bears responsibility for acts of all its departments of government, including its judiciary.[10]

2.8 In *Brazil – Retreaded Tyres*, the Panel found that a prohibition on the importation of used tyres was being applied in a manner that constituted unjustifiable discrimination under Article XX of the GATT, because certain tyres were still being imported as a result of injunctions granted by Brazilian courts in specific cases. The Panel took note of the Brazilian government's efforts, within its domestic legal system, to prevent, and then seek reversal of, those court injunctions. However, the Panel found that these governmental actions did not exonerate Brazil from the violation of its WTO obligations:

> While the Panel appreciates the practical difficulties that may be associated with the prevention of such imports within Brazil's domestic legal system, it is of the view that it remains incumbent upon Brazil to ensure that it applies its measure in a manner that is consistent with the requirements of Article XX. The fact that the imports arise from court rulings does not exonerate Brazil from its obligation to comply with the requirements of Article XX. Rather, as noted by the Appellate Body in *US – Shrimp*, a Member of the WTO 'bears responsibility for acts of all its departments of government, including its judiciary'.[1480]

[1480] See the Appellate Body Report on *US – Shrimp*, para. 173 and the references cited in the footnote 177 to that paragraph. See also Article 4 of the International Law Commission's Articles on Responsibility of States for Internationally Wrongful Acts (2001), which provides that 'The conduct of any State organ shall be considered an act of that State under international law, whether the organ exercises legislative, executive, judicial or any other functions,

---

[10] Appellate Body Report, *US – Shrimp*, para. 173 (citing Appellate Body Report, *US – Gasoline*, p. 28; R. Jennings and A. Watts (eds.), *Oppenheim's International Law*, 9th edn (Longman's, 1992), Vol. I, p. 545; I. Brownlie, *Principles of Public International Law*, 4th edn (Clarendon Press, 1990), p. 450).

whatever position it holds in the organization of the State, and whatever its character as an organ of the central Government or of a territorial unit of the State'. The Panel also notes in this context the provisions of Article XVI:4 of the WTO Agreement, requiring that: 'Each Member shall ensure the conformity of its laws, regulations and administrative procedures with its obligations as provided in the annexed agreements', and the terms of Article XXV:12 of GATT 1994, which foresees that 'Each Member shall take such reasonable measures as may be available to it to ensure observance of the provisions of this Agreement by the regional and local governments and authorities within its territories'.[11]

In the compliance proceedings in *US – Zeroing (Japan) (Article 21.5 – Japan)*, **2.9** the United States argued that liquidation of duty liability in the US retrospective system of duty assessment was outside the scope of US implementation obligations in the underlying dispute, particularly where liquidation was delayed due to domestic judicial proceedings and the timing of liquidation was controlled by an independent judiciary, not an administering authority. The Appellate Body disagreed:

> We note that a WTO Member 'bears responsibility for acts of all its departments of government, including its judiciary.' This is supported by Article 18.4 of the Anti-Dumping Agreement, Article XVI:4 of the WTO Agreement, and Article 27 of the *Vienna Convention*. The judiciary is a state organ and even if an act or omission derives from a WTO Member's judiciary, it is nevertheless still attributable to that WTO Member. Thus, the United States cannot seek to avoid the obligation to comply with the DSB's recommendations and rulings within the reasonable period of time, by relying on the timing of liquidation being 'controlled by the independent judiciary'.[12]

2.2.5　Individual government officials

The Panel in *Korea – Procurement* referred to 'long established principles of State **2.10** responsibility' in the context of rejecting Korea's argument that certain inaccurate information provided to the United States in the context of negotiations under the Agreement on Government Procurement (GPA) was the responsibility of a single individual in a single Ministry:

> [I]n our view, Korea is simply wrong in making such an argument. The Parties to the GPA did not expect incomplete or even possibly inaccurate answers from one portion of the Korean Government speaking only for itself. The answers *must* be on behalf of the whole of the Korean Government. Negotiations would be impossible otherwise. The Korean Government chose who was tasked with answering the questions and the Korean Government cannot avoid responsibility for the result. It cannot be a justifiable excuse for

---

[11] Panel Report, *Brazil – Retreaded Tyres*, para. 7.305.
[12] Appellate Body Report, *US – Zeroing (Japan) (Article 21.5 – Japan)*, para. 182 (citing Appellate Body Report, *US – Shrimp*, para. 173).

incomplete answers that an applicant for accession to the GPA gave responsibility to Ministry A to answer questions, but the projects and procurement
responsibilities were really the concern of Ministry B and Ministry A was
ignorant of the true situation when it provided answers. In our view, and as
we stated in the Findings, there is an affirmative duty on the part of a Party
or prospective Party to the GPA to answer such questions fully, comprehensively and on behalf of the whole government. This conclusion is supported
by the long established international law principles of State responsibility.
The actions and even omissions of State organs acting in that capacity are
attributable to the State as such and engage its responsibility under international law. [683]

---

[683] See the draft articles on State Responsibility drafted by the International Law
Commission, Articles 5 and 6 and Commentary, *Yearbook of the International
Law Commission* (1973), Vol. II, p. 173 *et seq.* See also *Corfu Channel Case,*
1949 ICJ Reports, p. 23; *US Diplomatic and Consular Staff in Tehran,* ICJ
Reports 1980, pp. 30–31 and 33. These principles of attributability of actions of
organs of the State must also function where it concerns communications of a
State organ, particularly in the context of negotiations of a plurilateral agreement
such as the GPA. Otherwise Parties to the GPA could not rely upon each other's
communications, which ultimately could result in the breakdown of the treaty
system itself.[13]

2.11 The Panel in *Thailand – Cigarettes (Philippines)* found that the actions of Thai
Customs and Thai Excise that were being challenged were attributable to
Thailand:

> The first element that needs to be established to prove the existence of an
> unpublished rule or norm is that the alleged rule or norm is *attributable* to the
> responding Member. The alleged Thai Customs' systematic refusal of transac-
> tion value and use of the deductive valuation method at issue is attributable to
> Thailand as Thai Customs and Thai Excise both consist of appointed govern-
> ment officials who are accountable to the Thai government. WTO Members are
> responsible for the actions of their government officials, where their action is
> inconsistent with the WTO covered agreements.[14]

2.2.6 State, provincial, and local governments

2.12 In *Australia – Salmon (Article 21.5 – Canada)*, the Panel concluded that a ban by
Tasmania was to be regarded as a measure taken by Australia, 'in the sense that it
is a measure for which Australia, under both general international law and
relevant WTO provisions, is responsible'.[15]

---

[13] Panel Report, *Korea – Procurement*, para. 6.5.
[14] Panel Report, *Thailand – Cigarettes (Philippines)*, para. 7.120 (citing Article 4(1) of the Articles on
  Responsibility of States for Internationally Wrongful Acts (2001); Appellate Body Report, *US –
  Gasoline*, p. 28).
[15] Panel Report, *Australia – Salmon (Article 21.5 – Canada)*, para. 7.12.

In *Brazil – Retreaded Tyres*, the Panel noted that 'the measures of Rio Grande **2.13**
do Sul, a state of the Federative Republic of Brazil, are attributable to Brazil as
a WTO Member and therefore should be considered as "measures" for the
purposes of Article 3.3 of the DSU'.[16]

In *Canada – Renewable Energy / Feed-In Tariff Program*, the Panel examined the **2.14**
WTO-consistency of certain measures adopted by the Province of Ontario, and
noted at the outset that '[i]t is not disputed that, under public international law,
Canada is responsible for the actions of the Government of the Province of
Ontario'.[17]

2.3   Entities exercising elements of governmental authority

Article 5 of the ILC Articles on State Responsibility, entitled 'Conduct of **2.15**
persons or entities exercising elements of governmental authority', states:

> The conduct of a person or entity which is not an organ of the State under
> article 4 but which is empowered by the law of that State to exercise elements of
> the governmental authority shall be considered an act of the State under
> international law, provided the person or entity is acting in that capacity in
> the particular instance.

Panels and the Appellate Body have considered when an entity may be considered an 'agency' of a government, and when the actions of a government
agency may be attributed to the State.

In *Canada – Dairy*, the Panel concluded that certain provincial marketing **2.16**
boards were government 'agencies' within the meaning of Article 9.1(a) of the
Agreement on Agriculture. In the course of its analysis, the Panel referred
to the precursor to Article 5 of the ILC Articles on State Responsibility:

> [T]hese boards act under the explicit authority delegated to them by either
> the federal or a provincial government. Accordingly, they can be presumed
> to be an 'agency' of one or more of Canada's governments in the sense of
> Article 9.1(a).[427]

---

[427] In this respect, we refer to Article 7:2 of the Draft Articles on State Responsibility of the International Law Commission (ILC) – which might be considered as
reflecting customary international law – which states: 'The conduct of an organ of
an entity which is not part of the formal structure of the State or of a territorial
governmental entity, but which is empowered by the internal law of that State to
exercise elements of the governmental authority, shall also be considered as an act

---

[16] Panel Report, *Brazil – Retreaded Tyres*, para. 7.400.
[17] Panel Report, *Canada – Renewable Energy / Feed-In Tariff Program*, footnote 37.

of the State under international law, provided that organ was acting in that capacity in the case in question' (Report of the ILC on the Work of its 48th Session, General Assembly, Official Records, 51st Session, Supplement No. 1 (A/51/10), under Chapter III).[18]

2.17 In *US – Gambling*, the Panel referred to 'customary principles of international law concerning attribution' in the context of concluding that, as an agency of the US government with specific responsibilities and powers, actions taken by the United States International Trade Commission (USITC) pursuant to those responsibilities and powers were attributable to the United States:

> We believe that, as an agency of the United States government with specific responsibilities and powers, actions taken by the USITC pursuant to those responsibilities and powers are attributable to the United States.
>
> This conclusion is supported by the International Law Commission ('ILC') *Articles on the Responsibility of States for Internationally Wrongful Acts*. Article 4, which is based on the principle of the unity of the State, defines generally the circumstances in which certain conduct is attributable to a State. This provision is not binding as such, but does reflect customary principles of international law concerning attribution. As the International Law Commission points out in its commentary on the Articles on State Responsibility, the rule that 'the State is responsible for the conduct of its own organs, acting in that capacity, has long been recognized in international judicial decisions.' As explained by the ILC, the term 'state organ' is to be understood in the most general sense. It extends to organs from any branch of the State, exercising legislative, executive, judicial or any other functions.
>
> The fact that certain institutions performing public functions and exercising public powers are regarded in internal law as autonomous and independent of the executive government does not affect their qualification as a state organ. Thus, the fact that the USITC is qualified as an 'independent agency' does not affect the attributability of its actions to the United States, because what matters is the activity at issue in a particular case, not the formal qualification of the body concerned.
>
> Consequently, official pronouncements by the USITC in an area where it has delegated powers are to be attributed to the United States.[19]

2.18 In *Canada – Renewable Energy/Feed-In Tariff Program*, the Appellate Body considered the meaning of the term 'government agency' in the context of Article III:8(a) of the GATT. Article III:8(a) provides that the non-discrimination obligation contained in Article III does not apply to laws, regulations or requirements governing the procurement 'by governmental agencies' of products purchased for governmental purposes and not with a view to commercial resale

---

[18] Panel Report, *Canada – Dairy*, para. 7.77, footnote 427 (citing the draft Articles on State Responsibility (2001) and ILC Commentaries thereto).
[19] Panel Report, *US – Gambling*, paras. 6.127–6.130.

or with a view to use in the production of goods for commercial sale. The Appellate Body stated:

> The term 'agency' is defined as '[a] business, body, or organization providing a particular service, or negotiating transactions on behalf of a person or group'. The word 'agency' is used in connection with the word 'governmental' and, accordingly, Article III:8(a) refers to entities acting for or on behalf of government. The Appellate Body has held that the meaning of 'government' is derived, in part, from the functions that it performs and, in part, from the authority under which it performs those functions. We therefore consider that the question of whether an entity is a 'governmental agency', in the sense of Article III:8(a), is determined by the competences conferred on the entity concerned and by whether that entity acts for or on behalf of government.
>
> We consider that Articles XVII:1 and XVII:2 of the GATT 1994 provide relevant context for the interpretation of the term 'governmental agency' in Article III:8(a). Article XVII:1 stipulates obligations for state trading enterprises and Article XVII:2 sets out a derogation from those obligations for certain government procurement transactions. In contrast to Article III:8(a), the provisions of Article XVII relate to 'state trading enterprises' and not to 'governmental agencies'. According to Article XVII:1, this includes state enterprises and enterprises that are conferred exclusive or special privileges from the state. It follows that the GATT 1994 recognizes that there is a public and a private realm, and that government entities may act in one, the other, or both. Governments may limit the actions of entities to the public realm or give entities competences to act in the private realm. In our view, the term 'governmental agencies' refers to those entities acting for or on behalf of government in the public realm within the competences that have been conferred on them to discharge governmental functions. This further confirms our understanding that a 'governmental agency' is an entity acting for or on behalf of government and performing governmental functions within the competences conferred on it.[20]

2.19   In *US – Anti-Dumping and Countervailing Duties (China)* (DS379), the Appellate Body reversed the Panel's finding that the term 'public body' in Article 1.1 (a)(1) of the SCM Agreement means any entity 'controlled' by a government (e.g. through ownership of shares), and found instead that the term covers only those entities that exercise or are vested with governmental authority. In this regard, the Appellate Body referred to Article 5 of the Articles on State Responsibility:

> [O]ur above interpretation of the term 'public body' coincides with the essence of Article 5. We have indicated that being vested with, and exercising, authority to perform governmental functions is a core feature of a 'public body' in the sense of Article 1.1(a)(1). Here, we note that the commentary on Article 5 explains that Article 5 refers to the true common feature of the entities covered

---

[20] Appellate Body Report, *Canada – Renewable Energy/Feed-In Tariff Program*, paras. 5.60–5.61 (citing Appellate Body Reports, *Canada – Dairy*, para. 97; *US – Anti-Dumping and Countervailing Duties (China)*, para. 290).

by that provision, namely that they are empowered, if only to a limited extent or in a specific context, to exercise specified elements of governmental authority. The commentary also states that the existence of a greater or lesser State participation in its capital, or ownership of its assets are not decisive criteria for the purpose of attribution of the entity's conduct to the State. This corresponds to our above interpretation of the term 'public body' in Article 1.1(a)(1). As we have said above, being vested with governmental authority is the key feature of a public body. State ownership, while not being a decisive criterion, may serve as evidence indicating, in conjunction with other elements, the delegation of governmental authority.

In this context, we observe that the United States acknowledges that the ILC Articles might reflect customary international law to some extent. Yet, the United States contends that given the 'fine line distinctions' constructed in Articles 5 to 8 of the ILC Articles, it remains an open and contested question whether all of these details and distinctions have risen to the status of customary international law. Our analysis, however, does not draw on any details or 'fine line distinctions' that might exist under Article 5 of the ILC Articles. Rather, we see similarities in the core principles and functions of the respective provisions. Our consideration of Article 5 of the ILC Articles does not contradict our analysis of Article 1.1(a)(1) above. Rather, it lends further support to that analysis. Yet, because the outcome of our analysis does not turn on Article 5, it is not necessary for us to resolve definitively the question of to what extent Article 5 of the ILC Articles reflects customary international law.[222]

---

[222] We recall that, with respect to Article 4 of the ILC Articles, the panel in *US – Gambling* stated that the principle set out in Article 4 of the ILC Articles reflects customary international law concerning attribution (Panel Report, *US – Gambling*, para. 6.128).[21]

2.4   Private parties

2.20 Article 8 of the ILC Articles on State Responsibility, entitled 'Conduct directed or controlled by a State', reads:

> The conduct of a person or group of persons shall be considered an act of a State under international law if the person or group of persons is in fact acting on the instructions of, or under the direction or control of, that State in carrying out the conduct.

There have been several cases in which GATT/WTO panels and the Appellate Body have considered the extent to which actions by or otherwise involving private parties may nonetheless be attributable to a government by virtue of some governmental connection to or endorsement of those actions.

---

[21] Appellate Body Report, *US – Anti-Dumping and Countervailing Duties (China)*, paras. 310–11 (also citing Commentary on Article 5 of the ILC Draft Articles, para. 3).

The Panel in *Japan – Film* characterized the problem of classifying private action **2.21** as a governmental 'measure' in the following terms:

> As the WTO Agreement is an international agreement, in respect of which only national governments and separate customs territories are directly subject to obligations, it follows by implication that the term *measure* in Article XXIII:1(b) and Article 26.1 of the DSU, as elsewhere in the WTO Agreement, refers only to policies or actions of governments, not those of private parties. But while this 'truth' may not be open to question, there have been a number of trade disputes in relation to which panels have been faced with making sometimes difficult judgments as to the extent to which what appear on their face to be private actions may nonetheless be attributable to a government because of some governmental connection to or endorsement of those actions.[22]

The Panel in *Japan – Film* had to determine whether certain 'administrative guidance' in Japan amounted to a governmental 'measure'. The Panel began by considering the ordinary meaning of the term 'measure':

> The ordinary meaning of *measure* as it is used in Article XXIII:1(b) certainly encompasses a law or regulation enacted by a government. But in our view, it is broader than that and includes other governmental actions short of legally enforceable enactments. At the same time, it is also true that not every utterance by a government official or study prepared by a non-governmental body at the request of the government or with some degree of government support can be viewed as a measure of a Member government.
>
> In Japan, it is accepted that the government sometimes acts through what is referred to as administrative guidance. In such a case, the company receiving guidance from the Government of Japan may not be legally bound to act in accordance with it, but compliance may be expected in light of the power of the government and a system of government incentives and disincentives arising from the wide array of government activities and involvement in the Japanese economy. As noted by the parties, administrative guidance in Japan takes various forms. Japan, for example, refers to what it calls 'regulatory administrative guidance', which it concedes effectively substitutes for formal government action. It also refers to promotional administrative guidance, where companies are urged to do things that are in their interest to do in any event. In Japan's view, this sort of guidance should not be assimilated to a measure in the sense of Article XXIII:1(b). For our purposes, these categories inform, but do not determine the issue before us. Thus, it is not useful for us to try to place specific instances of administrative guidance into one general category or another. It will be necessary for us, as it has been for GATT panels in the past, to examine each alleged 'measure' to see whether it has the particular attributes required of a measure for Article XXIII:1(b) purposes.[23]

---

[22] Panel Report, *Japan – Film*, para. 10.52.
[23] *Ibid.*, paras. 10.43–10.44 (citing the *Concise Oxford Dictionary*).

The Panel in *Japan – Film* reviewed prior GATT practice and defined 'sufficient government involvement' as the decisive criterion for whether actions taken by private parties may be deemed to be a governmental 'measure':

> [P]ast GATT cases demonstrate that the fact that an action is taken by private parties does not rule out the possibility that it may be deemed to be governmental if there is sufficient government involvement with it. It is difficult to establish bright-line rules in this regard, however. Thus, that possibility will need to be examined on a case-by-case basis.[24]

2.22 In *Canada – Autos*, the Panel examined the WTO-consistency of commitments undertaken by Canadian motor vehicle manufacturers, in letters addressed to the government, to increase Canadian value-added in the production of motor vehicles. Referring to prior GATT panel reports, the Panel analysed whether those commitments fell within the 'requirements' covered in Article III:4 of the GATT:

> [T]o qualify a private action as a 'requirement' within the meaning of Article III:4 means that in relation to that action a Member is bound by an international obligation, namely to provide no less favourable treatment to imported products than to domestic products.
>
> A determination of whether private action amounts to a 'requirement' under Article III:4 must therefore necessarily rest on a finding that there is a nexus between that action and the action of a government such that the government must be held responsible for that action. We do not believe that such a nexus can exist only if a government makes undertakings of private parties legally enforceable, as in the situation considered by the Panel on *Canada – FIRA*, or if a government conditions the grant of an advantage on undertakings made by private parties, as in the situation considered by the Panel on *EEC – Parts and Components*. We note in this respect that the word 'requirement' has been defined to mean '1. The action of requiring something; a request. 2. A thing required or needed, a want, a need. Also the action or an instance of needing or wanting something. 3. Something called for or demanded; a condition which must be complied with.' The word 'requirements' in its ordinary meaning and in light of its context in Article III:4 clearly implies government action involving a demand, request or the imposition of a condition but in our view this term does not carry a particular connotation with respect to the legal form in which such government action is taken. In this respect, we consider that, in applying the concept of 'requirements' in Article III:4 to situations involving actions by private parties, it is necessary to take into account that there is a broad variety of forms of government of action that can be effective in influencing the conduct of private parties.[25]

2.23 A series of panel and Appellate Body reports have interpreted Article 1.1(a)(1)(iv) of the SCM Agreement, which refers to the situation in which a government 'entrusts or directs a private body to carry out' certain functions. In the course of

---

[24] Panel Report, *Japan – Film*, paras. 10.55–10.56.
[25] Panel Report, *Canada – Autos*, paras. 10.106–10.107.

its analysis in *US – Countervailing Duty Investigation on DRAMS*, the Appellate Body stated:

> [Article 1.1(a)(1)(iv)] covers situations where a private body is being used as a proxy by the government to carry out one of the types of functions listed in paragraphs (i) through (iii). Seen in this light, the terms 'entrusts' and 'directs' in paragraph (iv) identify the instances where seemingly private conduct may be attributable to a government for purposes of determining whether there has been a financial contribution within the meaning of the *SCM Agreement*.[26]

Following a detailed analysis of Article 1.1(a)(1)(iv), the Appellate Body concluded:

> In sum, we are of the view that, pursuant to paragraph (iv), 'entrustment' occurs where a government gives responsibility to a private body, and 'direction' refers to situations where the government exercises its authority over a private body. In both instances, the government uses a private body as proxy to effectuate one of the types of financial contributions listed in paragraphs (i) through (iii). It may be difficult to identify precisely, in the abstract, the types of government actions that constitute entrustment or direction and those that do not. The particular label used to describe the governmental action is not necessarily dispositive. Indeed, as Korea acknowledges, in some circumstances, 'guidance' by a government can constitute direction. In most cases, one would expect entrustment or direction of a private body to involve some form of threat or inducement, which could, in turn, serve as evidence of entrustment or direction. The determination of entrustment or direction will hinge on the particular facts of the case.[188]

---

[188] The Commentaries to the ILC Draft Articles similarly state that 'it is a matter for appreciation in each case whether particular conduct was or was not carried out under the control of a State, to such an extent that conduct controlled should be attributed to it'. (Commentaries to the ILC Draft Articles, *supra*, footnote 104, Article 8, Commentary (5), p. 107).[27]

2.5   Conduct taken in the context of a customs union

2.5.1 General

In *Turkey – Textiles*, India brought a case against Turkey in respect of certain **2.24** measures applied by Turkey. However, Turkey argued that these were measures of 'another entity', namely, the EC–Turkey Customs Union. The Panel considered that, under public international law, Turkey could be held responsible for the measures taken pursuant to the customs union between itself and the

---

[26] Appellate Body Report, *US – Countervailing Duty Investigation on DRAMS*, para. 108.
[27] *Ibid.*, para. 116.

European Communities. The Panel began its analysis of this issue by reference to PCIJ jurisprudence regarding the legal personality of a customs union:

> As to the issue of whether the measures at issue should be considered to be measures of the Turkey–EC customs union as such, we note that according to the Permanent Court of International Justice[269], the assessment whether any customs union (or another legal entity) has a legal personality distinct from that of its constituent countries is to be based on an examination of the treaty forming such customs union and the relevant circumstances. Such determination will therefore always be made on a case by case basis. We note that the Turkey–EC customs union agreement does not have any legislative body which would have the constitutional authority to enact laws and regulations that would be, as such, applicable to the territory of the customs union. Under the Turkey–EC customs union, the only institutional body with legislative features is the Association Council, the powers of which were first defined in the Ankara Agreement. Paragraph 1 of Article 22 of the Ankara Agreement states that the Association Council shall have the power to take decisions. Although each of the two parties are 'bound to take the steps involved in the execution of the decisions adopted', these decisions 'shall be taken unanimously' (Article 23 of the Ankara Agreement) and there is no further enforcement process. The Turkey–EC Customs Union Joint Committee can only 'carry out exchange of views and information, formulate recommendations to the Association Council and deliver opinions with a view to ensuring the proper functioning of the Customs Union' (Article 52 of the Decision 1/95 of the Turkey–EC customs union). Article 55 imposes on Turkey and the European Communities the obligation to notify each other of the adoption of any new legislation that may affect each other or the functioning of the customs union. Article 58 also envisages the situation of 'discrepancies between Community and Turkish legislation'. This is a recognition that each party to the customs union may adopt measures, to some extent different, and which may not be fully consistent with one another; it provides confirmation of the ability of the parties to act independently and that Turkey maintains that sovereign right. Since the actions of the Association Council require independent implementation by the parties to the customs union without any enforcement process either individually or jointly; since the Association Council cannot force the parties to act[273]; and since there is no other provision that would lead us to conclude that either of the two parties, or some collective entity on behalf of them, could enact legislation applicable to both of them; we consider the measures at issue taken, implemented and enforced by the Turkish government itself, applied on Turkish territory only, can only be Turkish measures.

---

[269] The Permanent Court of International Justice (PCIJ) concluded in the *Customs Regime between Germany and Austria*, that the wording of the customs union was determinant as to whether a member lost its sovereignty. An example of a customs union where member states appear to have retained full sovereignty and independence *vis-à-vis* third countries is the customs union between the Czech Republic and the Slovak Republic. It can be noted that in such a customs union, the parties have not created any autonomous institution capable of enacting legislation or providing for the legal personality of the

customs union, independent and autonomous from that of each member state. Consequently, to take one example, when the Czech Republic and the Slovak Republic wanted to enter into a free trade agreement with Slovenia, Poland, Hungary and Romania, each of them (the Czech Republic and the Slovak Republic) signed individually and independently the so-called CEFTA. It is not the Czech–Slovak customs union, as an entity, which did so. The same is also true for the recent free trade agreement between Turkey and Lithuania, which is parallel to the EC–Lithuania free trade agreement. Again it is not the Turkey–EC customs union which concluded one single free trade agreement with Lithuania, but the EC and Turkey, individually, signed separate agreements. As far as the Turkey–EC custom union treaty is concerned, we have already concluded above, that the institutions existing in the context of the customs union do not have the legal capacity to legislate (there is only a provision that any legislation or measure adopted by either party (the EC or Turkey) must be notified to the other party and consulted upon). The terms of the Turkey–EC customs union agreement provide no indication of a transfer of sovereignty of the member states either to an institution established under the customs union, nor to the EC. In WTO terms, unless a customs union is provided with distinct rights and obligations (and therefore some WTO legal personality, such as the European Communities) each party to the customs union remains accountable for measures it adopts for application on its specific territory. See also Jennings, R., Watts, A., *Oppenheim's International Law* (1996), 9th edn, Vol. 1 (Peace), Introduction and Part 1, p. 255.
[273] In the *Reparations for Injuries* case, the ICJ stated that, where a group of states claims to be a legal entity distinct from its members, the test is whether it was in 'such a position that it possesses, in regard to its Members, rights which it is entitled to ask them to respect.' (See ICJ Rep (1949), p. 178 and also *Western Sahara* case (1975), p. 63; see Jennings, R., Watts, A., *Oppenheim's International Law* (1996), Op. cit., p. 119.)[28]

The Panel in *Turkey – Textiles* then applied the general international law principle that, where two or more States act through a common organ, each State may be separately answerable for a wrongful act of that organ:

> Finally, we note that in public international law, in the absence of any contrary treaty provision, Turkey could reasonably be held responsible for the measures taken by the Turkey–EC customs union. In the *Nauru* case one of the conclusions of Judge Shahabuddeen's separate opinion was:
>
> > '[T]he [International Law Commission] considered, that *where States act through a common organ, each State is separately answerable for the wrongful act of the common organ.* That view, it seems to me, runs in the direction of supporting Nauru's contention that each of the three States in this case is jointly and severally responsible for the way Nauru was administered on their behalf by Australia, whether or not Australia may be regarded as technically as a common organ . . .'. (Emphasis added.)

---

[28] Panel Report, *Turkey–Textiles*, para. 9.40.

The International Law Commission (ILC) had stated in its commentaries to
its adopted report:

> A similar conclusion is called for in cases of parallel attribution of
> single course of conduct to several States, as when the conduct in
> question has been adopted by an organ common to a number of States.
> According to the principles on which the articles of chapter II of the
> draft are based, *the conduct of the common organ cannot be considered
> otherwise than as an act of each of the States whose common organ it is. If
> that conduct is not in conformity with an international obligation, then the
> two or more States will concurrently have committed separate, although
> identical, internationally wrongful acts.* It is self-evident that the parallel
> commission of identical offences by two or more States is altogether
> different from participation by one of those States in an internationally
> wrongful act committed by the other. (Emphasis added.)[29]

2.5.2 Organs of the European Communities

2.25 In several cases, panels have considered that certain authorities and institutions
of the EC member States constitute organs of the European Communities.

2.26 In *EC – Trademarks and Geographical Indications*, the Panel examined a Council
Regulation and its related implementing and enforcement measures. The Panel
stated:

> The European Communities . . . indicates that Community laws are generally not
> executed through authorities at Community level but rather through recourse to
> the authorities of its member States which, in such a situation, 'act *de facto* as
> organs of the Community, for which the Community would be responsible under
> WTO law and international law in general'. The Panel accepts this explanation of
> what amounts to the European Communities' domestic constitutional arrange-
> ments and accepts that the submissions of the European Communities' delegation
> to this panel proceeding are made on behalf of all the executive authorities of the
> European Communities.[30]

2.27 In *EC – Approval and Marketing of Biotech Products*, the Panel examined certain
EC measures affecting the approval and marketing of biotech products, and
related measures taken by some of the EC member States. At the outset, the
Panel explained that:

> It is important to note that even though the member State safeguard measures
> were introduced by the relevant member States and are applicable only in the

---

[29] Panel Report, *Turkey – Textiles*, paras. 9.42–9.43 (citing *Nauru* case, Separate Opinion of Judge
Shahabuddeen, at 284; R. Clark, Book review of *Nauru: Environmental Damage Under Inter-
national Trusteeship* (C. Weeramantry), *The International Lawyer*, Vol. 28, No. 1, p. 186;
Yearbook of the International Law Commission (1978), Vol. II, Part Two, p. 99).

[30] *EC – Trademarks and Geographical Indications (US)*, para. 7.98 (citing Panel Report, *US – Section
301 Trade Act*, para. 7.123).

territory of the member States concerned, the European Communities as a whole is the responding party in respect of the member State safeguard measures. This is a direct consequence of the fact that the Complaining Parties have directed their complaints against the European Communities, and not individual EC member States.[275] The European Communities never contested that, for the purposes of this dispute, the challenged member State measures are attributable to it under international law and hence can be considered EC measures.[31]

In *EC – Selected Customs Matters*, the United States claimed that the European **2.28**
Communities acted inconsistently with Article X:3(b) of the GATT, which requires that Members maintain judicial, arbitral or administrative tribunals or procedures for the review and correction of administrative action. The United States argued that the provision of judicial, arbitral or administrative tribunals or procedures for the review and correction of administrative action by *individual member States* within the European Communities does not satisfy the *European Communities'* obligation under Article X:3(b) of the GATT. The Panel rejected this claim, and considered that the European Communities could comply with its obligations through organs in its member States:

> It is the Panel's view that the European Communities may comply with its obligations under Article X:3(b) of the GATT 1994 through organs in its member States. We consider that this follows from the fact that Article X:3(b) of the GATT 1994 does not contain any requirements regarding the institutional structure of the review mechanism required by that Article other than the requirement that the review be undertaken by judicial, arbitral or administrative tribunals.[932]

---

[932] The Panel considers that this also follows from Article 4 of the Draft Articles on Responsibility of States for Internationally Wrongful Acts, which provides that:

> '1. The conduct of any State organ shall be considered as an act of that State under international law, whether the organ exercises legislative, executive, judicial or any other functions, whatever position it holds in the organization of the State, and whatever its character as an organ of the central government or of a territorial unit of the State.'[32]

---

[31] Panel Report, *EC – Approval and Marketing of Biotech Products*, para. 7.101 (citing Panel Report, *EC – Asbestos*, paras. 2.3 and 3.4).
[32] Panel Report, *EC – Selected Customs Matters*, para. 7.552.

3

BREACH OF AN OBLIGATION

3.1   Introduction

Article 12 of the ILC Articles on State Responsibility, entitled 'Existence of a   **3.1**
breach of an international obligation', provides that:

> There is a breach of an international obligation by a State when an act of that
> State is not in conformity with what is required of it by that obligation,
> regardless of its origin or character.

This chapter covers statements by WTO adjudicators addressing five concepts
regarding the existence of a breach of an international obligation,[1] including:
(i) the concept of a breach; (ii) breaches arising from omissions; (iii) breaches
arising from legislation as such; (iv) breaches arising from composite measures;
and (v) the concept of harmless error.

3.2   Concept of a breach

WTO panels and the Appellate Body have used various terms interchangeably   **3.2**
when referring to measures that breach treaty obligations, including measures
that 'breach' an obligation, that are 'inconsistent' with an obligation, that
'violate' an obligation, that are 'incompatible' with an obligation, that are
'contrary' to an obligation, that are not 'in conformity' with an obligation,
and that 'fail to comply' with an obligation.

For example, in *EC – Asbestos*, the Appellate Body used at least four different   **3.3**
expressions interchangeably in the context of contrasting 'violation' complaints
and 'non-violation' complaints in paragraphs (a) and (b) of Article XXIII:1 of the
GATT (including "failed to carry out", "acted inconsistently with", "conflicts
with" and "violates"):

---

[1] See also Chapter 8.3.2 below ('Measures defeating the purpose of a treaty and/or expectations
derived therefrom').

Article XXIII:1(a) sets forth a cause of action for a claim that a Member has failed to carry out one or more of its obligations under the GATT 1994. A claim under Article XXIII:1(a), therefore, lies when a Member is alleged to have acted inconsistently with a provision of the GATT 1994. Article XXIII:1(b) sets forth a separate cause of action for a claim that, through the application of a measure, a Member has 'nullified or impaired' 'benefits' accruing to another Member, 'whether or not that measure conflicts with the provisions' of the GATT 1994. Thus, it is not necessary, under Article XXIII:1(b), to establish that the measure involved is inconsistent with, or violates, a provision of the GATT 1994.[2]

3.4 The Panel in *US – Gambling* examined Article 19.1 of the DSU, which provides that, where a panel or the Appellate Body concludes that a measure is 'inconsistent with a covered agreement', it shall recommend that the Member concerned bring the measure 'into conformity' with that agreement. The Panel noted:

> [A]t the risk of stating the obvious, the ordinary meaning of 'inconsistent' may be defined as '[n]ot in keeping, discordant, at variance. Foll. by *with*.' In other words, a measure 'inconsistent with' a covered agreement is not in 'conformity with' that agreement. The same is true of the terms used in the French and Spanish versions of the DSU, that are equally authentic, and that use the terms *'conforme'* and *'incompatible'*, and *'en conformidad'* and *'incompatible'*, respectively.[3]

3.3   Breaches arising from omissions

3.5 Article 2 of the ILC Articles on State Responsibility provides that there is an internationally wrongful act of a State when 'conduct consisting of an action or omission' is attributable to the State and constitutes a breach of an international obligation of the State. In the context of WTO dispute settlement, complaining parties often claim that respondents have violated a given obligation through an omission (i.e. the failure to do that which is required by the obligation). There is no case in which a party or adjudicator questioned the notion that a treaty obligation establishing a positive obligation (i.e. an obligation to do something, in contrast to an obligation to refrain from doing something) can be breached through an omission.

3.6 In *Guatemala – Cement I*, the Appellate Body noted that '[a] measure can also be an omission or a failure to act on the part of a Member' and cited, as an example, *India – Patents (US)*.[4] In that case, the Appellate Body had upheld the Panel's finding that India acted inconsistently with Articles 70.8(a) and Article 70.9 of the TRIPS Agreement by failing to have in place, as from

---

[2] Appellate Body Report, *EC – Asbestos*, para. 185.
[3] Panel Report, *US – Gambling*, para. 6.13 (citing the *New Shorter Oxford English Dictionary*).
[4] Appellate Body Report, *Guatemala – Cement I*, footnote 47.

the date of entry into force of the WTO Agreement, certain mechanisms relating to intellectual property rights.[5]

In *US – Corrosion-Resistant Steel Sunset Review*, the Appellate Body confirmed **3.7** that '[i]n principle, any act or omission attributable to a WTO Member can be a measure of that Member for purposes of dispute settlement proceedings'.[6]

In *Dominican Republic – Import and Sale of Cigarettes*, the Panel examined a **3.8** claim that the Dominican Republic had failed to administer a law in a reasonable manner, as required by Article X:3(a) of the GATT. The Panel stated:

> Honduras's claim centres on an alleged omissive conduct on the part of the Dominican Republic, constituted by its failure to comply with a positive obligation, that of administering its laws and regulations, of the kind described in Article X:1, in a uniform, impartial and reasonable manner.
>
> The Panel agrees that a Member may act in a manner inconsistent with its obligations under the covered WTO agreements, not only by adopting a particular positive conduct, but also by failing to adopt a conduct, i.e. by an omission, when the relevant rule imposes an obligation to adopt a specific action.[7]

3.4   Breaches arising from legislation as such

The commentary to Article 12 of the ILC Articles on State Responsibility **3.9** explains that '[t]he question often arises whether an obligation is breached by the enactment of legislation by a State (in cases where the content of the legislation *prima facie* conflicts with what is required by the international obligation), or whether the legislation has to be applied in a given case before the breach can be said to have occurred'.[8] In the context of WTO dispute settlement, it is well established that WTO treaty obligations may be breached by legislation mandating conduct that is inconsistent with WTO obligations, independently from the application of that legislation in any particular instance.

In *US – Section 301 Trade Act*, the Panel offered the following view on what it **3.10** termed 'traditional' public international law:

> [U]nder traditional public international law, legislation under which an eventual violation could, or even would, subsequently take place, does not normally in and of itself engage State responsibility. If, say, a State undertakes not to expropriate property of foreign nationals without appropriate compensation,

---

[5] Appellate Body Report, *India – Patents*, paras. 97(a) and (b).
[6] Appellate Body Report, *US – Corrosion-Resistant Steel Sunset Review*, para. 81.
[7] Panel Report, *Dominican Republic – Import and Sale of Cigarettes*, paras. 7.378–7.379.
[8] ILC Commentary to the Articles on State Responsibility, para. 12.

its State responsibility would normally be engaged only at the moment foreign property had actually been expropriated in a given instance.[9]

3.11 In *US – 1916 Act*, the Appellate Body observed the existence of a long line of GATT cases that 'firmly established' the principle that complaining parties were permitted to challenge legislation 'as such', and noted how, since the entry into force of the WTO, numerous panels had dealt with claims regarding legislation 'as such':

> Prior to the entry into force of the *WTO Agreement*, it was firmly established that Article XXIII:1(a) of the GATT 1947 allowed a Contracting Party to challenge legislation as such, independently from the application of that legislation in specific instances. While the text of Article XXIII does not expressly address the matter, panels consistently considered that, under Article XXIII, they had the *jurisdiction* to deal with claims against legislation as such. In *examining* such claims, panels developed the concept that mandatory and discretionary legislation should be distinguished from each other, reasoning that only legislation that mandates a violation of GATT obligations can be found as such to be inconsistent with those obligations . . .
>
> Thus, that a Contracting Party could challenge legislation as such before a panel was well-settled under the GATT 1947. We consider that the case law articulating and applying this practice forms part of the GATT *acquis* which, under Article XVI:1 of the *WTO Agreement*, provides guidance to the WTO and, therefore, to panels and the Appellate Body. Furthermore, in Article 3.1 of the DSU, Members affirm 'their adherence to the principles for the management of disputes heretofore applied under Articles XXII and XXIII of GATT 1947'. We note that, since the entry into force of the *WTO Agreement*, a number of panels have dealt with dispute settlement claims brought against a Member on the basis of its legislation as such, independently from the application of that legislation in specific instances.[10]

3.12 In *US – Oil Country Tubular Goods Sunset Reviews*, the Appellate Body discussed the characteristics of legislation and other measures that would be subject to 'as such' claims:

> By definition, an 'as such' claim challenges laws, regulations, or other instruments of a Member that have general and prospective application, asserting that a Member's conduct – not only in a particular instance that has occurred, but in future situations as well – will necessarily be inconsistent with that Member's WTO obligations. In essence, complaining parties bringing 'as such' challenges seek to prevent Members *ex ante* from engaging in certain conduct. The implications of such challenges are obviously more far-reaching than 'as applied' claims.[11]

3.13 In *US – Corrosion-Resistant Steel Sunset Review*, the Appellate Body explained the reasons for allowing complaining parties to challenge measures 'as such', irrespective of any individual instances of application:

---

[9] Panel Report, *US – Section 301 Trade Act*, para. 7.80.
[10] Appellate Body Report, *US – 1916 Act*, paras. 60–1.
[11] Appellate Body Report, *US – Oil Country Tubular Goods Sunset Reviews*, para. 172.

[I]n GATT and WTO dispute settlement practice, panels have frequently examined measures consisting not only of particular acts applied only to a specific situation, but also of acts setting forth rules or norms that are intended to have general and prospective application. In other words, instruments of a Member containing rules or norms could constitute a 'measure', irrespective of how or whether those rules or norms are applied in a particular instance. This is so because the disciplines of the GATT and the WTO, as well as the dispute settlement system, are intended to protect not only existing trade but also the security and predictability needed to conduct future trade. This objective would be frustrated if instruments setting out rules or norms inconsistent with a Member's obligations could not be brought before a panel once they have been adopted and irrespective of any particular instance of application of such rules or norms. It would also lead to a multiplicity of litigation if instruments embodying rules or norms could not be challenged as such, but only in the instances of their application. Thus, allowing claims against measures, as such, serves the purpose of preventing future disputes by allowing the root of WTO-inconsistent behaviour to be eliminated.[12]

3.5   Breaches arising from composite measures

Article 15 of the ILC Articles on State Responsibility, entitled 'Breach consisting   **3.14** of a composite act', defines the concept of a 'composite act' as 'a series of actions or omissions defined in the aggregate' as wrongful. Article 15 has not been referred to in WTO jurisprudence. However, there have been a number of cases in which WTO adjudicators have assessed whether several actions or omissions should be analysed collectively as a single 'measure'. In addition, there have been cases involving subsidies in which panels and the Appellate Body have undertaken an analysis of the 'aggregated effects' of a series of individual subsidies to determine whether such subsidies have, collectively, caused serious prejudice within the meaning of Article 6 of the SCM Agreement.

US – Tuna II (Mexico) is an example of a case in which the Panel decided to   **3.15** consider several measures jointly, and made findings based on their combined operation, rather than on the basis of each individual measure separately. In the course of its analysis, the Panel took into account prior WTO jurisprudence on this issue. The Panel began by noting that:

> In addressing this issue, we first note that it has not been suggested in these proceedings that any of these legal instruments taken in isolation would not constitute an 'act or omission of the organs of the state' attributable to the United States. We further note that the DPCIA and the implementing regulations constitute legislative or regulatory acts of the federal authorities, while the court ruling constitutes an act of the judicial branch. Each of these normative

---

[12] Appellate Body Report, *US – Corrosion-Resistant Steel Sunset Review*, para. 168.

instruments is *a priori* capable of constituting a measure attributable to the United States, which may be challenged in dispute settlement proceedings under the DSU.[13]

After reviewing how the various instruments functioned and related to each other, the Panel in *US – Tuna II (Mexico)* concluded that:

> To summarize, together and collectively, the various provisions in the different legal instruments identified by Mexico, including the *Hogarth* ruling, set out the terms of the US 'dolphin-safe' labelling scheme, as currently applied by the United States. We also note that the United States does not object to Mexico's request to consider the various instruments together and that it has articulated its defence in these proceedings on the basis of the measures taken together. In light of these elements, we see merit in considering these closely related instruments together as a single measure for the purposes of this dispute.
>
> We also note that a comparable issue has arisen in two cases relating to SPS measures (*Japan – Apples* and *Australia – Apples*), where the panels considered whether various requirements imposed by Japan and Australia respectively, and embodied in different instruments, should be treated as a single measure or as a combination of several individual measures. In these cases, in addition to considering whether the different requirements might constitute a single measure for the purposes of dispute settlement under the DSU, the panel also had to consider whether they constituted a 'phytosanitary measure' within the meaning of the *SPS Agreement*, an issue that is not before this Panel. Nonetheless, we find that the test developed by the panel in *Japan – Apples* provides useful guidance for our analysis. The panel in that case considered that the various requirements were interrelated and cumulatively constituted the measures actually applied by Japan to the importation of US apple fruit to protect against the entry, establishment or spread of fire blight within its territory. That panel therefore saw no legal, logical or factual obstacle to treating the requirements identified by the United States as a single phytosanitary measure within the meaning of the SPS Agreement.
>
> Similarly, we see no 'legal, factual or logical obstacle' to treating the various interrelated legal instruments identified by Mexico as the basis for its claims in these proceedings as a single measure for the purposes of our findings. Accordingly, we will consider them together throughout these findings. These measures taken together are hereafter referred to as 'the US dolphin-safe labelling provisions'.[14]

3.16 WTO panels and the Appellate Body have considered issues relating to aggregation in the context of analysing causation. Specifically, panels and the Appellate Body have examined the 'aggregate effects' of individual subsidies in the context of examining whether a series of individual subsidies have caused any of the adverse trade effects set forth in Article 6.3 of the SCM Agreement. In the

---

[13] Panel Report, *US – Tuna II (Mexico)*, para. 7.20.

[14] *Ibid.*, paras. 7.24–7.26 (citing Panel Report, *Japan – Apples*, para. 4.17; Panel Report, *Australia – Apples*, paras. 7.113–7.115; Panel Report, *US – Superfund*, para. 5.2.2; Panel Report, *Japan – Apples*, paras. 8.16–8.17).

context of addressing issues relating to the collective assessment of the subsidies at issue in *US – Large Civil Aircraft (2nd complaint)*, the Appellate Body offered the following observations:

> Articles 5(c) and 6.3 of the SCM Agreement do not require that a serious prejudice analysis 'clinically isolate each individual subsidy and its effects'. Rather, the way in which a panel structures its evaluation of a claim that multiple subsidies have caused serious prejudice will necessarily vary from case to case. Relevant circumstances that will bear upon the appropriateness of a panel's approach include the design, structure, and operation of the subsidies at issue, the alleged market phenomena, and the extent to which the subsidies are provided in relation to a particular product or products. A panel must also take account of the manner in which the claimant presents its case, and the extent to which it claims that multiple subsidies have similar effects on the same product, or that the effects of multiple subsidies manifest themselves collectively in the relevant market. A panel enjoys a degree of methodological latitude in selecting its approach to analyzing the collective effects of multiple subsidies for purposes of assessing causation. However, a panel is never absolved from having to establish a 'genuine and substantial relationship of cause and effect' between the impugned subsidies and the alleged market phenomena under Article 6.3, or from assessing whether such causal link is diluted by the effects of other factors. Moreover, a panel must take care not to segment unduly its analysis such that, when confronted with multiple subsidy measures, it considers the effects of each on an individual basis only and, as a result of such an atomized approach, finds that no subsidy is a substantial cause of the relevant adverse effects.[15]

3.6 Harmless error

To date, no WTO adjudicator has accepted a defence of 'harmless error'. In one **3.17** case, a panel stated that the concept of 'harmless error' had not attained the status of a general principle of public international law.

In *Guatemala – Cement II*, Guatemala argued that certain alleged violations **3.18** constituted harmless error, and argued that it is a general principle of law that, in case of a violation of a procedural rule, prejudice must be shown before a party obtains the right to be compensated for this procedural error. The Panel rejected Guatemala's defence:

> We do not consider that the concept of 'harmless error' as presented by Guatemala has attained the status of a general principle of public international

---

[15] Appellate Body Report, *US – Large Civil Aircraft (2nd complaint)*, para. 1284 (citing Panel Report, *US – Upland Cotton*, paras. 7.1192, 7.1194; Panel Report, *Indonesia – Autos*, para. 14.206; Panel Report, *Korea – Commercial Vessels*, paras. 7.560, 7.616; Appellate Body Report, *EC and certain member States – Large Civil Aircraft*, para. 1376; Appellate Body Report, *US – Upland Cotton*, para. 438; Appellate Body Report, *US – Upland Cotton (Article 21.5 – Brazil)*, paras. 368, 375).

law. In any event, we consider that our first task in this dispute is to determine whether Guatemala has acted consistently with its obligations under the relevant provisions of the AD Agreement. To the extent that Mexico can demonstrate that Guatemala has not respected its obligations under the relevant provisions of that Agreement, we must next consider arguments raised by Guatemala in respect of the nullification or impairment of benefits accruing to Mexico thereunder. Thus, while arguments regarding the existence and extent of the possible harm suffered by Mexico may be relevant to the issue of nullification or impairment, we do not consider that an argument of harmless error represents a defence in itself to an alleged infringement of a provision of the WTO Agreement.[16]

3.19 In *US – Stainless Steel (Korea)*, the Panel found that a factual error committed by the investigating authority in an anti-dumping investigation did not undermine the investigating authority's ultimate conclusion. In this regard, the Panel drew the following distinction with respect to the issue of 'harmless error':

> In our view, the factual error committed by the DOC does not undermine the validity of the DOC's resolution of this issue. Nor do we see any inconsistency between our ruling here and that in *Guatemala – Cement II*. The issue in that dispute was whether certain *violations* of the *AD Agreement* – failure to provide timely notice of initiation, to provide an appropriate public notice and to timely provide the text of the application – were harmless. Here, the question is rather whether certain *factual errors* vitiate a determination, thus giving rise to a violation.[17]

3.20 The Panel in *Argentina – Ceramic Tiles* drew a similar distinction in the context of rejecting harmless error as a defence to a treaty violation:

> Argentina raises as a final defence the concept of harmless error, and argues that the EC failed to demonstrate that the Italian exporters were prejudiced by the failure to determine an individual margin of dumping. In its answers to questions from the Panel, Argentina asserts that the concept of harmless error – i.e. an error that does not cause injury or affect the rights of one of the parties – has been accepted in WTO law. Argentina refers in particular to the Report of the Appellate Body in the *Korea – Dairy Safeguards* case.
>
> We note, however, that the Appellate Body Report in the *Korea – Dairy Safeguards* case, to which Argentina refers in support of its argument, dealt with the question of whether the request for establishment met the requirements of Article 6.2 of the DSU. The issue before the Appellate Body was whether Article 6.2 of the DSU was complied with or not. The Appellate Body, in deciding that question, concluded that one element to be considered was whether the defending Member was prejudiced in its ability to defend itself by a lack of clarity or specificity in the request for establishment. The Appellate Body did not address the question whether, once it had been established that a provision of the Agreement is violated, it needs in addition to be demonstrated that this violation

---

[16] Panel Report, *Guatemala – Cement II*, para. 8.22.
[17] Panel Report, *US – Stainless Steel (Korea)*, para. 5.5.

had prejudiced the rights of the complaining party. Thus, we do not agree that this Appellate Body decision supports Argentina's argument that the concept of harmless error has been accepted in WTO law.[18]

In *EC – Salmon (Norway)*, the Panel stated that 'an allegation of harmless **3.21** error … is not cognizable in our evaluation of the investigating authority's determination.'[19]

---

[18] Panel Report, *Argentina – Ceramic Tiles*, paras. 6.102–6.103.
[19] Panel Report, *EC – Salmon (Norway)*, footnote 763.

4

CONFLICTS BETWEEN TREATIES

4.1 Introduction

This chapter reviews WTO jurisprudence on general international law concepts **4.1** and principles concerning conflicts between treaties. The problem of treaty conflicts was discussed by the earliest writers on public international law,[1] and has attracted considerable attention in recent years.[2] In 2006, an ILC study group issued an analytical study addressing related concepts and principles of general international law, including but not limited to the principle of *lex specialis*, the rules governing conflicts between successive norms, and the principle of treaty interpretation reflected in Article 31(3)(c) of the Vienna Convention.[3] These and other concepts and principles relating to treaty conflicts have been the subject of extensive commentary in the context of WTO law,[4]

---

[1] In 1953, Jenks observed that '[w]hile the importance which has recently been assumed by the problem of the conflict of law-making treaties is a reflection of the progress made … of the intensive international legislative activity in recent years, the problem of the conflict of treaties arose at a much earlier date and is discussed in some detail by Grotius, Pufendorf, and Vattel'. C. W. Jenks, 'The Conflict of Law-Making Treaties' (1953) 30 *British Yearbook of International Law* 401, at p. 405.

[2] See e.g. J. B. Mus, 'Conflicts between Treaties in International Law' (1998) 45(2) *Netherlands International Law Review* 208; N. Metz-Luck, 'Treaties, Conflicts Between' (December 2010) in *Max Planck Encyclopedia of Public International Law*.

[3] ILC, *Fragmentation of International Law: Difficulties Arising from the Diversification and Expansion of International Law – Report of the Study Group of the International Law Commission* UN Doc. A/CN.4/L.682 (13 April 2006), as corrected UN Doc. A/CN.4/L.682/Corr.1 (11 August 2006) (finalized by Martti Koskenniemi). The study group's conclusions appear at Report of the International Law Commission, 58th Session, 1 May–9 June, 3 July–11 August 2006, pp. 407–23, UN Doc. A/61/10; GAOR, 61st Session, Supp. No. 10 (2006) (hereinafter 'Conclusions'). Neither the Report nor the Conclusions were adopted by the Commission. The Commission, however, 'decided to take note' of the Conclusions, 'commended them to the attention of the General Assembly', and requested that the Report be made available on the Commission's website and published in its *Yearbook* (*ibid.*, p. 402). Thereafter, the General Assembly also took note of the Conclusions 'together with' the Report on which they were based. GA Res. 61/34, UN GAOR, 61st Session, Supp. No. 10, UN Doc. A/RES/61/34, p. 2 (18 December 2006).

[4] For commentary, see J. Pauwelyn, *Conflict of Norms in Public International Law: How WTO Law Relates to Other Rules of International Law* (Cambridge University Press, 2003).

for two different reasons. First, the WTO Agreement is a complex treaty comprising a series of overlapping agreements and instruments, and therefore WTO adjudicators have had to address various questions about the relationship *among* the different agreements and instruments that constitute the overall WTO treaty.[5] Second, there have been several GATT/WTO proceedings in which the respondent argued that the challenged measure was required or permitted under a non-WTO treaty, or that the WTO obligation was superseded or otherwise rendered inapplicable by that treaty (e.g. a multilateral environmental agreement, a bilateral trade agreement and/or another international legal instrument). The WTO agreements contain some provisions for resolving conflicts *among* the agreements and instruments that comprise the WTO treaty.[6] However, many issues are left unregulated by the text of the WTO agreements including, for example, what constitutes a 'conflict'. This has left some scope for general international law concepts and principles relating to treaty conflicts to be taken into account by WTO adjudicators. This chapter reviews statements by WTO adjudicators related to seven different ways to avoid or resolve treaty conflicts: (i) applying the narrow definition of and presumption against 'conflict' in international law; (ii) applying the principle of treaty interpretation reflected in Article 31(3)(c) of the Vienna Convention; (iii) using treaties as evidence of facts; (iv) applying priority clauses; (v) applying the *lex specialis* principle; (vi) applying the *lex posterior* principle reflected in Article 30 of the Vienna Convention; and (vii) applying the rule in Article 41 of the Vienna Convention regarding the modification of multilateral treaties by certain parties only (*inter se* modifications).

4.2   Conflict avoidance

4.2.1 The narrow definition of and presumption against 'conflict' in international law[*]

4.2 In cases where questions relating to potential treaty conflicts have arisen, WTO adjudicators have often proceeded by first determining whether there is any actual 'conflict' which would trigger the application of any priority clauses, the

---

[5] For example, see E. Montaguti and M. Lugard, 'The GATT 1994 and Other Annex 1A Agreements: Four Different Relationships?' (2000) 3(3) *Journal of International Economic Law* 473.

[6] These provisions include the following: (i) Article XVI:3 of the WTO Agreement (conflicts between the Marrakesh Agreement and any of the Multilateral Trade Agreements); (ii) the General Interpretative Note to Annex 1A (conflicts between the GATT and other WTO agreements on trade in goods); (iii) Article 21.1 of the Agreement on Agriculture (conflicts between the Agreement on Agriculture and the other WTO agreements on trade in goods); and (iv) Article 1.2 of the DSU (conflicts between the DSU and special or additional rules and procedures in other WTO agreements).

[*] See also cases in Section 1.2.1. ('Restrictions on admissibility not lightly inferred').

lex specialis principle or Article 30 of the Vienna Convention. In that context, WTO adjudicators have developed and applied a fairly narrow definition of a 'conflict' and have found, in a number of cases, that overlapping obligations apply cumulatively. Panels and the Appellate Body have not lightly assumed the existence of conflicts among the WTO agreements, or between the WTO agreements and other international treaty obligations.[7]

In *Indonesia – Autos*, Indonesia invoked the principle of *lex specialis* in support of **4.3** its argument that the subsidy measures at issue were governed exclusively by Article XVI of the GATT and the SCM Agreement, and were not also subject to Article III of the GATT (or, for the same reason, the TRIMs Agreement). The Panel rejected Indonesia's argument on the grounds that there is no conflict between these sets of provisions:

> In considering Indonesia's defence that there is a general conflict between the provisions of the SCM Agreement and those of Article III of GATT, and consequently that the SCM Agreement is the only applicable law, we recall first that in public international law there is a presumption against conflict.[649] This presumption is especially relevant in the WTO context since all WTO agreements, including GATT 1994 which was modified by Understandings when judged necessary, were negotiated at the same time, by the same Members and in the same forum. In this context we recall the principle of effective interpretation pursuant to which all provisions of a treaty (and in the WTO system all agreements) must be given meaning, using the ordinary meaning of words.

---

[649] In international law for a conflict to exist between two treaties, three conditions have to be satisfied. First, the treaties concerned must have the same parties. Second, the treaties must cover the same substantive subject-matter. Were it otherwise, there would be no possibility for conflict. Third, the provisions must conflict, in the sense that the provisions must impose mutually exclusive obligations. '... [T]echnically speaking, there is a conflict when two (or more) treaty instruments contain obligations which cannot be complied with simultaneously ... Not every such divergence constitutes a conflict, however ... Incompatibility of contents is an essential condition of conflict'. (7 *Encyclopedia of Public International Law* (North-Holland 1984), page 468.) The *lex specialis derogat legi generali* principle 'which [is] inseparably linked with the question of conflict' (*Ibid.*, page 469) between two treaties or between two provisions (one arguably being more specific than the other), does not apply if the two treaties 'deal with the same subject from different points of view or [is] applicable in different circumstances, or one provision is more far-reaching than but not inconsistent with, those of the other' (Wilfred Jenks, 'The Conflict of Law-Making Treaties', *The British Yearbook of International Law* (BYIL) 1953, at 425 *et seq.*). For in such a case it is possible for a state which is a signatory

---

[7] For additional cases in which panels and the Appellate Body found that Article 30 was inapplicable because there was no inherent conflict between the provisions or instruments at issue, see Section 4.3.3 ('Article 30 of the Vienna Convention').

of both treaties to comply with both treaties at the same time. The presumption against conflict is especially reinforced in cases where separate agreements are concluded between the same parties, since it can be presumed that they are meant to be consistent with themselves, failing any evidence to the contrary. See also E. W. Vierdag, 'The Time of the "Conclusion" of a Multilateral Treaty: Article 30 of the Vienna Convention on the Law of Treaties and Related Provisions', BYIL, 1988, at 100; Sir Robert Jennings/Sir Arthur Watts (ed.), *Oppenheim's International Law*, Vol. I., Parts 2 to 4, 1992, at 1280; Sir Gerald Fitzmaurice, 'The Law and Procedure of the International Court of Justice', BYIL, 1957, at 237; Sir Ian Sinclair, *The Vienna Convention on the Law of Treaties*, 1984, at 97.[8]

4.4 In *EC – Bananas III*, the Panel examined the meaning of the term 'conflict' in the General Interpretative Note to Annex 1A to the WTO agreements, which provides that, in the event of a conflict between a provision of the GATT and a provision of the other WTO agreements on trade in goods, the latter prevails to the extent of the conflict. The Panel stated:

> As a preliminary issue, it is necessary to define the notion of 'conflict' laid down in the General Interpretative Note. In light of the wording, the context, the object and the purpose of this Note, we consider that it is designed to deal with (i) clashes between obligations contained in GATT 1994 and obligations contained in agreements listed in Annex 1A, where those obligations are mutually exclusive in the sense that a Member cannot comply with both obligations at the same time, and (ii) the situation where a rule in one agreement prohibits what a rule in another agreement explicitly permits.
>
> However, we are of the view that the concept of 'conflict' as embodied in the General Interpretative Note does not relate to situations where rules contained in one of the Agreements listed in Annex 1A provide for different or complementary obligations in addition to those contained in GATT 1994. In such a case, the obligations arising from the former and GATT 1994 can both be complied with at the same time without the need to renounce explicit rights or authorizations. In this latter case, there is no reason to assume that a Member is not capable of, or not required to, meet the obligations of both GATT 1994 and the relevant Annex 1A Agreement.[9]

The Panel offered the following example of a situation 'where a rule in one agreement prohibits what a rule in another agreement explicitly permits':

> For instance, Article XI:1 of GATT 1994 prohibits the imposition of quantitative restrictions, while Article XI:2 of GATT 1994 contains a rather limited catalogue of exceptions. Article 2 of the Agreement on Textiles and Clothing ('ATC') authorizes the imposition of quantitative restrictions in the textiles and clothing sector, subject to conditions specified in Article 2:1–21 of the ATC. In other words, Article XI:1 of GATT 1994 prohibits what Article 2 of the ATC permits in equally explicit terms. It is true that Members could theoretically

---

[8] Panel Report, *Indonesia – Autos*, para. 14.28.
[9] Panel Report, *EC – Bananas III (US)*, paras. 7.159–7.160.

comply with Article XI:1 of GATT, as well as with Article 2 of the ATC, simply by refraining from invoking the right to impose quantitative restrictions in the textiles sector because Article 2 of the ATC authorizes rather than mandates the imposition of quantitative restrictions. However, such an interpretation would render whole Articles or sections of Agreements covered by the WTO meaningless and run counter to the object and purpose of many agreements listed in Annex 1A which were negotiated with the intent to create rights and obligations which in parts differ substantially from those of the GATT 1994. Therefore, in the case described above, we consider that the General Interpretative Note stipulates that an obligation or authorization embodied in the ATC or any other of the agreements listed in Annex 1A prevails over the conflicting obligation provided for by GATT 1994.[10]

In *Guatemala – Cement I*, the Appellate Body examined Article 1.2 of the DSU, **4.5** which provides that the special and additional rules on dispute settlement contained in certain WTO agreements prevail over those in the DSU to the extent there is a 'difference' between them. The Appellate Body interpreted this to mean a conflict in the narrow sense:

> Article 1.2 of the DSU provides that the 'rules and procedures of this Understanding shall apply *subject to such special or additional rules and procedures* on dispute settlement contained in the covered agreements as are identified in Appendix 2 to this Understanding' (emphasis added). It states, furthermore, that these special or additional rules and procedures 'shall prevail' over the provisions of the DSU '[t]o the extent that there is a *difference* between' the two sets of provisions (emphasis added). Accordingly, if there is no 'difference', then the rules and procedures of the DSU apply *together with* the special or additional provisions of the covered agreement. In our view, it is only where the provisions of the DSU and the special or additional rules and procedures of a covered agreement *cannot* be read as *complementing* each other that the special or additional provisions are to *prevail*. A special or additional provision should only be found to *prevail* over a provision of the DSU in a situation where adherence to the one provision will lead to a violation of the other provision, that is, in the case of a *conflict* between them. An interpreter must, therefore, identify an *inconsistency* or a *difference* between a provision of the DSU and a special or additional provision of a covered agreement *before* concluding that the latter *prevails* and that the provision of the DSU does not apply.[11]

In *Argentina – Textiles and Apparel*, Argentina argued that its measures found to **4.6** be inconsistent with Article VII of the GATT were required as a result of its obligations to the IMF. The Appellate Body upheld the Panel's finding that Argentina had failed to identify any conflicting obligations. After reviewing the Panel's statements on this issue, the Appellate Body found:

> Implicit in the above statement is the Panel's belief that Argentina had not successfully shown that it was required under an agreement with the IMF to

---

[10] *Ibid.*, footnote 401.   [11] Appellate Body Report, *Guatemala – Cement I*, para. 65.

impose the statistical tax. Indeed, the Panel does not appear to have been convinced that Argentina had a legally binding agreement with the IMF at all. From the panel record in this case, it does not appear possible to determine the precise legal nature of this Memorandum on Economic Policy, nor the extent to which commitments undertaken by Argentina in this Memorandum constitute legally binding obligations. We note that page 7 of the Memorandum on Economic Policy refers to 'a temporary 3 percent surcharge on imports', which is not necessarily the same thing as the 3 per cent statistical tax levied on imports. Argentina did not show an irreconcilable conflict between the provisions of its 'Memorandum of Understanding' with the IMF and the provisions of Article VIII of the GATT 1994. We thus agree with the Panel's implicit finding that Argentina failed to demonstrate that it had a legally binding commitment to the IMF that would somehow supersede Argentina's obligations under Article VIII of the GATT 1994.[12]

4.7 In another dispute, *Argentina – Hides and Leather*, Argentina argued that its challenged measure was necessary to meet its commitments pursuant to an agreement between itself and the IMF. The Panel disagreed:

> Lastly, we turn to Argentina's assertion that no changes to the current pre-payment mechanisms are possible, as this could preclude Argentina from meeting its deficit commitments to the IMF. In support of its assertion, Argentina has referred us to an Economic Policy Memorandum and a Technical Memorandum, which Argentina says are part of an agreement with the IMF. However, in neither Memorandum is there a statement to the effect that Argentina is under an obligation to impose a discriminatory tax burden on importers. Nor do we see a requirement in those Memoranda which would bar Argentina from compensating importers for the discrimination suffered. Furthermore, Argentina has in any event not presented argument and evidence sufficient for us to find that it would be impossible for Argentina to meet its deficit targets if it were to compensate importers for the additional interest lost or paid. It should also be recalled in this context that Argentina has not invoked Article XX(d) on the basis that RG 3431 and RG 3543 are necessary to secure compliance with IMF commitments, but on the basis that they are necessary to secure compliance with the IVA Law and IG Law. For these reasons, we do not consider that, in the present case, Argentina's commitments to the IMF provide a justification for not compensating importers.[13]

4.8 In *Brazil – Retreaded Tyres*, the European Communities challenged the WTO-consistency of an import ban on retreaded tyres that provided for an exemption from the ban for tyres imported from MERCOSUR countries. Brazil introduced the MERCOSUR exemption to comply with a ruling issued by a MERCOSUR arbitral tribunal, which had found Brazil's restrictions on the importation of remoulded tyres to be a violation of its obligations under MERCOSUR. Before the WTO Panel, Brazil argued that the MERCOSUR exemption was neither

---

[12] Appellate Body Report, *Argentina – Textiles and Apparel*, para. 69.
[13] Panel Report, *Argentina – Hides and Leather*, para. 11.328.

'arbitrary' nor 'unjustifiable' discrimination within the meaning of the chapeau of Article XX of the GATT, because it was taken to implement the MERCO-SUR tribunal ruling. The Panel agreed with Brazil. However, the Appellate Body reversed the Panel's interpretation of Article XX, and concluded that the exemption from the import ban for MERCOSUR countries did indeed result in arbitrary or unjustifiable discrimination within the meaning of the chapeau of Article XX of the GATT.[14] In the course of its analysis, the Appellate Body indicated that it saw no necessary conflict between Brazil's MERCOSUR and WTO obligations:

> This being said, we observe, like the Panel, that, before the arbitral tribunal established under MERCOSUR, Brazil could have sought to justify the challenged Import Ban on the grounds of human, animal, and plant health under Article 50(d) of the Treaty of Montevideo.[443] Brazil, however, decided not to do so. It is not appropriate for us to second-guess Brazil's decision not to invoke Article 50(d), which serves a function similar to that of Article XX(b) of the GATT 1994. However, Article 50(d) of the Treaty of Montevideo, as well as the fact that Brazil might have raised this defence in the MERCOSUR arbitral proceedings, show, in our view, that the discrimination associated with the MERCOSUR exemption does not necessarily result from a conflict between provisions under MERCOSUR and the GATT 1994.[15]

4.2.2 Article 31(3)(c) of the Vienna Convention

Article 31(3)(c) of the Vienna Convention provides that a treaty interpreter shall **4.9** take account of 'any relevant rules of international law applicable in the relations between the parties'. In several cases, panels and the Appellate Body have declined to take account of non-WTO instruments to interpret WTO provisions on the grounds that those instruments did not qualify as 'relevant rules of international law applicable in the relations between the parties'; in some cases, panels and the Appellate Body have taken other international instruments and/or principles of customary international law into account, either on the basis that they did so qualify under Article 31(3)(c), or without any express reference to Article 31(3)(c). In those cases where WTO adjudicators have taken into account other treaties and/or international law concepts and principles pursuant to Article 31(3)(c), it has generally been to support an interpretation arrived at on the basis of the text, context and purpose of the provision at issue. To date, there is no case in which a WTO adjudicator has justified its interpretation of a WTO provision expressly and primarily on the basis of Article 31(3)(c).[16]

---

[14] Appellate Body Report, *Brazil – Retreaded Tyres*, paras. 224–34.   [15] *Ibid.*, para. 234.
[16] For additional statements by panels and the Appellate Body regarding the relationship between the WTO agreements and other rules of international law, see Section 13.3 ('Customary international law').

4.10 In *US – Gasoline*, the Appellate Body, without mentioning Article 31(3)(c), stated that Article 3.2 of the DSU, which provides that the WTO dispute settlement system serves to clarify the existing provisions of the covered agreements in accordance with customary rules of interpretation of public international law, 'reflects a measure of recognition that the *General Agreement* is not to be read in clinical isolation from public international law'.[17]

4.11 In *US – Shrimp*, the Appellate Body concluded that the meaning of the term 'exhaustible natural resources' in Article XX(g) of the GATT is not confined to non-living (e.g. mineral) resources. The Appellate Body, without referring to Article 31(3)(c) of the Vienna Convention, referred to several international conventions and international instruments as support for that view:

> From the perspective embodied in the preamble of the *WTO Agreement*, we note that the generic term 'natural resources' in Article XX(g) is not 'static' in its content or reference but is rather 'by definition, evolutionary'. It is, therefore, pertinent to note that modern international conventions and declarations make frequent references to natural resources as embracing both living and non-living resources. For instance, the 1982 United Nations Convention on the Law of the Sea ('UNCLOS'), in defining the jurisdictional rights of coastal states in their exclusive economic zones, provides:
>
> *Article 56*
> *Rights, jurisdiction and duties of the coastal State in the exclusive economic zone*
>
> > 1. In the exclusive economic zone, the coastal State has:
> >   (a) sovereign rights for the purpose of exploring and exploiting, conserving and managing the *natural resources, whether living or non-living*, of the waters superjacent to the sea-bed and of the sea-bed and its subsoil . . . (emphasis added)
>
> The UNCLOS also repeatedly refers in Articles 61 and 62 to 'living resources' in specifying rights and duties of states in their exclusive economic zones. The Convention on Biological Diversity uses the concept of 'biological resources'. Agenda 21 speaks most broadly of 'natural resources' and goes into detailed statements about 'marine living resources'. In addition, the Resolution on Assistance to Developing Countries, adopted in conjunction with the Convention on the Conservation of Migratory Species of Wild Animals, recites:
>
> > Conscious that an important element of development lies in the conservation and management of *living natural resources* and that migratory species constitute a significant part of these resources . . . (emphasis added)
>
> Given the recent acknowledgement by the international community of the importance of concerted bilateral or multilateral action to protect living natural

---

[17] Appellate Body Report, *US – Gasoline*, p. 17.

resources, and recalling the explicit recognition by WTO Members of the objective of sustainable development in the preamble of the *WTO Agreement*, we believe it is too late in the day to suppose that Article XX(g) of the GATT 1994 may be read as referring only to the conservation of exhaustible mineral or other non-living natural resources. Moreover, two adopted GATT 1947 panel reports previously found fish to be an 'exhaustible natural resource' within the meaning of Article XX(g). We hold that, in line with the principle of effectiveness in treaty interpretation, measures to conserve exhaustible natural resources, whether *living* or *non-living*, may fall within Article XX(g).'[18]

In *US – Shrimp*, the Appellate Body noted that most of the international instruments referred to above had been ratified or otherwise accepted by the parties to the dispute, and/or were regarded, in the case of UNCLOS, as reflecting customary international law:

> We note that India, Malaysia and Pakistan have ratified the UNCLOS. Thailand has signed, but not ratified the Convention, and the United States has not signed the Convention. In the oral hearing, the United States stated: '. . . we have not ratified this Convention although, with respect to fisheries law, for the most part we do believe that UNCLOS reflects international customary law.' Also see, for example, W. Burke, *The New International Law of Fisheries* (Clarendon Press, 1994), p. 40 . . .
>
> . . . We note that India, Malaysia and Pakistan have ratified the Convention on Biological Diversity, and that Thailand and the United States have signed but not ratified the Convention.
>
> . . . We note that India and Pakistan have ratified the Convention on the Conservation of Migratory Species of Wild Animals, but that Malaysia, Thailand and the United States are not parties to the Convention.[19]

In the subsequent compliance proceeding, the Panel in *US – Shrimp (Article* **4.12** *21.5 – Malaysia)* referred back to the Appellate Body's references to these international agreements, and made reference to Article 31(3)(c) of the Vienna Convention:

> [W]e note that the Appellate Body, like the Original Panel, referred to a number of international agreements, many of which have been ratified or otherwise accepted by the parties to this dispute. Article 31.3(c) of the Vienna Convention provides that, in interpreting a treaty, there shall be taken into account, together with the context, 'any relevant rule of international law applicable to the relations between the parties'. We note that, with the exception of the Bonn Convention on the Conservation of Migratory Species of Wild Animals (CMS), Malaysia and the United States have accepted or are committed to comply with all of the international instruments referred to by the Appellate Body in paragraph 168 of its Report.[20]

---

[18] Appellate Body Report, *US – Shrimp*, paras. 130–1.   [19] *Ibid.*, footnotes 110–13.
[20] Panel Report, *US – Shrimp (Article 21.5 – Malaysia)*, para. 5.57.

4.13 In *EC – Approval and Marketing of Biotech Products* the Panel stated, with regard to the Appellate Body's reference to these international instruments in *US – Shrimp*, that 'the Appellate Body did not suggest that it was looking to other rules of international law because it was required to do so pursuant to the provisions of Article 31(3)(c) of the *Vienna Convention*. Indeed, the Appellate Body did not even mention Article 31(3)(c).'[21]

4.14 The Panel in *US – Section 110(5) Copyright Act* stated, without reference to Article 31(3)(c), that, following the 'public international law presumption against conflicts', it would avoid interpreting the copyright provisions of the TRIPS Agreement to mean something different from the relevant provisions of the Berne Convention:

> In the area of copyright, the Berne Convention and the TRIPS Agreement form the overall framework for multilateral protection. Most WTO Members are also parties to the Berne Convention. We recall that it is a general principle of interpretation to adopt the meaning that reconciles the texts of different treaties and avoids a conflict between them. Accordingly, one should avoid interpreting the TRIPS Agreement to mean something different than the Berne Convention except where this is explicitly provided for. This principle is in conformity with the public international law presumption against conflicts, which has been applied by WTO panels and the Appellate Body in a number of cases. We believe that our interpretation of the legal status of the minor exceptions doctrine under the TRIPS Agreement is consistent with these general principles.[22]

4.15 In *Chile – Price Band*, the Panel found that the Economic Complementarity Agreement No. 35 (ECA 35), an international agreement between Chile and MERCOSUR, could not determine the meaning of Article 4.2 of the Agreement on Agriculture:

> Finally, Article 24 of ECA 35 does not constitute in our view a 'relevant rule of international law applicable in the relations between the parties'. Again, leaving aside the question of whether such a rule of international law should be applicable between *all* parties to the WTO Agreement, the language of ECA 35 itself makes clear that Article 24 cannot be 'relevant' to the interpretation of Article 4.2 of the Agreement on Agriculture. First, the Preamble states that the commercial policies and compromises of ECA 35 shall 'adjust to' the WTO framework of rights and obligations. *A fortiori*, Article 24 of ECA 35 cannot influence the interpretation of the WTO Agreement. Second, Chile's commitment regarding its PBS in Article 24 of ECA 35 has been explicitly made 'within the framework of ECA 35. Such language suggests that the parties to ECA 35 did not intend to exclude the possibility that different commitments regarding the Chilean PBS may have been or will be made in the context of other international agreements.[23]

---

[21] Panel Report, *EC – Approval and Marketing of Biotech Products*, footnote 271.
[22] Panel Report, *US – Section 110(5) Copyright Act*, para. 6.66.
[23] Panel Report, *Chile – Price Band*, para. 7.85.

In *Argentina – Poultry Anti-Dumping Duties*, Brazil challenged an Argentine **4.16**
anti-dumping measure before a MERCOSUR Tribunal and then initiated
WTO dispute settlement proceedings against the same measure. Argentina
argued that the earlier MERCOSUR ruling was part of the normative framework to be applied by the Panel as a result of Article 31(3)(c) of the Vienna
Convention (and/or that Brazil was 'estopped' from pursuing its claims before
the WTO panel – see para. 1.13 above). The Panel disagreed with Argentina:

> We note that Article 3.2 of the *DSU* is concerned with international rules of treaty
> interpretation. Article 31.3(c) of the *Vienna Convention* is similarly concerned
> with treaty interpretation. However, Argentina has not sought to rely on any law
> providing that, in respect of relations between Argentina and Brazil, the WTO
> agreements should be interpreted in a particular way. In particular, Argentina has
> not relied on any statement or finding in the MERCOSUR Tribunal ruling to
> suggest that we should interpret specific provisions of the WTO agreements in a
> particular way. Rather than concerning itself with the interpretation of the WTO
> agreements, Argentina actually argues that the earlier MERCOSUR Tribunal
> ruling requires us to rule in a particular way. In other words, Argentina would have
> us apply the relevant WTO provisions in a particular way, rather than interpret
> them in a particular way. However, there is no basis in Article 3.2 of the *DSU*, or
> any other provision, to suggest that we are bound to rule in a particular way, or
> apply the relevant WTO provisions in a particular way. We note that we are not
> even bound to follow rulings contained in adopted WTO panel reports, so we see
> no reason at all why we should be bound by the rulings of non-WTO dispute
> settlement bodies. Accordingly, we reject Argentina's alternative arguments
> regarding Article 31.3(c) of the *Vienna Convention*.[64]

> ---
> [64] Even if Argentina had relied on the MERCOSUR Tribunal ruling to argue
> that particular provisions of the WTO Agreement should be interpreted in a
> particular way, it is not entirely clear that Article 31.3(c) of the *Vienna Conven-
> tion* would apply. In particular, it is not clear to us that a rule applicable between
> only several WTO Members would constitute a relevant rule of international
> law applicable in the relations between the 'parties'.[24]

In *EC – Chicken Cuts*, the Appellate Body found that the consensus among **4.17**
Members to use the Harmonized System of tariff nomenclature as the basis for
their WTO Schedules constitutes an 'agreement' within the meaning of Article
31(2)(a) of the Vienna Convention (see para. 15.28 below). In light of this
conclusion, the Appellate Body, like the Panel in that dispute, did not find it
necessary to determine whether the Harmonized System could constitute a
'relevant rule of international law' within the meaning of Article 31(3)(c) of
the Vienna Convention.[25]

[24] Panel Report, *Argentina – Poultry Anti-Dumping Duties*, para. 7.41 (citing Appellate Body Report, *Japan – Alcoholic Beverages II*, p. 14).
[25] Appellate Body Report, *EC – Chicken Cuts*, footnote 384.

4.18 In *EC – Commercial Vessels*, the panel concluded that the European Communities acted inconsistently with Article 23.1 of the DSU, which provides that Members must have recourse to WTO dispute settlement procedures when seeking the redress of a violation of WTO obligations (as opposed to engaging in unilateral retaliation). The European Communities argued that measures not involving a suspension of concessions or other obligations fall outside of the scope of Article 23.1 of the DSU. In this regard, the European Communities argued that Article 23.1 should be interpreted in light of Article 60 of the Vienna Convention (concerning the termination or suspension of the operation of a treaty as a consequence of its breach). The Panel, without referring to Article 31(3)(c), found that the public international law concepts invoked by the European Communities could not justify reading this limitation into Article 23.1:

> The Panel recalls that it has concluded, based on an interpretation of Article 23.1 of the DSU in accordance with the ordinary meaning of its terms and in light of the object and purpose of the provision, that measures not involving a suspension of WTO concessions or other obligations are not excluded from its scope. While the Panel realizes that in a number of WTO dispute settlement and arbitration cases reference has been made to the public international law concepts invoked by the European Communities,[395] the Panel can see no basis for using these concepts to read into Article 23.1 a limitation that is unsupported by an interpretation based on its text, context and object and purpose.

---

[395] Thus, for example, the Appellate Body has referred to 'the rules of general international law on state responsibility, which require that countermeasures in response to breaches by states of their international obligations be commensurate with the injury suffered'. Appellate Body Report, *US – Cotton Yarn*, para. 120. See also Appellate Body Report, *US – Line Pipe*, para. 259. The concept of countermeasures as used in the international law on state responsibility has also been referred to in *US – FSC (Article 22.6 – US)*, paras. 5.58–5.60; *Brazil – Aircraft (Article 22.6 – Brazil)*, para. 3.44; and *EC – Bananas III (US) (Article 22.6 – EC)*, para. 6.16.[26]

4.19 In *Mexico – Taxes on Soft Drinks*, the Panel examined certain measures that Mexico characterized as countermeasures in response to an alleged US breach of the NAFTA. Mexico did not contest the United States' claim that the measures violated Article III of the GATT, but argued that they were justified under Article XX(d) of the GATT as measures 'necessary to secure compliance with laws or regulations which are not inconsistent with this Agreement'. At the outset of its analysis of Mexico's defence under Article XX(d), the Panel observed that, 'although Mexico has characterized its actions as an exercise of countermeasures, as recognized under international law, it does not seem to be

---

[26] Panel Report, *EC – Commercial Vessels*, para. 7.205.

suggesting that the international law rules governing such actions should affect the interpretation of Article XX(d)'.[27]

In *EC – Approval and Marketing of Biotech Products*, the disputing parties **4.20** disagreed on whether the Biosafety Protocol qualified as a relevant rule of international law, within the meaning of Article 31(3)(c), to be taken into account for the purpose of interpreting the SPS Agreement. In light of that disagreement, the Panel conducted a detailed analysis of Article 31(3)(c). In the course of its analysis, the Panel considered the sources of public international law covered by 'rules of international law', the meaning of the phrase 'applicable in the relations between the parties', what it considered to be the separate issue of having reference to other rules of international law for the purpose of determining the 'ordinary meaning' of a term under Article 31(1). The Panel also offered several observations on the function of Article 31(3)(c) more generally. Beginning with the sources of public international law covered by 'rules of international law', the Panel rejected a restrictive interpretation of these terms:

> In considering the provisions of Article 31(3)(c), we note, initially, that it refers to 'rules of international law'. Textually, this reference seems sufficiently broad to encompass all generally accepted sources of public international law, that is to say, (i) international conventions (treaties), (ii) international custom (customary international law), and (iii) the recognized general principles of law. In our view, there can be no doubt that treaties and customary rules of international law are 'rules of international law' within the meaning of Article 31(3)(c). We therefore agree with the European Communities that a treaty like the *Biosafety Protocol* would qualify as a 'rule of international law'. Regarding the recognized general *principles* of law which are applicable in international law, it may not appear self-evident that they can be considered as '*rules*' of international law' within the meaning of Article 31(3)(c). However, the Appellate Body in *US – Shrimp* made it clear that pursuant to Article 31(3)(c) general principles of international law are to be taken into account in the interpretation of WTO provisions. As we mention further below, the European Communities considers that the principle of precaution is a 'general principle of international law'. Based on the Appellate Body report on *US – Shrimp*, we would agree that if the precautionary principle is a general principle of international law, it could be considered a 'rule of international law' within the meaning of Article 31(3)(c).[28]

The Panel in *EC – Approval and Marketing of Biotech Products* then considered the meaning of the term 'the parties' in Article 31(3)(c):

> [I]mportantly, Article 31(3)(c) indicates that it is only those rules of international law which are 'applicable in the relations between the parties' that are to be taken into account in interpreting a treaty. This limitation gives rise to the

---

[27] Panel Report, *Mexico – Taxes on Soft Drinks*, para. 8.162.
[28] Panel Report, *EC – Approval and Marketing of Biotech Products*, para. 7.67 (citing Appellate Body Report, *US – Shrimp*, para. 158 and footnote 157).

question of what is meant by the term 'the parties'. In considering this issue, we note that Article 31(3)(c) does not refer to 'one or more parties'.[240] Nor does it refer to 'the parties to a dispute'.[241] We further note that Article 2.1(g) of the *Vienna Convention* defines the meaning of the term 'party' for the purposes of the *Vienna Convention*. Thus, 'party' means 'a State which has consented to be bound by the treaty and for which the treaty is in force'.[242] It may be inferred from these elements that the rules of international law applicable in the relations between 'the parties' are the rules of international law applicable in the relations between the States which have consented to be bound by the treaty which is being interpreted, and for which that treaty is in force. This understanding of the term 'the parties' leads logically to the view that the rules of international law to be taken into account in interpreting the WTO agreements at issue in this dispute are those which are applicable in the relations between the WTO Members.[243]

---

[240] We note that, by contrast, Article 31(2)(b) of the *Vienna Convention* refers to 'one or more parties'.

[241] By contrast, Article 66 of the *Vienna Convention*, which deals with procedures for judicial settlement, arbitration and conciliation, refers to 'the parties to a dispute'. We note that the absence of a reference to 'the parties to a dispute' in Article 31 is not surprising given that Article 31 does not purport to lay down rules of interpretation which are applicable solely in the context of international (quasi-)judicial proceedings.

[242] We are aware that Article 31(2)(a) of the *Vienna Convention* refers to 'all the parties'. However, we do not consider that Article 31(2)(a) rules out our interpretation of the term 'the parties' in Article 31(3)(c). In our view, the reference to 'all the parties' is used in Article 31(2)(a) to make clear the difference between the class of documents at issue in that provision (namely, agreements relating to a treaty which were made between 'all the parties') and the class of documents at issue in Article 31(2)(b) (namely, instruments made by 'one or more parties' and accepted by 'the other parties' as related to a treaty). In other words, we think that the use of the term 'all the parties' in Article 31(2)(a) is explained, and necessitated, by the existence of Article 31(2)(b). Consistent with this view, we think that the absence of a reference to 'all the parties' in Article 31(3)(c) is explained by the fact that Article 31(3) contains no provision like Article 31(2)(b), i.e. that Article 31(3) contains no provision which refers to 'one or more parties' and hence could render unclear or ambiguous the reference to 'the parties' in Article 31(3)(c). It is useful to note, in addition, that the view that the term 'the parties' in Article 31(3)(c) should be understood as referring to all the parties to a treaty has also been expressed by Mustafa Yasseen, 'L'interprétation des Traités d'après la Convention de Vienne sur le Droit des Traités', in *Recueil des Cours de l'Académie de Droit International* (1976), Vol. III, p. 63, para. 7.

[243] We find further support for this view in the provisions of Article 31(3)(b). Article 31(3)(b), which is part of the immediate context of Article 31(3)(c), provides that a treaty interpreter must take into account 'any subsequent practice in the application of the treaty which establishes the agreement of the parties regarding its interpretation'. Like Article 31(3)(c), this provision

makes reference to 'the parties'. In *EC – Chicken Cuts*, the Appellate Body appeared to agree with the panel in that case that the term 'the parties' in Article 31(3)(b) means the parties to a treaty and in the WTO context must be understood as meaning the WTO Members. Appellate Body Report, *EC – Chicken Cuts*, paras. 272 (referring to 'a treaty party' and agreement with a practice by 'other WTO Members') and 273 (referring to the 'issue of how to establish the agreement by Members that have not engaged in a practice'). See also Appellate Body Report, *Japan – Alcoholic Beverages II*, p. 13 (referring to 'the agreement of the parties [to a treaty] regarding its interpretation'). It is true that the Appellate Body found that 'the interpretation of a treaty provision on the basis of subsequent practice is binding on all parties, including those that have not actually engaged in such practice'. Appellate Body Report, *EC – Chicken Cuts*, para. 273. But it also found that it is necessary 'to establish agreement of those that have not engaged in a practice'. Appellate Body Report, *EC – Chicken Cuts*, para. 271. Thus, our interpretation of the term 'the parties' in Article 31(3)(c) is consistent with, and indeed supported by, the Appellate Body's interpretation of the same term in Article 31(3)(b). In our view, it would be incongruous to allow the interpretation of a treaty to be affected by rules of international law which are not applicable in the relations between all parties to the treaty, but not by a subsequent practice which does not establish the agreement of all parties to the treaty regarding the meaning of that treaty.[29]

The Panel in *EC – Approval and Marketing of Biotech Products* rejected the EC argument that it should interpret the WTO agreements at issue in light of other rules of international law even if those rules were not binding on all parties to the dispute:

> In addressing this argument, we first recall our view that Article 31(3)(c) should be interpreted to mandate consideration of rules of international law which are applicable in the relations between all parties to the treaty which is being interpreted. The parties to a dispute over compliance with a particular treaty are, of course, parties to that treaty. In relation to the present dispute it can thus be said that if a rule of international law is not applicable to one of the four WTO Members which are parties to the present dispute, the rule is not applicable in the relations between all WTO Members. Accordingly, based on our interpretation of Article 31(3)(c), we do not consider that in interpreting the relevant WTO agreements we are required to take into account other rules of international law which are not applicable to one of the Parties to this dispute. But even independently of our own interpretation, we think Article 31(3)(c) cannot reasonably be interpreted as the European Communities suggests. Indeed, it is not apparent why a sovereign State would agree to a mandatory rule of treaty interpretation which could have as a consequence that the interpretation of a treaty to which that State is a party is affected by other rules of international law which that State has decided not to accept.

---

[29] Panel Report, *EC – Approval and Marketing of Biotech Products*, para. 7.68.

Before applying our interpretation of Article 31(3)(c) to the present case, it is important to note that the present case is not one in which relevant rules of international law are applicable in the relations between all parties to the dispute, but not between all WTO Members, and in which all parties to the dispute argue that a multilateral WTO agreement should be interpreted in the light of these other rules of international law. Therefore, we need not, and do not, take a position on whether in such a situation we would be entitled to take the relevant other rules of international law into account.[30]

The Panel in *EC – Approval and Marketing of Biotech Products* also discussed what it considered to be the separate issue of having reference to other rules of international law for the purpose of determining the 'ordinary meaning' of a term under Article 31(1), and considered that this would permit consideration of international conventions that may not qualify as 'relevant rules of international law applicable between the relations between the parties' under Article 31(3)(c):

> The ordinary meaning of treaty terms is often determined on the basis of dictionaries. We think that, in addition to dictionaries, other relevant rules of international law may in some cases aid a treaty interpreter in establishing, or confirming, the ordinary meaning of treaty terms in the specific context in which they are used. Such rules would not be considered because they are legal rules, but rather because they may provide evidence of the ordinary meaning of terms in the same way that dictionaries do. They would be considered for their informative character. It follows that when a treaty interpreter does not consider another rule of international law to be informative, he or she need not rely on it.
>
> In the light of the foregoing, we consider that a panel may consider other relevant rules of international law when interpreting the terms of WTO agreements if it deems such rules to be informative. But a panel need not necessarily rely on other rules of international law, particularly if it considers that the ordinary meaning of the terms of WTO agreements may be ascertained by reference to other elements.
>
> This approach is consistent with the Appellate Body's approach in *US – Shrimp*, as we understand it. In that case, the Appellate Body had to interpret the term 'exhaustible natural resources' in Article XX(g) of the GATT 1994. The Appellate Body found that this term was by definition evolutionary and therefore found it 'pertinent to note that modern international conventions and declarations make frequent references to natural resources as embracing both living and non-living resources'. Thus, as we understand it, the Appellate Body drew on other rules of international law because it considered that they were informative and aided it in establishing the meaning and scope of the term 'exhaustible natural resources'. The European Communities correctly points out that the Appellate Body referred to conventions which were not applicable to all disputing parties. However, the mere fact that one or more disputing parties are not parties to a convention does not necessarily mean that a convention cannot shed light on the meaning and scope of a treaty term to be interpreted.[31]

---

[30] *Ibid.*, paras. 7.71–7.72.
[31] *Ibid.*, paras. 7.92–7.94 (citing Appellate Body Report, *US – Shrimp*, para. 130).

The Panel in *EC – Approval and Marketing of Biotech Products* offered several observations on the function of Article 31(3)(c) more generally:

It is important to note that Article 31(3)(c) mandates a treaty interpreter to take into account other rules of international law ('[t]here shall be taken into account'); it does not merely give a treaty interpreter the option of doing so.[244] It is true that the obligation is to 'take account' of such rules, and thus no particular outcome is prescribed. However, Article 31(1) makes clear that a treaty is to be interpreted 'in good faith'. Thus, where consideration of all other interpretative elements set out in Article 31 results in more than one permissible interpretation, a treaty interpreter following the instructions of Article 31(3)(c) in good faith would in our view need to settle for that interpretation which is more in accord with other applicable rules of international law.[245]

Taking account of the fact that Article 31(3)(c) mandates consideration of other applicable rules of international law, and that such consideration may prompt a treaty interpreter to adopt one interpretation rather than another, we think it makes sense to interpret Article 31(3)(c) as requiring consideration of those rules of international law which are applicable in the relations between all parties to the treaty which is being interpreted. Requiring that a treaty be interpreted in the light of other rules of international law which bind the States parties to the treaty ensures or enhances the consistency of the rules of international law applicable to these States and thus contributes to avoiding conflicts between the relevant rules.

---

[244] This view is confirmed by the negotiating history of Article 31(3). The International Law Commission, in its commentary to Article 27 of the draft *Vienna Convention*, which contained language identical to the current Article 31 of the *Vienna Convention*, stated that 'the three elements [the three subparagraphs of what is now Article 31(3)] are all of an obligatory character and by their very nature could not be considered to be norms of interpretation in any way inferior to those which precede them'. *Yearbook of the International Law Commission* (1966), Vol. II, p. 220, para. 9.

[245] We are not suggesting that other applicable rules of international law invariably or exclusively serve as a kind of 'tie-breaker' in the interpretative process.[32]

In *US / Canada – Continued Suspension*, the Panel suggested that the principle of **4.21** good faith in international legal relations could be taken into account via Article 31(3)(c):

We note that what the European Communities claims in this respect is the existence of a presumption of good faith compliance based on the international law principle of good faith. We are mindful of the position expressed by the United States that the impact of general international law on the DSU is limited to the application of the customary rules of interpretation of public international

---

[32] Panel Report, *EC – Approval and Marketing of Biotech Products*, paras. 7.69–7.70.

law embodied in the Vienna Convention on the Law of Treaties (cf. Article 3.2 of the DSU). However, we note that Article 31.3(c) provides that

> [t]here shall be taken into account, together with the context . . . (c) any relevant rule of international law applicable to the relations between the parties.

Having regard to the overarching nature of the principle of good faith in international legal relations, we deem it appropriate to determine first whether there is any basis in public international law for the principle to which the European Communities refers. If this is the case, we will then proceed with determining whether the WTO Agreement in general and the DSU in particular exclude the application of this principle.[33]

4.22 In *US – Anti-Dumping and Countervailing Duties (China)* (DS379), the Appellate Body interpreted the term 'public body' in Article 1.1(a)(1) of the SCM Agreement in light of the ILC Articles on State Responsibility. In that context, the Appellate Body engaged in a discussion of Article 31(3)(c):

> We note that Article 31(3)(c) of the *Vienna Convention*, quoted above, contains three elements. First, it refers to 'rules of international law'; second, the rules must be 'relevant'; and third, such rules must be 'applicable in the relations between the parties'. We will address these three elements in turn.
>
> First, the reference to 'rules of international law' corresponds to the sources of international law in Article 38(1) of the Statute of the International Court of Justice and thus includes customary rules of international law as well as general principles of law. Second, in order to be relevant, such rules must concern the same subject-matter as the treaty terms being interpreted. To the extent that Articles 4, 5, and 8 of the ILC Articles concern the same subject-matter as Article 1.1(a)(1) of the *SCM Agreement*, they would be 'relevant' in the sense of Article 31(3)(c) of the *Vienna Convention*. With respect to the third requirement, the question is whether the ILC Articles are 'applicable in the relations between the parties'. We observe that Articles 4, 5, and 8 of the ILC Articles are not binding *by virtue of* being part of an international treaty. However, insofar as they reflect customary international law or general principles of law, these Articles are applicable in the relations between the parties.[34]

The Appellate Body criticized the Panel's reluctance to take the ILC Articles on State Responsibility into account, as well as the Panel's understanding of prior WTO jurisprudence regarding Article 31(3)(c):

> In our view, the Panel misconstrued the role of the ILC Articles when it set out to analyze 'whether [the ILC Articles] would override [the Panel's] analysis and conclusions based on the text of the SCM Agreement itself'. The question is not

---

[33] Panel Reports, *US / Canada – Continued Suspension*, para. 7.310.

[34] Appellate Body Report, *US – Anti-Dumping and Countervailing Duties (China)*, paras. 308–9 (citing M. E. Villiger, *Commentary on the 1969 Vienna Convention on the Law of Treaties* (Martinus Nijhoff, 2009), p. 433; Appellate Body Reports, *US/Canada – Continued Suspension*, para. 382; Panel Report, *US – Gambling*, para. 6.128).

whether intermediate results of one element of the interpretative exercise 'override' the results of another. Rules of international law within the meaning of Article 31(3)(c) are one of several means to ascertain the common intention of the parties to a particular agreement reflected in Article 31 of the *Vienna Convention*.

> We are puzzled by the Panel's statement that the ILC Articles have been cited by panels and the Appellate Body 'as conceptual guidance only to supplement or confirm, but not to replace, the analyses based on the ordinary meaning, context and object and purpose of the relevant covered Agreements'. The Panel elaborated that, while in some WTO disputes the ILC Articles 'have been cited as containing similar provisions to those in certain areas of the WTO Agreement, in others they have been cited by way of contrast with the provisions of the WTO Agreement, as a way to better understand the possible meaning of the provisions of the WTO Agreement'. The Panel considered this to indicate that panels and the Appellate Body have not considered the ILC Articles to constitute rules of international law in the sense of Article 31(3)(c). To us, this demonstrates the opposite. If, as the Panel states, certain ILC Articles have been 'cited as containing similar provisions to those in certain areas of the WTO Agreement' or 'cited by way of contrast with the provisions of the WTO Agreement', this evinces that these ILC Articles have been 'taken into account' in the sense of Article 31(3)(c) by panels and the Appellate Body in these cases.[35]

Furthermore, the Appellate Body disagreed with the Panel's statement that the ILC Articles on State Responsibility had been 'superseded' by Article 1.1(a)(1) of the SCM Agreement as *lex specialis* pursuant to Article 55 of the ILC Articles. The Appellate Body drew a distinction between reference to other rules of international law to *interpret* a provision, versus the *direct application* of those other rules:

> As we see it, Article 55 of the ILC Articles does not speak to the question of whether, for the purpose of interpreting Article 1.1(a)(1) of the *SCM Agreement*, a panel or the Appellate Body can take into account provisions of the ILC Articles. Article 55 stipulates that '[t]hese articles do not apply where . . .'. Article 55 addresses the question of which rule to *apply* where there are multiple rules addressing the same subject-matter. The question in the present case, however, is not whether certain of the ILC Articles are to be *applied*, that is, whether attribution of conduct of the SOEs and SOCBs at issue to the Government of China is to be assessed pursuant to the ILC Articles instead of Article 1.1(a)(1) of the *SCM Agreement*. There is no doubt that the provision being applied in the present case is Article 1.1(a)(1). Rather, the question is, whether, when interpreting the terms of Article 1.1(a)(1), the relevant provisions of the ILC Articles may be taken into account as one among several interpretative elements. Thus, the treaty being *applied* is the *SCM Agreement*, and the attribution rules of the ILC Articles are to be *taken into account* in interpreting the meaning of the terms of that treaty. Article 55 of the ILC Articles does not speak to the issue of how the latter should be done.[36]

---

[35] Appellate Body Report, *US – Anti-Dumping and Countervailing Duties (China)*, paras. 312–13.
[36] Appellate Body Report, *US – Anti-Dumping and Countervailing Duties (China)*, para. 316.

4.23 In *EC and certain member States – Large Civil Aircraft*, the European Communities argued that the Panel should exclude all pre-1992 subsidies from its
analysis because, in a bilateral agreement between the European Communities
and the United States (the '1992 Agreement'), the parties had agreed to waive
their right to challenge any subsidies granted prior to 1992. In that regard, the
European Communities argued that the Panel should treat the 1992 Agreement
as a 'relevant rule of international law applicable in the relations between the
parties' under Article 31(3)(c) that should affect the 'interpretation' of the
'temporal scope of this proceeding' (and/or as a basis for estoppel or simply as
directly applicable law – see paras. 1.17 and 1.34 above). The Panel rejected
the European Communities' argument:

> The European Communities argues that the Panel should take the 1992 Agree-
> ment into consideration in its interpretation of the temporal scope of application
> of the SCM Agreement for purposes of this dispute. The European Commu-
> nities argues that Article 31(3)(c) of the VCLT provides a basis for us to do so,
> because the 1992 Agreement constitutes a relevant rule of international law
> applicable in the relations between the parties. Although presented as an
> argument relating to the 'interpretation' of the SCM Agreement, the European
> Communities has not specifically indicated how the 1992 Agreement should
> influence our interpretation of the actual terms in Article 5 of the SCM
> Agreement, other than to argue that we should 'interpret' a particular temporal
> scope of application of the SCM Agreement for this dispute because the parties
> agreed in Article 2 of the 1992 Agreement to exclude pre-1992 measures from
> GATT/WTO dispute settlement proceedings. In reality, this is an argument
> that a particular group of measures (i.e. support measures for large civil aircraft
> committed by either of the parties prior to 17 July 1992) should be excluded
> from the disciplines of the SCM Agreement based on the 1992 Agreement,
> rather than an argument about the interpretation of provisions of the SCM
> Agreement, or of specific terms within those provisions.
>
>   It is not necessary for us to determine whether, for purposes of Article 31(3)
> (c) of the VCLT, the 1992 Agreement constitutes applicable law between the
> parties that we must take into account in interpreting the SCM Agreement.[1911]
> Even if it were (and we emphasize that on this issue we express no view), as we
> have previously indicated, we do not agree with the European Communities that
> the 1992 Agreement constitutes an agreement between the parties to 'grand-
> father' pre-1992 measures of support for large civil aircraft for the purposes of
> subsequent GATT/WTO proceedings. Consequently, even if we were to inter-
> pret the temporal scope of the SCM Agreement 'taking into account' the
> 1992 Agreement pursuant to Article 31(3)(c) of the VCLT, there is nothing
> in the 1992 Agreement that would lead us to 'interpret' the SCM Agreement as
> not applying to measures of support to large civil aircraft committed by the
> parties prior to 17 July 1992.

[1911] In *EC – Approval and Marketing of Biotech Products*, the European Communities argued that provisions of the Convention on Biological Diversity and
the 2000 Cartagena Protocol on Biosafety to the Convention on Biodiversity

informed the meaning and effect of various provisions in the SPS Agreement and the GATT 1994. The Panel rejected this argument because not all of the parties to the dispute were parties to the conventions in question. That situation is different from the one before this Panel, where both parties to the dispute are parties to the 1992 Agreement. We note that, in *EC – Approval and Marketing of Biotech Products*, the Panel expressed the view (at para. 7.68 and footnote 243) that the term 'the parties' in Article 31(3)(c) of the VCLT suggests that the rules of international law to be taken into account in interpreting the WTO Agreements at issue in a dispute are those which are applicable in the relations between the WTO Members (and not merely the parties to the dispute). Panel Report, *EC – Approval and Marketing of Biotech Products*, para. 7.68 and footnote 243.[37]

In *EC and certain member States – Large Civil Aircraft*, the European Communities also argued that the Panel's assessment of whether launch aid/member State financing (LA/MSF) conferred a 'benefit' within the meaning of Article 1.1(b) of the SCM Agreement should be informed by the benchmark levels of support agreed to in the 1992 Agreement. In that regard, the European Communities again argued that the Panel should treat the 1992 Agreement as a 'relevant rule of international law applicable in the relations between the parties' under Article 31(3)(c). The Panel again rejected the European Communities' argument:

> Although the European Communities argues that Article 4 serves as relevant context for the *interpretation* of the notion of 'benefit', it has not explained exactly how it informs the *meaning* that must be given to this term. Rather, a large part of the European Communities' submissions on this subject are devoted to demonstrating that the post 1992 LA/MSF measures *comply* with the terms of Article 4 of the 1992 Agreement. In this light, it is not entirely clear to us how the European Communities believes the *meaning* of the word 'benefit' in Article 1.1(b) of the SCM Agreement is informed by Article 4 of the 1992 Agreement.
>
> As we have previously noted, Article 4 establishes a set of qualitative and quantitative parameters for the provision of support for the development of new LCA or derivative programmes. It identifies the dividing line that was agreed between the United States and the European Communities for acceptable and prohibited 'development support' under that Agreement. It contains no definition of a 'subsidy' nor does it make any reference to the notion of 'benefit'. Thus, we see nothing in the language of Article 4 to suggest that it informs the meaning of Article 1.1(b) of the SCM Agreement. Moreover, we cannot simply assume, on the basis of the arguments presented by the European Communities, that 'development support' measures taken in compliance with Article 4 of the 1992 Agreement do not have the characteristics of 'financial contributions' that confer a 'benefit', within the meaning of Article 1.1 of the SCM Agreement. Thus, even assuming that the 1992 Agreement were an instrument containing relevant rules of international law applicable between the parties, within the

[37] Panel Report, *EC and certain member States – Large Civil Aircraft*, paras. 7.99–7.100.

meaning of Article 31(3)(c) of the VCLT (and once again, we emphasize that on this question, we express no view), we are not convinced that Article 4 of that Agreement provides any guidance on how to interpret the concept of 'benefit' under Article 1.1(b) of the SCM Agreement. Consequently, we dismiss the European Communities' argument that the benchmark to be applied when assessing whether LA/MSF confers a 'benefit' should, in effect, be Article 4 of the 1992 Agreement.[38]

4.24 In *EC and certain member States – Large Civil Aircraft*, the Appellate Body agreed with the Panel that the 1992 Agreement was not relevant to the interpretation of Article 1.1(b) of the SCM Agreement. In the course of its analysis, the Appellate Body provided guidance on Article 31(3)(c). The Appellate Body began by stating:

> To qualify under Article 31(3)(c), the 1992 Agreement would therefore have to be a 'rule of international law', which is 'relevant' and 'applicable in the relations between the parties'. Moreover, even assuming the 1992 Agreement were to fulfil these conditions, the chapeau to Article 31(3)(c) specifies the normative weight to be ascribed to the 1992 Agreement, namely that it is to be 'taken into account' in interpreting the *SCM Agreement*.[39]

Regarding the extensive debate surrounding the meaning of the expression 'applicable in the relations between the parties' in Article 31(3)(c), in *EC and certain member States – Large Civil Aircraft* the Appellate Body offered the following observations:

> We note that the meaning of the term 'the parties' in Article 31(3)(c) of the *Vienna Convention* has in recent years been the subject of much academic debate and has been addressed by the ILC. While the participants refer to WTO panels that have addressed its meaning, the Appellate Body has made no statement as to whether the term 'the parties' in Article 31(3)(c) refers to *all* WTO Members, or rather to a subset of Members, such as the parties *to the dispute*.
>   An interpretation of 'the parties' in Article 31(3)(c) should be guided by the Appellate Body's statement that 'the purpose of treaty interpretation is to establish the *common* intention of the parties to the treaty.' This suggests that one must exercise caution in drawing from an international agreement to which not all WTO Members are party.[1916] At the same time, we recognize that a proper interpretation of the term 'the parties' must also take account of the fact that Article 31(3)(c) of the *Vienna Convention* is considered an expression of the 'principle of systemic integration' which, in the words of the ILC, seeks to ensure that 'international obligations are interpreted by reference to their normative environment' in a manner that gives 'coherence and meaningfulness' to the process of legal interpretation. In a multilateral context such as the WTO, when recourse is had to a non-WTO rule for the purposes of interpreting provisions of the WTO agreements, a delicate balance must be struck between, on the one

---

[38] *Ibid.*, paras. 7.388–7.389.
[39] Appellate Body Report, *EC and certain member States – Large Civil Aircraft*, para. 841.

hand, taking due account of an individual WTO Member's international obligations and, on the other hand, ensuring a consistent and harmonious approach to the interpretation of WTO law among all WTO Members.

[1916] We note that Article 31(3)(b) requires a treaty interpreter to take into account, together with context, 'any subsequent practice in the application of the treaty which establishes the agreement of *the parties* regarding its interpretation' (emphasis added). According to the Appellate Body in *EC – Chicken Cuts*, Article 31(3)(b) requires the agreement, whether express or tacit, of all WTO Members for a practice to qualify under that provision. The Appellate Body recognized that the agreement of the parties regarding a treaty's interpretation may be deduced, not only from the actions of those actually engaged in the relevant practice, but also from the acceptance of other parties to the treaty through their affirmative reactions, or depending on the attendant circumstances, their silence. (See Appellate Body Report, *EC – Chicken Cuts*, paras. 255–273.[40])

In *EC and certain member States – Large Civil Aircraft*, the Appellate Body concluded that the 1992 Agreement was not a 'relevant' rule of international law, as it was not relevant to the specific question that must be examined under Article 1.1(b) of the SCM Agreement. In the course of its analysis, the Appellate Body stated:

> In this dispute, the resolution of the European Union's arguments regarding the 1992 Agreement need not turn on the proper meaning to be ascribed to the term 'the parties'. Even accepting the European Union's argument that the 1992 Agreement is 'applicable in the relations between *the parties*', we recall that for the 1992 Agreement to qualify under Article 31(3)(c) of the *Vienna Convention*, it must be shown to be 'relevant'. A rule is 'relevant' if it concerns the subject-matter of the provision at issue. In this dispute, the essence of the European Union's claim is that Article 4 of the 1992 Agreement is relevant to the interpretation of the term 'benefit' in Article 1.1(b) of the *SCM Agreement*.[41]

The Panel in *China – Raw Materials* referred to Article 31(3)(c) in the context of **4.25** finding that the requirements of Article XX(g) of the GATT can be interpreted harmoniously with the international law principle of State sovereignty over its natural resources:

---

[40] *Ibid.*, paras. 844–5 (citing ILC Report on Fragmentation, paras. 410–80, in particular paras. 413, 419, and footnote 569; Panel Report, *EC – Approval and Marketing of Biotech Products*, paras. 7.65–7.89; Panel Report, *US – Shrimp (Article 21.5 – Malaysia)*, para. 5.57; Appellate Body Report, *EC – Computer Equipment*, para. 93; J. Combacau and S. Sur, 'Principe d'intégration', in *Droit international public* (Montchrestien, 2004), p. 175; C. McLachlan, 'The Principle of Systemic Integration and Article 31(3)(c) of the Vienna Convention' (2005) 54 *International and Comparative Law Quarterly* 279).

[41] Appellate Body Report, *EC and certain member States – Large Civil Aircraft*, para. 846 (citing M. E. Villiger, *Commentary on the 1969 Vienna Convention on the Law of Treaties* (Martinus Nijhoff, 2009), p. 433).

In our view, the Panel must take into account in interpreting Article XX(g) principles of general international law applicable to WTO Members. Article 31(3)(c) of the *Vienna Convention* provides that in interpreting a treaty, there shall be taken into account together with the context 'any relevant rules of international law applicable in the relations between the parties'.

One of the fundamental principles of international law is the principle of state sovereignty, denoting the equality of all states in competence and independence over their own territories and encompassing the right to make laws applicable within their own territories without intrusion from other sovereign states.[42]

4.26 The Panel in *China – Rare Earths*, a closely related case that also involved the interpretation and application of Article XX(g) of the GATT, stated:

Pursuant to Article 31(3)(c) of the Vienna Convention, the Panel next considers the international law principles of sovereignty over natural resources and sustainable development, which, in the Panel's opinion, should also be taken into account when interpreting subparagraph (g) and, for the purposes of this case, especially, the term 'conservation'. In the Panel's view there is no doubt that the general principle of States' sovereignty over their natural resources is a 'relevant' rule of international law applicable between the parties.[43]

4.2.3 Treaties as evidence of facts

4.27 In a number of cases, panels and the Appellate Body have referred to other international legal instruments, not for the purpose of *interpreting* a WTO provision (through Article 31(3)(c) or otherwise), but rather as *evidence* of one or more *factual conclusions*. In this regard, other international instruments have been referred to as evidence for the factual conclusions that unilateral measures are not the only means that States have to protect migratory species of animals, that certain product bans could have been foreseen at a given point in time, that States follow certain practices in the field of double taxation, that a particular problem is one encountered by developing countries, or that certain fees were set at a level which would be insufficient to cover the long-term operating costs and losses of certain export credit programmes.

4.28 In *US – Shrimp*, the Appellate Body stated that 'a significant number of other international instruments and declarations' recognized the fact that the protection and conservation of highly migratory species of sea turtles 'demands concerted and cooperative efforts on the part of the many countries whose

---

[42] Panel Report, *China – Raw Materials*, paras. 7.377–7.378 (citing Panel Report, *EC – Approval and Marketing of Biotech Products*, para. 7.67).
[43] Panel Report, *China – Rare Earths*, para. 7.262 (citing Panel Report, *EC – Approval and Marketing of Biotech Products*, para. 7.67; Appellate Body Report, *EC and certain member States – Large Civil Aircraft*, para. 841).

waters are traversed in the course of recurrent sea turtle migrations'.[44] Furthermore, the Appellate Body concluded that consensual and multilateral procedures to conserve sea turtles are 'available and feasible', and referred to the Inter-American Convention as evidence for this factual conclusion. As summarized by the Appellate Body in the subsequent compliance proceeding, it 'saw the Inter-American Convention as evidence that an alternative course of action based on cooperation and consensus was reasonably open to the United States'.[45]

In *EC – Asbestos*, Canada argued that the measure at issue could not reasonably **4.29** have been foreseen at the time of the tariff concession negotiations. The Panel disagreed. In support of its factual conclusion that the measure at issue could have reasonably been foreseen by Canada, the Panel recalled that chrysotile asbestos had been classified as a category I carcinogenic product by the WHO since 1977, and that a 1986 ILO convention encouraged governments to provide wherever possible for the replacement of certain types of asbestos or products containing asbestos by other materials or products.[46]

In *US – FSC (Article 21.5 – EC)*, both the Panel and the Appellate Body **4.30** reviewed the taxation practice of Members, and considered various international instruments (including but not limited to the UN Model Tax Convention and the OECD Model Tax Convention) as evidence of that practice. The Panel emphasized that:

> We want to be clear that when we refer to the OECD Model Tax Convention here and elsewhere in this Report, we are not suggesting that its provisions are somehow controlling of our interpretation of the WTO Agreement. Rather, we consider that the OECD Model Tax Convention can be relevant to the extent it is reflective of tax practices of certain WTO Members.[47]

In *EC – Tariff Preferences*, the Appellate Body examined the Enabling Clause, **4.31** which establishes conditions for granting tariff preferences to developing countries (which would otherwise violate the most-favoured-nation obligation in Article I of the GATT). The Appellate Body stated that a particular need cannot be characterized as one of the specified 'needs of developing countries', in the sense of paragraph 3(c) of the Enabling Clause, based merely on an assertion to that effect by a preference-granting country or a developing country benefitting from such a preference. Rather, the Appellate Body considered that '[b]road-based recognition of a particular need, set out in the *WTO Agreement* or in multilateral instruments

---

[44] Appellate Body Report, *US – Shrimp*, para. 168.
[45] Appellate Body Report, *US – Shrimp (Article 21.5 – Malaysia)*, para. 128 (discussing Appellate Body Report, *US – Shrimp*, para. 170).
[46] Panel Report, *EC – Asbestos*, paras. 8.247, 8.295.
[47] Panel Report, *US – FSC (Article 21.5 – EC)*, footnote 195.

adopted by international organizations' could serve as evidence that the particular need was a 'need of developing countries'.[48] In that connection, the Appellate Body noted that the European Communities had referred to 'several international conventions and resolutions that have recognized drug production and drug trafficking as entailing particular problems for developing countries'.[49]

4.32 In *EC – Commercial Vessels*, the Panel agreed with Korea that the measure at issue was a 'specific action against a subsidy of another Member' that was inconsistent with Article 32.1 of the SCM Agreement. In this context, the Panel referred to a related bilateral agreement between the European Communities and Korea in the context of finding a 'strong correlation and inextricable link' between the measure at issue and alleged subsidization by Korea. The Panel emphasized that its review of the bilateral agreement 'only serves the purpose of enabling [the Panel] to decide a factual issue on which the parties disagree', and clarified that it was 'not interpreting the [bilateral agreement] in order to determine the rights and obligations of the parties under that bilateral agreement'.[50]

4.33 In *US – Upland Cotton (Article 21.5 – Brazil)*, both the Panel and the Appellate Body found that certain provisions of the OECD Arrangement on Officially Supported Export Credits (the 'OECD Arrangement') were relevant, not as a 'legally binding benchmark' or rule that was 'directly applicable', but rather 'from an evidentiary point of view'. At issue was whether a US programme involved the 'provision . . . of export credit guarantee or insurance programmes . . . at premium rates which are inadequate to cover the long-term operating costs and losses of the programmes' within the meaning of item (j) of Annex I to the SCM Agreement (the 'Illustrative List of Export Subsidies'). In this context, Brazil presented the Panel with various financial data relating to the performance of the programme. This evidence included, among other things, a comparison between fees under the programme and the minimum premium rates (the 'MPRs') provided for in the OECD Arrangement. The Panel, observing that the MPR provisions of the OECD Arrangement do not provide a 'legally binding benchmark' for determining whether a programme constitutes an export subsidy within the scope of item (j), nevertheless opined that the MPRs are relevant 'from an evidentiary point of view' because the MPR 'may be regarded as representing an assessment, developed by and agreed upon by the export credit experts of the Participants to the Arrangement, of the premia levels that are necessary to ensure that export credit guarantee programmes cover their long-term operating costs and losses'; in light of the magnitude of the difference between the

---

[48] Appellate Body Report, *EC – Tariff Preferences*, para. 163.   [49] *Ibid.*, footnote 335.
[50] Panel Report, *EC – Commercial Vessels*, para. 7.131 and footnote 275.

MPRs and the fees under the revised GSM 102 programme (the MPRs were on average 106 per cent above GSM 102 fees), the Panel considered that 'the MPRs may provide an indication, on an informed basis, of the fact that GSM 102 fees are set at a level which is insufficient to cover the long term operating costs and losses'.[51] On appeal, the Appellate Body saw no error in the Panel's analysis.[52]

4.34 In *US – Clove Cigarettes*, the Panel relied on the WHO guidelines for implementation of certain provisions of the WHO Framework Convention on Tobacco Control as evidence to support the factual conclusion that flavoured cigarettes appeal to youth.[53]

4.35 In *US – Tuna II (Mexico)*, the Panel considered that the existence of dolphin mortality limits established by the Agreement on the International Dolphin Conservation Program, signed by the United States and Mexico, supported the factual conclusion that the practice of 'setting' on dolphins, even in controlled conditions, may result in some dolphin mortality.[54]

4.36 In *EC – Seal Products*, the Panel examined a ban on the sale of seal products that contained an exception for seal products resulting from hunts by Inuit and other indigenous communities. In the context of examining whether this distinction was justifiable, the Panel took account of certain provisions in the United Nations Declaration on the Rights of Indigenous Peoples and the ILO Convention concerning Indigenous and Tribal Peoples in Independent Countries. The Panel explained that these instruments were relevant as 'factual evidence' regarding seal hunting in those communities:

> In our view, these sources, taken in their entirety as factual evidence,[475] demonstrate the recognized interests of Inuit and indigenous peoples in preserving their traditions and cultures. More specifically, in the case of seal hunts, the evidence before us shows that seal hunting represents a vital element of the tradition, culture, and livelihood of Inuit and indigenous communities.

---

[475] In taking into account the recognition given by international instruments in the context of the United Nations and the ILO to the interests of Inuit and indigenous communities, the Panel is mindful that these instruments are not WTO instruments and they do not set out WTO obligations *per se*. We are considering the content of these instruments as part of the evidence submitted by the European Union to support its position concerning the interests of Inuit and indigenous communities, not as legal obligations of Members.[55]

---

[51] Panel Report, *US – Upland Cotton (Article 21.5 – Brazil)*, para. 14.97.
[52] Appellate Body Report, *US – Upland Cotton (Article 21.5 – Brazil)*, paras. 303–6.
[53] Panel Report, *US – Clove Cigarettes*, paras. 2.29–2.32, 7.229–7.232 and 7.414.
[54] Panel Report, *US – Tuna II (Mexico)*, footnote 686.
[55] Panel Report, *EC – Seal Products*, para. 7.295.

4.3   Conflict resolution

4.3.1 Priority clauses

4.37 Priority clauses clarify which provisions prevail in the event of a conflict among certain provisions contained within a treaty, or between provisions contained in different treaties. It is a common drafting convention for such priority clauses to state that one set of rules is 'subject to' the other.[56] Certain WTO provisions state that some WTO rights and obligations are 'subject to' others, and this phrase has been interpreted and applied by panels and the Appellate Body.

4.38 In *EC – Bananas III*, the Panel noted that:

> [P]ursuant to Article 21 of the Agreement on Agriculture, GATT rules apply 'subject to' the provisions of the Agreement on Agriculture, a wording that clearly suggests priority for the latter. But giving priority to Article 4.1 of the Agreement on Agriculture, which simply 'relates' market access concessions to Members' goods schedules as attached to GATT by the Marrakesh Protocol, does not necessitate, or even suggest, a limitation on the application of Article XIII. The provisions are complementary, and do not clash.[57]

4.39 Likewise, Article II:1(b) of the GATT states that market access concessions granted by a Member in one part of its goods schedule are 'subject to the terms, conditions or qualifications set forth' in another part of the Member's schedule. In *Canada – Dairy*, the Appellate Body stated:

> In our view, the ordinary meaning of the phrase 'subject to' is that such concessions are without prejudice to and are *subordinated to*, and are, therefore, *qualified by*, any 'terms, conditions or qualifications' inscribed in a Member's Schedule.[58]

4.3.2 The *lex specialis* principle

4.40 The latin maxim *lex specialis derogat legi generali* stands for the proposition that, in the event of a conflict, the specific law prevails over the general law. WTO panels and the Appellate Body have referred to and applied this principle in several cases when dealing with the relationship between two or more provisions of the WTO agreements.[59]

---

[56] For example, Article 30(2) of the Vienna Convention provides that '[w]hen a treaty specifies that it is *subject to*, or that it is not to be considered as incompatible with, an earlier or later treaty, the provisions of that other treaty prevail' (emphasis added).

[57] Panel Report, *EC – Bananas III (US)*, para. 7.126.

[58] Appellate Body Report, *Canada – Dairy*, para. 134.

[59] For additional statements by panels and the Appellate Body regarding *lex specialis* in the context of the relationship between the WTO agreements and customary international law, see Section 13.3.3. ('The relationship between treaties and customary international law').

In *EEC – Apples (US)*, a GATT panel proceeding, Chile claimed that the **4.41**
measures at issue were inconsistent with the most-favoured-nation obligation
in Article I of the GATT, and also with the non-discrimination obligations in
Article XIII of the GATT. The Panel stated:

> The Panel considered it more appropriate to examine the consistency of the
> EEC measures with the most-favoured-nation principles of the General
> Agreement in the context of Article XIII ... This provision deals with the
> non-discriminatory administration of quantitative restrictions and is thus the
> *lex specialis* in this particular case.[60]

As noted at paragraph 4.3 above, the Panel in *Indonesia – Autos* discussed the *lex* **4.42**
specialis principle and ultimately rejected the *lex specialis* argument advanced
by Indonesia in that case, on the grounds that there was no conflict between the
provisions at issue.

The Panel in *US – 1916 Act (Japan)* referred to the *lex specialis* principle in the **4.43**
context of setting forth its understanding of a prior Appellate Body statement,
in *EC – Bananas III*,[61] regarding the correct order of applying two WTO
agreements where one of them 'deals specifically, and in detail' with the matter
at issue. Referring to this statement, the Panel in *US – 1916 Act (Japan)* stated
that 'we view the Appellate Body statement as applying the general principle
of international law *lex specialis derogat legi generali*'.[62] The Panel noted:

> It is a general principle of international law that, when applying a body of norms
> to a given factual situation, one should consider that factual situation under the
> norm which most specifically addresses it.[344]

---

[344] See Appellate Body Report on *European Communities – Bananas*, Op. cit.,
para. 204, and the judgement of the Permanent Court of International Justice in
the *Serbian Loans* case (1929), where the PCIJ stated that 'the special words,
according to elementary principles of interpretation, control the general expression' (PCIJ, Series A, No. 20/21, at p. 30). See also György Haraszti, *Some
Fundamental Problems of the Law of Treaties* (1973), p. 191.[63]

In *US – Shrimp (Thailand) / US – Customs Bond Directive*, the Panel found that **4.44**
the challenged measure was inconsistent with Article 18.1 of the Anti-Dumping
Agreement and the Ad Note to Article VI:2 and VI:3 of the GATT. The Panel
declined to rule on certain additional claims under the GATT. In the course of
explaining why, the Panel referred to the *lex specialis* principle:

> [W]e consider the Panel's discussion in *US – 1916 Act (Japan)* further relevant
> to this issue. After finding a violation of Article VI of the *GATT 1994*, the Panel

---

[60] GATT Panel Report, *EEC – Apples (US)*, para. 12.28.
[61] Appellate Body Report, *EC – Bananas III*, para. 204.
[62] Panel Report, *US – 1916 Act (Japan)*, para. 6.269.   [63] *Ibid.*, para. 6.76.

considered whether it must also analyse a claim under Article III:4 of the *GATT 1994*. It held that, in the case before it, Article VI addressed the 'basic feature' of the measure at issue more directly than Article III:4. In doing so, the Panel referred to the international law principle *lex specialis derogat legi generali* in support of its reasoning. The Panel did so by virtue of the Appellate Body's finding in *EC – Bananas III* that:

> Although Article X:3(a) of the *GATT 1994* and Article 1.3 of the *Licensing Agreement* both apply, the Panel, in our view, should have applied the *Licensing Agreement* first, since this agreement deals specifically, and in detail, with the administration of import licensing procedures. If the Panel had done so, then there would have been no need for it to address the alleged inconsistency with Article X:3(a) of the *GATT 1994*.

We agree that the principle of *lex specialis* should apply in such circumstances. Since Article VI of the *GATT 1994*, including the Ad Note, 'deals specifically, and in detail', with the issue of security for definitive anti-dumping and countervailing duties, those provisions address the 'basic feature' of the measure at issue more directly than the other *GATT 1994* provisions cited by India. Article VI and the Ad Note therefore constitute *lex specialis* that should prevail over the more general *GATT 1994* provisions cited by India.[64]

4.45 In *Thailand – Cigarettes (Philippines)*, the Panel rejected the respondent's argument that Article 11.1 of the Customs Valuation Agreement is *lex specialis* in relation to Article X:3(b) of the GATT, such that the latter provision is not applicable in respect of appeals for certain types of decisions covered by the former provision. The Panel rejected this argument on the ground that the two provisions do not relate to the same subject-matter. At the outset of its analysis, the Panel made the following observations regarding the *lex specialis* principle:

> The *lex specialis* principle has been defined by the International Law Commission ('ILC') as 'a generally accepted technique of interpretation and conflict resolution in international law. It suggests that whenever two or more norms deal with the same subject-matter, priority should be given to the norm that is more specific'.[1760]

[1760] Report of the International Law Commission, Fifty-eighth session 1 May–9 June, 3 July–11 August 2006, General Assembly Official Records Sixty-first session Supplement No. 10 (A/61/10), p. 408 (Emphasis added). As an illustration, the ILC refers to two decisions. It first referred to the [decision] in *Bankovic* v. *Belgium and others* by the European Court of Human Rights, which held that 'the Convention [here the specific law] should be interpreted as far as possible in harmony with other principles of international law [here the general law] of which it forms part' (ECHR, *Bankovic* v. *Belgium and others*, Decision of 12 December 2001, Admissibility, ECHR 2001-XII, p. 351, para. 57). It also

---

[64] Panel Report, *US – Shrimp (Thailand)*, paras. 7.159–7.162 (citing Panel Report, *US – 1916 Act (Japan)*, para. 6.269; Appellate Body Report, *EC – Bananas III*, para. 204).

cited to the Panel statement in *Korea – Measures Affecting Government Procurement* that 'to the extent that there is no conflict or inconsistency, or an expression in a covered WTO agreement [here the specific law] that applies differently, we are of the view that the customary rules of international law [here the general law] apply to the WTO treaties and to the process of treaty formation under the WTO.' (Panel Report, *Korea – Measures Affecting Government Procurement*, para. 7.96.) We note that the Appellate Body has extensively relied on general principles of international law to interpret member's obligations. See for instance, Appellate Body Report, *US – Cotton Yarn*, para. 120, applying the general principle of proportionality as found in Article 51 of the International Law Commission Draft Articles on State's Responsibility.[65]

4.46 The Panel in *EU – Footwear (China)* addressed the relationship between Article 6.2 of the Anti-Dumping Agreement, which provides in general terms that an interested party be given a 'full opportunity' to defend its interests, and the more specific provisions of Article 6, including Article 6.4, which puts limits on the scope of an investigating authority's obligation to make information available to interested parties. The European Union argued that the limits established in Article 6.4 'may not be by-passed' through an expansive interpretation of Article 6.2. In the European Union's view, such an interpretation would be contrary to the rule of interpretation which requires that meaning and effect must be given to all the terms of a treaty 'and to the *lex specialis* principle which suggests that whenever two or more norms deal with the same subject-matter, priority should be given to the norm that is more specific.'[66] The Panel, without referring expressly to the *lex specialis* principle, agreed with the European Union's approach to the interpretation of these provisions:

> [W]hile a 'full opportunity' for the defence of a party's interests may well include, conceptually, the notion of access to information, in our view, the more specific provisions of Article 6, including Articles 6.1.2, 6.4, and 6.9, establish the obligations on investigating authorities in this regard. In our view, Article 6.2 does not add anything specific to the obligations on investigating authorities with respect to interested parties' ability to see or receive information in the hands of the investigating authorities established in other provisions of Article 6. Thus, while a failure to comply with one of the more specific provisions of Article 6 concerning access to or disclosure of information may establish a violation of Article 6.2, we find it difficult to imagine a situation where the more specific provision is complied with, but Article 6.2 is nonetheless violated as a result of an investigating authority's actions in connection with access to or disclosure of information to interested parties.[67]

4.47 The Panel in *US – Countervailing and Anti-Dumping Measures (China)* (DS449) opined that, in the event of a conflict between the obligation in Article X:2 of the GATT, which prohibits certain types of retroactive measures, and Articles

---

[65] Panel Report, *Thailand – Cigarettes (Philippines)*, para. 7.1047.
[66] Panel Report, *EU – Footwear (China)*, para. 7.598, footnote 1210.   [67] *Ibid.*, para. 7.604.

20 and 10 of the SCM and Anti-Dumping Agreements, which permit the retroactive levying of countervailing and anti-dumping duties in specified circumstances, the latter would function as *lex specialis*:

> These provisions would not be redundant if Article X:2 also applied in the situations covered by Articles 20.2 and 10.2. This is because even if Article X:2 applied in these situations, the SCM Agreement and the Anti-Dumping Agreement would be *leges speciales* in relation to Article X:2. Consequently, it is the provisions of these agreements that would be applied rather than Article X:2.[68]

4.3.3 Article 30 of the Vienna Convention

4.48 WTO adjudicators have considered Article 30 of the Vienna Convention in a number of cases. In several cases, Article 30 was found to be inapplicable because there was no inherent conflict between the instruments in question, or because the terms of one of the instruments specified their interrelationship (thereby obviating the need to have recourse to Article 30), or because the two instruments entered into force at the same time. In several cases, panels have found that, by virtue of Article 30, certain WTO obligations prevailed over earlier bilateral agreements between the disputing parties. Article 30 of the Vienna Convention, entitled 'Application of successive treaties relating to the same subject-matter', reads in relevant part[69] as follows:

> 2. When a treaty specifies that it is subject to, or that it is not to be considered as incompatible with, an earlier or later treaty, the provisions of that other treaty prevail.
> 3. When all the parties to the earlier treaty are parties also to the later treaty but the earlier treaty is not terminated or suspended in operation under article 59, the earlier treaty applies only to the extent that its provisions are compatible with those of the latter treaty.

4.49 In *EEC – Cotton Yarn*, the GATT Panel saw no conflict between certain provisions of the Tokyo Round Anti-Dumping Code and the Tokyo Round Multifibre Arrangement (MFA):

> Brazil had also argued that the MFA modified the requirements of Articles 3:2, 3:3 and 3:4 of the Anti-Dumping Agreement. The Panel noted that Article 30 of the Vienna Convention on the Law of Treaties dealt with the application of successive treaties relating to the same subject-matter. A precondition for the application of Article 30 of the Vienna Convention on the Law of Treaties was that the two treaties relate to the same subject-matter. The Panel was of the view that when Article 9:1 of the MFA spoke of 'additional trade measures' it

---

[68] Panel Report, *US – Countervailing and Anti-Dumping Measures (China)*, para. 7.114.
[69] There is no WTO jurisprudence concerning Article 30(1), 30(4) or 30(5).

included anti-dumping measures. For the purposes of analysing this argument by Brazil, the Panel assumed (but did not find it necessary to decide) that the Anti-Dumping Agreement and the MFA were treaties 'relating to the same subject-matter'.

The Panel was of the view that Article 30 of the Vienna Convention on the Law of Treaties assumes that obligations created by successive treaties relating to the same subject-matter would be incompatible obligations. Article 9:1 of the MFA provides:

> In view of the safeguards provided for in this Arrangement the participating countries shall, as far as possible, refrain from taking additional trade measures which may have the effect of nullifying the objectives of this Arrangement.

From examination of this Article, the Panel noted that the obligation contained therein was not mandatory in nature. It did not establish a prohibition on the use of other 'trade measures'. It simply provided that because of the safeguards established by the MFA (i.e. quantitative restrictions), participating countries shall as far as possible refrain from taking additional trade measures which may have the effect of nullifying the objectives of the MFA. Accordingly, Article 9:1 of the MFA did not as a matter of law prohibit the taking of additional trade measures.[70]

In *Japan – Film*, the Panel referred to Article 30 in the context of rejecting Japan's **4.50** argument that the schedules annexed to the WTO agreements prevail as a 'later agreement' over schedules that entered into force under GATT 1947. The Panel saw nothing 'inherently incompatible' between the two sets of provisions:

> In our view, such an interpretation would only make sense if the Marrakesh Protocol, referred to in paragraph 1(d) of GATT 1994, were viewed as later in time than the protocols referred to in paragraph 1(b)(i) thereof, and then, only to the extent of any conflict between tariff concessions annexed to the Marrakesh Protocol and the concessions in the other tariff protocols incorporated in GATT 1994. We consider that, as argued by the United States, Article 30 of the Vienna Convention, which is designed to resolve conflicts between provisions of successive treaties on the same subject-matter, is not applicable to the situation at hand because there is nothing inherently incompatible – in conflict – between the earlier and later agreed tariff concessions. Such a conflict would only seem to exist if the subsequent concessions were less favourable than prior concessions, which is not the situation in this case. Where tariff concessions have been progressively improved, the benefits – expectations of improved market access – accruing directly or indirectly under different tariff concession protocols incorporated in GATT 1994 can be read in harmony. This approach is in accordance with general principles of legal interpretation which, as the Appellate Body reiterated in *US – Gasoline*, teach that one should endeavour to give legal effect to all elements of a treaty and not reduce them to redundancy or inutility.[71]

---

[70] GATT Panel Report, *EEC – Cotton Yarn*, paras. 540–1.
[71] Panel Report, *Japan – Film*, para. 10.67.

4.51 In *EC – Poultry*, the European Communities argued that its bilateral agreement
with Brazil had been superseded by its Schedule under the rules of Article 59(1)
or, alternatively, Article 30(3) of the Vienna Convention. The Appellate Body
stated that 'it is not necessary to have recourse to either Article 59.1 or Article
30.3 of the *Vienna Convention*, because the text of the *WTO Agreement* and the
legal arrangements governing the transition from the GATT 1947 to the WTO
resolve the issue of the relationship between Schedule LXXX and the Oilseeds
Agreement in this case'.[72]

4.52 In *EC – Hormones (US) (Article 22.6 – EC)*, the Arbitrators applied Article 30 in
the context of declining to take certain bilateral agreements invoked by the
United States into account. The Arbitrators found that the relevant parts of
the EC schedule (which is an integral part of the WTO treaty) superseded and
prevailed over a prior agreement between the European Communities and the
United States:

> [T]he legal validity and enforceability of such rights and bilateral agreements
> invoked by the US is questionable for the following reasons.
>   Both bilateral agreements were concluded *before* the relevant EC schedules
> that explicitly allocated the quota to both the US and Canada. Moreover, both
> bilateral agreements were negotiated in a GATT/WTO context where conces-
> sions are normally negotiated first on a bilateral level and then 'multilateralized'
> through binding schedules. Once this is done, the bilateral agreement, as a result
> of which the concession is granted, is superseded by the multilateral schedule.
> Both the bilateral agreements and the relevant parts of the EC schedule deal with
> the same subject-matter. Considering the GATT/WTO specific circumstances
> of their conclusion, the bilateral agreements would appear to be incompatible
> with the multilateral EC schedule – a quota allocated to only one Member as
> opposed to a quota allocated to two Members. On these grounds we consider it
> appropriate to conclude that the EC schedule, in accordance with Article 30 of
> the Vienna Convention on the Law of Treaties, has superseded and prevails over
> the bilateral agreements.[73]

4.53 In *EC and certain member States – Large Civil Aircraft*, the Panel addressed
several issues relating to a 1992 bilateral agreement between the United States
and the European Communities (the '1992 Agreement'). In the context of
finding that the parties did not waive their rights to WTO dispute settlement
under the 1992 Agreement, the Panel observed that, in the event of a conflict, the
SCM Agreement would prevail over the 1992 Agreement by virtue of Article 30:

> Article 30(3) of the VCLT provides that, when all of the parties to an earlier
> treaty are also parties also to the later Agreement but the earlier treaty is not
> suspended in operation, the earlier treaty applies *only to the extent that its*

---

[72] Appellate Body Report, *EC – Poultry*, para. 79.
[73] Decision by the Arbitrators, *EC – Hormones (US) (Article 22.6 – EC)*, para. 50.

provisions are compatible with those of the later treaty. This is also consistent with
our view that, even if the 1992 Agreement could be considered a bilateral
Agreement expressly modifying the application of the GATT/Tokyo Round
subsidies rules in the way for which the European Communities contends, it
precedes the SCM Agreement, and in the absence of any provision in the SCM
Agreement to the effect that the SCM Agreement is subject to, or not to be
considered incompatible with, the 1992 Agreement, the SCM Agreement would
prevail over the 1992 Agreement to the extent of any inconsistency between
them.[74]

The Panel in *US – Section 110(5) Copyright Act* considered Article 30 to be **4.54**
inapplicable to situations involving treaty provisions that entered into force
at the same time, stating:

> [T]he question that arises is how the conditions for invoking exceptions pro-
> vided under the Berne Convention (1971), in particular under the minor
> exceptions doctrine and Article 11bis(2), and the conditions for invoking Article
> 13 of the TRIPS Agreement interrelate. We note that Article 30 of the Vienna
> Convention on the application of successive treaties is not relevant in this
> respect, because all provisions of the TRIPS Agreement – including the incorp-
> orated Articles 1–21 of the Berne Convention (1971) – entered into force at the
> same point in time.[75]

In *China – Rare Earths*, the Panel concluded that the obligation in Paragraph **4.55**
11.3 of China's Accession Protocol is not subject to the general exceptions
in Article XX of the GATT. China appealed certain aspects of the Panel's
reasoning, and presented a number of arguments relating to the relationship
between the provisions of its Accession Protocol and the provisions of the
GATT. One such argument concerned Article 30 of the Vienna Convention.
The Appellate Body did not consider Article 30 to be relevant to this issue:

> [W]e do not consider Article 30(3) of the Vienna Convention to be apposite for
> understanding the relationship between the different components of this single
> package of rights and obligations, all of which form part of 'the same treaty' to
> which China acceded in 2001.[76]

4.3.4 Article 41 of the Vienna Convention

WTO panels have referred to Article 41 of the Vienna Convention in two cases. **4.56**
In both cases, the panels considered whether a bilateral treaty effected an *inter se*
modification of the disputing parties' obligations under the WTO agreements.
The panels answered in the negative: in the first case, because the bilateral

---

[74] Panel Report, *EC and certain member States – Large Civil Aircraft*, para. 7.93, footnote 1906.
[75] Panel Report, *US – Section 110(5) Copyright Act*, para. 6.41.
[76] Appellate Body Report, *China – Rare Earths*, para. 5.70 (citing Appellate Body Report, *Argentina – Footwear (EC)*, para. 81).

agreement could not alter the rights and obligations of the complainants who were not parties to that agreement; in the second case, because the bilateral agreement in question had not yet entered into force. Article 41 of the Vienna Convention, entitled 'Agreements to modify multilateral treaties between certain of the parties only', provides in relevant part:

1. Two or more of the parties to a multilateral treaty may conclude an agreement to modify the treaty as between themselves alone if:
   (a) the possibility of such a modification is provided for by the treaty; or
   (b) the modification in question is not prohibited by the treaty and:
      (i) does not affect the enjoyment by the other parties of their rights under the treaty or the performance of their obligations;
      (ii) does not relate to a provision, derogation from which is incompatible with the effective execution of the object and purpose of the treaty as a whole.

4.57 In *Turkey – Textiles*, the respondent argued that it was required by the terms of its customs union agreement with the European Communities to adopt the latter's import restrictions on textiles and clothing. The Panel rejected this argument, stating that 'a bilateral agreement between two Members, such as that between the European Communities and Turkey, does not alter the legal nature of the measures at issue or the applicability of the relevant GATT/WTO provisions'. The Panel continued:

> We recall that in the *EC – Bananas III* dispute the European Communities raised similar arguments with regard to what it was required to do pursuant to the Lomé Convention with the ACP countries. The European Communities argued that the panel should not have examined the content of the Lomé Convention and should have deferred to the common understanding of the parties. In that case the panel and the Appellate Body did examine the Lomé convention (for the purpose of assessing the scope of the Lomé waiver) and concluded that unless explicitly authorized by the waiver the provisions of the Lomé convention could not alter the rights and obligations of WTO Members including those of the European Communities.
> We note in this context the relevance of Article 41 of the VCLT, which provides that:
>
> > Two or more parties to a multilateral treaty may conclude an agreement to modify the treaty as between themselves alone if . . . (b) the modification in question is not prohibited by the treaty and (i) does not affect the enjoyment by the other parties of their rights under the treaty or the performance of their obligations.[77]

4.58 In *Peru – Agricultural Products*, the respondent argued that a free trade agreement (FTA) between itself and Guatemala, the complainant in that case,

[77] Panel Report, *Turkey – Textiles*, paras. 9.178–9.181.

reflected the parties' agreement that Peru could maintain the challenged measures. Peru claimed that this FTA further provided that, in the event of a conflict, it prevailed over the WTO agreements. Peru argued that pursuant to Article 41 of the Vienna Convention, if the Panel were to find that the challenged measure was inconsistent with its obligations under the WTO agreements, the FTA resulted in the modification of WTO rights and obligations, as between the parties, to the extent that such rights and obligations were inconsistent with the provisions of the FTA. The Panel rejected this argument on the grounds that the agreement between Peru and Guatemala had not yet entered into force (the significance of which it had also addressed earlier in its report, in the context of examining an argument based on Article 18 of the Vienna Convention):

> Peru's argument that the relevant clauses in the FTA – i.e. paragraph 9 of Annex 2.3 and Article 1.3 – modified certain obligations between the parties under the WTO agreements presupposes that those provisions in the FTA are legally binding on Guatemala and Peru. For this to be the case, the FTA would have had to enter into force. It is, however, an undisputed fact that the FTA has not yet entered into force.
>
> As discussed above, a treaty signed by the parties but which has not yet entered into force has only limited legal effects. Inasmuch as the FTA has not entered into force, its relevant provisions are not currently legally binding on the parties.[78]

---

[78] Panel Report, *Peru – Agricultural Products*, paras. 7.526–7.527.

5

COUNTERMEASURES

5.1 Introduction

General international law concepts and principles governing countermeasures **5.1**
are codified in the ILC Articles on State Responsibility.[1] The WTO agreements establish a specific regime governing countermeasures,[2] and the commentary to the ILC Articles on State Responsibility identifies the WTO
dispute settlement system as an example of a *lex specialis* regime on countermeasures.[3] While certain aspects of the relationship between the WTO regime
of countermeasures and general international law may not be entirely clear,[4] it
is clear that at least some features of the WTO regime of countermeasures
differ from general international law principles. At the same time, this has
not prevented WTO adjudicators from applying and clarifying some
key general international law concepts and principles relating to countermeasures in the context of interpreting and applying WTO provisions governing

---

[1] Part Three, Chapter II ('Countermeasures').
[2] These are found in Article 22 of the DSU ('Compensation and the Suspension of Concessions')
and Articles 4 and 7 of the SCM Agreement ('Remedies'). Article 22.4 of the DSU provides that
'[t]he level of the suspension of concessions or other obligations authorized by the DSB shall be
equivalent to the level of the nullification or impairment'. In cases where a Member fails to
withdraw a subsidy ruled to be a prohibited subsidy within the meaning of Article 3 of the SCM
Agreement, Article 4 of the SCM Agreement grants the complaining Member the right to take
'appropriate countermeasures'; Article 4 clarifies that '[t]his expression is not meant to allow
countermeasures that are disproportionate in light of the fact that the subsidies dealt with under
these provisions are prohibited'. In the case of a subsidy causing adverse effects, Article 7.9 of the
SCM Agreement grants the right to take 'countermeasures, commensurate with the degree and
nature of the adverse effects determined to exist'.
[3] ILC Commentary to the Articles on State Responsibility, Article 55, para. 3.
[4] For commentary, see F. Perez-Aznar, *Countermeasures in the WTO Dispute Settlement System: An
Analysis of their Characteristics and Procedure in the Light of General International Law* (Graduate
Institute of International Studies, 2005), available at www.iadb.org/intal/intalcdi/PE/2009/02758.
pdf; P. Mavroidis, 'Remedies in the WTO Legal System: Between a Rock and a Hard Place'
(2000) 11 *European Journal of International Law* 763; J. Gomula, 'Responsibility and the World
Trade Organization', in J. Crawford, A. Pellet and S. Olleson (eds.), *The Law of International
Responsibility* (Oxford University Press, 2010), pp. 791–801, at pp. 797 *et seq.*

countermeasures. This chapter reviews WTO statements of wider applicability relating to three aspects of general international law: (i) the objects and limits of countermeasures; (ii) proportionality of countermeasures; and (iii) termination of countermeasures.

5.2 Object and limits of countermeasures

5.2 WTO adjudicators have considered the function of countermeasures in a number of cases, mostly in disputes regarding the permissible level of countermeasures under Article 22.6 of the DSU and/or Articles 4 and 7 of the SCM Agreement. In that context, adjudicators have considered the ILC Articles on State Responsibility, and in particular the guidance therein regarding the purpose of countermeasures. Article 49 of the ILC Articles on State Responsibility, entitled 'Object and limits of countermeasures', reads:

> 1. An injured State may only take countermeasures against a State which is responsible for an internationally wrongful act in order to induce that State to comply with its obligations under part two.
> 2. Countermeasures are limited to the non-performance for the time being of international obligations of the State taking the measures towards the responsible State.
> 3. Countermeasures shall, as far as possible, be taken in such a way as to permit the resumption of performance of the obligations in question.

5.3 In *Brazil – Aircraft (Article 22.6 – Brazil)*, the Arbitrator referred to the ILC Articles on State Responsibility in the context of interpreting the term 'countermeasures' in Articles 4.10 and 4.11 of the SCM Agreement, explaining that 'we use the Draft Articles as an indication of the agreed meaning of certain terms in general international law'.[5] The Arbitrator stated:

> While the parties have referred to dictionary definitions for the term 'countermeasures', we find it more appropriate to refer to its meaning in general international law[45] and to the work of the International Law Commission (ILC) on state responsibility, which addresses the notion of countermeasures.[46] We note that the ILC work is based on relevant state practice as well as on judicial decisions and doctrinal writings, which constitute recognized sources of international law.[47] When considering the definition of 'countermeasures' in Article 47 of the Draft Articles,[48] we note that countermeasures are meant to 'induce [the State which has committed an internationally wrongful act] to comply with its obligations under articles 41 to 46'. We note in this respect that the Article 22.6 arbitrators in the EC – Bananas (1999) arbitration made a similar statement. We conclude that a countermeasure is 'appropriate' *inter alia* if it effectively induces compliance.

---

[5] Decision by the Arbitrator, *Brazil – Aircraft (Article 22.6 – Brazil)*, footnote 48.

[45] See, e.g. the *Naulilaa* arbitral award (1928), UN Reports of International Arbitral Awards, Vol. II, p. 1028 and *Case Concerning the Air Services Agreement of 27 March 1946 (France v. United States of America)* (1978) International Law Reports, Vol. 54 (1979), p. 338. See also, *inter alia*, the *Draft Articles on State Responsibility With Commentaries Thereto Adopted by the International Law Commission on First Reading* (January 1997), hereinafter the 'Draft Articles' and the draft Articles provisionally adopted by the Drafting Committee on second reading, A/CN.4/L 600, 11 August 2000. Even though the latter modify a number of provisions of the Draft Articles, they do not affect the terms to which we refer in this report.

[46] We also note that, on the basis of the definition of 'countermeasures' in the Draft Articles, the notion of 'appropriate countermeasures' would be more general than the term 'equivalent to the level of nullification or impairment'. It would basically include it. Limiting its meaning to that given to the term 'equivalent to the level of nullification or impairment' would be contrary to the principle of effectiveness in interpretation of treaties.

[47] See Article 38 of the Statute of the ICJ.

[48] We note that Canada objects to us using the Draft Articles in this interpretation process. Canada argues that the Draft Articles are not 'relevant rules of international law applicable to the relations between the parties' within the meaning of Article 31.3(c) of the Vienna Convention. As already mentioned, we use the Draft Articles as an indication of the agreed meaning of certain terms in general international law.[6]

In *US – Upland Cotton (Article 22.6 – US I)*, the Arbitrators began their 5.4 analysis by interpreting the term 'countermeasures' in Article 4.10 of the SCM Agreement:

> We note that the term 'countermeasures' is the general term used by the ILC in the context of its *Draft Articles on State Responsibility*, to designate temporary measures that injured States may take in response to breaches of obligations under international law.
>
> We agree that this term, as understood in public international law, may usefully inform our understanding of the same term, as used in the *SCM Agreement*. Indeed, we find that the term 'countermeasures', in the *SCM Agreement*, describes measures that are in the nature of countermeasures as defined in the ILC's Draft Articles on State Responsibility.
>
> At this stage of our analysis, we therefore find that the term 'countermeasures' essentially characterizes the *nature* of the measures to be authorized, i.e. temporary measures that would otherwise be contrary to obligations under the WTO Agreement and that are taken in response to a breach of an obligation under the *SCM Agreement*. This is also consistent with the meaning of this term in public international law as reflected in the ILC Articles on State Responsibility.[7]

[6] *Ibid.*, para. 3.44.
[7] Decision by the Arbitrator, *US – Upland Cotton (Article 22.6 – US I)*, paras. 4.40–4.42.

In *US – Upland Cotton (Article 22.6 – US I)*, the Arbitrators further stated:

> This objective of suspension of concessions or other obligations under Article 22.4 of the DSU has been recently confirmed by the Appellate Body in *US – Continued Suspension*. Prior arbitrators have also found that the objective of countermeasures under Article 4.10 of the *SCM Agreement* is to 'induce compliance'.
>
> We agree that countermeasures under Article 4.10 of the *SCM Agreement* serve to 'induce compliance'. However, it seems abundantly clear that this purpose does not, in and of itself, distinguish Article 4.10 from the other comparable provisions in the WTO Agreement. 'Inducing compliance' appears rather to be the common purpose of retaliation measures in the WTO dispute settlement system, including in the context of Article 22.4 of the DSU. The fact that countermeasures under Article 4.10 of the *SCM Agreement* serve to induce compliance does not in and of itself provide specific indications as to the *level* of countermeasures that may be permissible under this provision.
>
> This distinction is also found under general rules of international law, as reflected in the ILC's Articles on State Responsibility, which have been referred to by Brazil in these proceedings. Article 49 of these Draft Articles defines 'inducing compliance' as the only legitimate object of countermeasures, while a separate provision, Article 51, addresses the question of the permissible level of countermeasures, which is defined in relation to proportionality to the injury suffered, taking into account the gravity of the breach.[8]

5.5 The Panel in *US – Certain EC Products* discussed the concept of retaliation under general international law in the context of examining a claim under Article 23 of the DSU:

> Under general international law, retaliation (also referred to as reprisals or counter-measures) has undergone major changes in the course of the XX century, specially, as a result of the prohibition of the use of force (*jus ad bellum*). Under international law, these types of countermeasures are now subject to requirements, such as those identified by the International Law Commission in its work on state responsibility (proportionality etc. ... see Article 43 of the Draft). However, in WTO, countermeasures, retaliations and reprisals are strictly regulated and can take place only within the framework of the WTO/DSU. Elagab Omer Youssif, 'The Legality of Non-Forcible Counter-Measures in International Law' (1988), Oxford University Press; Boisson de Charzournes Laurence, Les contre-mesures dans les relations économiques internationales (1992) A. Pedone; Henkin L, Pugh R. C., Schacter O. and Smit H., International Law (1993), West Publishing, p. 570–571 and Chapter 11.[9]

5.6 In *Mexico – Taxes on Soft Drinks*, the Panel distinguished international counter-measures from measures taken to enforce national laws or regulations falling within the scope of Article XX(d) of the GATT, and in that context stated:

> [T]he notion of enforcement contains a concept of action within a hierarchical structure that is associated with the relation between the state and its subjects,

---

[8] *Ibid.*, paras. 4.111–4.113. [9] Panel Report, *US – Certain EC Products*, footnote 100.

and which is almost entirely absent from international law (action under Chapter VII of the United Nations Charter is arguably an exception, but it has no relevance in the present dispute). The possibility for states to take countermeasures, that is to try by their own actions to persuade other states to respect their obligations, is itself an acknowledgement of the absence of any international body with enforcement powers.[10]

5.3 Proportionality of countermeasures

Article 51 of the ILC Articles on State Responsibility, entitled 'Proportionality', **5.7** provides that 'Countermeasures must be commensurate with the injury suffered, taking into account the gravity of the internationally wrongful act and the rights in question'. WTO adjudicators have considered the concept of proportionality in several different contexts, including in the context of countermeasures.

In *EC – Bananas III (US) (Article 22.6 – EC)*, the Arbitrator referred to the **5.8** 'general international law principle of proportionality of countermeasures' in the context of disallowing double-counting of the same nullification or impairment by different complainants in Article 22.6 proceedings:

> If we were to allow for such '*double-counting*' of the same nullification or impairment in arbitration proceedings under Article 22.6 of the DSU with different WTO Members, incompatibilities with the standard of '*equivalence*' as embodied in paragraphs 4 and 7 of Article 22 of the DSU could arise. Given that the *same* amount of nullification or impairment inflicted on *one* Member cannot simultaneously be inflicted on *another*, the authorizations to suspend concessions granted by the DSB to different WTO Members could exceed the overall amount of nullification or impairment caused by the Member that has failed to bring a WTO inconsistent measure into compliance with WTO law. Moreover, such *cumulative* compensation or *cumulative* suspension of concessions by different WTO Members for the *same* amount of nullification or impairment would run counter to the general international law principle of proportionality of countermeasures.[67]

---

[67] Draft Articles on State Responsibility with Commentaries Thereto Adopted by the International Law Commission on First Reading, January 1997, Article 49 on Proportionality: 'Countermeasures taken by an injured State shall not be out of proportion to the degree of gravity of the international wrongful act and the effects thereof on the injured State.' See also: I. Brownlie, International Law and the Use of Force by States, Oxford (1983), page 219; H. Kelsen, Principles of International Law, New York (1966), page 21.[11]

In *US – Cotton Yarn*, the Appellate Body examined a claim under Article 6.4 of **5.9** the ATC involving the application of a safeguard measure on certain imports.

---

[10] Panel Report, *Mexico – Taxes on Soft Drinks*, para. 8.178.
[11] Decision by the Arbitrator, *EC – Bananas III (US) (Article 22.6 – EC)*, para. 6.16.

The Appellate Body concluded that the part of the total serious damage attributed to an exporting Member must be proportionate to the damage caused by the imports from that Member. The Appellate Body stated:

> Our view is supported further by the rules of general international law on state responsibility, which require that countermeasures in response to breaches by states of their international obligations be commensurate with the injury suffered. In the same vein, we note that Article 22.4 of the DSU stipulates that the suspension of concessions shall be equivalent to the level of nullification or impairment. This provision of the DSU has been interpreted consistently as not justifying punitive damages. These two examples illustrate the consequences of breaches by states of their international obligations, whereas a safeguard action is merely a remedy to WTO-consistent 'fair trade' activity. It would be absurd if the breach of an international obligation were sanctioned by proportionate countermeasures, while, in the absence of such breach, a WTO Member would be subject to a disproportionate and, hence, 'punitive', attribution of serious damage not wholly caused by its exports. In our view, such an exorbitant derogation from the principle of proportionality in respect of the attribution of serious damage could be justified only if the drafters of the *ATC* had expressly provided for it, which is not the case.[12]

5.10 In *US – Line Pipe*, also in the context of reviewing the application of a safeguard measure, the Appellate Body emphasized the importance of the State responsibility rules which require proportionality when imposing countermeasures:

> If the pain inflicted on exporters by a safeguard measure were permitted to have effects beyond the share of injury caused by increased imports, this would imply that an exceptional remedy, which is not meant to protect the industry of the importing country from unfair or illegal trade practices, could be applied in a more trade-restrictive manner than countervailing and anti-dumping duties. On what basis should the *WTO Agreement* be interpreted to limit a countermeasure to the extent of the injury caused by unfair practices or a violation of the treaty but not so limit a countermeasure when there has not even been an allegation of a violation or an unfair practice?
>
> . . .
>
> We note as well the customary international law rules on state responsibility, to which we also referred in *US – Cotton Yarn*. We recalled there that the rules of general international law on state responsibility require that countermeasures in response to breaches by States of their international obligations be proportionate to such breaches. Article 51 of the International Law Commission's Draft Articles on Responsibility of States for Internationally Wrongful Acts provides that 'countermeasures must be commensurate with the injury suffered, taking into account the gravity of the internationally wrongful act and the rights in question'. Although Article 51 is part of the International Law Commission's Draft Articles, which do not constitute a binding legal instrument as such, this provision sets out a recognized principle

---

[12] Appellate Body Report, *US – Cotton Yarn*, paras. 119–20.

of customary international law. We observe also that the United States has acknowledged this principle elsewhere. In its comments on the International Law Commission's Draft Articles, the United States stated that 'under customary international law a rule of proportionality applies to the exercise of countermeasures'.[13]

In *US – FSC (Article 22.6 – US)*, the Arbitrator examined the concept of 'appropriate countermeasures' referred to in Articles 4.10 and 4.11 of the SCM Agreement, including the language in those provisions which clarifies that this concept is 'not meant to allow countermeasures that are disproportionate in light of the fact that the subsidies dealt with under these provisions are prohibited'. The Arbitrator stated: **5.11**

> The term 'disproportionate' can be defined as 'lacking proportion, poorly proportioned, out of proportion'. The term 'proportion' refers, *inter alia*, to a 'comparative relation or ratio between things in size, quantity, numbers' or a 'relation between things in nature. etc. The term 'disproportionate' thus suggests a lack of proper or due relationship between two elements.
>
> Based on the ordinary meaning of the terms, the concept involved is understood well enough in everyday experience. It is a manner of describing relationships adapted to the circumstances, where the instrument of measurement is perception by the naked eye rather than scrutiny under the microscope. It is not meant to entail a mathematically exact equation but soundly enough to respect the relative proportions at issue so that there is no manifest imbalance or incongruity. In short, there is a requirement to avoid a response that is disproportionate to the initial offence – to maintain a congruent relationship in countering the measure at issue so that the reaction is not excessive in light of the situation to which there is to be a response. But this does not require exact equivalence – the relationship to be respected is precisely that of 'proportion' rather than 'equivalence'.[14]

In *US – FSC (Article 22.6 – US)*, the Arbitrator considered that this negative formulation meant that strict proportionality was not required, and stated:

> We note in this regard the view of the commentator, Sir James Crawford, on the relevant Article of the ILC text on State Responsibility, reflected in a resolution adopted on 12 December 2001 by the UN General Assembly (A/RES/56/83), which expresses – but only in positive terms – a requirement of proportionality for countermeasures:
>
> > the positive formulation of the proportionality requirement is adopted in Article 51. A negative formulation might allow too much latitude.' (J. Crawford, The ILC's Articles on State Responsibility, Introduction, Text and Commentaries 2002, CUP, para. 5 on Article 51.) Article 51 of the ILC Articles on State responsibility (entitled *Proportionality*) reads as follows: 'countermeasures must be commensurate with the injury suffered,

---

[13] Appellate Body Report, *US – Line Pipe*, paras. 257 and 259.
[14] Decision by the Arbitrator, *US – FSC (Article 22.6 – US)*, paras. 5.17–5.18.

taking into account the gravity of the internationally wrongful act and the rights in question'. (emphasis added)

We also note in this respect that, while that provision expressly refers – contrary to footnote 9 of the *SCM Agreement* – to the injury suffered, it also requires the gravity of the wrongful act and the right in question to be taken into account. This has been understood to entail a qualitative element to the assessment, even where commensurateness with the injury suffered is at stake. We note the view of Sir James Crawford on this point in his Commentaries to the ILC Articles:

> Considering the need to ensure that the adoption of countermeasures does not lead to inequitable results, proportionality must be assessed taking into account not only the purely 'quantitative' element of the injury suffered, but also 'qualitative' factors such as the importance of the interest protected by the rule infringed and the seriousness of the breach. Article 51 relates proportionality primarily to the injury suffered but 'taking into account' two further criteria: the gravity of the internationally wrongful act, and the rights in question. The reference to 'the rights in question' has a broad meaning, and includes not only the effect of a wrongful act on the injured State but also on the rights of the responsible State. Furthermore, the position of other States which may be affected may also be taken into consideration.' (*op. cit.*, para. 6 of the commentaries on Article 51.)[15]

5.4   Termination of countermeasures

5.12 Article 53 of the ILC Articles on State Responsibility, entitled 'Termination of countermeasures', provides that 'Countermeasures shall be terminated as soon as the responsible State has complied with its obligations under part two in relation to the internationally wrongful act'. The Appellate Body has addressed the requirement to terminate countermeasures in one case.

5.13 In *US / Canada – Continued Suspension*, the European Communities claimed that the United States and Canada were acting inconsistently with certain provisions of the DSU by continuing their countermeasures against the European Communities notwithstanding that it had taken measures that, in its view, brought about compliance with its WTO obligations. Canada and the United States disagreed that the measures taken by the European Communities achieved compliance. The Appellate Body disagreed with the EC argument that a Member's adoption and notification of a compliance measure replacing the original measure is sufficient to establish compliance, and found instead that, where there is a disagreement, the duty to cease the application of countermeasures is not triggered until compliance is determined through the applicable dispute

---

[15] *Ibid.*, para. 5.27, footnote 52.

settlement proceedings. In the course of its analysis, the Appellate Body found
support for its conclusion in Article 53 of the Articles on State Responsibility:

> The European Communities additionally submits that its position is consistent
> with the approach taken in the Articles on Responsibility of States for Inter-
> nationally Wrongful Acts (the 'Articles on State Responsibility'), which require
> that countermeasures be suspended if the internationally wrongful act has ceased
> and the dispute is pending before a tribunal that has the authority to make
> decisions binding upon the parties. Yet, the Articles on State Responsibility do
> not lend support to the European Communities' position. For example, Article
> 53 provides that countermeasures must be terminated as soon as the State 'has
> complied with its obligations' in relation to the internationally wrongful act.
> Thus, relevant principles under international law, as reflected in the Articles on
> State Responsibility, support the proposition that countermeasures may con-
> tinue until such time as the responsible State has ceased the wrongful act by fully
> complying with its obligations.[16]

---

[16] Appellate Body Report, *US / Canada – Continued Suspension*, para. 382.

6

DUE PROCESS

6.1   Introduction

It has been suggested that the concept of due process 'is probably the greatest **6.1** contribution ever made to modern civilization by lawyers or perhaps any other professional group.'[1] It is a pervasive concept in international law. The United States' 2004 Model Bilateral Investment Treaty clarifies that the obligation to accord 'fair and equitable treatment' includes the obligation not to deny justice in criminal, civil, or administrative adjudicatory proceedings 'in accordance with the principle of due process embodied in the principal legal systems of the world'. Article 17.2 of the Rome Statute of the International Criminal Court refers to 'principles of due process recognized by international law'. Article 17(1) of the UNCITRAL Arbitration Rules, without referring to 'due process', requires that the parties be treated 'with equality', that each party be 'given a reasonable opportunity of presenting its case', and that the tribunal provide 'a fair and efficient process' for resolving the dispute. This chapter reviews WTO jurisprudence clarifying the requirements of due process.[2] The first part covers due process in the context of international dispute settlement proceedings. It then briefly reviews WTO jurisprudence on due process in the administration of domestic laws and regulations.

6.2   Due process in international dispute settlement proceedings

While the term 'due process' does not appear in the text of the DSU or the other **6.2** covered agreements at the time of writing, it has been referred to over 2,300 times in 189 different WTO reports, awards and decisions. Most of the references concern the requirements of due process in the context of international dispute settlement

---

[1] P. Atiyah, *Law and Modern Society* (Oxford University Press, 1983), p. 42.

[2] For commentary, see A. Mitchell, 'Due Process in WTO Disputes', in R. Yerxa and B. Wilson (eds.), *Key Issues in WTO Dispute Settlement* (Cambridge University Press, 2005), pp. 144–60.

proceedings. There has also been discussion of due process in the context of reviewing domestic countervailing and anti-dumping duty investigations (where there are not many statements of wider applicability), and in the administration of domestic law (where there are, and which are covered towards the end of this Chapter). The Appellate Body has equated due process with fairness, and has clarified that it is a fundamental and inherent right in international dispute settlement proceedings, and has explained that due process requires a balancing of interests on a case-by-case basis. The Appellate Body and panels have also articulated several elements of due process in international dispute settlement proceedings, including the right of response, compliance with established procedural requirements, the prompt and clear articulation of claims and defences, impartiality in the decision-making process, and the issuance of reasoned decisions. This is not an exhaustive list.

6.2.1 Nature of due process

6.3 In *EC – Hormones*, the Appellate Body referred to 'fundamental fairness, or what in many jurisdictions is known as due process of law or natural justice'.[3] The Appellate Body held that, while panels enjoy a margin of discretion to deal with situations that are not explicitly regulated, they must always act in accordance with due process:

> [T]he DSU, and in particular its Appendix 3, leave panels a margin of discretion to deal, always in accordance with due process, with specific situations that may arise in a particular case and that are not explicitly regulated. Within this context, an appellant requesting the Appellate Body to reverse a panel's ruling on matters of procedure must demonstrate the prejudice generated by such legal ruling.[4]

6.4 The Panel in *EC – Tariff Preferences* addressed the issue of the joint representation of a party and third party by the same legal counsel. The Panel considered that it had 'inherent authority' to manage the proceeding in accordance with due process:

> [F]lowing from its terms of reference and from the requirement . . . pursuant to Article 12 of the DSU, to determine and administer its Working Procedures, the Panel has the inherent authority – and, indeed, the duty – to manage the proceeding in a manner guaranteeing due process to all parties involved in the proceeding and to maintain the integrity of the dispute settlement system.[5]

6.5 In *Australia – Apples*, the respondent raised several concerns regarding the Panel's procedure for selecting and consulting scientific experts, and qualified

---

[3] Appellate Body Report, *EC – Hormones*, para. 133.   [4] *Ibid.*, footnote 138.
[5] Panel Report, *EC – Tariff Preferences*, para. 7.8.

these as concerns regarding 'the observance of due process'. In the course of addressing this issue, the Panel recalled prior Appellate Body statements regarding due process. The Panel distinguished 'minor procedural concerns' from those affecting 'due process', and considered that the latter merit 'special attention':

> Any legal proceeding, including WTO proceedings, may raise procedural concerns for the parties involved. By definition, due process concerns are of a procedural nature. However, not all procedural concerns necessarily affect due process. In response to a question by the Panel, Australia accepted the validity of a distinction between procedural concerns that affect due process and other 'minor procedural concerns'.[6]

Citing to prior WTO jurisprudence, the Panel continued:

> The concept of due process is implicit in WTO dispute settlement. In the words of the Appellate Body, due process constitutes 'an obligation inherent in the WTO dispute settlement system', and it is 'fundamental to ensuring a fair and orderly conduct of dispute settlement proceedings.' Due process ensures a fair hearing for the parties to a dispute, through an adequate opportunity to submit claims, arguments and evidence and to respond to the claims, arguments and evidence presented by the other party. Thus, due process also ensures procedural equality between the parties by 'guarantee[ing] that the proceedings are conducted with fairness and impartiality, and that one party is not unfairly disadvantaged with respect to other parties in a dispute.' Ultimately, due process ensures an objective assessment of the matter by panels, as mandated by Article 11 of the DSU.
>
> . . .
>
> If a procedural concern puts at risk the purpose and role of due process in WTO dispute settlement, it is effectively a due process concern, to which panels need to pay special attention. However, it is difficult to state in the abstract whether a specific type of procedural concern affects due process. Only by taking into account the specific circumstances of the case, can a panel assess whether a procedural concern affects due process and thus merits such special attention.[7]

In *Thailand – Cigarettes (Philippines)*, the Appellate Body discussed some **6.6** fundamental features of due process, recalling some of its prior jurisprudence:

> We note that Thailand couches its claim under Article 11 of the DSU as a 'due process claim'. Due process is a fundamental principle of WTO dispute settlement. It informs and finds reflection in the provisions of the DSU. In conducting an objective assessment of a matter, a panel is 'bound to ensure that due process is respected'. Due process is intrinsically connected to notions of

---

[6] Panel Report, *Australia – Apples*, para. 7.5.
[7] Panel Report, *Australia – Apples*, paras. 7.7–7.9 (citing Appellate Body Report, *Canada – Continued Suspension*, paras. 433–5; Appellate Body Report, *India – Patents (US)*, para. 94; Appellate Body Report, *Chile – Price Band System*, para. 176; Appellate Body Report, *Thailand – H-Beams*, para. 88; Appellate Body Report, *US – Gambling*, para. 273).

fairness, impartiality, and the rights of parties to be heard and to be afforded an adequate opportunity to pursue their claims, make out their defences, and establish the facts in the context of proceedings conducted in a balanced and orderly manner, according to established rules. The protection of due process is thus a crucial means of guaranteeing the legitimacy and efficacy of a rules-based system of adjudication.[8]

In *Thailand – Cigarettes (Philippines)*, the Appellate Body explained that ensuring due process requires a balancing of different interests, including both general and case-specific considerations:

> As a general rule, due process requires that each party be afforded a meaningful opportunity to comment on the arguments and evidence adduced by the other party. This was expressly acknowledged by the Appellate Body in *Australia – Salmon* when it stated that '[a] fundamental tenet of due process is that a party be provided with an opportunity to respond to claims made against it'. At the same time, due process may also require a panel to take appropriate account of the need to safeguard other interests, such as an aggrieved party's right to have recourse to an adjudicative process in which it can seek redress in a timely manner, and the need for proceedings to be brought to a close ... Accordingly, ensuring due process requires a balancing of various interests, including systemic interests as well as those of the parties, and both general and case-specific considerations. In our view, panels are best situated to determine how this balance should be struck in any given proceeding, provided that they are vigilant in the protection of due process and remain within the bounds of their duties under Article 11 of the DSU.
>
> ... As set out above, due process generally demands that each party be afforded a meaningful opportunity to comment on evidence adduced by the other party. At the same time, a number of different considerations will need to be factored into a panel's effort to protect due process in a particular dispute, and these may include the need for a panel, in pursuing prompt resolution of the dispute, to exercise control over the proceedings in order to bring an end to the back and forth exchange of competing evidence by the parties. In the context of this dispute, there are several considerations that are germane to our assessment of Thailand's claim under Article 11 of the DSU. These include: the conduct of the parties; the legal issue to which the evidence related and the circumstances surrounding the submission of the evidence relating to that issue; and the discretion afforded under the DSU to panels in their handling of the proceedings and appreciation of the evidence.[9]

---

[8] Appellate Body Report, *Thailand – Cigarettes (Philippines)*, para. 147 (citing Appellate Body Reports, *US/Canada – Continued Suspension*, para. 433; Appellate Body Report, *Thailand – H-Beams*, para. 88; Appellate Body Report, *Chile – Price Band System*, para. 176; Appellate Body Report, *Mexico – Corn Syrup (Article 21.5 – US)*, para. 107; Appellate Body Report, *India – Patents (US)*, para. 94).

[9] Appellate Body Report, *Thailand – Cigarettes (Philippines)*, paras. 150 and 155 (citing Appellate Body Report, *Australia – Salmon*, paras. 272, 278; Appellate Body Report, *US – Gambling*, para. 270).

6.2.2 The right of response

In *Australia – Salmon*, the Appellate Body warned that panels must 'be careful to   **6.7**
observe due process, which entails providing the parties adequate opportunity to
respond to the evidence submitted', and that '[a] fundamental tenet of due
process is that a party be provided with an opportunity to respond to claims
made against it'.[10]

In *Canada – Aircraft Credits and Guarantees (Article 22.6 – Canada)*, Brazil   **6.8**
advanced new arguments in its concluding remarks at the hearing with the
Arbitrator. Canada presented an additional submission to the Arbitrator to
respond to those arguments. The Arbitrator decided to accept this additional
submission in the interest of due process:

> A strict interpretation of our Working Procedures should lead us to disregard
> Canada's additional submission. However, we note that Brazil developed a
> rather new line of argumentation in its concluding remarks. It was in the interest
> of due process and of the information of the Arbitrator to hear what Canada had
> to say about it, if it wished to do so. We also note that, even if Canada decided
> to reply to Brazil's arguments, Brazil's right – as respondent – to speak last was
> preserved by the opportunity given to parties to comment on each other's replies
> to the questions of the Arbitrator. We saw no reason to formally intervene in
> that process as long as due process was ultimately respected. We also do not
> believe that our passivity in this respect could lead to an endless exchange of
> arguments since the comments on the replies to the questions were the last
> opportunity for parties to express their views, as provided by the Arbitrator at its
> hearing with the parties.[11]

In *Chile – Price Band System*, the Appellate Body concluded that the Panel had   **6.9**
made a finding on a claim not made by Argentina, i.e. *ultra petita*. The Appellate
Body ruled that, by doing so, the Panel had denied Chile a fair right of response:

> There is, furthermore, the requirement of due process. As Argentina made no
> claim under the second sentence of Article II:1(b) of the GATT 1994, Chile was
> entitled to assume that the second sentence was not in issue in the dispute, and
> that there was no need to offer a defence against a claim under that sentence. We
> agree with Chile that, by making a finding on the second sentence – a claim that
> was neither made nor argued – the Panel deprived Chile of a 'fair right of
> response'.
>   As we said in *India – Patents*, '. . . the demands of due process . . . are implicit
> in the DSU'. And, as we said in *Australia – Salmon* on the right of response,
> '[a] fundamental tenet of due process is that a party be provided with an
> opportunity to respond to claims made against it'. Chile contends that this
> fundamental tenet of due process was not observed on this issue.

---

[10] Appellate Body Report, *Australia – Salmon*, paras. 272, 278.
[11] Decision by the Arbitrator, *Canada – Aircraft Credits and Guarantees (Article 22.6 – Canada)*,
     para. 2.16.

As we said earlier, Article 11 imposes duties on panels that extend beyond the requirement to assess evidence objectively and in good faith, as suggested by Argentina. This requirement is, of course, an indispensable aspect of a panel's task. However, in making 'an objective assessment of the matter before it', a panel is also duty bound to ensure that due process is respected. Due process is an obligation inherent in the WTO dispute settlement system. A panel will fail in the duty to respect due process if it makes a finding on a matter that is not before it, because it will thereby fail to accord to a party a fair right of response. In this case, because the Panel did not give Chile a fair right of response on this issue, we find that the Panel failed to accord to Chile the due process rights to which it is entitled under the DSU.[12]

6.10 In *US – Tuna II (Mexico)*, the Panel received an unsolicited *amicus curiae* brief. The Panel stated that '[w]here the Panel considered the information presented in and the evidence attached to the *amicus curiae* brief relevant, it has sought the views of the parties in accordance with the requirements of due process'.[13] In the course of its analysis, the Panel reiterated that 'insofar as the Panel deemed this information to be relevant for the purposes of its assessment, it invited Mexico to comment on it in order to take full account of Mexico's right of response and defense in respect of due process considerations'.[14]

6.2.3 Compliance with established procedural requirements

6.11 In *Argentina – Textiles and Apparel* the Appellate Body recalled its view that 'detailed, standard working procedures for panels would help to ensure due process and fairness in panel proceedings'.[15]

6.12 In *US – Stainless Steel (Mexico)*, the Appellate Body emphasized the importance of participants complying with procedural requirements in the Appellate Body's Working Procedures:

> Compliance with established time periods by all participants regarding the filing of submissions is an important element of due process of law. The Appellate Body clarified in *India – Patents (US)* that due process requirements are implicit in the DSU. This is particularly important, given that, according to Rules 22(1) and 24(1) of the *Working Procedures*, the appellee's submission(s) and the third participant's submission(s) are filed contemporaneously. The late filing of a participant's submission could have implications for the other participants. Compliance with the procedural requirements relating to the timely filing of submissions is a matter of fairness and orderly procedure, which are referred to in Rule 16(1) of the *Working Procedures*.[16]

---

[12] Appellate Body Report, *Chile – Price Band System*, paras. 174–6.
[13] Panel Report, *US – Tuna II (Mexico)*, para. 7.9.   [14] *Ibid.*, footnote 559.
[15] Appellate Body Report, *Argentina – Textiles and Apparel*, footnote 68.
[16] Appellate Body Report, *US – Stainless Steel (Mexico)*, para. 164.

6.2.4 Prompt and clear articulation of claims and defences

In *Brazil – Desiccated Coconut*, the Appellate Body explained the importance of a **6.13**
panel's terms of reference in light of due process:

> A panel's terms of reference are important for two reasons. First, terms of
> reference fulfil an important due process objective – they give the parties and
> third parties sufficient information concerning the claims at issue in the dispute
> in order to allow them an opportunity to respond to the complainant's case.
> Second, they establish the jurisdiction of the panel by defining the precise claims
> at issue in the dispute.[17]

In *Thailand – H-Beams*, the Appellate Body elaborated on the due process **6.14**
objective behind the requirement that a panel identify the legal basis of the
complaint sufficient to present the problem clearly:

> Article 6.2 of the DSU calls for sufficient clarity with respect to the legal basis of
> the complaint, that is, with respect to the 'claims' that are being asserted by the
> complaining party. A defending party is entitled to know what case it has to
> answer, and what violations have been alleged so that it can begin preparing its
> defence. Likewise, those Members of the WTO who intend to participate as
> third parties in panel proceedings must be informed of the legal basis of the
> complaint. This requirement of due process is fundamental to ensuring a fair
> and orderly conduct of dispute settlement proceedings.[18]

In *EC – Computer Equipment*, the responding party argued that its right to due **6.15**
process during the course of the proceedings was violated because the panel
request failed to identify the specific products at issue. The Appellate Body stated:

> We do not see how the alleged lack of precision of the terms, LAN equipment
> and PCs with multimedia capability, in the request for the establishment of a
> panel affected the rights of defence of the European Communities in the course
> of the panel proceedings. As the ability of the European Communities to defend
> itself was not prejudiced by a lack of knowing the measures at issue, we do not
> believe that the fundamental rule of due process was violated by the Panel.[19]

In *US – Gambling*, the United States argued that the challenged measures were **6.16**
justified under the general exceptions in Article XIV of the GATS. The United
States did not raise this defence until its second written submission to the Panel,
which was filed on the same day as the complainant's second written submission.
On appeal, the complainant argued that the United States' delayed invocation of its
defence was an unfair litigation tactic, and that because the United States did not
invoke the defence at an earlier stage of the panel proceeding, Antigua was deprived
of a full and fair opportunity to respond to the defence. The Appellate Body stated:

---

[17] Appellate Body Report, *Brazil – Desiccated Coconut*, p. 21.
[18] Appellate Body Report, *Thailand – H-Beams*, para. 88.
[19] Appellate Body Report, *EC – Computer Equipment*, para. 70.

[T]he opportunity afforded to a Member to respond to claims and defences made against it is also a 'fundamental tenet of due process'. A party must not merely be given *an* opportunity to respond, but that opportunity must be meaningful in terms of that party's ability to defend itself adequately. A party that considers it was not afforded such an opportunity will often raise a due process objection before the panel. The Appellate Body has recognized in numerous cases that a Member's right to raise a claim or objection, as well as a panel's exercise of discretion, are circumscribed by the due process rights of other parties to a dispute. Those due process rights similarly serve to limit a responding party's right to set out its defence at *any* point during the panel proceedings.

Due process may be of particular concern in cases where a party raises *new facts* at a late stage of the panel proceedings. The Appellate Body has observed that, under the standard working procedures of panels, complaining parties should put forward their cases – with 'a full presentation of the facts on the basis of submission of supporting evidence' – during the *first* stage of panel proceedings. We see no reason why this expectation would not apply equally to responding parties, which, once they have received the first written submission of a complaining party, are likely to be aware of the defences they might invoke and the evidence needed to support them.

It follows that the principles of good faith and due process oblige a responding party to articulate its defence promptly and clearly. This will enable the complaining party to understand that a specific defence has been made, 'be aware of its dimensions, and have an adequate opportunity to address and respond to it.' Whether a defence has been made at a sufficiently early stage of the panel proceedings to provide adequate notice to the opposing party will depend on the particular circumstances of a given dispute.

Furthermore, as part of their duties, under Article 11 of the DSU, to 'make an objective assessment of the matter' before them, panels must ensure that the due process rights of parties to a dispute are respected. A panel may act inconsistently with this duty if it addresses a defence that a responding party raised at such a late stage of the panel proceedings that the complaining party had no meaningful opportunity to respond to it. To this end, panels are endowed with 'sufficient flexibility' in their working procedures, by virtue of Article 12.2 of the DSU, to regulate panel proceedings and, in particular, to adjust their timetables to allow for additional time to respond or for additional submissions where necessary.[20]

6.2.5 Impartiality in the decision-making process

6.17 In *US / Canada – Continued Suspension*, the Appellate Body found that the institutional affiliations of two outside scientific experts appointed by the Panel

---

[20] Appellate Body Report, *US – Gambling*, paras. 270–3 (citing Appellate Body Reports, *Australia – Salmon*, paras. 272, 278; *Chile – Price Band System*, paras. 164, 174–7; *US – FSC*, paras. 165–6; *Thailand – H-Beams*, paras. 88, 95; *EC – Tariff Preferences*, para. 113; *US – Oil Country Tubular Goods Sunset Reviews*, para. 161; *US – Carbon Steel*, para. 123; *Mexico – Corn Syrup (Article 21.5 – US)*, para. 50; *US – 1916 Act*, paras. 54, 150; *Argentina – Textiles and Apparel*, para. 79; *US – FSC (Article 21.5 – EC)*, para. 243).

compromised the adjudicative independence and impartiality of the Panel. The Appellate Body began its analysis by discussing due process:

> Fairness and impartiality in the decision-making process are fundamental guarantees of due process. Those guarantees would not be respected where the decision-makers appoint and consult experts who are not independent or impartial. Such appointments and consultations compromise a panel's ability to act as an independent adjudicator. For these reasons, we agree with the view of the European Communities that the protection of due process applies to a panel's consultations with experts. This due process protection applies to the process for selecting experts and to the panel's consultations with the experts, and continues throughout the proceedings.[21]

6.2.6 Issuing reasoned decisions

In *Mexico – Corn Syrup (Article 21.5 – US)*, the Appellate Body stated that 'as a   **6.18** matter of due process, and the proper exercise of the judicial function, panels are required to address issues that are put before them by the parties to a dispute'.[22] The Appellate Body further considered a panel's duty to provide a 'basic rationale' for its findings as per Article 12.7 of the DSU, and explained how this is linked to due process:

> In our view, the duty of panels under Article 12.7 of the DSU to provide a 'basic rationale' reflects and conforms with the principles of fundamental fairness and due process that underlie and inform the provisions of the DSU. In particular, in cases where a Member has been found to have acted inconsistently with its obligations under the covered agreements, that Member is entitled to know the reasons for such finding as a matter of due process. In addition, the requirement to set out a 'basic rationale' in the panel report assists such Member to understand the nature of its obligations and to make informed decisions about: (i) what must be done in order to implement the eventual rulings and recommendations made by the DSB; and (ii) whether and what to appeal. Article 12.7 also furthers the objectives, expressed in Article 3.2 of the DSU, of promoting security and predictability in the multilateral trading system and of clarifying the existing provisions of the covered agreements, because the requirement to provide 'basic' reasons contributes to other WTO Members' understanding of the nature and scope of the rights and obligations in the covered agreements.
>
> We do not believe that it is either possible or desirable to determine, in the abstract, the minimum standard of reasoning that will constitute a 'basic rationale' for the findings and recommendations made by a panel. Whether a panel has articulated adequately the 'basic rationale' for its findings and recommendations must be determined on a case-by-case basis, taking into account the facts of the case, the specific legal provisions at issue, and the particular findings and recommendations made by a panel. Panels must identify the relevant facts

---

[21] Appellate Body Report, *US/Canada – Continued Suspension*, para. 436.
[22] Appellate Body Report, *Mexico – Corn Syrup (Article 21.5 – US)*, para. 36.

and the applicable legal norms. In applying those legal norms to the relevant facts, the reasoning of the panel must reveal how and why the law applies to the facts. In this way, panels will, in their reports, disclose the essential or fundamental justification for their findings and recommendations.

This does not, however, necessarily imply that Article 12.7 requires panels to expound at length on the reasons for their findings and recommendations. We can, for example, envisage cases in which a panel's 'basic rationale' might be found in reasoning that is set out in other documents, such as in previous panel or Appellate Body reports – provided that such reasoning is quoted or, at a minimum, incorporated by reference. Indeed, a panel acting pursuant to Article 21.5 of the DSU would be expected to refer to the initial panel report, particularly in cases where the implementing measure is closely related to the original measure, and where the claims made in the proceeding under Article 21.5 closely resemble the claims made in the initial panel proceedings.[23]

6.3   Due process in the administration of domestic law

6.19 Article X of the GATT is entitled 'Publication and Administration of Trade Regulations'. The obligations contained in Article X, which are elaborated in the text of that provision, include the following: (i) measures of general application must be published promptly and in such a manner as to enable governments and traders to become acquainted with them (Article X:1); (ii) measures of general application may not be enforced before such measure has been officially published (Article X:2); and (iii) Members must maintain independent judicial, arbitral or administrative tribunals or procedures for the purpose, *inter alia*, of the prompt review and correction of administrative action (Article X:3(b)). While Article X does not expressly refer to 'due process', panels and the Appellate Body have linked all of these requirements of these provisions to the concept of due process.

6.20 In *EC – Selected Customs Matters*, the Panel discussed the 'due process theme' that underlies Article X of the GATT:

> The title as well as the content of the various provisions of Article X of the GATT 1994 indicate that that Article, at least in part, is aimed at ensuring that due process is accorded to traders when they import or export. In this regard, we note that Article X:1 of the GATT 1994 requires that customs laws, regulations etc. should be published 'in such a manner as to enable governments and traders to become acquainted with them' ... This due process theme, which would appear to be reflected in each of sub-paragraphs of Article X of the GATT 1994, has been referred to by the Appellate Body when interpreting that Article.[24]

---

[23] Appellate Body Report, *Mexico – Corn Syrup (Article 21.5 – US)*, paras. 107–9.
[24] Panel Report, *EC – Selected Customs Matters*, para. 7.107.

The Panel in *EC – IT Products* examined a claim of violation under Article X:1 **6.21** of the GATT. In the course of its analysis, the Panel offered the following observations on how this provision reflects due process concerns:

> Article X:1 of the GATT 1994 is primarily concerned with the publication of 'laws, regulations, judicial decisions and administrative rulings of general application' as opposed to the content of such measures. Paragraph 1 also reflects the 'due process' concerns that underlie Article X as a whole. In particular, Article X:1 addresses the due process notion of notice by requiring publication that is prompt and that ensures those who need to be aware of certain laws, regulations, judicial decisions and administrative rulings of general application can become acquainted with them.[25]

In *US – Underwear*, the Appellate Body described the policy underlying Article **6.22** X:2 as pertaining to transparency and due process:

> Article X:2, *General Agreement*, may be seen to embody a principle of fundamental importance – that of promoting full disclosure of governmental acts affecting Members and private persons and enterprises, whether of domestic or foreign nationality. The relevant policy principle is widely known as the principle of transparency and has obviously due process dimensions. The essential implication is that Members and other persons affected, or likely to be affected, by governmental measures imposing restraints, requirements and other burdens, should have a reasonable opportunity to acquire authentic information about such measures and accordingly to protect and adjust their activities or alternatively to seek modification of such measures.[26]

In *US – Shrimp*, the Appellate Body found that the procedures under which **6.23** US authorities were granting the certification that foreign countries were required to obtain to export shrimp into the United States were 'informal' and 'casual' and not 'transparent' and 'predictable'. In this regard, the Appellate Body referred to Article X of the GATT, and found that this provision established 'certain minimum standards' for transparency and 'procedural fairness' in the administration of trade regulations which, in its view, had not been met in this case:

> [W]ith respect to neither type of certification under [the measure at issue requiring certification] is there a transparent, predictable certification process that is followed by the competent United States government officials. The certification processes under Section 609 consist principally of administrative *ex parte* inquiry or verification by staff of the Office of Marine Conservation in the Department of State with staff of the United States National Marine Fisheries Service. With respect to both types of certification, there is no formal opportunity for an applicant country to be heard, or to respond to any arguments that may be made against it, in the course of the certification process

---

[25] Panel Reports, *EC – IT Products*, para. 7.1015.
[26] Appellate Body Report, *US – Underwear*, p. 21.

before a decision to grant or to deny certification is made. Moreover, no formal written, reasoned decision, whether of acceptance or rejection, is rendered on applications for either type of certification, whether under Section 609(b)(2) (A) and (B) or under Section 609(b)(2)(C). Countries which are granted certification are included in a list of approved applications published in the Federal Register; however, they are not notified specifically. Countries whose applications are denied also do not receive notice of such denial (other than by omission from the list of approved applications) or of the reasons for the denial. No procedure for review of, or appeal from, a denial of an application is provided.

The certification processes followed by the United States thus appear to be singularly informal and casual, and to be conducted in a manner such that these processes could result in the negation of rights of Members. There appears to be no way that exporting Members can be certain whether the terms of Section 609, in particular, the 1996 Guidelines, are being applied in a fair and just manner by the appropriate governmental agencies of the United States. It appears to us that, effectively, exporting Members applying for certification whose applications are rejected are denied basic fairness and due process, and are discriminated against, *vis-à-vis* those Members which are granted certification.

[T]he provisions of Article X:3 of the GATT 1994 bear upon this matter. In our view, Section 609 falls within the 'laws, regulations, judicial decisions and administrative rulings of general application' described in Article X:1. Inasmuch there are due process requirements generally for measures that are otherwise imposed in compliance with WTO obligations, it is only reasonable that rigorous compliance with the fundamental requirements of due process should be required in the application and administration of a measure which purports to be an exception to the treaty obligations of the member imposing the measure and which effectively results in a suspension *pro hac vice* of the treaty rights of other members.

It is also clear to us that Article X:3 of the GATT 1994 establishes certain minimum standards for transparency and procedural fairness in the administration of trade regulations which, in our view, are not met here. The non-transparent and *ex parte* nature of the internal governmental procedures applied by the competent officials in the Office of Marine Conservation, the Department of State, and the United States National Marine Fisheries Service throughout the certification processes under Section 609, as well as the fact that countries whose applications are denied do not receive formal notice of such denial, nor of the reasons for the denial, and the fact, too, that there is no formal legal procedure for review of, or appeal from, a denial of an application, are all contrary to the spirit, if not the letter, of Article X:3 of the GATT 1994.[27]

6.24 In *Thailand – Cigarettes (Philippines)*, the Appellate Body discussed the relationship between due process and procedures for the prompt review of administrative action under Article X:3(b):

---

[27] Appellate Body Report, *US – Shrimp*, paras. 180–3.

A basic object and purpose of the GATT 1994, as reflected in Article X:3(b), is to ensure due process in relation to customs matters. The Appellate Body referred to this due process objective in *EC – Selected Customs Matters*. In that vein, the panel in *EC – Selected Customs Matters* stated that Article X:3(b) seeks to 'ensure that a trader who has been adversely affected by a decision of an administrative agency has the ability to have that adverse decision reviewed'. In addition, relating more broadly to Article X:3 of the GATT 1994, the Appellate Body has found that this provision establishes certain minimum standards for transparency and procedural fairness in Members' administration of their trade regulations. While recognizing WTO Members' discretion to design and administer their own laws and regulations, Article X:3 also serves to ensure that Members afford the protection of due process to individual traders. As we see it, the obligation under Article X:3(b) to maintain tribunals or procedures for the prompt review and correction of administrative action relating to customs matters is an expression of this due process objective of Article X:3 . . .

[T]he due process objective reflected in Article X:3 of the GATT 1994 suggests that 'prompt review and correction' is to be understood as review and correction of administrative action that is performed in a quick and effective manner and without delay. What is quick or performed without delay depends on the context and particular circumstances, including the nature of the specific type of action to be reviewed and corrected.[28]

---

[28] Appellate Body Report, *Thailand – Cigarettes (Philippines)*, paras. 202–3 (citing Appellate Body Report, *EC – Selected Customs Matters*, para. 302; Panel Report, *EC – Selected Customs Matters*, para. 7.536; Appellate Body Report, *US – Shrimp*, para. 183).

7

EVIDENCE BEFORE INTERNATIONAL TRIBUNALS

7.1   Introduction

The written rules governing dispute settlement before international courts and tribunals are largely silent with regard to evidentiary issues.[1] As a consequence, pronouncements by international courts and tribunals have become a primary source for guidance on the principles that govern the treatment of evidence in international dispute settlement proceedings.[2] In the context of WTO dispute settlement, several specific issues relating to evidence are expressly regulated through rules found in the WTO agreements, or in the working procedures of panels.[3] WTO jurisprudence relating to these issues is largely context-specific, and probably therefore of limited relevance for other areas of international

7.1

---

[1] The *Max Planck Encyclopedia of Public International Law* observes: 'Evidentiary rules of international courts or tribunals adjudicating on inter-State claims mostly deal with formalities concerning the production and the taking of evidence (International Court of Justice, Rules and Practice Directions; International Courts and Tribunals, Rules and Practice Directions [ECJ, CFI, ECtHR, IACtHR, ICSID, ITLOS, WTO Panels and Appellate Body]). These rules give only limited indications concerning the burden of proof, the assessment of, or the weight to be given to particular forms of evidence.' See R. Wolfrum, 'International Courts and Tribunals, Evidence' (March 2006), in *Max Planck Encyclopedia of Public International Law*, para. 2.

[2] M. Benzing, 'Evidentiary Issues', in A. Zimmermann, K. Oellers-Frahm, C. Tomuschat and C. J. Tams (eds.), *The Statute of the International Court of Justice: A Commentary*, 2nd edn (Oxford University Press, 2012), pp. 1234–75, at pp. 1236–7. See generally D. V. Sandifer, *Evidence before International Tribunals* (University Press of Virginia, 1975); R. Lillich (ed.), *Fact-Finding before International Tribunals* (Transnational Publishers, 1992); M. Kazazi, *Burden of Proof and Related Issues: A Study on Evidence before International Tribunals* (Kluwer, 1996); C. F. Amerasinghe, *Evidence in International Litigation* (Brill, 2005); C. Brown, *A Common Law of International Adjudication* (Oxford University Press, 2007), Chapter 3 ('Aspects of Evidence in International Adjudication'), pp. 83–118; A. Riddell and B. Plant, *Evidence before the International Court of Justice* (British Institute of International and Comparative Law, 2009).

[3] These include the following: (i) Article 13 of the DSU grants panels the right to seek information from any source; (ii) Appendix 4 to the DSU, Article 11 of the SPS Agreement and Annex 2 to the TBT Agreement contain detailed rules governing experts appointed by the panel to advise on scientific or technical issues; (iii) the working procedures of panels (developed on a case-by-case basis) often contain deadlines for submitting factual evidence; and (iv) certain documents generated by Members pursuant to transparency obligations in the covered agreements cannot be used in dispute settlement proceedings.

dispute settlement. Beyond those specific provisions, however, Article 11 of the DSU simply instructs panels to make 'an objective assessment of the facts of the case', and WTO adjudicators have addressed many questions of evidence in light of general international law concepts and principles. WTO dispute settlement proceedings are often fact-intensive, and this has contributed to the development of a substantial body of WTO jurisprudence clarifying general principles of law relating to evidence.[4] This chapter reviews statements by WTO adjudicators of potentially wider applicability relating to: (i) the burden of proof; (ii) forms of evidence; and (iii) the standard of proof.

7.2   Burden of proof

7.2 It is well established in WTO jurisprudence that the burden of proof rests on the party that asserts the affirmative of a claim or defence, and that the party that asserts a particular fact is responsible for providing proof thereof. WTO panels and the Appellate Body have expressed their understanding that these and other principles governing the burden of proof in WTO dispute settlement proceedings reflect principles of general international law.[5] WTO jurisprudence offers support for the proposition that there are some situations in which the party that carries the burden of proof need not provide evidence to prove a particular factual assertion, including in some instances where this would involve proving a negative, where the other party admits a fact in a dispute settlement proceeding, where a given fact is widely known, or where the relevant documents and information are in the sole possession of the other party. It is well established that neither party carries the burden of proof on questions relating to the interpretation of WTO law.

7.2.1 General rule

7.3 In *US – Wool Shirts and Blouses*, the Appellate Body held that the burden of proof rests upon the party, whether complaining or defending, who asserts the affirmative of a particular claim or defence:

---

[4] For commentary, see M. Grando, *Evidence, Proof, and Fact-Finding in WTO Dispute Settlement* (Oxford University Press, 2009); J. Pauwelyn, 'Evidence, Proof and Persuasion in WTO Dispute Settlement: Who Bears the Burden?' (1998) 1(2) *Journal of International Economic Law* 227; Y. Taniguchi, 'Understanding the Concept of Prima Facie Proof in WTO Dispute Settlement', in M. E. Janow, V. Donaldson and A. Yanovich (eds.), *The WTO: Governance, Dispute Settlement & Developing Countries* (Juris Publishing Inc., 2008); G. Cook, 'Defining the Standard of Proof in WTO Dispute Settlement Proceedings: Jurists, Prudence and Jurisprudence' (2012) 1(2) *Journal of International Trade and Arbitration Law* 49.

[5] See also Section 13.4 ('General principles of law').

[W]e find it difficult, indeed, to see how any system of judicial settlement could work if it incorporated the proposition that the mere assertion of a claim might amount to proof. It is, thus, hardly surprising that various international tribunals, including the International Court of Justice, have generally and consistently accepted and applied the rule that the party who asserts a fact, whether the claimant or the respondent, is responsible for providing proof thereof.[15] Also, it is a generally accepted canon of evidence in civil law, common law and, in fact, most jurisdictions, that the burden of proof rests upon the party, whether complaining or defending, who asserts the affirmative of a particular claim or defence. If that party adduces evidence sufficient to raise a presumption that what is claimed is true, the burden then shifts to the other party, who will fail unless it adduces sufficient evidence to rebut the presumption.[16]

---

[15] M. Kazazi, *Burden of Proof and Related Issues: A Study on Evidence Before International Tribunals* (Kluwer Law International, 1996), p. 117.

[16] See M. N. Howard, P. Crane and D. A. Hochberg, *Phipson on Evidence*, 14th edn (Sweet & Maxwell, 1990), p. 52: 'The burden of proof rests upon the party, whether plaintiff or defendant, who substantially asserts the affirmative of the issue.' See also L. Rutherford and S. Bone (eds.), *Osborne's Concise Law Dictionary*, 8th edn (Sweet & Maxwell, 1993), p. 266; Earl Jowitt and C. Walsh, *Jowitt's Dictionary of English Law*, 2nd edn by J. Burke (Sweet & Maxwell, 1977), Vol. 1, p. 263; L. B. Curzon, *A Directory of Law*, 2nd edn (Macdonald and Evans, 1983), p. 47; Art. 9, Nouveau Code de Procédure Civile; J. Carbonnier, *Droit Civil*, Introduction, 20th edn (Presses Universitaires de France, 1991), p. 320; J. Chevalier and L. Bach, *Droit Civil*, 12th edn (Sirey, 1995), Vol. 1, p. 101; R. Guillien and J. Vincent, *Termes juridiques*, 10th edn (Dalloz, 1995), p. 384; O. Samyn, P. Simonetta and C. Sogno, *Dictionnaire des Termes Juridiques* (Editions de Vecchi, 1986), p. 250; J. González Pérez, *Manual de Derecho Procesal Administrativo*, 2nd edn (Editorial Civitas, 1992), p. 311; C. M. Bianca, S. Patti and G. Patti, *Lessico di Diritto Civile* (Giuffré Editore, 1991), p. 550; F. Galgano, *Diritto Privato*, 8th edn (Casa Editrice Dott. Antonio Milani, 1994), p. 873; and A. Trabucchi, *Istituzioni di Diritto Civile* (Casa Editrice Dott. Antonio Milani, 1991), p. 210.[6]

In *Japan – Apples*, the Appellate Body emphasized the distinction between the **7.4** two 'distinct' principles relating to the burden of proof:

It is important to distinguish, on the one hand, the principle that the complainant must establish a *prima facie* case of inconsistency with a provision of a covered agreement from, on the other hand, the principle that the party that asserts a fact is responsible for providing proof thereof. In fact, the principles are distinct.[7]

In *Canada – Dairy (Article 21.5 – New Zealand and US II)*, the Appellate Body **7.5** indicated that it would 'not readily find' that there are situations in which the usual rules on burden of proof in international proceedings do not apply:

---

[6] Appellate Body Report, *US – Wool Shirts and Blouses*, p. 14.

[7] Appellate Body Report, *Japan – Apples*, para. 157 (citing Appellate Body Report, *EC – Hormones*, para. 98; Appellate Body Report, *US – Wool Shirts and Blouses*, p. 14).

[W]e have consistently held that, as a general matter, the burden of proof rests upon the complaining Member. That Member must make out a *prima facie* case by presenting sufficient evidence to raise a presumption in favour of its claim. If the complaining Member succeeds, the responding Member may then seek to rebut this presumption. Therefore, under the usual allocation of the burden of proof, a responding Member's measure will be treated as WTO-*consistent*, until sufficient evidence is presented to prove the contrary. We will not readily find that the usual rules on burden of proof do not apply, as they reflect a 'canon of evidence' accepted and applied in international proceedings.[8]

7.6 In *Chile – Price Band (Article 21.5 – Argentina)*, the Appellate Body reiterated that in WTO dispute settlement 'as in most legal systems and international tribunals', the burden of proof rests on the party that asserts the affirmative of a claim or defence.[9]

7.7 The Panel in *US – Large Civil Aircraft (2nd complaint)* similarly stated that the 'normal international legal standards' governing the discharge of the burden of proof unquestionably apply to the WTO dispute settlement procedures, as an important element of its functions concerning dispute resolution under the rule of law and due process.[10]

7.8 In *Dominican Republic – Safeguard Measures*, the Panel characterized the foregoing as the application of 'general principles of law':

Although the DSU does not contain any express provision governing the burden of proof, by application of the general principles of law the WTO dispute settlement system has traditionally recognized that the burden of proof lies with the party asserting a fact, whether that party be the complainant or the defendant.[11]

7.9 The Panel in *US – Countervailing and Anti-Dumping Measures (China)* (DS449) considered it 'useful to recall certain principles that apply in WTO dispute settlement and international law more generally with respect to the burden of proof, the assessment of evidence, and the level of proof required'.[12]

7.2.2 Proving a negative

7.10 In *US – Gambling*, the Appellate Body confirmed that the general exceptions in the GATT and GATS cannot be interpreted as imposing an impossible burden of proof on the party invoking the exception:

---

[8] Appellate Body Report, *Canada – Dairy (Article 21.5 – New Zealand and US II)*, para. 66.
[9] Appellate Body Report, *Chile – Price Band (Article 21.5 – Argentina)*, para. 134.
[10] Panel Report, *US – Large Civil Aircraft (2nd complaint)*, para. 7.13.
[11] Panel Report, *Dominican Republic – Safeguard Measures*, para. 7.16.
[12] Panel Report, *US – Countervailing and Anti-Dumping Measures (China)*, para. 7.374 (citing Panel Report, *US – Large Civil Aircraft (2nd complaint)*, para. 7.13).

[T]he responding party must show that its measure is 'necessary' to achieve objectives relating to public morals or public order. In our view, however, it is not the responding party's burden to show, in the first instance, that there are no reasonably available alternatives to achieve its objectives. In particular, a responding party need not identify the universe of less trade-restrictive alternative measures and then show that none of those measures achieves the desired objective. The WTO agreements do not contemplate such an impracticable and, indeed, often impossible burden.[13]

In *Japan – Agricultural Products II*, the United States appealed the Panel's **7.11** finding under Article 2.2 of the SPS Agreement, arguing that, under the Panel's approach to the burden of proof, complaining parties would have the impossible task of proving a negative, i.e. that there is no scientific evidence which supports a measure. The Appellate Body suggested that requiring a complaining party to prove such a negative would be an 'erroneous burden of proof', but disagreed that the Panel had done so in that case:

> [W]e disagree with the United States that the Panel imposed on the United States an impossible and, therefore, erroneous burden of proof by requiring it to prove a negative, namely, that there are *no* relevant studies and reports which support Japan's varietal testing requirement. In our view, it would have been sufficient for the United States to raise a presumption that there are no relevant studies or reports. Raising a presumption that there are no relevant studies or reports is *not* an impossible burden. The United States could have requested Japan, pursuant to Article 5.8 of the *SPS Agreement*, to provide 'an explanation of the reasons' for its varietal testing requirement, in particular, as it applies to apricots, pears, plums and quince. Japan would, in that case, be obliged to provide such explanation. The failure of Japan to bring forward scientific studies or reports in support of its varietal testing requirement as it applies to apricots, pears, plums and quince, would have been a strong indication that there are no such studies or reports. The United States could also have asked the Panel's experts specific questions as to the existence of relevant scientific studies or reports or it could have submitted to the Panel the opinion of experts consulted by it on this issue. The United States, however, did not submit *any* evidence relating to apricots, pears, plums and quince.[14]

In *Guatemala – Cement II*, the Panel found that Guatemala violated Annex I(2) **7.12** of the Anti-Dumping Agreement by failing to inform the government of Mexico of the inclusion of non-governmental experts in the ministry's verification team. In the context of finding a violation, the Panel noted the impossibility of proving a negative:

> In principle, Mexico bears the burden to prove that the Ministry failed to inform it of the inclusion of non-governmental experts in the Ministry's verification team. As a practical matter, this burden is impossible for Mexico to meet: one

---

[13] Appellate Body Report, *US – Gambling*, para. 309.
[14] Appellate Body Report, *Japan – Agricultural Products II*, para. 137.

simply cannot prove that one was not informed of something. Although Mexico cannot establish definitively that it was not informed by the Ministry of the Ministry's intention to include non-governmental experts in its verification team, there is sufficient evidence before us to suggest strongly that it was not so informed. Although an investigating authority should normally be able to demonstrate that it complied with a formal requirement to inform the authorities of another Member, Guatemala has failed to rebut the strong suggestion that it failed to do so. In fact, Guatemala has simply referred to the very letter which suggests strongly that Mexico was not notified by Guatemala. In these circumstances, we do not consider that the evidence and arguments of the parties 'remain in equipoise'.[15]

7.13 In *Canada – Pharmaceutical Patents*, the Panel recognized that one of the conditions for justification under Article 30 of the TRIPS Agreement involves proving a negative:

> The third condition of Article 30 is the requirement that the proposed exception must not 'unreasonably prejudice the legitimate interests of the patent owner, taking into account the legitimate interests of third parties'. Although Canada, as the party asserting the exception provided for in Article 30, bears the burden of proving compliance with the conditions of that exception, the order of proof is complicated by the fact that the condition involves proving a negative. One cannot demonstrate that no legitimate interest of the patent owner has been prejudiced until one knows what claims of legitimate interest can be made. Likewise, the weight of legitimate third party interests cannot be fully appraised until the legitimacy and weight of the patent owner's legitimate interests, if any, are defined. Accordingly, without disturbing the ultimate burden of proof, the Panel chose to analyse the issues presented by the third condition of Article 30 according to the logical sequence in which those issues became defined.[16]

7.2.3 Admissions made by a party in a dispute settlement proceeding

7.14 The Panel in *US – Shrimp* observed that the United States did not dispute that the measure at issue amounted to a 'restriction' on the importation of shrimp within the meaning of Article XI:1 of GATT, and stated:

> This statement of the United States creates a particular situation where the defendant basically admits that a given measure amounts to a restriction prohibited by GATT 1994. It is usual legal practice for domestic and international tribunals, including GATT panels, to consider that, if a party admits a particular fact, the judge may be entitled to consider such fact as accurate.[17]

7.15 In *EC – Selected Customs Matters*, the Panel accepted a factual assertion unsupported by any evidence because it was admitted by the respondent:

---

[15] Panel Report, *Guatemala – Cement II*, para. 8.196.
[16] Panel Report, *Canada – Pharmaceutical Patents*, para. 7.60.
[17] Panel Report, *US – Shrimp*, para. 7.15.

The Panel notes that the United States has not provided any evidence to support its allegation of divergence in the tariff classification of drip irrigation products. Rather, it merely asserts the existence of a difference between French and Spanish BTI for drip irrigation products in its submissions. Nevertheless, the Panel is willing to accept this assertion in light of the fact that the European Communities does not dispute the existence of divergence in this regard.[18]

7.2.4 Judicial notice of facts widely known

7.16 In *Brazil – Aircraft*, the Panel applied Article 27.4 of the SCM Agreement, which prescribes a period during which developing countries are to phase out their export subsidies. Brazil argued before the Panel and the Appellate Body that for the purpose of applying this provision, which states that a developing country shall not 'increase the level' of its export subsidies, there should be a comparison between the level of export subsidies granted at the time of the entry into force of the SCM Agreement with the current level, and that the latter should be calculated in constant (i.e. adjusted for inflation) dollars. Brazil argued that calculating the current level in constant dollars is necessary because, if inflation is not taken into account, the phase-out period would be rendered meaningless. In advancing this argument, Brazil argued that 'the Appellate Body may take "judicial notice" that currencies tend to depreciate over time because of inflationary pressures, and these pressures are greatest in developing countries'.[19] The Appellate Body agreed with Brazil's argument, and stated, without reference to the concept of 'judicial notice' (but also without citation to any evidence), that 'to take no account of inflation in assessing the level of export subsidies granted by a developing country Member would render the special and differential provisions of Article 27 meaningless'.[20]

7.17 In *Egypt – Steel Rebar*, the Panel was reluctant to recognize any formal principle of 'judicial notice' in the WTO context, but then confirmed that it certainly had 'an awareness of matters pertaining to life, nature and society':

> Turkey also argues that if we should decide, in terms of Article 17.5(ii), that the record that we can take into account should ordinarily be limited to the facts made available to the Investigating Authority during the course of the investigation, we nevertheless should adopt the legal principle of taking 'judicial notice' of certain other facts. We are not aware of a principle of 'judicial notice' at the WTO level. Certainly, we as Panelists have an awareness of matters pertaining to life, nature and society.[21]

---

[18] Panel Report, *EC – Selected Customs Matters*, para. 7.215.
[19] Appellate Body Report, *Brazil – Aircraft*, para. 70.   [20] *Ibid.*, para. 162.
[21] Panel Report, *Egypt – Steel Rebar*, para. 7.19.

7.18 In *US – Shrimp (Viet Nam)*, the complaining party invited the Panel to take judicial notice of certain facts based on the factual findings in prior panel and Appellate Body reports. The Panel declined this invitation, and instead based its findings on the evidence in the record before it (which ultimately led it to the same factual findings). The Panel explained:

> We note that Viet Nam invites us to take judicial notice of the findings of prior panels and of the Appellate Body as to the existence and WTO-inconsistency of the US 'zeroing methodology', in particular those in *US – Zeroing (Japan)* and *US – Stainless Steel (Mexico)*, in which the US zeroing methodology, as it relates to the use of the weighted-average-to-transaction comparison method ('simple zeroing') in periodic reviews was found to be WTO-inconsistent … Viet Nam argues that we should apply an approach similar to that of the panels in *US – Shrimp (Ecuador)* and *US – Anti-Dumping Measures on PET Bags*. We note, though, that while the complainants in these disputes were allowed to rely on prior legal findings regarding the WTO-inconsistency of an identical measure in an earlier proceeding, the complainants were not dispensed from establishing, as a matter of fact, the existence of that measure. In addition, we note that the Appellate Body has cautioned, in *US – Continued Zeroing*, that findings of facts in one dispute are not binding in another dispute.[22]

7.2.5 Evidence in the sole possession of one party: adverse inferences

7.19 The Panel in *Argentina – Textiles and Apparel* discussed the requirement for collaboration of the parties in the presentation of the facts and evidence to the panel, and especially the role of the respondent in that process:

> Another incidental rule to the burden of proof is the requirement for collaboration of the parties in the presentation of the facts and evidence to the panel and especially the role of the respondent in that process. It is often said that the idea of peaceful settlement of disputes before international tribunals is largely based on the premise of co-operation of the litigating parties. In this context the most important result of the rule of collaboration appears to be that the adversary is obligated to provide the tribunal with relevant documents which are in its sole possession. This obligation does not arise until the claimant has done its best to secure evidence and has actually produced some *prima facie* evidence in support of its case. It should be stressed, however, that '"discovery" of documents, in its common-law system sense, is not available in international procedures'.[185] We shall, therefore, follow these general rules when addressing, for instance, the request of the United States to Argentina for production of documents and the fact that Argentina did not do so.

---

[185] See Mojtaba Kazazi, Op. Cit. and, for further discussions on the rule of collaboration, George Scelle, Yearbook of International Law Commission (1950), vol. II, p. 134 and other references in footnote 184 above.[23]

---

[22] Panel Report, *US – Shrimp (Viet Nam)*, footnote 166 (citing Appellate Body Report, *US – Continued Zeroing*, para. 190).

[23] Panel Report, *Argentina – Textiles*, para. 6.40.

In *Canada – Aircraft*, the Appellate Body also addressed the issue whether **7.20**
panels have the authority to draw 'adverse inferences' from a party's refusal
to provide information. In this dispute, Canada refused to provide Brazil,
during consultations, with information on the financing activities of a particular agency, such information being subsequently also requested by the
Panel. On appeal, Brazil submitted that the Panel erred by not drawing
the inference that the information withheld by Canada was adverse to
Canada and supportive of Brazil's claim that the agency's debt financing
was a prohibited export subsidy under Article 3.1(a) of the SCM Agreement.
The Appellate Body held that it is within the discretion of panels to draw
adverse inferences and that in this particular case the Panel, in deciding not
to draw adverse inferences, had not abused this discretion. In the context of
discussing the issue of 'adverse inferences', the Appellate Body noted the
practice of international tribunals relating to circumstantial evidence more
generally:

> There is no logical reason why the Members of the WTO would, in conceiving
> and concluding the *SCM Agreement*, have granted panels the authority to
> draw inferences in cases involving actionable subsidies that *may* be illegal
> *if* they have certain trade effects, but not in cases that involve prohibited
> export subsidies for which the adverse effects are presumed. To the contrary,
> the appropriate inference is that the authority to draw adverse inferences from
> a Member's refusal to provide information belongs *a fortiori* also to panels
> examining claims of prohibited export subsidies. Indeed, that authority seems
> to us an ordinary aspect of the task of all panels to determine the relevant facts
> of any dispute involving any covered agreement: a view supported by the
> general practice and usage of international tribunals.[120]

---

[120] See, for instance, *The Corfu Channel Case*, 1949, ICJ 4, p. 18, where the
International Court of Justice stated that '... the victim of a breach of
international law is often unable to furnish direct proof of facts giving rise to
responsibility. Such a State should be allowed a more liberal recourse to
inferences of fact and circumstantial evidence. This indirect evidence is admitted in all systems of law, and its use is recognized by international decisions.';
Case Concerning Military and Paramilitary Activities In and Against Nicaragua,
1986 ICJ 14, pp. 82–86, paras. 152, 154–156, where on the basis of the facts
before it, the International Court of Justice found that it could 'reasonably
infer' that certain aid had been provided from Nicaraguan territory; the
International Court of Justice also made use of inferences to conclude that
the scale of this aid ceased to be significant after the early months of 1981; *Case
Concerning The Barcelona Traction, Light and Power Company, Limited*,
1970 ICJ 3, p. 215, para. 97. Judge Jessup, in his separate opinion, opined
that '... if a party fails to produce on demand a relevant document which is in
its possession, there may be an inference that the document "if brought, would
have exposed facts unfavourable to the party ..."'. The Mexican–United States
General Claims Commissions stated, in *William A. Parker (USA.)* v. *United
Mexican States* (Reports of International Arbitral Awards, Vol. IV, 35, p. 39),

that '[i]n any case where evidence which would probably influence its decision is peculiarly within the knowledge of the claimant or of the respondent Government, the failure to produce it, unexplained, may be taken into account by the Commission in reaching a decision.' See also D. V. Sandifer, *Evidence Before International Tribunals*, Revised Edition, (University Press of Virginia, 1975), p. 153.[24]

7.21 In *US – Continued Zeroing*, the Panel cited to the Appellate Body's analysis in *Canada – Aircraft*, and stated that '[w]hile a panel has the authority to draw such inferences where information it requested is not provided, such an inference should not be drawn by a panel lightly, and only where the circumstances warrant, which they do not in this case'.[25]

7.22 In *US – Large Civil Aircraft (2nd complaint)*, the European Communities requested the Panel to draw adverse inferences as to the amounts of the alleged subsidies in light of alleged non-cooperation by the United States in disclosing certain information regarding the amount of funding provided to Boeing. The Panel suggested that the same result could be reached through the operation of the normal rules on burden of proof:

> For each of the challenged measures, the European Communities has presented the Panel with evidence and arguments in support of its estimate of the amount of the subsidy allegedly provided to Boeing. Where the United States disputes the European Communities' estimate of the amount of an alleged subsidy, it has provided the Panel with its own evidence and/or arguments to support its own, generally lower, estimate. If the Panel were to consider the evidence and/or arguments advanced by the United States to be insufficient to rebut the evidence and arguments presented by the European Communities, then the Panel would accept the European Communities' estimate. In such a situation, the Panel would accept the European Communities' estimate not by virtue of United States 'non-cooperation', and not as a matter of drawing 'adverse inferences', but simply by virtue of the operation of the normal principles regarding the burden of proof in WTO dispute settlement proceedings. Likewise, if the Panel were to consider the evidence and/or arguments advanced by the United States to be sufficient to rebut the evidence and arguments presented by the European Communities, then the Panel would accept the United States' estimate not by virtue of United States 'cooperation', but simply by virtue of the operation of the normal principles regarding the burden of proof in WTO dispute settlement proceedings.[26]

7.23 In *Argentina – Import Measures*, the Panel reached certain conclusions 'having drawn inferences from the refusal of Argentina to provide evidence in its possession which it has not denied'.[27] In the course of its analysis, the Panel stated:

---

[24] Appellate Body Report, *Canada – Aircraft*, para. 202.
[25] Panel Report, *US – Continued Zeroing*, para. 6.20.
[26] Panel Report, *US – Large Civil Aircraft (2nd complaint)*, para. 7.38.
[27] Panel Report, *Argentina – Import Measures*, paras. 6.155, 6.165.

The Panel is of the view that it was incumbent upon Argentina to provide copies of the agreements signed between the Argentine Government and importers or economic operators and of letters addressed by importers or economic operators to the Argentine Government, pursuant to the duty of collaboration stipulated in Article 13 of the DSU and confirmed by the Appellate Body on a number of occasions. As a party to these agreements and as the recipient of the letters, the Panel is of the view that Argentina was in the best position to do so.[28]

In *Chile – Alcoholic Beverages*, the Panel asked Chile to submit a copy of a study **7.24** commissioned by the Chilean pisco industry. Chile stated that it was unable to do so because it was the property of the pisco industry, which refused to make it available due to alleged flaws in the results and because confidential information was purportedly contained therein. The Panel stated:

> We find the decision of Chile and its industry regrettable . . . It is true that there is no compulsory discovery process in WTO dispute settlement proceedings. However, the overall dispute settlement process cannot work fairly and efficiently either at the consultation or panel stage if relevant evidence is withheld. In this case, the Chilean pisco industry decided to withhold this evidence. While it is the Chilean government which is party to this case, it would be unrealistic and artificial to argue that the panel should not address the issue based on this distinction given the direct underlying economic interest of the Chilean industry. Thus, Chile did not avail itself of the opportunity to rebut the evidence presented by the European Community. (See also the Panel Report on *Indonesia – Certain Measures Affecting the Automobile Industry*, adopted on 23 July 1998, WT/DS54, WT/DS55, WT/DS59, WT/DS64, paras. 14.230–14.235. We note that this case involved the failure of a complainant's industry to submit evidence supporting complainant's case, but we agree generally with the point that parties and their industries should not be able to withhold relevant evidence and expect panels to view it favourably.)[29]

7.2.6 Issues of law: *jura novit curia*

In *EC – Tariff Preferences*, the Appellate Body invoked the principle of *jura novit* **7.25** *curia* in support of the proposition that the burden of proof does not apply to questions of law or legal interpretation:

> Consistent with the principle of *jura novit curia*, it is not the responsibility of the European Communities to provide us with the legal interpretation to be given to a particular provision in the Enabling Clause; instead, the burden of the European Communities is to adduce sufficient evidence to substantiate its assertion that the Drug Arrangements comply with the requirements of the Enabling Clause.[30]

---

[28] *Ibid.*, paras. 6.58 (citing Panel Report, *Argentina – Textiles and Apparel*, para. 6.40).
[29] Panel Report, *Chile – Alcoholic Beverages*, footnote 390.
[30] Appellate Body Report, *EC – Tariff Preferences*, para. 105.

In a footnote to this passage, the Appellate Body quoted the International Court of Justice's interpretation of *jura novit curia*:

> The principle of *jura novit curia* has been articulated by the International Court of Justice as follows:
>
>> It being the duty of the Court itself to ascertain and apply the relevant law in the given circumstances of the case, the burden of establishing or proving rules of international law cannot be imposed upon any of the parties, for the law lies within the judicial knowledge of the Court.
>
> (International Court of Justice, Merits, *Case Concerning Military and Paramilitary Activities in and against Nicaragua (Nicaragua* v. *United States of America), 1986 ICJ Reports, p. 14, para. 29 (quoting International Court of Justice, Merits, Fisheries Jurisdiction Case (United Kingdom of Great Britain and Northern Ireland* v. *Iceland*), 1974 ICJ Reports, p. 9, para. 17)).[31]

7.26 In *EC – Export Subsidies on Sugar*, the Panel reiterated that the burden of proof is relevant when dealing with 'evidentiary' issues, but not with respect to questions of legal interpretation:

> In the Panel's view, what constitutes a Member's 'reduction commitment level' for the purpose of Article 10.3 of the *Agreement on Agriculture* or the 'reduction commitment' within the meaning of Article 9 or the 'commitment levels' within the meaning of Article 3.3 or the 'commitment as specified in a Member's schedule' within the meaning of Article 8 of the *Agreement on Agriculture* is an issue of legal interpretation, for which there is no burden of proof as such.[437]

---

[437] The Panel recalls the Appellate Body's conclusion in *EC – Hormones*, para. 156, that 'Panels are inhibited from addressing legal claims falling outside their terms of reference'. However, nothing in the *DSU* limits the faculty of a panel freely to use arguments submitted by any of the parties – or to develop its own legal reasoning – to support its own findings and conclusions on the matter under its consideration. Recently in *EC – Tariff Preferences*, para. 105, the Appellate Body clarified that the burden of proof is relevant when dealing with 'evidentiary' issues but not with 'legal' interpretation. Therefore, it is always for the panel to provide the appropriate legal interpretation independently of what is put forward by any party.[32]

7.27 The Panel in *US – Zeroing (Japan) (Article 21.5 – Japan)* referred to this prior jurisprudence and stated that '[w]e agree that there is no burden of proof for issues of legal interpretation of provisions of the covered agreements'.[33]

7.28 The principle of *jura novit curia* rests on the distinction between questions of law and questions of fact (as do certain other legal concepts and principles).

---

[31] *Ibid.*, footnote 220.   [32] Panel Report, *EC – Export Subsidies on Sugar (Australia)*, para. 7.121.
[33] Panel Report, *US – Zeroing (Japan) (Article 21.5 – Japan)*, para. 7.8.

The Appellate Body clarified the distinction between questions of law versus questions of fact in *EC – Hormones*, as follows:

> Under Article 17.6 of the DSU, appellate review is limited to appeals on questions of law covered in a panel report and legal interpretations developed by the panel. Findings of fact, as distinguished from legal interpretations or legal conclusions, by a panel are, in principle, not subject to review by the Appellate Body. The determination of whether or not a certain event did occur in time and space is typically a question of fact; for example, the question of whether or not Codex has adopted an international standard, guideline or recommendation on MGA is a factual question. Determination of the credibility and weight properly to be ascribed to (that is, the appreciation of) a given piece of evidence is part and parcel of the fact finding process and is, in principle, left to the discretion of a panel as the trier of facts. The consistency or inconsistency of a given fact or set of facts with the requirements of a given treaty provision is, however, a legal characterization issue. It is a legal question.[34]

In *EC – Hormones*, the Appellate Body also confirmed that, on questions of law, WTO panels and the Appellate Body are free to develop their own legal reasoning and are not confined to the arguments presented by the parties:

> Panels are inhibited from addressing legal claims falling outside their terms of reference. However, nothing in the DSU limits the faculty of a panel freely to use arguments submitted by any of the parties – or to develop its own legal reasoning – to support its own findings and conclusions on the matter under its consideration. A panel might well be unable to carry out an objective assessment of the matter, as mandated by Article 11 of the DSU, if in its reasoning it had to restrict itself solely to arguments presented by the parties to the dispute.[35]

7.3   Forms of evidence

7.29 WTO jurisprudence offers support for the proposition that international tribunals are generally free to admit and evaluate evidence of any kind (subject of course to any restrictions arising from the applicable procedural rules). Panels and the Appellate Body have confirmed that parties have wide latitude with regard to the forms of evidence that may be submitted to prove factual assertions, including circumstantial and indirect evidence, statements against interest by government and/or company officials, press reports and newspapers, and affidavit evidence. This is hardly an exhaustive list. There is also some support in WTO jurisprudence for the proposition that a presumption of authenticity applies to evidence submitted by a State.

---

[34] Appellate Body Report, *EC – Hormones*, para. 132.   [35] *Ibid.*, para. 156.

7.3.1 The distinction between admissibility and weight

7.30 In *EC – Bed Linen*, India provided the panel with an account of statements made during the consultations between the parties which took place before the establishment of the Panel. The European Communities objected. Although the Panel ultimately considered it unnecessary to rule on the EC objection, it provided its views on the difference between questions concerning the admissibility of evidence, on the one hand, and questions concerning the weight to be accorded to the evidence:

> [W]e consider that, as a general rule, panels have wide latitude in admitting evidence in WTO dispute settlement. The DSU contains no rule that might restrict the forms of evidence that panels may consider. Moreover, international tribunals are generally free to admit and evaluate evidence of every kind, and to ascribe to it the weight that they see fit. As one legal scholar has noted:
>
>> 'The inherent flexibility of the international procedure, and its tendency to be free from technical rules of evidence applied in municipal law, provide the "evidence" with a wider scope in international proceedings . . . Generally speaking, international tribunals have not committed themselves to the restrictive rules of evidence in municipal law. They have found it justified to receive every kind and form of evidence, and have attached to them the probative value they deserve under the circumstances of a given case'.[36]

7.3.2 Inferences and circumstantial evidence

7.31 The Panel in *Argentina – Textiles and Apparel* expressed the view that international tribunals may rely upon inferences where direct evidence is not available:

> For international disputes it seems normal that tribunals, in evaluating claims, are given considerable flexibility. Inference (or judicial presumption) is a useful means at the disposal of international tribunals for evaluating claims. In situations where direct evidence is not available, relying on inferences drawn from relevant facts of each case facilitates the duty of international tribunals in determining whether or not the burden of proof has been met. It would therefore appear to be the prerogative of an international tribunal, in each given case, to determine whether applicable and unrebutted inferences are sufficient for satisfying the burden of proof. In this respect, the International Court of Justice, in some cases, found it difficult to assert stringent rules of evidence.[37]

---

[36] Panel Report, *EC – Bed Linen*, para. 6.34 (citing M. Kazazi, *Burden of Proof and Related Issues: A Study on Evidence before International Tribunals* (Kluwer, 1996), pp. 180, 184).

[37] Panel Report, *Argentina – Textiles and Apparel*, para. 6.39 (citing K. Highet, 'Evidence and Proof of Facts', in Lori Fisler Damrosch (ed.), *The International Court of Justice at a Crossroads* (Transnational Publishers Inc., 1987), p. 355; and M. Kazazi, *Burden of Proof and Related Issues: A Study on Evidence before International Tribunals* (Kluwer, 1996)).

In *Canada – Aircraft*, the Appellate Body confirmed that panels may draw **7.32**
inferences from facts placed on the record, and this is an 'inherent and unavoidable aspect' of fact-finding:

> The DSU does not purport to state in what detailed circumstances inferences,
> adverse or otherwise, may be drawn by panels from infinitely varying combin-
> ations of facts. Yet, in all cases, in carrying out their mandate and seeking to
> achieve the 'objective assessment of the facts' required by Article 11 of the DSU,
> panels routinely draw inferences from the facts placed on the record. The
> inferences drawn may be inferences of fact: that is, from fact A and fact B, it
> is reasonable to infer the existence of fact C. Or the inferences derived may be
> inferences of law: for example, the ensemble of facts found to exist warrants the
> characterization of a 'subsidy' or a 'subsidy contingent ... in fact ... upon
> export performance'. The facts must, of course, rationally support the inferences
> made, but inferences may be drawn whether or not the facts already on the
> record deserve the qualification of a *prima facie* case. The drawing of inferences
> is, in other words, an inherent and unavoidable aspect of a panel's basic task of
> finding and characterizing the facts making up a dispute.[38]

The Panel in *Argentina – Hides and Leather* found that the complainant had **7.33**
failed to demonstrate that certain actions resulted in export restrictions. In this
context, the Panel offered the following observations on circumstantial evidence:

> The European Communities has advanced several theories as to why the presence
> alone of ADICMA representatives might result in export restrictions. However,
> the European Communities as complainant cannot rely on mere theories alone.
> This should not be construed to mean that a complaining party may not establish
> the existence of an export restriction largely on the basis of circumstantial
> evidence. It clearly may. However, in our view, a panel cannot, consistently with
> its obligation to make an objective assessment of the matter before it, draw
> inferences from the circumstantial evidence placed on record, unless that evidence
> clearly and convincingly sustains the complainant's suggested conclusion.[340]

---

[340] For an analogous approach to the proper weight to be given to circumstantial
evidence see the judgement of the International Court of Justice (ICJ) in the
Corfu Channel Case (Merits), Judgement of 9 April 1949, ICJ Rep. 1949, p. 18.
We recognize that there are distinctions between that case and the present
dispute. In the *Corfu Channel* case, the question was whether circumstantial
evidence could support a finding with respect to a factual aspect of the case
rather than a legal conclusion as here. However, as that factual point was so
central and led so directly, if established, to the legal conclusion, we believe the
reference is useful.[39]

In *Japan – Apples*, the Panel considered the arguments put forward by the parties **7.34**
regarding the inclusion or exclusion of 'direct' versus 'indirect' evidence as

---

[38] Appellate Body Report, *Canada – Aircraft*, para. 198.
[39] Panel Report, *Argentina – Hides and Leather*, para. 11.28.

'scientific evidence' within the meaning of Article 2.2 of the SPS Agreement. The Panel stated:

> [R]equiring 'scientific evidence' does not limit the field of scientific evidence available to Members to support their measures. 'Direct' or 'indirect' evidence may be equally considered. The only difference is not one of scientific quality, but one of probative value within the legal meaning of the term, since it is obvious that evidence which does not directly prove a fact might not have as much weight as evidence directly proving it, if it is available.[40]

7.35 In *US – Countervailing Duty Investigation on DRAMS*, the Panel and the Appellate Body reviewed the US investigating authority's determination that the government of Korea had 'entrusted or directed' certain Korean financial institutions to provide subsidies to a private firm within the meaning of Article 1.1(a)(1)(iv) of the SCM Agreement. The United States argued that the Panel erred in effectively requiring every piece of evidence 'to be direct evidence of entrustment or direction and thereby precluded legitimate inferences drawn from circumstantial and secondary evidence'. The Appellate Body agreed:

> In our view, having accepted an investigating authority's approach, a panel normally should examine the probative value of a piece of evidence in a similar manner to that followed by the investigating authority. Moreover, if, as here, an investigating authority relies on individual pieces of circumstantial evidence viewed together as support for a finding of entrustment or direction, a panel reviewing such a determination normally should consider that evidence in its totality, rather than individually, in order to assess its probative value with respect to the agency's determination. Indeed, requiring that each piece of circumstantial evidence, on its own, establish entrustment or direction effectively precludes an agency from finding entrustment or direction on the basis of circumstantial evidence. Individual pieces of circumstantial evidence, by their very nature, are not likely to establish a proposition, unless and until viewed in conjunction with other pieces of evidence.[41]

The Appellate Body faulted the Panel in that case on the following grounds:

> [W]hat is absent from the Panel's 'global' assessment, in our view, is a consideration of the *inferences* that might reasonably have been drawn by the USDOC on the basis of the *totality* of the evidence. As we have already observed, individual pieces of circumstantial evidence are unlikely to establish entrustment or direction; the significance of individual pieces of evidence may become clear only when viewed together with other evidence. In other words, a piece of evidence that may initially appear to be of little or no probative value, when viewed in isolation, *could*, when placed beside another piece of evidence of the same nature, form part of an overall picture that gives rise to a reasonable inference of entrustment or direction.[42]

---

[40] Panel Report, *Japan – Apples*, para. 8.98.
[41] Appellate Body Report, *US – Countervailing Duty Investigation on DRAMS*, para. 150.
[42] *Ibid.*, para. 154.

A similar conclusion was reached by the Panel in *EC – Countervailing Measures* **7.36**
on DRAM Chips, which examined the EC investigating authority's determination in respect of the same measures. The Panel stated:

> [E]ntrustment or direction can be demonstrated by all means of evidence as long
> as the overall conclusion is reasonable and adequately explained. In the absence
> of a clear and explicit government order, the evidence to be relied on will
> inevitably be circumstantial.[43]

In *US – Continued Zeroing*, the Appellate Body concluded that there was **7.37**
sufficient evidence to conclude that US investigating authorities were using
the so-called 'zeroing' methodology in the context of dumping calculations:

> The fact that there is no direct evidence establishing the use of simple zeroing
> does not absolve a panel from examining submitted evidence in its totality. We,
> however, come to this question not as the original reviewer of that evidence, but
> against the standard of whether the factual findings and uncontested facts on the
> Panel record adequately support completion. On that basis, we decide not to
> complete the analysis to reach a finding that the United States applied simple
> zeroing in these two periodic reviews. We emphasize that the nature and scope
> of the evidence that might be reasonably expected by an adjudicator in order to
> establish a fact or claim in a particular case will depend on a range of factors,
> including the type of evidence that is made available by a Member's regulating
> authority. Because the design and operation of national regulatory systems will
> vary, we believe that, in a specific case, a panel may have a sufficient basis to
> reach an affirmative finding regarding a particular fact or claim on the basis of
> inferences that can be reasonably drawn from circumstantial rather than direct
> evidence.[44]

In *China – X-Ray Equipment*, the European Union argued that there was **7.38**
evidence on the record indicating that the injury to the domestic industry was
caused by a voluntary aggressive pricing policy pursued by a domestic firm, but
that China's investigating authority did not address this causal factor in its final
determination. China responded that there was no direct evidence on the record
to support the contention that the firm adopted an aggressive pricing policy, and
therefore its investigating authority was not under an obligation to address this
argument. The Panel considered that:

> The Panel notes that the evidence on the record relied upon by the European
> Union to support its argument is not direct evidence of the existence of an
> aggressive pricing policy on the domestic market. However, given the highly
> confidential nature of a company's pricing strategies, any evidence from a
> competitor regarding the existence of a particular pricing policy will necessarily
> be circumstantial.[45]

[43] Panel Report, *EC – Countervailing Measures on DRAM Chips*, para. 7.105.
[44] Appellate Body Report, *US – Continued Zeroing*, para. 357.
[45] Panel Report, *China – X-Ray Equipment*, para. 7.291.

7.3.3 Statements against interest by government and/or company officials

7.39 The Panel in *Australia – Automotive Leather II* examined the WTO-consistency of a subsidy granted to a company. In the course of its analysis, the Panel observed that public reports at the time contained information on the design and grant of the subsidy at issue, in the form of statements by individuals. The Panel stated:

> [W]e consider the reports, both press and company, submitted by the United States as relevant to our analysis of the facts and circumstances surrounding the design and grant of that assistance. Moreover, to the extent that Australia has not specifically challenged the truth of the facts (or statements by individuals) reported, we conclude that we may consider these articles, and make our own judgment as to their appropriate weight and probative value. A commentator on the International Court of Justice's consideration of evidence and proof of facts has stated:
>
>> 'It appears to be the case that press reports, when significant but not denied by the responsible state, or when reporting other events such as official statements by responsible officials and agencies of that state, are accepted; [footnote omitted] but when they are uncorroborated or do not otherwise contain material with an independent title of credibility and persuasiveness, the tendency of the Court is to discount them almost entirely.'
>
> Highet, 'Evidence and Proof of Facts', in Damrosch, *The International Court of Justice at a Crossroads*, 1987. Similarly, we take into account the circumstances in which the reported remarks were made, the source, and whether the information is corroborated elsewhere or contrary evidence is offered, in assessing the value of these Exhibits as evidence.[46]

7.40 In *Chile – Alcoholic Beverages*, the Panel examined whether certain directly competitive or substitutable products were not similarly taxed 'so as to afford protection to domestic production' within the meaning of Article III:2 of the GATT. Based on prior Appellate Body reports, the Panel discussed the kinds of evidence that may be relevant to an examination under this element of Article III:2. In that context, the Panel stated:

> Statements by a government against WTO interests (e.g. indicating a protective purpose or design) are most probative. Correspondingly, it is less likely that self-serving comments by a government attempting to justify its measure would be particularly probative. To put it another way, dissimilar taxation applied so as to afford protection to domestic production cannot be justified as WTO-consistent because of good intentions.[47]

7.41 In *EC – Approval and Marketing of Biotech Products*, the European Communities argued that various statements by EC and member State officials, submitted by

---

[46] Panel Report, *Australia – Automotive Leather II*, footnote 210.
[47] Panel Report, *Chile – Alcoholic Beverages*, para. 7.119.

the complainants along with other evidence to prove the existence of a *de facto* moratorium on biotech products, were expressions of personal opinion associated with specific persons or reflected the views of individual EC member States. The Panel noted the following:

> The Panel begins by noting that there appears to be no disagreement among the parties that EC documents or statements by EC or member State officials may constitute evidence of the existence of a measure. The European Communities referred in this respect to the GATT panel report on *Japan – Semi-conductors*. In that case, the panel considered a position paper of the responding party which described the measure at issue as well as the responding party's statements before the panel and found that they provided 'further confirmation' of a certain fact. In the Panel's view, it cannot be inferred from this that such documents or statements may be relied on to confirm facts that have already been found to exist based on other evidence, but that they may not be relied on, together with other evidence, to establish facts. At a minimum, such an inference would appear unwarranted in a case such as this one where the existence of a *de facto* measure is alleged. In such cases, it is often inevitable that Complaining Parties base their complaints largely on circumstantial evidence. This said, it is clear that statements by individual government officials and similar evidence must be given proper weight, which weight can only be determined in the specific circumstances of each case.[48]

In *EC and certain member States – Large Civil Aircraft*, the United States **7.42** submitted various public statements by member State officials and company executives, as evidence that Airbus would not have been able to launch its aircraft without the subsidies at issue. Citing the prior panel report in *Australia – Automotive Leather II*, the Panel stated:

> In considering the above evidence, we recognize that the public statements of Airbus or participant company executives and public officials as to the need for LA/MSF in order to launch a given aircraft may involve a degree of self-interest. For example, comments attributed to Sir Austin Pearce appear to have been made in the midst of efforts by British Aerospace to lobby the government of the United Kingdom for additional support. In these circumstances, it may well have been in the interest of the company to suggest that its participation in the A320 project would come to a halt without further commitment from the UK government. Having committed public monies, it is also possible that public officials would be inclined to describe government participation in Airbus projects as essential. However, we note that the Decision letter of the European Commission seems to us to be in the nature of a quasi-judicial evaluation and finding, rather than mere statements by public officials, and therefore the same concerns do not arise in evaluating that decision. In any event, we consider it appropriate to take this evidence into account, making our own judgements as to its weight and probative value, together with other evidence in our evaluation of the United States claims.[49]

---

[48] Panel Report, *EC – Approval and Marketing of Biotech Products*, para. 7.522.
[49] Panel Report, *EC and certain member States – Large Civil Aircraft*, para. 7.1919.

7.43 The Panel in *Argentina – Import Measures* engaged in an analysis of the evidentiary value of statements by Argentine government officials, taking into account prior WTO and ICJ jurisprudence. The complainants referred in their submissions to numerous statements by high-ranking Argentine officials, including the President, the Minister of Economy and Public Finance, the Minister of Industry, the Minister of Agriculture, the Secretary of Domestic Trade, and the President of the Central Bank of Argentina. Argentina objected to the probative value of these statements, on the ground that they were non-binding. The Panel stated:

> In the Panel's view, caution is warranted when assessing the probative value of any statement, including those made by public officials. Having said that, previous panels have considered that public statements of government officials, even when reported in the press, may serve as evidence to assess the facts in dispute.[183]

---

[183] See, for example, Panel Reports, *Australia – Automotive Leather II*, fn 210 to para. 9.65; *EC – Approval and Marketing of Biotech Products*, para. 7.532; *Mexico – Taxes on Soft Drinks*, paras. 8.76–8.77; *Turkey – Rice*, paras. 7.78–7.79 and fn 367. Other international courts, such as the ICJ, for example, also accord value to public statements by government officials. The ICJ has said that 'statements of this kind, emanating from high-ranking official political figures, sometimes indeed of the highest rank, are of particular probative value when they acknowledge facts or conduct unfavourable to the State represented by the person who made them. They may then be construed as a form of admission. However, it is natural also that the Court should treat such statements with caution . . . The Court must take account of the manner in which the statements were made public; evidently, it cannot treat them as having the same value irrespective of whether the text is to be found in an official national or international publication, or in a book or newspaper.' ICJ, Merits, Military and Paramilitary Activities In and Against Nicaragua (Nicaragua v. United States of America) (1986), paras. 64–65. See also, ICJ, Fisheries Case (United Kingdom v. Norway) (1951), pp. 23–24. In its judgment on *Nuclear Tests*, the ICJ accorded legal value to 'a number of consistent public statements' made by certain French authorities (such as the President of the French Republic and the Office of the President; the Minister for Foreign Affairs; the Minister of Defence; and, the French Embassy in Wellington); some of these statements had been made in speeches, at press conferences, or in interviews on television. ICJ, Judgment, Nuclear Tests (New Zealand v. France) (1974), paras. 33–44. In its judgment on Armed Activities, the ICJ considered the legal value of a statement made by Rwanda's Minister of Justice at the United Nations Commission on Human Rights. The ICJ rejected Rwanda's argument that the Minister could not, by her statement, bind the Rwandan State internationally. The ICJ noted in this regard that the statement had been made in the officer's capacity as Minister and on behalf of her country, and that the subject-matter fell within the purview of the minister. The ICJ subsequently considered the circumstances and the terms in which the statement had been made (including whether the terms were clear and specific). The ICJ concluded that the statement could only be taken as a declaration of intent, very general in scope. ICJ, Jurisdiction of

the Court and Admissibility of the Application, Armed Activities on the Territory
of the Congo (Democratic Republic of the Congo v. Rwanda), (2006), paras.
45–55. In a judgment on a frontier dispute, the ICJ found that a single statement
made by Mali's head of State during an interview, in light of the factual
circumstances in which it occurred, did not constitute a unilateral act with legal
implications in the case. ICJ, Judgment, Frontier Dispute (Burkina Faso v. Mali)
(1986), paras. 36–40.[50]

The Panel in *Argentina – Import Measures* continued:

> Consistent public statements made on the record by a public official cannot be
> devoid of importance, especially when they relate to a topic in which that official
> has the authority to design or implement policies. That is the case for the
> Argentine officials that have been cited, such as the President, the Minister of
> Economy and Public Finance, the Minister of Industry, the Minister of Agri-
> culture, the Secretary of Domestic Trade, and the President of the Central Bank
> of Argentina. It is appropriate for the Panel to assume that these officials have
> authority to make statements in the matters that relate to their respective
> competences. In many cases, the statements were prepared speeches delivered
> at formal events or were contained in notes issued by the press office of agencies
> of the Argentine Government; these cannot be dismissed as casual statements.
> While the Panel notes Argentina's assertion that statements made by public
> officials, and even by the President of Argentina, have limited legal value, 'a
> panel must not lightly cast doubt on the good faith underlying governmental
> declarations and on the veracity of these declarations'. Indeed, Argentina itself
> cited and relied upon statements made by its high-ranking officials, including
> some made by the Argentine President.
>
> Moreover, as has been noted by the International Court of Justice, statements
> made by public officials, 'are of particular probative value when they acknow-
> ledge facts or conduct unfavourable to the State represented by the person who
> made them'. Additionally, account must be taken as to the manner in which the
> statements are made, including the medium in which they are made public, but
> also whether the statements are unambiguous and, in the case of plural state-
> ments, whether they are consistent and repeated over time.
>
> Accordingly, the Panel will not disregard the evidence of public statements
> made by high-ranking officials.[51]

7.3.4 Press reports

7.44 The Panel in *Indonesia – Autos* found that the complaining parties failed to
provide enough evidence to establish that the effect of subsidies granted by
Indonesia was to displace or impede imports of like passenger cars from the

---

[50] Panel Report, *Argentina – Import Measures*, para. 6.78.
[51] *Ibid.*, paras. 6.79–6.81 (citing Panel Report, *EC – Approval and Marketing of Biotech Products*,
paras. 7.480, 7.532; International Court of Justice, Merits, *Military and Paramilitary Activities In
and Against Nicaragua (Nicaragua v. United States of America)* (1986), paras. 64–5; Panel Report,
China – Intellectual Property Rights, paras. 7.617, 7.628–7.629 and 7.658; International Court of
Justice, *Fisheries Case (United Kingdom v. Norway)* (1951), p. 26).

Indonesian market. The Panel noted that the evidence presented by the complainants was very general, and supporting documentation was non-existent, with the exception of newspaper reports and letters prepared by GM, Ford and Chrysler for the purpose of this dispute. The Panel observed that:

> We do not mean to suggest that in WTO dispute settlement there are any rigid evidentiary rules regarding the admissibility of newspaper reports or the need to demonstrate factual assertions through contemporaneous source information. However, we are concerned that the complainants are asking us to resolve core issues relating to adverse trade effects on the basis of little more than general assertions. This situation is particularly disturbing, given that the affected companies certainly had at their disposal copious evidence in support of the claims of the complainants, such as the actual business plans relating to the new models, government documentation indicating approval for such plans (assuming the 'approval' referred to by the complainants with respect to the Optima means approval by the Indonesian government), and corporate minutes or internal decision memoranda relating both to the initial approval, and the subsequent abandonment, of the plans in question.[52]

7.45 In *China – Intellectual Property Rights*, the Panel was presented with evidence on one point in the form of various newspaper and magazine articles. The Panel explained why it did not give any weight to that evidence or consider the information that these press articles contained to be adequate:

> The Panel has reviewed the press articles and notes that none of them are corroborated, nor do they refer to events or statements that would not require corroboration. Whilst the publications are reputable, most of these particular articles are brief and are quoted either for general statements or random pieces of information. Most are anecdotal in tone, some repeating casual remarks about prices of fake goods, anonymous statements or speculation. They have titles including *'Fake Pens Write Their Own Ticket'*, *'Chasing copycats in a tiger economy'*, *'Hollywood takes on fake Chinese DVDs'*, *'Film not out yet on DVD? You can find it in China'* and *'Inside China's teeming world of fake goods'*. Most of the press articles are printed in US or other foreign English-language media that are not claimed to be authoritative sources of information on prices and markets in China. There are four press articles from Chinese sources, one from Xinhua News Agency and three from the English-language *China Daily*. Two are quoted simply to demonstrate the existence of certain goods in China; another quotes a vague statement from unnamed 'market insiders' on how illegal publishers tend to work; and the other quotes an 'insider' for the maximum and minimum prices of a range of pirated and genuine goods. One other alleged 'recent news account' is not attributed to any source at all.
>
> The Panel emphasizes that, in the absence of more reliable and relevant data, it has reviewed the evidence in the press articles with respect to a central point in this claim that is highly contested. The credibility and weight of that evidence are therefore critical to the Panel's task. For the reasons set out above, the Panel

---

[52] Panel Report, *Indonesia – Autos*, para. 14.234.

does not ascribe any weight to the evidence in the press articles and finds that, even if it did, the information that these press articles contain is inadequate to demonstrate what is typical or usual in China for the purposes of the relevant treaty obligation.[607]

---

[607] The Panel's approach is consistent with the approach of other international tribunals, notably the International Court of Justice: see Rosenne, S., *The Law and Practice of the International Court 1920–2005* (M. Nijhoff, 2006), Volume III at para. 257, and Highet, K., 'Evidence and Proof of Facts', in Damrosch, L., *The International Court of Justice at a Crossroads* (Transnational, 1987) cited in the Panel Report in *Australia – Automotive Leather II* at para. 9.65, fn. 210. The Panel's approach in the present dispute is also consistent with the approach in the Arbitrator's Award in *EC – The ACP–EC Partnership Agreement II*, at paras. 57–58. Whilst the Appellate Body Report in *Brazil – Retreaded Tyres* referred to a newspaper article in a footnote, it did so after referencing two substantial reports on point, and the point was not central to the findings in that dispute: see Appellate Body Report, para. 207, fn. 393, citing the Panel Report, para. 7.201, fn. 1358.[53]

The Panel in *Argentina – Import Measures* engaged in an analysis of the **7.46** evidentiary value of newspaper and magazine articles (reporting on statements by government officials), taking into account prior WTO jurisprudence, along with prior ICJ jurisprudence. With regard to these press reports, Argentina objected to the probative value of certain articles on the grounds that the printed media reports originated from two media companies that were biased against the Argentine government. The Panel stated:

> Previous panels have taken into account information contained in articles published in newspapers or magazines. In some cases, however, the probative value of the information contained in press articles has been rejected; for example, because the information was 'too little and too random', it consisted of a 'single, anecdotal newspaper article', or it was limited to foreign press or originated from non-authoritative sources of information on the country at issue.
>
> Newspapers or magazine articles may sometimes be a reflection of personal opinions by their authors. However, they can be useful sources of information, particularly when dealing with unwritten measures and when corroborating facts asserted through other forms of evidence[175] ...
>
> A panel must assess the credibility and persuasiveness of newspapers or magazine articles submitted as evidence, taking into account that the articles may reflect personal opinions, and assess the information contained in those articles contrasting it with the other evidence on the record. Ultimately, the Panel's task of making an objective assessment of the facts of the case consists in a holistic consideration of all the available evidence that has probative value. Furthermore, if an article submitted as evidence by one party is thought

---

[53] Panel Report, *China – Intellectual Property Rights*, paras. 7.628–7.629.

to contain incorrect information, nothing prevents another party from presenting evidence to rebut that information or to seek to demonstrate that it is
incorrect.

Accordingly, in the absence of sound legal reasons to disregard specific
exhibits, the Panel rejects Argentina's argument that journalistic material,
regardless of its source, cannot be 'considered to have any probative value'.'

---

[175] In one case, for example, the International Court of Justice (ICJ) accorded
probative value to information contained *inter alia* in newspaper, radio and
television reports considering that the information 'is wholly consistent and
concordant as to the main facts and circumstances of the case'. The ICJ also
took into account that the facts had not been denied or called into question by
the other party. ICJ, Judgment, United States Diplomatic and Consular Staff in
Tehran (United States v. Iran) (1980), para. 13. In another case, the ICJ
indicated it had 'been careful to treat [reports in press articles] with great
caution; even if they seem to meet high standards of objectivity, the Court
regards them not as evidence capable of proving facts, but as material which can
nevertheless contribute, in some circumstances, to corroborating the existence of
a fact, i.e. as illustrative material additional to other sources of evidence'. ICJ,
Merits, Military and Paramilitary Activities In and Against Nicaragua (Nicaragua v. United States of America) (1986), para. 62.[54]

7.3.5 Affidavit evidence

7.47 In *US – Softwood Lumber V*, the Panel observed that the Anti-Dumping
Agreement does not prescribe the nature and form of the information or
evidence applicants are required to submit, and which the investigating
authority must consider in deciding whether to initiate an investigation.
The Panel stated:

> We note that the *AD Agreement* does not contain any guidance on this issue and
> that affidavits are accepted in the legal systems of many jurisdictions as evidence.
> In light of the explanations submitted by the United States, we therefore see no
> reason why affidavits regarding price information may not be considered as
> relevant evidence in deciding whether there is sufficient evidence to justify the
> initiation of the investigation.[55]

7.48 In *US – Large Civil Aircraft (2nd complaint)*, the Panel reviewed the evidence
presented by the parties concerning the technology effects of certain research and
development subsidies provided to Boeing. In that context, the Panel noted that:

---

[54] Panel Report, *Argentina – Import Measures*, paras. 6.69–6.72 (also citing Panel Report, *Brazil –
Aircraft*, para. 7.84; Panel Report, *US – Countervailing Duty Investigation on DRAMS*, para. 7.117;
Panel Report, *Australia – Automotive Leather II*, para. 9.65, footnote 210; Panel Report, *Turkey –
Rice*, footnote 367; Panel Report, *Australia – Automotive Leather II*, footnote 210; Panel Report,
China – Intellectual Property Rights, paras. 7.617. 7.628–7.629, 7.658).
[55] Panel Report, *US – Softwood Lumber V*, para. 7.117.

The United States refers to statements by various Boeing engineers as 'affidavits'. The Panel's use of the titles assigned to these statements by the United States does not imply that the Panel considers these statements to be affidavits.[56]

In *Argentina – Import Measures*, the complainants submitted statements made by **7.49** the officials of companies operating in Argentina, as evidence of the existence and operation of certain trade-related requirements imposed by the Argentine government. These included statements by a notary public attesting to having been shown copies of certain documents by company officials (who wished not to be identified for fear of retaliation by the Argentine government). Argentina argued that the Panel should exercise caution when evaluating whether, and to what extent, assertions made by public notaries should be given any evidentiary weight in the absence of any ability by the Panel to corroborate those assertions. The Panel stated:

> The Panel will exercise caution in considering the probative value of all of these documents with respect to the facts described therein.[204] At the same time, the Panel finds no reason to completely disregard the notarized statements or the transcripts of earnings conference calls as evidence. Indeed, Argentina has not specifically challenged the veracity of the facts described in these documents, nor offered valid reasons for the Panel to disregard the statements. The Panel notes that previous panels have considered evidence submitted in the form of statements and affidavits.[205]

---

[204] The Panel agrees with Argentina's statement that 'the Panel should exercise caution' in considering the probative value of the notarized statements and other statements from company officials. Indeed, neither the Panel nor the respondent had an opportunity to pose questions to the declarants or, in the case of some of the documents, to have information on the declarants' identity. At the same time, the Panel must assume that the complainants have provided these documents in good faith. As noted by the Appellate Body, in dispute settlement, 'every Member of the WTO must assume the good faith of every other Member'. Appellate Body Report, *EC – Sardines*, para. 278. Moreover, as noted above, despite its attempts to seek more information from the parties and even a proposal for special procedures, the Panel has been stymied in its efforts to obtain additional evidence related to the matters dealt with in the report. See paras. 6.44–6.51 above.

[205] For example, the panel in *US – COOL* took into account affidavits submitted as exhibits, as evidence of certain facts. These findings were appealed and not reversed by the Appellate Body. See Panel Report, *US – COOL*, paras. 7.364–7.368; and Appellate Body Report, *US – COOL*, para. 310.[57]

7.3.6 Authenticity of evidence

In *EC – Bed Linen*, the Panel had to consider issues relating to good faith, fraud **7.50** and the authenticity of evidence in the context of examining an alleged

---

[56] Panel Report, *US – Large Civil Aircraft (2nd complaint)*, footnote 3670.
[57] Panel Report, *Argentina – Import Measures*, para. 6.91.

violation of the requirement, in Article 5.4 of the Anti-Dumping Agreement, that no anti-dumping investigation shall be initiated when domestic producers expressly supporting the application account for less than 25 per cent of total production of the like product produced by the domestic industry. The European Communities provided the Panel with photocopies, and in some cases photocopies of photocopies, of faxes of the letters of support received by various producers and domestic industry associations. The dates in the fax headers and footers in the photocopied documents submitted to the Panel were inconsistent with one another, and with the dates of the letters themselves. India asked the Panel to conclude that these letters were not in fact received by the EC investigating authority prior to initiation, that the EC investigating authority did not in fact examine them prior to initiation, and that the European Communities had 'tried to cover this fundamental error by manufacturing evidence *post hoc* and misrepresenting the facts' before the Panel. The Panel declined India's request, and stated:

> As noted above, India bears the burden of coming forward with sufficient evidence to make a *prima facie* case that the European Communities failed to act consistently with its obligations under Article 5.4 to determine the necessary level of support prior to initiation. We presume that Members act in good faith in the context of dispute settlement proceedings, and are unwilling to assume possible malfeasance in the absence of evidence to that effect. We consider that the 'doubts' which India has as to the European Communities' actions in this regard do not establish the necessary *prima facie* case in this context – the 'evidence' of the fax headers relied on by India does not, in our view, constitute evidence of fraud sufficient to overcome the presumption of good faith. Moreover, we believe it is more probable that these inconsistencies in the photocopies are attributable to the photocopying itself, rather than to the perpetration of a massive fabrication of fax headers and footers by the EC investigating authority to hide a failure to make a determination of standing prior to initiation. We therefore do not consider it necessary to examine the originals of the documents in question.[58]

7.51 In *Brazil – Aircraft (Article 22.6 – Brazil)*, the Arbitrators applied 'a presumption of good faith to statements and evidence originating in subjects of international law':

> A related problem faced by the Arbitrators in this case was that, in many instances, the original data necessary for the calculations or assessments was solely in the hands of Brazil. When this information originated in the Brazilian government, we assumed good faith and accepted the information and the supporting evidence provided by Brazil to the extent Canada also accepted it or did not provide sufficient evidence to put in doubt the accuracy of Brazil's statements and/or evidence.

---

[58] Panel Report, *EC – Bed Linen*, para. 6.216.

However, since this case relates to subsidies granted for the purchase of aircraft produced by the Brazilian aircraft manufacturer, Embraer, a large number of data essential for the resolution of our task is only available to that company. We assumed that Embraer was independent from the Brazilian government and, for that reason, we could not treat statements from that company as we would have if they had originated from a subject of international law.[15] When Brazil only provided statements regarding information available solely to Embraer, we requested that Brazil support those statements with materials usually regarded as evidence, such as articles or statements reproduced in the specialized press, company annual reports or any other certified information originating in Embraer or other reliable sources. When Brazil was not in a position to provide documentary evidence, we requested a detailed explanation of the reasons why such evidence was not available and expressed our willingness to consider written declarations from authorized Embraer officials, if duly certified. We then weighed this evidence against the evidence submitted by Canada.

---

[15] See preceding paragraph, where we apply a presumption of good faith to statements and evidence originating in subjects of international law; on production and appraisal of evidence, see, *inter alia*, International Court of Justice ('ICJ') judgement of 9 April 1949 *Corfu Channel Case*, ICJ Reports 1949, p. 32; ICJ judgement of 11 September 1992 *Land, Island and Maritime Frontier Dispute (El Salvador* v. *Honduras, Nicaragua intervening)*, ICJ Reports 1992, p. 399, para. 63; ICJ judgement on merits *Military and Paramilitary Activities In and Against Nicaragua (Nicaragua* v. *United States of America)*, ICJ Reports 1986, p. 40, para. 60.[59]

In *US – Continued Zeroing*, the Appellate Body found that the Panel committed **7.52** certain factual and legal errors when concluding that the European Communities had not shown that simple zeroing was used in seven of the periodic reviews at issue. Among other things, the Appellate Body criticized the Panel's insistence that only 'authenticated USDOC documents', and not other evidence, could be relied upon to demonstrate the use of zeroing. In that case, the Appellate Body reasoned that 'the absence of authentication does not negate the evidentiary significance of the documents'.[60] The Appellate Body ultimately concluded:

We agree with the United States that the issue of whether documents submitted by the European Communities were authenticated as USDOC-generated appears to have been 'pivotal' to the Panel's finding regarding the seven periodic reviews. While the Panel does not explain the extent to which the probative value of submitted evidence was, in its view, undermined by its non-authentication, the fact of non-authentication was one of two factors, and at times the *only* factor, cited by the Panel for its conclusion that the European

---

[59] Decision by the Arbitrators, *Brazil – Aircraft (Article 22.6 – Brazil)*, paras. 2.10–2.11.
[60] Appellate Body Report, *US – Continued Zeroing*, para. 339.

Communities had failed to demonstrate the use of simple zeroing in particular periodic reviews. We therefore consider that the Panel, by insisting on authenticated USDOC documents to demonstrate or show the use of simple zeroing, also failed to make an objective assessment by allowing a challenge to the authenticity of evidence originating from the USDOC, but later reproduced by interested parties, to skew its consideration of the probative value of that evidence.[61]

7.4   The standard of proof

7.53   There are different approaches to the standard of proof in common law and civil law systems, and it may be for this reason that panels and the Appellate Body have been cautious in formulating a generally applicable standard of proof. However, there are multiple panel and Appellate Body statements articulating the standard of proof in terms of a 'balance of probabilities'.

7.54   In *US – Wool Shirts and Blouses*, the Appellate Body confirmed that the burden of proof rests upon the party, whether complaining or defending, who asserts the affirmative of a particular claim or defence. The Appellate Body then set forth the standard of 'evidence sufficient to raise a presumption that what is claimed is true'. Specifically, the Appellate Body stated:

> [I]t is a generally accepted canon of evidence in civil law, common law and, in fact, most jurisdictions, that the burden of proof rests upon the party, whether complaining or defending, who asserts the affirmative of a particular claim or defence. If that party adduces evidence sufficient to raise a presumption that what is claimed is true, the burden then shifts to the other party, who will fail unless it adduces sufficient evidence to rebut the presumption.
>
> In the context of the GATT 1994 and the WTO Agreement, precisely how much and precisely what kind of evidence will be required to establish such a presumption will necessarily vary from measure to measure, provision to provision, and case to case.[62]

7.55   The Panel in *US – Section 301 Trade Act* referred to a situation where 'all the evidence and arguments remain in equipoise'. The Panel stated:

> Since, in this case, both parties have submitted extensive facts and arguments in respect of the [European Communities'] claims, our task will essentially be to balance all evidence on record and decide whether the EC, as [the] party bearing the original burden of proof, has convinced us of the validity of its claims. In case of uncertainty, i.e. in case all the evidence and arguments remain in equipoise, we have to give the benefit of the doubt to the [United States] as defending party.[63]

---

[61] *Ibid.*, para. 341.   [62] Appellate Body Report, *US – Wool Shirts and Blouses*, p. 14.
[63] Panel Report, *US – Section 301 Trade Act*, para. 7.14.

The Panel in *US – 1916 Act* articulated a similar standard, and distinguished the **7.56** burden of proof from the standard of proof:

> This rule [regarding the burden of proof in WTO dispute settlement proceedings] however is only applicable to determine whether and when a party bears the burden of proof. Once both parties have submitted evidence meeting those requirements, it is up to the Panel to weigh the evidence as a whole. In cases where the evidence as a whole regarding a particular claim or defence remains in equipoise, the issue must be decided against the party bearing the burden of proof on that claim or defence.[64]

In the context of addressing a disputed issue of municipal law, the Panel stated:

> If, after having applied the above methodology, we could not reach certainty as to the most appropriate court interpretation, i.e. if the evidence remains in equipoise, we shall follow the interpretation that favours the party against which the claim has been made, considering that the claimant did not convincingly support its claim.[65]

The Panel in *US – Section 211 Appropriations Act* stated that 'the Panel's task **7.57** becomes a matter of weighing the arguments and evidence available to it to determine whether, on balance, the Panel is convinced that the US measures are inconsistent with the provisions of the TRIPS Agreement'.[66]

The Panel in *Argentina – Hides and Leather* observed that it 'may be an open **7.58** question' as to whether the 'quantum of evidence' necessary to support a violation under a particular provision of the WTO agreements is the same as that required to support a case in a domestic court:

> The evidence before us is quite thin. We have a newspaper article and opinion piece, a press release … and a statement by a member of the *Congreso de la Nación*. Such evidence would certainly not support a case in a domestic court. While it may be an open question whether the same quantum of evidence is necessary to support such allegations in a WTO dispute under Article XI of the GATT 1994, surely the difference cannot be that great. What is clear is that whatever level of proof may be required, it was not reached here.[67]

The Panel in *Canada – Dairy (Article 21.5 – New Zealand and US II)*, without **7.59** attempting to formulate the standard of proof applicable in WTO dispute settlement proceedings, defined in negative terms what it is *not*:

> [W]e consider that Canada's proposed focus on the cost of production of individual producers would require a government to have access to, and make available, information on the cost of production of each producer and on whether or not the individual producer participates in the CEM market. It

---

[64] Panel Report, *US – 1916 Act (Japan)*, para. 6.25.   [65] *Ibid.*, para. 6.57.
[66] Panel Report, *US – Section 211 Appropriations Act*, para. 8.19.
[67] Panel Report, *Argentina – Hides and Leather*, para. 11.52.

seems to us that only on rare occasion would a government have record-keeping of this magnitude. Quite apart from the administrative cost and unworkability of this approach, we note that even Canada has expressed doubts that the Appellate Body could have intended a benchmark for determining the existence of payments that entails a standard of proof akin to the 'beyond a reasonable doubt' standard under criminal law.[68]

7.60 In *US – Countervailing Duty Investigation on DRAMS*, the Panel was presented with the question of whether the evidence before the US investigating author-ities in the underlying countervailing duty investigation demonstrated that the Korean government had 'entrusted or directed' private bodies to provide subsidies within the meaning of Article 1.1(a)(1)(iv) of the SCM Agreement. In the context of addressing this issue, the Panel stated that the evidence of entrustment or direction must in all cases be 'probative and compelling'. On appeal, the United States challenged the Panel's articulation and application of this evidentiary standard (thus, the issue in this case was not the standard of proof to be applied by WTO panels; rather, it was what standard of proof should be applied by domestic investigating authorities when making a particular type of determination in the context of a countervailing duty investigation). The Appellate Body offered the following observations:

> [N]either the *SCM Agreement* nor the DSU explicitly articulates a standard for the evidence required to substantiate a finding of entrustment or direction under Article 1.1(a)(1)(iv). Article 12 of the *SCM Agreement*, entitled 'Evidence', specifies in paragraph 2 that a decision of the investigating authority as to the existence of a subsidy 'can only be based on' evidence on the record of that agency; this applies equally to evidence used to support a finding of a financial contribution under Article 1.1(a)(1)(iv). Beyond this requirement, however, we see no basis in the *SCM Agreement* or in the DSU to impose upon an investi-gating authority a particular standard for the evidence supporting its finding of entrustment or direction.
>
> The Panel explained that, in using the terms 'probative' and 'compelling', it was expressing the view that the total evidence relied upon by an agency must 'demonstrate' entrustment or direction with respect to each private body in a given financial contribution. In so stating, the Panel, in our view, did not require that the evidence relied upon by the USDOC be 'irrefutable', nor did it require the evidence to be of such quality or quantity so as to 'force' the USDOC to arrive at a finding of entrustment or direction. Indeed, after reviewing the USDOC's evidence, the Panel concluded that the USDOC 'could not properly have found that there was sufficient evidence to *support* [its] finding of entrust-ment or direction.' It appears to us, on balance, that the Panel did not apply the term 'compelling' in the manner suggested by the United States; had it done so, it would have erroneously imposed a qualitative standard higher than that contemplated by the *SCM Agreement*.[69]

---

[68] Panel Report, *Canada – Dairy (Article 21.5 – New Zealand and US II)*, para. 5.67.
[69] Appellate Body Report, *US – Countervailing Duty Investigation on DRAMS*, paras. 138–9.

In *US – Upland Cotton (Article 21.5 – Brazil)*, the Appellate Body was called **7.61**
upon to address a number of complex issues. One was whether the Panel erred
in its assessment of the evidence relating to the profitability of a US programme,
in the context of applying item (j) of the Illustrative List of Export Subsidies
contained in Annex I to the SCM Agreement. Item (j) refers to the provision of
export credit guarantee or insurance programmes 'at premium rates which are
inadequate to cover the long-term operating costs and losses of the programmes'.
In the context of addressing this issue, the Appellate Body stated that 'the
quantitative evidence submitted by Brazil and the United States support two
plausible conclusions that one could draw regarding the profitability of the
revised GSM 102 programme', and that the question was whether the evidence
as assessed by the Panel makes one of the two probable outcomes that emerge
from the quantitative evidence 'more likely than not'.[70] After reviewing the
evidence, the Appellate Body concluded that 'it is more likely than not that the
revised GSM 102 programme operates at a loss', and that '[t]herefore,
we consider that Brazil has succeeded in establishing that the revised GSM
102 programme is provided at premiums that are inadequate to cover its long-
term operating costs and losses'.[71]

In *US – Continued Zeroing*, the Panel found that the European Communities **7.62**
had not proven that the United States used the so-called 'zeroing' methodology
in seven of the anti-dumping administrative reviews at issue in that dispute. On
appeal, the European Communities argued that the Panel applied an 'unreasonable burden of proof in this case' because it required 'evidence "necessarily
showing" (i.e. without any trace of doubt) that zeroing was "actually used" in
the seven administrative reviews at issue'. The Appellate Body stated:

> If evidence 'necessarily showing' a particular fact were required, this would
> suggest that the evidence must in no circumstance permit of a conclusion *other
> than* the existence of that fact. We agree that such a standard is more stringent
> than the assessment of whether the evidence meets the required burden of
> proof.[72]

The Panel in *US – Countervailing and Anti-Dumping Measures (China)* (DS449) **7.63**
concluded that the USDOC failed to investigate so-called 'double remedies' in
twenty-five concurrent anti-dumping and countervailing duty (CVD) investigations
and reviews, based on the following facts: (i) USDOC imposed CVDs concurrently
with anti-dumping duties in twenty-five successive investigations and reviews
over a four-year period without making any adjustment or offset to avoid possible
double remedies, either on the anti-dumping or the CVD side; and (ii)

---

[70] Appellate Body Report, *US – Upland Cotton (Article 21.5 – Brazil)*, para. 301.
[71] *Ibid.*, para. 321.   [72] Appellate Body Report, *US – Continued Zeroing*, para. 335.

double remedies are 'likely' to arise from the concurrent imposition of CVDs and anti-dumping duties calculated under the United States' methodology for calculating dumping margins. The Panel stated:

> We acknowledge that these two facts do not *necessarily* lead to this (and only this) conclusion. That is to say, we are not suggesting that these facts permit of no conclusion *other than* this conclusion … It is hypothetically conceivable that USDOC would have investigated whether double remedies arose in the investigations and reviews at issue, and determined – in respect of 25 successive proceedings, and in respect of every subsidy at issue in each one of those proceedings – that none of these subsidies had any effect on the export price for any of the products in question. However … it is a remote possibility that USDOC investigated and, based on such an investigation, determined on the basis of positive evidence that none of the subsidies at issue in any of the investigations had any effect on the export price of any of the products at issue (and then justifiably imposed CVDs concurrently with anti-dumping duties in 25 successive investigations and reviews without making any adjustments on account of double remedies). We consider that to reject China's claim on the basis of a remote possibility that USDOC might have investigated whether double remedies arose (when 100% CVDs were concurrently imposed with 100% anti-dumping duties without making any adjustments on either the CVD side or the anti-dumping side to offset for double remedies, in 25 successive investigations and reviews, which comprise every CVD investigation on imports from China over a period of more than four years) would not be in keeping with the standard of proof that applies in WTO panel proceedings. We consider that 'such a standard [would be] more stringent' than is required of China to meet 'the required burden of proof'.[73]

---

[73] Panel Report, *US – Countervailing and Anti-Dumping Measures (China)*, para. 7.378 (citing Appellate Body Report, *US – Continued Zeroing*, para. 335).

8

GOOD FAITH

8.1 Introduction

This chapter reviews WTO jurisprudence on good faith, a fundamental concept **8.1**
that permeates the law of treaties and international dispute settlement.[1] This
concept is 'ambiguous if not amorphous or elusive'.[2] In *General Principles of
Law as Applied by International Courts and Tribunals*, Cheng wrote:

> What exactly this principle implies is perhaps difficult to define. As an English
> judge once said, such rudimentary terms applicable to human conduct as 'Good
> Faith', 'Honesty', or 'Malice' elude *a priori* definition. 'They can be illustrated
> but not defined.' [This part] will be an attempt to illustrate, by means of
> international judicial decisions, the application of this essential principle of
> law in the international legal order.[3]

WTO adjudicators have been confronted with various arguments and issues
relating to 'good faith', and have generated a substantial body of related juris
prudence as a result.[4] This chapter reviews statements by WTO adjudicators
of wider applicability concerning: (i) good faith pending the entry into force of
treaties; (ii) good faith and the performance and interpretation of treaties; and
(iii) good faith in international dispute settlement.

---

[1] E. Zoller, *La bonne foi en droit international public* (Pedone, 1977); J. F. O'Connor, *Good Faith in
International Law* (Aldershot, 1991); R. Kolb, *La bonne foi en droit international public* (Bruylant,
1998).

[2] M. Kotzur, 'Good Faith' (January 2009) in *Max Planck Encyclopedia of Public International Law*,
para. 1.

[3] B. Cheng, *General Principles of Law as Applied by International Courts and Tribunals* (Stevens &
Sons, 1953), Part Two, p. 105.

[4] For commentary, see T. Cottier and K. Nadakavukaren Schefer, 'Good Faith and the Protection of
Legitimate Expectations in the WTO', in M. Bronckers and R. Quick (eds.), *New Directions in
International Economic Law: Essays in Honour of John Jackson* (Kluwer, 2000), pp. 47–68;
M. Panizzon, *Good Faith in the Jurisprudence of the WTO: The Protection of Legitimate Expectations,
Good Faith Interpretation and Fair Dispute Settlement* (Hart, 2006); A. Mitchell, 'Good Faith in
WTO Dispute Settlement' (2006) 7 *Melbourne Journal of International Law* 339.

8.2   Good faith pending the entry into force of treaties

8.2   Article 18 of the Vienna Convention, entitled 'Obligation not to defeat
the object and purpose of a treaty prior to its entry into force', provides that
a State 'is obliged to refrain from acts which would defeat the object and
purpose of a treaty' pending its entry into force. Several panels have expressed
the view that Article 18 summarizes the concept of good faith, and several
panels have examined the consistency of certain actions with the obligation in
Article 18.

8.3   In *US – Shrimp*, the Panel stated that it understood prior statements by the
Appellate Body regarding the interpretation of the general exceptions in Article
XX of the GATT to be an application of the international law principle
according to which international agreements must be applied in good faith, in
light of the *pacta sunt servanda* principle in Article 26 of the Vienna Convention.
In that context, the Panel expressed the view that the formulation of Article
18 of the Vienna Convention informs the meaning of good faith in the context
of Article 26 of the Vienna Convention:

> The concept of good faith is explained in Article 18 of the Vienna Convention
> which states that 'A State is obliged to refrain from acts which would defeat the
> object and purpose of a treaty'.[645]

---

[645] This rule, which applies to the period between the moment when a State has
expressed its consent to be bound by a treaty and its entry into force, nevertheless seems to express a generally applicable principle. See Patrick Daillier & Alain
Pellet, Droit International Public (1994), p. 216.[5]

8.4   The Panel in *US – Offset Act (Byrd Amendment)*, in the context of examining
claims under the parallel provisions of Article 5.4 of the Anti-Dumping Agreement and Article 11.4 of the SCM Agreement, offered similar observations
regarding the principle of good faith. Specifically, the Panel also considered that
the obligation in Article 18 of the Vienna Convention shed light on the meaning
of good faith:

> The importance of the principle of good faith as a general rule of conduct in
> international relations is well established.[313] Good faith requires a party to a
> treaty to refrain from acting in a manner which would defeat the object and
> purpose of the treaty as a whole or the treaty provision in question.[314]

---

[313] Also see: V. D. Degan, Sources of International Law, Martinus Nijhoff,
1997, p. 401.

[5] Panel Report, *US – Shrimp*, para. 7.41.

[314] One prominent scholar states that Article 18 of the Vienna Convention on the Law of Treaties, 'while not explicitly referring to the principle of good faith, summarizes its substance by providing that a signatory "is obliged to refrain from acts which would defeat the object and purpose" of the treaty.' A. D'Amato, 'Good Faith', in 'Encyclopaedia of International Law', p. 599. The International Law Commission commenting on the principle of good faith stated that '[s]ome members felt that there would be an advantage in also stating that a party must abstain from acts calculated to frustrate the object and purpose of the treaty. The Commission however considered that this was clearly implicit in the obligation to perform the treaty in good faith and preferred to state the *pacta sunt servanda* rule in as simple a form as possible' (Yearbook International Law Commission, 1966, Vol. II, p. 211).[6]

In *Argentina – Poultry Anti-Dumping Duties*, the Panel referred to Article 18 in **8.5** the context of finding that Brazil was not estopped from requesting a panel under the WTO agreements with respect to a measure that had already been the subject of a dispute before a MERCOSUR tribunal. The Protocol of Olivos allowed MERCOSUR members to choose the forum in which they wished disputes to be settled, but stipulated that, once a procedure has been initiated in one forum, this precluded resorting to any of the other forums provided for in the Protocol. The Panel noted:

> The Protocol of Olivos was signed on 18 February 2002 and has not entered into force yet. According to the European Communities, the question might be raised whether the request for the establishment of the panel made by Brazil on 25 February 2002, i.e. after the signature of the Protocol of Olivos, was consistent with Brazil's obligation under Article 18 of the *Vienna Convention* not to defeat the object and purpose of a signed treaty prior to its entry into force. However, Article 50 of the Protocol of Olivos appears to suggest that it does not apply to disputes already decided in accordance with the Protocol of Brasilia.[7]

In *EC – Marketing and Approval of Biotech Products*, the Panel observed that the **8.6** mere fact that the United States had signed the Convention on Biological Diversity did not mean that the CBD was applicable to it as such. The Panel noted:

> We note that pursuant to Article 18 of the *Vienna Convention* a State which has signed a treaty must refrain from acts which would defeat the object and purpose of that treaty, at least until it has made its intention clear not to become a party. Initially, we note that there is an issue whether the provisions of Article 18 reflect customary international law. Even disregarding this issue, we note that Article 18 refers to 'acts' which rise to the level of 'defeat[ing] the object and purpose' of a treaty, not to acts which are inconsistent with specific terms of that treaty. It does not follow from Article 18 that a State which has signed a treaty has

---

[6] Panel Report, *US – Offset Act (Byrd Amendment)*, para. 7.64.
[7] Panel Report, *Argentina – Poultry Anti-Dumping Duties*, footnote 49.

obligations pursuant to the specific terms of that treaty and that the treaty is applicable to it as such.[8]

8.7 In *Peru – Agricultural Products*, the respondent argued that a free trade agreement between itself and Guatemala, the complainant in that case, reflected the parties' agreement that Peru could maintain the challenged measures. Peru argued that, in these circumstances, the Panel should find that Guatemala had not acted in good faith in initiating the dispute. In the context of addressing this argument, the Panel considered Article 18 of the Vienna Convention:

> To begin with, the parties agree that the FTA has not yet entered into force. Peru's argument to the effect that paragraph 9 of Annex 2.3 to the FTA contains an undertaking by Guatemala not to challenge the PRS is limited by this undisputed fact. An international treaty only begins to produce legal effects and bind the parties from the moment it enters into force. The mere signing of a treaty, before it enters into force, imposes only limited obligations on the parties, fundamentally that of refraining from acting in such a way as to defeat the object and purpose of the treaty. To impose, as an effect of the signing of a treaty, legal consequences that go beyond those indicated in Article 18 of the Vienna Convention would blur the difference between a treaty in force and one that is not yet in force. Thus, the Panel cannot attribute to the FTA a legal value that it does not currently possess.
>
> The Panel has also taken note of Peru's argument according to which, by having challenged the PRS through the present procedure, Guatemala is defeating the object and purpose of the FTA, within the meaning of Article 18 of the Vienna Convention. In this connection, Peru has pointed out that its argument does not mean that it is asking the Panel to determine whether or not Guatemala is defeating the object and purpose of the FTA.
>
> The relevant part of Article 18 of the Vienna Convention provides as follows:
>
> > A State is obliged to refrain from acts which would defeat the object and purpose of a treaty when:
> >
> > (a) it has signed the treaty or has exchanged instruments constituting the treaty subject to ratification, acceptance or approval, until it shall have made its intention clear not to become a party to the treaty . . .
>
> In the opinion of some scholars, the obligation contained in Article 18 of the Vienna Convention is in the nature of a customary rule of public international law. In the circumstances of this dispute, it is not necessary for the Panel to rule on the applicability of this obligation. In any case, as emerges from the text, the provision does not require a signatory to comply with the terms of a treaty which it has not yet ratified, and does not even require the signatory not to act in a manner inconsistent with that treaty. The only obligation is to refrain from acts which would prevent it from being in a position to comply with the treaty once

---

[8] Panel Report, *EC – Marketing and Approval of Biotech Products*, footnote 251.

the latter enters into force or which would invalidate the object and purpose of the treaty.

The Panel is not convinced that the violation by a Member of the obligation contained in Article 18 of the Vienna Convention with respect to a treaty that does not form part of the WTO covered agreements can constitute evidence of lack of the good faith required by Articles 3.7 and 3.10 of the DSU. In any event, and even assuming for the sake of argument that this were so, Peru's argument would require it to be shown that Guatemala's action, in initiating the present procedure, constitutes an act which has the effect of defeating the object and purpose of the FTA. This, in turn, would require the Panel to determine what is the object and purpose of the FTA. The Panel notes that the parties hold significantly divergent opinions on this issue. In any event, to make a determination as to what is the object and purpose of the FTA would be to go beyond the terms of reference entrusted to this Panel by the DSB.[9]

8.3   Good faith in the performance and interpretation of treaties

Article 26 of the Vienna Convention, entitled '*Pacta sunt servanda*', states that **8.8** '[e]very treaty in force is binding upon the parties to it and must be performed by them in good faith'. Furthermore, Article 31(1) of the Vienna Convention provides that a treaty 'shall be interpreted in good faith'. WTO adjudicators have discussed various interrelated aspects of the principle of good faith in Articles 26 and 31(1), including: (i) reasonableness and *abus de droit*; (ii) measures defeating the purpose of a treaty and/or expectations derived therefrom; (iii) the presumption that States act in good faith; (iv) measures threatening prohibited conduct; and (v) withdrawal of measures based on errors.

8.3.1 Reasonableness and *abus de droit*

In several cases, panels and the Appellate Body have relied on authorities linking **8.9** the concept of good faith to the concepts of reasonableness and *abus de droit*.

In *US – Shrimp*, the Panel stated that it understood prior statements by **8.10** the Appellate Body regarding the interpretation of the general exceptions in Article XX of the GATT 'to be an application of the international law principle

---

[9] Panel Report, *Peru – Agricultural Products*, paras. 7.88–7.92 (citing P. Palchetti, 'Article 18 of the 1969 Vienna Convention: A Vague and Ineffective Obligation or a Useful Means for Strengthening Legal Cooperation?', in: E. Cannizzaro (ed.), *The Law of Treaties beyond the Vienna Convention* (Oxford University Press, 2011), p. 25; M. Villiger, *Commentary on the 1969 Vienna Convention on the Law of Treaties* (Martinus Nijhoff Publishers, 2009), p. 252; International Law Commission, Report on the Work of its Eighteenth Session (4 May-19 July 1966), GAOR, 21st Session, Supp. No. 9, UN Doc. A/6309/Rev.1, p. 202; A. Aust, *Modern Treaty Law and Practice*, 3rd edn (Cambridge University Press, 2013), pp. 107 and 118–19; International Law Commission, Report on the Work of its Fifty-Ninth Session (7 May–5 June 2007), GAOR, 62nd Session, Supp. No. 10, UN Doc. A/62/10, p. 56; Appellate Body Report, *Mexico – Taxes on Soft Drinks*, paras. 56, 78).

according to which international agreements must be applied in good faith, in light of the *pacta sunt servanda* principle'. The Panel noted:

> Good faith in the application of treaties is generally considered as a fundamental principle of treaty law. See Article 26 (*Pacta Sunt Servanda*) of the Vienna Convention, which provides that 'Every treaty in force is binding upon the parties to it and must be performed by them in good faith.' See judgement of the International Court of Justice of 27 August 1952 in the *Case Concerning Rights of Nationals of the United States of America in Morocco (France v. United States)*, ICJ Report 1952, p. 176, at p. 212, where the Court stated that 'The power of making the valuation [a power granted by the 1906 Act of Algesiras] rests with the customs authorities, but it is a power *which must be exercised reasonably and in good faith*' (emphasis added).[10]

8.11 In *US – Shrimp*, the Appellate Body held that the chapeau of Article XX of the GATT was 'but one expression of good faith' and also reflected the notion of '*abus de droit*':

> The chapeau of Article XX is, in fact, but one expression of the principle of good faith. This principle, at once a general principle of law and a general principle of international law, controls the exercise of rights by states. One application of this general principle, the application widely known as the doctrine of *abus de droit*, prohibits the abusive exercise of a state's rights and enjoins that whenever the assertion of a right 'impinges on the field covered by [a] treaty obligation, it must be exercised *bona fide*, that is to say, reasonably.'[156] An abusive exercise by a Member of its own treaty right thus results in a breach of the treaty rights of the other Members and, as well, a violation of the treaty obligation of the Member so acting. Having said this, our task here is to interpret the language of the chapeau, seeking additional interpretative guidance, as appropriate, from the general principles of international law.[157]

---

[156] B. Cheng, *General Principles of Law as Applied by International Courts and Tribunals* (Stevens & Sons, 1953), Chapter 4, in particular, p. 125 elaborates:

> . . . A reasonable and *bona fide* exercise of a right in such a case is one which is appropriate and necessary for the purpose of the right (i.e. in furtherance of the interests which the right is intended to protect). It should at the same time be *fair and equitable as between the parties* and not one which is calculated to procure for one of them an unfair advantage in the light of the obligation assumed. A reasonable exercise of the right is regarded as compatible with the obligation. But the exercise of the right in such a manner as to prejudice the interests of the other contracting party arising out of the treaty is unreasonable and is considered as inconsistent with the *bona fide* execution of the treaty obligation, and a breach of the treaty . . . (emphasis added)

Also see, for example, Jennings and Watts (eds.), *Oppenheim's International Law*, 9th edn Vol. I (Longman's, 1992), pp. 407–410, *Border and Transborder Armed Actions Case*, (1988) ICJ Rep. 105; *Rights of Nationals of the United States*

---

[10] Panel Report, *US – Shrimp*, footnote 644.

in Morocco Case (1952) ICJ Rep. 176; *Anglo-Norwegian Fisheries Case* (1951)
ICJ Rep. 142.
[157] Vienna Convention, Article 31(3)(c).[11]

In *US – Hot-Rolled Steel*, the Appellate Body stated that the principle of good **8.12**
faith restrained investigating authorities from imposing unreasonable burdens on
exporters:

> This provision requires investigating authorities to strike a balance between the
> effort that they can expect interested parties to make in responding to question-
> naires, and the practical ability of those interested parties to comply fully with all
> demands made of them by the investigating authorities. We see this provision as
> another detailed expression of the principle of good faith, which is, at once, a
> general principle of law and a principle of general international law, that informs
> the provisions of the *Anti-Dumping Agreement*, as well as the other covered
> agreements. This organic principle of good faith, in this particular context,
> restrains investigating authorities from imposing on exporters burdens which,
> in the circumstances, are not reasonable.[12]

The Panel in *US – Gambling*, quoting Sinclair's book on the law of treaties, **8.13**
stated that '[w]e also note that "the principle of good faith in the process of
interpretation underlies the concept that interpretation should not lead to a
result which is manifestly absurd or unreasonable".'[13]

In *Peru – Agricultural Products*, the Panel referred to the Appellate Body's **8.14**
discussion of *abus de droit* in *US – Shrimp*, and stated:

> The Appellate Body's approach indicates that a right will be exercised abusively
> when its assertion unreasonably interferes with the sphere covered by an
> obligation arising out of a treaty. This would occur when a Member initiates a
> dispute settlement procedure in a manner contrary to good faith, along the lines
> described above.[14]

8.3.2 Measures defeating the purpose of a treaty and/or expectations
derived therefrom

The principle that treaties must be performed 'in good faith' raises the question **8.15**
of whether there can be situations in which a State can breach a treaty provision
through actions that, while not in breach of the terms thereof, are calculated to

[11] Appellate Body Report, *US – Shrimp*, para. 158.
[12] Appellate Body Report, *US – Hot-Rolled Steel*, para. 101.
[13] Panel Report, *US – Gambling*, para. 6.49 (citing I. Sinclair, *The Vienna Convention on the Law of Treaties*, 2nd edn (Manchester University Press, 1984), p. 120).
[14] Panel Report, *Peru – Agricultural Products*, para. 7.95.

defeat its object and purpose.[15] WTO jurisprudence supports the proposition that the threshold would be very high for finding any breach on that basis, and would require exceptional circumstances.

8.16 In *Korea – Procurement*, the Panel explained that the 'non-violation' complaint provided for in Article XXIII:1(b) of the GATT is 'further development' of the principle of *pacta sunt servanda* is expressed in Article 26 of the Vienna Convention, and that both concern measures that have been taken that frustrate the object and purpose of the treaty and the reasonably expected benefits that flow therefrom:

> In our view, the non-violation remedy as it has developed in GATT/WTO jurisprudence should not be viewed in isolation from general principles of customary international law. As noted above, the basic premise is that Members should not take actions, even those consistent with the letter of the treaty, which might serve to undermine the reasonable expectations of negotiating partners. This has traditionally arisen in the context of actions which might undermine the value of negotiated tariff concessions. In our view, this is a further development of the principle of *pacta sunt servanda* in the context of Article XXIII:1(b) of the GATT 1947 and disputes that arose thereunder, and subsequently in the WTO Agreements, particularly in Article 26 of the DSU. The principle of *pacta sunt servanda* is expressed in Article 26 of the *Vienna Convention*[751] in the following manner:
>
> > Every treaty in force is binding upon the parties to it and must be performed by them in good faith.
>
> It seems clear that good faith performance has been agreed by the WTO Members to include subsequent actions which might nullify or impair the benefits reasonably expected to accrue to other parties to the negotiations in question. The consistency of such an interpretation with the general principles of customary international law is confirmed by reference to the negotiating history of the *Vienna Convention*. According to the Report of the International Law Commission to the General Assembly, this issue was considered by the members negotiating the Convention in the following manner:
>
> > 'Some members felt that there would be advantage in also stating that a party must abstain from acts calculated to frustrate the object and purpose of the treaty. The Commission, however, considered that this was clearly implicit in the obligation to perform the treaty in good faith and preferred to state the *pacta sunt servanda* rule in as simple a form as possible.'[752]
>
> The non-violation doctrine goes further than just respect for the object and purpose of the treaty as expressed in its terminology. One must respect actual provisions (i.e. concessions) as far as their material effect on competitive

---

[15] For example, see H. Thirlway, 'The Law and Procedure of the International Court of Justice 1960–1989, Part Four' (1992) 63 *British Yearbook of International Law* 1, at 48–54 (under the heading 'Duty Not to Deprive a Treaty of its Object and Purpose').

opportunities is concerned. It is an extension of the good faith requirement in this sense.

. . .

In our view, these observations by previous panels are entirely in line with the concept of *pacta sunt servanda*. The vast majority of actions taken by Members which are consistent with the letter of their treaty obligations will also be consistent with the spirit. However, upon occasion, it may be the case that some actions, while permissible under one set of rules (e.g. the Agreement on Subsidies and Countervailing Measures is a commonly referenced example of rules in this regard), are not consistent with the spirit of other commitments such as those in negotiated Schedules. That is, such actions deny the competitive opportunities which are the reasonably expected effect of such commitments. However, we must also note that, while the overall burden of proof is on the complainant, we do not mean to introduce here a new requirement that a complainant affirmatively prove actual bad faith on the part of another Member. It is fairly clear from the history of disputes prior to the conclusion of the Uruguay Round that such a requirement was never established and there is no evidence in the current treaty text that such a requirement was newly imposed. Rather, the affirmative proof should be that measures have been taken that frustrate the object and purpose of the treaty and the reasonably expected benefits that flow therefrom.

---

[751] A reference to the rule of *pacta sunt servanda* also appears in the preamble to the Vienna Convention.
[752] Yearbook of the International Law Commission (1966), Vol. II at p. 211.[16]

The Panel in *Japan – Film* explained that non-violation complaints should be   **8.17** approached with caution and treated as an exceptional concept:

Although the non-violation remedy is an important and accepted tool of WTO/ GATT dispute settlement and has been 'on the books' for almost 50 years, we note that there have only been eight cases in which panels or working parties have substantively considered Article XXIII:1(b) claims. This suggests that both the GATT contracting parties and WTO Members have approached this remedy with caution and, indeed, have treated it as an exceptional instrument of dispute settlement. We note in this regard that both the European Communities and the United States in the *EEC – Oilseeds* case, and the two parties in this case, have confirmed that the non-violation nullification or impairment remedy should be approached with caution and treated as an exceptional concept. The reason for this caution is straightforward. Members negotiate the rules that they agree to follow and only exceptionally would expect to be challenged for actions not in contravention of those rules.[17]

In *India – Patents (US)*, the Appellate Body reversed the Panel's finding that   **8.18** India acted inconsistently with Article 70.8 of the TRIPS Agreement. The Panel

---

[16] Panel Report, *Korea – Procurement*, paras. 7.93–7.99.
[17] Panel Report, *Japan – Film*, para. 10.36.

had framed the issue before it in terms of whether or not the measures taken by India 'achieve the object and purpose of Article 70.8 and thereby protect the legitimate expectations of other WTO Members'. The Appellate Body considered that any finding of violation should have been based on the text of the provisions at issue. The Appellate Body found that the Panel erred by importing the concept of 'reasonable expectations' from the context of non-violation complaints into cases of alleged violation:

> The doctrine of protecting the 'reasonable expectations' of contracting parties developed in the context of 'non-violation' complaints brought under Article XXIII:1(b) of the GATT 1947. Some of the rules and procedures concerning 'non-violation' cases have been codified in Article 26.1 of the DSU. 'Non-violation' complaints are rooted in the GATT's origins as an agreement intended to protect the reciprocal tariff concessions negotiated among the contracting parties under Article II. In the absence of substantive legal rules in many areas relating to international trade, the 'non-violation' provision of Article XXIII:1(b) was aimed at preventing contracting parties from using non-tariff barriers or other policy measures to negate the benefits of negotiated tariff concessions. Under Article XXIII:1(b) of the GATT 1994, a Member can bring a 'non-violation' complaint when the negotiated balance of concessions between Members is upset by the application of a measure, whether or not this measure is inconsistent with the provisions of the covered agreement. The ultimate goal is not the withdrawal of the measure concerned, but rather achieving a mutually satisfactory adjustment, usually by means of compensation.
>
>   . . . This case involves allegations of violation of obligations under the *TRIPS Agreement*. However, the Panel's invocation of the 'legitimate expectations' of Members relating to conditions of competition melds the legally distinct bases for 'violation' and 'non-violation' complaints under Article XXIII of the GATT 1994 into one uniform cause of action.[18]

The Appellate Body further found that the Panel erred in its understanding of good faith. The Panel considered that 'good faith' interpretation requires the protection of 'legitimate expectations derived from' the protection of intellectual property rights provided for in the Agreement. The Appellate Body disagreed:

> The Panel misapplies Article 31 of the *Vienna Convention*. The Panel misunderstands the concept of legitimate expectations in the context of the customary rules of interpretation of public international law. The legitimate expectations of the parties to a treaty are reflected in the language of the treaty itself. The duty of a treaty interpreter is to examine the words of the treaty to determine the intentions of the parties. This should be done in accordance with the principles of treaty interpretation set out in Article 31 of the *Vienna Convention*. But these

---

[18] Appellate Body Report, *India – Patents (US)*, paras. 41–2 (citing E.-U. Petersmann, 'Violation Complaints and Non-Violation Complaints in International Law' (1991) *German Yearbook of International Law* 175).

principles of interpretation neither require nor condone the imputation into a treaty of words that are not there or the importation into a treaty of concepts that were not intended.[19]

In *EC – Computer Equipment*, the Panel considered the requirement of 'good **8.19** faith' treaty interpretation to mean that it should interpret the meaning of a tariff concession in the EC Schedule in light of the 'legitimate expectations' of an exporting Member. The Appellate Body again disagreed:

> [W]e do not agree with the Panel that interpreting the meaning of a concession in a Member's Schedule in the light of the 'legitimate expectations' of exporting Members is consistent with the principle of good faith interpretation under Article 31 of the *Vienna Convention*. Recently, in *India – Patents*, the panel stated that good faith interpretation under Article 31 required 'the protection of legitimate expectations'. We found that the panel had misapplied Article 31 of the *Vienna Convention* . . .
>
> The purpose of treaty interpretation under Article 31 of the *Vienna Convention* is to ascertain the *common* intentions of the parties. These *common* intentions cannot be ascertained on the basis of the subjective and unilaterally determined 'expectations' of *one* of the parties to a treaty. Tariff concessions provided for in a Member's Schedule – the interpretation of which is at issue here – are reciprocal and result from a mutually advantageous negotiation between importing and exporting Members. A Schedule is made an integral part of the GATT 1994 by Article II:7 of the GATT 1994. Therefore, the concessions provided for in that Schedule are part of the terms of the treaty. As such, the only rules which may be applied in interpreting the meaning of a concession are the general rules of treaty interpretation set out in the *Vienna Convention*.[20]

In *US – Offset Act (Byrd Amendment)*, the Appellate Body reversed the Panel's **8.20** finding that the United States had acted inconsistently with Article 5.4 of the Anti-Dumping Agreement and Article 11.4 of the SCM Agreement by taking a measure that 'defeated the purpose' of those provisions. Those provisions require that authorities determine that support for an investigation has been expressed by a specified percentage of domestic producers before initiating an anti-dumping or countervailing duty investigation. The Panel found that the measure at issue, which redistributed duties collected from imports to domestic firms that expressed support for initiating the investigation, defeated the purpose of these provisions, and that 'the United States may be regarded as not having acted in good faith in promoting this outcome'. The Appellate Body reversed the Panel's analysis and conclusion. The Appellate Body considered that the Panel erred in using the object and purpose of Articles 5.4 and 11.4, rather than the

---

[19] Appellate Body Report, *India – Patents (US)*, para. 45.
[20] Appellate Body Report, *EC – Computer Equipment*, paras. 83–4.

terms of those provisions, as the basis for finding a violation. The Appellate Body stated:

> At the outset, we express our concern with the Panel's approach in interpreting Article 5.4 of the *Anti-Dumping Agreement* and Article 11.4 of the *SCM Agreement*. Specifically, we fail to see how the Panel's interpretation of those provisions may be said to be based on the ordinary meaning of the words found in those provisions, and hence we do not believe the Panel properly applied the principles of interpretation codified in the *Vienna Convention* . . .
>
> . . .
>
> [I]t seems that, on the basis of a textual analysis of Articles 5.4 and 11.4, the Panel did not find that the CDSOA constitutes a violation of those provisions. The Panel went on to note, however, that this was not the 'matter at issue'. Instead, according to the Panel, the question was whether the CDSOA 'defeats' what it identified as the object and purpose of Article 5.4 of the *Anti-Dumping Agreement* and Article 11.4 of the *SCM Agreement*.
> As mentioned above, we have difficulty with the Panel's approach.[21]

After rejecting the Panel's conclusion that the United States violated the provisions at issue by taking a measure that allegedly defeated the purpose of those provisions, the Appellate Body then took issue with the Panel's conclusion that the United States had not acted in 'good faith':

> We observe that Article 31(1) of the Vienna Convention directs a treaty interpreter to interpret a treaty in good faith in accordance with the ordinary meaning to be given to the terms of the treaty in their context and in the light of the treaty's object and purpose. The principle of good faith may therefore be said to inform a treaty interpreter's task. Moreover, the performance of treaties is also governed by good faith. Hence, Article 26 of the *Vienna Convention*, entitled *Pacta Sunt Servanda*, to which several appellees referred in their submissions, provides that '[e]very treaty in force is binding upon the parties to it and must be performed by them in good faith.' The United States itself affirmed 'that WTO Members must uphold their obligations under the covered agreements in good faith'.
> We have recognized the relevance of the principle of good faith in a number of cases. Thus, in *US – Shrimp*, we stated:
>
> > The chapeau of Article XX is, in fact, but one expression of the principle of good faith. This principle, at once a general principle of law and a general principle of international law, controls the exercise of rights by states.
>
> In *US – Hot-Rolled Steel*, we found that:
>
> > . . . the principle of good faith . . . informs the provisions of the *Anti-Dumping Agreement*, as well as the other covered agreements.
>
> Clearly, therefore, there is a basis for a dispute settlement panel to determine, in an appropriate case, whether a Member has not acted in good faith.

---

[21] Appellate Body Report, *US – Offset Act (Byrd Amendment)*, paras. 281, 284–5.

Nothing, however, in the covered agreements supports the conclusion that simply because a WTO Member is found to have violated a substantive treaty provision, it has therefore not acted in good faith. In our view, it would be necessary to prove more than mere violation to support such a conclusion.

The evidence in the Panel record does not, in our view, support the Panel's statement that the United States 'may be regarded as not having acted in good faith'. We are of the view that the Panel's conclusion is erroneous and, therefore, we reject it.[22]

In *EC – Bed Linen (Article 21.5 – India)*, India argued that the European **8.21** Communities had applied the provision at issue in 'bad faith' by allegedly advocating one interpretation before its municipal courts in the context of litigation concerning the corresponding provision of EC law, and another interpretation before the WTO panel. The Panel rejected India's claim, and stated:

> [W]e reject the assertion that a WTO dispute settlement panel should find a violation of a provision of a covered agreement, not on the basis of inconsistency of a Member's measure with a provision of a covered agreement, but rather on the basis that a provision of a covered agreement is 'being applied in bad faith'. Whatever may be the implications of national court decisions for the arguments of Members before WTO dispute settlement panels, a question which we neither address nor resolve here, 'estoppel' based on national court decisions interpreting municipal law does not limit the decisions of WTO panels interpreting a covered agreement. A WTO panel is obligated to interpret the terms of covered agreements in accordance with customary rules of interpretation of public international law. We know of no basis in international law, and India has not cited any, that would require us to conclude that a measure which is consistent with a Member's obligations under a provision of a covered agreement that we have interpreted in accordance with customary rules of interpretation of public international law could nonetheless be found to be in violation of that provision on the basis of alleged 'bad faith'.[23]

8.3.3 The presumption that States act in good faith[24]

While Article 26 of the Vienna Convention provides for an obligation and not a **8.22** presumption, WTO panels and the Appellate Body have consistently held that States must be presumed to act in good faith.

In *EC – Sardines*, the Appellate Body examined a claim under Article 2.4 of the **8.23** TBT Agreement, which provides in relevant part that a Member's technical regulations must be based on international standards except when such standards would be an ineffective or inappropriate means for the fulfilment of the objectives pursued through the regulation. The Appellate Body found that a complainant seeking to establish a violation had to demonstrate that the

---

[22] Appellate Body Report, *US – Offset Act (Byrd Amendment)*, paras. 296–9.
[23] Panel Report, *EC – Bed Linen (Article 21.5 – India)*, para. 6.91.
[24] See also Section 7.3.6 ('Authenticity of evidence').

international standard in question is effective and appropriate to fulfil the legitimate objectives pursued by the respondent. Peru argued that the burden of proof should be on the respondent, because a complainant cannot 'spell out' the 'legitimate objectives' of the technical regulation. The Appellate Body rejected that argument, on the ground that a complainant may obtain relevant information about a technical regulation from a respondent under Article 2.5 of the TBT Agreement, which establishes a compulsory mechanism requiring the supplying of information by the regulating Member. Peru countered that a Member may not respond fully or adequately to a request for information under Article 2.5, and that, therefore, it was inappropriate to rely on this obligation to support assigning the burden of proof under Article 2.4 to the complainant. The Appellate Body was not persuaded by this argument, and in that context it stated:

> We must assume that Members of the WTO will abide by their treaty obligations in good faith, as required by the principle of *pacta sunt servanda* articulated in Article 26 of the *Vienna Convention*. And, always in dispute settlement, every Member of the WTO must assume the good faith of every other Member.[25]

8.24 In *US / Canada – Continued Suspension*, the Appellate Body addressed issues relating to the termination of countermeasures in situations where a Member declared that it had taken steps to bring its measures into conformity with its WTO obligations (and that the countermeasures were therefore no longer justified). In that context, the Appellate Body accepted that the Member should be presumed to act in good faith, but reasoned that this did not provide a sufficient basis to resolve the matter, because the complaining party should also be presumed to act in good faith. In the course of its analysis, the Appellate Body stated:

> The Member required to implement the DSB's recommendations and rulings may be presumed to have acted in good faith when adopting the implementing measure. However, the presumption of good faith attaches to the actor, but not to the action itself. Thus, whilst the presumption of good faith concerns the reasons for which a Member acts, such a presumption does not answer the question whether the measure taken by the implementing Member has indeed brought about substantive compliance. Similarly, the suspending Member can also be presumed to act in good faith in maintaining the suspension of concessions, but that does not entail that the suspension of concessions is necessarily consistent with Article 22.8. When a disagreement arises as to whether the implementing measure achieves substantive compliance and whether the suspension of concessions may continue, it should be submitted for adjudication in dispute settlement proceedings. In sum, a presumption of good faith, which can be claimed by both parties, does not offer a clear answer to the question of when inconsistencies arising from the original measure should be considered to have been removed within the meaning of Article 22.8 of the DSU.[26]

---

[25] Appellate Body Report, *EC – Sardines*, para. 278.
[26] Appellate Body Report, *US/Canada – Continued Suspension*, para. 315.

The Panel in *Thailand – Cigarettes (Philippines)*, referring to Article 26 and prior   **8.25**
jurisprudence, considered that, in the absence of solid evidence to prove the
contrary, there is no reason to assume that government officials would act in a
manner contrary to their WTO obligations:

> In addition, we note that the Appellate Body has recognized that the good faith
> principle has an implication for the Panels' interpretation of the Members
> obligations. (Appellate Body Report, *US – Offset Act (Byrd Amendment)*,
> para. 297.) The Panel in *Canada – Continued Suspension* also found that one
> aspect of the good faith principle applied to the context of WTO disputes was to
> grant members a presumption of WTO consistency in the application of their
> domestic laws:
>
> > It is implicit from the duty to perform treaty obligations in good faith that
> > a party to an international agreement should be deemed to have acted in
> > good faith in the performance of its treaty obligations. More generally,
> > even though Article 26 provides for an obligation and not a presumption,
> > *pacta sunt servanda* is but only one expression of the principle of good
> > faith. Good faith is a general principle of international law that governs all
> > reciprocal actions of States. We are therefore inclined to agree with the
> > European Communities that every party to an international agreement
> > must be presumed to be performing its obligation under that agreement in
> > good faith (Panel Report, *Canada – Continued Suspension*, para. 7.317).
>
> In the absence of solid evidence to prove the contrary, there is no reason to
> assume that TTM directors, who are Thai government officials, would act in
> contradiction to their WTO obligations.[27]

In *US – COOL*, the Panel referred to Article 26 in the context of presuming the   **8.26**
truthfulness of the information contained in a Member's official notification of
the measure to the relevant WTO committee:

> [T]he complainants' argument implies that what the United States has expressly
> identified as the objective pursued in its official WTO notification of the COOL
> measure is not true. The United States' notification to the TBT Committee of
> the COOL measure indicates 'consumer information' as the objective. While we
> are not saying that this constitutes definite and determinative evidence that the
> objective pursued through the COOL measure is not trade protectionism, we do
> consider that it is one of the objective circumstances that will inform the
> complainants of the objective of the COOL measure. Moreover, according to
> the Appellate Body, under the principle of good faith under general inter-
> national law as embodied in Article 26 of the Vienna Convention on the Law
> of Treaties, parties to an international agreement enjoy a presumption that they
> will perform their treaty obligations in good faith, including their WTO
> obligations. Thus, the United States must be presumed to have truthfully
> notified the TBT Committee of the objective it was seeking to pursue through
> its COOL measure. The presumption of good faith can, of course, be rebutted

---

[27] Panel Report, *Thailand – Cigarettes (Philippines)*, footnote 1543.

by solid evidence, in this case demonstrating that trade protectionism is indeed the objective pursued by the United States through the COOL measure. However, we have not been presented with such evidence.[28]

8.27 In *US – Anti-Dumping and Countervailing Duties (China)* (DS379), the Appellate Body reversed the Panel's finding that the term 'public body' in Article 1.1(a)(1) of the SCM Agreement means 'any entity controlled by a government', and found instead that the term 'public body' in the context of Article 1.1(a)(1) of the SCM Agreement covers only those entities that possess, exercise or are vested with governmental authority. In the course of its analysis, the Appellate Body stated:

> [A]ccording to Article 31 of the *Vienna Convention*, a treaty is to be interpreted in good faith. That means, *inter alia*, that terms of a treaty are not to be interpreted based on the assumption that one party is seeking to evade its obligations and will exercise its rights so as to cause injury to the other party. Yet, the United States' argument that 'a government would be able to hide behind its ownership interest in an entity and engage in entrustment or direction behind closed doors' pleads for an interpretation founded on this very assumption, and the above statement by the Panel reveals an interpretation on this basis. A proper interpretation in accordance with Article 31 of the *Vienna Convention*, however, cannot proceed based on such an assumption.[29]

8.3.4 Measures threatening prohibited conduct

8.28 The Panel in *US – Section 301 Trade Act* found that a measure threatening WTO-inconsistent conduct could give rise to a violation. The Panel based this conclusion, in part, on the principle of 'good faith'. The Panel began with the general observation that:

> It is notoriously difficult, or at least delicate, to construe the requirement of the Vienna Convention that a treaty shall be interpreted in good faith in third party dispute resolution, not least because of the possible imputation of bad faith to one of the parties. We prefer, thus, to consider which interpretation suggests 'better faith' and to deal only briefly with this element of interpretation. Applying the good faith requirement to Article 23 may not lead to a conclusive result but impels us in the direction suggested by our examination of the ordinary meaning of the raw text.[30]

The Panel in *US – Section 301 Trade Act* proceeded to develop a 'good faith' interpretation of the requirement, in Article 23 of the DSU, to have recourse to and abide by the multilateral dispute settlement rules and procedures of the DSU instead of making a unilateral determination that another Member's measure is WTO-inconsistent. The Panel stated:

[28] Panel Report, *US – COOL*, para. 7.605.
[29] Appellate Body Report, *US – Anti-Dumping and Countervailing Duties (China)*, para. 326.
[30] Panel Report, *US – Section 301 Trade Act*, para. 7.64.

Imagine two farmers with adjacent land and a history of many disputes concerning real and alleged mutual trespassing. In the past, self help through force and threats of force has been used in their altercations. Naturally, exploitation of the lands close to the boundaries suffers since it is viewed as dangerous terrain. They now sign an agreement under which they undertake that henceforth in any case of alleged trespassing they will abjure self help and always and exclusively make recourse to the police and the courts of law. They specifically undertake never to use force when dealing with alleged trespass. After the entry into force of their agreement one of the farmers erects a large sign on the contested boundary: 'No Trespassing. Trespassers may be shot on sight'.

One could, of course, argue that since the sign does not say that trespassers *will* be shot, the obligations undertaken have not been violated. But would that be the 'better faith' interpretation of what was promised? Did they not after all promise *always and exclusively* to make recourse to the police and the courts of law?

Likewise, is it a good faith interpretation to construe the obligations in Article 23 to allow a Member that promised its WTO partners – under Articles 23.1 and 23.2(a) – that it will generally, including in its legislation, have recourse to and abide by the rules and procedures of the DSU which specifically contain an undertaking not to make a determination of inconsistency prior to exhaustion of DSU proceedings, to put in place legislation the language of which explicitly, *urbi et orbi*, reserves to its Executive Branch the right to make a determination of inconsistency – that which it promised it would not do? This Panel thinks otherwise.

The good faith requirement in the Vienna Convention suggests, thus, that a promise to have recourse to and abide by the rules and procedures of the DSU, also in one's legislation, includes the undertaking to refrain from adopting national laws which threaten prohibited conduct.[31]

8.3.5 Withdrawal/correction of measures based on errors

In *US – Cotton Yarn*, the Appellate Body explained that under the standard of **8.29** review that panels must follow when reviewing safeguard investigations and determinations, a panel cannot take into account evidence that was not known to the investigating authority at the time of its determination, as this would amount to *de novo* review. However, the Appellate Body then referred to the 'pervasive' general principle of good faith and discussed the possibility that a Member might be under an obligation to withdraw a measure if new evidence (i.e. 'post-determination evidence') emerged demonstrating that the determination rested on a critical factual error:

> There is no need for the purpose of this appeal to express a view on the question whether an importing Member would be under an *obligation*, flowing from the 'pervasive' general principle of *good faith* that underlies all treaties, to *withdraw* a safeguard measure if post-determination evidence relating to pre-determination facts were to emerge revealing that a determination was based on such a critical

---

[31] Panel Report, *US – Section 301 Trade Act*, paras. 7.65–7.68.

factual error that one of the conditions required by Article 6 turns out never to have been met.[32]

8.4   Good faith in international dispute settlement proceedings

8.30 Article 3.10 of the DSU states that 'all members will engage in these procedures in good faith in an effort to resolve the dispute'. WTO jurisprudence offers support for the proposition that good faith in international dispute settlement proceedings precludes a party from among other things withholding, for tactical reasons, arguments and information that should have been raised at an earlier stage of the proceeding.

8.31 In *US – 1916 Act (EC)*, the Panel stated:

> Article 3.10 provides that parties must engage in dispute settlement in good faith. This implies that they should not withhold until the interim review stage arguments that they could be legitimately expected to have raised at a much earlier stage of the proceedings, in light of the claims developed in the first submissions.[33]

8.32 In *US – FSC*, the Appellate Body laid down the general principle that '[t]he procedural rules of WTO dispute settlement are designed to promote, not the development of litigation techniques, but simply the fair, prompt and effective resolution of trade disputes'. The Appellate Body stated:

> Article 3.10 of the DSU commits Members of the WTO, if a dispute arises, to engage in dispute settlement procedures 'in good faith in an effort to resolve the dispute'. This is another specific manifestation of the principle of good faith which, we have pointed out, is at once a general principle of law and a principle of general international law. This pervasive principle requires both complaining and responding Members to comply with the requirements of the DSU (and related requirements in other covered agreements) in good faith. By good faith compliance, complaining Members accord to the responding Members the full measure of protection and opportunity to defend, contemplated by the letter and spirit of the procedural rules. The same principle of good faith requires that responding Members seasonably and promptly bring claimed procedural deficiencies to the attention of the complaining Member, and to the DSB or the Panel, so that corrections, if needed, can be made to resolve disputes. The procedural rules of WTO dispute settlement are designed to promote, not the development of litigation techniques, but simply the fair, prompt and effective resolution of trade disputes.[34]

---

[32] Appellate Body Report, *US – Cotton Yarn*, para. 81.
[33] Panel Report, *US – 1916 Act (EC)*, para. 5.18.
[34] Appellate Body Report, *US – FSC*, para. 166 (citing Appellate Body Report, *US – Shrimp*, para. 158).

In *EC – Asbestos*, the Panel indicated that, while neither party claimed during the   **8.33**
interim review stage of the proceeding (at which time the disputing parties may
provide comments on a non-final version of the panel's decision) that the Panel
had made any substantive error in its assessment of the facts, the letter attached
to Canada's interim review comments indicated that its request for review was
'without prejudice to Canada's position on all the aspects of the Panel's Report'.
The Panel considered that:

> [I]f it had misunderstood or misrepresented some of the factual aspects of the
> case in its findings, the parties would need the interim review stage in order to
> make the necessary corrections or clarifications because, unlike errors of law,
> errors of fact cannot usually be modified on appeal. The parties should take
> advantage of this last opportunity to rectify the factual assessments of the
> Panel[,] otherwise the Panel could unnecessarily be at risk of being accused of
> not having made an objective evaluation of the facts. It might be claimed that
> the fact that a party does not inform the Panel of a factual error in its findings
> may be contrary to the obligation in Article 3.10 of the Understanding, which
> provides *inter alia* that 'all Members will engage in these procedures [settlement
> of disputes] in good faith in an effort to resolve the dispute'.[35]

In *US – Upland Cotton*, the Panel applied the principle that good faith requires   **8.34**
that responding Members bring alleged procedural deficiencies to the attention
of the complaining Member promptly:

> If a Member is uncertain as to the scope of the measures referred to by another
> Member in a request for consultations, and chooses not to seek clarification, it
> cannot rely on its own uncertainty as a jurisdictional bar to a Panel finding on
> the measures. Members have an obligation under Article 3.10 of the *DSU* to
> engage in WTO dispute settlement procedures in good faith in an effort to
> resolve the dispute.[36]

The Panel in *EC – Fasteners (China)* stated that Article 3.10 of the DSU was   **8.35**
inconsistent with 'inappropriate legal manoeuvres to avoid dispute settlement.'[37]

---

[35] Panel Report, *EC – Asbestos*, para. 7.2.   [36] Panel Report, *US – Upland Cotton*, para. 7.67.
[37] Panel Report, *EC – Fasteners (China)*, footnote 205.

9

JUDICIAL ECONOMY

9.1 Introduction

Judicial economy is a 'general canon' of adjudication.[1] For instance, the ICJ has **9.1** confirmed that 'it retains the freedom to select the ground upon which it will base its judgment, and is under no obligation to examine all of the considerations advanced by the Parties if other considerations appear to it to be sufficient for its purpose'.[2] In *The Development of International Law by the International Court*, Lauterpacht touched on the related issues of 'Judicial Limitation of the Scope of Decision', 'Judicial Caution and Economy of Expression' and 'Considerations of Economy in the Work of the Court'.[3] Likewise, in *The Development of International Law by the European Court of Human Rights*, Merrills included a related discussion on the 'Limitation of the scope of the decision'.[4] These and other judicial techniques and concepts are captured in the concept of 'judicial economy', broadly defined. There is a substantial body of WTO jurisprudence relating to judicial economy.[5]

---

[1] In F. M. Palombino, 'Judicial Economy and Limitation of the Scope of the Decision in International Adjudication' (2010) 23(4) *Leiden Journal of International Law* 909, at 910, the author writes: 'The absence of specific provisions in the matter, however, does not prevent the principle of judicial economy from guiding and affecting the international judge's activity. It belongs, in fact, to the general canons of adjudication – that is, those canons which are inherent in the judicial function and that the judge takes into account in the exercise of his duties, regardless of what the written procedural law establishes.'

[2] International Court of Justice, *Application of the Convention of 1902 Governing the Guardianship of Infants (Netherlands v. Sweden)*, Judgment, 1958 ICJ Reports, p. 55, at 62. See also H. Thirlway, 'Reflections on the Articulation of International Judicial Decisions and the Problem of "Mootness"', in R. St John MacDonald (ed.), *Essays in honour of Wang Tieya* (Martinus Nijhoff Publishers, 1994), pp. 789–812, at p. 789; M. Weller, 'Modesty Can be a Virtue – Judicial Economy in the ICJ Kosovo Opinion?' (2011) 24(1) *Leiden Journal of International Law* 127.

[3] H. Lauterpacht, *The Development of International Law by the International Court* (Stevens & Sons, 1958), pp. 77–84, 89–91, 130–4.

[4] J. G. Merrills, *The Development of International Law by the European Court of Human Rights* (Manchester University Press, 1988), pp. 36–8.

[5] For commentary, see W. J. Davey, 'Has the WTO Dispute Settlement System Exceeded its Authority? A Consideration of Deference Shown by the System to Member Government Decisions and Its Use of Issue-Avoidance Techniques' (2001) 4(1) *Journal of International Economic Law* 17; and J. Bohanes and A. Sennekamp, 'Reflections on the Concept of "Judicial Economy" in WTO

This jurisprudence does not seem to be derived from any special features of the WTO dispute settlement system, and seems to relate instead to certain inherent aspects of the judicial function exercised by WTO adjudicators and other international courts and tribunals. This chapter reviews WTO pronouncements of wider applicability relating to three forms of judicial economy: (i) judicial economy in the strict sense of refraining from making findings on whether a given measure, having been found to violate one or more obligations, is also inconsistent with other obligations; (ii) judicial economy in a broader sense (including the use of *arguendo* assumptions to reject a claim or defence, leaving the precise boundaries of certain legal concepts undefined, declining to rule on issues rendered moot, and focusing on issues in dispute between the parties); and (iii) judicial economy with respect to procedural issues (e.g. early preliminary rulings and proceedings involving multiple complainants).

9.2   *Stricto sensu*: alleged violations of multiple obligations arising out of the same measure

9.2   In the context of WTO dispute settlement, judicial economy has been understood *stricto sensu* to refer to the principle that an adjudicator, having found that a measure is inconsistent with one or more obligations, may refrain from making further findings on whether the same measure is inconsistent with other obligations invoked by the complaining party. In deciding whether to exercise such judicial economy in respect of one or more claims, the general guideline that has been articulated is whether additional findings of violation could affect how the responding Member would have to bring its challenged measure into conformity with its treaty obligations: if the actions that the responding Member would need to take to bring the challenged measure into conformity with the obligations in respect of which a violation has been found would necessarily cure any inconsistency with other obligations, an adjudicator may invoke judicial economy in respect of claims under those other obligations. It is well established that panels may exercise judicial economy in this respect, and panels do so regularly.

9.2.1 Generally

9.3   The Panel in *US – Wool Shirts and Blouses* decided to exercise judicial economy with respect to some of India's claims in that dispute. The Appellate Body upheld the finding of the Panel and discussed the legal basis for judicial economy, and in the course of its analysis stated:

Dispute Settlement', in G. Sacerdoti, A. Yanovich and J. Bohanes (eds.), *The WTO at Ten: The Contribution of the Dispute Settlement System* (Cambridge University Press, 2006), pp. 424–49.

Previous GATT 1947 and WTO panels have frequently addressed only those issues that such panels considered necessary for the resolution of the matter between the parties, and have declined to decide other issues. Thus, if a panel found that a measure was inconsistent with a particular provision of the GATT 1947, it generally did not go on to examine whether the measure was also inconsistent with other GATT provisions that a complaining party may have argued were violated. In recent WTO practice, panels likewise have refrained from examining each and every claim made by the complaining party and have made findings only on those claims that such panels concluded were necessary to resolve the particular matter.

Although a few GATT 1947 and WTO panels did make broader rulings, by considering and deciding issues that were not absolutely necessary to dispose of the particular dispute, there is nothing anywhere in the *DSU* that requires panels to do so.

...

Given the explicit aim of dispute settlement that permeates the *DSU*, we do not consider that Article 3.2 of the *DSU* is meant to encourage either panels or the Appellate Body to 'make law' by clarifying existing provisions of the *WTO Agreement* outside the context of resolving a particular dispute. A panel need only address those claims which must be addressed in order to resolve the matter in issue in the dispute.[6]

In *Canada – Wheat Exports and Grain Imports*, the Appellate Body stated: **9.4**

The practice of judicial economy, which was first employed by a number of GATT panels, allows a panel to refrain from making multiple findings that the same measure is *inconsistent* with various provisions when a single, or a certain number of findings of inconsistency, would suffice to resolve the dispute. Although the doctrine of judicial economy *allows* a panel to refrain from addressing claims beyond those necessary to resolve the dispute, it does not *compel* a panel to exercise such restraint.[7]

In *Brazil – Retreaded Tyres*, the Appellate Body confirmed that the concept of **9.5** judicial economy *stricto sensu* applies only where there is a finding of violation:

[W]e observe that it might have been appropriate for the Panel to address the European Communities' separate claims that the MERCOSUR exemption was inconsistent with Article I:1 and Article XIII:1. We have previously indicated that the principle of judicial economy 'allows a panel to refrain from making multiple findings that the same measure is inconsistent with various provisions when a single, or a certain number of findings of inconsistency, would suffice to resolve the dispute', and it seems that the Panel assumed this to be the case in the present dispute. However, the Panel found that the MERCOSUR exemption resulted in the Import Ban being applied *consistently* with the requirements of the chapeau of Article XX. In view of this finding, we must acknowledge that we have difficulty seeing how the Panel could have been justified in not addressing the separate claims of inconsistency under Article I:1 and Article XIII:1 directed at the MERCOSUR exemption.[8]

---

[6] Appellate Body Report, *US – Wool Shirts and Blouses*, pp. 18–19 (citing GATT Panel Report, *EEC – Dessert Apples*, para. 12.20).
[7] Appellate Body Report, *Canada – Wheat Exports and Grain Imports*, para. 133.
[8] Appellate Body Report, *Brazil – Retreaded Tyres*, para. 257.

9.6 In *Canada – Renewable Energy/Feed-In Tariff Program*, the Appellate Body stated that 'panels have a margin of discretion with respect to the exercise of judicial economy'.[9]

9.2.2 Judicial economy and transparency

9.7 In *Canada – Autos*, the Appellate Body admonished the Panel for not stating explicitly that it was exercising judicial economy when it did not address a particular claim:

> In our view, it was not necessary for the Panel to make a determination on the European Communities' *alternative* claim relating to the CVA requirements under Article 3.1(a) of the *SCM Agreement* in order 'to secure a positive solution' to this dispute. The Panel had already found that the CVA requirements violated both Article III:4 of the GATT 1994 and Article XVII of the GATS. Having made these findings, the Panel, in our view, exercising the discretion implicit in the principle of judicial economy, could properly decide not to examine the *alternative* claim of the European Communities that the CVA requirements are inconsistent with Article 3.1(a) of the *SCM Agreement*.
>
> We are bound to add that, for purposes of transparency and fairness to the parties, a panel should, however, in all cases, address expressly those claims which it declines to examine and rule upon for reasons of judicial economy. Silence does not suffice for these purposes.[10]

9.2.3 False judicial economy

9.8 In *Australia – Salmon*, the Appellate Body held that the right to exercise judicial economy could not be exercised where this would lead to only a partial resolution of a dispute:

> The principle of judicial economy has to be applied keeping in mind the aim of the dispute settlement system. This aim is to resolve the matter at issue and 'to secure a positive solution to a dispute'. To provide only a partial resolution of the matter at issue would be false judicial economy. A panel has to address those claims on which a finding is necessary in order to enable the DSB to make sufficiently precise recommendations and rulings so as to allow for prompt compliance by a Member with those recommendations and rulings 'in order to ensure effective resolution of disputes to the benefit of all Members'.[11]

9.9 In *Japan – Agricultural Products*, the Appellate Body found an error of law in the Panel's exercise of judicial economy. The Appellate Body found that

---

[9] Appellate Body Report, *Canada – Renewable Energy/Feed-In Tariff Program*, para. 5.93.
[10] Appellate Body Report, *Canada – Autos*, paras. 116–17.
[11] Appellate Body Report, *Australia – Salmon*, para. 223.

the Panel had exercised 'false' judicial economy and had provided only a partial resolution of the dispute before it:

> We note that there is an error of logic in the Panel's finding in paragraph 8.63. The Panel stated that it had found earlier in its Report that the varietal testing requirement violates Article 2.2, and that there was, therefore, no need to examine whether the measure at issue was based on a risk assessment in accordance with Articles 5.1 and 5.2 of the *SPS Agreement*. We note, however, that the Panel's finding of inconsistency with Article 2.2 only concerned the varietal testing requirement as it applies to apples, cherries, nectarines and walnuts. With regard to the varietal testing requirement as it applies to apricots, pears, plums and quince, the Panel found that there was insufficient evidence before it to conclude that this measure was inconsistent with Article 2.2. The Panel, therefore, made an error of logic when it stated, in general terms, that there was no need to examine whether the varietal testing requirement was consistent with Article 5.1 because this requirement had already been found to be inconsistent with Article 2.2. With regard to the varietal testing requirement as it applies to apricots, pears, plums and quince, there was clearly still a need to examine whether this measure was inconsistent with Article 5.1. By not making a finding under Article 5.1 with regard to the varietal testing requirement as it applies to apricots, pears, plums and quince, the Panel improperly applied the principle of judicial economy. We believe that a finding under Article 5.1 with respect to apricots, pears, plums and quince is necessary 'in order to ensure effective resolution' of the dispute.[12]

In *US – Large Civil Aircraft (2nd complaint)*, the Appellate Body found that the **9.10** Panel erred in failing to provide a more comprehensive analysis of a legal issue before it, and stated:

> By refusing to undertake a more comprehensive analysis of the legal issue of how the DSB is to initiate an Annex V procedure, the Panel deprived Members of the benefit of   'a clear enunciation of the relevant WTO law' and failed to advance a key objective of WTO dispute settlement, namely, the resolution of disputes 'in a manner that preserves the rights and obligations of WTO Members and clarifies existing provisions of the covered agreements in accordance with the customary rules of interpretation of public international law'. We also recall that, when a panel's findings provide 'only a partial resolution of the matter at issue', this amounts to 'false judicial economy' and an error of law.[13]

9.3   Judicial economy in a broader sense

While the term 'judicial economy' seems to be used in WTO adjudication and **9.11** jurisprudence only in the narrow sense reviewed above, i.e. situations in which a tribunal may refrain from making multiple findings of violation in respect of the

---

[12] Appellate Body Report, *Japan – Agricultural Products II*, para. 111.
[13] Appellate Body Report, *US – Large Civil Aircraft (2nd complaint)*, para. 500 (citing Appellate Body Report, *China – Publications and Audiovisual Products*, para. 213; Appellate Body Report, *Australia – Salmon*, paras. 223–6).

same measure, there are various other ways in which WTO adjudicators exercise judicial economy, understood in a broader sense. WTO jurisprudence provides some support for the proposition that, in principle, an international tribunal must address only those issues and arguments that are necessary to resolve a particular claim or defence, may rely on *arguendo* assumptions, may leave the precise boundaries of certain legal concepts undefined, may decline to rule on issues rendered moot by other findings or developments, and may also decline to rule on (or engage in any lengthy analysis of) issues in respect of which the parties to a dispute agree.

9.3.1 Judicial economy in respect of arguments

9.12 In *EC – Fasteners (China)*, the Appellate Body recalled that, while the concept of 'judicial economy' applies *stricto sensu* only in respect of *claims*, panels are also required to address only those *arguments* that are necessary to resolve a particular claim:

> [T]he issue of judicial economy is only relevant to the manner in which a panel deals with a party's *claims*. Moreover, as the Appellate Body has found, a panel has the discretion 'to address only those arguments it deems necessary to resolve a particular claim' and 'the fact that a particular argument relating to that claim is not specifically addressed in the "Findings" section of a panel report will not, in and of itself, lead to the conclusion that that panel has failed to make the "objective assessment of the matter before it" required by Article 11 of the DSU'.[14]

9.3.2 *Arguendo* assumptions

9.13 In *Mexico – Corn Syrup (Article 21.5 – US)*, the Appellate Body made certain findings assuming, *arguendo*, that the requirements in Article 6.2 of the DSU apply in the context of compliance panel proceedings. The Appellate Body did not make a finding whether they actually applied in the context of compliance proceedings and, if so, to what extent.[15]

9.14 In *US – Oil Country Tubular Goods Sunset Reviews*, the Appellate Body stated:

> [E]ven assuming *arguendo* that a 'practice' may be challenged as a 'measure' in WTO dispute settlement – an issue on which we express no view here – we *find* that the record does not allow us to complete the analysis of Argentina's conditional appeal with respect to the 'practice' of the USDOC regarding the likelihood determination in sunset reviews.[16]

---

[14] Appellate Body Report, *EC – Fasteners (China)*, para. 511 (citing Appellate Body Report, *EC – Poultry*, para. 135).
[15] Appellate Body Report, *Mexico – Corn Syrup (Article 21.5 – US)*, paras. 52–3, 67.
[16] Appellate Body Report, *US – Oil Country Tubular Goods Sunset Reviews*, para. 220.

In *US – Shrimp (Thailand)* / *US – Customs Bond Directive*, the Appellate Body **9.15** considered it unnecessary to resolve the issue of whether Article XX(d) of the GATT can be invoked as a defence to justify a violation of Article 18.1 of the Anti-Dumping Agreement. The Appellate Body found that '[a]ssuming, *arguendo*, that such a defence is available to the United States',[17] the measure at issue was not 'necessary' within the meaning of Article XX(d)' of the GATT. Having made that finding, the Appellate Body stated that 'we do not express a view on the question of whether a defence under Article XX(d) of the GATT 1994 was available to the United States'.[18]

In *China – Publications and Audiovisual Products*, the Appellate Body offered the **9.16** following general guidance on the use of *arguendo* assumptions by panels:

> We observe that reliance upon an assumption *arguendo* is a legal technique that an adjudicator may use in order to enhance simplicity and efficiency in decision-making. Although panels and the Appellate Body may choose to employ this technique in particular circumstances, it may not always provide a solid foundation upon which to rest legal conclusions. Use of the technique may detract from a clear enunciation of the relevant WTO law and create difficulties for implementation. Recourse to this technique may also be problematic for certain types of legal issues, for example, issues that go to the jurisdiction of a panel or preliminary questions on which the substance of a subsequent analysis depends. The purpose of WTO dispute settlement is to resolve disputes in a manner that preserves the rights and obligations of WTO Members and clarifies existing provisions of the covered agreements in accordance with the customary rules of interpretation of public international law. In doing so, panels and the Appellate Body are not bound to favour the most expedient approach or that suggested by one or more of the parties to the dispute. Rather, panels and the Appellate Body must adopt an analytical methodology or structure appropriate for resolution of the matters before them, and which enables them to make an objective assessment of the relevant matters and make such findings as will assist the DSB in making the recommendations or in giving the rulings provided for in the covered agreements.[19]

In that case, the Appellate Body concluded that it was not appropriate to proceed on the basis of an *arguendo* assumption on the question of whether the defence in Article XX(a) of the GATT could be invoked in respect of paragraph 5.1 of China's Accession Protocol:

> In our view, assuming *arguendo* that China can invoke Article XX(a) could be at odds with the objective of promoting security and predictability through dispute settlement, and may not assist in the resolution of this dispute, in particular because such an approach risks creating uncertainty with respect to China's implementation obligations.[20]

---

[17] Appellate Body Report, *US – Shrimp (Thailand)/US – Customs Bond Directive*, para. 310.
[18] *Ibid.*, para. 319.
[19] Appellate Body Report, *China – Publications and Audiovisual Products*, para. 213.
[20] *Ibid.*, para. 215.

9.17 In *US – Large Civil Aircraft (2nd complaint)*, the Panel found that, assuming
arguendo that the allocation of intellectual property rights under NASA and
Department of Defense contracts and agreements with Boeing involved a
subsidy within the meaning of Article 1 of the SCM Agreement, the European
Communities had failed to demonstrate that any such subsidy was specific
within the meaning of Article 2 of the SCM Agreement. With respect to its
use of this *arguendo* assumption, the Panel recalled the Appellate Body's
guidance in *China – Publications and Audiovisual Products*, and explained that:

> We have relied upon the *arguendo* assumption that the allocation of patent rights is
> a subsidy within the meaning of Article 1 of the SCM Agreement and proceeded
> directly to the issue of specificity under Article 2 of the SCM Agreement for the
> following reasons. First, the question of whether the allocation of patent rights
> under NASA/DOD R&D contracts and agreements with Boeing constitutes a
> financial contribution, whether in the form of a provision of goods within the
> meaning of Article 1.1(a)(1)(iii) of the SCM Agreement or otherwise, is a poten-
> tially difficult one; in contrast, the question of whether the alleged subsidy is
> specific is more straightforward ... In other words, we have relied upon this
> *arguendo* assumption to 'enhance simplicity and efficiency' in our decision-making.
> Second, having found that the alleged subsidy is not specific under Article 2, our
> reliance upon this *arguendo* assumption creates no issues or difficulties from the
> point of view of the 'implementation' of DSB recommendations and rulings.
> Third, the question of whether or not the allocation of patent rights constitutes
> a subsidy does not 'go to the jurisdiction' of the Panel. Finally, the substance of our
> analysis under Article 2 does not depend on whether the measures at issue are
> properly characterized as subsidies within the meaning of Article 1.[21]

9.18 In *US – Large Civil Aircraft (2nd complaint)*, the Appellate Body faulted the
Panel for relying on the *arguendo* assumption with respect to this particular issue.
The Appellate Body stated:

> The chapeau of Article 2.1 of the *SCM Agreement* states that the analysis of
> specificity is directed at 'a subsidy, as defined in paragraph 1 of Article 1'. We
> understand that this is a reference to the measure that has been determined to be a
> subsidy under Article 1.1 because the measure is a financial contribution that
> confers a benefit. This suggests that the 'subsidy, as defined in paragraph 1 of Article
> 1' is the starting point of the assessment of specificity. The analysis of specificity
> called for in Article 2.1 presupposes that the subsidy has already been found to exist.
> No such finding was made here given that the Panel never performed an analysis
> under Article 1 but, rather, chose to start its assessment with the issue of specificity.
> The Panel thought that its adoption of an *arguendo* approach was consistent with
> the Appellate Body's guidance in *China – Publications and Audiovisual Products*.
> However, in that case, the Appellate Body identified precisely the same problem that
> arises here when it said that recourse to an *arguendo* approach 'may also be
> problematic for certain types of legal issues, for example, issues that go to the

---

[21] Panel Report, *US – Large Civil Aircraft (2nd complaint)*, footnote 2933.

jurisdiction of a panel or preliminary questions on which the substance of a subsequent analysis depends.' As we have explained, the assessment of specificity under Article 2.1 depends on how the subsidy was defined under Article 1.1, leaving little, if any, room for the adoption of an *arguendo* approach.[22]

9.3.3 Leaving the precise boundaries of certain legal concepts undefined

In *Korea – Alcoholic Beverages*, the Appellate Body examined the requirement, in **9.19** Article 12.7 of the DSU, that a panel report must set out 'the basic rationale' behind any findings and recommendations that it makes. The Appellate Body stated:

> In this case, we do not consider it either necessary, or desirable, to attempt to define the scope of the obligation provided for in Article 12.7 of the DSU. It suffices to state that the Panel has set out a detailed and thorough rationale for its findings and recommendations in this case. The Panel went to some length to take account of competing considerations and to explain why, nonetheless, it made the findings and recommendations it did. The rationale set out by the Panel may not be one that Korea agrees with, but it is certainly more than adequate, on any view, to satisfy the requirements of Article 12.7 of the DSU. We, therefore, conclude that the Panel did not fail to set out the basic rationale for its findings and recommendations as required by Article 12.7 of the DSU.[23]

In *Mexico – Corn Syrup (Article 21.5 – US)*, the Appellate Body returned to this **9.20** same issue and, citing the passage from *Korea – Alcoholic Beverages* reproduced above, stated:

> We do not believe that it is either possible or desirable to determine, in the abstract, the minimum standard of reasoning that will constitute a 'basic rationale' for the findings and recommendations made by a panel. Whether a panel has articulated adequately the 'basic rationale' for its findings and recommendations must be determined on a case-by-case basis, taking into account the facts of the case, the specific legal provisions at issue, and the particular findings and recommendations made by a panel.[24]

In *EC and certain member States – Large Civil Aircraft*, the Panel declined to offer **9.21** a 'precise or absolute definition' of certain terms 'in the abstract'. The provision at issue was Article 1.1(a)(1)(iii) of the SCM Agreement, which provides that a government financial contribution (potentially constituting a subsidy) exists when 'a government provides goods or services other than general infrastructure'. The Panel developed an interpretation of the concept of 'general infrastructure', but stated in the course of its analysis that 'it is difficult if not impossible' to define the

---

[22] *Ibid.*, para. 739 (citing Appellate Body Report, *China – Publications and Audiovisual Products*, para. 213).
[23] Appellate Body Report, *Korea – Alcoholic Beverages*, para. 168.
[24] Appellate Body Report, *Mexico – Corn Syrup (Article 21.5 – US)*, para. 108.

concept of general infrastructure 'in the abstract'. Citing to examples from prior panel and Appellate Body reports, the Panel noted:

> Other disputes involving questions of interpretation of Article 1.1(a)(1) of the SCM Agreement have similarly not resulted in precise or absolute definitions of terms, in the abstract. Thus, the Panel in *US – FSC*, para. 6.7, addressing the definition of 'otherwise due' in Article 1.1(a)(1)(ii) noted that 'the application of the concept of "otherwise due" in other disputes would require panels to apply their best judgement on a case-by-case basis' and at paragraph 7.93 observed 'In the foregoing sections, we have concluded that whether revenue foregone is "otherwise due" is to be determined on the basis of an examination of the fiscal treatment that would be applicable "but for" the measures in question. Of course, as in other areas under the WTO Agreement, the application of this test requires panels to apply their best judgment on a case-by-case basis.' Panel Report, *United States – Tax Treatment for 'Foreign Sales Corporations'* (*'US – FSC'*), WT/DS108/R, adopted 20 March 2000, as modified by Appellate Body Report WT/DS108/AB/R, DSR 2000:IV[1675] (emphasis added). Similarly, in *US – DRAMS*, para. 116, the Appellate Body acknowledged the difficulty in formulating precise, abstract definition of 'entrusts or directs' in the context of Article 1.1(a)(1)(iv) ('It may be difficult to identify precisely, in the abstract, the types of government actions that constitute entrustment or direction and those that do not. The particular label used to describe the governmental action is not necessarily dispositive. Indeed, as Korea acknowledges, in some circumstances, "guidance" by a government can constitute direction. In most cases, one would expect entrustment or direction of a private body to involve some form of threat or inducement, which could, in turn, serve as evidence of entrustment or direction. The determination of entrustment or direction will hinge on the particular facts of the case.' (emphasis added, footnote omitted) Appellate Body Report, *United States – Countervailing Duty Investigation on Dynamic Random Access Memory Semiconductors (DRAMS) from Korea* (*'US – Countervailing Duty Investigation on DRAMS'*), WT/DS296/AB/R, adopted 20 July 2005, DSR 2005:XVI, 8131.)[25]

9.3.4 Declining to rule on issues rendered moot by other findings or developments

9.22 In *US – Countervailing and Anti-Dumping Measures (China)* (DS449), the United States requested that the Panel make a preliminary ruling that China's panel request did not comply with the requirements of Article 6.2 of the DSU. China subsequently represented that it did not intend to pursue some of the claims at issue. In these circumstances, the Panel decided that it was not necessary for it to rule on whether, insofar as those claims were concerned, the panel request complied with Article 6.2 of the DSU. In the course of its reasoning, the Panel stated:

> [W]e note that other panels confronting issues that they determined were moot responded by not examining them further. In the particular circumstances of

---

[25] Panel Report, *EC and certain member States – Large Civil Aircraft*, footnote 3868.

this case, we consider that the aim of the WTO dispute settlement mechanism, which is to 'secure a positive solution to a dispute', does not require us to rule on an Article 6.2 issue that we have determined is moot. Indeed, it appears futile to offer a ruling linked to claims that the complaining party no longer deems fruitful to pursue. We likewise consider that a ruling on the Article 6.2 issue that pertains to the abandoned claims is not necessary to 'assist the DSB in making the recommendations or in giving the rulings provided for' in the covered agreements. As explained, it follows from China's statement before this Panel that the abandoned claims will not result in DSB recommendations or rulings of any kind.[26]

9.3.5 Issues in respect of which the parties agree

In *US – Gasoline*, all parties and third parties accepted that measures 'relating to'   **9.23** conservation in Article XX(g) of the GATT had to be 'primarily aimed at' conservation. The Appellate Body stated:

> All the participants and the third participants in this appeal accept the propriety and applicability of the view of the Herring and Salmon report and the Panel Report that a measure must be 'primarily aimed at' the conservation of exhaustible natural resources in order to fall within the scope of Article XX(g). Accordingly, we see no need to examine this point further, save, perhaps, to note that the phrase 'primarily aimed at' is not itself treaty language and was not designed as a simple litmus test for inclusion or exclusion from Article XX(g).[27]

Along the same lines, in *EC – Seal Products*, another case dealing with Article XX   **9.24** of the GATT, the Appellate Body noted that it was not necessary to determine whether there is any implied territorial limitation that applies to the scope of the exceptions in Article XX, because all participants in that case agreed that the measure at issue had a 'sufficient nexus' with the European Union (see para. 14.31 below).

In *US – Clove Cigarettes*, the Panel noted that the parties agreed that the first   **9.25** sentence of Article 2.2 of the TBT Agreement sets out a general principle, the meaning of which is explained and defined in the second sentence of Article 2.2 – in other words, that the first sentence of Article 2.2 does not create a separate and distinct obligation from that found in the second sentence of that provision. The Panel indicated that it saw no reason to disagree, and that '[g]iven that the parties in this case agree on this point, there is no need for this Panel to address the point in any detail'.[28]

---

[26] Preliminary Ruling by the Panel in *US – Countervailing and Anti-Dumping Measures (China)*, circulated as WT/DS449/4, para. 3.10 (citing Panel Report, *China – X-Ray Equipment*, para. 7.410; Panel Report, *US – Hot-Rolled Steel*, paras. 7.52 and 7.60; Panel Report, *US – Lamb*, para. 5.65; Panel Report, *Guatemala – Cement II*, para. 8.171).
[27] Appellate Body Report, *US – Gasoline*, pp. 18–19.
[28] Panel Report, *US – Clove Cigarettes*, footnote 618.

9.4   Judicial economy regarding procedural issues

9.26 In addition to exercising judicial economy in respect of *substantive* legal questions, panels and the Appellate Body have also given weight to considerations of
procedural economy. In some domestic contexts, the term 'judicial economy' is
used primarily in this sense, i.e. to mean procedural economy in the conduct of
a proceeding. For example, *Black's Law Dictionary* defines 'judicial economy' to
mean:

> Efficiency in the operation of the courts and the judicial system esp., the
> efficient management of litigation so as to minimize duplication of effort and
> to avoid wasting the judiciary's time and resources. A court can enter a variety of
> orders to promote judicial economy. For instance, a court may consolidate
> two cases for trial to save the court and the parties from having two trials,
> or it may order a separate trial on certain issues if doing so would provide
> the opportunity to avoid a later trial that would be more complex and time-
> consuming.[29]

Panels and the Appellate Body have taken considerations of procedural economy
into account in the context of resolving various procedural issues, including with
respect to the conduct of proceedings involving multiple complaining parties,
and with respect to the timing of preliminary rulings on jurisdiction and/or
admissibility.[30]

9.27 In *EC – Hormones*, the Panel decided to hold a joint meeting with the scientific
experts for the panel proceeding initiated against the European Communities by
Canada, and for the parallel panel proceeding initiated against the European
Communities by the United States. The alternative option would have been to
hold two separate meetings. After reviewing the Panel's reasoning underlying
this decision, the Appellate Body concluded that the Panel's decision was
justified, and stated:

> We consider the explanation of the Panel quite reasonable, and its decision to
> hold a joint meeting with the scientific experts consistent with the letter and
> spirit of Article 9.3 of the DSU. Clearly, it would be an uneconomical use of
> time and resources to force the Panel to hold two successive but separate

---

[29] B. Garner (ed.), *Black's Law Dictionary*, 8th edn (Thomson West, 2004), p. 863.
[30] While the rules of some international courts and tribunals provide guidance on how to address
requests for preliminary rulings (see e.g. Article 79 of the Rules of Court of the International
Court of Justice), no such provision is found in the DSU. As a consequence, panels have
a measure of discretion on whether to make preliminary rulings. One panel has observed that
'there is no established jurisprudence nor is there any established practice on whether panels
need to rule on the scope of their mandate on a preliminary basis, i.e. before the issuance
of its Interim Report to the parties'. See Panel Report, *Colombia – Ports of Entry*, paras.
7.13–7.14.

meetings gathering the same group of experts twice, expressing their views twice regarding the same scientific and technical matters related to the same contested EC measures.[31]

In *Mexico – Taxes on Soft Drinks*, the Panel explained that an early preliminary **9.28** ruling on jurisdiction and admissibility was justified in that case on the basis of considerations relating to procedural economy:

> In order to issue its preliminary ruling, the Panel considered Mexico's request as well as the arguments presented by the United States, the complaining party in the case, and by the third parties. Nothing in the DSU, or in the Panel's working procedures, required the Panel to address Mexico's request in a preliminary ruling. Instead, the Panel could have waited to rule on the request until its final report. It was the Panel's opinion, however, that both the parties and the panel proceeding were better served by an early ruling on the request. Had it been appropriate for the Panel to decline to exercise its jurisdiction, an early decision to this effect would have saved time and resources. On the other hand, if the Panel – as in the event it did – rejected Mexico's request, an early decision would allow the parties to concentrate on the other aspects of the dispute.[32]

---

[31] Appellate Body Report, *EC – Hormones*, para. 152.
[32] Panel Report, *Mexico – Taxes on Soft Drinks*, para. 7.2.

10

MUNICIPAL LAW

10.1 Introduction

In the context of WTO jurisprudence, the term 'municipal law' is used interchangeably with the terms 'national law' and 'domestic law', in the same way that one finds these terms being used interchangeably elsewhere.[1] WTO adjudicators have been confronted with a range of different issues relating to municipal law, one reason being that many of the measures challenged in WTO dispute settlement proceedings are municipal laws.[2] The WTO agreements contain some specific provisions that speak to the relationship between those agreements and municipal law. For instance, Article XVI:4 of the WTO Agreement establishes that '[e]ach Member shall ensure the conformity of its laws, regulations and administrative procedures with its obligations as provided in the annexed Agreements',[3] and a small number of provisions in the covered agreements establish a '*renvoi*' to each Member's national law to define certain terms.[4] Otherwise, when confronted with questions relating to municipal

---

[1] For example, I. Brownlie and J. Crawford, *Brownlie's Principles of Public International Law*, 8th edn (Oxford University Press, 2012), Chapter 3 ('The Relations of International and National Law'); M. N. Shaw, *International Law*, 6th edn (Cambridge University Press, 2008), Chapter 4 ('International Law and Municipal Law'). See also P. Dupuy, 'International Law and Domestic (Municipal) Law' (April 2011) in *Max Planck Encyclopedia of Public International Law*.

[2] For commentary, see S. Bhuiyan, *National Law in WTO Law: Effectiveness and Good Governance in the World Trading System* (Cambridge University Press, 2011).

[3] Similar language is used in Article 32.5 of the SCM Agreement and Article 18.4 of the Anti-Dumping Agreement.

[4] For example: (i) Article 2(i) of the Agreement on Rules of Origin provides that, when introducing changes to their rules of origin or new rules of origin, they shall not apply such changes retroactively 'as defined in, and without prejudice to, their laws or regulations'; (ii) Article XXVIII(k) of the GATS defines 'natural person of another Member' to mean a person who 'under the law of that other Member' is a national or has the right of permanent residence; and (iii) footnote 6 to Article XIV(d) of the GATS provides that '[t]ax terms or concepts in paragraph (d) of Article XIV and in this footnote are determined according to tax definitions and concepts, or equivalent or similar definitions and concepts, under the domestic law of the Member taking the measure'.

law, WTO adjudicators have often fallen back on general international law concepts and principles of wider applicability. This chapter reviews WTO statements of wider applicability relating to: (i) the relevance of municipal law concepts and classifications to treaty interpretation; (ii) the invocation of municipal law as a justification for a failure to perform a treaty obligation; (iii) alleged violations of municipal law; (iv) the interpretation of municipal law by international tribunals; (v) the implementation of international obligations in municipal law; and (vi) representations made by a State regarding the operation of its municipal law.

10.2   Relevance of municipal law concepts and classifications to treaty interpretation

10.2 There are many examples of WTO adjudicators stating that a Member's municipal law concepts and classifications may be of limited relevance in the context of treaty interpretation. One of the stated reasons for this reluctance to rely on a Member's municipal law concepts and classifications is the concern that it would be inappropriate to characterize, for purposes of applying multilateral treaty provisions, the same thing differently depending on its legal categorization within the jurisdictions of different States. The foregoing does not apply to municipal law concepts and principles that transcend particular municipal law systems and rise to the level of 'general principles of law' within the meaning of Article 38(1)(d) of the ICJ statute (and which, by definition, do not vary from State to State).[5] WTO jurisprudence offers some support for the proposition that certain international law concepts, such as the determination of certain issues relating to nationality, must be applied by reference to each State's municipal law (i.e. *renvoi* to municipal law).

10.3 In the context of setting out its standard of review, the Panel in *US – Cotton Yarn* stated that it would examine whether the factual findings of the investigating authority was justifiable. The Panel noted that there were several reasons why it used the term 'justifiable', including the following:

> We have recourse to this term also in order to avoid terms such as 'reasonableness' or 'wide margin of discretion' which are used in national systems of administrative law and which inevitably carry with them many connotations from these national legal systems.[6]

---

[5] See Section 13.4.1 ('General principles of law').
[6] Panel Report, *US – Cotton Yarn*, footnote 193.

In *US – Countervailing Measures on Certain EC Products*, the Panel rejected the **10.4** relevance of municipal law distinctions between a company and its shareholders for purposes of determining the existence of a benefit under Article 1.1(b) of the SCM Agreement. According to the Panel, '[t]he concept of benefit is independent of the legal business structure established pursuant to national corporate law'.[7] Likewise, the Appellate Body considered that, if the corporate law distinction between a corporation and its shareholders were to be determinative of the existence of 'benefit' under the SCM Agreement, this would essentially enable subsidizing governments to circumvent the provisions of the SCM Agreement by providing financial contributions to a corporation's shareholders, rather than the corporation itself. The Appellate Body concluded that 'the legal distinction between firms and their owners that may be recognized in a domestic legal context is not necessarily relevant, and certainly not conclusive, for the purpose of determining whether a "benefit" exists under the SCM Agreement'.[8]

In *US – Corrosion-Resistant Steel Sunset Review*, the Appellate Body found that **10.5** the phrase 'laws, regulations and administrative procedures' in Article 18.4 of the Anti-Dumping Agreement encompasses the entire body of generally applicable rules, norms and standards adopted by Members in connection with the conduct of anti-dumping investigations. The Appellate Body cautioned against relying on the label given to instruments under municipal law in this context:

> We observe that the scope of each element in the phrase 'laws, regulations and administrative procedures' must be determined for purposes of WTO law and not simply by reference to the label given to various instruments under the domestic law of each WTO Member. This determination must be based on the content and substance of the instrument, and not merely on its form or nomenclature. Otherwise, the obligations set forth in Article 18.4 would vary from Member to Member depending on each Member's domestic law and practice.[9]

In *US – Softwood Lumber IV*, the Appellate Body rejected Canada's argument **10.6** that standing timber should be excluded from the definition of 'goods' in Article 1.1(a)(1)(iii) of the SCM Agreement. In that context, the Appellate Body cautioned against reliance on municipal law concepts for the purpose of interpreting or applying WTO provisions:

> [W]e observe that the arguments put forward by Canada relating to the nature of 'personal property', raise issues concerning the relevance, for WTO dispute settlement, of the way in which the municipal law of a WTO Member classifies or regulates things or transactions. Previous Appellate Body Reports confirm

[7] Panel Report, *US – Countervailing Measures on Certain EC Products*, para. 7.50.
[8] Appellate Body Report, *US – Countervailing Measures on Certain EC Products*, para. 115.
[9] Appellate Body Report, *US – Corrosion-Resistant Steel Sunset Review*, footnote 87.

that an examination of municipal law or particular transactions governed by it might be relevant, as evidence, in ascertaining whether a financial contribution exists. However, municipal laws – in particular those relating to property – vary amongst WTO Members. Clearly, it would be inappropriate to characterize, for purposes of applying any provisions of the WTO covered agreements, the same thing or transaction differently, depending on its legal categorization within the jurisdictions of different Members. Accordingly, we emphasize that municipal law classifications are not determinative of the issues raised in this appeal.

> . . .

In seeking to exclude 'standing timber' from the definition of 'goods' in Article 1.1(a)(1)(iii), Canada contends in the alternative that, even if we find that the term is not limited to 'tradable items with an actual or potential tariff classification', standing timber is still not 'goods' as the Panel has defined them, because it is neither 'personal property' nor an 'identified thing to be severed from real property'. The concepts of 'personal' and 'real' property are, in the context Canada raises them, creatures of municipal law that are not reflected in Article 1.1(a)(1)(iii) itself. As we have said above, the manner in which the municipal law of a WTO Member classifies an item cannot, in itself, be determinative of the interpretation of provisions of the WTO covered agreements. As such, we do not believe that the distinction drawn by Canada is dispositive of the issues raised in this appeal.[10]

10.7 In *China – Auto Parts*, the Appellate Body upheld the Panel's finding that the measure was an 'internal charge' falling within the scope of Article III:2 of the GATT, and not an 'ordinary customs duty' falling under Article II:1(b) of the GATT. The Appellate Body stated:

> [W]e first observe that the way in which a Member's domestic law characterizes its own measures, although useful, cannot be dispositive of the characterization of such measures under WTO law . . . In addition, as the Panel recognized, and as is the case with all of the criteria we have just mentioned, a degree of caution must be exercised in attributing decisive weight to characteristics that fall exclusively within the control of WTO Members, 'because otherwise Members could determine by themselves which of the provisions would apply to their charges.'[11]

10.8 In *US – Anti-Dumping and Countervailing Duties (China)* (DS379), the Appellate Body rejected the Panel's interpretation of the term 'public body' in Article 1.1(a)(1) of the SCM Agreement. In the course of its analysis, the Appellate

---

[10] Appellate Body Report, *US – Softwood Lumber IV*, paras. 56, 65 (citing Appellate Body Report, *US – FSC*, para. 90; Appellate Body Report, *India – Patents (US)*, paras. 65–71; Appellate Body Report, *US – Section 211 Appropriations Act*, paras. 103–6; Appellate Body Report, *US – Corrosion-Resistant Steel Sunset Review*, footnote 87).

[11] Appellate Body Report, *China – Auto Parts*, para. 178 (citing Appellate Body Report, *US – Softwood Lumber IV (Article 21.5 – Canada)*, para. 82; Appellate Body Report, *US – Softwood Lumber IV*, para. 56; GATT Panel Report, *EEC – Parts and Components*, paras. 5.6 and 5.7; Panel Report, *US – 1916 Act (Japan)*, paras. 6.58, 6.63, 6.134 and 6.152(a) and footnotes 461, 464, 504 and 518).

Body expressed concern with the Panel's reliance on municipal law concepts in its interpretative analysis:

> [W]e recall that dictionaries are not, as the Appellate Body has previously recognized, the sole source of information for determining the meaning of a treaty term. Nonetheless, we have some reservations relating to the way in which the Panel had recourse to usages of the term 'public body' or similar terms in the municipal law of a number of jurisdictions in this dispute. First, the Panel did not clearly explain why it considered that an examination of the understanding of the concept of a public body in municipal law would assist in answering the particular interpretative question with which it was confronted. Second, while the Panel refers to the definition of 'public body' or similar terms in four different jurisdictions, it is not clear whether the Panel assessed the usage of the relevant terms only in these four jurisdictions or whether the Panel surveyed other jurisdictions as well. If the former, it is not evident why the Panel picked those particular jurisdictions; if the latter, the Panel did not disclose or discuss the results of its survey in their entirety. Nor did the Panel, as it might usefully have done, seek input from the parties and third parties as to which municipal law usages of the term 'public body' were of assistance, if any, and why.[12]

10.9 The Panel in *China – Electronic Payment Services* expressed its reservations about relying on municipal legal instruments to interpret the terms in China's Schedule to the GATS (which, as an integral element of the WTO Agreement, is treaty text and subject to the general rule of interpretation in Article 31 of the Vienna Convention). The Panel stated:

> In considering the above-mentioned United States and Chinese legal documents, we observe that they emanate from, and reflect the particular objectives and needs of, the domestic legal systems of the United States and China. It is therefore important to be cautious when interpreting the treaty term 'FFIs' that we do not attribute undue weight to these documents for the purposes of our interpretative task. In particular, as regards the legal definitions provided in some of these documents, we consider that it would be inappropriate to draw, from these context-specific definitions, general conclusions as to the meaning and scope of the term 'FFIs' as it appears in China's Schedule.[13]

10.10 In *Canada – Renewable Energy/Feed-In Tariff Program*, the Panel interpreted the term 'purchase', and stated that the notion of a 'purchase', in the context of Article 1.1(a)(1)(iii) of the SCM Agreement, should involve some kind of payment (usually monetary) in exchange for a good. As to whether a purchase must involve 'consideration', the Panel stated:

> We note that the notion of 'consideration' is derived from common law, where it plays a critical role in determining the existence of a contract. However, the

---

[12] Appellate Body Report, *US – Anti-Dumping and Countervailing Duties (China)*, para. 335.
[13] Panel Report, *China – Electronic Payment Services*, para. 7.556.

word 'consideration' does not appear in the above dictionary definitions. More-over, the notion of 'consideration' is not a necessary element of contracts executed under civil law (and possibly other legal) systems. Thus, to the extent that the concept of 'consideration' may inform the meaning of the term 'purchase [of] goods' under Article 1.1(a)(1)(iii) of the SCM Agreement, it needs to be recalled that it is a legal construct that cannot be found in the legal systems of many WTO Members.[14]

10.11 In *EC – Trademarks and Geographical Indications*, the Panel referred to public international law principles governing nationality in the context of interpreting the term 'nationals' in Article 1.3 of the TRIPS Agreement. After reviewing the practice followed under the Paris Convention, the Panel stated:

> This is consistent with the position under public international law.[216] With respect to the meaning of 'nationals of other Members' for the purposes of the TRIPS Agreement, WTO Members have, through Article 1.3 of the TRIPS Agreement, incorporated the meaning of 'nationals' as it was understood in the Paris Convention (1967) and under public international law. With respect to natural persons, they refer first to the law of the Member of which nationality is claimed.[217] With respect to legal persons, each Member first applies its own criteria to determine nationality.

---

[216] See, for example, A. A. Fatouros, 'National Legal Persons in International Law' in R. Bernhardt (ed.), *Encyclopedia of Public International Law*, Volume III (1997), pp. 495–501; and I. Brownlie, *Principles of Public International Law* (5th edition, Oxford, 1998), p. 426, submitted to the Panel by the European Communities in Exhibits EC-88 and EC-115, respectively.

[217] With respect to natural persons, the Panel also notes that a State may not be bound to recognize a grant of nationality if it does not represent a genuine connection between the natural person and the State granting the nationality: see the judgement of the International Court of Justice in the *Nottebohm case (Liechtenstein* v. *Guatemala)* (second phase), ICJ Reports (1955), 4.[15]

10.3   Respondent invoking municipal law as a justification for a failure to perform a treaty obligation

10.12 Article 27 of the Vienna Convention, entitled 'Internal law and observance of treaties', provides that 'A party may not invoke the provisions of its internal law as justification for its failure to perform a treaty'. There are numerous examples of GATT/WTO adjudicators applying the general principle codified in Article 27 of the Vienna Convention, including but not limited to situations in which

---

[14] Panel Reports, *Canada – Renewable Energy/Feed-In Tariff Program*, footnote 442.
[15] Panel Report, *EC – Trademarks and Geographical Indications (US)*, para. 7.148.

a respondent has invoked its constitutional law requirements or its private contractual obligations.

In *Canada – Gold Coins*, the GATT Panel referred to Article 27 of the Vienna **10.13** Convention in the context of applying Article XXIV:12 of the GATT:

> The Panel noted that it is a well-established principle of international law that a party to a treaty may not invoke the provisions of its internal law, including its constitutional law, as justification for the failure to perform the treaty (see Article 27 of the Vienna Convention on the Law of Treaties). According to this principle, Canada would be fully responsible for any actions, taken by any State organs, having international trade policy effects, and would have an unqualified obligation to ensure the observance of the General Agreement by regional and local governments and authorities, unless some specific provision of the General Agreement determined otherwise.[16]

In *Brazil – Aircraft (Article 21.5 – Canada)*, the compliance Panel found that the **10.14** continued issuance of bonds by Brazil pursuant to letters of commitment issued prior to the modification of the programme at issue was inconsistent with WTO obligations. In the course of its analysis, the Panel rejected Brazil's argument that it had a contractual obligation to issue those bonds pursuant to commitments already entered into, and that it would be liable to damages for breach of contract if it failed to do so. The Panel noted that:

> Although a Panel may examine municipal law in order to determine whether a Member has complied with the *WTO Agreement*, (See, e.g. *India – Patent Protection for Pharmaceutical and Agricultural Chemical Products*, Report of the Appellate Body adopted on 16 January 1998, WT/DS50/AB/R, para. 66), we are reluctant to enter into such an examination here, as the issues are complex, not fully briefed, and ultimately not essential to our resolution of the case at hand. In any event, we recall that, under Article 27 of the *Vienna Convention on the Law of Treaties*, a party to a treaty may not invoke the provisions of its internal law as justification for its failure to perform a treaty.[17]

In *Brazil – Aircraft (Article 21.5 – Canada)*, the Appellate Body endorsed the **10.15** Panel's above finding without mentioning Article 27:

> We note Brazil's argument before the Article 21.5 Panel that Brazil has a contractual obligation under domestic law to issue PROEX bonds pursuant to commitments that have already been made, and that Brazil could be liable for damages for breach of contract under Brazilian law if it failed to respect its contractual obligations. In response to a question from us at the oral hearing, however, Brazil conceded that a WTO Member's domestic law does not excuse that Member from fulfilling its international obligations. Like the Article 21.5 Panel, we do not consider that any private contractual obligations, which Brazil

---

[16] GATT Panel Report, *Canada – Gold Coins*, para. 53.
[17] Panel Report, *Brazil – Aircraft (Article 21.5 – Canada)*, footnote 23.

may have under its domestic law, are relevant to the issue of whether the DSB's recommendation to 'withdraw' the prohibited export subsidies permits the continued issuance of NTN-I bonds under letters of commitment issued before 18 November 1999.[18]

10.16 In a subsequent Article 22.6 proceeding in the same case, *Brazil – Aircraft (Article 22.6 – Brazil)*, the Arbitrators stated that '[w]e do not consider the arguments based on Brazil's contractual obligations to be compelling. Obligations under internal law are no justification for not performing international obligations'.[19]

10.17 In *Argentina – Textiles and Apparel*, the responding Member referred to domestic legal procedures and remedies that were allegedly available, in the context of defending an alleged violation of Article II of the GATT. In the course of its analysis, the Panel stated:

> There is a general rule of international law that a state cannot plead provisions of its own law (or deficiencies in that law) as a defence to a claim against it for an alleged breach of its obligations under international law. Thus, in the *Free Zones of Upper Savoy and the District of Gex*, the Permanent Court of International Justice said: 'It is certain that France cannot rely on her own legislation to limit the scope of her international obligations'. (1932, PCIJ, Series A/B, case No. 46, p. 167.)[20]

10.18 In *Mexico – Telecoms*, the Panel confirmed that a requirement imposed by a Member under its domestic competition law cannot unilaterally erode its international commitments made in its schedule to other WTO Members:

> The Panel is aware that, pursuant to doctrines applicable under the competition laws of some Members, a firm complying with a specific legislative requirement of such a Member (e.g. a trade law authorizing private market-sharing agreements) may be immunized from being found in violation of the general domestic competition law. The reason for these doctrines is that, in most jurisdictions, domestic legislatures have the legislative power to limit the scope of competition legislation. International commitments made under the GATS 'for the purpose of preventing suppliers . . . from engaging in or continuing anti-competitive practices' are, however, designed to limit the regulatory powers of WTO Members. Reference Paper commitments undertaken by a Member are international obligations owed to all other Members of the WTO in all areas of the relevant GATS commitments. In accordance with the principle established in Article 27 of the Vienna Convention, a requirement imposed by a Member under its internal law on a major supplier cannot unilaterally erode its international commitments made in its schedule to other WTO Members to prevent major suppliers from

---

[18] Appellate Body Report, *Brazil – Aircraft (Article 21.5 – Canada)*, para. 46.
[19] Decision by the Arbitrators, *Brazil – Aircraft (Article 22.6 – Brazil)*, para. 3.65.
[20] Panel Report, *Argentina – Textiles and Apparel*, footnote 198.

'continuing anti-competitive practices'. The pro-competitive obligations in Section 1 of the Reference Paper do not reserve any such unilateral right of WTO Members to maintain anticompetitive measures.[21]

10.4   Alleged violations of municipal law

Under the standard terms of reference, the subject-matter jurisdiction of WTO panels is limited to claims under the WTO agreements, and would not extend to claims directly based on alleged violations of a Member's municipal law. There have been several cases in which panels rejected interpretations of WTO provisions that would, if accepted, have required an assessment, by a panel, of whether the respondent's conduct was consistent with its own municipal law.   **10.19**

In *US – Hot-Rolled Steel*, the Panel rejected certain claims under Article X:3(a) of the GATT, which requires that laws and regulations be administered in a uniform, impartial and reasonable manner. In the course of its analysis, the Panel stated: **10.20**

> Some of Japan's arguments concerning the alleged lack of uniform, impartial, and reasonable administration of the US anti-dumping law assert that USDOC made different decisions in this case than it has made in other cases, or that the decisions were in violation of controlling US legal authority. It is not, in our view, properly a panel's task to consider whether a Member has acted consistently with its own domestic legislation.[22]

In *US – Stainless Steel (Korea)*, the Panel also rejected certain claims under Article X:3(a) of the GATT, and stated: **10.21**

> [Article X:3(a)] was not in our view intended to function as a mechanism to test the consistency of a Member's particular decisions or rulings with the Member's own domestic law and practice; that is a function reserved for each Member's domestic judicial system, and a function WTO panels would be particularly ill-suited to perform. An incautious adoption of the approach advocated by Korea could however effectively convert every claim that an action is inconsistent with domestic law or practice into a claim under the *WTO Agreement*.[23]

The Panel in *EU – Footwear (China)* addressed a number of claims under the Anti-Dumping Agreement. In the course of its analysis of one issue, the Panel stated: **10.22**

> Even accepting China's assertion to be true, and the European Union does not deny that the domestic industry was defined as complainant EU producers in the original investigation, we note that China's arguments in this regard appear

---

[21] Panel Report, *Mexico – Telecoms*, para. 7.244.
[22] Panel Report, *US – Hot-Rolled Steel*, para. 7.267.
[23] Panel Report, *US – Stainless Steel (Korea)*, para. 6.50.

to be based on EU law. The requirements of EU law in this respect, whatever they may be, are irrelevant to our consideration of whether the European Union has acted inconsistently with its obligations under the AD Agreement.[24]

Elsewhere in its analysis, the Panel in *EU – Footwear (China)* stated that 'we agree [with the EU] that whether or not EU law requires an explanation of a change in methodology is irrelevant to our analysis, as it is not our role to enforce EU law'.[25]

10.5   The interpretation of municipal law by international tribunals

10.23   WTO jurisprudence offers support for the proposition that an international tribunal must determine the content and meaning of a respondent's municipal law insofar as necessary to determine the consistency of that law (or related measures) with the international obligations at issue in a dispute. WTO jurisprudence also offers support for the proposition that a tribunal may not simply defer to the respondent's assertions regarding the meaning of its own law; rather, questions relating to the content and interpretation of municipal law are treated as questions of fact. In accordance with the normal principles regarding the allocation of the burden of proof, a party advancing an assertion about the content and meaning of the respondent's municipal law bears the burden of proving its assertion on the basis of evidence. The Appellate Body has explained that the nature of such evidence will vary from case to case, but will typically be produced in the form of the text of the relevant legislation or legal instruments, which may be supported by evidence of the consistent application of such laws, the pronouncements of domestic courts on the meaning of such laws, the opinions of legal experts and the writings of recognized scholars.

10.24   In *India – Patents (US)*, India argued that the Panel should have given India the benefit of the doubt as to the operation of an aspect of Indian law, and that the Panel should have sought guidance from India on matters relating to the interpretation of Indian law. The Appellate Body stated:

> In public international law, an international tribunal may treat municipal law in several ways. Municipal law may serve as evidence of facts and may provide evidence of state practice. However, municipal law may also constitute evidence of compliance or non-compliance with international obligations. For example, in *Certain German Interests in Polish Upper Silesia*, the Permanent Court of International Justice observed:

---

[24] Panel Report, *EU – Footwear (China)*, para. 7.423.   [25] *Ibid.*, para. 7.858.

'It might be asked whether a difficulty does not arise from the fact that the Court would have to deal with the Polish law of July 14th, 1920. This, however, does not appear to be the case. From the standpoint of International Law and of the Court which is its organ, municipal laws are merely facts which express the will and constitute the activities of States, in the same manner as do legal decisions and administrative measures. *The Court is certainly not called upon to interpret the Polish law as such; but there is nothing to prevent the Court's giving judgment on the question whether or not, in applying that law, Poland is acting in conformity with its obligations towards Germany under the Geneva Convention.*' (emphasis added)

... It is clear that an examination of the relevant aspects of Indian municipal law and, in particular, the relevant provisions of the Patents Act as they relate to the 'administrative instructions', is essential to determining whether India has complied with its obligations under Article 70.8(a). There was simply no way for the Panel to make this determination without engaging in an examination of Indian law. But, as in the case cited above before the Permanent Court of International Justice, in this case, the Panel was not interpreting Indian law 'as such'; rather, the Panel was examining Indian law solely for the purpose of determining whether India had met its obligations under the *TRIPS Agreement*. To say that the Panel should have done otherwise would be to say that only India can assess whether Indian law is consistent with India's obligations under the *WTO Agreement*. This, clearly, cannot be so.'[26]

The Panel in *US – Section 301 Trade Act* explained its approach to examining **10.25** aspects of municipal law. After recalling the Appellate Body's statements above, the Panel stated:

In this case, too, we have to examine aspects of municipal law, namely Sections 301–310 of the US Trade Act of 1974. Our mandate is to examine Sections 301–310 solely for the purpose of determining whether the US meets its WTO obligations. In doing so, we do not, as noted by the Appellate Body in *India – Patents (US)*, interpret US law 'as such', the way we would, say, interpret provisions of the covered agreements. We are, instead, called upon to establish the meaning of Sections 301–310 as factual elements and to check whether these factual elements constitute conduct by the US contrary to its WTO obligations. The rules on burden of proof for the establishment of facts referred to above also apply in this respect.[635]

---

[635] In this respect, the International Court of Justice ('ICJ'), referring to an earlier judgment by the Permanent Court of International Justice ('PCIJ') noted the following: 'Where the determination of a question of municipal law is essential to the Court's decision in a case, the Court will have to weigh the jurisprudence of the municipal courts, and "If this is uncertain or divided, it will rest with the Court to select the interpretation which it considers most in conformity with the law" (*Brazilian Loans*, PCIJ, Series

---

[26] Appellate Body Report, *India – Patents (US)*, paras. 65–6 (citing 1926, PCIJ, Series A, No. 7, p. 19).

A, Nos. 20/21, p. 124)' (*Elettronica Sicula SpA (ELSI)*, Judgment, ICJ Reports 1989, p. 47, para. 62).[27]

10.26 In *US – 1916 Act*, the Panel stated:

> [B]oth parties rely, in order to support their claims, on a number of judgements by US courts which have applied and interpreted the 1916 Act since the 1970's. In many Members, final judicial decisions regarding the interpretation of a given law may not be contested any further, whereas administrative interpretations of a law may generally be overruled by a domestic judge called upon to review that law. However, an administrative interpretation will normally provide one single interpretation. In contrast, depending on the judicial structure of a Member, judicial interpretations may emanate from several courts positioned at different levels in the judicial order. The diversity of the sources of the case-law may make it more difficult to assess the respective value of the judgements of which that case-law is composed.
>
> We recall that the International Court of Justice, in the *Elettronica Sicula SpA (ELSI)* case, referred to the judgement of the Permanent Court of International Justice in the *Brazilian Loans* case – to which the United States also refers in its submissions – and noted that:
>
> > 'Where the determination of a question of municipal law is essential to the Court's decision in a case, the Court will have to weigh the jurisprudence of the municipal courts, and "If this is uncertain or divided, it will rest with the Court to select the interpretation which it considers most in conformity with the law" (*Brazilian Loans*, PCIJ, Series A, Nos. 20/21, p. 124).'
>
> We are fully aware that our role is to clarify the existing provisions of the covered agreements so as to determine the compatibility of a domestic law with those agreements. We are also aware that, in the *Brazilian Loans* case, the PCIJ was asked to apply domestic legislation to a given case. We are nevertheless of the view that there is nothing in the text of the DSU, nor in the practice of the Appellate Body, that prevents us from 'weigh[ing] the jurisprudence of municipal [US] courts' if it is 'uncertain or divided'. This would not require us to develop our own independent interpretation of US law, but simply to select among the relevant judgements the interpretation most in conformity with the US law, as necessary in order to resolve the matter before us.[456]

---

[456] We do not consider that this would be engaging into *interpreting* US law, with the risks highlighted by the United States in its submissions. Our approach is in line with the reasoning of the PCIJ in the *Brazilian Loans* case, which, even though it had to apply domestic law, was prudent in its approach of the domestic case law:

> 'It follows that the Court must pay the utmost regard to the decisions of the municipal courts of a country, for it is with the aid of their

---

[27] Panel Report, *US – Section 301 Trade Act*, para. 7.18.

jurisprudence that it will be enabled to decide what are the rules which, in actual fact, are applied in the country the law of which is recognized as applicable in a given case' (PCIJ, Series A, Nos. 20/21, p. 124).[28]

10.27 The Panel in *US – Countervailing Measures on Certain EC Products* observed that where the measure giving rise to the alleged violation is legislation, an examination of the relevant aspects of municipal law is essential to determining whether a Member has complied with its obligations. The Panel added:

> It is a well-established practice of legal interpretation in international jurisprudence that 'where the determination of a question of municipal law is essential to the Court's decision in a case, the Court will have to weigh the jurisprudence of the municipal courts.'[29]

10.28 In *US – Carbon Steel*, the Appellate Body identified several types of evidence that may be taken into account to determine the scope and meaning of municipal law:

> The party asserting that another party's municipal law, as such, is inconsistent with relevant treaty obligations bears the burden of introducing evidence as to the scope and meaning of such law to substantiate that assertion. Such evidence will typically be produced in the form of the text of the relevant legislation or legal instruments, which may be supported, as appropriate, by evidence of the consistent application of such laws, the pronouncements of domestic courts on the meaning of such laws, the opinions of legal experts and the writings of recognized scholars. The nature and extent of the evidence required to satisfy the burden of proof will vary from case to case.[30]

10.29 The Panel in *US – Zeroing (EC)* was presented with a claim that certain legislation was inconsistent as such with WTO obligations. The Panel recalled prior Appellate body pronouncements on how such an analysis is to be conducted, and stated:

> WTO panels and the Appellate Body have applied the principle, articulated by the Permanent Court of International Justice, that municipal laws are facts before international tribunals. One aspect of this is the need for an international tribunal to take account of decisions of domestic courts on the meaning of municipal law.[157]

---

[157] 'Interpretation of their own laws by national courts is binding on an international tribunal'. Ian Brownlie, *Principles of Public International Law*, 5th Ed. (1998), p. 40.[31]

---

[28] Panel Report, *US – 1916 Act (EC)*, paras. 6.52–6.53 (also citing *Case Concerning Elettronica Sicula SpA (ELSI) (United States of America* v. *Italy)*, 1989 ICJ Reports, p. 15, at 47, para. 62).

[29] Panel Report, *US – Countervailing Measures on Certain EC Products*, para. 7.124 (citing *Brazilian Loans*, PCIJ, Series A, Nos. 20/21, p. 124 cited in *Elettronica Sicula SpA (ELSI)*, Judgment, 1989 ICJ Reports, p. 47, para. 62).

[30] Appellate Body Report, *US – Carbon Steel*, para. 157.

[31] Panel Report, *US – Zeroing (EC)*, para. 7.53.

10.6   Implementation of international obligations in municipal law

10.30 Article 1.1 of the TRIPS Agreement expressly provides that Members 'shall be free to determine the appropriate method of implementing the provisions of this Agreement within their own legal system and practice'.[32] In various other contexts, WTO adjudicators have found that, where a particular obligation is in the nature of an 'obligation of result', a State is free to determine the means to implement and comply with that obligation. Several WTO panels have also commented on the concept of 'direct effect', in the sense of certain international legal obligations becoming enforceable within the domestic legal system of a State without any implementing legislation.

10.6.1 Obligations of result

10.31 In *US – Section 301 Trade Act*, the Panel explained its general methodology for evaluating the conformity of municipal law with WTO obligations. In the course of its discussion, the Panel stated:

> When evaluating the conformity of national law with WTO obligations in accordance with Article XVI:4 of the WTO Agreement account must be taken of the wide-ranging diversity in the legal systems of the Members. Conformity can be ensured in different ways in different legal systems. It is the end result that counts, not the manner in which it is achieved. Only by understanding and respecting the specificities of each Member's legal system, can a correct evaluation of conformity be established.[33]

10.32 In *US – Tyres (China)*, the Panel noted that the WTO Agreement 'does not prescribe any particular manner in which a Member's WTO obligations and commitments must be transposed into its domestic law'.[34]

10.33 In *US – Line Pipe*, the Appellate Body stated that the obligations in the Agreement on Safeguards (or at least the obligations that were at issue in that dispute) concern the ultimate determinations made by a Member. Without using the terminology of an 'obligation of result', the Appellate Body explained that how the competent authorities reached their determinations 'is entirely up to WTO Members in the exercise of their sovereignty':

> We note also that we are not concerned with how the competent authorities of WTO Members reach their determinations in applying safeguard measures. The *Agreement on Safeguards* does not prescribe the internal decision-making

---

[32] See Appellate Body Report, *India – Patents (US)*, para. 59.
[33] Panel Report, *US – Section 301 Trade Act*, para. 7.24.
[34] Panel Report, *US – Tyres (China)*, para. 7.136.

process for making such a determination. That is entirely up to WTO Members in the exercise of their sovereignty. We are concerned only with the determination itself, which is a singular act for which a WTO Member may be accountable in WTO dispute settlement. It is of no matter to us whether that singular act results from a decision by one, one hundred, or – as here – six individual decision-makers under the municipal law of that WTO Member. What matters to us is whether the determination, however it is decided domestically, meets the requirements of the *Agreement on Safeguards.*[35]

Article 19.1 of the DSU provides that a Member found to have acted inconsistently with its obligations under one of the covered agreements is under an obligation 'to bring the measure into conformity with that agreement'. Numerous arbitration awards under Article 21.3(c) of the DSU, the purpose of which is to determine the reasonable period of time for implementation, have established that this language creates an 'obligation of result', and that the Member concerned is in principle free to choose the means for achieving that result. For example, the Arbitrator in *Chile – Alcohol (Article 21.3(c))* stated: **10.34**

> The European Communities also suggests that the urgency procedures available under the Constitution could be used by the President. It is my belief, however, that the Member concerned, has the sovereign prerogative and responsibility of determining for itself the most appropriate, and probably effective, method of implementing the recommendations and rulings of the DSB by securing the passage of the amendatory law.[36]

10.6.2 The concept of direct effect

In *US – Section 301 Trade Act*, the Panel offered a number of observations on the question of 'direct effect', in the sense of treaty obligations becoming legally enforceable rights and obligations within a municipal legal order in the absence of any implementing legislation: **10.35**

> Under the doctrine of direct effect, which has been found to exist most notably in the legal order of the EC but also in certain free trade area agreements, obligations addressed to States are construed as creating legally enforceable rights and obligations for individuals. Neither the GATT nor the WTO has so far been interpreted by GATT/WTO institutions as a legal order producing direct effect.[661] Following this approach, the GATT/WTO did *not* create a new legal order the subjects of which comprise both contracting parties or Members and their nationals.

---

[661] We make this statement as a matter of fact, without implying any judgment on the issue. We note that whether there are circumstances where obligations in

---

[35] Appellate Body Report, *US – Line Pipe*, para. 158.
[36] Award of the Arbitrator, *Chile – Alcohol (Article 21.3(c))*, para. 42.

any of the WTO agreements addressed to Members would create rights for individuals which national courts must protect, remains an open question, in particular in respect of obligations following the exhaustion of DSU procedures in a specific dispute (see Eeckhout, P., The Domestic Legal Status of the WTO Agreement: Interconnecting Legal Systems, *Common Market Law Review*, 1997, p. 11; Berkey, J., The European Court of Justice and Direct Effect for the GATT: A Question Worth Revisiting, *European Journal of International Law*, 1998, p. 626). The fact that WTO institutions have not to date construed any obligations as producing direct effect does not necessarily preclude that in the legal system of any given Member, following internal constitutional principles, some obligations will be found to give rights to individuals. Our statement of fact does not prejudge any decisions by national courts on this issue.[37]

10.36 In *Mexico – Taxes on Soft Drinks*, the Appellate Body observed that '[i]n some WTO Members, certain international rules may have direct effect within their domestic legal systems without requiring implementing legislation. In such circumstances, these rules also become part of the domestic law of that Member.'[38]

10.37 In *Mexico – Anti-Dumping Measures on Rice*, the Panel considered Mexico's argument that, in Mexican law, international agreements such as the WTO agreements are 'self-executing' and automatically applicable in Mexico, and that its law must be applied in a manner compatible with Mexico's WTO treaty obligations. The Panel stated:

> While we understand the important role given to Mexico's international commitments by providing for the direct effect of international agreements such as the WTO Agreements in Mexican law, we do not consider that for this reason, Mexico's laws would be shielded from any review of the consistency of these laws with the WTO Agreements or that such laws can never be found to be inconsistent with the WTO Agreements. The fact that provision is made for the direct effect of the WTO Agreements does not automatically and inevitably ensure a correct interpretation of the WTO Agreements, at least not in a situation where there is also a distinct domestic legal provision which manifestly conflicts with the terms of the Agreements. In our view, the direct effect of the WTO Agreements in Mexican law may prove important in case the domestic law leaves the authority with discretion to apply the law in a WTO consistent manner. However, in case the domestic law which implements Mexico's international commitments with regard to for example the AD Agreement and SCM Agreement, as does the Act, is clear and manifestly conflicts with and effectively impairs the enjoyment of the rights which the affected party is unconditionally entitled to under the WTO Agreement, as is the case here, then the direct effect of the WTO Agreements cannot shield the domestic law from such scrutiny by WTO panels.[39]

[37] Panel Report, *US – Section 301 Trade Act*, para. 7.72.
[38] Appellate Body Report, *Mexico – Taxes on Soft Drinks*, footnote 148.
[39] Panel Report, *Mexico – Anti-Dumping Measures on Rice*, para. 7.224.

10.7   Representations made by a State regarding the operation of its municipal law

There have been several cases in which WTO panels have found that a disputing **10.38** party was legally bound by representations made before the panel regarding the operation of its municipal law. In some of these cases, panels have considered and applied the criteria developed by the ICJ in the *Nuclear Tests* case regarding the binding effect of unilateral undertakings.

In *US – Section 301 Trade Act*, the Panel found that certain undertakings given **10.39** by the United States regarding the operation of the law at issue effectively resolved the dispute. More precisely, the Panel found that '[a]s a matter of international law, the effect of the US undertakings is to anticipate, or discharge, any would-be State responsibility that could have arisen'. In the course of its analysis, the Panel stated:

> Attributing international legal significance to unilateral statements made by a State should not be done lightly and should be subject to strict conditions. Although the legal effects we are ascribing to the US statements made to the DSB through this Panel are of a more narrow and limited nature and reach compared to other internationally relevant instances in which legal effect was given to unilateral declarations, we have conditioned even these limited effects on the fulfilment of the most stringent criteria. A sovereign State should normally not find itself legally affected on the international plane by the casual statement of any of the numerous representatives speaking on its behalf in today's highly interactive and inter-dependant world[692] nor by a representation made in the heat of legal argument on a State's behalf. This, however, is very far from the case before us.

---

[692] In the *Nuclear Test* case (Australia v. France), the ICJ held that France was legally bound by publicly given undertakings, made on behalf of the French Government, to cease the conduct of atmospheric nuclear tests. The criteria of obligation were: the intention of the state making the declaration that it should be bound according to its terms; and that the undertaking be given publicly:

> 'It is well recognized that declarations made by way of unilateral acts, concerning legal or factual situations, may have the effect of creating legal obligations. Declarations of this kind may be, and often are, very specific. When it is the intention of the State making the declaration that it should become bound according to its terms, that intention confers on the declaration the character of a legal undertaking, the State being henceforth legally required to follow a course of conduct consistent with the declaration. An undertaking of this kind, if given publicly, and with an intent to be bound, even though not made within the context of international negotiations, is binding'.

(ICJ Reports (1974), p. 253 at pp. 267–271, quoted above from para. 43; see also *Nuclear Test* case (New Zealand v. France), ICJ Reports (1974), p. 457, at pp. 472–475; *Legal Status of Eastern Greenland* case, PCIJ Reports, Series

A/B, No. 53, where a statement was found to have legal effects even though
it was not made publicly but in the course of conversations with the Norwegian
Foreign Minister; *Nicaragua* case (Merits), ICJ Reports (1986), p. 14, at p. 132;
Case Concerning the Frontier Dispute, ICJ Reports (1986), p. 554, at
pp. 573–574).

In this case, the legal effect of the US statements does not go as far as creating a
new legal obligation. Nonetheless we have applied to them the same, and perhaps
even more, stringent conditions. Subsequent to the *Nuclear test* case, some authors
criticized giving legal effect to declarations not directed to a specific State or States
but expressed *erga omnes* (see Rubin, A., The International Legal Effects of
Unilateral Declarations, American Journal of International Law, 1977, p. 1 and
Franck, T., Word Made Law: The Decision of the ICJ in the Nuclear Test Cases,
American Journal of International Law, 1975, p. 612). In this case the US
statements had explicit recipients and were made in the context of a specific
dispute settlement procedure.[40]

The Panel in *US – Section 301 Trade Act* proceeded to identify additional
circumstances that led it to give weight to the undertaking given by the United
States in that proceeding:

> The statements made by the US before this Panel were a reflection of official US
> policy, intended to express US understanding of its international obligations as
> incorporated in domestic US law. The statements did not represent a new US
> policy or undertaking but the bringing of a pre-existing US policy and under-
> taking made in a domestic setting into an international forum.
>
> The representations and statements by the representatives of the US
> appearing before us were solemnly made, in a deliberative manner, for the
> record, repeated in writing and confirmed in the Panel's second hearing. There
> was nothing casual about these statements nor were they made in the heat of
> argument. There was ample opportunity to retract. Rather than retract, the US
> even sought to deepen its legal commitment in this respect.
>
> We are satisfied that the representatives appearing before us had full powers to
> make such legal representations and that they were acting within the authority
> bestowed on them. Panel proceedings are part of the DSB dispute resolution
> process. It is inconceivable except in extreme circumstances that a panel would
> reject the power of the legal representatives of a Member to state before a panel,
> and through the panel to the DSB, the legal position of a Member as regards its
> domestic law read in the light of its WTO obligations. The panel system would
> not function if such a power could not be presumed.
>
> We are equally satisfied, as a matter of fact, that the statements made to us
> were intended to be part of the record in the full knowledge and understand-
> ing that they could, as any other official submission, be made part of our
> Report; that they were made with the intention not only that we rely on
> them but also that the EC and the third parties to the dispute as well as all
> Members of the DSB – effectively all WTO Members – place such reliance
> on them.

---

[40] Panel Report, *US – Section 301 Trade Act*, para. 7.118.

Accordingly, we find that these statements by the US express the unambiguous and official position of the US representing, in a manner that can be relied upon by all Members, an undertaking that the discretion of the USTR has been limited so as to prevent a determination of inconsistency before exhaustion of DSU proceedings. Although this representation does not create a new international legal obligation for the US – after all the US was already bound by Article 23 in becoming a WTO Member – it clarifies and gives an undertaking, at an international level, concerning aspects of domestic US law, in particular, the way the US has implemented its obligations under Article 23.2(a) of the DSU.

... As a matter of international law, the effect of the US undertakings is to anticipate, or discharge, any would-be State responsibility that could have arisen had the national law under consideration in this case consisted of nothing more than the statutory language.[41]

In *US – 1916 Act (EC)*, the European Communities argued that certain **10.40** statements made by US officials regarding the law at issue should be treated as admissions that the law at issue was GATT-inconsistent. The Panel declined to attach much weight to these statements, based in part on the circumstances in which they had been made:

[W]e should determine whether they could actually generate legal obligations for the United States under international law. For instance, since they are subsequent to the notification by the United States of its 'grandfathered' legislation under the GATT 1947, it might be argued that they implicitly modified that notification by stating that the 1916 Act was 'grandfathered'. We recall that the International Court of Justice has developed, *inter alia* in its judgement in the *Nuclear tests* case, criteria on when a statement by a representative of a State could generate international obligations for that State. In the present case, we are reluctant to consider the statements made by senior US officials in testimonies or letters to the US Congress or to members thereof as generating international obligations for the United States. First, we recall that the constitution of the United States provides for a strict separation of the judicial and executive branches. With the exception of criminal prosecutions, the application of the 1916 Act falls within the exclusive responsibility of the federal courts. Under those circumstances, a statement by the executive branch of government in a domestic forum can only be of limited value. Second, with the possible exception of the statement of US Trade Representative Clayton Yeutter, they were not made at a sufficiently high level compared with the statements considered by the International Court of Justice in the *Nuclear Tests* case, where essentially declarations by a head of State and of members of the French government were at issue. Moreover, the statements referred to in the present case were not directly addressed to the general public. Finally, they were not made on behalf of the United States, but – at best – on behalf of the executive branch of government. This aspect would not be essential if the statements had been made in an international forum, where the executive

[41] *Ibid.*, paras. 7.119–7.126.

branch represents the State. However, in the present case, the statements were addressed to the US legislative branch. Therefore, we cannot consider them as creating obligations for the United States under international law.[42]

10.41 In *EC – Trademarks and Geographical Indications*, the Panel considered that certain statements regarding aspects of EC law made by agents of the European Commission before the Panel 'commit and engage the European Communities':

> The European Communities' delegation to this panel proceeding confirms that the statements made by agents of the European Commission before the Panel commit and engage the European Communities. It indicates that Community laws are generally not executed through authorities at Community level but rather through recourse to the authorities of its member States which, in such a situation, 'act *de facto* as organs of the Community, for which the Community would be responsible under WTO law and international law in general'. The Panel accepts this explanation of what amounts to the European Communities' domestic constitutional arrangements and accepts that the submissions of the European Communities' delegation to this panel proceeding are made on behalf of all the executive authorities of the European Communities.[43]

10.42 In *US – Gambling*, the Panel suggested that the United States was 'bound' by certain statements it had made at DSB meetings regarding the operation of US law:

> During two successive DSB meetings, the United States stated that a prohibition on the 'cross-border supply of gambling and betting services under US laws' exists in the United States. The panel's decision in *US – Section 301 Trade Act* appears to support the view that the United States should be bound by these statements. The statements were made by representatives of the United States to express their understanding of US law. They were made in the context of a formal WTO meeting for the record. The United States has not argued that the representatives were acting outside the authority bestowed upon them in making these statements.[44]

---

[42] Panel Report, *US – 1916 Act (EC)*, para. 6.63 (citing *Nuclear Tests case*, Judgments of 20 December 1974, 1974 ICJ Reports, p. 253 (*Australia* v. *France*), p. 457 (*New Zealand* v. *France*); P. Daillier and A. Pellet, *Droit international public*, 5th edn (1994), pp. 354–8; Article 7 of the Vienna Convention).
[43] Panel Report, *EC – Trademarks and Geographical Indications (US)*, para. 7.98.
[44] Panel Report, *US – Gambling*, para. 6.161 (citing Panel Report, *US – Section 301 Trade Act*, paras. 7.118–7.125).

11

NON-RETROACTIVITY

11.1   Introduction

It has been said that '[t]emporal jurisdiction has long been a source of conten- **11.1** tion between states in international adjudication', and '[i]nternational tribunals have faced such questions for over a century and have developed a jurisprudence of continuing circumstances'.[1] Certain provisions of the WTO agreements specify their temporal scope and application,[2] and other provisions deal with issues of retroactivity in the context of the administration of domestic trade regulations.[3] However, most of the WTO agreements are silent on their temporal scope, and WTO adjudicators have therefore been called upon to clarify WTO rights and obligations in light of concepts and principles found in general international law. This chapter reviews WTO pronouncements relating to: (i) the non-retroactivity of treaties (Article 28 of the Vienna Convention); (ii) the non-retroactive consequences of treaty termination (Article 70 of the Vienna Convention); (iii) Article 14 of the ILC Articles on State Responsibility; and (iv) other inter-temporal rules of international law.

11.2   Non-retroactivity of treaties

A number of WTO decisions have considered and applied the general principle in **11.2** Article 28 of the Vienna Convention, entitled 'Non-retroactivity of treaties'. It reads:

---

[1] S. Blanchard, 'State Consent, Temporal Jurisdiction, and the Importation of Continuing Circumstances Analysis into International Investment Arbitration' (2011) 10(3) *Washington University Global Studies Law Review* 419, at 422.

[2] For example, Article 32.3 of the SCM Agreement (and the parallel provision in Article 18.3 of the Anti-Dumping Agreement) provides that 'the provisions of this Agreement shall apply to investigations, and reviews of existing measures, initiated pursuant to applications which have been made on or after the date of entry into force for a Member of the WTO Agreement'.

[3] These include: (i) Article X:2 of the GATT; (ii) Article 10 of the Anti-Dumping Agreement; (iii) Article 20 of the SCM Agreement; and (iv) Article 2(i) of the Agreement on Rules of Origin.

> Unless a different intention appears from the treaty or is otherwise established, its provisions do not bind a party in relation to any act or fact which took place or any situation which ceased to exist before the date of the entry into force of the treaty with respect to that party.

11.3 In *US – Non-Rubber Footwear*, the GATT Panel examined the temporal scope of the United States' obligations under the Tokyo Round Subsidies Code with respect to countervailing duties collected after the entry into force of the Code, pursuant to investigations completed prior to the entry into force of the Code. Prior to the entry into force of the Code in 1980, the United States did not conduct an injury determination with respect to imports from certain GATT parties, including Brazil; with the entry into force of the Code, the United States became subject to the injury determination requirement in Article VI:6(a) of the GATT, at least *vis-à-vis* other Code signatories, including Brazil. In 1981, Brazil requested the US authorities to conduct an injury determination with respect to the pre-existing countervailing duties being applied to imports of footwear from Brazil. The US authorities did so, and made a negative injury determination. The United States revoked the countervailing duties as from the date of the request. Brazil claimed that the United States should have revoked the duties as from the date of the entry into force of the relevant treaty obligation in the Code (1980), and not only from the later date that Brazil made its request pursuant to that obligation (1981). The Panel rejected Brazil's claim:

> [T]he existence of a valid decision on the one hand, and the entry into effect of a new obligation on the other, required that this decision be re-examined in the light of this new obligation. This interpretation was confirmed by the general principles of international law governing the application of treaties as codified in the Vienna Convention on the Law of Treaties. Under Article 28 of that Convention new treaty provisions did not bind parties in relation to any act or fact which had taken place before the date of entry into force of the treaty. However, the treaty provisions did bind parties in relation to a situation which had arisen from a previous act (decision to impose countervailing duties) which situation (levying of countervailing duties) continued to exist.
>
> In general terms, the Panel considered that the obligation regarding injury determination of a Code signatory with respect to pre-existing decisions to impose countervailing duties would be satisfied as long as the signatory subject to such a decision had a right to an injury examination as of entry into force, through the Code, of the Article VI:6(a) obligations. If such an examination were to be made on the initiative of the investigating authorities, it would have to cover the period starting on that date; if there were a finding of no injury it would have to apply as of that date. However, the Panel noted that nothing in Article VI excluded another procedure for the injury examination, i.e. an examination upon request. Indeed, as noted in paragraph 4 above, such a procedure had been used under the pre-selection system to implement the continuing obligation regarding the determination of injury. This procedure could, therefore, be used provided the right to an injury examination as of the date of entry into force were observed. To this effect, the Panel considered that

the examination procedure would comply with obligations under Article VI:6(a) as long as the request for an examination could be made as of the date of entry into force of the Article VI obligations for the parties concerned and, if a finding of no injury were made, countervailing duties could be revoked as of the date of the request. If, however, the signatory subject to the pre-existing countervailing duty decision were to choose not to invoke its right as of that date but made its request at a later date, again there was nothing in Article VI or in its subsequent interpretation in the Code to imply that any earlier date than the date of the request would be relevant for an injury determination and possible revocation of countervailing duties.[4]

In *Brazil – Desiccated Coconut*, the Panel examined the temporal scope of the **11.4** SCM Agreement *vis-à-vis* countervailing duty measures. The Panel found that the text of the SCM Agreement (in particular Article 32.3 thereof) spelled out the precise temporal application of the SCM Agreement with respect to countervailing duties imposed pursuant to investigations initiated prior to its entry into force. Accordingly, the Panel found it unnecessary to base its decision on the principle contained in Article 28 of the Vienna Convention. The Panel opined that the application of Article 28 to the factual circumstances of that case would have been a matter of 'great legal delicacy':

> The imposition of that duty, it is argued, constitutes an independent act which, since it takes place after the entry into force of the WTO Agreement, should be subject to its strictures. The problem in this case is that the circumstances underlying Brazil's imposition of a countervailing duty on imports of desiccated coconut are part of a process which straddled the date of entry into force of the WTO Agreement. It is an accepted principle of customary international law, reflected in Article 28 of the Vienna Convention, that rights and obligations under a new treaty do not apply retroactively. How to apply that principle to the particular case of a countervailing measure based on a process begun before, but completed after, the date of entry into force of the WTO Agreement, is a matter of great legal delicacy. We note that the parties to the dispute and certain third parties presented extensive arguments regarding the application in this case of the principle reflected in Article 28 of the Vienna Convention. But it should be noted that the principle set forth in Article 28 applies '[u]nless a different intention appears from the treaty or is otherwise established ...'. In this case, the Panel has reached its conclusions on the basis of the intention of the drafters as evidenced in the text of the WTO Agreement itself. Accordingly, we have not addressed the parties' arguments regarding customary principles of international law, nor do we express any view regarding the application of such principles in other contexts under the WTO Agreement. In our view, the SCM Agreement recognizes the principle of non-retroactivity, and taking into account the complexities of applying this general principle in the context of countervailing duties, resolves the difficult question of the operation of the general principle

---

[4] GATT Panel Report, *US – Non-Rubber Footwear*, para. 4.5.

in this specific context through transition rules which spell out the precise temporal application of the SCM Agreement, as described above.[5]

11.5 In *Brazil – Desiccated Coconut*, the Appellate Body upheld the Panel's conclusion, and offered the following observations on Article 28 of the Vienna Convention:

> The fundamental question in this case is one of the temporal application of one set of international legal norms, or the successor set of norms, to a particular measure taken during the period of co-existence of the GATT 1947 and the *Tokyo Round SCM Code* with the *WTO Agreement*. Article 28 of the *Vienna Convention* contains a general principle of international law concerning the non-retroactivity of treaties.
>
> . . .
>
> Article 28 states the general principle that a treaty shall not be applied retroactively 'unless a different intention appears from the treaty or is otherwise established'. Absent a contrary intention, a treaty cannot apply to acts or facts which took place, or situations which ceased to exist, before the date of its entry into force. Article 32.3 of the *SCM Agreement* is an express statement of intention which we will now examine.[6]

11.6 In *EC – Bananas III*, the European Communities argued before the Panel that, because the GATS entered into force on 1 January 1995, only the EC banana import regime as it existed in late 1994 and afterwards (rather than 1992 and before) should be examined in light of Articles II and XVII of GATS. The Panel responded:

> We are not certain of the precise relevance of this argument. The EC does not argue that the introduction of the EC common market organization for bananas resulted in a single, non-recurring adjustment of the market which was completed by 31 December 1994. To the contrary, the EC banana regulations remained in force or were enacted or amended also after 1 January 1995 (e.g. Regulation 478/95 on the export certificate requirement) and, more importantly, they foresee a recurring and ongoing process of import licence allocations according to annually recalculated reference quantities on the basis of operator categories and activity functions. Consequently, the fact that the EC common market organization was introduced in 1993, prior to the entry into force of the GATS, is not relevant for our legal analysis. Thus, we examine the consistency of the EC banana regulations as they currently stand with the EC's obligations arising from the GATS. Therefore, the scope of our legal examination includes only actions which the EC took or continued to take, or measures that remained in force or continued to be applied by the EC, and thus did not cease to exist after the entry into force of the GATS.[486] Likewise, any finding of consistency or inconsistency with the requirements of Articles II and XVII of GATS would be made with respect to the period after the entry into force of the GATS.

---

[5] Panel Report, *Brazil – Desiccated Coconut*, para. 279.
[6] Appellate Body Report, *Brazil – Desiccated Coconut*, p. 14.

Moreover, in this connection we note that there is no grandfather clause in the WTO Agreement that would permit Members to maintain indefinitely national legislation that is inconsistent with WTO rules. Indeed, Article XVI:4 of the WTO Agreement provides that '[e]ach Member shall ensure the conformity of its laws, regulations and administrative procedures with its obligations as provided in the annexed Agreements'.

---

[486] Article 28 of the Vienna Convention embodies the general international law principle that '[u]nless a different intention appears from the treaty or is otherwise established, its provisions do not bind a party in relation to ... any situation which ceased to exist before the date of entry into force of the treaty ...'. Under this rule, the EC measures at issue may be considered as continuing measures, which in some cases were enacted before the entry into force of GATS but which did *not* cease to exist after that date (the opposite of the situation envisaged in Article 28).[7]

On appeal, the European Communities argued that the Panel erred by finding **11.7** *de facto* discrimination under Articles II and XVII of the GATS on the basis of factual data related to 1992, that is, before the entry into force of the GATS in 1995. In the European Communities' view, this established only that there was *de facto* discrimination in 1992, and that there was no basis for the assumption that this discrimination continued to exist after entry into force of the GATS. The European Communities argued that the non-retroactivity principle in Article 28 of the Vienna Convention invalidated the Panel's finding of a violation on the basis of that data. The Appellate Body considered this finding to be a question of fact, not a question of law, stating:

> It is, however, evident from the terms of its finding that the Panel concluded, as a matter of fact, that the *de facto* discrimination did continue to exist after the entry into force of the GATS. This factual finding is beyond review by the Appellate Body. Thus, we do not reverse or modify the Panel's conclusion in paragraph 7.308 of the Panel Reports.[8]

In *EC – Hormones*, the Appellate Body examined the Panel's finding that the **11.8** obligations in Articles 5.1 and 5.5 of the SPS Agreement apply to measures enacted before the entry into force of the WTO Agreement on 1 January 1995, insofar as the measures continued to exist after that date. The Appellate Body stated:

> We agree with the Panel that the *SPS Agreement* would apply to situations or measures that did not cease to exist, such as the 1981 and 1988 Directives, unless the *SPS Agreement* reveals a contrary intention. We also agree with the Panel that the *SPS Agreement* does not reveal such an intention. The *SPS Agreement* does not contain any provision limiting the temporal application of

---

[7] Panel Report, *EC – Bananas III (US)*, para. 7.308.
[8] Appellate Body Report, *EC – Bananas III*, paras. 235–7.

the *SPS Agreement*, or of any provision thereof, to SPS measures adopted after 1 January 1995. In the absence of such a provision, it cannot be assumed that central provisions of the *SPS Agreement*, such as Articles 5.1 and 5.5, do not apply to measures which were enacted before 1995 but which continue to be in force thereafter. If the negotiators had wanted to exempt the very large group of SPS measures in existence on 1 January 1995 from the disciplines of provisions as important as Articles 5.1 and 5.5, it appears reasonable to us to expect that they would have said so explicitly. Articles 5.1 and 5.5 do not distinguish between SPS measures adopted before 1 January 1995 and measures adopted since; the relevant implication is that they are intended to be applicable to both.[9]

11.9 In *Canada – Patent Term*, the Appellate Body interpreted Article 70.1 of the TRIPS Agreement, which provides that '[t]his Agreement does not give rise to obligations in respect of acts which occurred before the date of application of the Agreement for the Member in question'. At issue was whether the 20-year patent term provided for under the TRIPS Agreement applied to patents that had already been granted prior to the entry into force of the TRIPS Agreement, but which had not yet expired when the TRIPS Agreement entered into force. Canada argued that the 20-year patent term requirement did not apply to such patents, as they constituted 'acts which occurred' before the entry into force of the TRIPS Agreement. The Appellate Body disagreed:

> [I]n the realm of intellectual property rights, it is of fundamental importance to distinguish between 'acts' and the 'rights' created by those 'acts' . . .
>
> With respect to Article 70.1, the crucial question for consideration before us is, therefore: if patents created by 'acts' of public authorities under the Old Act continue to be in force on the date of application of the *TRIPS Agreement* for Canada (that is, on 1 January 1996), can Article 70.1 operate to exclude those patents from the scope of the *TRIPS Agreement*, on the ground that they were created by 'acts which occurred' before that date?
>
> The ordinary meaning of the term 'acts' suggests that the answer to this question must be no. An 'act' is something that is 'done', and the use of the phrase 'acts which occurred' suggests that what was done is now complete or ended.[10]

In *Canada – Patent Term*, the Appellate Body found that Article 28 of the Vienna Convention provided further support for its interpretation of Article 70 of the TRIPS Agreement:

> We wish to point out that our interpretation of Article 70 does not lead to a 'retroactive' application of the TRIPS Agreement. Article 70.1 alone addresses 'retroactive' circumstances, and it excludes them generally from the scope of the Agreement. The application of Article 33 to inventions protected under Old Act patents is justified under Article 70.2, not Article 70.1. A treaty applies to

---

[9] Appellate Body Report, *EC – Hormones*, para. 128.
[10] Appellate Body Report, *Canada – Patent Term*, paras. 56–8.

existing rights, even when those rights result from 'acts which occurred' before the treaty entered into force.

This conclusion is supported by the general principle of international law found in the *Vienna Convention*, which establishes a presumption against the retroactive effect of treaties in the following terms ...

Article 28 of the *Vienna Convention* covers not only any 'act', but also any 'fact' or 'situation which ceased to exist'. Article 28 establishes that, in the absence of a contrary intention, treaty provisions do *not* apply to 'any situation which ceased to exist' before the treaty's entry into force for a party to the treaty. Logically, it seems to us that Article 28 also necessarily implies that, absent a contrary intention, treaty obligations *do* apply to any 'situation' which has *not* ceased to exist – that is, to any situation that arose in the past, but continues to exist under the new treaty. Indeed, the very use of the word 'situation' suggests something that subsists and continues over time; it would, therefore, include 'subject-matter existing ... and which is protected', such as Old Act patents at issue in this dispute, even though those patents, and the rights conferred by those patents, arose from 'acts which occurred' before the date of application of the *TRIPS Agreement* for Canada.

This interpretation is confirmed by the Commentary on Article 28, which forms part of the preparatory work of the *Vienna Convention*:

> If, however, an act or fact or situation which took place or arose prior to the entry into force of a treaty continues to occur or exist after the treaty has come into force, it will be caught by the provisions of the treaty. The non-retroactivity principle cannot be infringed by applying a treaty to matters that occur or exist when the treaty is in force, even if they first began at an earlier date.

This point is further explained by the Special Rapporteur:

> The main point ... was that 'the non-retroactivity principle cannot be infringed by applying a treaty to matters that occur or exist when the treaty is in force, even if they first began at an earlier date'. In these cases, the treaty does not, strictly speaking, apply to a fact, act or situation falling partly within and partly outside the period during which it is in force; it applies only to the fact, act or situation which occurs or exists after the treaty is in force. *This may have the result that prior facts, acts or situations are brought under consideration for the purpose of the application of the treaty; but this is only because of their causal connexion with the subsequent facts, acts or situations to which alone in law the treaty applies.* (emphasis added)

We note that Article 28 of the *Vienna Convention* is not applicable if 'a different intention appears from the treaty or is otherwise established'. We see no such 'different intention' in Article 70. Despite some differences in wording and structure from Article 28, we do not see Article 70.1 as in any way establishing 'a different intention' within the meaning of Article 28 of the *Vienna Convention*.[11]

---

[11] *Ibid.*, paras. 70–4 (citing D. Raushning (ed.), *Vienna Convention on the Law of Treaties, Travaux Préparatoires* (Alfred Metzner Verlag, 1978), observation 3 on Article 28 of the International Law Commission Final Draft, p. 220; observation 3 on the Waldock Report VI, p. 218).

11.10 In *EC – Sardines*, the Appellate Body addressed the temporal scope of the TBT Agreement with respect to technical regulations enacted prior to its entry into force. In the course of its analysis, the Appellate Body stated:

> We recall that Article 28 of the *Vienna Convention on the Law of Treaties* (the 'Vienna Convention') provides that treaties generally do not apply retroactively. Article 28 provides . . . As we have said in previous disputes, the interpretation principle codified in Article 28 is relevant to the interpretation of the covered agreements'.
>
> . . .
>
> Like the sanitary measure in *EC – Hormones*, the EC Regulation is currently in force. The European Communities has conceded that the EC Regulation is an act or fact that has not 'ceased to exist'. Accordingly, following our reasoning in *EC – Hormones*, Article 2.4 of the *TBT Agreement* applies to existing measures unless that provision 'reveals a contrary intention'. As we have said, we see nothing in Article 2.4 which would suggest that the provision does not apply to existing measures.[12]

11.11 In *EC and certain member States – Large Civil Aircraft*, the Appellate Body considered the principle of non-retroactivity in Article 28 in the context of interpreting Article 5 of the SCM Agreement. The Appellate Body began by recalling that it 'has previously confirmed that the principle of non-retroactivity under Article 28 of the *Vienna Convention* is a general principle of law, which is relevant to the interpretation of the WTO covered agreements'.[13] The Appellate Body then explained that:

> As a general proposition, a treaty does not apply to acts or facts that took place, or situations that ceased to exist, before the date of its entry into force. As we have noted above, in order to determine the temporal scope of Article 5 of the *SCM Agreement*, regard must be had to the *text of the treaty at issue* and, importantly, to the subject-matter of the treaty in question and to the nature of the *treaty obligations* undertaken. We therefore disagree with the European Union to the extent that it suggests that it is the pre-1995 *measures* that are to be interpreted consistently with the principle of non-retroactivity reflected in Article 28 of the *Vienna Convention*. Rather, as the Panel found, it is, as set out in Article 5, the causing through the use of any subsidy of adverse effects to the interests of other Members that is the subject of that provision. Thus, even assuming that the European Union was correct in its assertion that the pre-1995 *measures* challenged by the United States could be properly characterized as 'completed acts', this would not mean that such measures are precluded from challenge under Article 5 of the *SCM Agreement*, as the European Union suggests.[14]
>
> . . .
>
> In practice, it is often difficult to distinguish between, on the one hand, an act or fact that was 'completed' before the entry into force of the new treaty and, on

---

[12] Appellate Body Report, *EC – Sardines*, paras. 200, 207 (citing Appellate Body Report, *Brazil – Desiccated Coconut*, p. 15; Appellate Body Report, *Canada – Periodicals*, paras. 71–2; Appellate Body Report, *EC – Hormones*, para. 128).

[13] Appellate Body Report, *EC and certain member States – Large Civil Aircraft*, para. 672 (citing Appellate Body Report, *EC – Sardines*, para. 200).

[14] Appellate Body Report, *EC and certain member States – Large Civil Aircraft*, para. 675.

the other hand, an act, fact, or situation that 'continues' or has 'continuing effect'. In order to draw the line between these concepts, we turn to the text of Article 28 of the *Vienna Convention*.

Article 28 refers to 'acts or facts which took place', as well as to 'situations which ceased to exist'. The Appellate Body has previously described the word 'act' within the meaning of Article 28 as 'something that is "done"'. In assessing the temporal scope of a treaty provision that is directed at 'acts' or 'facts', the relevant question is whether the act or fact 'occurred' or 'took place' prior to the entry into force of the treaty. By contrast, with regard to treaty provisions that are directed at a 'situation', Article 28 does not ask whether the 'situation' 'took place', but rather whether it 'ceased to exist' prior to the entry into force of the treaty. As the Appellate Body found in *Canada – Patent Term*, the use of the word 'situation' in Article 28 'suggests something that subsists and continues over time'. The reference to 'ceased to exist' supports the notion that a 'situation' may continue to exist over a period of time, rather than simply occur at a particular instant in time, after which the 'situation' may 'cease to exist'.

In response to questioning at the oral hearing, the participants agreed that, as a general proposition, there is a certain degree of overlap between the concepts of 'act', 'fact', and 'situation'. To us, it would appear that almost any 'situation' can be said to have arisen from one or more past 'acts' or 'facts', including ones that have been 'completed'. Moreover, it would seem that a 'situation' may consist of more than a distinct set of repeated acts, such as the use of subsidies under a scheme.[15]

The Appellate Body then explained that:

[W]e agree with the Panel that Article 5 addresses a 'situation' that consists of causing, through the use of any subsidy, adverse effects to the interests of another Member. It is this 'situation', which is subject to the requirements of Article 5 of the *SCM Agreement*, that is to be construed consistently with the non-retroactivity principle reflected in Article 28 of the *Vienna Convention*. The relevant question for purposes of determining the temporal scope of Article 5 is whether the causing of adverse effects has 'ceased to exist' or continues as a 'situation'. We consequently disagree with the European Union that, by virtue of Article 28 of the *Vienna Convention*, no obligation arising out of Article 5 of the *SCM Agreement* is to be imposed on a Member in respect of subsidies granted or brought into existence prior to the entry into force of the *SCM Agreement*. This may mean that a subsidy granted prior to 1 January 1995 falls within the scope of Article 5 of the *SCM Agreement*, but this is only because of its possible nexus to the continuing situation of causing, through the use of this subsidy, adverse effects to which Article 5 applies. In reaching this conclusion, we are *not* saying that the causing of adverse effects, through the use of pre-1995 subsidies, can necessarily be characterized as a 'continuing' situation in this case. Rather, we simply find that a challenge to pre-1995 subsidies is not *precluded* under the terms of the *SCM Agreement*.[16]

---

[15] *Ibid.*, paras. 677–9 (citing Appellate Body Report, *Canada – Patent Term*, paras. 58, 72; P. Reuter, *Introduction to the Law of Treaties* (Kegan Paul International, 1995), p. 100).

[16] Appellate Body Report, *EC and certain member States – Large Civil Aircraft*, paras. 686 (citing Sir Humphrey Waldock, Special Rapporteur, Sixth Report on the Law of Treaties, UN Doc. A/CN.4/186 and Add.1–7, *Yearbook of the International Law Commission* (1966), Vol. II, p. 63).

11.3   Non-retroactive consequences of treaty termination

11.12 Article 70(1)(b) of the Vienna Convention, entitled 'Consequences of the termination of a treaty', provides that unless the treaty otherwise provides or the parties otherwise agree, the termination of a treaty 'does not affect any right, obligation or legal situation of the parties created through the execution of the treaty prior to its termination'. This principle, i.e. that the termination of a treaty does not have retroactive consequences, has been expressly referred to and applied in one case.

11.13 In *Brazil – Aircraft (Article 22.6 – Brazil)*, Canada and Brazil entered into a bilateral agreement regarding recourse to Articles 21 and 22 of the DSU and Article 4 of the SCM Agreement, which extended the deadline, set forth in Article 22.6 of the DSU, for Canada to request authorization from the WTO to retaliate against Brazil's non-compliance with the original rulings. Brazil subsequently declared that it had terminated the bilateral agreement because of a material breach by Canada, and referred to Article 60 of the Vienna Convention. Brazil stated that, pursuant to Article 22.6 of the DSU, the Arbitrators should determine that the proposed countermeasures were not permitted under the SCM Agreement on the ground that the time within which they may be authorized had expired. The Arbitrators stated:

> We note that Article 60 of the Vienna Convention provides for the 'termination' of a treaty by one party in response to a 'material breach' by the other party. Article 70 of the Vienna Convention nevertheless provides that the termination of a treaty does not affect any right, obligation or legal situation of the parties created through the execution of the treaty prior to its termination. We conclude that, even assuming that the Bilateral Agreement has been terminated by Brazil on 14 July 2000, the request by Canada under Article 4.10 of the SCM Agreement, to the extent it was made in accordance with the terms of the Bilateral Agreement, remains unaffected by the termination. We therefore do not find it necessary to address further this question.[17]

11.4   Other inter-temporal principles of international law

11.14 While most issues relating to non-retroactivity and the temporal scope of WTO obligations have been resolved on the basis of Article 28 of the Vienna Convention, in one case reference was also made to two other closely related principles of international law: (i) the *Island of Palmas Arbitration* principle; and (ii) the inter-temporal principle codified in Article 14 of the ILC Articles on State

---

[17] Decision by the Arbitrators, *Brazil – Aircraft (Article 22.6 – Brazil)*, para. 3.10.

Responsibility, which is entitled 'Extension in time of the breach of an international obligation' and reads as follows:

1. The breach of an international obligation by an act of a State not having a continuing character occurs at the moment when the act is performed, even if its effects continue.
2. The breach of an international obligation by an act of a State having a continuing character extends over the entire period during which the act continues and remains not in conformity with the international obligation.
3. The breach of an international obligation requiring a State to prevent a given event occurs when the event occurs and extends over the entire period during which the event continues and remains not in conformity with that obligation.

In *EC and certain member States – Large Civil Aircraft*, the Panel considered **11.15** Article 28 of the Vienna Convention in the context of interpreting Article 5 of the SCM Agreement. In the course of its analysis, the Panel also addressed the European Communities' separate argument that, pursuant to the 'inter-temporal rules of international law', certain older measures could not be assessed for compliance with the SCM Agreement, but should instead be measured against the standards that were contained in the Tokyo Round Subsidies Code, which was the international legal framework in force when the challenged measures were taken. The Panel stated:

> As we understand it, the doctrine of inter-temporal application of international law, as it was pronounced in the *Island of Palmas Arbitration*, has two elements: first, that acts should be judged in the light of the law contemporary with their creation; and second, that rights acquired in a valid manner according to the law contemporaneous with their creation may be lost if not maintained in accordance with changes in international law. Although doubts have been expressed about the status of the second element as a principle of international law, the first element, which is the foundation of the European Communities' argument, appears to have obtained wide acceptance. However, in the circumstances of the present case, we find the European Communities' reliance on this aspect of the doctrine to be misguided.
>
> We recall that in our preliminary ruling, we concluded that Article 5 of the SCM Agreement establishes an obligation on Members not to cause adverse effects to the interests of other Members through the use of subsidies. In doing so, we dismissed the European Communities' contention that Article 5 does not apply to subsidies granted prior to 1 January 1995. In this light, the European Communities' reliance on the doctrine is misconceived. The very fact that Article 5 addresses adverse effects caused by the use of subsidies, which may have been granted prior to 1 January 1995, means that such measures must necessarily fall within the scope of the SCM Agreement and therefore be assessed on the basis of the rules of that agreement. In other words, because Article 5 of the SCM Agreement applies to pre-1995 subsidies that cause adverse effects after entry into force of the WTO Agreement, the doctrine of inter-temporal

application of international law cannot operate to preclude the application of the SCM Agreement to such subsidies.[18]

11.16 In *EC and certain member States – Large Civil Aircraft*, the Appellate Body also rejected the European Union's argument based on 'the rules on inter-temporal application of international law', and framed the issue in terms of Article 28 of the Vienna Convention:

> As we see it, the European Union's argument is based on the assumption that subsidies that were granted or brought into existence before 1 January 1995 amount to completed 'acts' or 'situations' and, thus, are outside the temporal scope of application of the *SCM Agreement*. We have disagreed with that proposition above, and do not consider our approach to lead to a retroactive application of Article 5 of the *SCM Agreement*. As the ILC has explained, '[t]he non-retroactivity principle cannot be infringed by applying a treaty to matters that occur or exist when the treaty is in force, *even if they first began at an earlier date*'.[19]

In *EC and certain member States – Large Civil Aircraft*, the Appellate Body considered Article 28 of the Vienna Convention in the context of interpreting the effects-based disciplines in Article 5 of the SCM Agreement, but in response to certain EC arguments referred to Article 14 of the ILC Articles on State Responsibility:

> As we have noted above, Article 5 of the *SCM Agreement* sets out an obligation not to cause, through the use of any subsidy, adverse effects to the interests of other Members. It is the 'causing' of such effects that is relevant for purposes of Article 5, and the conclusion as to retroactivity will hinge on whether that situation continues or has been completed, rather than on when the act of granting a subsidy occurred.
>
> Article 14(1) of the ILC Articles stipulates that '[t]he breach of an international obligation by an act of a State not having a continuing character occurs at the moment when the act is performed, even if its effects continue.' In other words, Article 14(1) distinguishes between *acts* and the *effects* of such acts. Referring to the ILC's Commentary on this provision, the European Union observes that '[a] completed act occurs "at the moment when the act is performed", even though its effects or consequences may continue.' We agree

---

[18] Panel Report, *EC and certain member States – Large Civil Aircraft*, paras. 7.322–7.323 (citing the *Island of Palmas* arbitration, 2 RIAA (1928) 829, 845; the *Grisbadarna* case, 11 RIAA 155 (1909); the *North Atlantic Coast Fisheries* case, 11 RIAA 167 (1910); the *Fisheries Case (United Kingdom v. Norway)*, 1951 ICJ Reports, p. 116; the *Minquiers and Ecrehos* case, 1953 ICJ Reports, p. 47; and the *Aegean Sea Continental Shelf* case, 1978 ICJ Reports, p. 3; A. D'Amato, 'International Law, Intertemporal Problems', in *Encyclopaedia of Public International Law*, 1992, pp. 1234–6, at p. 1235; P. C. Jessup, 'The Palmas Island Arbitration' (1928) 22 *American Journal of International Law* 735–52, at 740; T. O. Elias, 'The Doctrine of Intertemporal Law' (1980) 74 *American Journal of International Law* 285–307; I. Brownlie, *Principles of Public International Law*, 5th edn (Clarendon Press, 1998), pp. 126–8).

[19] Appellate Body Report, *EC and certain member States – Large Civil Aircraft*, paras. 689 (citing *Yearbook of the International Law Commission* (1966), Vol. II, p. 212, para. 3).

with the European Union that it is important to distinguish between an act and its effects. Article 5 of the *SCM Agreement* is concerned, however, with a 'situation' that continues over time, rather than with specific 'acts'. Thus, although the act of granting a subsidy may have been completed prior to 1 January 1995, the situation of causing adverse effects may continue.[20]

---

[20] Appellate Body Report, *EC and certain member States – Large Civil Aircraft*, paras. 684–5.

12

REASONABLENESS

12.1 Introduction

The concept of reasonableness is 'present in many of international law's primary **12.1** rules, across a wide range of subject areas', including international human rights law, the law of the sea, and international environmental law.[1] In the *Barcelona Traction Case*, the ICJ held that 'it is necessary that the law be applied reasonably' in the field of diplomatic protection 'as in all other fields of international law'.[2] The term 'reasonable' appears more than 200 times in the WTO agreements, and there are more than 8,000 references to this term (and its variants) in WTO decisions. This chapter reviews WTO jurisprudence relating to the three different aspects of reasonableness as a legal standard: (i) the meaning of the term 'reasonable' in various provisions of the WTO agreements; (ii) reasonableness as an unwritten legal test in different contexts; and (iii) reasonableness in treaty interpretation.

12.2 The meaning of the term 'reasonable'

12.2.1 Reasonable administration of laws

WTO panels and the Appellate Body have been called upon to interpret and **12.2** apply the term 'reasonable' in the context of Article X:3(a) of the GATT, which

---

[1] O. Corten, 'Reasonableness in International Law' (May 2006) in *Max Planck Encyclopedia of Public International Law*, para. 3; A. Adinolfi, 'The Principle of Reasonableness in EU Law', in G. Bongiovanni, G. Sartor and V. C. Giovanni (eds.), *Reasonableness and Law* (Springer: 2009), pp. 383–403; J. Salmon, 'Le concept de raisonnable en droit international public', in D. Bardonnet (ed.), *Mélanges Paul Reuter* (Pedone, 1981), pp. 447–78; I. Gallala, 'La notion de caution raisonnable dans la jurisprudence du tribunal international du droit de la mer' (2001) 105 *Revue générale de droit international public* 931–68; and C. B. Andersen, 'Reasonable Time in Article 39(1) of the CISG – Is Article 39(1) Truly a Uniform Provision?' (1998), available at http://cisgw3.law.pace.edu/cisg/biblio/andersen.html.
[2] 1970 ICJ Reports, p. 48, para. 93.

provides that WTO Members 'shall administer in a uniform, impartial and reasonable manner all its laws, regulations, decisions and rulings'.

12.3 In *US – COOL*, a dispute involving a claim under Article X:3(a), the Panel stated:

> The term 'reasonable' is defined as 'in accordance with reason', 'not irrational or absurd', 'proportionate', 'sensible', and 'within the limits of reason, not greatly less or more than might be thought likely or appropriate'. We assess the parties' claims of not reasonable administration in light of these definitions.
>
> In our view, whether an act of administration can be considered reasonable within the meaning of Article X:3(a) entails a consideration of factual circumstances specific to each case. This is confirmed by previous disputes where the requirement of reasonable administration was understood as requiring the examination of the features of the administrative act at issue in the light of its objective, cause or the rationale behind it.[1080]

[1080] In *Argentina – Hides and Leather*, for example, the panel considered access to confidential information by a competitor in the market to be a relevant factor in determining reasonableness of the administrative action in that dispute (para. 11.86). We further recall the Appellate Body's analysis in *Brazil – Retreaded Tyres* that 'the analysis of whether the application of a measure results in arbitrary or unjustifiable discrimination should focus on the cause of the discrimination, or the rationale put forward to explain its existence' (Appellate Body Report, *Brazil – Retreaded Tyres*, para. 226; Panel Report, *Thailand – Cigarettes*, para. 7.291). In *Thailand – Cigarettes (Philippines)*, the Philippines claimed that the appointment of dual function officials as directors of a company under administrative proceedings constituted unreasonable administration because the officials were in a position where they could gather and reveal confidential information on Philippines industries' direct competitors. The panel found that Thailand did not act inconsistently with Article X:3(a). However, the overall delays in the administrative proceedings shown throughout the course of the review process of customs valuation were considered by the panel '*not* appropriate or proportionate' considered against the nature of the circumstances concerned, and therefore, the administration was considered to be 'unreasonable' (Panel Report, *Thailand – Cigarettes*, para. 7.969). In *Dominican Republic – Import and Sale of Cigarettes*, the Panel found that the Dominican Republic had administered the provisions governing the Selective Consumption Tax in a manner that was 'unreasonable' and therefore inconsistent with Article X:3(a) of GATT 1994 (paras. 7.365–7.394).[3]

12.2.2 Reasonable period of time

12.4 WTO adjudicators have been called upon to interpret and apply the term 'reasonable' in the context of provisions referring to a 'reasonable period of

---

[3] Panel Report, *Thailand – Cigarettes (Philippines)*, paras. 7.850–7.851.

time', including Article 6.8 of the Anti-Dumping Agreement, Article 21.3 of the DSU and Article 5.7 of the SPS Agreement.

In *US – Hot-Rolled Steel*, the Appellate Body interpreted the terms 'reasonable **12.5** period' and 'reasonable time'. Article 6.8 of the Anti-Dumping Agreement provides that, if any interested party refuses access to necessary information 'within a reasonable period' in an anti-dumping investigation, the determination may be made on the basis of the facts available. Annex II:1 to the Anti-Dumping Agreement provides in relevant part that the authorities should ensure that interested parties are aware that, if information is not supplied 'within a reasonable time', the authorities will be free to make determinations on the basis of the facts available. The Appellate Body stated:

> The word 'reasonable' implies a degree of flexibility that involves consideration of all of the circumstances of a particular case. What is 'reasonable' in one set of circumstances may prove to be less than 'reasonable' in different circumstances. This suggests that what constitutes a reasonable period or a reasonable time, under Article 6.8 and Annex II of the *Anti-Dumping Agreement*, should be defined on a case-by-case basis, in the light of the specific circumstances of each investigation.
>
> In sum, a 'reasonable period' must be interpreted consistently with the notions of flexibility and balance that are inherent in the concept of 'reasonableness', and in a manner that allows for account to be taken of the particular circumstances of each case. In considering whether information is submitted within a reasonable period of time, investigating authorities should consider, in the context of a particular case, factors such as: (i) the nature and quantity of the information submitted; (ii) the difficulties encountered by an investigated exporter in obtaining the information; (iii) the verifiability of the information and the ease with which it can be used by the investigating authorities in making their determination; (iv) whether other interested parties are likely to be prejudiced if the information is used; (v) whether acceptance of the information would compromise the ability of the investigating authorities to conduct the investigation expeditiously; and (vi) the numbers of days by which the investigated exporter missed the applicable time-limit.[4]

Article 21 of the DSU provides that a WTO Member has a 'reasonable period of **12.6** time' to comply in the event of an adverse dispute settlement ruling. In *US – Hot-Rolled Steel (Article 21.3(c))*, the Arbitrator considered that the essence of 'reasonableness' as articulated by the Appellate Body in *US – Hot-Rolled Steel* in the context of Article 6.8 of the Anti-Dumping Agreement (see above) is 'equally pertinent for an arbitrator faced with the task of determining what constitutes "a reasonable period of time" in the context of the DSU'.[5] Along the same lines, the Arbitrator in *US – Offset Act (Byrd Amendment) (Article 21.3(c))* stated:

---

[4] Appellate Body Report, *US – Hot-Rolled Steel*, paras. 85–6.
[5] Award of the Arbitrator, *US – Hot-Rolled Steel (Article 21.3(c))*, para. 26.

The final sentence of Article 21.3(c), moreover, makes clear that the 'reasonable period of time' cannot be determined in the abstract, but rather has to be established on the basis of the particular circumstances of each case. I therefore agree, in principle, with the Arbitrator in *US – Hot-Rolled Steel*, who found that the term 'reasonable' should be interpreted as including 'the notions of flexibility and balance', in a manner which allows for account to be taken of the particular circumstances of each case.[6]

12.7 In *Japan – Agricultural Products II*, the Appellate Body considered the phrase 'reasonable period of time' in the context of Article 5.7 of the SPS Agreement, which provides that, where relevant scientific evidence is insufficient, a Member may provisionally adopt sanitary or phytosanitary measures on the basis of available pertinent information; the provision goes on to state that, in such circumstances, Members shall seek to obtain the additional information necessary for a more objective assessment of risk, and review the SPS measure accordingly 'within a reasonable period of time'. The Appellate Body stated:

> In our view, what constitutes a 'reasonable period of time' has to be established on a case-by-case basis and depends on the specific circumstances of each case, including the difficulty of obtaining the additional information necessary for the review *and* the characteristics of the provisional SPS measure. In the present case, the Panel found that collecting the necessary additional information would be relatively easy. Although the obligation 'to review' the varietal testing requirement has only been in existence since 1 January 1995, we agree with the Panel that Japan has not reviewed its varietal testing requirement 'within a reasonable period of time'.[7]

12.2.3 Reasonable terms and conditions

12.8 In *Mexico – Telecoms*, the Panel interpreted paragraph 5(a) of the GATS Annex on Telecommunications, which provides in relevant part that each Member shall ensure that any service supplier of any other Member is accorded access to and use of public telecommunications transport networks and services 'on reasonable and non-discriminatory terms and conditions' for the supply of a service included in its Schedule. The Panel stated:

> The dictionary meaning of the word 'reasonable' means 'being in accordance with reason', 'not extreme or excessive'. The word 'reasonable' implies a degree of flexibility that involves consideration of the circumstances of a particular case. What is 'reasonable' in one set of circumstances may prove to be less than 'reasonable' in different circumstances. The elements of 'balance' and

---

[6] Award of the Arbitrator, *US – Offset Act (Byrd Amendment) (Article 21.3(c))*, para. 42.
[7] Appellate Body Report, *Japan – Agricultural Products II*, para. 93.

'flexibility', as well as the need for a 'case-by-case analysis', are inherent in the notion of 'reasonable'.[1029]

[1029] The Appellate Body in *US – Hot-Rolled Steel*, paragraphs 84–85, stated that '[i]n sum, a "reasonable period" must be interpreted consistently with the notions of flexibility and balance that are inherent in the concept of "reasonableness", and in a manner that allows for account to be taken of the particular circumstances of each case'. Although the Appellate Body was interpreting a 'reasonable' period of time in the context of a different WTO Agreement, we consider that the same basic elements of the word 'reasonable' also apply in the present context.[8]

12.3 Reasonableness as an unwritten legal test

WTO panels and the Appellate Body have sometimes applied reasonableness **12.9** tests in the absence of any express reference to the term in the provision at issue, including: (i) sometimes applying 'reasonableness relationship' tests when applying provisions that envisage a connection between two things; (ii) developing the concept of 'reasonable expectations' in the context of examining 'non-violation' claims under Article 26 of the DSU and Article XXIII:1(b) of the GATT; and (iii) reasonableness as a standard of review.

12.3.1 Reasonable relationship tests

When interpreting provisions that envisage a relationship between two things **12.10** (for example, a provision requiring that A be 'based on' B, that A be 'related to' B, or that A be 'for the purpose' of B), WTO adjudicators have sometimes applied a 'rational relationship' test as the relevant legal standard.

In *EC – Hormones*, the Appellate Body examined Article 5.1 of the SPS **12.11** Agreement, which provides that Members shall ensure that their sanitary or phytosanitary measures are 'based on' a risk assessment. The Appellate Body stated that this requires a 'rational relationship' (using 'rational relationship' interchangeably with 'reasonable relationship').[9] In the course of its analysis, the Appellate Body stated:

> We believe that Article 5.1, when contextually read as it should be, in conjunction with and as informed by Article 2.2 of the *SPS Agreement*, requires that the results of the risk assessment must sufficiently warrant – that is to say, reasonably support – the SPS measure at stake. The requirement that an SPS measure be 'based on' a risk assessment is a substantive requirement that there be a rational relationship between the measure and the risk assessment.[10]

---

[8] Panel Report, *Mexico – Telecoms*, para. 7.328 (citing the Merriam Webster Online Dictionary).
[9] See e.g. Appellate Body Report, *EC – Hormones*, paras. 193–4.   [10] *Ibid.*, para. 193.

12.12 In *Thailand – Cigarettes (Philippines)*, the Appellate Body interpreted the phrase 'action relating to customs matters' in the context of Article X:3(b) of the GATT. Recalling its prior interpretation of the terms 'relating to' in the context of Article XX(g) of the GATT,[11] the Appellate Body explained:

> Turning to the term 'relating to', we note that 'relate to' is defined, *inter alia*, as '[h]ave some connection with, be connected to'. The Panel also referred to the Appellate Body's interpretation of the term 'related to' in the context of Article XX of the GATT 1994, where the Appellate Body found that for a measure to be 'related to' a particular objective, there must be a rational relationship between the measure and the objective pursued. For such a rational relationship to exist, the measure must not be disproportionately wide in its scope and reach in relation to its objective. Similarly, in the context of Article X:3(b), we consider that measures must have a rational connection with customs matters to fall within the scope of that provision.[12]

12.13 In *Canada – Renewable Energy/Feed-In Tariff Program*, the Appellate Body examined Article III:8(b) of the GATT, which provides that the non-discrimination obligation in Article III does not apply to laws, regulations or requirements governing the procurement by governmental agencies of products purchased 'for governmental purposes'. In the context of interpreting the phrase 'for governmental purposes', the Appellate Body stated:

> Finally, we recall that Article III:8(a) refers to purchases '*for* governmental purposes'. The word 'for' relates the term 'products purchased' to 'governmental purposes', and thus indicates that the products purchased must be intended to be directed at the government or be used for governmental purposes. Thus, Article III:8(a) requires that there be a rational relationship between the product and the governmental function being discharged.[13]

12.3.2 Reasonable expectations

12.14 The concept of 'reasonable expectations' was developed by GATT panels in the context of adjudicating non-violation complaints under Article XXIII:1(b) of the GATT. The concept of 'reasonable expectations' has subsequently been applied by WTO panels and the Appellate Body notwithstanding the absence of any textual reference to 'reasonable expectations' in Article XXIII:1(b) of the GATT or in Article 26 of the DSU.[14]

---

[11] See also Section 16.7.3 ('"Affecting", "based on", "governing", "relating to"') for additional WTO jurisprudence on the words 'relating to'.

[12] Appellate Body Report, *Thailand – Cigarettes (Philippines)*, para. 194 (citing Appellate Body Report, *US – Shrimp*, para. 141).

[13] Appellate Body Report, *Canada – Renewable Energy/Feed-In Tariff Program*, para. 5.68.

[14] Article XXIII:3 of the GATS codifies this concept, providing that '[i]f any Member considers that any benefit it could reasonably have expected to accrue to it under a specific commitment of another Member under Part III of this Agreement is being nullified or impaired as a result of the

In this regard, the Panel in *Japan – Film* observed that '[t]he text of Article **12.15**
XXIII:1(b) simply refers to "a benefit accruing, directly or indirectly, under this
Agreement" and does not further define or explain what benefits are referred to.
Past GATT panel reports have considered that such benefits include those that a
Member reasonably expects to obtain from a tariff negotiation.'[15] The Panel
observed that 'the issue of reasonable anticipation needs to be addressed on a
case-by-case basis'.[16]

The subsequent Panel in *Korea – Procurement* recalled the elements of the text of **12.16**
Article XXIII:1(b), and then stated that '[t]o this we would add the notion that
has been developed in all these cases that the nullification or impairment of the
benefit as a result of the measure must be contrary to the reasonable expectations
of the complaining party at the time of the agreement'.[17]

12.3.3 Reasonableness as a standard of review

In the context of reviewing factual findings by investigating authorities in anti- **12.17**
dumping and countervailing duty determinations, panels and the Appellate
Body have sometimes formulated the applicable standard of review in terms of
reasonableness.

In *EC – Tube or Pipe Fittings*, which involved factual findings by national **12.18**
investigating authorities in an anti-dumping investigation, the Panel stated that
'[a] reasonable and objective authority could have reached this determination on
the basis of the record of this investigation. It is not our task to substitute our
judgement for that of the investigating authority.'[18]

With respect to the applicable standard of review to apply to factual findings **12.19**
by national investigating authorities in a countervailing duty case, the Panel in
EC – Countervailing Measures on DRAM Chips stated along the same lines that:

> We are, therefore, fully conscious of the fact that it is not the role of the Panel to
> perform a *de novo* review of the evidence which was before the investigating
> authority at the time it made its determination. We will, therefore, examine
> whether on the basis of the record before it, a reasonable and objective investi-
> gating authority could have reached the conclusions the EC investigating
> authority reached with regard to the determination of subsidization and
> injury.[19]

---

application of any measure which does not conflict with the provisions of this Agreement, it may
have recourse to the DSU'.
[15] Panel Report, *Japan – Film*, para. 10.72.   [16] *Ibid.*, para. 10.79.
[17] Panel Report, *Korea – Procurement*, para. 7.85.
[18] Panel Report, *EC – Tube or Pipe Fittings*, para. 7.296.
[19] Panel Report, *EC – Countervailing Measures on DRAM Chips*, para. 7.6.

12.20 In *US – Softwood Lumber VI (Article 21.5 – Canada)*, the Appellate Body found that the Panel had applied an excessively deferential and passive standard of review when examining the factual findings of the investigating authority. The Panel repeatedly characterized various findings of the investigating authority as 'not unreasonable'. In the course of its analysis, the Appellate Body stated:

> [A]lthough we consider that a panel would be acting consistently with the applicable standard of review if it sets out to determine whether an objective and unbiased authority could reasonably find that a particular piece of evidence supports an intermediate factual finding, we are not persuaded that this is the same as the Panel's version of this standard, which appears simply to involve testing whether the USITC's conclusions were 'not unreasonable'. In our view, the Panel's repeated references to the USITC's conclusions as 'not unreasonable' suggest that the Panel applied an insufficient degree of scrutiny to the Section 129 Determination and failed to engage in the type of critical and searching analysis called for by Article 11 of the DSU.[20]

12.21 In *EC – Asbestos*, the Panel considered a different type of factual question, namely, whether certain products posed a risk to human health. In that context, the Panel relied on the standard of what a decision-maker for taking public health measures might reasonably conclude:

> The Panel therefore considers that the evidence before it tends to show that handling chrysotile-cement products constitutes a risk to health rather than the opposite. Accordingly, a decision-maker responsible for taking public health measures might reasonably conclude that the presence of chrysotile-cement products posed a risk because of the risks involved in working with those products.[21]

12.22 The Appellate Body is sometimes presented with claims that a panel failed to make an 'objective assessment of the facts' as required by Article 11 of the DSU. In dealing with such claims, the Appellate Body has sometimes examined the issue in terms of whether a panel's factual finding was 'unreasonable'.

12.23 For example, in *Mexico – Anti-Dumping Measures on Rice*, the Appellate Body stated that 'it appears to us that it was not unreasonable for the Panel to conclude that the criterion of positive evidence set out in Article 3.1 of the *Anti-Dumping Agreement* was not met'.[22]

12.24 In *US – Upland Cotton*, the Appellate Body stated that '[i]t was not unreasonable' for the Panel to conclude that the effect of the price-contingent subsidies

---

[20] Appellate Body Report, *US – Softwood Lumber VI (Article 21.5 – Canada)*, para. 113.
[21] Panel Report, *EC – Asbestos*, para. 8.193.
[22] Appellate Body Report, *Mexico – Anti-Dumping Measures on Rice*, para. 168.

was significant price suppression, even if some other factor might also have price-suppressive effects.[23]

When reviewing the manner in which a panel deals with an issue that is not **12.25** explicitly regulated by the DSU (or by a panel's *ad hoc* working procedures), the Appellate Body has sometimes applied a reasonableness test.

In *EC – Hormones*, the Panel decided to hold a joint meeting with the scientific **12.26** experts for the two parallel panel proceedings initiated by Canada and the United States against the European Communities. The alternative would have been to hold two separate meetings. After reviewing the Panel's reasoning underlying this decision, the Appellate Body concluded that 'the explanation of the Panel [was] quite reasonable'.[24]

In *US – Offset Act (Byrd Amendment)*, another dispute involving multiple **12.27** complainants, the United States requested, at a late stage of the proceeding, that the Panel issue separate panel reports in respect of each complaining party. The Appellate Body found that the Panel acted within its discretion by denying the US request. In this connection, the Appellate Body stated that '[w]e do not believe that we should lightly disturb panels' decisions on their procedure, particularly in cases such as the one at hand, in which the Panel's decision appears to have been reasonable and in accordance with due process'.[25]

In some cases, the Appellate Body has applied a reasonableness standard when **12.28** presented with procedural issues that are not explicitly regulated by its own working procedures. For example, in *EC – Sardines*, the European Communities conditionally withdrew its notice of appeal, and then re-filed an amended notice of appeal. At the time, the Appellate Body's working procedures did not explicitly regulate such a situation (they were subsequently revised to regulate this situation). After reviewing the circumstances under which the European Communities withdrew its notice of appeal subject to the condition of filing a replacement notice of appeal, the Appellate Body concluded that '[i]n our view, attaching the condition to the withdrawal was not unreasonable under the circumstances'.[26]

12.4   Reasonableness in treaty interpretation[*]

WTO adjudicators have rejected interpretations resulting in consequences **12.29** labelled 'unreasonable' or 'absurd'. WTO adjudicators have also used a variety

---

[23] Appellate Body Report, *US – Upland Cotton*, para. 455.
[24] Appellate Body Report, *EC – Hormones*, para. 152.
[25] Appellate Body Report, *US – Offset Act (Byrd Amendment)*, paras. 315–16.
[26] Appellate Body Report, *EC – Sardines*, para. 144.
[*] See also the cases in Section 8.3 ('Good faith in the performance and interpretation of treaties'), especially Section 8.3.1. ('Reasonableness and *abus de droit*').

of other labels when characterizing unacceptable consequences, including 'anomalous', 'bizarre', 'contradictory', 'curious', 'extreme', 'far-reaching', 'illogical', 'impractical', 'inconceivable', 'incongruous', 'irrational', 'ludicrous', 'nonsensical', 'obviously wrong', 'ominous', 'outlandish', 'surprising', 'unacceptable' and 'unworkable'. Two categories of results that WTO adjudicators have frequently regarded as unreasonable are irrational distinctions and inverted outcomes.

12.4.1 Irrational distinctions

12.30 There have been many cases in which an interpretation has been rejected on the grounds that it would lead to a distinction in the treatment of two things that are materially the same.

12.31 In *Korea – Alcoholic Beverages*, the Panel quoted prior jurisprudence stating that the obligation in the first sentence of Article III:2 of the GATT protects expectations on the competitive relationship between imported and domestic products, and noted:

> We do not consider it a meaningful distinction on this issue that this quote refers to the first sentence of Article III:2 rather than the second sentence. To find otherwise would be to imply that one could refer to expectations with respect to determining the market conditions for examining like products but not for examining whether products are directly competitive or substitutable. Given that like products are a subset of directly competitive or substitutable products, this would be illogical.[27]

12.32 In *Canada – Dairy (Article 21.5 – New Zealand and US II)*, the Appellate Body reasoned that the provision at issue should be interpreted in a manner that avoided what was, in its view, an 'incongruous' distinction:

> [I]t would be incongruous if the costs of family labour and management were excluded from the [cost of production] standard when provided by family, but included when provided by others. Likewise, it would be curious if the cost of capital, of which equity is one type, were excluded from the [cost of production] standard when capital is provided through the owner's equity, but included when it is provided through, for instance, debt, merely because the cost of debt is expressed in recurring cash outlays for interest payments. In each case, the dairy enterprise is incurring an economic cost and that cost should be appropriately reflected in the costs of production.[28]

12.33 The Panel in *US – Gambling* examined a claim under Article XVI:2(a) of the GATS, which prohibits limitations on the number of service suppliers whether

---

[27] Panel Report, *Korea – Alcoholic Beverages*, footnote 364.
[28] Appellate Body Report, *Canada – Dairy (Article 21.5 – New Zealand and US II)*, para. 105.

in the form of numerical quotas, monopolies, exclusive service suppliers or certain other requirements. The Panel reasoned that:

> [A] measure that is not expressed in the form of a numerical quota or economic needs test may still fall within the scope of Article XVI:2(a). To hold that only restrictions explicitly couched in numerical terms fall within Article XVI:2(a) would produce absurd results. It would, for example, allow a law that explicitly provides that 'all foreign services are prohibited' to escape the application of Article XVI, because it is not expressed in numerical terms.[29]

12.4.2 Inverted outcomes

There have been many cases in which an interpretation has been rejected **12.34** on the grounds that it would result in an inverted or upside down outcome, i.e. acts or omissions deserving better treatment receiving worse treatment and *vice versa*.

In *US – Shrimp*, the Appellate Body referred to Article X of the GATT in **12.35** the context of analysing whether the measure at issue was applied in a manner that constituted 'arbitrary or unjustifiable' discrimination under Article XX of the GATT. Article X establishes certain transparency and due process obligations for trade regulations. In the course of its analysis the Appellate Body stated:

> [T]he provisions of Article X:3 of the GATT 1994 bear upon this matter . . . Inasmuch there are due process requirements generally for measures that are otherwise imposed in compliance with WTO obligations, it is only reasonable that rigorous compliance with the fundamental requirements of due process should be required in the application and administration of a measure which purports to be an exception to the treaty obligations of the member imposing the measure and which effectively results in a suspension *pro hac vice* of the treaty rights of other members.[30]

The Panel in *Australia – Salmon (Article 21.5 – Canada)* considered that a **12.36** narrow interpretation of the terms 'measures taken to comply' in Article 21.5 of the DSU could lead to an upside down result:

> The question of whether a measure is one in the direction of WTO conformity or, on the contrary, maintains the original violation or aggravates it, can, in our view, not determine whether a measure is one 'taken to comply'. If this were so, one would be faced with an absurd situation: if the implementing Member introduces a 'better' measure – in the direction of WTO conformity – it would be subject to an expedited Article 21.5 procedure; if it introduces a 'worse'

---

[29] Panel Report, *US – Gambling*, para. 6.332.
[30] Appellate Body Report, *US – Shrimp*, para. 182.

measure – maintaining or aggravating the violation – it would have a right to a completely new WTO procedure.[31]

12.37 In *Mexico – Olive Oil*, the Panel rejected the European Communities' argument that the definition of 'domestic industry' in Article 16.1 of the SCM Agreement requires an enterprise to be producing actual output of the like product at the time of application and/or during the period of investigation, in order to be considered producers for the purpose of that provision. After referring to the ordinary meaning of the term and various contextual arguments, the Panel rejected this interpretation to avoid an inverted outcome:

> Most importantly, in our view, the European Communities' interpretation could lead to the result that an industry may be so badly injured by subsidized imports as to be forced to cease production for some period, but would be disqualified from obtaining the very remedy aimed at addressing such injury. We believe that this outcome would be absurd and contrary to the intention of the drafters of the *SCM Agreement*.[32]

---

[31] Panel Report, *Australia – Salmon (Article 21.5 – Canada)*, para. 7.10.
[32] Panel Report, *Mexico – Olive Oil*, para. 7.203.

13

SOURCES OF INTERNATIONAL LAW

13.1 Introduction

International law treatises typically devote a chapter to the 'sources of inter- **13.1**
national law',[1] and it has been said that '[f]ew provisions of treaty law, if any,
have called for as many comments, debates, criticisms, praises, warnings,
passions, as Art. 38 of the Statute'.[2] Article 38(1) of the ICJ Statute reads:

> The Court, whose function is to decide in accordance with international law
> such disputes as are submitted to it, shall apply:
>
> a. international conventions, whether general or particular, establishing rules
>   expressly recognized by the contesting states;
> b. international custom, as evidence of a general practice accepted as law;
> c. the general principles of law recognized by civilized nations;
> d. subject to the provisions of Article 59, judicial decisions and the teachings of
>   the most highly qualified publicists of the various nations, as subsidiary
>   means for the determination of rules of law.

In the process of discharging their function of clarifying the provisions of the
WTO agreements, WTO adjudicators have offered useful statements on all
of the different sources of international law. This chapter reviews WTO pronouncements of wider applicability relating to: (i) Article 38(1) generally; (ii)
customary international law; (iii) general principles of law; (iv) judicial decisions;
and (v) the teachings of publicists.

---

[1] For example, I. Brownlie and J. Crawford, *Brownlie's Principles of Public International Law*, 8th
edn (Oxford University Press, 2012), Chapter 2 ('The Sources of International Law'); M. N.
Shaw, *International Law*, 6th edn (Cambridge University Press, 2008), Chapter 3 ('Sources').

[2] A. Pellet, 'Article 38', in A. Zimmermann, K. Oellers-Frahm, C. Tomuschat and C. J. Tams (eds.),
The Statute of the International Court of Justice: A Commentary, 2nd edn (Oxford University Press,
2012), pp. 731–870, at p. 733.

13.2 Article 38(1) of the ICJ Statute

13.2 WTO panels and the Appellate Body have relied on Article 38(1) of the ICJ Statute as a general and authoritative definition of the accepted sources of international law.

13.3 In *EC – Approval and Marketing of Biotech Products*, the Panel stated that the reference to 'rules of international law' in the context of Article 31(3)(c) of the Vienna Convention seems sufficiently broad to encompass 'all generally accepted sources of public international law'. The Panel did not make express reference to Article 38(1), but the 'generally accepted sources of public international law' that the Panel identified corresponded to those set out therein:

> In considering the provisions of Article 31(3)(c), we note, initially, that it refers to 'rules of international law'. Textually, this reference seems sufficiently broad to encompass all generally accepted sources of public international law, that is to say, (i) international conventions (treaties), (ii) international custom (customary international law), and (iii) the recognized general principles of law.[3]

13.4 In *US – Anti-Dumping and Countervailing Duties (China)* (DS379), the Appellate Body stated, along the same lines, that the reference to 'rules of international law' in Article 31(3)(c) of the Vienna Convention 'corresponds to the sources of international law in Article 38(1) of the Statute of the International Court of Justice and thus includes customary rules of international law as well as general principles of law'.[4]

13.3 Customary international law

13.5 In a number of decisions, panels and the Appellate Body have linked the concept of 'customary international law' to 'general international law'. Panels and the Appellate Body have referred to different types of evidence for the purpose of assessing whether a norm is established as customary international law, including the views of the PCIJ/ICJ, other international courts and tribunals, the ILC, commentators, and statements made by a disputing party on previous occasions and/or in the context of the proceeding in question. In several cases, panels and the Appellate Body have considered it unnecessary to resolve definitely whether a particular norm had attained the status of customary international law. Panels and the Appellate Body have stated that treaty provisions normally prevail over

---

[3] Panel Report, *EC – Approval and Marketing of Biotech Products*, para. 7.67.

[4] Appellate Body Report, *US – Anti-Dumping and Countervailing Duties (China)*, para. 309 (citing M. E. Villiger, 'Commentary on the 1969 Vienna Convention on the Law of Treaties' (Martinus Nijhoff, 2009), p. 433).

norms of customary international law, but that, to the extent there is no conflict or inconsistency, treaty provisions must be read against the background of customary international law.

13.3.1 The concept(s) of 'general' and 'customary' international law

In its first decision, *US – Gasoline*, the Appellate Body stated that the general **13.6** rule of interpretation contained in Article 31 of the Vienna Convention had attained the status of 'customary or general international law'.[5]

In *US – Line Pipe*, the Appellate Body appeared to use the two terms inter- **13.7** changeably when it said:

> We note as well the customary international law rules on state responsibility, to which we also referred in *US – Cotton Yarn*. We recalled there that the rules of general international law on state responsibility require that countermeasures in response to breaches by States of their international obligations be proportionate to such breaches.[6]

In *EC – Hormones*, the Appellate Body equated 'general' international law with **13.8** 'customary' international law, which it then contrasted with what it termed 'customary international environmental law'.[7] The Appellate Body stated:

> The status of the precautionary principle in international law continues to be the subject of debate among academics, law practitioners, regulators and judges. The precautionary principle is regarded by some as having crystallized into a general principle of customary international *environmental* law. Whether it has been widely accepted by Members as a principle of *general* or *customary international law* appears less than clear. We consider, however, that it is unnecessary, and probably imprudent, for the Appellate Body in this appeal to take a position on this important, but abstract, question. We note that the Panel itself did not make any definitive finding with regard to the status of the precautionary principle in international law and that the precautionary principle, at least outside the field of international environmental law, still awaits authoritative formulation.[8]

13.3.2 Establishing customary/general international law

Article 3.2 of the DSU states that the WTO dispute settlement system serves to **13.9** clarify the existing provisions of those agreements 'in accordance with customary rules of interpretation of public international law'. The WTO Appellate Body has confirmed that Articles 31, 32 and 33 of the Vienna Convention are all rules of 'customary international law', based on the jurisprudence of international

---

[5] Appellate Body Report, *US – Gasoline*, p. 17.
[6] Appellate Body Report, *US – Line Pipe*, paras. 257, 259.
[7] Appellate Body Report, *EC – Hormones*, para. 124.   [8] *Ibid.*, para. 124.

courts and tribunals and secondary sources. In *US – Gasoline*, the Appellate Body stated that the general rule of interpretation contained in Article 31 of the Vienna Convention had attained the status of 'customary or general international law', and gave the following sources:

> See, e.g. *Territorial Dispute Case (Libyan Arab Jamahiriya* v. *Chad)*, (1994), ICJ Reports p. 6 (International Court of Justice); *Golder* v. *United Kingdom*, ECHR, Series A, (1995) no. 18 (European Court of Human Rights); *Restrictions to the Death Penalty Cases*, (1986) 70 International Law Reports 449 (Inter-American Court of Human Rights); Jiménez de Aréchaga, 'International Law in the Past Third of a Century' (1978-I) 159 Recueil des Cours 1, p. 42; D. Carreau, Droit International (3è ed., 1991), p. 140; Oppenheim's International Law (9th edn, Jennings and Watts, eds. 1992) Vol. 1, pp. 1271–1275.[9]

13.10 In *Japan – Alcoholic Beverages II*, the Appellate Body confirmed that Article 32 of the Vienna Convention has also attained the status of a rule of 'customary or general international law', and gave the following sources:

> See e.g.: Jiménez de Aréchaga, 'International Law in the Past Third of a Century' (1978-I) 159 Recueil des Cours p. 1 at 42; *Territorial Dispute (Libyan Arab Jamahiriya/Chad), Judgment*, (1994), ICJ Reports, p. 6 at 20; *Maritime Delimitation and Territorial Questions between Qatar and Bahrain, Jurisdiction and Admissibility, Judgment*, (1995), ICJ Reports, p. 6 at 18; *Interpretation of the Convention of 1919 Concerning Employment of Women during the Night* (1932), PCIJ, Series A/B, No. 50, p. 365 at 380; cf. the *Serbian and Brazilian Loans Cases* (1929), PCIJ, Series A, Nos. 20–21, p. 5 at 30; *Constitution of the Maritime Safety Committee of the IMCO* (1960), ICJ Reports, p. 150 at 161; *Air Transport Services Agreement Arbitration (United States of America* v. *France)* (1963), International Law Reports, 38, p. 182 at 235–43.[10]

13.11 In *US – Offset Act (Byrd Amendment)*, the Appellate Body examined Article 26 of the Vienna Convention, which several complainants had referred to in their submissions. The Appellate Body noted that the United States 'said, in response to questioning at the oral hearing, that it has no difficulty with the notion that Article 26 of the *Vienna Convention* expresses a customary international law principle'.[11]

13.12 In *US – Line Pipe*, the Appellate Body stated that Article 51 of the ILC Articles on State Responsibility sets out a 'recognized principle of customary international law', and referred in this regard to decisions by international courts and tribunals, and a disputing party's prior statements recognizing the same:

> Article 51 of the International Law Commission's Draft Articles on Responsibility of States for Internationally Wrongful Acts provides that 'countermeasures

---

[9] Appellate Body Report, *US – Gasoline*, footnote 34.
[10] Appellate Body Report, *Japan – Alcoholic Beverages II*, footnote 17.
[11] Appellate Body Report, *US – Offset Act (Byrd Amendment)*, footnote 247.

must be commensurate with the injury suffered, taking into account the gravity of the internationally wrongful act and the rights in question'. Although Article 51 is part of the International Law Commission's Draft Articles, which do not constitute a binding legal instrument as such, this provision sets out a recognized principle of customary international law.[256] We observe also that the United States has acknowledged this principle elsewhere. In its comments on the International Law Commission's Draft Articles, the United States stated that 'under customary international law a rule of proportionality applies to the exercise of countermeasures'.[257]

---

[256] See, *Case Concerning Military and Paramilitary Activities in and against Nicaragua* (Nicaragua v. United States of America), Merits, Judgment of 27 June 1986, (1986) ICJ Rep., p. 14, at p. 127, para. 249; and, *Case Concerning the Gabcikovo-Nagymaros Project* (Hungary v. Slovakia), (1997) ICJ Rep., p. 7, at p. 220.

[257] See, *Draft Articles on State Responsibility: Comments of the Government of the United States of America*, dated 22 October 1997, in response to the United Nations Secretary General's request of 12 February 1997 for comments and observations on the draft articles on State responsibility adopted provisionally on first reading by the International Law Commission, reprinted in, M. Nash, 'Contemporary Practice of the United States Relating to International Law', *American Journal of International Law*, Vol. 92, No. 2 (1998), p. 251, at pp. 252 and 254.

The United States has also acknowledged this principle before the Arbitral Tribunal established by the Compromis of 11 July 1978 in the *Case Concerning the Air Services Agreement of 27 March 1946 (United States vs. France)*. See, *Reply of the United States to the Memorial Submitted by France*, excerpted in M. Nash, *Digest of United States Practice in International Law 1978* (Office of the Legal Adviser, Department of State, 1980), at p. 776.[12]

In *Korea – Procurement*, the Panel considered the concept of error in treaty **13.13** formation under Article 48 of the Vienna Convention, which it considered to be customary international law based on the fact that it was 'derived largely from case law of the relevant jurisdiction, the PCIJ and the ICJ'. The Panel stated:

Error in respect of a treaty is a concept that has developed in customary international law through the case law of the Permanent International Court of Justice[764] and of the International Court of Justice.[765] Although these cases are concerned primarily with the question in which circumstances of error *cannot* be advanced as a reason for invalidating a treaty, it is implicitly accepted that error can be a ground for invalidating (part) of a treaty. The elements developed by the case law mentioned above have been codified by the International Law Commission in what became the *Vienna Convention on the Law of Treaties of 1969*. The relevant parts of Article 48 of the Convention read as follows . . .

---

[12] Appellate Body Report, *US – Line Pipe*, para. 259.

Since this article has been derived largely from case law of the relevant
jurisdiction, the PCIJ and the ICJ, there can be little doubt that it presently
represents customary international law and we will apply it to the facts of
this case.

---

[764] *Legal Status of Eastern Greenland* (1933) PCIJ, series A/B, No. 53, p. 22,
at p. 71 and dissenting opinion of Judge Anzilotti, at pp. 91–92.
[765] Case concerning the *Temple of Preah Vihear*, ICJ Reports 1962, p. 6, at
pp. 26–27.[13]

13.14 As noted at paragraph 13.8 above, in *EC – Hormones* the Appellate Body
considered it unnecessary to rule on whether the precautionary principle has
become a principle of customary international law. In that context, the Appellate
Body referred to the works of several authors:

> Authors like P. Sands, J. Cameron and J. Abouchar, while recognizing that the
> principle is still evolving, submit nevertheless that there is currently sufficient state
> practice to support the view that the precautionary principle is a principle of
> customary international law. See, for example, P. Sands, *Principles of International
> Environmental Law*, Vol. I (Manchester University Press 1995), p. 212;
> J. Cameron, 'The Status of the Precautionary Principle in International Law', in
> J. Cameron and T. O'Riordan (eds.), *Interpreting the Precautionary Principle*
> (Cameron May, 1994) 262, p. 283; J. Cameron and J. Abouchar, 'The Status
> of the Precautionary Principle in International Law', in D. Freestone and E. Hey
> (eds.), *The Precautionary Principle in International Law* (Kluwer, 1996) 29, p. 52.
> Other authors argue that the precautionary principle has not yet reached the status
> of a principle of international law, or at least, consider such status doubtful,
> among other reasons, due to the fact that the principle is still subject to a great
> variety of interpretations. See, for example, P. Birnie and A. Boyle, *International
> Law and the Environment* (Clarendon Press, 1992), p. 98; L. Gündling, 'The
> Status in International Law of the Precautionary Principle' (1990), 5:1,2,3
> *International Journal of Estuarine and Coastal Law* 25, p. 30; A. de Mestral
> (et al.), *International Law Chiefly as Interpreted and Applied in Canada*, 5th edn
> (Emond Montgomery, 1993), p. 765; D. Bodansky, in *Proceedings of the 85th
> Annual Meeting of the American Society of International Law* (ASIL, 1991),
> p. 415.[14]

With respect to its statement that the precautionary principle still awaits
'authoritative formulation', at least outside the field of international environmental law, the Appellate Body referred to an ICJ decision:

> In *Case Concerning the Gabcíkovo-Nagymaros Project (Hungary/Slovakia)*, the
> International Court of Justice recognized that in the field of environmental
> protection '... new norms and standards have been developed, set forth in a great
> number of instruments during the last two decades. Such new norms have to be
> taken into consideration, and such new standards given proper weight ...'.

---

[13] Panel Report, *Korea – Procurement*, para. 7.123.
[14] Appellate Body Report, *EC – Hormones*, footnote 92.

However, we note that the Court did not identify the precautionary principle as one of those recently developed norms. It also declined to declare that such principle could override the obligations of the Treaty between Czechoslovakia and Hungary of 16 September 1977 concerning the construction and operation of the Gabcíkovo/Nagymaros System of Locks. See, *Case Concerning the Gabcíkovo-Nagymaros Project (Hungary/Slovakia)*, ICJ Judgement, 25 September 1997, paras. 140, 111–114. Not yet reported in the ICJ Reports but available on Internet at http://www.icj-cij.org/idecis.htm.[15]

The Panel in *EC – Approval and Marketing of Biotech Products* declined to uphold the European Communities' contention that the precautionary principle has 'by now become a fully fledged and general principle of international law', and opted to refrain from expressing any view on the issue. With reference to the Appellate Body's statement that the precautionary principle still awaits 'authoritative formulation', the Panel observed: **13.15**

> The Appellate Body made this statement in January 1998. It appears to us from the Parties' arguments and other available materials that the legal debate over whether the precautionary principle constitutes a recognized principle of general or customary international law is still ongoing. Notably, there has, to date, been no authoritative decision by an international court or tribunal which recognizes the precautionary principle as a principle of general or customary international law. It is correct that provisions explicitly or implicitly applying the precautionary principle have been incorporated into numerous international conventions and declarations, although, for the most part, they are environmental conventions and declarations. Also, the principle has been referred to and applied by States at the domestic level, again mostly in domestic environmental law. On the other hand, there remain questions regarding the precise definition and content of the precautionary principle. Finally, regarding doctrine, we note that many authors have expressed the view that the precautionary principle exists as a general principle in international law. At the same time, as already noted by the Appellate Body, others have expressed scepticism and consider that the precautionary principle has not yet attained the status of a general principle in international law.
>
> Since the legal status of the precautionary principle remains unsettled, like the Appellate Body before us, we consider that prudence suggests that we not attempt to resolve this complex issue, particularly if it is not necessary to do so. Our analysis below makes clear that for the purposes of disposing of the legal claims before us, we need not take a position on whether or not the precautionary principle is a recognized principle of general or customary international law. Therefore, we refrain from expressing a view on this issue.[16]

In a different section of its analysis, the Panel in *EC – Approval and Marketing of Biotech Products* recalled several ways in which a sovereign State can decide not to **13.16**

---

[15] Appellate Body Report, *EC – Hormones*, footnote 93.
[16] Panel Report, *EC – Approval and Marketing of Biotech Products*, paras. 7.88–7.89.

'accept' other rules of international law, as regards both treaties and customary international law. The Panel then noted:

> It is useful to recall that there are several ways in which a sovereign State can decide not to accept other rules of international law. Thus, in the case of other rules of international law embodied in a treaty, a State may have decided not to participate in the negotiation of the treaty; it may have decided not to sign the final text of the treaty in question; or the legislature of a State may have decided not to ratify the treaty after it had been signed by its executive branch. There are also cases of ratifications with objections/exceptions. In the case of customary rules of international law, a State may have persistently objected to such a rule during its formation.[17]

13.17 In *US – Anti-Dumping and Countervailing Duties (China)* (DS379), the Appellate Body concluded that 'it is not necessary for us to resolve definitively the question of to what extent Article 5 of the ILC Articles reflects customary international law'.[18]

13.3.3 The relationship between treaties and customary international law

13.18 In *EC – Hormones*, the Appellate Body concluded that, while it was not necessary to definitively rule on whether the precautionary principle had attained the status of customary international law, the Panel was correct in finding that it 'does not override the provisions of Articles 5.1 and 5.2 of the *SPS Agreement*'. The Panel had concluded:

> To the extent that this principle could be considered as part of customary international law ... we consider that this principle would not override the explicit wording of Articles 5.1 and 5.2 outlined above, in particular since the precautionary principle has been incorporated and given a specific meaning in Article 5.7 of the SPS Agreement.[19]

13.19 The Panel in *US – 1916 Act* stated:

> It is well established under general international law that treaty provisions normally prevail over norms of customary international law.[546]

---

[546] See, e.g. ICJ judgement *Military and Paramilitary Activities in and against Nicaragua* (Nicaragua v. United States of America), ICJ Reports 1986, p. 137, which stated at paragraph 274 that:

> 'In general, treaty rules being *lex specialis*, it would not be appropriate that a State should bring a claim based on a customary-law rule if it has by treaty already provided means for settlement of such a claim'.[20]

---

[17] *Ibid.*, footnote 248.
[18] Appellate Body Report, *US – Anti-Dumping and Countervailing Duties (China)*, para. 311.
[19] Panel Report, *EC – Hormones (US)*, para. 8.157.
[20] Panel Report, *US – 1916 Act (Japan)*, para. 6.189.

The Panel in *Korea – Procurement* stated that customary rules of international **13.20** law apply to the WTO treaties. The Panel stated:

> We take note that Article 3.2 of the DSU requires that we seek within the context of a particular dispute to clarify the existing provisions of the WTO agreements in accordance with customary rules of interpretation of public international law. However, the relationship of the WTO Agreements to customary international law is broader than this. Customary international law applies generally to the economic relations between the WTO Members. Such international law applies to the extent that the WTO treaty agreements do not 'contract out' from it. To put it another way, to the extent there is no conflict or inconsistency, or an expression in a covered WTO agreement that implies differently, we are of the view that the customary rules of international law apply to the WTO treaties and to the process of treaty formation under the WTO.[21]

The Panel in *US – Certain EC Products* stated, in the context of addressing issues **13.21** relating to countermeasures and reprisals, that 'in the WTO context, the provision of Article 60 of the Vienna Convention on the Law of Treaties (1969) on this matter does not apply since the adoption of the more specific provisions of Article 23 of the DSU'.[22]

In *US – Upland Cotton (Article 22.6 – US I)*, the Arbitrators relied on the ILC **13.22** Articles on State Responsiblity to inform their understanding of the meaning of 'countermeasures' as used in the SCM Agreement, but noted:

> We also note however that, by their own terms, the Articles of the ILC on State Responsibility do not purport to prevail over any specific provisions relating to the areas it covers that would be contained in specific legal Instruments. We note in particular the following Commentary of the ILC:
>
>> In common with other chapters of these articles, the provisions on countermeasures are residual and may be excluded or modified by a special rule to the contrary (see article 55). Thus, a treaty provision precluding the suspension of performance of an obligation under any circumstances will exclude countermeasures with respect to the performance of the obligation. Likewise, a regime for dispute resolution to which States must resort in the event of a dispute, especially if (as with the WTO dispute settlement system) it requires an authorization to take measures in the nature of countermeasures in response to a proven breach.[23]

In *US – Anti-Dumping and Countervailing Duties (China)* (DS379), the Appel- **13.23** late Body disagreed with the Panel's statement that the ILC Articles on State Responsibility would be 'superseded' by Article 1.1(a)(1) of the SCM Agreement

---

[21] Panel Report, *Korea – Procurement*, para. 7.96.
[22] Panel Report, *US – Certain EC Products*, footnote 170.
[23] Decision by the Arbitrators, *US – Upland Cotton (Article 22.6 – US I)*, footnote 129.

as a consequence of Article 55 of the ILC Articles. The Appellate Body drew a distinction between reference to other rules of international law to interpret a provision versus the direct application of those other rules:

> As we see it, Article 55 of the ILC Articles does not speak to the question of whether, for the purpose of interpreting Article 1.1(a)(1) of the *SCM Agreement*, a panel or the Appellate Body can take into account provisions of the ILC Articles. Article 55 stipulates that '[t]hese articles do not apply where . . .'. Article 55 addresses the question of which rule to *apply* where there are multiple rules addressing the same subject-matter. The question in the present case, however, is not whether certain of the ILC Articles are to be *applied*, that is, whether attribution of conduct of the SOEs and SOCBs at issue to the Government of China is to be assessed pursuant to the ILC Articles instead of Article 1.1(a)(1) of the *SCM Agreement*. There is no doubt that the provision being applied in the present case is Article 1.1(a)(1). Rather, the question is, whether, when interpreting the terms of Article 1.1(a)(1), the relevant provisions of the ILC Articles may be taken into account as one among several interpretative elements. Thus, the treaty being *applied* is the *SCM Agreement*, and the attribution rules of the ILC Articles are to be *taken into account* in interpreting the meaning of the terms of that treaty. Article 55 of the ILC Articles does not speak to the issue of how the latter should be done.[24]

13.4   General principles of law

13.24 Panels and the Appellate Body have referred to 'general principles of law' and also, more frequently, to 'general principles of international law'. Express references to 'general principles of law' within the meaning of Article 38(1)(c) of the ICJ Statute are scarce in WTO jurisprudence, but a prominent example relates to the allocation of the burden of proof. There are a number of references to 'general principles of international law' in WTO jurisprudence.

13.4.1 'General principles of law'

13.25 In *US – Wool Shirts and Blouses*, the Appellate Body held that the burden of proof rests upon the party, whether complaining or defending, who asserts the affirmative of a particular claim or defence. In a frequently cited passage, the Appellate Body referred to 'generally accepted canon[s] of evidence in civil law, common law and, in fact, most jurisdictions':

> [W]e find it difficult, indeed, to see how any system of judicial settlement could work if it incorporated the proposition that the mere assertion of a claim might

---

[24] Appellate Body Report, *US – Anti-Dumping and Countervailing Duties (China)*, para. 316.

amount to proof. It is, thus, hardly surprising that various international tribunals, including the International Court of Justice, have generally and consistently accepted and applied the rule that the party who asserts a fact, whether the claimant or the respondent, is responsible for providing proof thereof.[15] Also, it is a generally accepted canon of evidence in civil law, common law and, in fact, most jurisdictions, that the burden of proof rests upon the party, whether complaining or defending, who asserts the affirmative of a particular claim or defence. If that party adduces evidence sufficient to raise a presumption that what is claimed is true, the burden then shifts to the other party, who will fail unless it adduces sufficient evidence to rebut the presumption.[16]

---

[15] M. Kazazi, Burden of Proof and Related Issues: A Study on Evidence Before International Tribunals (Kluwer Law International, 1996), p. 117.

[16] See M. N. Howard, P. Crane and D. A. Hochberg, *Phipson on Evidence*, 14th edn (Sweet & Maxwell, 1990), p. 52: 'The burden of proof rests upon the party, whether plaintiff or defendant, who substantially asserts the affirmative of the issue.' See also L. Rutherford and S. Bone (eds.), *Osborne's Concise Law Dictionary*, 8th edn (Sweet & Maxwell, 1993), p. 266; Earl Jowitt and C. Walsh, *Jowitt's Dictionary of English Law*, 2nd edn by J. Burke (Sweet & Maxwell, 1977), Vol. 1, p. 263; L. B. Curzon, *A Directory of Law*, 2nd edn (Macdonald and Evans, 1983), p. 47; Art. 9, Nouveau Code de Procédure Civile; J. Carbonnier, *Droit Civil*, Introduction, 20th edn (Presses Universitaires de France, 1991), p. 320; J. Chevalier and L. Bach, *Droit Civil*, 12th edn (Sirey, 1995), Vol. 1, p. 101; R. Guillien and J. Vincent, *Termes juridiques*, 10th edn (Dalloz, 1995), p. 384; O. Samyn, P. Simonetta and C. Sogno, *Dictionnaire des Termes Juridiques* (Editions de Vecchi, 1986), p. 250; J. González Pérez, *Manual de Derecho Procesal Administrativo*, 2nd edn (Editorial Civitas, 1992), p. 311; C. M. Bianca, S. Patti and G. Patti, *Lessico di Diritto Civile* (Giuffré Editore, 1991), p. 550; F. Galgano, *Diritto Privato*, 8th edn (Casa Editrice Dott. Antonio Milani, 1994), p. 873; and A. Trabucchi, *Istituzioni di Diritto Civile* (Casa Editrice Dott. Antonio Milani, 1991), p. 210.[25]

In *Dominican Republic – Safeguard Measures*, the Panel understood that the Appellate Body's ruling in *US – Wool Shirts and Blouses* as involving the 'application of ... general principles of law'.[26] **13.26**

In *EC – Hormones*, the Appellate Body referred to 'what in many jurisdictions' is known as due process of law or natural justice.[27] **13.27**

The Panel in *EC – Tariff Preferences* addressed the issue of the joint representation of a party and a third party by the same legal counsel. In the context of **13.28**

---

[25] Appellate Body Report, *US – Wool Shirts and Blouses*, p. 14.
[26] Panel Report, *Dominican Republic – Safeguard Measures*, para. 7.16.
[27] Appellate Body Report, *EC – Hormones*, para. 133.

exercising this 'inherent authority' to manage the proceeding 'in a manner guaranteeing due process'[28] to all parties involved, the Panel in *EC – Tariff Preferences* then took into account rules of conduct elaborated by bar associations in many jurisdictions, and discerned a principle common to all such ethical rules. Without referring expressly to a 'general principle of law', the Panel stated:

> As a general matter, the Panel considers that it is the responsibility of legal counsel to ensure that it is not placing itself in a position of actual or potential conflict of interest when agreeing to represent, and thereafter representing, one or more WTO Members in a dispute under the DSU. In this regard, the Panel notes that bar associations in many jurisdictions have elaborated rules of conduct dealing explicitly with conflicts of interest through joint representation.[250]
>
> ───────────
> [250] See, e.g. American Bar Association, Model Rules of Professional Conduct, Rule 1.7; State Bar of California, Rules of Conduct, Rule 3-310; New York State Bar Association, Lawyer's Code of Professional Responsibility, DR 5-105; Canadian Bar Association, Code of Professional Conduct, Chapter V; Law Society of Upper Canada, Rule of Professional Conduct, Rule 2.04; Council of the Bars and Law Societies of the European Union, Code of Conduct for Lawyers in the European Union, Rule 3.2; Barreau de Paris, Règles professionnelles, Article 155; Bar of England and Wales, Code of Conduct, Rules 603 and 608.
>
> Common to all such ethical rules of conduct is the principle that counsel shall not accept or continue representation of more than one client in a matter in which the interests of the clients actually or potentially conflict.[29]

13.4.2 'General principles of international law'

13.29 In *US – Shrimp*, the Appellate Body stated that the principle of good faith is 'at once a general principle of law and a general principle of international law'.[30] In *US – Shrimp*, the Appellate Body further stated that 'our task here is to interpret the language of the chapeau [of Article XX of the GATT], seeking additional interpretative guidance, as appropriate, from the general principles of international law'.[31]

13.30 The Panel in *India – Autos* referred to 'widely recognized principles of international law', in the context of observing that 'it is certainly true that certain widely recognized principles of international law have been found to be applicable in WTO dispute settlement, particularly concerning fundamental procedural matters'.[32]

───────────

[28] Panel Report, *EC – Tariff Preferences*, para. 7.8. [29] *Ibid.*, paras. 7.9–7.10.
[30] Appellate Body Report, *US – Shrimp*, para. 158. [31] *Ibid.*, para. 158 and footnote 157.
[32] Panel Report, *India – Autos*, para. 7.57.

The Panel in *Guatemala – Cement II* rejected the defence of 'harmless error', **13.31**
finding among other things that the concept of 'harmless error' as presented
by Guatemala had not attained the status of a 'general principle of public
international law'.[33]

In *Thailand – Cigarettes (Philippines)*, the Panel observed that 'the Appellate **13.32**
Body has extensively relied on general principles of international law to interpret
member's obligations'.[34]

In *EC – Approval and Marketing of Biotech Products*, the Panel commented as **13.33**
follows on the meaning of the expression 'general principle of international law':

> We note that this term may be understood as encompassing either rules of
> customary law or the recognized general principles of law or both. Given this, we
> are prepared to consider whether the precautionary principle fits within either of
> these categories.[35]

13.5   Judicial decisions

WTO jurisprudence relating to the precedential effect[36] of international judicial **13.34**
decisions can be divided into three categories: (i) precedents of other international courts and tribunals on general international law concepts and principles; (ii) precedents by the same body on questions of treaty interpretation; and
(iii) *res judicata*. As to the first category, there are numerous examples of panels
and the Appellate Body taking into account the 'prevailing practice' of other
international courts and tribunals in respect of certain issues related to international dispute settlement, including PCIJ/ICJ jurisprudence and a wide range
of decisions by other international courts and tribunals. As to the second
category, the Appellate Body and several panels have applied the principle that,
absent cogent reasons, WTO panels are expected to follow prior legal interpretations developed by the Appellate Body. As to the third category, issues relating
to *res judicata* have been raised in a number of different cases, mostly in the
context of compliance proceedings under Article 21.5 of the DSU; without
necessarily using the term '*res judicata*', panels and the Appellate Body have held,
in that context, that a disputing party (either complainant or respondent) is

---

[33] Panel Report, *Guatemala – Cement II*, para. 8.22.
[34] Panel Report, *Thailand – Cigarettes (Philippines)*, footnote 1760.
[35] Panel Report, *EC – Approval and Marketing of Biotech Products*, para. 7.86 (citing I. Brownlie, *Principles of Public International Law*, 5th edn (Clarendon Press, 1998), pp. 18–19).
[36] The expression 'precedential effect' is used here in the broadest sense. For example, *res judicata* precludes judging the same matter between the same parties again, and therefore relates more to the admissibility of a claim (see Chapter 1) than to the precedential effect of the prior decision.

precluded from re-litigating the same claims, issues or defences that had already been ruled on by the panel and/or Appellate Body in the original proceeding.

13.5.1 Precedents of other international tribunals on general issues

13.35 In *EC – Bananas III*, Saint Lucia requested that the Appellate Body permit its non-governmental legal advisers to participate in the oral hearing. Saint Lucia submitted that, as a matter of customary international law, no international organization has the right to interfere with a government's sovereign right to decide whom it may accredit as officials and members of its delegation. The Appellate Body agreed, and referred to 'the prevailing practice of international tribunals' in this regard:

> [W]e can find nothing in the Marrakesh Agreement Establishing the World Trade Organization (the 'WTO Agreement'), the DSU or the Working Procedures, nor in customary international law or the prevailing practice of international tribunals, which prevents a WTO Member from determining the composition of its delegation in Appellate Body proceedings.[37]

13.36 In *Argentina – Poultry Anti-Dumping Duties*, Brazil challenged an Argentine anti-dumping measure before a MERCOSUR Tribunal and then initiated WTO dispute settlement proceedings against the same measure. Argentina argued that the Panel should be bound by this ruling, but the Panel noted that Argentina had 'made it clear that it was not invoking the principle of *res judicata*'.[38] In the course of its analysis, the Panel stated:

> We note that we are not even bound to follow rulings contained in adopted WTO panel reports, so we see no reason at all why we should be bound by the rulings of non-WTO dispute settlement bodies.[39]

13.37 In *EC – Approval and Marketing of Biotech Products*, the European Communities argued that it is a legal principle recognized in jurisdictions around the world, and commonly applied by international tribunals including the ICJ, that a tribunal should not rule on a measure no longer in existence. The Panel responded:

> We would agree with the European Communities that it may be appropriate for panels to look to the practice of international tribunals for inspiration, particularly in situations where the WTO agreements, GATT/WTO jurisprudence or practice provide no useful guidance. But we do not find ourselves in a situation of this kind. As is clear from the above remarks, there is specific GATT/WTO

---

[37] Appellate Body Report, *EC – Bananas III*, para. 10.
[38] Panel Report, *Argentina – Poultry Anti-Dumping Duties*, footnote 53.
[39] *Ibid.*, para. 7.41 (citing Appellate Body Report, *Japan – Alcoholic Beverages II*, p. 14).

jurisprudence and practice to guide us. In these circumstances, we see no need to draw on the jurisprudence of the International Court of Justice.[40]

In *US – 1916 Act*, the Panel recalled that an earlier Appellate Body report had **13.38** considered whether certain judgments of the International Court of Justice 'establish[ed] a general rule that in all international litigation, a complaining party must have a legal interest in order to bring a case'. This led the Panel in *US – 1916 Act* to state:

> We assume from that report that if the judgements of the International Court of Justice had established a general rule on demonstration of legal interest, and the terms of the WTO Agreement did not prevent its application to dispute settlement, the Appellate Body would have applied that principle.[41]

Elsewhere in its decision, the Panel in *US – 1916 Act* observed that the DSU does not expressly provide guidance on how panels should interpret domestic legislation, and stated that 'both Article 3.2 of the DSU and the practice of the Appellate Body make it clear that we should, whenever appropriate, take into consideration the practice of international tribunals in this respect'.[42]

In *China – Rare Earths*, the Panel considered the meaning of 'even-handedness' **13.39** in the context of an earlier statement by the Appellate Body that Article XX(g) of the GATT, in requiring that trade-restrictive measures be made effective in conjunction with domestic restrictions, is essentially a requirement of 'even-handedness'. In the course of its analysis, the Panel stated:

> The Panel has sought to illuminate its understanding of the principle of even-handedness by reference to different sources of international law. The only explicit reference to the even handedness principle is available in international investment law. The Panel does observe however that in substance, its own understanding of even-handedness or fairness is not essentially different from that of other international tribunals ... The Panel has not relied on these sources to clarify the meaning of even-handedness, because they do not add any further clarification to the existing jurisprudence on Article XX(g).[43]

13.5.2 Precedents by the same body on questions of treaty interpretation

In *Japan – Alcoholic Beverages II*, the Appellate Body clarified that adopted **13.40** GATT/WTO panel reports 'are not binding, except with respect to resolving the particular dispute between the parties to that dispute'. The Appellate Body then noted that:

---

[40] Panel Report, *EC – Approval and Marketing of Biotech Products*, para. 7.1663.
[41] Panel Report, *US – 1916 Act (Japan)*, para. 5.8.   [42] *Ibid.*, para. 6.36.
[43] Panel Report, *China – Rare Earths*, para. 7.322.

It is worth noting that the Statute of the International Court of Justice has an explicit provision, Article 59, to the same effect. This has not inhibited the development by that Court (and its predecessor) of a body of case law in which considerable reliance on the value of previous decisions is readily discernible.[44]

13.41 In *US – Stainless Steel (Mexico)*, the Appellate Body explained that, absent cogent reasons, an adjudicatory body should resolve the same legal question in the same way in a subsequent case. Recalling its prior jurisprudence and various international legal materials, the Appellate Body stated:

> It is well settled that Appellate Body reports are not binding, except with respect to resolving the particular dispute between the parties. This, however, does not mean that subsequent panels are free to disregard the legal interpretations and the *ratio decidendi* contained in previous Appellate Body reports that have been adopted by the DSB. In *Japan – Alcoholic Beverages II*, the Appellate Body found that:
>
>> [a]dopted panel reports are an important part of the GATT *acquis*. They are often considered by subsequent panels. They create legitimate expectations among WTO Members, and, therefore, should be taken into account where they are relevant to any dispute.
>
> In *US – Shrimp (Article 21.5 – Malaysia)*, the Appellate Body clarified that this reasoning applies to adopted Appellate Body reports as well. In *US – Oil Country Tubular Goods Sunset Reviews*, the Appellate Body held that 'following the Appellate Body's conclusions in earlier disputes is not only appropriate, but is what would be expected from panels, especially where the issues are the same.'
>
> Dispute settlement practice demonstrates that WTO Members attach significance to reasoning provided in previous panel and Appellate Body reports. Adopted panel and Appellate Body reports are often cited by parties in support of legal arguments in dispute settlement proceedings, and are relied upon by panels and the Appellate Body in subsequent disputes. In addition, when enacting or modifying laws and national regulations pertaining to international trade matters, WTO Members take into account the legal interpretation of the covered agreements developed in adopted panel and Appellate Body reports. Thus, the legal interpretation embodied in adopted panel and Appellate Body reports becomes part and parcel of the *acquis* of the WTO dispute settlement system. Ensuring 'security and predictability' in the dispute settlement system, as contemplated in Article 3.2 of the DSU, implies that, absent cogent reasons, an adjudicatory body will resolve the same legal question in the same way in a subsequent case.[313]

---

[313] See H. Lauterpacht, 'The so-called Anglo-American and Continental Schools of Thought in International Law' (1931) 12 *British Yearbook of International Law* 53, who points out that adherence to legal decisions 'is imperative if the law is to fulfil one of its primary functions, i.e. the maintenance of security and stability'. Consistency of jurisprudence is valued

[44] Appellate Body Report, *Japan – Alcoholic Beverages II*, footnote 30.

also in dispute settlement in other international fora. In this respect we note the Decision of the International Criminal Tribunal for the Former Yugoslavia, Case No. IT-95-14/1-A, *Prosecutor* v. *Aleksovski*, Judgement of 24 March 2000, para. 113, which states that 'the right of appeal is ... a component of the fair trial requirement, which is itself a rule of customary international law and gives rise to the right of the accused to have like cases treated alike. This will not be achieved if each Trial Chamber is free to disregard decisions of law made by the Appeals Chamber, and decide the law as it sees fit.' Furthermore, we note the Decision of 21 March 2007 of the ICSID (International Centre for Settlement of Investment Disputes) Arbitration Tribunal, Case No. ARB/05/07, *Saipem SpA* v. *The People's Republic of Bangladesh*, ICSID IIC 280 (2007), p. 20, para. 67, which states that '[t]he Tribunal considers that it is not bound by previous decisions. At the same time, it is of the opinion that it must pay due consideration to earlier decisions of international tribunals. It believes that, subject to compelling contrary grounds, it has a duty to adopt solutions established in a series of consistent cases. It also believes that, subject to the specifics of a given treaty and of the circumstances of the actual case, it has a duty to seek to contribute to the harmonious development of investment law and thereby to meet the legitimate expectations of the community of States and investors towards certainty of the rule of law.'[45]

In *US – Stainless Steel (Mexico)*, the Appellate Body explained its deep concern regarding the Panel's decision to depart from well-established Appellate Body jurisprudence clarifying the interpretation of the same legal issues:

In the hierarchical structure contemplated in the DSU, panels and the Appellate Body have distinct roles to play. In order to strengthen dispute settlement in the multilateral trading system, the Uruguay Round established the Appellate Body as a standing body. Pursuant to Article 17.6 of the DSU, the Appellate Body is vested with the authority to review 'issues of law covered in the panel report and legal interpretations developed by the panel'. Accordingly, Article 17.13 provides that the Appellate Body may 'uphold, modify or reverse' the legal findings and conclusions of panels. The creation of the Appellate Body by WTO Members to review legal interpretations developed by panels shows that Members recognized the importance of consistency and stability in the interpretation of their rights and obligations under the covered agreements. This is essential to promote 'security and predictability' in the dispute settlement system, and to ensure the 'prompt settlement' of disputes. The Panel's failure to follow previously adopted Appellate Body reports addressing the same issues undermines the development of a coherent and predictable body of jurisprudence clarifying Members' rights and obligations under the covered agreements as contemplated under the DSU. Clarification, as envisaged in Article 3.2 of the DSU, elucidates the scope and meaning of the provisions of the covered

[45] Appellate Body Report, *US – Stainless Steel (Mexico)*, paras. 158–60 (also citing Appellate Body Report, *Japan – Alcoholic Beverages II*, p. 14; Appellate Body Report, *US – Shrimp (Article 21.5 – Malaysia)*, para. 109; Appellate Body Report, *US – Oil Country Tubular Goods Sunset Reviews*, para. 188).

agreements in accordance with customary rules of interpretation of public international law. While the application of a provision may be regarded as confined to the context in which it takes place, the relevance of clarification contained in adopted Appellate Body reports is not limited to the application of a particular provision in a specific case.

We are deeply concerned about the Panel's decision to depart from well-established Appellate Body jurisprudence clarifying the interpretation of the same legal issues. The Panel's approach has serious implications for the proper functioning of the WTO dispute settlement system, as explained above.[46]

13.42 In *China – Rare Earths*, China argued that the Panel should find, contrary to the Appellate Body's interpretation in an earlier case, that a particular obligation in China's Accession Protocol is subject to the general exceptions in Article XX of the GATT. The Panel recalled the Appellate Body's statements in *US – Stainless Steel (Mexico)* (see paragraph 13.41 above), and then set forth its understanding of the concept of 'cogent reasons' in light of the jurisprudence of two other international courts. In the course of its analysis, the Panel stated:

> [W]e consider the relevant legal question to be whether those arguments present 'cogent reasons' for departing from the prior adopted finding, by the Appellate Body, on the same question of law presented to this Panel. The Appellate Body has not attempted to define the concept of 'cogent reasons'. The word 'cogent' means '[a]ble to compel assent or belief; *esp.* (of an argument, explanation, etc.) persuasive, expounded clearly and logically, convincing'. The Panel considers that the expression 'cogent reasons' may be understood as referring generally to a high threshold.[127]

---

[127] We note that the Appellate Body introduced the concept of 'cogent reasons' in *US – Stainless Steel (Mexico)*, and the footnote accompanying this passage of the Appellate Body report . . . referred to the Judgement of the Appeals Chamber of the International Criminal Tribunal for the Former Yugoslavia in *Prosecutor* v. *Aleksovski*. While the Appeals Chamber in that case did not attempt to define the concept of 'cogent reasons' in the abstract, the following passage from that judgement suggests that the threshold is high:

> Instances of situations where cogent reasons in the interests of justice require a departure from a previous decision include cases where the previous decision has been decided on the basis of a wrong legal principle or cases where a previous decision has been given *per incuriam*, that is a judicial decision that has been 'wrongly decided, usually because the judge or judges were ill-informed about the applicable law.' (Appeals Chamber of the International Criminal Tribunal for the Former Yugoslavia, Case No. IT-95-14/1-A, *Prosecutor* v. *Aleksovski*, Judgement of 24 March 2000, para. 108 (internal footnote omitted).)

---

[46] Appellate Body Report, *US – Stainless Steel (Mexico)*, paras. 161–2.

Likewise, it appears that the European Court of Human Rights has adopted a high threshold for finding that 'cogent reasons' exist for it to depart from one of its prior decisions. In the *Cossey Case*, the Court stated:

> It is true that … the Court is not bound by its previous judgments … However, it usually follows and applies its own precedents, such a course being in the interests of legal certainty and the orderly development of the Convention case law. Nevertheless, this would not prevent the Court from departing from an earlier decision if it was persuaded that there were cogent reasons for doing so. Such a departure might, for example, be warranted in order to ensure that the interpretation of the Convention reflects societal changes and remains in line with present-day conditions. (European Court of Human Rights, Cossey Judgement of 27 September 1990, Series A, vol. 184, para. 35.)[47]

13.43 In *US – Countervailing and Anti-Dumping Measures (China)* (DS449), the United States argued that the Panel should find, contrary to the Appellate Body's interpretation in an earlier case, that the imposition of double remedies through the concurrent imposition of countervailing and anti-dumping duties does not violate the obligation, in Article 19.3 of the SCM Agreement, to levy countervailing duties in the 'appropriate amounts'. The Panel recalled the Appellate Body's statements in *US – Stainless Steel (Mexico)* (see paragraph 13.41 above), and then identified a non-exhaustive list of circumstances that might justify a panel deviating from a prior Appellate Body interpretation:

> To our minds, 'cogent' reasons, i.e. reasons that could in appropriate cases justify a panel in adopting a different interpretation, would encompass, *inter alia*: (I) a multilateral interpretation of a provision of the covered agreements under Article IX:2 of the WTO Agreement that departs from a prior Appellate Body interpretation; (ii) a demonstration that a prior Appellate Body interpretation proved to be unworkable in a particular set of circumstances falling within the scope of the relevant obligation at issue; (iii) a demonstration that the Appellate Body's prior interpretation leads to a conflict with another provision of a covered agreement that was not raised before the Appellate Body; or (iv) a demonstration that the Appellate Body's interpretation was based on a factually incorrect premise.[48]

13.5.3 *Res judicata*

13.44 In *India – Autos*, India argued that the United States had already obtained a ruling that certain measures were inconsistent with Article XI of the GATT in a prior dispute, and that the scope of that earlier ruling also covered the measure

---

[47] Panel Report, *China – Rare Earths*, para. 7.61 (citing the *Shorter Oxford English Dictionary*).
[48] Panel Report, *US – Countervailing and Anti-Dumping Measures (China)*, para. 7.317.

being challenged in the instant case. India argued that the Panel should dismiss the US claims on the grounds of *res judicata*. The Panel stated:

> The general question as to the applicability of the doctrine of *res judicata* to WTO dispute settlement is of systemic importance. It does not appear to have been explicitly considered in WTO dispute settlement. A general principle of *res judicata* has also not been otherwise referred to or endorsed by any WTO panel or by the Appellate Body, although it is certainly true that certain widely recognized principles of international law have been found to be applicable in WTO dispute settlement, particularly concerning fundamental procedural matters.[332]

[332] See for instance *US – Shrimp*, Report of the Appellate Body, WT/DS58/AB/R, para. 158, on the principle of good faith as a general principle of law and general principle of international law, or *Indonesia – Autos*, Panel Report, WT/DS54/R, WT/DS55/R, WT/DS59/R, WT/DS64/R, para. 14.28 concerning the 'presumption against conflict' in international law.[49]

The Panel in *India – Autos* reviewed prior ICJ jurisprudence on the doctrine of *res judicata* with a view to identifying the conditions that must be satisfied in order to render a claim inadmissible:

> In international jurisdictions where it is applicable, the doctrine is generally understood to mean that an issue that has been decided on in a final adjudication, that is, after exhaustion of any available appeal rights, must be considered as a settled matter between the parties to the dispute. Consequently the issue previously resolved cannot be re-opened in subsequent proceedings. This doctrine has found application in the jurisprudence of the International Court of Justice, whose Statute contains express provisions concerning the binding and final character of its judgments.[336]

[336] In the context of the International Court of Justice, two provisions of its Statute, Articles 59 and 60, as referred to by India, are frequently cited as the source of the principle of *res judicata* concerning its own decisions, although some divergences appear to emerge among commentators as to the exact role of either of the two provisions or even the need to consider them as the source of this principle since it is arguably a general principle of law in any case (see Collier and Lowe, *The Settlement of Disputes in International Law. Institutions and Procedures*, Oxford University Press, p. 177).

In the words of Sir Gerald Fitzmaurice,

> A judgment of the [International] Court [of Justice] has, internationally, the authority of *res judicata*, and this covers all matters which are actually the subject of decision in the judgment. Thus in the *Haya de la Torre* case, the Court (ICJ, 1951, 77) referred to

[49] Panel Report, *India – Autos*, para. 7.57.

'... questions which the Judgment of November 20th, 1950, had already decided with the authority of *res judicata*'

... Unless, however, the point is duly covered by the previous decision, there is no *res judicata*, and therefore nothing (on that particular score) to prevent it being raised in later proceedings. Thus, again in the *Haya* case, the Court said (*ibid.*, 80):

'As mentioned above, the question of the surrender of the refugee was not decided by the judgment of November 20th. This question is new; it was raised by Peru in its Note to Colombia of November 28th, 1950, and was submitted to the Court by the Application of Colombia of December 13th, 1950. There is consequently no *res judicata* upon the question of surrender."

(in *The Law and Procedure of the International Court of Justice*, Sir Gerald Fitzmaurice, Volume Two, Cambridge, Grotius Publications Limited, 1986, pp. 584–585).[50]

In *EC – Bed Linen (Article 21.5 – India)*, the original panel rejected a claim (on **13.45** the grounds that India failed to make a *prima facie* case). The panel's findings on that claim were not appealed. India then reasserted the same claim in the subsequent compliance proceeding under Article 21.5 of the DSU. The respondent argued that the decision of the original panel rejecting India's claim 'has *res judicata* effects' between the parties, and therefore India was precluded from reasserting the same claim before the subsequent panel. The Appellate Body agreed with the respondent that the claim 'was not properly before' the subsequent Panel, and stated:

In our view, the effect, for the parties, of findings adopted by the DSB as part of a panel report is the same, regardless of whether a panel found that the complainant failed to establish a *prima facie* case that the measure is inconsistent with WTO obligations, that the Panel found that the measure is fully consistent with WTO obligations, or that the Panel found that the measure is not consistent with WTO obligations. A complainant that, in an original proceeding, fails to establish a *prima facie* case should not be given a 'second chance' in an Article 21.5 proceeding, and thus be treated more favourably than a complainant that did establish a *prima facie* case but, ultimately, failed to prevail before the original panel, with the result that the panel did not find the challenged measure to be inconsistent with WTO obligations. Nor should a defending party be subject to a second challenge of the measure found not to be inconsistent with WTO obligations, merely because the complainant failed to establish a *prima facie* case, as opposed to failing ultimately to persuade the original panel.[51]

[50] Panel Report, *India – Autos*, para. 7.62.
[51] Appellate Body Report, *EC – Bed Linen (Article 21.5 – India)*, para. 96.

13.46 In *US – Upland Cotton (Article 21.5 – Brazil)*, the Appellate Body recalled some of its prior statements on this issue, and distinguished the situation in that case from the situation addressed in *EC – Bed Linen (Article 21.5 – India)*:

> As the Appellate Body found in *EC – Bed Linen (Article 21.5 – India)*, a complainant who had failed to make out a *prima facie* case in the original proceedings regarding an element of the measure that remained unchanged since the original proceedings may not re-litigate the same claim with respect to the unchanged element of the measure in the Article 21.5 proceedings. Similarly, a complainant may not reassert the same claim against an unchanged aspect of the measure that had been found to be *WTO-consistent* in the original proceedings. Because adopted panel and Appellate Body reports must be accepted by the parties to a dispute, allowing a party in an Article 21.5 proceeding to re-argue a claim that has been decided in adopted reports would indeed provide an unfair 'second chance' to that party. The situation before us is different. Brazil's claims against export credit guarantees provided under the original GSM 102 programme to pig meat and poultry meat were not resolved on the merits in the original proceedings, because the Appellate Body was unable to complete the analysis as a result of there being insufficient factual findings or undisputed facts on the record. Thus, allowing Brazil's claims in this case would not raise the due process concerns identified by the United States. Brazil is not unfairly getting a 'second chance' to make a case that it failed to make out in the original proceedings such that the finality of the DSB's recommendations and rulings would be compromised.[52]

13.47 In *US – Gambling*, the Appellate Body concluded that the United States failed to demonstrate that the measure at issue was justified under the general exceptions in Article XIV of the GATS. In *US – Gambling (Article 21.5 – Antigua and Barbuda)*, the United States argued that it had brought the measure into conformity with its obligations by adducing new arguments and evidence to demonstrate that the measure, which remained unchanged, was in fact justified under Article XIV of the GATS. The compliance Panel rejected the US argument. In the course of its analysis of this issue, the compliance Panel stated that the United States was not 'entitled to another opportunity to demonstrate before this compliance panel that the measures in fact *do* meet the requirements of the chapeau of Article XIV',[53] and that 'the adopted Appellate Body report entails more than a final ruling on the evidence presented. It entails a final decision on the claims and defences ruled upon with respect to the measures at issue as they existed at the time of the original proceeding'.[54] The compliance Panel further considered that Article 17.14 of the DSU, which states that an

---

[52] Appellate Body Report, *US – Upland Cotton (Article 21.5 – Brazil)*, para. 210 (citing Appellate Body Report, *US – Shrimp (Article 21.5 – Malaysia)*, paras. 96–7; Appellate Body Report, *EC – Bed Linen (Article 21.5 – India)*, para. 93).
[53] Panel Report, *US – Gambling (Article 21.5 – Antigua and Barbuda)*, para. 6.28.
[54] *Ibid.*, para. 6.56.

adopted Appellate Body report shall be 'unconditionally accepted' by the parties to the dispute 'precludes re-argument of the same defence in relation to the same measure without any change relevant to the measure' at the compliance stage of the proceeding.[55]

13.6 Teachings of the most highly qualified publicists

13.6.1 Generally

There are very few instances in which WTO adjudicators have referred to **13.48** commentaries or scholarly writings for the purpose of interpreting the provisions of the WTO agreements. However, for the purpose of clarifying the content and status of other rules of international law that do not fall within the exclusive jurisdiction of the WTO dispute settlement system, e.g. general international law concepts and principles, WTO adjudicators have frequently referred to and relied on such secondary sources.

In one case, a panel referred expressly to Article 38(1)(d) of the Statute. **13.49** After citing an author's commentary on the Berne Convention, the Panel in *US – Section 110(5) Copyright Act* explained that:

> We are ready to take into account 'teachings of the most highly qualified publicists of the various nations' as a 'subsidiary source for the determination of law'. We refer to this phrase in the sense of Article 38(d) of the Statute of the International Court of Justice which refers to such 'teachings' (or, in French 'la doctrine') as 'subsidiary means for the determination of law'.[56]

13.6.2 International Law Commission

Many WTO decisions refer to the work of the International Law Commission, **13.50** most notably to its commentaries on its draft articles on the law of treaties (which subsequently became the Vienna Convention on the Law of Treaties), and to the ILC Articles on State Responsibility and its commentary thereon. Decisions have also referred to ILC draft articles on other topics,[57] as well as reports by individual ILC Special Rapporteurs and ILC study groups.[58]

---

[55] *Ibid.*, para. 6.59.   [56] Panel Report, *US – Section 110(5) US Copyright Act*, footnote 114.
[57] For example, Panel Report, *EC – Tariff Preferences*, footnote 441 (citing ILC draft Articles on Most-Favoured-Nation Clauses).
[58] For example, Panel Report, *Canada – Patent Term*, para. 73 (citing the Sixth Report of H. Waldock, Special Rapporteur on the Law of Treaties); Appellate Body Report, *EC and certain member States – Large Civil Aircraft*, para. 845 (citing the Report of the ILC Study Group on the Fragmentation of International Law, finalized by M. Koskenniemi).

13.51 In *Brazil – Aircraft (Article 22.6 – Brazil)*, the Arbitrators referred to the ILC Articles on State Responsibility in the context of interpreting the term 'countermeasures' in Articles 4.10 and 4.11 of the SCM Agreement, explaining that it would use them as an indication of the agreed meaning of certain terms in general international law. The Arbitrators stated that, while the parties had referred to dictionary definitions for the term 'countermeasures', the Arbitrators found it more appropriate to refer to its meaning in general international law 'and to the work of the International Law Commission on state responsibility, which addresses the notion of countermeasures'. In this context, the Arbitrators noted 'that the ILC work is based on relevant state practice as well as on judicial decisions and doctrinal writings, which constitute recognized sources of international law', and referred to Article 38 of the Statute of the ICJ.[59]

13.52 Along the same lines, in *US – FSC (Article 22.6 – US)*, the Arbitrator also referred to the ILC draft articles on State responsibility, and also explained that '[w]e note that the ILC's work is based on relevant State practice as well as on judicial decisions and doctrinal writings, which constitute recognized sources of international law under Article 38 of the Statute of the International Court of Justice'.[60]

---

[59] Decision by the Arbitrators, *Brazil – Aircraft (Article 22.6 – Brazil)*, para. 3.44.
[60] Decision by the Arbitrators, *US – FSC (Article 22.6 – US)*, footnote 68.

14

SOVEREIGNTY

14.1   Introduction

The concept of State sovereignty 'is a pivotal principle of modern international **14.1**
law', and '[m]ost of the other, if not all institutions and principles of international law rely, directly or indirectly, on State sovereignty'.[1] Sir Hersch
Lauterpacht dedicated a significant part of *The Development of International
Law by the International Court* to a discussion of various issues under the rubric
of 'The Court and State Sovereignty'.[2] This chapter follows suit and reviews
statements by WTO adjudicators of wider applicability relating to: (i) treaties as
acts of sovereignty; (ii) sovereignty and treaty interpretation; (iii) the sovereign
right to regulate; (iv) sovereignty and taxation; (v) sovereignty and extraterritoriality; and (vi) permanent sovereignty over natural resources. It then reviews the
paucity of statements by WTO adjudicators regarding: (vii) sovereign equality;
and (viii) the domestic jurisdiction. There are some theoretical disagreements
among academics as to whether 'sovereignty' is or is not a founding assumption
of international trade law, and whether international trade law therefore is or is
not in some way fundamentally different from other areas of public international
law.[3] It is hard to see anything in the statements of WTO adjudicators to
support the proposition that the concept of 'sovereignty' has been understood
to mean something different in the WTO context as compared with other areas
of international law, or with regard to the 'classic' understanding of sovereignty;
to the contrary, panels and the Appellate Body have relied quite heavily on some
classic formulations of the concept developed by the PCIJ in the 1920s.

---

[1] S. Besson, 'Sovereignty' (April 2011) in *Max Planck Encyclopedia of Public International Law*,
paras. 1–2.
[2] H. Lauterpacht, *The Development of International Law by the International Court* (Stevens & Sons,
1958), Part V.
[3] D. McRae, 'The Contribution of International Trade Law to the Development of International
Law' (1996) 250 *Recueil des cours de l'Académie de droit international* 99; J. Pauwelyn, *Conflict of
Norms in Public International Law: How WTO Law Relates to Other Rules of International Law*
(Cambridge University Press, 2003), pp. 29 *et seq.*

14.2   Treaties as acts of sovereignty

14.2   In several cases, panels and the Appellate Body emphasized that States may exercise their sovereignty by negotiating and entering into treaties. In this regard, there is support in WTO jurisprudence for the proposition that the right of entering into international engagements is an attribute of State sovereignty, such that restrictions on the exercise of sovereign rights that a State voluntarily accepts through a treaty cannot be considered as an infringement of its sovereignty.

14.3   In *Japan – Alcoholic Beverages II*, the Appellate Body stated:

> The *WTO Agreement* is a treaty – the international equivalent of a contract. It is self-evident that in an exercise of their sovereignty, and in pursuit of their own respective national interests, the Members of the WTO have made a bargain. In exchange for the benefits they expect to derive as Members of the WTO, they have agreed to exercise their sovereignty according to the commitments they have made in the *WTO Agreement*.[4]

14.4   In *China – Raw Materials*, the Panel stated that 'the ability to enter into international agreements – such as the WTO Agreement – is a quintessential example of the exercise of sovereignty'.[5] In response to China's argument that the WTO agreements affirm the inherent and sovereign right of every WTO Member to regulate trade, the Panel also stated:

> The Panel agrees with China that WTO Members have an inherent and sovereign right to regulate trade. WTO Members and China have exercised this right, *inter alia*, in negotiating and ratifying the WTO Agreement. China has exercised its inherent and sovereign right to regulate trade in negotiating, among other actions, the terms of its accession into the WTO.
>
> To the Panel, the implication of China's argument is that because it has an inherent right to regulate trade, this right prevails over WTO rules intended to govern the exercise of that right. In the Panel's view, it is China's sovereign right to regulate trade that enabled it to negotiate and agree with the provisions of Paragraph 11.3 of its Accession Protocol. Thus, there is no contradiction between China's sovereign right to regulate trade, the rights acquired, and the commitments undertaken by China that are contained in its Accession Protocol, including in its Paragraph 11.3. On the contrary, China's Accession Protocol and its various rights and obligations, are the ultimate expression of China's sovereignty.[6]

Later in its decision, the Panel in *China – Raw Materials* returned to the concept of sovereignty, and stated:

> One of the fundamental principles of international law is the principle of state sovereignty, denoting the equality of all states in competence and independence

---

[4] Appellate Body Report, *Japan – Alcoholic Beverages II*, p. 15.
[5] Panel Report, *China – Raw Materials*, para. 7.382.   [6] *Ibid.*, para. 7.156.

over their own territories and encompassing the right to make laws applicable within their own territories without intrusion from other sovereign states. Independent decisions can be taken with regard to matters including the choice of political, economic and social systems. The principle of state sovereignty is also exercised whenever states choose to enter into an international agreement with other sovereign states.

   This was first established by the Permanent Court of International Justice (PCIJ) in the case of the *SS Wimbledon* (1923), where it confirmed that 'the right of entering into international engagements is an attribute of State sovereignty'. This principle was further elaborated in the PCIJ's advisory opinion on the *Exchange of Greek and Turkish Populations* (1925). We find especially instructive for our purposes the PCIJ's consideration of the principle in the case on *Jurisdiction of the European Danube Commission between Galatz and Braila* (1927), where the Court stated that 'restrictions on the exercise of sovereign rights accepted by treaty by the State concerned cannot be considered as an infringement of sovereignty'.[7]

The Panel in *Argentina – Import Measures* observed that: **14.5**

> [T]he WTO agreements highlight the positive role international trade can play as part of the development policies of developing and least developed country Members. This realization explains why sovereign nations, such as Argentina, voluntarily accept the international obligations that are the result of subscribing to the WTO Agreement and becoming Members of the World Trade Organization.[8]

14.3   Sovereignty and treaty interpretation: *in dubio mitius*

The Appellate Body referred to the principle of *in dubio mitius* in a footnote in   **14.6** one of its early decisions. It has not subsequently been applied by the Appellate Body or any panel.

In *EC – Hormones*, the Appellate Body referred to the principle of *in dubio mitius*   **14.7** and the notion of interpreting treaties 'in deference to the sovereignty of states' in a footnote, and characterized this as a 'supplementary means of interpretation':

> The interpretative principle of *in dubio mitius*, widely recognized in international law as a 'supplementary means of interpretation', has been expressed in the following terms:
>   The principle of *in dubio mitius* applies in interpreting treaties, in deference to the sovereignty of states. If the meaning of a term is ambiguous, that meaning is to be preferred which is less onerous to the party assuming an obligation, or

---

[7] *Ibid.*, para. 7.378–7.379 (citing the PCIJ in the *SS Wimbledon* case, p. 25; *Exchange of Greek and Turkish Populations*, 1925, PCIJ, Series B, No. 10, p. 21; *Jurisdiction of the European Danube Commission between Galatz and Braila*, 1927, PCIJ, Series B, No. 14, p. 36).

[8] Panel Report, *Argentina – Import Measures*, para. 6.5.

which interferes less with the territorial and personal supremacy of a party, or involves less general restrictions upon the parties.

> R. Jennings and A. Watts (eds.), *Oppenheim's International Law*, 9th edn, Vol. I (Longman, 1992), p. 1278. The relevant case law includes: *Nuclear Tests Case (Australia* v. *France)*, (1974), ICJ Reports, p. 267 (International Court of Justice); *Access of Polish War Vessels to the Port of Danzig* (1931) PCIJ Rep., Series A/B, No. 43, p. 142 (Permanent Court of International Justice); *USA–France Air Transport Services Arbitration* (1963), 38 International Law Reports 243 (Arbitral Tribunal); *De Pascale Claim* (1961), 40 International Law Reports 250 (Italian – United States Conciliation Commission). See also: I. Brownlie, *Principles of Public International Law*, 4th edn (Clarendon Press, 1990), p. 631; C. Rousseau, *Droit International Public*, Vol. I (1990), p. 273; D. Carreau, *Droit International*, 4th edn (Editions A. Pedone, 1994), p. 142; M. Díez de Velasco, *Instituciones de Derecho Internacional Público*, 9th edn, Vol. I (Editorial Tecnos, 1991), pp. 163–164; and B. Conforti, *Diritto Internazionale*, 3rd edn (Editoriale Scientifica, 1987), pp. 99–100.[9]

14.8   In response to China invoking this principle in *China – Publications and Audiovisual Products*, the Appellate Body stated 'even if the principle of *in dubio mitius* were relevant in WTO dispute settlement', there was no scope for its application in that dispute:

> We have found above that the Panel did not err in its interpretation of 'Sound recording distribution services' in accordance with Article 31 of the *Vienna Convention*. We have expressed the view that the Panel's recourse to Article 32 of the *Vienna Convention* was not in error, but that it was also not necessary, given that the application of Article 31 yielded a conclusion on the proper interpretation of this entry in China's GATS Schedule. We have also observed that we see no error in the Panel's analysis under Article 32. We therefore do not accept China's contention that the Panel should have found that the meaning of the entry 'Sound recording distribution services' remains inconclusive or ambiguous after its analysis under Articles 31 and 32 of the *Vienna Convention*. Consequently, even if the principle of *in dubio mitius* were relevant in WTO dispute settlement, there is no scope for its application in this dispute.[10]

14.9   In *China – Intellectual Property Rights*, China argued that the United States should carry a significantly higher burden of proof on a claim concerning domestic criminal law matters, and that the Panel should treat 'sovereign jurisdiction over police powers' as a powerful default norm, departure from which can be authorized only in light of explicit and unequivocal consent of State parties. The Panel stated that 'concerns regarding sovereignty' may be expected 'to find reflection in the text and scope of treaty obligations':

> The Panel acknowledges the sensitive nature of criminal matters and attendant concerns regarding sovereignty. These concerns may be expected to find

---

[9] Appellate Body Report, *EC – Hormones*, footnote 154.
[10] Appellate Body Report, *China – Publications and Audiovisual Products*, para. 411.

reflection in the text and scope of treaty obligations regarding such matters as negotiated by States and other Members. Section 5 of Part III of the TRIPS Agreement, dedicated to criminal procedures and remedies, is considerably briefer and less detailed than the other Sections on enforcement in Part III. Brief as it is, the text of Section 5 also contains significant limitations and flexibilities. The customary rules of treaty interpretation oblige the treaty interpreter to take these limitations and flexibilities into account in interpreting the relevant provision.[11]

14.4   Sovereign right to regulate

The concept of a 'sovereign right to regulate' has been referred to by panels and **14.10** the Appellate Body in a number of cases, including with respect to such diverse matters as foreign direct investment, the administration of export laws and regulations, telecommunications, Internet gambling, environmental protection, public morals, and human health. In all such cases, panels and the Appellate Body have also underscored that a State's sovereign right to regulate must be exercised in accordance with its international obligations.

In *Canada – FIRA*, the GATT Panel referred to the 'sovereign right to regulate **14.11** foreign direct investments':

> In view of the fact that the General Agreement does not prevent Canada from exercising its sovereign right to regulate foreign direct investments, the Panel examined the purchase and export undertakings by investors subject to the Foreign Investment Review Act of Canada solely in the light of Canada's trade obligations under the General Agreement. This approach is in accordance with the Chairman of the Council's conclusions at the close of the discussion of this question at the Council meeting of 2 November 1982.[12]

In *Argentina – Hides and Leather*, the Panel found the appointment of individ- **14.12** uals from the private sector as customs officials to violate the 'reasonable' administration requirement under Article X:3(a) of the GATT, because the individuals were direct competitors to the importer and 'had no legal relationship' to the custom operations. The Panel contrasted this with the government, stating that the latter did have 'a relevant legal interest in the transaction based on the sovereign right to regulate and tax exports.'[13]

In *Mexico – Telecoms*, the Panel observed that: **14.13**

> Members maintain the sovereign right to regulate within the parameters of Article VI of the GATS. Members' regulatory sovereignty is an essential pillar

---

[11] Panel Report, *China – Intellectual Property Rights*, para. 7.501.
[12] GATT Panel Report, *Canada – FIRA*, para. 5.1.
[13] Panel Report, *Argentina – Hides and Leather*, para. 7.915.

of the progressive liberalization of trade in services, but this sovereignty ends whenever rights of other Members under the GATS are impaired.[14]

14.14 In *US – Gambling*, the United States argued that a finding that its measures were inconsistent with the GATS could be read as 'supporting the criticisms levelled by numerous groups against the GATS as being overreaching and an unjustified intrusion into the sovereign ability of Members to regulate in the area of services'.[15] The Panel responded by reiterating that:

> We have not decided that WTO Members do not have a right to regulate, including a right to prohibit, gambling and betting activities. In this case, we came to the conclusion that the US measures at issue prohibit the cross-border supply of gambling and betting services in the United States in a manner inconsistent with the GATS. We so decided, not because the GATS denies Members such a right but, rather, because we found, *inter alia*, that, in the particular circumstances of this case, the measures at issue were inconsistent with the United States' scheduled commitments and the relevant provisions of the GATS.[16]

14.15 In *US – Shrimp*, a case that concerned the WTO-consistency of US regulations relating to the protection of endangered sea turtles, the Appellate Body stated:

> In reaching these conclusions, we wish to underscore what we have *not* decided in this appeal. We have *not* decided that the protection and preservation of the environment is of no significance to the Members of the WTO. Clearly, it is. We have *not* decided that the sovereign nations that are Members of the WTO cannot adopt effective measures to protect endangered species, such as sea turtles. Clearly, they can and should. And we have *not* decided that sovereign states should not act together bilaterally, plurilaterally or multilaterally, either within the WTO or in other international fora, to protect endangered species or to otherwise protect the environment. Clearly, they should and do.[17]

14.16 In *China – Intellectual Property Rights*, the Panel stated that it agreed with an interpretation, set out in a World Intellectual Property Organization guide to the Berne Convention, regarding the 'sovereignty of member countries' to take the necessary steps to maintain public order:

> China draws the Panel's attention to the WIPO Guide to the Berne Convention, which states as follows regarding Article 17 of the Berne Convention (1971):
>
> > It covers the right of governments to take the necessary steps to maintain public order. On this point, the sovereignty of member countries is not affected by the rights given by the Convention. Authors may exercise their rights only if that exercise does not conflict with

---

[14] Panel Report, *Mexico – Telecoms*, para. 6.316.   [15] Panel Report, *US – Gambling*, para. 5.16.
[16] *Ibid.*, para. 5.17.   [17] Appellate Body Report, *US – Shrimp*, para. 185.

public order. The former must give way to the latter. The Article therefore gives Union countries certain powers to control.

The Panel agrees with this interpretation. A government's right to permit, to control, or to prohibit the circulation, presentation, or exhibition of a work may interfere with the exercise of certain rights with respect to a protected work by the copyright owner or a third party authorized by the copyright owner. However, there is no reason to suppose that censorship will eliminate those rights entirely with respect to a particular work.'[18]

In *US – Clove Cigarettes*, the Panel examined the consistency of a tobacco- **14.17** control measure adopted by the United States for reasons of public health. The Panel ultimately found that the measure was inconsistent with the non-discrimination obligation in Article 2.1 of the TBT Agreement, by virtue of the fact that the measure banned the sale of clove cigarettes and certain other flavoured cigarettes, but not of menthol-flavoured cigarettes. The Panel stated:

At the outset, this Panel would like to emphasize that measures to protect public health are of the utmost importance, and that the WTO Agreements fully recognize and respect the sovereign right of Members to regulate in response to legitimate public health concerns.[19]

In *US – Clove Cigarettes*, the Appellate Body concluded that 'the object and purpose **14.18** of the *TBT Agreement* is to strike a balance between, on the one hand, the objective of trade liberalization and, on the other hand, Members' right to regulate'.[20]

In *China – Rare Earths*, the Panel examined whether a particular obligation in **14.19** China's Accession Protocol was subject to the general exceptions in Article XX of the GATT are applicable to the export duty commitments. The Panel found that these exceptions were not available, but stated:

The Panel agrees with China that an interpretation of the covered agreements that resulted in sovereign States being legally prevented from taking measures that are necessary to protect the environment or human, animal or plant life or health would likely be inconsistent with the object and purpose of the WTO Agreement. In the Panel's view, such a result could even rise to the level of being 'manifestly absurd or unreasonable'.[21]

14.5   Sovereignty and taxation

Panels and the Appellate Body have made a number of statements linking **14.20** taxation powers to sovereignty. However, WTO jurisprudence makes clear that

---

[18] Panel Report, *China – Intellectual Property Rights*, paras. 7.131–7.132.
[19] Panel Report, *US – Clove Cigarettes*, para. 7.2.
[20] Appellate Body Report, *US – Clove Cigarettes*, para. 174.
[21] Panel Report, *China – Rare Earths*, para. 7.111.

State sovereignty regarding taxation is subject to, and must be exercised in accordance with, international treaty obligations.

14.21 In *US – Anti-Dumping and Countervailing Duties (China)* (DS379), the Appellate Body stated that taxation 'is an integral part of the sovereign function'.[22]

14.22 In *Chile – Alcoholic Beverages*, the Appellate Body upheld the Panel's finding that the measure at issue was inconsistent with the non-discrimination obligation in Article III:2 of the GATT. In that context, the Appellate Body stated that 'Members of the WTO have sovereign authority to determine the basis or bases on which they will tax goods, such as, for example, distilled alcoholic beverages, and to classify such goods accordingly, provided of course that the Members respect their WTO commitments'.[23]

14.23 In *US – FSC*, the United States argued that a WTO Member is free to maintain a worldwide or territorial tax system, and that, in recognition of 'principles of tax sovereignty', a country using a worldwide system is free to incorporate elements of a territorial system (or *vice versa*). The Panel stated:

> We agree with the United States that neither the SCM Agreement specifically, nor the WTO Agreement generally, is intended to dictate the type of tax system that should be maintained by a Member. On the other hand, certain WTO rules do have implications for specific tax practices of Members. In the area of subsidies, it is clear from Article 1 of the SCM Agreement itself that tax measures of a WTO Member may give rise to subsidies subject to the disciplines of the SCM Agreement. It is further clear that, to the extent that a subsidy is contingent upon export performance, it is a prohibited export subsidy. Thus, the United States is free to maintain a world wide tax system, a territorial tax system or any other type of system it sees fit. This is not the business of the WTO. What it is not free to do is to establish a regime of direct taxation, provide an exemption from direct taxes specifically related to exports, and then claim that it is entitled to provide such an export subsidy because it is necessary to eliminate a disadvantage to exporters created by the US tax system itself.[24]

14.24 In *US – FSC (Article 21.5 – EC)*, the Appellate Body also referred to sovereignty in the context of the question of providing relief from double taxation (i.e. in two different jurisdictions). The Appellate Body stated:

> We also recognize that Members are not obliged by the covered agreements to provide relief from double taxation. Footnote 59 to the *SCM Agreement* simply preserves the prerogative of Members to grant such relief, at their discretion, for 'foreign-source income'. Accordingly, we do not believe that measures falling under footnote 59 must grant relief from *all* double tax burdens. Rather,

---

[22] Appellate Body Report, *US – Anti-Dumping and Countervailing Duties (China)*, para. 296.
[23] Appellate Body Report, *Chile – Alcoholic Beverages*, para. 60.
[24] Panel Report, *US – FSC*, para. 7.122.

Members retain the sovereign authority to determine for themselves whether, and to what extent, they will grant such relief.[25]

In *US – FSC*, the Appellate Body referred to Members' sovereignty in the field of taxation in the context of interpreting Article 1.1(a)(1)(ii) of the SCM Agreement. Article 1.1(a)(1) lists four different forms of financial contribution that may give rise to a subsidy, the second of which is identified in Article 1.1(a)(1)(ii) as the foregoing of government revenue 'otherwise due'. The Appellate Body stated:

> To accept the argument of the United States that the comparator in determining what is 'otherwise due' should be something other than the prevailing domestic standard of the Member in question would be to imply that WTO obligations somehow compel Members to choose a particular kind of tax system; this is not so. A Member, in principle, has the sovereign authority to tax any particular categories of revenue it wishes. It is also free *not* to tax any particular categories of revenues.[26]

In *US – Large Civil Aircraft (2nd complaint)*, the Appellate Body stated that **14.25** 'WTO Members are sovereign in determining the structure and rates of their domestic tax regimes'.[27]

14.6 Sovereignty and extraterritoriality

The terms 'extraterritoriality' and 'extraterritorial jurisdiction' have been under- **14.26** stood to refer to the competence of a State to make, apply and enforce rules of conduct in respect of persons, property or events beyond its territory.[28] In several GATT/WTO cases, panels and the Appellate Body have examined trade measures that restricted or banned imports of products that were harvested in a manner that did not meet the importing country's requirements for protecting certain marine species (e.g. tuna, sea turtles, seals). The requirements at issue applied irrespective of where those marine species were located (i.e. inside or outside of the importing country's territory). One of the issues that arose in these cases was whether such measures, insofar as they were aimed to conserve exhaustible natural resources located outside of the importing country's territory, were permissible under WTO obligations and exceptions. In some of those cases, panels and the Appellate Body considered whether any such restriction existed in light of general international law and/or international legal

---

[25] Appellate Body Report, *US – FSC (Article 21.5 – EC)*, para. 148.
[26] Appellate Body Report, *US – FSC*, para. 90.
[27] Appellate Body Report, *US – Large Civil Aircraft (2nd complaint)*, para. 811.
[28] For commentary, see M. Kamminga, 'Extraterritoriality' (November 2012) in *Max Planck Encyclopedia of Public International Law*.

instruments. To date, the Appellate Body has avoided making any definitive ruling on this issue.

14.27 In *US – Tuna (EEC)*, the GATT Panel concluded that it could see 'no valid reason' supporting the conclusion that the general exception in Article XX(g) of the GATT, concerning measures relating to the conservation of exhaustible natural resources, would apply 'only to policies related to the conservation of exhaustible natural resources located within the territory of the contracting party invoking the provision'. The Panel consequently found that the US policy to conserve dolphins in the eastern tropical Pacific Ocean fell within the range of policies covered by Article XX(g). In the course of its analysis, the GATT Panel referred to general international law regarding the rights of States *vis-à-vis* their nationals:

> The Panel further observed that, under general international law, states are not in principle barred from regulating the conduct of their nationals with respect to persons, animals, plants and natural resources outside of their territory. Nor are states barred, in principle, from regulating the conduct of vessels having their nationality, or any persons on these vessels, with respect to persons, animals, plants and natural resources outside their territory. A state may in particular regulate the conduct of its fishermen, or of vessels having its nationality or any fishermen on these vessels, with respect to fish located in the high seas.[29]

14.28 In *US – Shrimp*, the Appellate Body examined a US import ban on shrimp that was harvested in a manner that did not meet US requirements aimed at protecting endangered sea turtles. The Appellate Body ultimately found that the measure, which aimed to protect such marine resources located (at least partially) outside of the territory of the importing country, could in principle be justified under Article XX(g) of the GATT. The Appellate Body considered it unnecessary, in the circumstances of that case, to consider the issue of whether there was any basis for finding an implied jurisdictional limitation, on the grounds that there was a 'sufficient nexus' on the facts of that case:

> The sea turtle species here at stake, i.e. covered by Section 609, are all known to occur in waters over which the United States exercises jurisdiction. Of course, it is not claimed that all populations of these species migrate to, or traverse, at one time or another, waters subject to United States jurisdiction. Neither the appellant nor any of the appellees claims any rights of exclusive ownership over the sea turtles, at least not while they are swimming freely in their natural habitat – the oceans. We do not pass upon the question of whether there is an implied jurisdictional limitation in Article XX(g), and if so, the nature or extent of that limitation. We note only that in the specific circumstances of the case before us, there is a sufficient nexus between the migratory and endangered marine populations involved and the United States for purposes of Article XX(g).[30]

---

[29] GATT Panel Report, *US – Tuna (EEC)*, para. 5.17.
[30] Appellate Body Report, *US – Shrimp*, para. 133.

Later in its analysis, in the context of examining whether that measure was applied in a manner that constituted arbitrary or unjustifiable discrimination under the chapeau of Article XX, the Appellate Body referred to various international instruments stating that measures seeking to conserve resources outside of a State's territorial jurisdiction should as far as possible be based on international consensus and cooperation:

> As stated earlier, the Decision on Trade and Environment, which provided for the establishment of the CTE and set out its terms of reference, refers to both the Rio Declaration on Environment and Development and Agenda 21. Of particular relevance is Principle 12 of the Rio Declaration on Environment and Development, which states, in part:
>
> > Unilateral actions to deal with environmental challenges outside the jurisdiction of the importing country should be avoided. Environmental measures addressing transboundary or global environmental problems should, as far as possible, be based on international consensus (emphasis added).
>
> In almost identical language, paragraph 2.22(i) of Agenda 21 provides:
>
> > Governments should encourage GATT, UNCTAD and other relevant international and regional economic institutions to examine, in accordance with their respective mandates and competences, the following propositions and principles . . .
>
> > (i) Avoid unilateral action to deal with environmental challenges outside the jurisdiction of the importing country. *Environmental measures addressing transborder problems should, as far as possible, be based on an international consensus* (emphasis added).
>
> Moreover, we note that Article 5 of the Convention on Biological Diversity states.
>
> > . . . each contracting party shall, as far as possible and as appropriate, cooperate with other contracting parties directly or, where appropriate, through competent international organizations, in respect of areas beyond national jurisdiction and on other matters of mutual interest, for the conservation and sustainable use of biological diversity.
>
> The Convention on the Conservation of Migratory Species of Wild Animals, which classifies the relevant species of sea turtles in its Annex I as 'Endangered Migratory Species', states:
>
> > The contracting parties [are] convinced that conservation and effective management of migratory species of wild animals requires the concerted action of all States within the national boundaries of which such species spend any part of their life cycle.[31]

---

[31] *Ibid.*, para. 168.

14.29 In *US – Shrimp (Article 21.5 – Malaysia)*, Malaysia argued that the United States, by imposing a unilaterally defined standard of protection to protect resources located outside of its territory, violated the sovereign right of Malaysia to determine its own sea turtles protection and conservation policy. The Panel responded:

> We are mindful of the problem caused by the type of measure applied by the United States to pursue its environmental policy objectives. We recall that Principle 12 of the Rio Declaration on Environment and Development states in part that:
>
>> unilateral actions to deal with environmental challenges outside the jurisdiction of the importing country should be avoided. Environmental measures addressing transboundary or global environmental problems should, as far as possible, be based on international consensus.
>
> However, it is the understanding of the Panel that the Appellate Body Report found that, while a WTO Member may not impose on exporting members to apply the same standards of environmental protection as those it applies itself, this Member may legitimately require, as a condition of access of certain products to its market, that exporting countries commit themselves to a regulatory programme deemed comparable to its own. At present, Malaysia does not have to comply with the US requirements because it does not export to the United States. If Malaysia exported shrimp to the United States, it would be subject to requirements that may distort Malaysia's priorities in terms of environmental policy. As Article XX of the GATT 1994 has been interpreted by the Appellate Body, the WTO Agreement does not provide for any recourse in the situation Malaysia would face under those circumstances. While we cannot, in light of the interpretation of Article XX made by the Appellate Body, find in favour of Malaysia on this 'sovereignty' issue, we nonetheless consider that the 'sovereignty' question raised by Malaysia is an additional argument in favour of the conclusion of an international agreement to protect and conserve sea turtles which would take into account the situation of all interested parties.[32]

14.30 In *US – Shrimp (Article 21.5 – Malaysia)*, the Appellate Body considered the meaning of the phrase 'as far as possible' in the context of Principle 12 of the Rio Declaration, stating:

> As we stated in *United States – Shrimp*, 'the protection and conservation of highly migratory species of sea turtles ... demands concerted and cooperative efforts on the part of the many countries whose waters are traversed in the course of recurrent sea turtle migrations'. Further, the 'need for, and the appropriateness of, such efforts have been recognized in the WTO itself as well as in a significant number of other international instruments and declarations'. For example, Principle 12 of the Rio Declaration on Environment and Development states, in part, that '[e]nvironmental measures addressing transboundary or global environmental problems

---

[32] Panel Report, *US – Shrimp (Article 21.5 – Malaysia)*, para. 5.103.

should, as far as possible, be based on international consensus'. Clearly, and 'as far as possible', a multilateral approach is strongly preferred. Yet it is one thing to *prefer* a multilateral approach in the application of a measure that is provisionally justified under one of the subparagraphs of Article XX of the GATT 1994; it is another to require the *conclusion* of a multilateral agreement as a condition of avoiding 'arbitrary or unjustifiable discrimination' under the chapeau of Article XX. We see, in this case, no such requirement.[33]

In *EC – Seal Products*, the Appellate Body examined an import ban on seal **14.31** products designed to address seal hunting activities occurring within and outside the European Union. The Appellate Body found that the measure was justified under Article XX(a) of the GATT as a measure necessary for the protection of public morals. In the course of its analysis, the Appellate Body noted that the disputing parties in that case agreed that there was a 'sufficient nexus' between the importing country and the public moral concerns and activities addressed by the measure, and considered it unnecessary to address the question further:

> [W]e note that, in *US – Shrimp*, the Appellate Body stated that it would not 'pass upon the question of whether there is an implied jurisdictional limitation in Article XX(g), and if so, the nature or extent of that limitation'. The Appellate Body explained that, in the specific circumstances of that case, there was 'a sufficient nexus between the migratory and endangered marine populations involved and the United States for purposes of Article XX(g)'. As set out in the preamble of the Basic Regulation, the EU Seal Regime is designed to address seal hunting activities occurring 'within and outside the Community' and the seal welfare concerns of 'citizens and consumers' in EU member States. The participants did not address this issue in their submissions on appeal.[1191] Accordingly, while recognizing the systemic importance of the question of whether there is an implied jurisdictional limitation in Article XX(a), and, if so, the nature or extent of that limitation, we have decided in this case not to examine this question further.

> ---
> [1191] In response to questioning at the oral hearing, the participants expressed their agreement that there is a sufficient nexus between the public moral concerns and activities addressed by the measure, on the one hand, and the European Union, on the other hand. The participants also indicated that, because the parties did not dispute that there was a sufficient nexus, the Appellate Body need not explore this issue further.[34]

14.7   Sovereignty over natural resources

The general international law principle of 'permanent sovereignty over **14.32** natural resources' is reflected in a number of international legal

---

[33] Appellate Body Report, *US – Shrimp (Article 21.5 – Malaysia)*, para. 124 (citing Appellate Body Report, *US – Shrimp*, para. 168).

[34] Appellate Body Report, *EC – Seal Products*, para. 5.173 (citing Appellate Body Report, *US – Shrimp*, para. 133).

instruments.[35] This principle was discussed in two WTO cases concerning measures taken to limit exports of certain natural resources.

14.33 In *China – Raw Materials*, the Panel considered that the requirements of Article XX(g) of the GATT can be interpreted harmoniously with the international law principle of State sovereignty over its natural resources:

> An important element of the principle of state sovereignty is the principle of sovereignty over natural resources, recognized as a principle of international law, and allowing states to 'freely use and exploit their natural wealth and resources wherever deemed desirable by them for their own progress and economic development'. The principle of sovereignty over natural resources is embodied in a number of international agreements, including in the Preamble of the *Convention on Biological Diversity*, which '[reaffirms] that States have sovereign rights over their biological resources'.[36]

14.34 In *China – Rare Earths*, the Panel considered the principle of permanent sovereignty over natural resources, again in the context of interpreting and applying Article XX(g) of the GATT. The Panel considered that States' sovereignty over their natural resources is a 'relevant rule of international law applicable between the parties' within the meaning of Article 31(3)(c) of the Vienna Convention, and took account of the same UN Resolutions referred to by the Panel in *China – Raw Materials*:

> As indicated above, the Panel believes that the international law principles of sovereignty over natural resources and sustainable development, which allow States to 'freely use and exploit their natural wealth and resources wherever deemed desirable by them for their own progress and economic development', are relevant to our interpretive exercise in this dispute. These two principles, which the Panel considers to be closely interrelated, are embodied in a number of international agreements. For example, the 1992 Rio Declaration on Environment and Development provides in Principles 2 and 4 that:
>
> > 2. States have, in accordance with the Charter of the United Nations and the principles of international law, the sovereign right to exploit their own resources pursuant to their own environmental and developmental policies, and the responsibility to ensure that activities within their jurisdiction or control do not cause damage to the environment of other States or of areas beyond the limits of national jurisdiction.
> >
> > . . .

---

[35] For commentary, see N. J. Schrijver, 'Permanent Sovereignty over Natural Resources' (June 2008) in *Max Planck Encyclopedia of Public International Law*.

[36] Panel Report, *China – Raw Materials*, para. 7.380 (citing UNGA Res. 1803 (XVII), 'Permanent Sovereignty Over Natural Resources' (14 December 1962); UNGA Res. 626 (VII), 'Right to Exploit Freely Natural Wealth and Resources' (21 December 1952); and the Convention on Biological Diversity, Rio de Janeiro, 1992, 1760 UNTS 79; 31 ILM s).

4. In order to achieve sustainable development, environmental protection shall constitute an integral part of the development process and cannot be considered in isolation from it.

Similarly, UN General Assembly Resolution 626 (VII) provides that States may freely exploit their natural resources 'wherever deemed desirable by them for their own progress and economic development'; and UN General Assembly Resolution 2158 (XXI) recognizes that:

> The natural resources of the developing countries constitute a basis of their economic development in general and of their industrial progress in particular ... it is essential that their exploitation and marketing should be aimed at securing the highest possible rate of growth of the developing countries ... this aim can better be achieved if the developing countries are in a position to undertake themselves the exploitation and marketing of their natural resources.

The principle of sovereignty over natural resources thus recognizes that WTO Members have the right to use their natural resources to promote their own development while also encouraging the regulation of such use to ensure sustainable development. According to the principle, then, conservation and economic development are not mutually exclusive policy goals; they can operate in harmony.

The Panel recognizes the permanent sovereignty that every WTO Member has, as a matter of fundamental principle, over its own natural resources. As noted above, the Panel believes that the principle of sovereignty over natural resources is a relevant rule of international law applicable in this case, and that it assists us with our interpretation of Article XX(g), and especially the word 'conservation'. The Panel acknowledges that, pursuant to their permanent sovereignty over natural resources, WTO Members may adopt conservation measures that are not merely concerned with 'preserv[ing] the natural resources in their current state'. Resource-endowed WTO Members are entitled to develop conservation policies on the basis of, or taking into account, a full range of policy considerations and goals, including the need to preserve resources in their current state as well as the need to use them in a sustainable manner. Moreover, given States' permanent sovereignty over natural resources, WTO Members, of course including China, are entitled to determine their own conservation objectives. Additionally, a Member's permanent sovereignty over its natural resources means that, in principle, it is entirely in that Member's discretion whether its conservation measures should 'decrease the absolute quantity' of materials extracted or 'control the speed' of such extraction, provided that its measures do not cause damage to the environment of other States or of areas beyond the limits of the regulating Member's national jurisdiction. Thus, understood in the light of every State's permanent sovereignty over their own natural resources, the Panel believes that conservation as used in Article XX(g) does not simply mean placing a moratorium on the exploitation of natural resources, but includes also measures that regulate and control such exploitation in accordance with a Member's development and conservation objectives. In this connection, we agree with China that 'conservation' as used in Article XX(g) is not limited to mere 'preservation of natural resources'.

In recognition of the permanent sovereignty that every Member exercises over its natural resources, WTO law recognizes the right of Members to adopt conservation measures should they wish to do so, in the light of their own objectives and policy goals, including economic and sustainable development. In other words, resource-endowed WTO Members are entitled to design conservation policies that meet their development needs, determine how much of a resource should be exploited today and how much should be preserved for the future, including for use by future generations, in a manner consistent with their sustainable development needs and their international obligations.

This permanent sovereignty over natural resources and the right of WTO Members to adopt conservation programmes pursuant to Article XX(g) allows WTO Members to develop and implement processes, means, or tools that put into practice a conservation policy in a way that responds to a Member's development and conservation concerns. It is not, however, a general right to regulate and control a natural resource market for any purpose. As the Appellate Body recognized in *US – Softwood Lumber IV*, natural resource products that will necessarily enter the market and are available for sale are subject to GATT disciplines in the same way as any other product. As such, no WTO Member has, under WTO law, the right to dictate or control the allocation or distribution of rare earth resources to achieve an economic objective. WTO Members' right to adopt conservation programmes is not a right to control the international markets in which extracted products are bought and sold.[37]

14.8   Sovereign equality

14.35 Article 2(1) of the Charter of the United Nations states that the UN is based on the 'sovereign equality' of all of its Members.[38] There is only one case to date in which a WTO adjudicator referred to the concept of 'sovereign equality' *per se*, suggesting that WTO adjudicators might understand 'sovereign equality' to either mean the same thing as, or to be subsumed within, the concept of 'sovereignty'.

14.36 In *EC – Bananas (US) (Article 22.6 – EC)*, the Arbitrator concluded that, for the purpose of determining the level of countermeasures that the United States could apply, the benchmark for the calculation of nullification or impairment of US trade flows should be losses in US exports of goods to the European

---

[37] Panel Report, *China – Rare Earths*, paras. 7.263–7.268 (citing UNGA Res. 1803 (XVII), 'Permanent Sovereignty Over Natural Resources' (14 December 1962); UNGA Res. 626 (VII), 'Right to Exploit Freely Natural Wealth and Resources' (21 December 1952); Rio Declaration on Environment and Development, Rio de Janeiro, 14 June 1992, 31 ILM 874).

[38] For commentary, see J. Kokott, 'States, Sovereign Equality' (April 2011) in *Max Planck Encyclopedia of Public International Law*.

Communities and losses by US service suppliers in services supply in or to the European Communities. In the course of its analysis, the Arbitrator stated:

> A right to seek redress for that amount of nullification or impairment does exist under the DSU for the WTO Members which are the countries of origin for these bananas, but not for the United States. In fact, a number of these WTO Members have been in the recent past, or are currently, in the process of exercising their rights under the DSU. Moreover, our concern with the protection of rights of other WTO Members is in conformity with public international law principles of sovereign equality of states and the non-interference with the rights of other states. Consequently, there is no right and no need under the DSU for one WTO Member to claim compensation or request authorization to suspend concessions for the nullification or impairment suffered by another WTO Member with respect to goods bearing the latter's origin or service suppliers owned or controlled by it.[39]

14.37 In *US – Clove Cigarettes*, the Panel rejected Indonesia's claim, under Article 2.2 of the TBT Agreement, that the challenged US measure to address youth smoking was more trade restrictive than necessary to fulfil a legitimate objective. In support of its claim, Indonesia argued that other countries had adopted less trade restrictive measures to address youth smoking. While it did not expressly refer to the 'sovereign equality' of States, the Panel made clear that it did not accept that the laws implemented to date by other countries should serve as some kind of benchmark for the United States or any other 'sovereign' WTO Member:

> In addition, we consider that Indonesia's reliance upon non-trade restrictive measures to address youth smoking allegedly adopted by certain other countries, including Australia and Singapore, is misplaced. For one thing, Indonesia has only provided some selective references to the practices of a few other countries, and has not made reference to other Members that have banned clove cigarettes. More importantly, however, is that it is not clear that the laws implemented to date by other countries should serve as some kind of benchmark for the United States or any other sovereign WTO Member, particularly where Indonesia has not established the objectives of these foreign measures and at what level those measures fulfil their respective objectives, and whether the objectives of the foreign measures are the same as the US objective and that the foreign countries seek to achieve that objective at the same level the United States does.[40]

14.9   The domestic jurisdiction

14.38 Article 2(7) of the Charter of the United Nations provides that nothing therein shall authorize the United Nations to intervene 'in matters which are essentially

---

[39] Decision by the Arbitrator, *EC – Bananas (Article 22.6 – US)*, para. 6.14.
[40] Panel Report, *US – Clove Cigarettes*, para. 7.426.

within the domestic jurisdiction of any state'.[41] In the context of WTO dispute settlement, there have been no cases in which a respondent argued that the challenged measure concerned a matter 'essentially within the domestic jurisdiction' of that State, and there have been no cases in which the Appellate Body or any panel or arbitrator has referred to the concept of 'domestic jurisdiction'.

[41] For commentary, see K. S. Ziegler, 'Domaine Réservé' (April 2008) in *Max Planck Encyclopedia of Public International Law*.

15

TREATY INTERPRETATION

15.1 Introduction

The number of books written on treaty interpretation in recent years speaks to [15.1] the importance of the topic.[1] It has been said that '[o]f all the issues raised by the Vienna Convention on the Law of Treaties, there can be few which combine the theoretical interest and practical importance to the same degree as the question of treaty interpretation'.[2] The reason is that '[m]ost disputes submitted to international adjudication involve some problem of treaty interpretation', and therefore '[j]ust as the interpretation of legislation is the constant concern of any government lawyer, treaty interpretation forms a significant part of the day-to-day work of a foreign ministry legal adviser'.[3] Article 3.2 of the DSU states that the WTO dispute settlement system serves to clarify the existing provisions of the WTO agreements 'in accordance with customary rules of interpretation of public international law'. WTO panels and the Appellate Body have confirmed the customary international law status of Articles 31, 32 and 33 of the Vienna Convention, and there is now a very substantial body of WTO jurisprudence regarding the various elements of these provisions. As far back as 1999, one WTO panel observed that '[i]n recent years, the jurisprudence of the Appellate

---

[1] R. Kolb. *Interprétation et création du droit international. Esquisse d'une herméneutique juridique moderne pour le droit international public* (Bruylant, 2006); U. Linderfalk, *On the Interpretation of Treaties: The Modern International Law as Expressed in the 1969 Vienna Convention on the Law of Treaties* (Springer, 2007); A. Orakhelashvili, *The Interpretation of Acts and Rules in Public International Law* (Oxford University Press, 2008); R. Gardiner, *Treaty Interpretation* (Oxford University Press, 2008); M. Villiger, *Commentary on the 1969 Vienna Convention on the Law of Treaties* (Martinus Nijhoff, 2009); M. Fitzmaurice, O. Elias and P. Merkouris (eds.), *Treaty Interpretation and the Vienna Convention on the Law of Treaties: 30 Years On* (Brill, 2010); O. Corten and P. Klein, *The Vienna Conventions on the Law of Treaties: A Commentary* (Oxford University Press, 2011); O. Dörr and K. Schmalenbach, *Vienna Convention on the Law of Treaties: A Commentary* (Springer, 2012), pp. 521–604; J. R. Weeramantry, *Treaty Interpretation in Investment Arbitration* (Oxford University Press, 2012).
[2] F. Jacobs, 'Varieties of Approach to Treaty Interpretation' (1969) 19 *International and Comparative Law Quarterly* 321, at 321.
[3] A. Aust, *Modern Treaty Law and Practice*, 2nd edn (Cambridge University Press, 2007), p. 230.

Body and WTO panels has become one of the richest sources from which to receive guidance on their application'.[4] Statements by WTO adjudicators relating to Articles 31, 32 and 33 of the Vienna Convention are of wider relevance because those provisions reflect the general principles of interpretation that apply to any treaty, irrespective of its subject-matter. As the Appellate Body explained in *US – Hot-Rolled Steel*:

> [T]he rules of treaty interpretation in Articles 31 and 32 of the *Vienna Convention* apply to *any* treaty, in *any* field of public international law, and not just to the WTO agreements. These rules of treaty interpretation impose certain common disciplines upon treaty interpreters, irrespective of the content of the treaty provision being examined and irrespective of the field of international law concerned.[5]

This chapter reviews statements by WTO adjudicators clarifying the various elements of Articles 31, 32 and 33 of the Vienna Convention, as well as certain ancillary concepts and principles of treaty interpretation. In keeping with the focus of this book, it does not cover statements by WTO adjudicators relating to any special rules of treaty interpretation contained in the WTO agreements.[6]

15.2   Good faith

15.2   See Section 8.3 above for WTO jurisprudence relating to good faith in the performance and interpretation of treaties.

15.3   Ordinary meaning

15.3   Article 31(1) of the Vienna Convention provides that a treaty shall be interpreted 'in accordance with the ordinary meaning to be given to the terms'. WTO jurisprudence offers support for the proposition that interpretation should be founded on the text of the provision at issue, and that dictionaries are a useful starting point for establishing the ordinary meaning of terms. To date, there have been few cases in which a WTO adjudicator found that a particular term should be given a 'special meaning' in the sense of Article 31(4)

---

[4] Panel Report, *US – Section 301 Trade Act*, para. 7.21. See also M. Lennard, 'Navigating by the Stars: Interpreting the WTO Agreements' (2002) 5(1) *Journal of International Economic Law* 17; I. Van Damme, *Treaty Interpretation by the WTO Appellate Body* (Oxford University Press, 2009); D. McRae, 'Treaty Interpretation and the Development of International Trade Law by the WTO Appellate Body', in G. Sacerdoti, A. Yanovich and J. Bohanes, *The WTO at Ten: The Contribution of the Dispute Settlement System* (Cambridge University Press, 2006), p. 360.

[5] Appellate Body Report, *US – Hot-Rolled Steel*, para. 60.

[6] These include Article 17.6(ii) of the Anti-Dumping Agreement and Article IX:2 of the WTO Agreement.

of the Vienna Convention. In several cases, the Appellate Body has concluded that, insofar as the meaning of a generic term at issue had evolved between the conclusion of the treaty and the time of interpretation, it should be given its contemporary meaning and field of application.

15.3.1 Text as the foundation of interpretation

In *US – Gasoline*, the Appellate Body considered the principle of effective treaty interpretation (*ut res magis valeat quam pereat*) as 'one of the corollaries of the "general rule of interpretation" in the *Vienna Convention*'. In particular, the Appellate Body stated: **15.4**

> One of the corollaries of the 'general rule of interpretation' in the *Vienna Convention* is that interpretation must give meaning and effect to all the terms of a treaty. An interpreter is not free to adopt a reading that would result in reducing whole clauses or paragraphs of a treaty to redundancy or inutility.[7]

In *Japan – Alcoholic Beverages II*, the Appellate Body stressed that 'Article 31 of the *Vienna Convention* provides that the words of the treaty form the foundation for the interpretative process: "interpretation must be based above all upon the text of the treaty".'[8] **15.5**

In *EC – Hormones*, the Appellate Body stated that '[t]he fundamental rule of treaty interpretation requires a treaty interpreter to read and interpret the words actually used by the agreement under examination, not words the interpreter may feel should have been used'.[9] **15.6**

In *India – Patents (US)*, the Appellate Body emphasized that the principles of treaty interpretation 'neither require nor condone' the importation into a treaty of 'words that are not there' nor of 'concepts that were not intended': **15.7**

> The duty of a treaty interpreter is to examine the words of the treaty to determine the intentions of the parties. This should be done in accordance with the principles of treaty interpretation set out in Article 31 of the *Vienna Convention*. But these principles of interpretation neither require nor condone the imputation into a treaty of words that are not there or the importation into a treaty of concepts that were not intended . . . These rules must be respected and applied in interpreting the *TRIPS Agreement* or any other covered agreements . . . Both panels and the

---

[7] Appellate Body Report, *US – Gasoline*, p. 23 (citing *Corfu Channel* case, 1949 ICJ Reports, p. 24; *Territorial Dispute Case (Libyan Arab Jamahiriya* v. *Chad)*, 1994 ICJ Reports, p. 23; *Yearbook of the International Law Commission* (1966), Vol. II, p. 219; R. Jennings and A. Watts (eds.), *Oppenheim's International Law*, 9th edn (Longman's, 1992), Vol. 1, pp. 1280–1; P. Daillier and A. Pellet, *Droit international public*, 5th edn (1994), para. 17.2; D. Carreau, *Droit international* (1994), para. 369).

[8] Appellate Body Report, *Japan – Alcoholic Beverages II*, p. 11.

[9] Appellate Body Report, *EC – Hormones*, para. 181.

Appellate Body must be guided by the rules of treaty interpretation set out in the *Vienna Convention*, and must not add to or diminish rights and obligations provided in the *WTO Agreement*.[10]

15.8 In *US – Carbon Steel*, the Appellate Body reiterated that 'the task of interpreting a treaty provision must begin with its specific terms'.[11]

15.9 In *Canada – Patent Term*, the Appellate Body recalled that 'we look first, as always, at the text of the treaty provision, in accordance with the general rule of interpretation in Article 31 of the *Vienna Convention*'.[12]

15.3.2 Dictionaries

15.10 Panels and the Appellate Body routinely refer to dictionary definitions (most frequently the *Shorter Oxford English Dictionary*) when interpreting the terms of the WTO agreements. In *China – Publications and Audiovisual Products*, the Appellate Body recalled some of its previous pronouncements pertaining to the use of dictionaries for the purpose of establishing the ordinary meaning of a term:

> The Appellate Body has previously held that, while a panel may start with the dictionary definitions of the terms to be interpreted, in the process of discerning the ordinary meaning, dictionaries alone are not necessarily capable of resolving complex questions of interpretation because they typically catalogue all meanings of words. Dictionaries are important guides to, but not dispositive of, the meaning of words appearing in treaties. For these reasons, the Appellate Body has cautioned panels against equating the 'ordinary meaning' of a term with the definition provided by dictionaries. Under Article 31 of the *Vienna Convention*, the 'ordinary meaning' of treaty terms may be ascertained only in their context and in the light of the object and purpose of the treaty. In this respect, the Appellate Body has explained that interpretation pursuant to the customary rule codified in Article 31 of the *Vienna Convention* is ultimately a holistic exercise that should not be mechanically subdivided into rigid components.[13]

---

[10] Appellate Body Report, *India – Patents (US)*, paras. 45–6. See also Appellate Body Report, *India – Quantitative Restrictions*, footnote 23, para. 94.
[11] Appellate Body Report, *US – Carbon Steel*, para. 62.
[12] Appellate Body Report, *Canada – Patent Term*, para. 53.
[13] Appellate Body Report, *China – Publications and Audiovisual Products*, para. 348 (citing Appellate Body Report, *US – Gambling*, para. 164; Appellate Body Report, *US – Softwood Lumber IV*, para. 59; Appellate Body Report, *Canada – Aircraft*, para. 153; Appellate Body Report, *EC – Asbestos*, para. 92; Appellate Body Report, *US – Offset Act (Byrd Amendment)*, para. 248; Appellate Body Report, *US – Gambling*, paras. 166, 167; Appellate Body Report, *EC – Chicken Cuts*, para. 176).

15.3.3 Special meaning

Article 31(4) of the Vienna Convention states that a 'special meaning shall be   **15.11**
given to a term if it is established that the parties so intended'. The Panel in
India – Quantitative Restrictions explained that:

> We identified the ordinary meaning of the terms which is confirmed by their
> context and the object and purpose of the WTO Agreement, whereas India's
> interpretation could be considered rather to support a special meaning (within
> the meaning of Article 31.4 of the Vienna Convention . . .), in respect of which
> it has not proved that there was an agreement of the negotiators.[14]

In *Mexico – Telecoms*, the Panel, in the process of considering the meaning of   **15.12**
various telecommunications terms (such as 'linking' and 'interconnection'),
decided that they should be given a 'special meaning' within the meaning of
Article 31(4) of the Vienna Convention. The Panel concluded that, given that
the provision at issue was a technical one that appeared in a specialized service
sector, the Panel was 'entitled to examine what "special meaning" it may have in
the telecommunications context'.[15] The Panel stated that '[w]e consider that
Article 31(4) includes cases in which the term at issue is a technical one that is in
common use in its field, and which the parties can be presumed to have been
aware of'.[16]

The Panel in *EC – Approval and Marketing of Biotech Products* conducted a   **15.13**
detailed analysis of Article 31(3)(c), and in the course of that analysis it made
passing reference to Article 31(4):

> A treaty interpreter would have to keep in mind, of course, that other rules of
> international law may be negotiated rules and, as such, may assign meanings to
> particular terms which may not be reflective of the ordinary meaning of those
> terms. We note that this possibility is recognized in Article 31(4) of the *Vienna
> Convention*, which states that '[a] special meaning shall be given to a term if it is
> established that the parties so intended'.[17]

The Panel in *China – Intellectual Property Rights* considered that certain terms   **15.14**
should be understood as a composite term when used together, but that this
did not amount to saying that they had a 'special meaning' in the sense of
Article 31(4):

> The Panel observes that the general rule of treaty interpretation in Article 31 of
> the Vienna Convention refers in paragraph 1 to the ordinary meaning of the
> terms of the treaty, read in context. Where the terms are a single term, or
> ordinarily used together, then the treaty interpreter should refer to the ordinary

---

[14] Panel Report, *India – Quantitative Restrictions*, para. 4.12.
[15] Panel Report, *Mexico – Telecoms*, paras. 7.108–7.117, 7.169–7.177.
[16] Panel Report, *Mexico – Telecoms*, para. 7.169.
[17] Panel Report, *EC – Approval and Marketing of Biotech Products*, footnote 269.

meaning of that single term, or of each term in the particular context of each other. This is a distinct exercise from that in paragraph 4 of Article 31 of the Vienna Convention which requires a 'special meaning' to be given to a term if it is established that the parties so intended. No party to this dispute considers that a 'special meaning' should be given to the phrase 'on a commercial scale', and nor does the Panel.[18]

15.3.4 Evolutionary interpretation

15.15 In *US – Shrimp*, the Appellate Body concluded that the meaning of the term 'exhaustible natural resources' in Article XX(g) of the GATT is not confined to non-living (e.g. mineral) resources. In the course of its analysis, the Appellate Body stated:

> From the perspective embodied in the preamble of the *WTO Agreement*, we note that the generic term 'natural resources' in Article XX(g) is not 'static' in its content or reference but is rather 'by definition, evolutionary'.[109]
>
> . . .
>
> Given the recent acknowledgement by the international community of the importance of concerted bilateral or multilateral action to protect living natural resources, and recalling the explicit recognition by WTO Members of the objective of sustainable development in the preamble of the *WTO Agreement*, we believe it is too late in the day to suppose that Article XX(g) of the GATT 1994 may be read as referring only to the conservation of exhaustible mineral or other non-living natural resources. Moreover, two adopted GATT 1947 panel reports previously found fish to be an 'exhaustible natural resource' within the meaning of Article XX(g). We hold that, in line with the principle of effectiveness in treaty interpretation, measures to conserve exhaustible natural resources, whether *living* or *non-living*, may fall within Article XX(g).

---

[109] See *Namibia (Legal Consequences) Advisory Opinion* (1971) ICJ Rep., p. 31. The International Court of Justice stated that where concepts embodied in a treaty are 'by definition, evolutionary', their 'interpretation cannot remain unaffected by the subsequent development of law … Moreover, an international instrument has to be interpreted and applied within the framework of the entire legal system prevailing at the time of the interpretation.' See also *Aegean Sea Continental Shelf Case* (1978) ICJ Rep., p. 3; Jennings and Watts (eds.), *Oppenheim's International Law*, 9th edn, Vol. I (Longman's, 1992), p. 1282 and E. Jimenez de Aréchaga, 'International Law in the Past Third of a Century' (1978-I) 159 *Recueil des Cours* 1, p. 49.[19]

15.16 In *China – Publications and Audiovisual Products*, the Appellate Body rejected China's argument that the Panel should have relied on the meaning of 'sound recording' and 'distribution' at the time of China's accession to the WTO in

---

[18] Panel Report, *China – Intellectual Property Rights*, para. 7.558.
[19] Appellate Body Report, *US – Shrimp*, paras. 130–1.

2001. First, the Appellate Body was not persuaded that the meaning of the terms had changed between 2001 and the time of the dispute (2009). Second, the Appellate Body stated:

> More generally, we consider that the terms used in China's GATS Schedule ('sound recording' and 'distribution') are sufficiently generic that what they apply to may change over time. In this respect, we note that GATS Schedules, like the GATS itself and all WTO agreements, constitute multilateral treaties with continuing obligations that WTO Members entered into for an indefinite period of time, regardless of whether they were original Members or acceded after 1995.[705]

---

[705] We consider such reading of the terms in China's GATS Schedule to be consistent with the approach taken in *US – Shrimp*, where the Appellate Body interpreted the term 'exhaustible natural resources' in Article XX(g) of the GATT 1994. (Appellate Body Report, *US – Shrimp*, paras. 129 and 130)

We observe that the International Court of Justice, in *Costa Rica* v. *Nicaragua*, found that the term '*comercio*' ('commerce'), contained in an 1858 'Treaty of Limits' between Costa Rica and Nicaragua, should be interpreted as referring to both trade in goods and trade in services, even if, at the time of the conclusion of the treaty, such term was used to refer only to trade in goods. (International Court of Justice, Judgment, *Case concerning the Dispute regarding Navigational and Related Rights (Costa Rica* v. *Nicaragua)*, 13 July 2009)[20]

15.4 Context: general principles

15.17 Article 31(1) of the Vienna Convention provides that a treaty shall be interpreted in accordance with the meaning to be given to the terms 'in their context'. WTO adjudicators rely heavily on different forms of contextual reasoning when interpreting treaty provisions. While it would be quite difficult to catalogue all of the different forms of contextual reasoning that are reflected in WTO jurisprudence, in general it may be said that contextual reasoning in WTO jurisprudence rests on the principle of harmonious interpretation, and often involves drawing inferences about the meaning of one provision based on a comparison with the content and/or wording of other parts of that provision, or other provisions. WTO adjudicators routinely rely on inferences drawn from immediately surrounding words, other sentences of the same paragraph of a provision, other paragraphs in a provision, the title of a provision, immediately adjacent articles, other articles in the same part of the treaty, or other articles in other parts of the treaty. In the course of contextual reasoning, WTO adjudicators have frequently applied the presumption that the use of different wording in different provisions must be given meaning.

---

[20] Appellate Body Report, *China – Publications and Audiovisual Products*, para. 396.

15.4.1 Harmonious interpretation

15.18 In *Korea – Dairy*, the Appellate Body emphasized the general principle that the provisions of a treaty should be interpreted harmoniously, with reference to various international legal materials:

> In light of the interpretive principle of effectiveness, it is the *duty* of any treaty interpreter to 'read all applicable provisions of a treaty in a way that gives meaning to *all* of them, harmoniously.' An important corollary of this principle is that a treaty should be interpreted as a whole, and, in particular, its sections and parts should be read as a whole.[44]

---

[44] The duty to interpret a treaty as a whole has been clarified by the Permanent Court of International Justice in *Competence of the ILO to Regulate Agricultural Labour* (1922), PCIJ, Series B, Nos. 2 and 3, p. 23. This approach has been followed by the International Court of Justice in *Ambatielos Case* (1953) *ICJ Reports*, p. 10; *Reservations to the Convention on the Prevention and Punishment of the Crime of Genocide* (1951) *ICJ Reports*, p. 15; and *Case Concerning Rights of United States Nationals in Morocco* (1952) *ICJ Reports*, pp. 196–199. See also I. Brownlie, *Principles of Public International Law*, 5th edn (Clarendon Press, 1998), p. 634; G. Fitzmaurice, 'The Law and Procedure of the International Court of Justice 1951–1954: Treaty Interpretation and Other Treaty Points', 33 *British Yearbook of International Law* (1957), p. 211 at p. 220; A. McNair, *The Law of Treaties* (Clarendon Press, 1961), pp. 381–382; I. Sinclair, *The Vienna Convention on the Law of Treaties* (Manchester University Press, 1984), pp. 127–129; M. O. Hudson, *La Cour Permanente de Justice Internationale* (Editions A Pedone, 1936), pp. 654–659; and L. A. Podesta Costa and J. M. Ruda, *Derecho Internacional Público*, Vol. 2 (Tipográfica, 1985), p. 105.[21]

15.19 The Panel in *US – Section 110(5) Copyright Act* stated:

> Reading treaty terms in their context requires that the text of the treaty must of course be read as a whole. One cannot simply concentrate on a paragraph, an article, a section, a chapter or a part. (Cf. Ian Sinclair, The Vienna Convention on the Law of Treaties (2nd edn), Manchester (1984), p. 127.) See also: Competence of Assembly regarding admission to the United Nations, Advisory Opinion, ICJ Reports 1950, p. 8; Arbitral Award of 31 July 1989, Judgment, ICJ Reports 1991, p. 69; Polish Postal Service in Danzig, PCIJ Series B, No. 11, p. 39. Yasseen notes that '[d]'autres dispositions plus ou moins éloignées risquent d'apporter une exception à la disposition qu'il s'agit d'interpréter ou de poser une condition à la mise en *œuvre* de cette disposition'. See Yasseen, L'interprétation des traités d'aprés la Convention de Vienne sur le Droit des Traités, 151 Recueil des Cours (1976-III), p. 34.[22]

---

[21] Appellate Body Report, *Korea – Dairy*, para. 81.
[22] Panel Report, *US – Section 110(5) Copyright Act*, footnote 49.

15.4.2 Different words, different meanings

In its first decision, *US – Gasoline*, the Appellate Body emphasized that it is **15.20** necessary to give meaning to the fact that different words are used in the different paragraphs of Article XX of the GATT:

> Applying the basic principle of interpretation that the words of a treaty, like the General Agreement, are to be given their ordinary meaning, in their context and in the light of the treaty's object and purpose, the Appellate Body observes that the Panel Report failed to take adequate account of the words actually used by Article XX in its several paragraphs. In enumerating the various categories of governmental acts, laws or regulations which WTO Members may carry out or promulgate in pursuit of differing legitimate state policies or interests outside the realm of trade liberalization, Article XX uses different terms in respect of different categories:
>
> 'necessary' – in paragraphs (a), (b) and (d);
> 'essential' – in paragraph (j);
> 'relating to' – in paragraphs (c), (e) and (g);
> 'for the protection of' – in paragraph (f);
> 'in pursuance of' – in paragraph (h); and
> 'involving' – in paragraph (i).
>
> It does not seem reasonable to suppose that the WTO Members intended to require, in respect of each and every category, the same kind or degree of connection or relationship between the measure under appraisal and the state interest or policy sought to be promoted or realized.[23]

In *EC – Hormones*, the Appellate Body faulted the Panel for failing to give **15.21** meaning to the use of different terms in different provisions of the SPS Agreement:

> Article 2.2 uses 'based on', while Article 2.4 employs 'conform to'. Article 3.1 requires the Members to 'base' their SPS measures on international standards; however, Article 3.2 speaks of measures which 'conform to' international standards. Article 3.3 once again refers to measures 'based on' international standards. The implication arises that the choice and use of different words in different places in the *SPS Agreement* are deliberate, and that the different words are designed to convey different meanings. A treaty interpreter is not entitled to assume that such usage was merely inadvertent on the part of the Members who negotiated and wrote that Agreement. Canada has suggested the use of different terms was 'accidental' in this case, but has offered no convincing argument to support its suggestion. We do not believe this suggestion has overturned the inference of deliberate choice.[24]

In *Japan – Alcoholic Beverages II*, the Appellate Body explained that the same **15.22** term (in that case, 'like products') may carry different meanings in different

---

[23] Appellate Body Report, *US – Gasoline*, pp. 17–18.
[24] Appellate Body Report, *Japan-Alcoholic Beverages II* p. 21.

provisions – including, in that case, in different paragraphs of the same article. The Appellate Body stated:

> The concept of 'likeness' is a relative one that evokes the image of an accordion. The accordion of 'likeness' stretches and squeezes in different places as different provisions of the WTO Agreement are applied. The width of the accordion in any one of those places must be determined by the particular provision in which the term 'like' is encountered as well as by the context and the circumstances that prevail in any given case to which that provision may apply. We believe that, in Article III:2, first sentence of the GATT 1994, the accordion of 'likeness' is meant to be narrowly squeezed.[25]

15.5   Context: agreements and instruments under Article 31(2)

15.23   Context is defined in Article 31(2) of the Vienna Convention to comprise, in addition to the text, including its preamble and annexes: (a) any agreement relating to the treaty which was made between all the parties in connection with the conclusion of the treaty; and (b) any instrument which was made by one or more parties in connection with the conclusion of the treaty and accepted by the other parties as an instrument related to the treaty. There have been a number of cases in which WTO panels and the Appellate Body examined whether certain agreements, instruments and documents qualified as 'context' within the meaning of Article 31(2)(a) or (b).

15.5.1   Generally

15.24   In *US – Gambling*, the Appellate Body found that the Panel erred in categorizing certain documents prepared by the GATT Secretariat in connection with the negotiation of the Members' GATT Schedules ('W/120' and the '1993 Scheduling Guidelines') as evidencing 'agreement' within the meaning of Article 31(2)(a) or 31(2)(b):

> We note that Article 31(2) refers to the *agreement* or *acceptance* of the parties. In this case, both W/120 and the 1993 Scheduling Guidelines were drafted by the GATT Secretariat rather than the parties to the negotiations. It may be true that, on its own, authorship by a delegated body would not preclude specific documents from falling within the scope of Article 31(2). However, we are not persuaded that in this case the Panel could find W/120 and the 1993 Scheduling Guidelines to be context. Such documents can be characterized as context only where there is sufficient evidence of their constituting an 'agreement relating to the treaty' between the parties or of their 'accept[ance by the parties] as an instrument related to the treaty'.
>
> We do not accept, as the Panel appears to have done, that, simply by requesting the preparation and circulation of these documents and using them in preparing their offers, the parties in the negotiations have accepted them as agreements or instruments related to the treaty. Indeed, there are indications to the contrary. As the United States pointed out before the Panel, the United

---

[25] Appellate Body Report, *Japan – Alcoholic Beverages II*, p. 21.

States and several other parties to the negotiations clearly stated, at the time W/ 120 was proposed, that, although Members were encouraged to follow the broad structure of W/120, it was never meant to bind Members to the CPC definitions, nor to any other 'specific nomenclature', and that 'the composition of the list was not a matter for negotiations'. Similarly, the Explanatory Note that prefaces the Scheduling Guidelines itself appears to contradict the Panel in this regard, as it expressly provides that, although it is intended to assist 'persons responsible for scheduling commitments', that assistance 'should not be considered as an authoritative legal interpretation of the GATS.'[26]

In *EC – Chicken Cuts*, the Panel referred to several authorities regarding the principles underlying Article 31(2):   **15.25**

> Regarding other agreements or instruments that may qualify under Article 31(2), the International Law Commission stated:
>
> > '[T]he principle on which [Article 31(2)] is based is that a unilateral document cannot be regarded as forming part of the context … *unless not only was it made in connexion with the conclusion of the treaty, but its relation to the treaty was accepted in the same manner by the other parties …* What is proposed in paragraph 2 is that, for purposes of interpreting the treaty, these categories of documents should not be treated as mere evidence to which recourse may be had for the purpose of resolving an ambiguity or obscurity, but as part of the context for the purpose of arriving at the ordinary meaning of the terms of the treaty.' (emphasis added)
>
> Further, a leading international law commentator suggests that, in order to be related to the treaty, and thus be part of the 'context' as opposed to the negotiating history, which is dealt with in Article 32 of the Vienna Convention, an instrument 'must be concerned with the substance of the treaty and clarify certain concepts in the treaty or limit its field of application. It must equally be drawn up on the occasion of the conclusion of the treaty.'[27]

15.5.2 Agreements under Article 31(2)(a)

In *US – Section 110(5) Copyright Act*, the Panel found that an 'agreement' **15.26** within the meaning of Article 31(2)(a) existed in connection with the Berne Convention, through an agreed statement, made by a Rapporteur-General, reflected in a general report formally adopted by the parties to that treaty. The Panel noted that this was not merely a statement made by a chair of a drafting group in his or her personal capacity:

---

[26] Appellate Body Report, *US – Gambling*, paras. 175–6.
[27] Panel Report, *EC – Chicken Cuts (Brazil)*, paras. 7.153–7.154 (citing *Yearbook of the International Law Commission* (1966), Vol. II, p. 221, para. 13; I. Sinclair, *The Vienna Convention on the Law of Treaties*, 2nd edn (Manchester University Press, 1984), p. 129).

When ascertaining the legal status of the minor exceptions doctrine, it is important to note that the General Report states that the Rapporteur-General had been '*entrusted with making an express mention* of the possibility available to national legislation to make what is commonly called minor reservations'.[62] We believe that the choice of these words reflects an agreement within the meaning of Article 31(2)(a) of the Vienna Convention between the Berne Union members at the Brussels Conference to retain the possibility of providing minor exceptions in national law. We arrive at this conclusion for the following reasons. First, the introduction of Articles 11*bis*(1)(iii) and 11(1)(ii) occurred simultaneously with the adoption of the General Report expressly mentioning the minor exceptions doctrine. Second, this doctrine is closely related to the substance of the amendment of the Berne Convention in that it limits the scope of the exclusive rights introduced by Articles 11*bis*(1)(iii) and 11(1)(ii) of the Berne Convention. Third, an 'agreement' between all the parties exists because, on the one hand, the Rapporteur-General is being 'entrusted to expressly mention' minor exceptions and, on the other hand, the General Report of the Brussels Conference reflecting this express mentioning was formally adopted by the Berne Union members. We therefore conclude that an agreement within the meaning of Article 31(2)(a) of the Vienna Convention between all the parties on the possibility to provide minor exceptions was made in connection with the conclusion of a revision of the Convention introducing additional exclusive rights, including those contained in Articles 11*bis*(1)(iii) and 11(1)(ii), to which these limitations were to apply, and that this agreement is relevant as context for interpreting these Articles.

---

[62] This is not merely a statement by a chair of a drafting group made in his/her personal capacity.[28]

15.27 The Panel in *EC – Tariff Preferences* found that an instrument adopted in the context of UNCTAD qualified as an 'agreement', within the meaning of Article 31(2)(a), for purposes of interpreting the 1971 waiver adopted by GATT Contracting Parties known as the Enabling Clause (subsequently incorporated by reference into the WTO agreements). The Agreed Conclusions of the United Nations Conference on Trade and Development ('UNCTAD') Special Committee on Preferences (the 'Agreed Conclusions'), recognized that preferential tariff treatment accorded under a generalized scheme of preferences was key for developing countries. The Agreed Conclusions also made clear that the achievement of these objectives through the adoption of preferences by developed countries required a GATT waiver, in particular, with respect to the MFN obligation in Article I:1. Accordingly, the GATT parties adopted the 1971 Waiver Decision in order to waive the obligations of Article I of the GATT 1947 and thereby authorize the granting of tariff preferences to developing countries. Following its review of the facts surrounding these instruments, the Panel in *EC – Tariff Preferences* concluded

[28] Panel Report, *US – Section 110(5) Copyright Act*, para. 6.53.

that Agreed Conclusions established an 'agreement relating to the conclusion of the 1971 Waiver Decision; therefore, they are context for the 1971 Waiver Decision in the sense of Article 31.2(a) of the Vienna Convention'.[29]

In *EC – Chicken Cuts*, the Appellate Body found that the consensus among Members to use the Harmonized System of tariff nomenclature as the basis for their WTO Schedules constitutes an 'agreement' within the meaning of Article 31(2)(a) of the Vienna Convention. More precisely, the Appellate Body established that the Harmonized System serves as 'context' under Article 31(2)(a) for the purpose of interpreting Member's Schedules based on a 'close link' between the Harmonized System and those Schedules, and 'broad consensus' among GATT parties to use the Harmonized System when preparing their Schedules. The Appellate Body stated:

15.28

> We note that, in 1983, the GATT Contracting Parties took a Decision setting out guidelines and 'special procedures' to facilitate the 'wide adoption of the Harmonized System'; later, in 1991, they took a Decision on Procedures to Implement Changes in the Harmonized System. The close link between the Harmonized System and the WTO agreements is also clear. A number of WTO agreements that resulted from the Uruguay Round negotiations use the Harmonized System for specific purposes; the *Agreement on Rules of Origin* (in Article 9), the *Agreement on Subsidies and Countervailing Measures* (in Article 27), and the *Agreement on Textiles and Clothing* (in Article 2 and the Annex thereto) refer to the Harmonized System for purposes of defining product coverage of the agreement or the products subject to particular provisions of the agreement.
>
> This close link to the Harmonized System is particularly true for agricultural products. Annex 1 to the *Agreement on Agriculture*, which forms an integral part of that Agreement, defines the product coverage of that Agreement by reference to headings of the Harmonized System, both at the level of whole chapters and at the four-digit level in respect of specific products. Moreover, it is undisputed that the Uruguay Round tariff negotiations for agricultural products were held on the basis of the Harmonized System and that all WTO Members have followed the Harmonized System in their Schedules to the GATT 1994 with respect to agricultural products.
>
> The above circumstances confirm that, prior to, during, as well as after the Uruguay Round negotiations, there was broad consensus among the GATT Contracting Parties to *use* the Harmonized System as the basis for their WTO Schedules, notably with respect to agricultural products. In our view, this consensus constitutes an 'agreement' between WTO Members 'relating to' the *WTO Agreement* that was 'made in connection with the conclusion of' that Agreement, within the meaning of Article 31(2)(a) of the *Vienna Convention*. As such, this agreement is 'context' under Article 31(2)(a) for the purpose of interpreting the WTO agreements, of which the EC Schedule is an integral part. In this light, we consider that the Harmonized System is relevant for

---

[29] Panel Report, *EC – Tariff Preferences*, para. 7.86.

purposes of interpreting tariff commitments in the WTO Members' Schedules.[30]

15.29 In *China – Raw Materials*, the Panel had some difficulty treating a discussion among GATT negotiators as an Article 31(2)(a) 'agreement' for the purpose of interpreting Article XI:2(a) of the GATT. Specifically, the Panel did not accept China's argument that there was an agreement that a product may be 'essential' to a Member within the meaning of Article XI:2(a) of the GATT because of its importance for domestic processing industries:

> Nor does the Panel find much assistance in the negotiators' agreement that Article XI:2(a) would cover Australia's ban on the export on live merino sheep. China posits that this demonstrates that a product may be essential to a Member because of its importance for domestic processing industries. Even if the Panel were to agree that the drafters' agreement constitutes context within the meaning of Article 31(2)(a) of the *Vienna Convention* as an 'agreement relating to the treaty which was made between all parties in connection with the conclusion of the treaty', the Panel does not consider China's identification of Australia's restriction on merino sheep particularly useful to the Panel's interpretative exercise.[468] In the documents submitted to the Panel, Australia sought clarification on whether Article XI:2 would permit it to apply a ban on sheep exports if a drought were to threaten its flocks. There does not appear to be any objection to applying Article XI:2(a) in such situation. It appears beyond debate that Australia considered then (and maintains today) that merino sheep are 'essential' products. However, there is no evidence before the Panel that the drafters expressly discussed the notion of products for use by the downstream industry, or the meaning of 'essential' products, when addressing Australia's concern with the potential application of a ban on the export of merino sheep.
>
> ---
> [468] The Panel finds it difficult to regard this discussion amongst negotiators concerning live merino sheep as an 'agreement relating to the treaty which was made between all parties in connection with the conclusion of the treaty' pursuant to Article 31.2(a) of the VCLT.[31]

15.5.3 Instruments under Article 31(2)(b)

15.30 In *EC – Chicken Cuts*, the Panel stated that the outcome of its interpretative exercise would not be affected depending on whether the Harmonized System of tariff nomenclature was classified as an agreement under Article 31(2)(a) or, instead, as an instrument under Article 31(2)(b):

> We do not consider that the outcome of the interpretative exercise we are undertaking with respect to heading 02.10 of the EC Schedule will be affected depending upon whether we classify the HS as 'context' under Article 31(2)(b)

---

[30] Appellate Body Report, *EC – Chicken Cuts*, paras. 197–9.
[31] Panel Report, *China – Raw Materials*, para. 7.281.

of the *Vienna Convention* as submitted by Brazil, or as 'context' under Article 31
(1) as submitted by Thailand, or as a 'relevant rule of international law' under
Article 31(3)(c) as submitted by Thailand and the European Communities.
Therefore, we will treat the HS as if it qualifies as 'context' under Article 31(2),
recalling that the Appellate Body in *EC – Computer Equipment* indicated that
the HS should be taken into consideration for the interpretation of a Member's
schedule.[32]

In *EC – IT Products*, the Panel concluded that the Information Technology **15.31**
Agreement (ITA), an agreement among a subset of WTO Members to modify
their individual Schedules (which are integral parts of the WTO agreements),
qualifies as an Article 31(2)(b) 'instrument' for the purpose of interpreting those
Schedules. The Panel began by stating:

> Setting aside for the moment whether the ITA is a treaty or not, Article 31(2)
> recognizes that both 'agreements' and 'instruments' may qualify as context as
> long as they meet certain conditions. The Vienna Convention refers to the
> concepts of 'agreement' and 'instrument' within the definition of 'treaty'
> above.[525] The statement by the International Law Commission above implies
> that a qualifying 'instrument' may even be a unilateral 'document' so long as it
> complies with the additional requirements in Article 31(2)(b) that it was 'made
> in connection with the conclusion of the treaty', and 'its relation to the treaty
> was accepted in the same manner by the other parties'. In light of this, it is useful
> to consider whether the ITA is concerned with the substance of the treaty,
> clarifies concepts in the *WTO Agreement*, or otherwise limits its field of applica-
> tion, and the extent to which it was drawn up on the occasion of the conclusion
> of the treaty.

---

[525] Specifically, the definition in Article 2(1) seems to imply that an 'agreement'
may itself be composed of one or more 'instruments'.[33]

The Panel in *EC – IT Products* explained why the ITA qualified as an 'instrument' within the meaning of Article 31(2)(b):

> At a minimum, the ITA qualifies as an 'instrument' for the purposes of Article
> 31(2)(b).[527] The ITA was proposed, drafted and agreed to by a subset of WTO
> Members and states or separate customs territories in the process of acceding to
> the WTO. ITA participants in turn modified their WTO Schedules, which
> themselves form part of the WTO Agreement, following the conclusion and
> signing of the ITA. In this sense, the parties recognized the ITA as an 'instru-
> ment' as we understand that term.

---

[527] In *US – FSC* (para. 7.58), the panel considered the ordinary meaning of the
term 'instrument' as follows:

---

[32] Panel Report, *EC – Chicken Cuts (Brazil)*, para. 7.189.
[33] Panel Report, *EC – IT Products*, paras. 7.376–7.377 (citing Panel Report, *EC – Chicken Cuts*,
para. 7.154; I. Sinclair, *The Vienna Convention on the Law of Treaties*, 2nd edn (Manchester
University Press, 1984), p. 129).

'In this respect, we note that the word "instrument" has been defined by one dictionary as follows: "Law. A formal legal document whereby a right is created or confirmed, or a fact recorded; a formal writing of any kind, as an agreement, deed, charter, or record, drawn up and executed in legal form"... Similarly, a legal dictionary has defined the word "instrument" to mean, *inter alia*, "[a] document or writing which gives formal expression to a legal act or agreement, for the purpose of creating, securing, modifying or terminating a right; a writing executed and delivered as the evidence of an act or agreement" ... Thus, the term "legal instrument" in its ordinary meaning involves the existence of a formal legal text that has a binding effect in determining the rights and/or obligations of the parties thereto, which in this case would be all GATT 1947 contracting parties.'[34]

In *EC – IT Products*, the Panel concluded that this instrument had been 'made by one or more parties in connection with the conclusion of the treaty' within the meaning of Article 31(2)(b):

The ITA also represents an instrument 'made by one or more parties in connection with the conclusion of the treaty', where the term 'parties' refers to WTO Members. The ITA (formally the Ministerial Declaration on Trade in Information Technology Products) was agreed upon on 13 December 1996 by 15 WTO Members (counting the then 15 EC member States as one), as well as States or separate customs territories in the process of acceding to the WTO. Pursuant to the provisions in the ITA, participants modified their schedules of concessions, which themselves form part of the *WTO Agreement*. Because the original ITA participants expressly agreed to a process for incorporating ITA-related concessions into their WTO Schedules, the Panel considers that the ITA was clearly made 'in connection with the conclusion of the treaty', as the WTO Members amended their Schedules (which form part of the WTO Agreement) in order to give effect to the ITA.

The ITA also meets the requirement of having being 'accepted by the other parties as an instrument related to the treaty.' At least three elements demonstrate this. First, the ITA was recognized under paragraph 18 of the Singapore Ministerial Declaration of 13 December 1996 which was adopted by *all* WTO Members:

'Taking note that a number of Members have agreed on a Declaration on Trade in Information Technology Products, *we welcome* the initiative taken by a number of WTO Members and other States or separate customs territories which have applied to accede to the WTO, who have agreed to tariff elimination for trade in information technology products on an MFN basis ...' (emphasis added)

This express reference to the ITA in a WTO Ministerial Declaration adopted by consensus by all WTO Members constitutes, in our view, acceptance by WTO Members that the ITA is an instrument related to the *WTO Agreement*.

---

[34] Panel Report, *EC – IT Products*, para. 377.

Second, following the ministerial declaration, ITA participants modified their WTO Schedules of concessions to reflect commitments undertaken pursuant to the ITA. No objections were raised by other WTO Members within the three-month period provided for such purpose to the ITA-related modifications that were proposed by the European Communities and these were, therefore, certified by the Director General of the WTO in document WT/Let/156.

Third, the EC headnote of the Annex to the EC Schedule, which forms part of the *WTO Agreement*, makes express reference to the ITA, further suggesting that the ITA is related to the *WTO Agreement*.[35]

15.6   Object and purpose

WTO adjudicators routinely assess the consequences of opting for a particular **15.32** interpretation in light of the object and purpose of the provision and/or agreement at issue. Reasoning by reference to the object and purpose of a treaty can take many different forms. WTO adjudicators have been wary of certain forms of reasoning by reference to object and purpose, and have generally been cautious about attaching too much weight to the object and purpose of a treaty as a basis for its interpretation. However, one form of reasoning by reference to the object and purpose of a treaty that has been employed fairly regularly by WTO panels and the Appellate Body is to avoid interpretations that would enable Members to easily 'circumvent' or 'evade' their obligations.

In *US – Norwegian Salmon AD*, the GATT Panel considered that statements of **15.33** objectives in the preamble to a treaty generally do not create substantive legal commitments:

> The Panel considered that the statement in the preamble relied upon by Norway could guide the Panel's interpretation of specific operative provisions of the Agreement and noted in this respect that Article 31:2 of the Vienna Convention on the Law of Treaties expressly referred to the preamble of a treaty as part of 'the context for the purpose of the interpretation of a treaty'. However, this statement in the preamble did not by itself constitute a legal obligation of Parties to the Agreement.[463]

---

[463] 'Preambular provisions, cast in general wording are generally not intended to constitute substantive stipulations. Since they are mere statements, preambles do not create any legal commitment above and beyond the actual text of the treaty.' Treviranus, in Encyclopaedia of Public International Law, Vol. 7, p. 394 (1984).[36]

---

[35] *Ibid.*, paras. 7.378–7.382.   [36] GATT Panel Report, *US – Norwegian Salmon AD*, para. 369.

15.34 In *Japan – Alcoholic Beverages II*, the Appellate Body stated that the object and purpose of a treaty are to be taken into account in determining the meaning of its provisions, and then noted:

> That is, the treaty's 'object and purpose' is to be referred to in determining the meaning of the 'terms of the treaty' and not as an independent basis for interpretation: Harris, Cases and Materials on International Law (4th edn, 1991), p. 770; Jiménez de Aréchaga, 'International Law in the Past Third of a Century' (1978-I) 159 Recueil des Cours p. 1 at 44; Sinclair, *The Vienna Convention and the Law of Treaties* (2nd edn 1984), p. 130. See e.g. Oppenheim's International Law (9th edn, Jennings and Watts, eds., 1992) Vol. I, p. 1273; *Competence of the ILO to Regulate the Personal Work of the Employer* (1926), PCIJ, Series B, No. 13, p. 6 at 18; *International Status of South West Africa* (1962), ICJ Reports, p. 128 at 336; *Re Competence of Conciliation Commission* (1955), 22 International Law Reports, p. 867 at 871.[37]

15.35 In *US – Shrimp*, the Appellate Body stated that the object and purpose of a treaty may shed useful light on the meaning of a provision when the meaning imparted by the text itself is equivocal or inconclusive:

> A treaty interpreter must begin with, and focus upon, the text of the particular provision to be interpreted. It is in the words constituting that provision, read in their context, that the object and purpose of the states parties to the treaty must first be sought. Where the meaning imparted by the text itself is equivocal or inconclusive, or where confirmation of the correctness of the reading of the text itself is desired, light from the object and purpose of the treaty as a whole may usefully be sought.[38]

15.36 In *Canada – Aircraft*, the Panel noted that the SCM Agreement does not contain any express statement of its object and purpose, and stated that '[w]e therefore consider it unwise to attach undue importance to arguments concerning the object and purpose of the SCM Agreement'.[39]

15.37 In *EC – Chicken Cuts*, the Appellate Body discussed the relationship between the object and purpose of particular provisions and that of the treaty as a whole:

> It is well accepted that the use of the singular word 'its' preceding the term 'object and purpose' in Article 31(1) of the *Vienna Convention* indicates that the term refers to the treaty as a whole; had the term 'object and purpose' been preceded by the word 'their', the use of the plural would have indicated a reference to particular 'treaty terms'. Thus, the term 'its object and purpose' makes it clear that the starting point for ascertaining 'object and purpose' is the treaty itself, in its entirety. At the same time, we do not believe that Article 31(1) excludes taking into account the object and purpose of particular treaty terms, if doing so assists the interpreter in determining the treaty's object and purpose on the whole. We do not see why it would be necessary to divorce a treaty's object and purpose from

---

[37] Appellate Body Report, *Japan – Alcoholic Beverages II*, footnote 20.
[38] Appellate Body Report, *US – Shrimp*, para. 114.
[39] Panel Report, *Canada – Aircraft*, para. 9.119.

the object and purpose of specific treaty provisions, or *vice versa*. To the extent that one can speak of the 'object and purpose of a treaty provision', it will be informed by, and will be in consonance with, the object and purpose of the entire treaty of which it is but a component.[40]

However, the Appellate Body in *EC – Chicken Cuts* cautioned against evaluating the 'object and purpose' of specific provisions of a treaty in isolation from the treaty in its entirety:

> Having said this, we caution against interpreting WTO law in the light of the purported 'object and purpose' of specific provisions, paragraphs or subparagraphs of the WTO agreements, or tariff headings in Schedules, in isolation from the object and purpose of the treaty on the whole. Even if, *arguendo*, one could rely on the specific 'object and purpose' of heading 02.10 of the EC Schedule in isolation, we would share the Panel's view that 'one Member's unilateral object and purpose for the conclusion of a tariff commitment cannot form the basis' for an interpretation of that commitment, because interpretation in the light of Articles 31 and 32 of the Vienna Convention must focus on ascertaining the common intentions of the parties.[41]

In *US – Anti-Dumping and Countervailing Duties (China)* (DS379), the Panel **15.38** reviewed some prior panel and Appellate Body statements regarding the importance of avoiding interpretations enabling the circumvention of treaty obligations:

> In their discussions of the object and purpose of the SCM Agreement, including in respect of predictability and certainty, the Appellate Body and various panels have emphasized the importance of avoiding overly narrow interpretations of the Agreement that would create loopholes by which Members could largely, if not entirely, escape the reach of these disciplines. For example, the Appellate Body stated in *US – Softwood Lumber IV* that:
>
> > 'It is in furtherance of [the Agreement's] object and purpose [of strengthening GATT disciplines] that Article 1.1(a)(1)(iii) recognizes that subsidies may be conferred, not only through monetary transfers, but also by the provision of non-monetary inputs. Thus, to interpret the term 'goods' in Article 1.1(a)(1)(iii) narrowly, as Canada would have us do, would permit the circumvention of subsidy disciplines in cases of financial contributions granted in a form other than money . . .'.
>
> Similarly, the panel in *US – FSC (Article 21.5 – EC)* stated:
>
> > '[I]t is evident that the interpretation [of 'revenue foregone'] advanced by the United States would be irreconcilable with th[e] object and purpose [of disciplining trade distorting subsidies in a way that provides security to

---

[40] Appellate Body Report, *EC – Chicken Cuts*, para. 238 (citing I. Sinclair, *The Vienna Convention on the Law of Treaties*, 2nd edn (Manchester University Press, 1984), pp. 130–5; Appellate Body Report, *Argentina – Textiles and Apparel*, para. 47).

[41] Appellate Body Report, *EC – Chicken Cuts*, para. 239 (citing Appellate Body Report, *EC – Computer Equipment*, para. 84; I. Sinclair, *The Vienna Convention on the Law of Treaties*, 2nd edn (Manchester University Press, 1984), pp. 130–1).

Members], given that it would offer governments '*carte-blanche*' to evade any effective disciplines, thereby creating fundamental uncertainty and unpredictability. In short, such an approach would eviscerate the subsidies disciplines in the SCM Agreement'. (emphasis original)

In keeping with this object and purpose, we consider it important to read Article 1.1(a)(1) in a manner that does not allow avoidance of the SCM Agreement's disciplines by excluding whole categories of government non-commercial behaviour undertaken by government-controlled entities.[42]

15.7   Subsequent agreements

15.39 Article 31(3)(a) of the Vienna Convention provides that a treaty shall be interpreted taking into account 'any subsequent agreement between the parties regarding the interpretation of the treaty or the application of its provisions'. There have been several cases in which WTO adjudicators examined whether particular instruments qualified as subsequent agreements within the meaning of Article 31(3)(a).

15.40 In *Brazil – Desiccated Coconut*, the Panel considered that, while the 1979 Tokyo Round Subsidies Code may have constituted a subsequent agreement under Article 31(3)(a) regarding the interpretation of Article VI of the GATT 1947, it could not be so regarded in respect of Article VI of the GATT (i.e. the current version of the GATT incorporated by reference into the WTO agreements):

> In any event, we do not consider that it would be appropriate to interpret Article VI of GATT 1994 in light of the Tokyo Round SCM Code. Article 31:3(a) of the Vienna Convention on the Law of Treaties . . . which is generally held to reflect customary principles of international law regarding treaty interpretation, provides that 'any subsequent agreement between the parties to a treaty regarding its interpretation or the application of its provisions' may be taken into account when interpreting a treaty. The Tokyo Round SCM Code may constitute such a subsequent agreement among Tokyo Round SCM Code signatories regarding the interpretation of Article VI of GATT 1947. However, Article II:4 of the WTO Agreement provides that the GATT 1994 is 'legally distinct' from the GATT 1947. While GATT 1994 consists of, *inter alia*, 'decisions of the CONTRACTING PARTIES to GATT 1947', the Tokyo Round SCM Code is not a 'decision' of the CONTRACTING PARTIES. Thus, the Tokyo Round SCM Code does not represent a subsequent agreement regarding interpretation of Article VI of GATT 1994. For the Panel to conclude to the contrary would in effect convert that Code into a 'covered agreement'

---

[42] Panel Report, *US – Anti-Dumping and Countervailing Duties (China)*, paras. 8.75–8.76 (citing Appellate Body Report, *US – Softwood Lumber IV*, para. 64; Panel Report, *US – FSC (Article 21.5 – EC)*, para. 8.39).

under Appendix 1 of the DSU. If such an approach were followed, WTO Members that were Tokyo Round Code signatories would find that their Code obligations were now enforceable under the WTO dispute settlement system.[43]

In *Canada – Patent Term*, the Panel considered that the NAFTA did not qualify **15.41** as a subsequent agreement relevant to the interpretation of Article 33 of the TRIPS Agreement. The Panel stated:

> We note Canada's argument that the parties to the North American Free Trade Agreement ('NAFTA') accepted the substantive equivalence of the protection offered by two types of protection term. The relevant NAFTA provision cited by Canada states that '[e]ach party shall provide a term of protection for patents of at least twenty years from the date of filing or seventeen years from the date of grant.' We do not consider that the NAFTA provision means that Section 45 of the Canadian *Patent Act* and Article 33 of the *TRIPS Agreement* have substantive equivalence of protection. In this regard, we note that the Panel in *United States – Restrictions on Imports of Tuna*, GATT Doc. DS29/R, 20 May 1994 (unadopted), stated, in relation to Article 31.3(a) of the *Vienna Convention*, the following:
>
> > The Panel recalled that the Vienna Convention provides for a general rule of interpretation (Article 31) and a supplementary means of interpretation (Article 32). The Panel first examined whether, under the *general* rule of interpretation of the Vienna Convention, the treaties referred to might be taken into account for the purposes of interpreting the General Agreement. The general rule provides that 'any subsequent agreement between the parties regarding the interpretation of the treaty or the application of its provisions' is one of the elements relevant to the interpretation of a treaty. However the Panel observed that the agreements cited by the parties to the dispute were bilateral or plurilateral agreements that were not concluded among the contracting parties to the General Agreement, and that they did not apply to the interpretation of the General Agreement or the application of its provisions. Indeed, many of the treaties referred to could not have done so, since they were concluded prior to the negotiation of the General Agreement. The Panel also observed that under the general rule of interpretation in the Vienna Convention account should be taken of 'any subsequent practice in the application of the treaty which established the agreement of the parties regarding its interpretation.' However, the Panel noted that practice under the bilateral and plurilateral treaties cited could not be taken as practice under the General Agreement, and therefore could not affect the interpretation of it. The Panel therefore found that under the general rule contained in Article 31 of the Vienna Convention, these treaties were not relevant as a primary means of interpretation of the text of the General Agreement.[44]

---

[43] Panel Report, *Brazil – Desiccated Coconut*, para. 255.
[44] Panel Report, *Canada – Patent Term*, footnote 49.

15.42 In *US – Section 211 Appropriations Act*, the Panel was faced with a situation in which a previously 'agreed interpretation' may have been reduced in value as a possible interpretative tool under Article 31(3)(a) as a consequence of supervening developments:

> The documents concerning the Lisbon Conference of 1958 provided by WIPO in response to our request make it unequivocally clear that from the very beginning of the Paris Convention's history, the predecessor provisions to Article 6 *quinquies* had been largely drafted in the same wording but had been since considered somewhat opaque. As a matter of fact, it was necessary, in order to arrive at the final adoption of the predecessor provisions, to adopt an agreed interpretation of that provision in the form of paragraph 4 of the final Protocol of 1883. This agreed interpretation is very clear in stating that the predecessor provision of Article 6 *quinquies* is an exception to the rule that the legislation of the Members of the Union remains applicable and is restricted only to the form of the trademark. Later on, this agreed interpretation was set aside at the Washington Conference of 1911 and this may have reduced its value as a possible interpretative tool under Article 31(3)(a) of the Vienna Convention.[45]

15.43 In *EC – Bananas III (Article 21.5 – Ecuador II) / EC – Bananas III (Article 21.5 – US)*, the Appellate Body discussed the relationship between Article 31(3)(a) and Article IX:2 of the WTO Agreement, which governs the adoption of interpretations of the WTO agreements by the WTO Ministerial Conference:

> Multilateral interpretations of provisions of WTO law are the next method identified above. Article IX:2 of the *WTO Agreement* sets out specific requirements for decisions that may be taken by the Ministerial Conference or the General Council to adopt interpretations of provisions of the Multilateral Trade Agreements. Such multilateral interpretations are meant to clarify the meaning of existing obligations, not to modify their content. Article IX:2 emphasizes that such interpretations 'shall not be used in a manner that would undermine the amendment provisions in Article X'. A multilateral interpretation should also be distinguished from a waiver, which allows a Member to depart from an existing WTO obligation for a limited period of time. We consider that a multilateral interpretation pursuant to Article IX:2 of the *WTO Agreement* can be likened to a subsequent agreement regarding the interpretation of the treaty or the application of its provisions pursuant to Article 31(3)(a) of the *Vienna Convention*, as far as the interpretation of the WTO agreements is concerned.[46]

The Appellate Body provided further guidance on Article 31(3)(a):

> We further observe that, in its commentary on the Draft Articles on the Law of Treaties, the International Law Commission (the 'ILC') describes a subsequent agreement within the meaning of Article 31(3)(a) of the *Vienna Convention* 'as a further *authentic element of interpretation* to be taken into account together with

---

[45] Panel Report, *US – Section 211 Appropriations Act*, para. 8.82.
[46] Appellate Body Report, *EC – Bananas III (Article 21.5 – Ecuador II)/EC – Bananas III (Article 21.5 – US)*, para. 383.

the context'. In our view, by referring to 'authentic interpretation', the ILC
reads Article 31(3)(a) as referring to agreements bearing specifically upon the
interpretation of a treaty. In the WTO context, multilateral interpretations
adopted pursuant to Article IX:2 of the *WTO Agreement* are most akin to
subsequent agreements within the meaning of Article 31(3)(a) of the *Vienna
Convention*, but not waivers adopted pursuant to Articles IX:3 and 4 of the
WTO Agreement.

    ... In our view, the term 'application' in Article 31(3)(a) relates to the
situation where an agreement specifies how existing rules or obligations in force
are to be 'applied'; the term does not connote the creation of new or the
extension of existing obligations that are subject to a temporal limitation and
are to expire. We find the Panel's conclusion that the Doha Article I Waiver
extended the duration of the tariff quota concession beyond 31 December 2002,
and thereby modified or changed the content of the European Communities'
Schedule, difficult to reconcile with its conclusion that the Waiver should be
considered an agreement on the *application* of existing commitments contained
in that Schedule. As such, we do not consider that the Doha Article I Waiver
could be regarded as an agreement on the application of the tariff quota
concession in the European Communities' Schedule within the meaning of
Article 31(3)(a) of the *Vienna Convention*.[47]

In *US – Clove Cigarettes*, the Appellate Body upheld the Panel's finding that, by **15.44**
allowing only three months between the publication and the entry into force of
the technical regulation at issue, the United States acted inconsistently with
Article 2.12 of the TBT Agreement, which, when interpreted in the context of
Paragraph 5.2 of the 'Doha Ministerial Decision on Implementation-Related
Issues and Concerns', requires a minimum of six months between the publication and the entry into force of a technical regulation.[48] In reaching this
conclusion, the Appellate Body found that, in the absence of evidence of the
existence of a specific recommendation from the relevant council concerning
the interpretation of Article 2.12 of the TBT Agreement, paragraph 5.2 of the
Doha Ministerial Decision did not constitute a multilateral interpretation
adopted pursuant to the procedural requirements specified in Article IX:2 of
the WTO Agreement. However, the Appellate Body agreed with the Panel that
paragraph 5.2 of the Doha Ministerial Decision nonetheless constitutes a
'subsequent agreement between the parties' within the meaning of Article 31
(3)(a). In the course of its analysis, the Appellate Body discussed the elements of
Article 31(3)(a):

Based on the text of Article 31(3)(a) of the *Vienna Convention*, we consider that
a decision adopted by Members may qualify as a 'subsequent agreement
between the parties' regarding the interpretation of a covered agreement or the
application of its provisions if: (i) the decision is, in a temporal sense, adopted
subsequent to the relevant covered agreement; and (ii) the terms and content of

---

[47] *Ibid.*, paras. 390–1.   [48] Appellate Body Report, *US – Clove Cigarettes*, paras. 241–75.

the decision express an *agreement* between Members on the *interpretation* or *application* of a provision of WTO law.

With regard to the first element, we note that the Doha Ministerial Decision was adopted by consensus on 14 November 2001 on the occasion of the Fourth Ministerial Conference of the WTO. Thus, it is beyond dispute that paragraph 5.2 of the Doha Ministerial Decision was adopted subsequent to the relevant WTO agreement at issue, the *TBT Agreement*. With regard to the second element, the key question to be answered is whether paragraph 5.2 of the Doha Ministerial Decision expresses an *agreement* between Members on the *interpretation* or *application* of the term 'reasonable interval' in Article 2.12 of the *TBT Agreement*.

We recall that paragraph 5.2 of the Doha Ministerial Decision provides:

> Subject to the conditions specified in paragraph 12 of Article 2 of the Agreement on Technical Barriers to Trade, the phrase 'reasonable interval' shall be understood to mean normally a period of not less than 6 months, except when this would be ineffective in fulfilling the legitimate objectives pursued.

In addressing the question of whether paragraph 5.2 of the Doha Ministerial Decision expresses an agreement between Members on the interpretation or application of the term 'reasonable interval' in Article 2.12 of the *TBT Agreement*, we find useful guidance in the Appellate Body reports in *EC – Bananas III (Article 21.5 – Ecuador II)/EC – Bananas III (Article 21.5 – US)*. The Appellate Body observed that the International Law Commission (the 'ILC') describes a subsequent agreement within the meaning of Article 31(3)(a) of the *Vienna Convention* as 'a further *authentic element of interpretation* to be taken into account together with the context'. According to the Appellate Body, 'by referring to "authentic interpretation", the ILC reads Article 31(3) (a) as referring to *agreements bearing specifically upon the interpretation of the treaty.*' Thus, we will consider whether paragraph 5.2 bears specifically upon the interpretation of Article 2.12 of the *TBT Agreement*.

Paragraph 5.2 of the Doha Ministerial Decision refers explicitly to the term 'reasonable interval' in Article 2.12 of the *TBT Agreement* and defines this interval as 'normally a period of not less than 6 months, except when this would be ineffective in fulfilling the legitimate objectives pursued' by a technical regulation. In the light of the terms and content of paragraph 5.2, we are unable to discern a function of paragraph 5.2 *other than* to interpret the term 'reasonable interval' in Article 2.12 of the *TBT Agreement*. We consider, therefore, that paragraph 5.2 *bears specifically* upon the interpretation of the term 'reasonable interval' in Article 2.12 of the *TBT Agreement*. We turn now to consider whether paragraph 5.2 of the Doha Ministerial Decision reflects an 'agreement' among Members – within the meaning of Article 31(3)(a) of the *Vienna Convention* – on the interpretation of the term 'reasonable interval' in Article 2.12 of the *TBT Agreement*.

We note that the text of Article 31(3)(a) of the *Vienna Convention* does not establish a requirement as to the form which a 'subsequent agreement between the parties' should take. We consider, therefore, that the term 'agreement' in Article 31(3)(a) of the *Vienna Convention* refers, fundamentally, to substance rather than to form. Thus, in our view, paragraph 5.2 of the Doha Ministerial

Decision can be characterized as a 'subsequent agreement' within the meaning of Article 31(3)(a) of the *Vienna Convention* provided that it clearly expresses a common understanding, and an acceptance of that understanding among Members with regard to the meaning of the term 'reasonable interval' in Article 2.12 of the *TBT Agreement*. In determining whether this is so, we find the terms and content of paragraph 5.2 to be dispositive. In this connection, we note that the understanding among Members with regard to the meaning of the term 'reasonable interval' in Article 2.12 of the *TBT Agreement* is expressed by terms – '*shall be understood to mean*' – that cannot be considered as merely hortatory.[49]

For the foregoing reasons, in *US – Clove Cigarettes* the Appellate Body upheld the Panel's finding that paragraph 5.2 of the Doha Ministerial Decision constitutes a subsequent agreement between the parties, within the meaning of Article 31(3)(a), on the interpretation of the term 'reasonable interval' in Article 2.12 of the TBT Agreement. Based on that characterization, the Appellate Body then stated:

> We observe that, in its commentaries on the *Draft articles on the Law of Treaties*, the ILC states that a subsequent agreement between the parties within the meaning of Article 31(3)(a) 'must be read into the treaty for purposes of its interpretation'. As we see it, while the terms of paragraph 5.2 must be 'read into' Article 2.12 for the purpose of interpreting that provision, this does not mean that the terms of paragraph 5.2 replace or override the terms contained in Article 2.12. Rather, the terms of paragraph 5.2 of the Doha Ministerial Decision constitute an interpretative clarification to be taken into account in the interpretation of Article 2.12 of the *TBT Agreement*.[50]

In *US – Tuna II (Mexico)*, the Appellate Body reversed the Panel's finding that **15.45** the 'dolphin-safe' definition and certification developed within the framework of the Agreement on the International Dolphin Conservation Program ('AIDCP') is a 'relevant international standard' within the meaning of Article 2.4 of the TBT Agreement.[51] In the context of interpreting the terms 'relevant international standard' in Article 2.4, the Appellate Body relied on the TBT Committee 'Decision on Principles for the Development of International Standards, Guides and Recommendations with Relation to Articles 2, 5, and Annex 3 to the Agreement', which it considered to be a 'subsequent agreement between the parties' within the meaning of Article 31(3)(a). In the course of its analysis, the Appellate Body stated:

> Pursuant to Article 3.2 of the DSU, panels and the Appellate Body are to 'clarify' the provisions of the covered agreements 'in accordance with

---

[49] *Ibid.*, paras. 262–7 (citing Appellate Body Reports, *EC – Bananas III (Article 21.5 – Ecuador II)/ EC – Bananas III (Article 21.5 – US)*, para. 390).

[50] Appellate Body Report, *US – Clove Cigarettes*, para. 269 (citing *Yearbook of the International Law Commission* (1966), Vol. II, p. 221, para. 14).

[51] Appellate Body Report, *US – Tuna II (Mexico)*, paras. 343–401.

customary rules of interpretation of public international law'. This raises the question on what basis we can take into account the TBT Committee Decision in the interpretation and application of Article 2.4 of the *TBT Agreement*. In particular, the issue is whether the Decision can qualify as a 'subsequent agreement between the parties regarding the interpretation of the treaty or the application of its provisions' within the meaning of Article 31(3)(a) of the *Vienna Convention on the Law of Treaties* … In this respect, we note that the Decision was adopted by the TBT Committee in the context of the Second Triennial Review of the Operation and Implementation of the *TBT Agreement*, which took place in the year 2000. It was thus adopted subsequent to the conclusion of the *TBT Agreement*. We further note that the membership of the TBT Committee comprises all WTO Members and that the Decision was adopted by consensus.

With respect to the question of whether the terms and content of the Decision express an agreement between Members on the interpretation or application of a provision of WTO law, we note that the title of the Decision expressly refers to 'Principles for the Development of International Standards, Guides and Recommendations *with Relation to Articles 2, 5 and Annex 3 of the Agreement*'. We further note that the TBT Committee undertook the activities leading up to the adoption of the Decision '[w]ith a view to developing a better understanding of international standards within the Agreement' and decided to develop the principles contained in the Decision, *inter alia*, 'to ensure the effective application of the Agreement' and to 'clarify and strengthen the concept of international standards under the Agreement'. We therefore consider that the TBT Committee Decision can be considered as a 'subsequent agreement' within the meaning of Article 31(3)(a) of the *Vienna Convention*. The extent to which this Decision will inform the interpretation and application of a term or provision of the *TBT Agreement* in a specific case, however, will depend on the degree to which it 'bears specifically' on the interpretation and application of the respective term or provision. In the present dispute, we consider that the TBT Committee Decision bears directly on the interpretation of the term 'open' in Annex 1.4 to the *TBT Agreement*, as well as on the interpretation and application of the concept of 'recognized activities in standardization'.[52]

15.8   Subsequent practice

15.46 Article 31(3)(b) of the Vienna Convention provides that a treaty shall be interpreted taking into account '(b) any subsequent practice in the application of the treaty which establishes the agreement of the parties regarding its interpretation'. WTO jurisprudence supports the proposition that, to qualify as subsequent practice under Article 31(3)(b), there must be a concordant,

[52] *Ibid.*, paras. 371–2 (citing Appellate Body Report, *US – Clove Cigarettes*, para. 265 (in turn citing Appellate Body Reports, *EC – Bananas III (Article 21.5 – Ecuador II)/EC – Bananas III (Article 21.5 – US)*, para. 390)).

common and consistent sequence of acts or pronouncements which is sufficient to establish a discernible pattern implying the agreement of the parties regarding its interpretation. The WTO Agreement had many parties when it entered into force in 1995, and to date WTO adjudicators have found that those conditions were not fulfilled in most of the cases in which arguments based on 'subsequent practice' were advanced by a party. However, there have been several cases in which panels or the Appellate Body referred to 'practice' to support or arrive at an interpretation.

In *Japan – Alcoholic Beverages II*, the Panel found that 'panel reports adopted by the CONTRACTING PARTIES constitute subsequent practice in a specific case'. The Appellate Body disagreed and, in reversing the Panel's findings on this issue, considered 'subsequent practice' to mean a 'concordant, common and consistent' sequence of acts: **15.47**

> Article 31(3)(b) of the *Vienna Convention* states that 'any subsequent practice in the application of the treaty which establishes the agreement of the parties regarding its interpretation' is to be 'taken into account together with the context' in interpreting the terms of the treaty. Generally, in international law, the essence of subsequent practice in interpreting a treaty has been recognized as a 'concordant, common and consistent' sequence of acts or pronouncements which is sufficient to establish a discernable pattern implying the agreement of the parties regarding its interpretation. An isolated act is generally not sufficient to establish subsequent practice; it is a sequence of acts establishing the agreement of the parties that is relevant.[53]

The Panel in *Brazil – Desiccated Coconut* concluded that the Tokyo Round Subsidies Code did not constitute 'subsequent practice' of the Contracting Parties to the GATT 1947, based in part on its view that Article 31(3) clearly distinguishes the use of subsequent agreements from the use of subsequent practice as interpretive tools: **15.48**

> We recognize that the Pork Panel had indicated, in passing, that the Tokyo Round SCM Code represents 'practice' under Article VI of GATT 1947. Article 31.3(b) of the Vienna Convention provides that there may be taken into account, when interpreting a treaty, '[a]ny subsequent practice in the application of the treaty which establishes the agreement of the parties regarding its interpretation'. Article 31.3 clearly distinguishes between the use of subsequent agreements and of subsequent practice as interpretive tools. The Tokyo Round SCM Code is, in our view, in the former category and cannot itself reasonably be deemed to represent 'customary practice' of the GATT 1947 CONTRACT-ING PARTIES. In any event, while the practice of Code signatories might be of some interpretive value in establishing their agreement regarding the

[53] Appellate Body Report, *Japan – Alcoholic Beverages II*, pp. 12–13 (citing *Yearbook of the International Law Commission* (1966), Vol. II, p. 222; I. Sinclair, *The Vienna Convention on the Law of Treaties*, 2nd edn (Manchester University Press, 1984), p. 138).

interpretation of the Tokyo Round SCM Code (and arguably through Article
XVI:1 of the WTO Agreement in interpreting provisions of that Code that were
carried over into the successor SCM Agreement), it is clearly not relevant to the
interpretation of Article VI of GATT 1994 itself; rather, only practice under
Article VI of GATT 1947 is legally relevant to the interpretation of Article VI of
GATT 1994.[54]

15.49 In *India – Patents (US)*, the Panel found that India had failed to demonstrate
that the 'subsequent practice' of developing country Members established the
agreement of all WTO Members regarding the interpretation of Article 70.9 of
the TRIPS Agreement. The Panel stated:

> On the contrary, the record showed that there had been no agreement on this
> issue in the Council for TRIPS; at most meetings of the Council, concern had
> been expressed by some Members about the absence of notifications or the
> limited information content of notifications related to the implementation of
> Article 70.9. Moreover, the matter had also been the subject of another recourse
> to the DSU in 'Pakistan – Patent Protection for Pharmaceutical and Agricultural
> Chemical Products' (WT/DS36). In any event, to paraphrase an Appellate Body
> report, the Panel felt that it was much too early for practice to have arisen under
> the TRIPS regime which had commenced only on 1 January 1995.[55]

15.50 In *Turkey – Textiles*, Turkey referred to the practice of the GATT contracting
parties to support its view that, on the occasion of the creation of a customs
union, individual GATT contracting parties and now WTO Members have
been authorized to introduce new, otherwise GATT/WTO-incompatible,
import restrictions. The Panel reviewed the historical evidence before it and
found no subsequent practice within the meaning of Article 31(3)(b). In this
regard, the Panel considered that it was 'quite evident that no consensus was
reached, nor was any practice agreed upon regarding Article XXIV of GATT',
that '[t]hese actions were not universally accepted' by GATT contracting parties,
and that:

> In light of these positions taken by individual GATT contracting parties[372]
> before the entry into force of the WTO Agreement and therefore the ATC, we
> cannot conclude that there is 'subsequent practice' (as that term is used in the
> VCLT) or 'customary practices' (as used in Article XVI:1 of the WTO Agree-
> ment) that could be regarded as an agreement or acceptance (even implicit) that
> paragraphs 5(a) or 8(a)(ii) of Article XXIV authorize or require the introduction
> of otherwise GATT/WTO inconsistent measures upon the formation of a
> customs union.

---

[372] It is also worth recalling the conclusions of the following GATT Panel
Report which, although not adopted, confirm that some contracting parties

---

[54] Panel Report, *Brazil – Desiccated Coconut*, para. 256.
[55] Panel Report, *India – Patents (US)*, para. 6.17 (citing Appellate Body Report, *US – Underwear*, p. 17).

opposed interpretations such as those suggested by Turkey, thereby denying the existence of any international customary practice. In the non-adopted Panel Report on *EEC – Tariff Treatment of Citrus Products from Certain Mediterranean Countries*, L/5776, paras. 3.12–3.22, the EEC argued that the non-recommendations by Working Parties which had examined the Treaty of Rome itself and other related agreements constituted tacit acceptance by the CONTRACTING PARTIES as a whole as well as the individual contracting parties that these agreements were in conformity with the provisions of Article XXIV, and that therefore the United States could not contest its preferential trade agreement with the Mediterranean Region. The United States' statement in response to the European Communities' argument was that the failure of the CONTRACTING PARTIES to reject the agreements did not imply acceptance nor did it constitute a legal finding of GATT consistency with Article XXIV.[56]

The Panel in *US – FSC* rejected the argument that a 1981 understanding among **15.51** the GATT contracting parties amounted to subsequent practice within the meaning of Article 31(3)(b). The Panel reasoned:

> In its first submission, the United States contends not only that the 1981 understanding is an 'other decision' that is thus part of GATT 1994, but also that it constitutes a 'subsequent practice' within the meaning of Article 31(3)(b) of the Vienna Convention on the Law of Treaties 'with respect to GATT Article XVI:4, as amended by the Subsidies Code.' Of course, the 1981 understanding could not represent a subsequent practice with respect to GATT 1994, but at most only with respect to GATT 1947. In any event, we consider that the 1981 understanding is not 'subsequent practice' within the meaning of the Vienna Convention for the same reason as it is not a 'part' of GATT 1994. In this respect, we recall that, under Article 31(3)(b) of the Vienna Convention, an interpreter must take into account, together with the context, '[a]ny subsequent practice in the application of the treaty which establishes the agreement of the parties regarding its interpretation'. Here, we have seen that the 1981 understanding was conditioned by the statement of the Chairman of the GATT 1947 Council that the understanding 'did not affect the rights and obligations of contracting parties under the General Agreement', and it is clear that many contracting parties considered that significant caveat as central to the adoption of the understanding. To treat the 1981 understanding as subsequent practice 'establishing the agreement of the parties regarding the interpretation' of GATT 1947 would not be consistent with that explicit qualification.[57]

In *Canada – Pharmaceutical Patents*, Canada pointed out that, after the conclu- **15.52** sion of the TRIPS Agreement, four other WTO Members adopted legislation containing similar regulatory review exceptions to those being challenged, and that two other Members adopted interpretations of existing patent law which confirmed certain exemptions for regulatory review. Canada argued that these actions were subsequent practice by parties to the agreement within the meaning of Article 31(3)(b) that confirmed its interpretation that regulatory review

---

[56] Panel Report, *Turkey – Textiles*, paras. 9.164–9.169.   [57] Panel Report, *US – FSC*, para. 7.75.

exceptions at issue were authorized by Article 30 of the TRIPS Agreement. The
Panel was not convinced:

> In reaching this conclusion, the Panel also considered Canada's additional
> arguments that both the negotiating history of Article 30 of the TRIPS Agree-
> ment and the subsequent practices of certain WTO Member governments
> supported the view that Article 30 was understood to permit regulatory review
> exceptions similar to Section 55.2(1). The Panel did not accord any weight to
> either of those arguments, however, because there was no documented evidence
> of the claimed negotiating understanding, and because the subsequent acts by
> individual countries did not constitute 'practice in the application of the treaty
> which establishes the agreement of the parties regarding its interpretation'
> within the meaning of Article 31.3(b) of the Vienna Convention.[58]

15.53 In *Chile – Price Band System*, the complainants argued that Chile acted inconsistently with its obligations under the Agreement on Agriculture by failing to
convert its price band system into ordinary customs duties. Chile argued that it
was highly relevant that no country that had a price band system in place before
the conclusion of the WTO agreements actually converted it into ordinary
customs duties. The Appellate Body stated:

> Neither the Panel record nor the participants' submissions on appeal suggests
> that there is a discernible pattern of acts or pronouncements implying an
> agreement among WTO Members on the interpretation of Article 4.2. Thus,
> in our view, this alleged practice of some Members does not amount to
> 'subsequent practice' within the meaning of Article 31(3)(b) of the *Vienna
> Convention*.[59]

In *Chile – Price Band System*, the Appellate Body also criticized the Panel's
conclusion that certain activities amounted to subsequent practice:

> We also find it difficult to understand how the Panel could find 'normative'
> support for its reasoning by examining the Schedules of WTO Members. We
> have observed in a previous case that '[t]he ordinary meaning of the term
> "concessions" suggests that a Member may yield rights and grant benefits, but
> it cannot diminish its obligations'. A Member's Schedule imposes obligations on
> the Member who has made the concessions. The Schedule of one Member, and
> even the scheduling practice of a number of Members, is not relevant in
> interpreting the meaning of a treaty provision, unless that practice amounts to
> 'subsequent practice in the application of the treaty' within the meaning of
> Article 31(3)(b) of the *Vienna Convention*. In this case the Panel Report contains
> no support for the conclusion that the scheduling activity of WTO Members
> amounts to 'subsequent practice'.[60]

[58] Panel Report, *Canada – Pharmaceutical Patents*, para. 7.47.
[59] Appellate Body Report, *Chile – Price Band System*, paras. 213–14.   [60] *Ibid.*, para. 272.

In *US – Gambling*, the Appellate Body clarified that establishing 'subsequent **15.54** practice' within the meaning of Article 31(3)(b) involves two elements:

> [I]n order for 'practice' within the meaning of Article 31(3)(b) to be established: (i) there must be a common, consistent, discernible pattern of acts or pronouncements; and (ii) those acts or pronouncements must imply agreement on the interpretation of the relevant provision.
>
> We have difficulty accepting Antigua's position that the 2001 Scheduling Guidelines constitute 'subsequent practice' revealing a common understanding that Members' specific commitments are to be construed in accordance with W/ 120 and the 1993 Scheduling Guidelines. Although the 2001 Guidelines were explicitly adopted by the Council for Trade in Services, this was in the context of the negotiation of *future* commitments and in order to assist in the preparation of offers and requests in respect of such commitments. As such, they do not constitute evidence of Members' understanding regarding the interpretation of *existing* commitments. Furthermore, as the United States emphasized before the Panel, in its Decision adopting the 2001 Guidelines, the Council for Trade in Services explicitly stated that they were to be 'non-binding' and 'shall not modify any rights or obligations of the Members under the GATS'. Accordingly, we do not consider that the 2001 Guidelines, in and of themselves, constitute 'subsequent practice' within the meaning of Article 31(3)(b) of the *Vienna Convention.*[61]

In *EC – Chicken Cuts*, the Appellate Body engaged in an extensive analysis of **15.55** Article 31(3)(b). The Appellate Body explained that 'common' and 'concordant' practice does not necessarily require practice by all parties to a treaty:

> We share the Panel's view that not each and every party must have engaged in a particular practice for it to qualify as a 'common' and 'concordant' practice. Nevertheless, practice by some, but not all parties is obviously not of the same order as practice by only one, or very few parties. To our mind, it would be difficult to establish a 'concordant, common and discernible pattern' on the basis of acts or pronouncements of one, or very few parties to a multilateral treaty, such as the WTO Agreement. We acknowledge, however, that, if only some WTO Members have actually traded or classified products under a given heading, this circumstance may reduce the availability of such 'acts and pronouncements' for purposes of determining the existence of 'subsequent practice' within the meaning of Article 31(3)(b).[62]

In *EC – Chicken Cuts*, the Appellate Body addressed the question of how agreement of the parties regarding the interpretation of a treaty term may occur when certain parties have not engaged in a practice:

> We agree with the Panel that, in general, agreement may be deduced from the affirmative reaction of a treaty party. However, we have misgivings about deducing, without further inquiry, agreement with a practice from a party's

---

[61] Appellate Body Report, *US – Gambling*, paras. 192–3.
[62] Appellate Body Report, *EC – Chicken Cuts*, para. 259.

'lack of reaction'. We do not exclude that, in specific situations, the 'lack of reaction' or silence by a particular treaty party may, in the light of attendant circumstances, be understood as acceptance of the practice of other treaty parties.[515] Such situations may occur when a party that has not engaged in a practice has become or has been made aware of the practice of other parties (for example, by means of notification or by virtue of participation in a forum where it is discussed), but does not react to it. However, we disagree with the Panel that 'lack of protest' against one Member's classification practice by other WTO Members may be understood, on its own, as establishing agreement with that practice by those other Members.

---

[515] 'It is not necessary to show that each party has engaged in a practice, only that all have accepted it, albeit tacitly.' (A. Aust, *Modern Treaty Law and Practice* (Cambridge University Press, 2000), p. 195.) See also D. Anzilotti, *Corso di Diritto Internazionale* ['International Law Course'], Vol. 1, IV Edizione (CEDAM, 1955), p. 292:

> These conclusive facts also include silence, the value of which, as a manifestation of will, obviously cannot be reduced to general rules, because such value depends on the factual circumstances in which the silence is observed ... It is easy, moreover, to envisage circumstances in which silence on the part of a State cannot be construed as anything but indifference or failure to express its will in any form: The recently expressed view that, in international law, the principle of *qui tacet consentire videtur* is entirely valid cannot be accepted in such general terms.

(Unofficial English translation from available French translation by G. Gidel, *Cours de droit international*, Vol. 1, III édition (Librairie du Recueil Sirey, 1929), p. 344);

J. P. Cot, 'La Conduite subséquente des Parties à un traité' ['Subsequent Conduct of the Parties to a Treaty'], in *Revue Générale de Droit International Public* (1966), 3rd series, Vol. 37, p. 645:

> ... the various facets of the subsequent conduct of the Parties in the law of treaties: Where it is the subject of tacit agreement, subsequent conduct should undoubtedly be approved by all the Parties; on the other hand, where it is merely indicative of the will of the Parties, it may be accepted even if it stems from a single State. *Its probative value then depends on the circumstances of the case.*

(Unofficial English translation; emphasis added);

W. Karl, *Vertrag und spätere Praxis im Völkerrecht* ['Treaty and Subsequent Practice in International Law'] (Springer Verlag, 1983), pp. 113 and 127; and F. Capotorti, 'Sul Valore della Prassi Applicativa dei Trattati Secondo la Convenzione di Vienna' ['On the Value of Practice in the Application of Treaties under the Vienna Convention'], in *Le Droit international à l'heure de sa codification*, Studi in onore di Roberto Ago (Giuffré, 1987), Vol. I, pp. 197.[63]

---

[63] *Ibid.*, para. 272.

In *EC – Chicken Cuts*, the Appellate Body rejected the view that Article IX:2 of the WTO Agreement, which provides for the possibility of WTO Members adopting a multilateral interpretation, exhausts the manner in which Members may agree to an interpretation established through subsequent practice:

> To our mind, the existence of Article IX:2 of the *WTO Agreement* is not dispositive for resolving the issue of how to establish the agreement by Members that have not engaged in a practice. We fail to see how the express authorization in the WTO Agreement for Members to adopt interpretations of WTO provisions – which requires a three-quarter majority vote and not a unanimous decision – would impinge upon recourse to subsequent practice as a tool of treaty interpretation under Article 31(3)(b) of the *Vienna Convention*. In any case, we are mindful that the Appellate Body, in *Japan – Alcoholic Beverages II*, cautioned that relying on 'subsequent practice' for purposes of interpretation must not lead to interference with the 'exclusive authority' of the Ministerial Conference and the General Council to adopt interpretations of WTO agreements that are binding on all Members. In our view, this confirms that 'lack of reaction' should not lightly, without further inquiry into attendant circumstances of a case, be read to imply agreement with an interpretation by treaty parties that have not themselves engaged in a particular practice followed by other parties in the application of the treaty. This is all the more so because the interpretation of a treaty provision on the basis of subsequent practice is binding on all parties to the treaty, including those that have not actually engaged in such practice.[64]

15.56 In *US – Zeroing (EC)*, the European Communities asserted that its interpretation of Article 2.4.2 of the Anti-Dumping Agreement was consistent with the information contained in notifications provided by seventy-six Members regarding their domestic anti-dumping legislation. The European Communities argued that this established 'subsequent practice' within the meaning of Article 31(3)(b). The Panel disagreed:

> We note that the argument of the European Communities with respect to subsequent practice is based on the fact that the particular provisions in domestic laws and/or regulations that have been notified to the Committee on Anti-Dumping Practices that in the view of the European Communities correspond to Article 2.4.2 of the *AD Agreement* either do not include the phrase 'during the investigation phase' or use the phrase 'during the investigation period.' In our view, this is simply not a sufficient basis to draw a conclusion as to whether or not it is the practice of a particular Member to apply Article 2.4.2 to the assessment of the amount of anti-dumping duties within the meaning of Article 9.3. Many Members have notified legislation that predates the WTO Agreement. We also note that in many cases, the legislation identified by the European Communities makes no or little mention of duty assessment at all, and it is therefore difficult to draw any conclusion regarding the specific methodology applied. We note, however, that many Members provide in their

---

[64] *Ibid.*, para. 273.

domestic anti-dumping legislation for the collection of anti-dumping duties through a system of variable duties. The transaction-specific character of such a duty assessment system would appear to suggest that those Members do not apply the symmetrical comparison methods foreseen in Article 2.4.2 to determine the amount of liability for payment of anti-dumping duties.

In any event, even if it were established conclusively that all the 76 Members referred to by the European Communities have adopted a practice of applying Article 2.4.2 to duty assessment, this would only mean that a considerable number of WTO Members have adopted an approach different from that of the United States. We fail to see how one can conclude on this basis that there exists 'a discernible pattern of acts or pronouncements *implying an agreement among WTO Members* on the interpretation of' Article 2.4.2. We note that one third party in this proceeding submitted arguments contesting the view of the European Communities that Article 2.4.2 applies to the imposition and collection of anti-dumping duties. Therefore, we conclude that even if the documentation provided by the European Communities were relevant as evidence of 'practice' within the meaning of Article 31(3)(b) of the *Vienna Convention*, that practice is not a practice 'which establishes the agreement between the parties regarding the interpretation' of Article 2.4.2. Consequently, the reference by the European Communities to 'subsequent practice' does not undermine the conclusion we have reached based on an interpretation of Article 2.4.2 in accordance with Article 31(1) of the *Vienna Convention*.[65]

15.57 In *China – Auto Parts*, China argued that there is widespread and consistent practice among WTO Members that demonstrates that a charge is 'on … importation' of a product if the charge bears an objective relationship to the administration and enforcement of a valid customs liability. The Panel disagreed:

The Panel starts by recalling that the Appellate Body has found that to establish 'subsequent practice' within Article 31(3)(b) of the *Vienna Convention*, the following two elements must be shown: (i) there must be a common, consistent, discernible pattern of acts or pronouncements; and (ii) those acts or pronouncements must imply agreement among WTO Members. Applying this standard, the Panel fails to observe subsequent practice establishing the agreement of the parties regarding China's interpretation of Article II:1(b), first sentence, of the GATT 1994. The practices of other Members described by China are not similar to the Chinese measure and do not support China's interpretation of Article II:1(b), first sentence, of the GATT 1994. We have reviewed the examples of customs practices from the complainants and other Members submitted by China on this issue and consider, as the United States and Canada correctly argue, that these practices, in fact, reinforce the evidence that WTO Members impose ordinary customs duties based on the state of the products as they are presented at the border and that they routinely *collect or assess* these duties after the products have entered the customs territory of the importing country. This supports our conclusion above that the ordinary meaning of 'on

---

[65] Panel Report, *US – Zeroing (EC)*, paras. 7.217–7.218.

their importation' in the first sentence of Article II:1(b) of the GATT 1994 indicates a *strict temporal element*.[66]

In *China – Auto Parts*, the Panel also rejected an argument based on certain Canadian measures, stating that '[i]n any event, even if Canada's measure were directly comparable to the measures at issue, this measure alone would not amount to "subsequent practice" within the meaning of Article 31(1)(b) of the *Vienna Convention*, which can be established only by a pattern of common, consistent, and concordant actions by WTO Members'.[67] In the context of addressing a different issue, the Panel in *China – Auto Parts* stated that, 'on the basis of the guidance provided as above by the Appellate Body on the assessment of subsequent practice for interpreting a treaty provision (China's commitments under its Schedule), the Panel will consider how China has been classifying CKD and SKD kits since its accession to the WTO as well as how the complainants and other WTO Members have been classifying such kits'.[68] The Panel ultimately concluded that, 'based on the available evidence before it . . . the classification practices of at least some WTO Members show that CKD and SKD kits are classified as motor vehicles'.[69]

In *EC – IT Products*, the Panel dealt extensively with the European Communities' arguments on the classification practice of itself and other Members regarding a tariff heading in its Schedule.[70] The Panel ultimately concluded that: **15.58**

> We observe that it is incumbent on a party asserting the existence of a 'common' and 'concordant' practice among WTO Members to provide sufficient evidence – which clearly is something beyond a handful of classification exercises in one Member – to establish such a 'consistent, common and concordant' classification practice. The European Communities has not met this burden here.[71]

In the context of addressing a different issue, the Panel in *EC – IT Products* stated that 'we do not think that the evidence adduced by the complainants or the European Communities satisfies the conditions for being considered subsequent practice'.[72]

The Panel in *US – Section 110(5) Copyright Act* referred to 'state practice' as reflected in national copyright laws: **15.59**

> We note that the parties and third parties have brought to our attention several examples from various countries of limitations in national laws based on the minor exceptions doctrine. In our view, state practice as reflected in the national copyright laws of Berne Union members before and after 1948, 1967 and 1971,

---

[66] Panel Report, *China – Auto Parts*, para. 7.182. [67] *Ibid.*, para. 7.481.
[68] *Ibid.*, para. 7.706. [69] *Ibid.*, para. 7.721.
[70] Panel Report, *EC – IT Products*, paras. 7.557–7.565. [71] *Ibid.*, para. 7.565.
[72] *Ibid.*, para. 7.1352.

as well as of WTO Members before and after the date that the TRIPS Agreement became applicable to them, confirms our conclusion about the minor exceptions doctrine.[68]

---

[68] By enunciating these examples of state practice we do not wish to express a view on whether these are sufficient to constitute 'subsequent practice' within the meaning of Article 31(3)(b) of the Vienna Convention. See description by the Appellate Body in its report on *Japan – Alcoholic Beverages*, op. cit., p. 13 . . .[73]

15.60 The Panel in *US – Shrimp (Article 21.5 – Malaysia)* found that conclusions formulated in a 1996 report of the Committee on Trade and Environment were relevant, leaving aside whether they qualified as 'subsequent practice':

> We also have evidence in the context of Article XX showing that preference must be given to a multilateral approach in terms of protection of the environment. In this respect, we note the content of the 1996 Report of the CTE, where the CTE endorsed and supported 'multilateral solutions based on international cooperation and consensus as the best and most effective way for governments to tackle environmental problems of a transboundary or global nature.' Insofar as this report can be deemed to embody the opinion of the WTO Members, it could be argued that it records evidence of 'subsequent practice in the application of the treaty which establishes the agreement of the parties regarding its interpretation' (Article 31.3(b) of the Vienna Convention) and as such should be taken into account in the interpretation of the provisions concerned. However, even if it is not to be considered as evidence of a subsequent practice, it remains the expression of a common opinion of Members and is therefore relevant in assessing the scope of the chapeau of Article XX.[74]

15.61 In *Mexico – Telecoms*, the Panel referred to the 'consistent practice of WTO Members' in respect of a particular issue:

> Article XX:1(d) permits Members who wish to depart from this general rule to specify a 'time-frame' within which they implement their commitments. We consider that the words 'where appropriate' in that subparagraph must be understood to refer to situations where the date of implementation differs from the date of entry into force of a commitment. The consistent practice of WTO Members in the scheduling of commitments supports this understanding.[75]

15.62 In *Canada – Patent Term*, the Panel did not consider it necessary to reach any decision on whether there was subsequent practice in order to resolve the issue before it:

---

[73] Panel Report, *US – Section 110(5) Copyright Act*, para. 6.55.
[74] Panel Report, *US – Shrimp (Article 21.5 – Malaysia)*, para. 5.56.
[75] Panel Report, *Mexico – Telecoms*, para. 7.368.

The United States argued that Article 31(3)(b) of the *Vienna Convention* allows treaty interpreters to take into account 'subsequent practice' to 'establish the agreement of the parties regarding its interpretation' and referred to six developed country Members, including itself, that amended their laws to implement the *TRIPS Agreement*. In connection with 'subsequent practice', the Appellate Body stated in *Japan – Alcoholic Beverages* that 'the essence of subsequent practice in interpreting a treaty has been recognized as a "concordant, common and consistent" sequence of acts ... which is sufficient to establish a discernable pattern implying the agreement of the parties regarding its interpretation.' For the purpose of this dispute, we do not consider it necessary to make a finding as to whether there is 'subsequent practice' to determine the requirement under Article 33 of the *TRIPS Agreement* and to ascertain whether Section 45 of Canada's *Patent Act* is in conformity with Article 33.[76]

In *US – FSC (Article 21.5 – EC)*, both the Panel and the Appellate Body **15.63** interpreted the concept of 'foreign-source income', in the context of footnote 59 to the SCM Agreement, based on a detailed review of the practice of Members in the field of taxation, and considered various international instruments (including but not limited to the UN Model Tax Convention, the OECD Model Tax Convention and a wide range of bilateral tax treaties) as evidence of that practice. The Appellate Body referred to a wide range of international tax treaties and instruments, as evidence of 'widely recognized principles which many States generally apply':

Although there is no universally agreed meaning for the term 'foreign-source income' in international tax law, we observe that many States have adopted bilateral or multilateral treaties to address double taxation. The United States, for instance, has more than fifty bilateral tax treaties addressing double taxation. Frequently, bilateral tax treaties have been based on multilaterally developed model tax conventions dealing with double taxation. In addition, the respective member States of the Andean Community and of the Caribbean Community have adopted multilateral agreements, binding on the members of each community, that seek to avoid double taxation.

Although these instruments do not define 'foreign-source income' uniformly, it appears to us that certain widely recognized principles of taxation emerge from them. In seeking to give meaning to the term 'foreign-source income' in footnote 59 to the *SCM Agreement*, which is a tax-related provision in an international trade treaty, we believe that it is appropriate for us to derive assistance from these widely recognized principles which many States generally apply in the field of taxation. In identifying these principles, we bear in mind that the measure at issue seeks to address foreign-source income of United States citizens and residents – that is, income earned by these taxpayers in 'foreign' States where the taxpayers are not resident.

---

[76] Panel Report, *Canada – Patent Term*, footnote 48.

We recognize, of course, that the detailed rules on taxation of non-residents differ considerably from State-to-State, with some States applying rules which may be more likely to tax the income of non-residents than the rules applied by other States. However, despite the differences, there seems to us to be a widely accepted common element to these rules. The common element is that a 'foreign' State will tax a non-resident on income which is generated by activities of the non-resident that have some link with that State. Thus, whether a 'foreign' State decides to tax non-residents on income generated by a permanent establishment or whether, absent such an establishment, it decides to tax a non-resident on income generated by the conduct of a trade or business on its territory, the 'foreign' State taxes a non-resident only on income generated by activities linked to the territory of that State. As a result of this link, the 'foreign' State treats the income in question as domestic-source, under its source rules, and taxes it. Conversely, where the income of a non-resident does not have any links with a 'foreign' State, it is widely accepted that the income will be subject to tax only in the taxpayer's State of residence, and that this income will not be subject to taxation by a 'foreign' State.[77]

15.9   Relevant rules of international law

15.64 For WTO jurisprudence on the requirement to interpret a treaty taking into account 'any relevant rules of law applicable in the relations between the parties', see Section 4.2.2 above.

15.10   Supplementary means of interpretation

15.65 Article 32 of the Vienna Convention, entitled 'Supplementary means of interpretation', provides that:

> Recourse may be had to supplementary means of interpretation, including the preparatory work of the treaty and the circumstances of its conclusion, in order to confirm the meaning resulting from the application of article 31, or to determine the meaning when the interpretation according to article 31:

---

[77] Appellate Body Report, *US – FSC (Article 21.5 – EC)*, paras. 141–3 (citing the OECD Model Tax Convention on Income and Capital; United Nations Double Taxation Convention between Developed and Developing Countries; B. J. Arnold and M. J. McIntyre, *International Tax Primer* (Kluwer Law International, 1995), p. 100; A. H. Qureshi, *The Public International Law of Taxation* (Graham & Trotman, 1994), p. 371; Andean Community Standard Agreement to Avoid Double Taxation between Member Countries and Other States Outside the Subregion; Caribbean Community Agreement Among the Governments of the Member States of the Caribbean Community for the Avoidance of Double Taxation and the Prevention of Fiscal Evasion with Respect to Taxes on Income, Profits or Gains and Capital Gains and for the Encouragement of Regional Trade and Investment).

(a) leaves the meaning ambiguous or obscure; or
(b) leads to a result which is manifestly absurd or unreasonable.

WTO jurisprudence offers support for the proposition that preparatory work and the circumstances of a treaty's conclusion do not exhaust the supplementary means that may potentially be taken into account, and that a potentially wide range of materials may be taken into account as part of the 'preparatory work' and/or 'circumstances' of a treaty's conclusion, but that, to form the basis for an interpretation, any such materials must at minimum establish or shed sufficient light on the common intentions of the parties. The terms 'preparatory work' and 'negotiating history' have been used interchangeably in WTO jurisprudence. In the vast run of cases, WTO panels and the Appellate Body have arrived at a conclusion regarding the meaning of the treaty provision at issue based on Article 31 of the Vienna Convention, but panels and the Appellate Body have typically nonetheless also addressed any arguments by the parties relating to supplementary means of interpretation. There have been very few cases in which supplementary means of interpretation have been relied upon to determine the meaning of a term, as opposed to confirming the meaning already arrived at on the basis of Article 31, and most of those cases have involved the interpretation of terms in Members' Schedules.

15.10.1 Generally

15.66 In *EC – Chicken Cuts*, the Appellate Body explained that the application of Article 31 of the Vienna Convention will usually allow a treaty interpreter to establish the meaning of a term:

> The application of these rules in Article 31 of the *Vienna Convention* will usually allow a treaty interpreter to establish the meaning of the term. However, if after applying Article 31 the meaning of the term remains ambiguous or obscure, or leads to a result which is manifestly absurd or unreasonable, Article 32 allows a treaty interpreter to have recourse to:
>
> > '... supplementary means of interpretation, including the preparatory work of the treaty and the circumstances of its conclusion.'
>
> With regard to 'the circumstances of [the] conclusion' of a treaty, this permits, in appropriate cases, the examination of the historical background against which the treaty was negotiated.[78]

In *EC – Chicken Cuts*, the Appellate Body also confirmed that the list of supplementary means of interpretation identified in Article 32 is not exhaustive:

---

[78] Appellate Body Report, *EC – Computer Equipment*, para. 86.

We stress, moreover, that Article 32 does not define exhaustively the supplementary means of interpretation to which an interpreter may have recourse. It states only that they *include* the preparatory work of the treaty and the circumstances of its conclusion. Thus, an interpreter has a certain flexibility in considering relevant supplementary means in a given case so as to assist in ascertaining the common intentions of the parties.[531]

---

[531] We agree with Yasseen who says:

> Let us not forget that the list of supplementary means of interpretation contained in Article 32 of the Vienna Convention is not exhaustive. If the circumstances in which the treaty was concluded are expressly mentioned, it is to underline their importance in the elaboration of the Treaty, and not to exclude the possibility of wider-ranging and more thorough historical research into a period preceding that of the conclusion of the treaty.

(Yasseen, *supra*, footnote 70, p. 92, paras. 10–11 (quoted in Panel Reports, footnote 570 to para. 7.342))[79]

15.67 The Panel in *EC – IT Products* recalled the passages above, and stated:

> It follows therefore that the fact that the HS2007 is not preparatory work of the treaty or circumstances of the conclusion of the treaty, does not *per se* disqualify it from being considered supplementary means of interpretation under Article 32. Nor can the fact that the HS2007 occurred subsequently to the conclusion of the treaty be *per se* a reason to disqualify it under Article 32, so long as it serves to indicate what were the 'common intentions of the parties' at the time of the conclusion of the treaty, i.e. at the time they bound their Schedules.[80]

15.68 In *Canada – Dairy*, the Appellate Body considered that it was 'appropriate, indeed necessary' in that case to have recourse to supplementary means of interpretation to interpret a term in a Member's Schedule:

> In our view, the language in the notation in Canada's Schedule is *not* clear on its face. Indeed, the language is general and ambiguous, and, therefore, requires special care on the part of the treaty interpreter. For this reason, it is appropriate, indeed necessary, in this case, to turn to 'supplementary means of interpretation' pursuant to Article 32 of the *Vienna Convention*.[81]

15.69 In *US – Gambling*, the Appellate Body concluded that it was necessary to have recourse to supplementary means of interpretation, again in that case to interpret an entry in a Member's Schedule:

> [A] proper interpretation pursuant to the principles codified in Article 31 of the *Vienna Convention* does not yield a clear meaning as to the scope of the commitment made by the United States in the entry 'Other recreational services

---

[79] Appellate Body Report, *EC – Chicken Cuts*, para. 283.
[80] Panel Report, *EC – IT Products*, para. 7.694.
[81] Appellate Body Report, *Canada – Dairy*, para. 138.

(except sporting)'. Accordingly, it is appropriate to have recourse to the supplemental means of interpretation identified in Article 32 of the *Vienna Convention*. These means include W/120, the 1993 Scheduling Guidelines, and a cover note attached to drafts of the United States' Schedule.[82]

In *China – Intellectual Property Rights*, the Panel considered it necessary to have **15.70** recourse to preparatory work to determine the meaning of the terms 'such requests' in the context of the third sentence of Article 46 of the TRIPS Agreement. The Panel stated:

> The third sentence of Article 46 refers to 'such requests' although the previous sentences do not refer expressly to any requests. The content of the third sentence clearly relates to materials and implements as addressed in the second sentence but it could equally relate to infringing goods as addressed in the first sentence. The text is ambiguous on this point. This ambiguity can be resolved by reference to the records of the negotiation of the TRIPS Agreement.[83]

In *China – Publications and Audiovisual Products*, the Appellate Body stated: **15.71**

> The elements to be examined under Article 32 are distinct from those to be analyzed under Article 31, but it is the same elements that are examined under Article 32 irrespective of the outcome of the Article 31 analysis. Instead, what may differ, depending on the results of the application of Article 31, is the weight that will be attributed to the elements analyzed under Article 32.[84]

15.10.2 Preparatory work

In *Canada – Periodicals*, the Appellate Body referred to the preparatory work of **15.72** Article III:8(b) of the GATT to support its understanding of the object and purpose of that provision:

> Our textual interpretation is supported by the context of Article III:8(b) examined in relation to Articles III:2 and III:4 of the GATT 1994. Furthermore, the object and purpose of Article III:8(b) is confirmed by the drafting history of Article III. In this context, we refer to the following discussion in the Reports of the Committees and Principal Sub-Committees of the Interim Commission for the International Trade Organization concerning the provision of the Havana Charter for an International Trade Organization that corresponds to Article III:8(b) of the GATT 1994:
>
> > 'This sub-paragraph was redrafted in order to make it clear that nothing in Article 18 could be construed to sanction the exemption of domestic products from internal taxes imposed on like imported products or the remission of such taxes. At the same time the Sub-Committee recorded its

---

[82] Appellate Body Report, *US – Gambling*, para. 197.
[83] Panel Report, *China – Intellectual Property Rights*, para. 7.260.
[84] Appellate Body Report, *China – Publications and Audiovisual Products*, para. 403.

view that nothing in this sub-paragraph or elsewhere in Article 18 would override the provisions of Section C of Chapter IV.'[85]

15.73 In *India – Quantitative Restrictions*, the Appellate Body found it difficult to give weight to arguments on negotiating history in the absence of a record of the negotiations:

> We note India's arguments relating to the negotiating history of the *BOP Understanding*. However, in the absence of a record of the negotiations on footnote 1 to the *BOP Understanding*, we find it difficult to give weight to these arguments. We do not exclude that footnote 1 to the *BOP Understanding* was 'heavily negotiated', and that it tries to accommodate opposing views held by different parties to the negotiations on the *BOP Understanding*. We are convinced, however, that the second sentence of footnote 1 does not accord with the position held by India. To interpret the sentence as proposed by India would require us to read into the text words which are simply not there. Neither a panel nor the Appellate Body is allowed to do so.[86]

15.74 In *US – Carbon Steel*, the Appellate Body considered that, even if it were appropriate to rely on a document constituting preparatory work to the SCM Agreement, 'in accordance with the rules of interpretation set forth in the *Vienna Convention*, selective reliance on such a document does not provide a proper basis for the conclusion reached by the Panel in this regard'.[87]

15.10.3 Circumstances of the treaty's conclusion

15.75 In *EC – Computer Equipment*, the Appellate Body stated that '[w]ith regard to "the circumstances of [the] conclusion" of a treaty, this permits, in appropriate cases, the examination of the historical background against which the treaty was negotiated'.[88] In *EC – Computer Equipment*, the Appellate Body further considered that the tariff classification practice of the European Communities with respect to the product at issue prior to the negotiation of its Schedule was part of the 'circumstances of the conclusion' of the WTO agreements and that this may be used as a supplementary means of interpretation to interpret the terms of that Schedule:

> In the light of our observations on 'the circumstances of [the] conclusion' of a treaty as a supplementary means of interpretation under Article 32 of the *Vienna Convention*, we consider that the classification practice in the European Communities during the Uruguay Round is part of 'the circumstances of [the] conclusion' of the *WTO Agreement* and may be used as a supplementary means of interpretation within the meaning of Article 32 of the *Vienna Convention*.[89]

---

[85] Appellate Body Report, *Canada – Periodicals*, pp. 33–4.
[86] Appellate Body Report, *India – Quantitative Restrictions*, para. 94.
[87] Appellate Body Report, *US – Carbon Steel*, para. 78.
[88] Appellate Body Report, *EC – Computer Equipment*, para. 86.   [89] *Ibid.*, para. 92.

With respect to the question whether the classification practice of one country at the time of tariff negotiation was relevant for the interpretation of a country's Schedule of concessions, the Appellate Body emphasized that, while it was of more limited value than evidence of the practice followed by all of the parties, such unilateral practice was not irrelevant. However, the Appellate Body found that, where such unilateral practice of one Member was inconsistent, it could not be considered relevant:

> We note that the Panel examined the classification practice of only the European Communities, and found that the classification of LAN equipment by the United States during the Uruguay Round tariff negotiations was not relevant. The purpose of treaty interpretation is to establish the *common* intention of the parties to the treaty. To establish this intention, the prior practice of only *one* of the parties may be relevant, but it is clearly of more limited value than the practice of all parties. In the specific case of the interpretation of a tariff concession in a Schedule, the classification practice of the importing Member, in fact, may be of great importance. However, the Panel was mistaken in finding that the classification practice of the United States was *not* relevant.
>
> . . .
>
> Then there is the question of the *consistency* of prior practice. Consistent prior classification practice may often be significant. Inconsistent classification practice, however, *cannot* be relevant in interpreting the meaning of a tariff concession.[90]

15.76 In *EC – Poultry*, the Appellate Body found that a bilateral agreement between two WTO Members could serve as 'supplementary means' of interpretation for a provision of a covered agreement, as part of the 'historical background':

> [T]he Oilseeds Agreement may serve as a *supplementary means* of interpretation of Schedule LXXX pursuant to Article 32 of the *Vienna Convention*, as it is part of the historical background of the concessions of the European Communities for frozen poultry meat.[91]

15.77 In *EC – Chicken Cuts*, the Appellate Body engaged in an extensive analysis of what may be taken into account as part of the 'circumstances of the conclusion' of a treaty. The Appellate Body clarified that a 'direct link' to the treaty text and 'direct influence' on the common intentions is not necessary for an event, act or instrument to qualify as a 'circumstance of the conclusion' of a treaty under Article 32 of the Vienna Convention, explaining:

> An 'event, act or instrument' may be relevant as supplementary means of interpretation not only if it has actually influenced a specific aspect of the treaty text in the sense of a relationship of cause and effect; it may also qualify as a 'circumstance of the conclusion' when it helps to discern what the common intentions of the parties were at the time of the conclusion with respect to the

---

[90] *Ibid.*, paras. 93–5.   [91] Appellate Body Report, *EC – Poultry*, para. 83.

treaty or specific provision . . . [I]t should not be misconstrued as introducing a concept that an act, event, or instrument qualifies as a circumstance only when it has influenced the intent of all the parties. Thus, not only 'multilateral' sources, but also 'unilateral' acts, instruments, or statements of individual negotiating parties may be useful in ascertaining 'the reality of the situation which the parties wished to regulate by means of the treaty' and, ultimately, for discerning the common intentions of the parties.[542]

---

[542] Sinclair, *supra*, footnote 36, p. 141. Sinclair adds that it may also be necessary to take into account 'the individual attitudes of the parties – their economic, political and social conditions, their adherence to certain groupings or their status, for example, as importing or exporting country in the particular case of a commodity agreement – in seeking to determine the reality of the situation which the parties wished to regulate by means of the treaty.' (*Ibid.*)[92]

The Appellate Body in *EC – Chicken Cuts* pointed out that 'relevance', as opposed to 'direct influence' or 'link', is the 'more appropriate criterion' to judge the extent to which a particular event, act, or other instrument should be relied upon or taken into account when interpreting a treaty provision in light of the 'circumstances of its conclusion'.[93] In light of this, the Appellate Body explained that interpreters should employ an objective approach to determine the relevance of circumstances for interpretation:

> In our view, the relevance of a circumstance for interpretation should be determined on the basis of objective factors, and not subjective intent. We can conceive of a number of objective factors that may be useful in determining the degree of relevance of particular circumstances for interpreting a specific treaty provision. These include the type of event, document, or instrument and its legal nature; temporal relation of the circumstance to the conclusion of the treaty;[546] actual knowledge or mere access to a published act or instrument; subject-matter of the document, instrument, or event in relation to the treaty provision to be interpreted; and whether or how it was used or influenced the negotiations of the treaty.

---

[546] We note that the term 'conclusion' has a temporal connotation that may give contextual guidance for interpreting the relevance of 'circumstances'. (See infra, para. 293)[94]

In *EC – Chicken Cuts*, the Appellate Body warned that the precise date of the conclusion of a treaty should not be confused with the circumstances that were prevailing at the point in time at which a treaty was concluded, thereby acknowledging that an interpreter should ascertain the circumstances of the conclusion of the treaty over a period of time:

---

[92] Appellate Body Report, *EC – Chicken Cuts*, para. 289.   [93] *Ibid.*, para. 290.
[94] *Ibid.*, para. 291.

Events, acts, and instruments may form part of the 'historical background against which the treaty was negotiated', even when these circumstances predate the point in time when the treaty is concluded, but continue to influence or reflect the common intentions of the parties at the time of conclusion. We also agree with the Panel that there is 'some correlation between the timing of an event, act or other instrument ... and their relevance to the treaty in question',[549] in the sense that 'the further back in time that an event, act or other instrument took place, was enacted or was adopted relative to the conclusion of a treaty', the less relevant it will be for interpreting the treaty in question. What should be considered 'temporally proximate will vary from treaty provision to treaty provision' and may depend on the structure of the negotiating process. Accordingly, we see no error in the Panels finding that the circumstances of the conclusion should be ascertained over a period of time ending on the date of the conclusion of the WTO Agreement.

---

[549] Panel Reports, para. 7.344. We recall, in this vein, that the panel and the Appellate Body in *EC – Computer Equipment* examined customs classification practice during the Uruguay Round when interpreting the relevant part of the EC Schedule. (Appellate Body Report, *EC – Computer Equipment*, para. 93) In considering 'supplementary means of interpretation' in *Canada – Dairy*, the Appellate Body observed that the terms and conditions at issue 'were incorporated into Canada's Schedule after lengthy negotiations' between Canada and the United States regarding 'reciprocal market access opportunities for dairy products'. (Appellate Body Report, *Canada – Dairy*, para. 139) The Appellate Body also recognized in *US – Gambling* that certain Scheduling Guidelines 'were drafted in parallel with the GATS itself' and, in that sense, could be considered to have been 'drawn up on the occasion of the conclusion of the treaty'. (Appellate Body Report, *US – Gambling*, footnote 244 to para. 196.)[95]

In *EC – Chicken Cuts*, the Appellate Body explained that official publication of an act or instrument, which provides interested parties with an opportunity to acquire knowledge about it, is sufficient for it to qualify as 'circumstances of conclusion' under Article 32 of the Vienna Convention:

> We understand the Panel's notion of 'constructive knowledge' to mean that 'parties have deemed notice of a particular event, act or instrument through publication'. We note the European Communities' view that 'deemed knowledge' on the basis of general 'access' to a publication cannot substitute the need for demonstrating a direct link between a circumstance and the common intentions of the parties. However, we consider that the European Communities conflates the preliminary question of what may qualify as a 'circumstance' of a treaty's conclusion with the separate question of ascertaining the degree of relevance that may be ascribed to a given circumstance, for purposes of interpretation under Article 32. As far as an act or instrument originating from an individual party may be considered to be a circumstance under Article 32 for ascertaining the parties' intentions, we consider that the fact that this act or

---

[95] *Ibid.*, para. 293.

instrument was officially published, and has been publicly available so that any interested party could have acquired knowledge of it, appears to be enough. Of course, proof of actual knowledge will increase the degree of relevance of a circumstance for interpretation.[96]

Finally, as to whether a Member's court judgments may be considered as supplementary means of interpretation under Article 32, the Appellate Body in *EC – Chicken Cuts* noted that domestic court judgments may be considered if they assist in ascertaining the common intentions of the parties:

> [J]udgments of domestic courts are not, in principle, excluded from consideration as 'circumstances of the conclusion' of a treaty if they would be of assistance in ascertaining the common intentions of the parties for purposes of interpretation under Article 32. It is necessary to point out, however, that judgments deal basically with a specific dispute and have, by their very nature, less relevance than legislative acts of general application (although judgments may have some precedential effect in certain legal systems).[97]

15.11 Treaties authenticated in two or more languages

15.78 Article 33 of the Vienna Convention is entitled 'Interpretation of treaties authenticated in two or more languages', and reads:

> 1. When a treaty has been authenticated in two or more languages, the text is equally authoritative in each language, unless the treaty provides or the parties agree that, in case of divergence, a particular text shall prevail.
> 2. A version of the treaty in a language other than one of those in which the text was authenticated shall be considered an authentic text only if the treaty so provides or the parties so agree.
> 3. The terms of the treaty are presumed to have the same meaning in each authentic text.
> 4. Except where a particular text prevails in accordance with paragraph 1, when a comparison of the authentic texts discloses a difference of meaning which the application of articles 31 and 32 does not remove, the meaning which best reconciles the texts, having regard to the object and purpose of the treaty, shall be adopted.

There is no WTO jurisprudence concerning Article 33(1) and/or (2); the WTO Agreement (along with an explanatory note to the GATT) expressly states that it was done in the English, French and Spanish languages, each text being authentic. There are a number of references to Article 33(3) in WTO jurisprudence. In the context of treaty interpretation, disputing parties and WTO adjudicators often compare the terms used in the English version of the agreements (the language in which most dispute settlement proceedings

---

[96] *Ibid.*, para. 297.   [97] *Ibid.*, para. 309.

are conducted) with those used in the French and Spanish versions. In most cases, reference to the different language versions is made only to confirm the meaning arrived at; in a few cases, however, the comparison of the different language versions has been central to the reasoning for adopting a particular interpretation.

In *US – Softwood Lumber IV*, the Appellate Body confirmed that Article 33(3) of **15.79** the Vienna Convention reflects customary international law:

> [I]n accordance with the customary rule of treaty interpretation reflected in Article 33(3) of the *Vienna Convention on the Law of Treaties* . . . the terms of a treaty authenticated in more than one language – like the *WTO Agreement* – are presumed to have the same meaning in each authentic text.[49] It follows that the treaty interpreter should seek the meaning that gives effect, simultaneously, to all the terms of the treaty, as they are used in each authentic language.[50]

---

[49] Article 33(3) of the Vienna Convention . . . provides: '[t]he terms of the treaty are presumed to have the same meaning in each authentic text'.

[50] See Appellate Body Report, *EC – Bed Linen (Article 21.5 – India)*, footnote 153 to para. 123. We also note that, in discussing the draft article that was later adopted as Article 33(3) of the *Vienna Convention*, the International Law Commission observed that the 'presumption [that the terms of a treaty are intended to have the same meaning in each authentic text] requires that every effort should be made to find a common meaning for the texts before preferring one to another'. (*Yearbook of the International Law Commission* (1966), Vol. II, p. 225) With regard to the application of customary rules of interpretation in respect of treaties authenticated in more than one language, see also International Court of Justice, Merits, *Case Concerning Elettronica Sicula SpA (ELSI) (United States* v. *Italy)* 1989, ICJ Reports, para. 132, where, in interpreting a provision of the Treaty of Friendship, Commerce and Navigation between the United States of America and the Italian Republic of 1948, the International Court of Justice noted that it was possible to interpret the English and Italian versions 'as meaning much the same thing', despite a potential divergence in scope.[98]

In *US – Anti-Dumping and Countervailing Duties (China)* (DS379), the Appel- **15.80** late Body reversed the Panel's interpretation of the term 'public body' in Article 1.1(a)(1) of the SCM Agreement. In the course of its analysis, the Appellate Body concluded that the Panel failed to properly address China's argument based on Article 33(3) of the Vienna Convention, which involved a comparison between the English and Spanish translations of the same term in two different sets of provisions:

> As a preliminary matter, we do not consider it determinative that the term used in Article 9.1 of the *Agreement on Agriculture* and Article 1.1(a)(1) of the *SCM*

---

[98] Appellate Body Report, *US – Softwood Lumber IV*, para. 59.

Agreement, '*organismo público*', is the same only in the Spanish version. The covered agreements are authentic in all three languages. Therefore, pursuant to Article 33(3) of the *Vienna Convention*, the terms of the treaty are presumed to have the same meaning in each authentic text. Nonetheless, specific terms may not have identical meanings in every covered agreement. Where the ordinary meaning of the term is broad enough to allow for different interpretations, and the context as well as the object and purpose of the relevant agreements point in different directions, the meaning of a term used in different places of the covered agreements may differ.

We note that the Panel rejected China's argument relating to the harmonious interpretation of 'government or any public body' in Article 1.1(a)(1) of the *SCM Agreement* and 'governments or their agencies' in Article 9.1 of the *Agreement on Agriculture*, because it had found definitions and usages showing a broader possible scope of the term 'public body'. However, we do not see that China argued simply that the term 'public body' or '*organismo público*' in itself has a narrow scope. Rather, we understand China's argument to be that the same term '*organismo público*' is used in Article 1.1(a)(1) of the *SCM Agreement* and Article 9.1 of the *Agreement on Agriculture*, and that, since the Appellate Body has interpreted the term '*organismo público*' in Article 9.1 of the *Agreement on Agriculture* to mean an entity which exercises powers vested in it by a government for the purpose of performing functions of a governmental character, the same term, albeit identical only in the Spanish version of the covered agreements, should be interpreted in the same way in the context of Article 1.1(a)(1) of the *SCM Agreement*.

In any event, for the purpose of the present appeal, it suffices to note that the Panel's statement that it had 'found other definitions and usages showing a broader possible scope' of the term 'public body' than the definitions suggested by China, provides no support to the conclusion of the Panel's analysis under Article 1.1(a)(1) of the *SCM Agreement*. In our view, the Panel failed to address properly the substance of China's argument about a harmonious interpretation of the term '*organismo público*' in the *SCM Agreement* and in the *Agreement on Agriculture*.[99]

15.81 In *US – Countervailing and Anti-Dumping Duties (China)* (DS449), the Appellate Body resolved an ambiguity in the English text of Article X:2 of the GATT based on the wording used in the French and Spanish versions of that provision:

This meaning of the preposition 'under' is reinforced by the French and Spanish versions of the text of Article X:2. We recall that, according to Article XVI:6 of the Marrakesh Agreement Establishing the World Trade Organization (WTO Agreement), the texts of the WTO covered agreements are authentic in each of the three WTO official languages, and that, in previous disputes, the Appellate Body has confirmed the ordinary meaning of terms in the English version by reference to the French and Spanish language versions of the relevant provision. The phrase 'under an established and uniform practice' reads in French '*en vertu d'usages établis et uniformes*' and in Spanish '*en virtud del uso establecido y*

[99] Appellate Body Report, *US – Anti-Dumping and Countervailing Duties (China)*, paras. 330–2.

uniforme'. In French and in Spanish, '*en vertu de*' and '*en virtud de*' describe the manner, the means, or how something is done. Moreover, '*en vertu de*' and '*en virtud de*' can be translated literally into English as 'by virtue of'. The term 'by virtue of' can be reconciled with those definitions of 'under', such as 'in the form of' and 'in the guise of'. In contrast, translating literally the French and the Spanish texts into English, we fail to see how the term 'by virtue of' can qualify the preceding term 'rate of duty' so that the phrase 'effecting an advance in a rate of duty or other charge *by virtue of* an established and uniform practice' could be read as referring to a *comparison between* a new higher rate and a prior rate.

The French and Spanish versions of the covered agreements cannot be read as connoting the phrase 'under an established and uniform practice' as the baseline of comparison as the Panel did. Rather, the French and Spanish versions of Article X:2 suggest that the phrase 'under an established and uniform practice' describes how the measure of general application effects an advance in a rate of duty or other charge on imports, in order to fall within the scope of Article X:2. Accordingly, the Panel's interpretation of the English text of Article X:2 is not reconcilable with the meaning of the provision in the two other authentic languages of the GATT 1994. In case of differences of meanings among authentic texts, Article 33 of the Vienna Convention on the Law of Treaties (Vienna Convention) requires an interpreter to adopt 'the meaning which best reconciles the texts, having regard to the object and purpose of the treaty'. In our view, the meanings of 'under' that best reconcile the texts of Article X:2 in English, French, and Spanish are 'in the form of' and 'in the guise of'.[442]

---

[442] According to Article 33 of the Vienna Convention, '(w)hen a treaty has been authenticated in two or more languages, the text is equally authoritative in each language' and '(t)he terms of the treaty are presumed to have the same meaning in each authentic text.' Moreover, 'when a comparison of the authentic texts discloses a difference of meaning which the application of Articles 31 and 32 does not remove, the meaning which best reconciles the texts, having regard to the object and purpose of the treaty, shall be adopted.'[100]

---

[100] Appellate Body Report, *US – Countervailing and Anti-Dumping Duties (China)*, paras. 4.76–4.77 (citing Appellate Body Report, *US – Upland Cotton*, para. 424, footnote 510; Appellate Body Reports, *US – Countervailing Duty Investigation on DRAMS*, para. 111, footnote 176; *EC – Tariff Preferences*, para. 147).

16

WORDS AND PHRASES CONSIDERED

16.1   Introduction

In his book, *The Law of Treaties*, Lord McNair included an appendix with the **16.1**
snappy title 'Some words and phrases occurring in, or in connection with,
Treaties, and considered by International and National Courts and Tribunals
and in the Reports of the Law Officers'.[1] While this appendix was rudimentary
as compared with the various encyclopaedic digests of 'words and phrases
judicially considered' that one encounters in the domestic context,[2] at least
one reviewer at the time considered McNair's mini-digest to be 'extremely
useful'.[3] In that spirit, this chapter reviews WTO statements relating to a range
of words and phrases under the following headings: (i) mandatory and discretionary terms; (ii) obligations of conduct; (iii) self-judging standards; (iv) normative standards; (v) timing language; and (vi) common English words.
Pronouncements about the meaning of a term in one particular context cannot
necessarily be transposed to a different context – there are numerous statements
by WTO adjudicators to that effect.[4] However, WTO jurisprudence is replete
with general guidance on the ordinary meaning of many English words and
phrases that are commonly found in treaties and other international legal
instruments, and in many instances such guidance does not seem to be context-specific.

---

[1]   A. D. McNair, *The Law of Treaties*, 2nd edn (Clarendon Press, 1961), Annex B.
[2]   For example, see H. DeVille, *The Australian Digest, Consolidated Words and Phrases* (LBC Information Services, 1996–); R. Blackburn (ed.), *Words & Phrases Judicially Defined in Canadian
Courts and Tribunals* (Carswell, 1993–); S. Malik, *Supreme Court on Words and Phrases* (India)
(Eastern Book Co., 1993); *Words and phrases. Permanent ed. 1658 to date. All judicial constructions
and definitions of words and phrases by the State and Federal courts from the earliest times, alphabetic-
ally arranged and indexed* (West Publishing Co., 1940–).
[3]   Book review of A. D. McNair, *The Law of Treaties*, 2nd edn (Clarendon Press, 1961) in (1962) 11
International and Comparative Law Quarterly 596–601, at 597.
[4]   For example, see *Japan – Alcoholic Beverages II*, quoted at para. 15.22 above.

16.2   Mandatory and discretionary terms

16.2 Panels and the Appellate Body have considered the difference between mandatory and discretionary terms in a wide range of contexts, including the terms 'shall', 'should' and 'may', and the terms 'guidelines' and 'principles', as well as qualifying language such as 'normally', 'as far as possible' and 'unless impracticable'.

16.2.1 'Shall', 'should' and 'may'

16.3 In *Japan – Alcoholic Beverages II*, the Panel examined a claim under Article III:2 of the GATT. The Panel compared and contrasted the 'general principles' of Article III:1 with the 'legally binding obligation' in Article III:2:

> The words 'recognize' and 'should' in Article III:1, as well as the wording of Article III:2, second sentence, ('the principles'), make it clear that Article III:1 does not contain a legally binding obligation but rather states general principles. In contrast, the use of the word 'shall' in Article III:2, both sentences, makes it clear that Article III:2 contains two legally binding obligations.[5]

16.4 In *EC – Sardines*, the Panel examined a claim under Article 2.4 of the TBT Agreement and commented on the use of the word 'shall' in that provision:

> Article 2.4 states that Members '*shall* use' international standards 'as a basis' for their technical regulation. The use of the word 'shall' denotes a requirement that is obligatory in nature and that goes beyond mere encouragement.[6]

16.5 In *India – Patents (EC)*, the Panel contrasted the 'directory or recommendatory' wording of Article 9.1 of the DSU with 'mandatory' language:

> Given their ordinary meaning, the terms of Article 9.1 are directory or recommendatory, not mandatory. They direct that a single panel *should* (not 'shall') be established, and that direction is limited to cases where it is *feasible*.[7]

16.6 In *Canada – Aircraft*, the Appellate Body interpreted Article 13.1 of the DSU, which provides that a Member 'should respond promptly and fully' to any request by a panel for such information as the panel considers necessary and appropriate. The Appellate Body concluded that Members were under a duty and an obligation to respond promptly and fully to any such request:

> Although the word 'should' is often used colloquially to imply an exhortation, or to state a preference, it is not always used in those ways. It can also be used 'to express a duty [or] obligation'.[120] The word 'should' has, for instance, previously been interpreted by us as expressing a 'duty' of panels in the context of Article 11

---

[5] Panel Report, *Japan – Alcoholic Beverages II*, para. 6.12.
[6] Panel Report, *EC – Sardines*, para. 7.110.   [7] Panel Report, *India – Patents (EC)*, para. 7.14.

of the DSU. Similarly, we are of the view that the word 'should' in the third sentence of Article 13.1 is, in the context of the whole of Article 13, used in a normative, rather than a merely exhortative, sense. Members are, in other words, under a duty and an obligation to 'respond promptly and fully' to requests made by panels for information under Article 13.1 of the DSU.

---

[120] *The Concise Oxford English Dictionary*, (Clarendon Press, 1995), p. 1283. See also *The Shorter Oxford English Dictionary*, (Clarendon Press, 1993), Vol. II, p. 2808, and *Black's Law Dictionary*, (West Publishing Co., 1990), p. 1379, which states that 'should' 'ordinarily impl[ies] duty or obligation; although usually no more than an obligation of propriety or expediency, or moral obligation, thereby distinguishing it from "ought".'[8]

In *EC – Bed Linen (Article 21.5 – India)*, the Panel concluded that, in the **16.7** context of Article 21.2 of the DSU, the hortatory word 'should' did not have the mandatory meaning of 'shall'. The Panel explained that:

India merely argues that in another case, the Appellate Body found that the word 'should' had the meaning of 'shall', and asserts, without more, that the same result is appropriate in this case. We disagree. The case India relies upon, *Canada – Aircraft*, involved a very different provision of a different agreement, concerning the duty of Members to respond promptly and fully to requests for information from Panels. Moreover, even in that case, the Appellate Body noted the dictionary definition of 'should' 'ordinarily impl[ies] duty or obligation; although usually no more than an obligation of propriety or expediency, or moral obligation, thereby distinguishing it from "ought"'. In addition, the fact that there is no specific action set out in Article 21.2 makes it unlikely that Members intended the provision to be mandatory – the lack of specificity in this regard implies rather a hortatory use of should.[9]

In *EC – Tariff Preferences*, the Panel commented on the use of the word 'may' in **16.8** paragraph 1 of the Enabling Clause:

There is no legal obligation in the Enabling Clause itself requiring the developed country Members to provide GSP to developing countries. The word 'may' in paragraph 1 of the Enabling Clause makes the granting of GSP clearly an *option* rather than an obligation.[10]

Along the same lines, the Panel in *Argentina – Poultry Anti-Dumping Duties* **16.9** stated:

[B]y virtue of Article 19.1 of the DSU, panels have discretion ('may') to suggest ways in which a Member could implement the relevant recommendation. Clearly, however, a panel is not required to make a suggestion should it not deem it appropriate to do so.[11]

---

[8] Appellate Body Report, *Canada – Aircraft*, para. 187.
[9] Panel Report, *EC – Bed Linen (Article 21.5 – India)*, para. 6.267.
[10] Panel Report, *EC – Tariff Preferences*, para. 7.38.
[11] Panel Report, *Argentina – Poultry Anti-Dumping Duties*, para. 8.5.

16.10 In *United States – 1916 Act*, the Panel observed that there are several different dictionary definitions of the word may, including a definition of 'may' which, in the interpretation of some statutes, establishes a mandatory obligation:

> See The New Shorter Oxford English Dictionary (1993), p. 1721. It is evident that while we review the ordinary meaning, our reading of the dictionary is already made selective by the broad context of the term. For instance, we left aside the definition of 'may' as 'have the possibility, opportunity or suitable conditions to . . .' or the definition of 'may' which, in the interpretation of some statutes means 'shall, must'.[12]

16.11 The Panel in *US – Upland Cotton* did not consider that the word 'may' gives rise to any discretion in the context of Article 6.3 of the SCM Agreement, or at least not in the sense argued by the respondent in that case. Article 5(c) of the SCM Agreement provides that no Member should cause, through the use of any specific subsidy, 'serious prejudice to the interests of another Member', and Article 6.3 of the SCM Agreement then clarifies that 'serious prejudice' in the sense of paragraph (c) of Article 5 '*may* arise in any case where one or several of the following apply', and then proceeds to enumerate a list of trade effects (e.g. lost sales). The interpretative issue that arose in *US – Upland Cotton* was whether a demonstration of one or more of those trade effects in Article 6.3(c) is sufficient to establish the existence of 'serious prejudice' within the meaning of Article 5(c). Notwithstanding the use of the term 'may', the Panel found that, where there is a demonstration of one or more of the trade effects in Article 6.3(c) is sufficient, serious prejudice within the meaning of Article 5(c) is deemed to exist. In the course of its reasoning on this issue, the Panel explained that:

> The ordinary meaning of the word 'may' in the chapeau of Article 6.3 of the *SCM Agreement* may express 'possibility' or 'permission'. We agree with the United States that the use of the word 'may' in the chapeau of Article 6.3(c) may, at least, play such a permissive role. In this sense, the ordinary meaning of the chapeau of Article 6.3 would be that there is a 'possibility' or 'opportunity' for serious prejudice in the sense of Article 5(c) to arise where one or more of the effects-based situations listed in Article 6.3 is found. A panel would be permitted to find serious prejudice upon finding that one of these listed effects-based situations exists.
>
> . . .
>
> [T]he text of the chapeau of Article 6.3 of the *SCM Agreement* is silent as to any factors which would guide an examination under its term 'may'. We do not believe that, in light of this relatively detailed express guidance that is available on certain aspects relevant to the Article 6.3 examination, there is *another* set of entirely *undefined* requirements or conditions that must also guide our examination and that must also be demonstrated in order to find serious prejudice within the meaning of Article 5(c).[13]

---

[12] Panel Report, *US – 1916 Act (Japan)*, footnote 562.
[13] Panel Report, *US – Upland Cotton*, paras. 7.1370, 7.1374.

16.2.2 'Guidelines' and 'principles'

In *US – Softwood Lumber IV*, the Appellate Body examined Article 14 of the **16.12**
SCM Agreement, which provides that any method used by an investigating
authority to calculate the amount of a subsidy 'shall' be consistent with the
'guidelines' contained in that provision. The Appellate Body stated:

> We agree with the Panel that the term 'shall' in the last sentence of the chapeau
> of Article 14 suggests that calculating benefit consistently with the guidelines is
> mandatory. We also agree that the term 'guidelines' suggests that Article
> 14 provides the 'framework within which this calculation is to be performed',
> although the 'precise detailed method of calculation is not determined'. Taken
> together, these terms establish mandatory parameters within which the benefit
> must be calculated, but they do not require using only one methodology for
> determining the adequacy of remuneration for the provision of goods by a
> government. Thus, we find merit in the United States' submission that the
> use of the term 'guidelines' in Article 14 suggests that paragraphs (a) through (d)
> should not be interpreted as 'rigid rules that purport to contemplate every
> conceivable factual circumstance'.[14]

In *Chile – Alcoholic Beverages (Article 21.3(c))*, the Arbitrator emphasized the use **16.13**
of the term 'guideline' in Article 21.3(c) of the DSU:

> What Article 21.3(c) of the DSU provides arbitrators with is a '*guide*line', not a
> fixed command, that the reasonable period should be not more than 15 months
> from the date of adoption by the DSB of the pertinent Panel and Appellate
> Body Reports. Article 21.3(c) evidently contemplates a case-specific approach
> and authorizes the consideration of the 'particular circumstances' of a given case,
> which may warrant a longer or shorter period.[15]

In *China – Intellectual Property Rights*, the Panel considered the ordinary **16.14**
meaning of the term 'principles' in the context of Article 59 of the TRIPS
Agreement, and stated:

> Article 59 refers to the 'principles' set out in Article 46. Therefore, it is necessary
> to determine what precisely that refers to in the first, third and fourth sentences
> of Article 46. The word 'principles' can be defined as 'a general law or rule
> adopted or professed as a guide to action.' Each of these sentences of Article
> 46 contains language that is a guide to action by authorities and none dictate the
> precise terms of orders in specific cases.[16]

In *EC – Approval and Marketing of Biotech Products*, the Panel concluded that **16.15**
'general principles of law' within the meaning of Article 38(1)(c) of the ICJ
Statute may qualify as relevant 'rules' of international law within the meaning of
Article 31(3)(c) of the Vienna Convention:

[14] Appellate Body Report, *US – Softwood Lumber IV*, para. 92.
[15] Award of the Arbitrator, *Chile – Alcoholic Beverages (Article 21.3(c))*, para. 39.
[16] Panel Report, *China – Intellectual Property Rights*, para. 7.264.

Regarding the recognized general *principles* of law which are applicable in international law, it may not appear self-evident that they can be considered as '*rules* of international law' within the meaning of Article 31(3)(c). However, the Appellate Body in *US – Shrimp* made it clear that pursuant to Article 31(3)(c) general principles of international law are to be taken into account in the interpretation of WTO provisions. As we mention further below, the European Communities considers that the principle of precaution is a 'general principle of international law'. Based on the Appellate Body report on *US – Shrimp*, we would agree that if the precautionary principle is a general principle of international law, it could be considered a 'rule of international law' within the meaning of Article 31(3)(c).[17]

16.16 In *US – Anti-Dumping and Countervailing Duties (China)* (DS379) the Appellate Body addressed Article 2 of the SCM Agreement, which requires an investigating authority to apply the 'principles' set out therein for the purpose of determining whether a subsidy is specific to certain enterprises. As regards the use of the term 'principles', the Appellate Body stated:

> The chapeau of Article 2.1 offers interpretative guidance with regard to the scope and meaning of the subparagraphs that follow. The chapeau frames the central inquiry as a determination as to whether a subsidy is specific to 'certain enterprises' within the jurisdiction of the granting authority and provides that, in an examination of whether this is so, the 'principles' set out in subparagraphs (a) through (c) 'shall apply'. We consider that the use of the term 'principles' – instead of, for instance, 'rules' – suggests that subparagraphs (a) through (c) are to be considered within an analytical framework that recognizes and accords appropriate weight to each principle. Consequently, the application of one of the subparagraphs of Article 2.1 may not by itself be determinative in arriving at a conclusion that a particular subsidy is or is not specific.[18]

16.2.3 'As far as possible', 'unless impracticable', 'normally'

16.17 In *US – Shrimp (Article 21.5 – Malaysia)*, the Appellate Body applied the ordinary meaning of the phrase 'as far as possible' in the context of Principle 12 of the Rio Declaration:

> Principle 12 of the Rio Declaration on Environment and Development states, in part, that '[e]nvironmental measures addressing transboundary or global environmental problems should, as far as possible, be based on international consensus'. Clearly, and 'as far as possible', a multilateral approach is strongly preferred. Yet it is one thing to *prefer* a multilateral approach in the application of a measure that is provisionally justified under one of the subparagraphs of Article XX of the GATT 1994; it is another to require the *conclusion* of a multilateral

---

[17] Panel Report, *EC – Approval and Marketing of Biotech Products*, para. 7.67.
[18] Appellate Body Report, *US – Anti-Dumping and Countervailing Duties (China)*, para. 366.

agreement as a condition of avoiding 'arbitrary or unjustifiable discrimination' under the chapeau of Article XX. We see, in this case, no such requirement.[19]

In *US – Softwood Lumber IV (Article 21.5 – Canada)*, the Appellate Body again **16.18** equated the expression 'as far as possible' with the concept of a preference, this time in the context of Article 21.5 of the DSU:

> [T]he end of the first sentence of Article 21.5 indicates that where there is disagreement regarding measures taken to comply, there should be recourse to the original panel 'wherever possible', thus expressing a preference for dealing with these 'disagreements' before the original panel that made the original recommendations and rulings in the dispute, rather than starting over again in new proceedings before a new panel.[20]

In *Chile – Alcoholic Beverages (Article 21.3(c))*, the Arbitrator contrasted the term **16.19** 'impracticable' with the term 'impossible' in the context of examining Article 21.3 of the DSU, which provides that a Member is entitled to a reasonable period of time to comply with DSB recommendations and rulings if it is 'impracticable' for a Member to comply immediately:

> The DSU clearly stressed the systemic interest of all WTO Members in the Member concerned complying 'immediately' with the recommendations and rulings of the DSB. Reading Articles 21.1 and 21.3 together, 'prompt' compliance is, in principle, 'immediate' compliance. At the same time, however, should 'immediate' compliance be 'impracticable' – it may be noted that the DSU does not use the far more rigorous term 'impossible' – the Member concerned becomes entitled to a 'reasonable period of time' to bring itself into a state of conformity with its WTO obligations.[21]

In *EC – Bananas III (Ecuador) (Article 22.6 – EC)*, the Arbitrator examined the **16.20** principle, set forth in Article 22.3(b) and (c) of the DSU, that, when a complaining party is suspending concessions or other obligations in a case of non-compliance, it should do so in the same sector/agreement under which a violation was found unless that party considers that this is 'not practicable' or effective:

> Several of these issues require the party seeking suspension to consider whether an alternative suspension with respect to the same sectors or agreements under which a violation was found is 'not practicable or effective'. In this regard, we note that the ordinary meaning of 'practicable' is 'available or useful in practice; able to be used' or 'inclined or suited to action as opposed to speculation etc.'. In other words, an examination of the 'practicability' of an alternative suspension concerns the question whether such an alternative is available for application in practice as well as suited for being used in a particular case.

---

[19] Appellate Body Report, *US – Shrimp (Article 21.5 – Malaysia)*, para. 124.
[20] Appellate Body Report, *US – Softwood Lumber IV*, para. 68.
[21] Award of the Arbitrator, *Chile – Alcoholic Beverages (Article 21.3(c))*, para. 38.

To give an obvious example, suspension of commitments in service sub-sectors or in respect of modes of service supply which a particular complaining party has not bound in its GATS Schedule is not available for application in practice and thus cannot be considered as practicable. But also other case-specific and country-specific situations may exist where suspension of concessions or other obligations in a particular trade sector or area of WTO law may not be 'practicable'.[22]

16.21 In *US – Clove Cigarettes*, the Appellate Body considered Paragraph 5.2 of the 'Doha Decision on Implementation-Related Issues', which provides in relevant part that the phrase 'reasonable interval' in Article 2.12 of the TBT Agreement 'shall be understood to mean normally a period of not less than 6 months, except when this would be ineffective in fulfilling the legitimate objectives pursued'. Regarding the word 'normally', the Appellate Body stated:

> On appeal, the United States argues that the use of the term 'normally' in paragraph 5.2 of the Doha Ministerial Decision does not support the conclusion that paragraph 5.2 represents a rule. We observe that the ordinary meaning of the term 'normally' is defined as 'under normal or ordinary conditions; as a rule'. In our view, the qualification of an obligation with the adverb 'normally' does not, necessarily, alter the characterization of that obligation as constituting a 'rule'. Rather, we consider that the use of the term 'normally' in paragraph 5.2 indicates that the rule establishing that foreign producers require a minimum of 'not less than 6 months' to adapt to the requirements of a technical regulation admits of derogation under certain circumstances.[23]

16.3   Obligations of conduct

16.22 In several cases, WTO adjudicators have examined obligations of conduct that require Members to 'take account' of certain circumstances, 'explore' certain courses of action, or 'seek to obtain' certain information. WTO jurisprudence offers support for the proposition that such language creates an obligation of conduct and generally does not prescribe any specific result.

16.23 Article 10.1 of the SPS Agreement provides that, in the preparation of SPS measures, Members 'shall take account' of the special needs of developing countries. Article 12.3 of the TBT Agreement contains a similar obligation in respect of technical regulations. In *EC – Approval and Marketing of Biotech Products*, the Panel found that this language does not prescribe a specific result to be achieved:

---

[22] Decision by the Arbitrator, *EC – Bananas III (Ecuador) (Article 22.6 – EC)*, paras. 70–1 (citing the *Shorter Oxford English Dictionary*).
[23] Appellate Body Report, *US – Clove Cigarettes*, para. 273.

[T]he obligation laid down in Article 10.1 is for the importing Member to 'take account' of developing country Members' needs. The dictionary defines the expression 'take account of' as 'consider along with other factors before reaching a decision'. Consistent with this, Article 10.1 does not prescribe a specific result to be achieved. Notably, Article 10.1 does not provide that the importing Member must invariably accord special and differential treatment in a case where a measure has lead, or may lead, to a decrease, or a slower increase, in developing country exports.[24]

In *EC – Bed Linen*, the Panel examined a claim under Article 15 of the Anti-Dumping Agreement, which provides that possibilities of constructive remedies 'shall be explored' before applying anti-dumping duties affecting the essential interests of developing country Members. The Panel concluded that, 'while the exact parameters of the term are difficult to establish, the concept of "explore" clearly does not imply any particular outcome'.[25] **16.24**

Article 5.7 of the SPS Agreement provides that, in cases where relevant scientific evidence is insufficient, a Member may provisionally adopt SPS measures on the basis of available pertinent information, but that, in such circumstances, Members 'shall seek to obtain' the additional information necessary for a more objective assessment of risk and review the sanitary or phytosanitary measure accordingly within a reasonable period of time. In *US / Canada – Continued Suspension*, the Appellate Body stated: **16.25**

> The requirement that the WTO Member 'shall seek to obtain the additional information necessary for a more objective assessment of risk' implies that, as of the adoption of the provisional measure, a WTO Member must make best efforts to remedy the insufficiencies in the relevant scientific evidence with additional scientific research or by gathering information from relevant international organizations or other sources ... A Member is required under Article 5.7 to seek to obtain additional information but is not expected to guarantee specific results.[26]

16.4   Self-judging standards

In several cases, WTO adjudicators have examined language creating a self-judging standard, for example, measures 'deemed appropriate' by a Member. WTO jurisprudence supports the proposition that the parties to a treaty may establish self-judging standards through the use of such language, but that legal rights and obligations are not presumed to be self-judging in the absence of such language. **16.26**

---

[24] Panel Report, *EC – Approval and Marketing of Biotech Products*, para. 7.1620 (citing the *Concise Oxford Dictionary*).
[25] Panel Report, *EC – Bed Linen*, para. 6.233.
[26] Appellate Body Report, *US / Canada – Continued Suspension*, para. 679.

16.27 In *EC – Hormones*, the Panel examined Annex A, paragraph 5, of the SPS Agreement, which refers to the level of protection 'deemed appropriate by the Member' establishing an SPS measure to protect human, animal or plant life or health within its territory. With reference to the phrase 'deemed appropriate by the Member', the Panel stated:

> The parties to this dispute seem to agree that the establishment of an 'appropriate level of sanitary protection' by a Member is a sovereign act, namely, as the definition in paragraph 5 of Annex A of the SPS Agreement provides, the level of protection '*deemed appropriate by the Member* establishing a sanitary . . . measure' (emphasis added). As outlined above, we note, however, that Members have agreed, in exercising their sovereign right to set their appropriate levels of protection, to observe the provisions of the SPS Agreement, in particular Articles 5.4 and 5.5 thereof. Furthermore, in choosing a measure to achieve that appropriate level of protection Members have agreed to observe the provisions of Articles 2, 5.1 to 5.3 and 5.6.[27]

16.28 In *EC – Bananas III*, the Appellate Body found that Members are expected to be 'self-regulating' in deciding whether to initiate a WTO dispute, taking into account the wording of Article XXIII:1 of the GATT and Article 3.7 of the DSU:

> The chapeau of Article XXIII:1 of the GATT 1994 provides:
>
> > If any Member should consider that any benefit accruing to it directly or indirectly under this Agreement is being nullified or impaired or that the attainment of any objective of the Agreement is being impeded . . .
>
> Of special importance for determining the issue of standing, in our view, are the words '[i]f any Member should consider . . .'. This provision in Article XXIII is consistent with Article 3.7 of the DSU, which states:
>
> > Before bringing a case, a Member shall exercise its judgement as to whether action under these procedures would be fruitful . . .
>
> Accordingly, we believe that a Member has broad discretion in deciding whether to bring a case against another Member under the DSU. The language of Article XXIII:1 of the GATT 1994 and of Article 3.7 of the DSU suggests, furthermore, that a Member is expected to be largely self-regulating in deciding whether any such action would be 'fruitful'.[28]

16.29 In *EC – Bananas III (Ecuador) (Article 22.6 – EC)*, Ecuador argued that it was the prerogative of the Member suffering nullification or impairment from ongoing non-compliance to decide whether it is 'practicable or effective' to choose the same sector, another sector or another agreement, for the purposes of retaliation. The Arbitrators held that the phrase 'if that party considers'

---

[27] Panel Report, *EC – Hormones (US)*, para. 8.164.
[28] Appellate Body Report, *EC – Bananas III*, paras. 134–5.

in subparagraphs (b) and (c) of Article 22.3 of the DSU, granted a certain margin of appreciation, but that a decision by a Member was nevertheless subject to review by the Arbitrators regarding whether the Member had considered the necessary facts objectively:

> It follows from the choice of the words 'if that party *considers*' in subparagraphs (b) and (c) that these subparagraphs leave a certain margin of appreciation to the complaining party concerned in arriving at its conclusions in respect of an evaluation of certain factual elements, i.e. of the practicability and effectiveness of suspension within the same sector or under the same agreement and of the seriousness of circumstances. However, it equally follows from the choice of the words 'in considering what concessions or other obligations to suspend, the complaining party *shall* apply the following principles and procedures' in the chapeau of Article 22.3 that such margin of appreciation by the complaining party concerned is subject to review by the Arbitrators. In our view, the margin of review by the Arbitrators implies the authority to broadly judge whether the complaining party in question has considered the necessary facts objectively and whether, on the basis of these facts, it could plausibly arrive at the conclusion that it was not practicable or effective to seek suspension within the same sector under the same agreements, or only under another agreement provided that the circumstances were serious enough.[29]

In *Argentina – Footwear (EC)*, Argentina argued on appeal that the Panel erred **16.30** by not acceding to the request of the parties to seek information from and consult with the IMF concerning certain aspects of the statistical tax. The Appellate Body disagreed, noting that Article 13.1 of the DSU grants a panel the right to seek information 'which it deems appropriate':

> Article 13.1 of the DSU gives a panel '... the right to seek information and technical advice from any individual or body which *it deems appropriate*.' (emphasis added) Pursuant to Article 13.2 of the DSU, a panel may seek information from any relevant source and may consult experts to obtain their opinions on certain aspects of the matter at issue. This is a grant of discretionary authority: a panel is not duty-bound to seek information in each and every case or to consult particular experts under this provision. We recall our statement in *EC Measures Concerning Meat and Meat Products (Hormones)* that Article 13 of the DSU enables a panel to seek information and technical advice as it deems appropriate in a particular case, and that the DSU leaves 'to the sound discretion of a panel the determination of whether the establishment of an expert review group is necessary or appropriate.' Just as a panel has the discretion to determine how to seek expert advice, so also does a panel have the discretion to determine whether to seek information or expert advice at all.[30]

The Panel in *China – Raw Materials* examined Article XI:2(a) of the GATT, **16.31** which provides that the obligation in Article X:1 of the GATT to eliminate

---

[29] Decision by the Arbitrator, *EC – Bananas III (Ecuador) (Article 22.6 – EC)*, para. 52.
[30] Appellate Body Report, *Argentina – Footwear (EC)*, para. 84.

quantitative restrictions on the importation and exportation of goods does not extend to export prohibitions or restrictions temporarily applied to prevent or relieve critical shortages of foodstuffs or 'other products essential to the exporting Member'. The Panel found that the concept of an 'essential product to the exporting Member' is *not* a self-judging standard, and contrasted the language of Article X:2(a) with the self-judging language found in Article XXI(b) of the GATT:

> The phrase 'essential to' is defined as 'affecting the essence of anything; "material", important', 'constituting, or forming part of, the essence of anything', and 'absolutely necessary, indispensably requisite'. The phrase 'to the exporting' Member appears to have been added to the initial draft of Article XI:2(a) to clarify that 'the importance of any product should be judged in relation to the particular country concerned'. Thus, a product may fall within the meaning of Article XI:2(a) when it is 'important' or 'necessary' or 'indispensable' to a particular Member.
>
> The Panel does not consider that the terms of Article XI:2, nor the statement made in the context of negotiating the text of Article XI:2 that the importance of a product 'should be judged in relation to the particular country concerned', means that a WTO Member may, on its own, determine whether a product is essential to it. If this were the case, Article XI:2 could have been drafted in a way such as Article XXI(b) of the GATT 1994, which states: 'Nothing in this Agreement shall be construed . . . to prevent any contracting party from taking any action *which it considers necessary* for the protection of its essential security interests' (emphasis added). In the Panel's view, the determination of whether a product is 'essential' to that Member should take into consideration the particular circumstances faced by that Member at the time when a Member applies a restriction or prohibition under Article XI:2(a).[31]

16.5   Normative standards

16.32   WTO adjudicators have interpreted and applied a range of normative standards, including the terms 'appropriate', 'discrimination', 'fair', 'legitimate' and 'necessary', and have focused on the circumstance-specific nature of some of these standards.

16.5.1 'Appropriate'

16.33   In *EC – Hormones*, the Appellate Body examined a claim under Article 5.1 of the SPS Agreement, which requires that SPS measures be based on a risk assessment, 'as appropriate to the circumstances'. The Appellate Body stated that 'this makes clear that the Members have a certain degree of flexibility in meeting the requirements of Article 5.1'.[32] Subsequently, the Panel in *Australia – Salmon*

---

[31] Panel Report, *China – Raw Materials*, paras. 7.275–7.276.
[32] Appellate Body Report, *EC – Hormones*, para. 129.

held that the phrase 'as appropriate to the circumstances' did not alleviate the duty to base a measure on a risk assessment:

> As to the product coverage of Article 5.1, the reference contained in Article 5.1 to base sanitary measures on an assessment 'as appropriate to the circumstances' cannot, in our view, annul or supersede the substantive obligation resting on Australia to base the sanitary measure in dispute (irrespective of the products that measure may cover) on a risk assessment. We consider that the reference 'as appropriate to the circumstances' relates, rather, to the way in which such risk assessment has to be carried out. Only Article 5.7 allows for an exception to the obligation to base sanitary measures on a risk assessment.[33]

In *US – Clove Cigarettes*, the Panel rejected a claim under Article 2.8 of the TBT **16.34** Agreement, which provides that technical regulations must be specified in terms of product performance rather than design or descriptive characteristics '[w]herever appropriate'. In that case the measure at issue (a ban on clove and certain other flavoured cigarettes) was specified in terms of 'design or descriptive characteristics', and not in terms of 'performance', but the Panel agreed with the United States that Indonesia had failed to demonstrate that the alternative approach was 'appropriate'. The Panel recalled prior panel and Appellate Body statements on the meaning of the term 'appropriate' in several other contexts:

> While there is no jurisprudence relating to the terms '[w]herever appropriate' in the context of Article 2.8 of the *TBT Agreement*, the Panel is mindful that the term 'appropriate' appears in numerous other provisions found in the WTO Agreements and that there is substantial and broadly consistent jurisprudence relating to the ordinary meaning of this term. Panels and the Appellate Body have relied upon ordinary dictionary definitions, and given the term 'appropriate' its ordinary meaning. For example, the Panel in *Mexico – Telecoms* observed that:
>
> > The word 'appropriate', in its general dictionary sense, means 'specially suitable, proper'. This suggests that 'appropriate measures' are those that are suitable for achieving their purpose.
>
> Along the same lines, the Panel in *EC   Tube or Pipe Fittings* considered that:
>
> > The ordinary meaning of the term 'appropriate' refers to something which is 'especially suitable or fitting'. 'Suitable', in turn, is defined as 'fitted for or appropriate to a purpose, occasion . . .' or 'adapted to a use or purpose'. 'Fitting' is defined as 'of a kind appropriate to the situation' . . . The term is consistent with an intent not to prejudge what the circumstances might be in the context of a given case. It is necessary for such appropriateness to be judged on a case by case basis . . . There is an element of flexibility,

---

[33] Panel Report, *Australia – Salmon*, para. 8.57. See also Appellate Body Report: *Australia – Salmon*, para. 130; *US/Canada – Continued Suspension*, para. 562; and *Australia – Apples*, paras. 237 and 244.

in that there are no predetermined rigid factors, indices, levels or requirements.

More recently, in *US – Anti-Dumping and Countervailing Duties (China)*, the Appellate Body relied on the same dictionary definitions in the context of interpreting the term 'appropriate amounts' in Article 19.3 of the *SCM Agreement*:

> Beginning with the term 'appropriate amounts', we note that relevant dictionary definitions of the term 'appropriate' include 'proper', 'fitting' and 'specially suitable (for, to)'. These definitions suggest that what is 'appropriate' is not an autonomous or absolute standard, but rather something that must be assessed by reference or in relation to something else.

We would also observe that in *EC – Sardines*, the Appellate Body agreed with the panel that the term 'inappropriate' in the context of Article 2.4 of the *TBT Agreement* 'refers to something which is not "specially suitable", "proper", or "fitting"', and that the question of appropriateness relates more to the nature of the means employed'.[34]

16.35 In *US – FSC (Article 22.6 – US)*, the Arbitrator interpreted the phrase 'appropriate countermeasures' in the context of Article 4.10 and 4.11 of the SCM Agreement. These provisions concern a complaining Member's right to take 'appropriate countermeasures' in the event that the responding Member does not follow a DSB recommendation to withdraw a prohibited subsidy. The Arbitrator stated:

> The ordinary dictionary meaning of the term 'appropriate' refers to something which is 'especially suitable or fitting'. 'Suitable', in turn, can be defined as 'fitted for or appropriate to a purpose, occasion …' or 'adapted to a use or purpose'. 'Fitting' can be defined as 'of a kind appropriate to the situation'.
>
>   As far as the amount or level of countermeasures is concerned, the expression 'appropriate' does not in and of itself predefine, much less does it do so in some mathematically exact manner, the precise and exhaustive conditions for the application of countermeasures. That is, in itself, surely significant. There would have been no *a priori* reason why some defined and/or formulaic approach could not have been set down in advance for the application of countermeasures. The terms of the *SCM Agreement* on this point manifestly eschew any such approach. But the provisions actually used do not become any the less meaningful or of lower legal status by reason of that fact. Much less can there be some kind of inherent presumption that they must be contorted to fit some kind of procrustean bed in the proportions of a formula when it is manifestly not present in the text itself.

---

[34] Panel Report, *US – Clove Cigarettes*, paras. 7.486–7.489 (citing Panel Report, *Mexico – Telecoms*, paras. 7.265, 7.367–7.368; Panel Report, *EC – Tube or Pipe Fittings*, paras. 7.240–7.241; Panel Report, *Argentina – Poultry Anti-Dumping Duties*, paras. 7.191, 7.365; Panel Report, *EC – Sardines*, para. 7.116; Panel Report, *US – Steel Plate*, para. 7.72; Panel Report, *Australia – Salmon*, paras. 8.57 and 8.71; Appellate Body Report, *US – Anti-Dumping and Countervailing Duties (China)*, para. 552; Appellate Body Report, *EC – Sardines*, para. 285).

It is, after all, scarcely a matter for debate that not all situations can be imagined in advance. But even if one takes the view that, as a consequence, there can be no manual which offers a precise course of action for a given situation, that does not mean that one is completely bereft of guidance or, as the case may be, that there are no bounds set to permissible action. This is clearly enough the situation we are dealing with here, where a Member might find itself resorting to countermeasures. The relevant provisions are not designed to lay down a precise formula or otherwise quantified benchmark or amount of countermeasures which might be legitimately authorized in each and every instance. Rather, the notion of 'appropriateness' is used.

Based on the plain meaning of the word, this means that countermeasures should be adapted to the particular case at hand. The term is consistent with an intent not to prejudge what the circumstances might be in the specific context of dispute settlement in a given case. To that extent, there is an element of flexibility, in the sense that there is thereby an eschewal of any rigid *a priori* quantitative formula. But it is also clear that there is, nevertheless, an objective relationship which must be absolutely respected: the countermeasures must be suitable or fitting by way of response to the case at hand.[35]

16.5.2 'Discrimination'

In *US – Shrimp*, the Appellate Body examined the meaning of the word **16.36** 'discrimination' in the context of the chapeau of Article XX of the GATT, which refers to 'arbitrary or unjustifiable discrimination' in application of measures falling within the scope of the general exceptions contained therein. In the course of its analysis, the Appellate Body stated:

> We believe that discrimination results not only when countries in which the same conditions prevail are differently treated, but also when the application of the measure at issue does not allow for any inquiry into the appropriateness of the regulatory program for the conditions prevailing in those exporting countries.[36]

In *Canada – Pharmaceutical Patents*, the Panel considered the concept of **16.37** 'discrimination', in the context of examining the obligation, in Article 27.1 of the TRIPS Agreement, to make patents available and patent rights enjoyable 'without discrimination' as to the place of invention, the field of technology, or whether products are imported or locally produced. The Panel stated:

> The primary TRIPS provisions that deal with discrimination, such as the national treatment and most-favoured-nation provisions of Articles 3 and 4, do not use the term 'discrimination'. They speak in more precise terms. The ordinary meaning of the word 'discriminate' is potentially broader than these

---

[35] Decision by the Arbitrator, *US – FSC (Article 22.6 – US)*, paras. 5.9–5.12 (citing *Webster's New Encyclopaedic Dictionary* and the *New Shorter Oxford English Dictionary*).
[36] Appellate Body Report, *US – Shrimp*, para. 165.

more specific definitions. It certainly extends beyond the concept of differential treatment. It is a normative term, pejorative in connotation, referring to results of the unjustified imposition of differentially disadvantageous treatment. Discrimination may arise from explicitly different treatment, sometimes called '*de jure* discrimination', but it may also arise from ostensibly identical treatment which, due to differences in circumstances, produces differentially disadvantageous effects, sometimes called '*de facto* discrimination'. The standards by which the justification for differential treatment is measured are a subject of infinite complexity. 'Discrimination' is a term to be avoided whenever more precise standards are available, and, when employed, it is a term to be interpreted with caution, and with care to add no more precision than the concept contains.

. . .

In considering how to address these conflicting claims of discrimination, the Panel recalled that various claims of discrimination, *de jure* and *de facto*, have been the subject of legal rulings under GATT or the WTO. These rulings have addressed the question whether measures were in conflict with various GATT or WTO provisions prohibiting variously defined forms of discrimination. As the Appellate Body has repeatedly made clear, each of these rulings has necessarily been based on the precise legal text in issue, so that it is not possible to treat them as applications of a general concept of discrimination. Given the very broad range of issues that might be involved in defining the word 'discrimination' in Article 27.1 of the TRIPS Agreement, the Panel decided that it would be better to defer attempting to define that term at the outset, but instead to determine which issues were raised by the record before the Panel, and to define the concept of discrimination to the extent necessary to resolve those issues.

. . .

As noted above, *de facto* discrimination is a general term describing the legal conclusion that an ostensibly neutral measure transgresses a non-discrimination norm because its actual effect is to impose differentially disadvantageous consequences on certain parties, and because those differential effects are found to be wrong or unjustifiable. Two main issues figure in the application of that general concept in most legal systems. One is the question of *de facto* discriminatory effect – whether the actual effect of the measure is to impose differentially disadvantageous consequences on certain parties. The other, related to the justification for the disadvantageous effects, is the issue of purpose – not an inquiry into the subjective purposes of the officials responsible for the measure, but an inquiry into the objective characteristics of the measure from which one can infer the existence or nonexistence of discriminatory objectives.[37]

16.38 In *EC – Tariff Preferences*, the Appellate Body examined the term 'non-discriminatory' in footnote 3 to paragraph 2(a) of the Enabling Clause, which requires that preference schemes for developing countries be 'generalized, non-reciprocal and non discriminatory'. Before the Panel, the parties offered competing definitions of

---

[37] Panel Report, *Canada – Pharmaceutical Patents*, paras. 94, 99 and 101.

the word 'discriminate': India advanced the broader definition of 'to make or constitute a difference in or between; distinguish' and 'to make a distinction in the treatment of different categories of peoples or things'; the European Communities advanced the narrower definition of 'to make a distinction in the treatment of different categories of people or things, sp. *unjustly* or *prejudicially* against people on grounds of race, colour, sex, social status, age, etc.'. The Appellate Body stated the term can carry either meaning, depending on the context:

> Both definitions can be considered as reflecting ordinary meanings of the term 'discriminate' and essentially exhaust the relevant ordinary meanings. The principal distinction between these definitions, as the Panel noted, is that India's conveys a '*neutral* meaning of making a distinction', whereas the European Communities' conveys a '*negative* meaning carrying the connotation of a distinction that is unjust or prejudicial.' Accordingly, the ordinary meanings of 'discriminate' point in conflicting directions with respect to the propriety of according differential treatment. Under India's reading, any differential treatment of GSP beneficiaries would be prohibited, because such treatment necessarily makes a distinction between beneficiaries. In contrast, under the European Communities' reading, differential treatment of GSP beneficiaries would not be prohibited *per se*. Rather, distinctions would be impermissible only where the basis for such distinctions was improper. Given these divergent meanings, we do not regard the term 'non-discriminatory', on its own, as determinative of the permissibility of a preference-granting country according different tariff preferences to different beneficiaries of its GSP scheme.[38]

In *Canada – Wheat Exports and Grain Imports*, the Appellate Body revisited the **16.39** same question, this time in the context of Article XVII(a) of the GATT, which provides that State trading enterprises (STEs) must act in a manner consistent with 'the general principles of non-discriminatory treatment' prescribed in the GATT:

> This requirement, which lies at the core of subparagraph (a), is a requirement that STEs not engage in certain types of discriminatory conduct. When viewed in the abstract, the concept of discrimination may encompass both the making of distinctions between similar situations, as well as treating dissimilar situations in a formally identical manner. The Appellate Body has previously dealt with the concept of discrimination and the meaning of the term 'non-discriminatory', and acknowledged that, at least insofar as the making of distinctions between similar situations is concerned, the ordinary meaning of discrimination can accommodate both drawing distinctions *per se*, and drawing distinctions *on an improper basis*. Only a full and proper interpretation of a provision containing a prohibition on discrimination will reveal which type of differential treatment is prohibited. In all cases, a claimant alleging *discrimination* will need to establish that differential treatment has occurred in order to succeed in its claim.[39]

---

[38] Appellate Body Report, *EC – Tariff Preferences*, paras. 151–2.
[39] Appellate Body Report, *Canada – Wheat Exports and Grain Imports*, para. 87.

16.5.3 'Fair'

16.40 In *EC – Bananas III*, the Appellate Body considered the phrase 'neutral . . . fair and equitable' to be interchangeable with the phrase 'uniform, impartial and reasonable':

> We attach no significance to the difference in the phrases 'neutral in application and administered in a fair and equitable manner' in Article 1.3 of the *Licensing Agreement* and 'administer in a uniform, impartial and reasonable manner' in Article X:3(a) of the GATT 1994. In our view, the two phrases are, for all practical purposes, interchangeable. We agree, therefore, with the Panel's interpretation that the provisions of Article X:3(a) of the GATT 1994 and Article 1.3 of the *Licensing Agreement* have identical coverage.[40]

16.41 In *US – Softwood Lumber V*, the Appellate Body examined the requirement, in Article 2.4 of the Anti-Dumping Agreement, that an investigating authority undertake a 'fair comparison' of export price and normal value when determining the existence of dumping:

> The term 'fair' is generally understood to connote impartiality, even-handedness, or lack of bias. For the reasons stated below, we consider that the use of zeroing under the transaction-to-transaction comparison methodology is difficult to reconcile with the notions of impartiality, even-handedness, and lack of bias reflected in the 'fair comparison' requirement in Article 2.4.[41]

16.42 In *US – Zeroing (EC)*, the Panel considered the 'fair comparison' requirement in Article 2.4 of the Anti-Dumping Agreement, and concluded that '[t]he meaning of "fair" in a legal rule must necessarily be determined having regard to the particular context within which that rule operates':

> We have carefully considered the arguments of the European Communities and some of the third parties regarding the ordinary meaning of the word 'fair' in light of dictionary definitions. We recall that we have already expressed our reservations earlier in this Report with respect to an approach to treaty interpretation that focuses on particular words divorced from their context in the *AD Agreement* and that equates 'ordinary meaning' as used in the *Vienna Convention* with dictionary definitions of words. We consider that caution with respect to such an approach is especially warranted where, as in the case of the first sentence of Article 2.4, a legal rule is expressed in terms of a standard that by its very nature is more abstract and less determinate than most other rules in the *AD Agreement*. The meaning of 'fair' in a legal rule must necessarily be determined having regard to the particular context within which that rule operates. Whereas words like 'fair' are also frequently used in connection with obligations of a procedural nature, in Article 2.4 of

---

[40] Appellate Body Report, *EC – Bananas III*, para. 203.
[41] Appellate Body Report, *US – Softwood Lumber V*, para. 138.

the *AD Agreement* 'fair' is used in a substantive obligation relating to the determination of dumping. Thus, a claim that a particular methodology is not 'fair' within the meaning of Article 2.4 is a claim that the methodology is not a fair method of determining dumping. The fairness of the methodology logically cannot be divorced from the underlying conception of what dumping means. To determine whether an approach is unfair there must be a discernible standard of appropriateness or rightness within the four corners of the *AD Agreement* which would provide a basis for reliably judging that there has been an unfair departure from that standard.

In *China – Rare Earths*, the Panel was called upon to consider the meaning of **16.43** 'even-handedness' in the context of the Appellate Body's prior statement that Article XX(g) of the GATT, in requiring that trade-restrictive measures be made effective in conjunction with domestic restrictions, is essentially a requirement of 'even-handedness'. In the course of its analysis, the Panel stated:

> In the English language, words such as 'fair', 'impartial' or 'balanced' are used as synonyms for even-handedness. Some international investment tribunals have acknowledged that the ordinary meaning of the terms 'fair' and 'equitable' in a 'fair and equitable' clause commonly found in bilateral investment treaties would include 'even-handedness'.
>
> The Panel also notes that the concepts of equity and even-handedness are quite closely related inasmuch as the Oxford English Dictionary defines 'equity' with reference to fairness, impartiality and even-handedness. International courts and tribunals including the International Court of Justice have had occasion to apply principles of equity, considering in one case that the principle of equity required 'an equitable result'.
>
> . . .
>
> The Panel has sought to illuminate its understanding of the principle of even-handedness by reference to different sources of international law . . . In international investment arbitration cases, in applying even-handedness requirements, for example, tribunals have been willing to show a degree of deference to the fact that governments have the right to choose the way in which they resolve their national problems. They have nevertheless assessed whether the processes governments adopt to resolve their problems are fair to foreign interests or show a predisposition towards favouring domestic interests. Moreover, tribunals have found that host state measures violate the even-handedness standard when no justifiable explanation for the uneven treatment is available. The Panel has not relied on these sources to clarify the meaning of even-handedness, because they do not add any further clarification to the existing jurisprudence on Article XX(g).[42]

---

[42] Panel Report, *China – Rare Earths*, paras. 7.319–7.322 (citing the *New Shorter Oxford English Dictionary*; Arbitral Tribunal, Award on Merits, *MTD Equity Sdn. Bhd. And MTD Chile S. A.*, ICSID Case No. ARB/01/7, para. 13; *Continental Shelf (Libya v. Malta)*, 1982 ICJ Reports, para. 70; Permanent Court of Arbitration, Partial Award, *Saluka Investments BV v. The Czech Republic*, UNCITRAL, paras. 411, 416).

16.5.4 'Legitimate'

16.44 In *Canada – Pharmaceutical Patents*, the Panel examined Article 30 of the TRIPS Agreement, which provides that Members may provide limited exceptions to the exclusive rights conferred by a patent, provided that such exceptions do not unreasonably conflict with a normal exploitation of the patent and do not unreasonably prejudice the 'legitimate interests' of the patent owner, taking account of the 'legitimate interests' of third parties. After quoting a dictionary definition of the word 'legitimate', the Panel stated:

> To make sense of the term 'legitimate interests' in this context, that term must be defined in the way that it is often used in legal discourse – as a normative claim calling for protection of interests that are 'justifiable' in the sense that they are supported by relevant public policies or other social norms. This is the sense of the word that often appears in statements such as 'X has no legitimate interest in being able to do Y'. We may take as an illustration one of the most widely adopted Article 30-type exceptions in national patent laws – the exception under which use of the patented product for scientific experimentation, during the term of the patent and without consent, is not an infringement. It is often argued that this exception is based on the notion that a key public policy purpose underlying patent laws is to facilitate the dissemination and advancement of technical knowledge and that allowing the patent owner to prevent experimental use during the term of the patent would frustrate part of the purpose of the requirement that the nature of the invention be disclosed to the public. To the contrary, the argument concludes, under the policy of the patent laws, both society and the scientist have a 'legitimate interest' in using the patent disclosure to support the advance of science and technology. While the Panel draws no conclusion about the correctness of any such national exceptions in terms of Article 30 of the TRIPS Agreement, it does adopt the general meaning of the term 'legitimate interests' contained in legal analysis of this type.[43]

16.45 In *US – COOL*, the Panel examined a claim under Article 2.2 of the TBT Agreement, which provides that technical regulations shall not be more trade-restrictive than necessary to fulfil 'a legitimate objective'. The Panel stated:

> The word 'legitimate' is defined as '2. a. Conformable to, sanctioned by or authorized by, law or principle; lawful; justifiable; proper. b. Normal, regular; conformable to a recognized standard type'. Based on the ordinary meaning, therefore, we need to assess whether 'providing consumer information on origin' is 'conformable to law or principle', 'justifiable and proper', or 'conformable to a recognized standard type'.
> This understanding is supported by the panel's analysis in this respect in *EC – Sardines*. Touching upon the meaning of the term 'legitimate' in the context of a legitimate objective as referred to in Articles 2.2 and 2.4, the panel in *EC – Sardines* suggested that the term 'legitimate' refers to the genuine nature of the objective. It further noted the statement of the panel in

---

[43] Panel Report, *Canada – Pharmaceutical Patents*, para. 7.69.

Canada – Pharmaceutical Patents, in defining the term 'legitimate interests' in the context of Article 30 of the TRIPS Agreement, that it must be defined 'as a normative claim calling for protection of interests that are "justifiable" in the sense that they are supported by relevant public policies or other social norms'.

The third sentence of Article 2.2 provides a non-exhaustive list of legitimate objectives under Article 2.2: national security requirements; the prevention of deceptive practices; protection of human health or safety; animal or plant life or health; or the environment. The use of the term '*inter alia*' in Article 2.2 of the TBT Agreement indicates that the objectives covered extend beyond the objectives specifically mentioned in Article 2.2. The type of objectives explicitly listed in Article 2.2 nonetheless demonstrates that the legitimacy of a given objective must be found in the '*genuine nature*' of the objective, which is 'justifiable' and 'supported by relevant public policies or other social norms'.[44]

Along the same lines, in *US – Tuna II (Mexico)* the Appellate Body stated, also in the context of examining a claim under Article 2.2 of the TBT Agreement, that: **16.46**

> Considering, first, the meaning of the term 'legitimate objective' in the sense of Article 2.2 of the *TBT Agreement*, we note that the word 'objective' describes a 'thing aimed at or sought; a target, a goal, an aim'. The word 'legitimate', in turn, is defined as 'lawful; justifiable; proper'. Taken together, this suggests that a 'legitimate objective' is an aim or target that is lawful, justifiable, or proper. Furthermore, the use of the words '*inter alia*' in Article 2.2 suggests that the provision does not set out a closed list of legitimate objectives, but rather lists several examples of legitimate objectives. We consider that those objectives expressly listed provide a reference point for which other objectives may be considered to be legitimate in the sense of Article 2.2. In addition, we note that the sixth and seventh recitals of the preamble of the *TBT Agreement* specifically recognize several objectives, which to a large extent overlap with the objectives listed in Article 2.2. Furthermore, we consider that objectives recognized in the provisions of other covered agreements may provide guidance for, or may inform, the analysis of what might be considered to be a legitimate objective under Article 2.2 of the *TBT Agreement*.[45]

16.5.5 'Necessary'

In *Korea – Various Measures on Beef*, the Appellate Body examined the meaning of the term 'necessary' in the context of Article XX(d) of the GATT, which contains a general exception for measures necessary to secure compliance with laws and regulations not inconsistent with the GATT: **16.47**

---

[44] Panel Report, *US – COOL*, paras. 7.630–7.632 (citing the *Shorter Oxford English Dictionary*; Panel Report, *EC – Sardines*, para. 7.121; Panel Report, *Canada – Pharmaceutical Patents*, para. 7.69; Panel Report, *US – Section 110(5) Copyright Act*, para. 6.224; Appellate Body Report, *EC – Sardines*, para. 286).

[45] Appellate Body Report, *US – Tuna II (Mexico)*, para. 313 (citing the *Shorter Oxford English Dictionary*).

The word 'necessary' normally denotes something 'that cannot be dispensed with or done without, requisite, essential, needful'. We note, however, that a standard law dictionary cautions that:

> '[t]his word must be considered in the connection in which it is used, as it is a word susceptible of various meanings. It may import absolute physical necessity or inevitability, or it may import that which is only convenient, useful, appropriate, suitable, proper, or conducive to the end sought. It is an adjective expressing degrees, and may express mere convenience or that which is indispensable or an absolute physical necessity'.

We believe that, as used in the context of Article XX(d), the reach of the word 'necessary' is not limited to that which is 'indispensable' or 'of absolute necessity' or 'inevitable'. Measures which are indispensable or of absolute necessity or inevitable to secure compliance certainly fulfil the requirements of Article XX(d). But other measures, too, may fall within the ambit of this exception. As used in Article XX(d), the term 'necessary' refers, in our view, to a range of degrees of necessity. At one end of this continuum lies 'necessary' understood as 'indispensable'; at the other end, is 'necessary' taken to mean as 'making a contribution to.' We consider that a 'necessary' measure is, in this continuum, located significantly closer to the pole of 'indispensable' than to the opposite pole of simply 'making a contribution to'.[46]

16.48 In *US – Gambling*, the Appellate Body examined the necessity standard in the context of the general exceptions in Article XIV of the GATS. In the course of its analysis, the Appellate Body noted the objective nature of the standard:

> We note, at the outset, that the standard of 'necessity' provided for in the general exceptions provision is an *objective* standard. To be sure, a Member's characterization of a measure's objectives and of the effectiveness of its regulatory approach – as evidenced, for example, by texts of statutes, legislative history, and pronouncements of government agencies or officials – will be relevant in determining whether the measure is, objectively, 'necessary'. A panel is not bound by these characterizations, however, and may also find guidance in the structure and operation of the measure and in contrary evidence proffered by the complaining party. In any event, a panel must, on the basis of the evidence in the record, independently and objectively assess the 'necessity' of the measure before it.[47]

16.49 In *Korea – Certain Paper*, the Panel examined the concept of 'necessary information' in the context of Article 6.8 of the Anti-Dumping Agreement, and touched upon the circumstance-specific nature of a necessity analysis:

> Article 6.8 of the Agreement stipulates that failure to provide necessary information within a reasonable period may allow the [investigating authority] to

---

Appellate Body Report, *Korea – Various Measures on Beef*, paras. 160–1.
Appellate Body Report, *US – Gambling*, para. 304.

resort to facts available. In our view, the decision as to whether or not a given piece of information constitutes 'necessary information' within the meaning of Article 6.8 has to be made in light of the specific circumstances of each investigation, not in the abstract. A particular piece of information that may play a critical role in an investigation may not be equally relevant in another one. We shall therefore determine whether or not CMI's financial statements and accounting records constituted necessary information in the circumstances of the investigation at issue.[48]

16.6   Timing language

WTO jurisprudence offers guidance on the meaning of words and phrases relating to timing, including 'as soon as', 'immediately', 'promptly', 'reasonable period of time' and 'without delay'. **16.50**

16.6.1 'As soon as'

In *Guatemala – Cement II*, the Panel examined a claim under Article 6.1.3 of the Anti-Dumping Agreement, which requires an investigating authority to take certain steps '[a]s soon as an investigation has been initiated'. The Panel stated: **16.51**

> We note that Article 6.1.3 does not specify the number of days within which the text of the application shall be provided. What it does specify is that the text of the application be provided 'as soon as' the investigation has been initiated. In this regard, the term 'as soon as' conveys a sense of substantial urgency. In fact, the terms 'immediately' and 'as soon as' are considered to be interchangeable. We do not consider that providing the text of the application 24 or even 18 days after the date of initiation fulfils the requirement of Article 6.1.3 that the text be provided 'as soon as an investigation has been initiated'.[49]

16.6.2 'Immediately'

In *US – Wheat Gluten*, the Appellate Body examined a claim under Article 12.1 of the Agreement on Safeguards, which requires a Member to 'immediately notify' the Committee on Safeguards upon the initiation of a safeguards investigation and/or certain other acts. The Appellate Body stated: **16.52**

> As regards the meaning of the word 'immediately' in the chapeau to Article 12.1, we agree with the Panel that the ordinary meaning of the word 'implies a

---

[48] Panel Report, *Korea – Certain Paper*, para. 7.43.
[49] Panel Report, *Guatemala – Cement II*, para. 8.101.

certain urgency'. The degree of urgency or immediacy required depends on a
case-by-case assessment, account being taken of the administrative difficulties
involved in preparing the notification, and also of the character of the information supplied. As previous panels have recognized, relevant factors in this
regard may include the complexity of the notification and the need for
translation into one of the WTO's official languages. Clearly, however, the
amount of time taken to prepare the notification must, in all cases, be kept to a
minimum, as the underlying obligation is to notify 'immediately'.[50]

16.6.3 'Promptly'

16.53 The Arbitrator in *Chile – Alcoholic Beverages (Article 21.3(c))* considered the
meaning of the word 'prompt' in the context of Article 21.1 of the DSU, which
states that '[p]rompt compliance with recommendations or rulings of the DSB
is essential in order to ensure effective resolution of disputes to the benefit of all
Members'. The Arbitrator stated:

> The DSU clearly stressed the systemic interest of all WTO Members in the
> Member concerned complying 'immediately' with the recommendations and
> rulings of the DSB. Reading Articles 21.1 and 21.3 together, 'prompt' compli-
> ance is, in principle, 'immediate' compliance. At the same time, however, should
> 'immediate' compliance be 'impracticable' – it may be noted that the DSU does
> not use the far more rigorous term 'impossible' – the Member concerned
> becomes entitled to a 'reasonable period of time' to bring itself into a state of
> conformity with its WTO obligations. Clearly, a certain element of flexibility in
> respect of time is built into the notion of compliance with the recommendations
> and rulings of the DSB. That element would appear to be essential if 'prompt'
> compliance, in a world of sovereign states, is to be a balanced conception and
> objective.[51]

16.54 In *EC – IT Products*, the Panel examined a claim under Article X:1 of the
GATT, which requires that trade regulations 'shall be published promptly in
such a manner as to enable governments and traders to become acquainted with
them'. The Panel stated:

> It does not, however, specify what 'promptly' means, i.e. what is the permissible
> time span *between* the moment that such measure is 'made effective' and the
> time it is 'published'. In this regard, we note that the adverb 'promptly' is
> defined as '[i]n a prompt manner; readily, quickly; at once, without delay;
> directly, forthwith, there and then.' The word 'prompt', as an adjective, means,
> *inter alia*, '2. a. Ready in action; quick to act when occasion arises; acting with
> alacrity, or without undue delay; ready and willing; quick *to* do something.' In
> our view, the meaning of prompt is not an absolute concept, i.e. a pre-set period
> of time applicable in all cases. Rather, an assessment of whether a measure has

---

[50] Appellate Body Report, *US – Wheat Gluten*, para. 105.
[51] Award of the Arbitrator, *Chile – Alcoholic Beverages (Article 21.3(c))*, para. 38.

been published 'promptly', that is 'quickly' and 'without undue delay', necessarily requires a case-by-case assessment. Accordingly, we will look at the time span between the moment the CNEN amendments were 'made effective' and the time they were 'published', and assess whether this is prompt in light of the facts of the case.[52]

In *EU – Footwear (China)*, the Panel examined a claim under Article 6.1.2 of the **16.55** Anti-Dumping Agreement, which states that evidence provided by one interested party in an anti-dumping investigation 'shall be made available promptly to other interested parties participating in the investigation'. The Panel stated:

> The word 'promptly' is defined as 'in a prompt manner, without delay' and '[i]n a prompt manner; readily, quickly; at once, without delay; directly, forthwith, there and then'. In our view, these definitions do not support the conclusion that information must be made available immediately in order to comply with Article 6.1.2. We consider that to make evidence available promptly must be understood in the context of the proceeding in question. In the context of a proceeding lasting months, where there are numerous opportunities for the parties to participate in the investigation after the evidence has been made available, we consider that the delays in this case do not establish a violation of Article 6.1.2, and we therefore reject China's claim with respect to Companies B, C and G.[53]

16.6.4 'Reasonable period of time'

For WTO jurisprudence relating to the phrase 'reasonable period of time', see **16.56** Section 12.2.2.

16.6.5 'Without delay'

As regards the phrase 'without delay', the Panel in *Canada – Autos* considered **16.57** Article 4.7 of the SCM Agreement, which provides that, where a measure is found to constitute a 'prohibited subsidy' under the SCM Agreement, the subsidizing Member shall 'withdraw the subsidy without delay'. The Panel stated:

> The noun 'delay' has been defined to mean, *inter alia*, 'the action or process of delaying; procrastination; lingering; putting off', while the verb to 'delay' has been defined, *inter alia*, as to 'put off to a later time; postpone, defer'. Thus, in its ordinary meaning, the phrase 'without delay' suggests that the Member must not put off, postpone or defer action, but must rather act as quickly as possible to withdraw the prohibited subsidy.[54]

---

[52] Panel Reports, *EC – IT Products*, para. 7.1074 (citing the *Shorter Oxford English Dictionary* and the *Merriam-Webster Online Dictionary*; GATT Panel Report, *EEC – Apples (US)*, para. 5.21; Appellate Body Report, *US – Wheat Gluten*, para. 105).

[53] Panel Report, *EU – Footwear (China)*, para. 7.583 (citing the *New Shorter Oxford English Dictionary* and the *Oxford English Dictionary* (on-line edition)).

[54] Panel Report, *Canada – Autos*, para. 11.6 (citing the *New Shorter Oxford English Dictionary*).

16.58 The Panel in *EC – Approval and Marketing of Biotech Products* interpreted the requirement, in Annex C(1)(a) to the SPS Agreement, that Members ensure that their approval procedures are 'undertaken and completed without undue delay'. The Panel interpreted this to mean 'with no unjustifiable loss of time':

> It is clear from the text of Annex C(1)(a), first clause, that not every delay in the undertaking or completion of approval procedures which is caused by a Member is contrary to the provisions of Annex C(1)(a), first clause. Only 'undue' delay is. Regarding the meaning of the phrase 'undue delay', we consider that of the dictionary meanings of the term 'delay' which have been identified by the United States, there is one which fits naturally with the provisions of Annex C(1)(a), first clause, namely, '(a period of) time lost by inaction or inability to proceed'. So far as concerns the term 'undue', of the dictionary meanings referred to by the United States we find two to be particularly relevant in the specific context of Annex C(1)(a), first clause – '[g]oing beyond what is warranted . . .' and 'unjustifiable'. We note that the United States, Canada and the European Communities have all identified 'unjustifiable' as a relevant meaning of 'undue'. This view is supported also by the French version of Annex C(1)(a), first clause, which refers to 'retard injustifié'. Thus, based on the ordinary meaning of the phrase 'without undue delay', we consider that Annex C(1)(a), first clause, requires that approval procedures be undertaken and completed with no unjustifiable loss of time.[55]

16.59 The Panel in *EC – Seal Products* interpreted the parallel obligation in Article 5.2.1 of the TBT Agreement, which provides that conformity assessment procedures are to be undertaken and completed 'as expeditiously as possible'. The Panel stated:

> [T]he adverb 'expeditiously' indicates that the obligation relates to the speed and/or timing of the performance of a CAP. At the same time, the term 'expeditiously' is qualified by the phrase 'as possible'. We take this qualification to be based on the fundamental purpose of any CAP to secure 'a positive assurance of conformity with technical regulations' [in Article 5.1 of the TBT Agreement], and recognition that doing so may necessarily entail some time to determine that relevant requirements are fulfilled.
>
> In this connection, we also take note of the interpretation by the panel in *EC – Approval and Marketing of Biotech Products* of the phrase 'without undue delay' to mean that approval procedures were required to be undertaken and completed 'with no unjustifiable loss of time'. The panel similarly accounted for the function of approval procedures to check and ensure fulfilment of SPS requirements, and reasoned on this basis that 'Members applying such procedures must in principle be allowed to take the time that is reasonably needed to determine with adequate confidence whether their relevant SPS requirements are fulfilled'.
>
> We agree with the approach of the panel in *EC – Approval and Marketing of Biotech Products*. While the duty of expeditious conformity assessment

---

[55] Panel Report, *EC – Approval and Marketing of Biotech Products*, para. 7.1495.

prescribed in Article 5.2.1 must be carried out so as not to create an unnecessary obstacle to trade, such duty of the regulating Members must be balanced against the regulating Members' need and practical ability to make an adequate conformity assessment. Therefore, in our view, Article 5.2.1 permits the time that is reasonably required to assess conformity with technical requirements.[56]

16.7 Common English words

WTO jurisprudence offers guidance on the meaning and function of common **16.60** English words found in almost all international legal instruments, including definite and indefinite articles ('a', 'the', 'any'), conjunctions ('and', 'or'), prepositions ('affecting', 'based on', 'governing', 'relating to') and definitional terms ('including', 'such as', 'i.e.').

16.7.1 'A', 'the', 'any'

In *US – Gambling (Article 21.3(c))*, the Arbitrator considered the meaning of the **16.61** indefinite article 'a' in the phrase 'a reasonable period of time' in Article 21.3(c) of the DSU, and stated:

> I am not persuaded that the mere use of the indefinite article 'a' in the phrase 'a reasonable period of time' suffices, as the United States suggests, to establish definitively that an arbitrator is authorized only to determine a *single* reasonable period of time for implementation in a dispute. At the same time, conceptually, I have difficulty accepting that it may be possible to determine, as Antigua seems to request me to do, two separate reasonable periods of time in respect of the *same* measure. I would not, however, want to exclude *a priori*, and without having carried out a thorough interpretative analysis of the relevant provisions of the DSU, the possibility that an arbitrator might be able to fix separate reasonable periods of time for separate measures.[57]

In *Argentina – Poultry Anti-Dumping Duties*, the Panel considered the require- **16.62** ment, in Article 2.4.2 of the Anti-Dumping Agreement, that the existence of margins of dumping shall normally be established on the basis of a comparison of '*a* weighted average normal value with a weighted average of prices of exports'. The Panel stated:

> Article 2.4.2 refers to a weighted average normal value, and not the weighted average normal value. In our view, use of the word 'a' simply means that there are various ways of establishing a weighted average.[58]

---

[56] Panel Report, *EC – Seal Products*, paras. 7.564–7.566 (citing the *Shorter Oxford English Dictionary*; Panel Report, *EC – Approval and Marketing of Biotech Products*, paras. 7.1495, 7.1498).
[57] Award of the Arbitrator, *US – Gambling (Article 21.3(c))*, para. 41.
[58] Panel Report, *Argentina – Poultry Anti-Dumping Duties*, para. 7.273.

The Panel in *Argentina – Poultry Anti-Dumping Duties* reasoned along the same lines when considering Article 4.1 of the Anti-Dumping Agreement. This provision defines what is meant by the 'domestic industry', for the purpose of determining whether dumped imports are causing injury to the domestic industry. The definition includes, *inter alia*, domestic producers whose collective output of the like product 'constitutes *a* major proportion of the total domestic production'. The Panel reasoned:

> Article 4.1 refers to producers of a major proportion of total domestic production. If Article 4.1 had referred to the major proportion, the requirement would clearly have been to define the 'domestic industry' as producers constituting 50+ per cent of total domestic production. However, the reference to a major proportion suggests that there may be more than one 'major proportion' for the purpose of defining 'domestic industry'.[59]

16.63 In *US – Softwood Lumber IV*, the Appellate Body examined Article 14 of the SCM Agreement, which states that 'any method' used by an investigating authority to calculate the amount of the benefit arising from the subsidy at issue shall be provided for in the national legislation or implementing regulations of the Member concerned. The Appellate Body stated:

> The chapeau of Article 14 requires that '*any*' method used by investigating authorities to calculate the benefit to the recipient shall be provided for in a WTO Member's legislation or regulations, and it requires that its application be transparent and adequately explained. The reference to '*any*' method in the chapeau clearly implies that more than one method consistent with Article 14 is available to investigating authorities for purposes of calculating the benefit to the recipient.[60]

16.64 Along the same lines, in *US – Anti-Dumping and Countervailing Duties (China)* (DS379) the Appellate Body examined the definition of a 'subsidy' in Article 1 of the SCM Agreement, and in particular the element of the definition referring to a financial contribution by 'a government or any public body'. The Appellate Body noted its agreement with the Panel that 'the word "any" before "public body" suggests that there may be different kinds of public bodies, and that all such entities fall within the scope of the collective term "government"'.[61]

16.65 In *US – Shrimp (Viet Nam)*, the Panel examined a claim under Article 6.8 of the Anti-Dumping Agreement, which provides that, in cases in which 'any interested party' refuses access to or otherwise does not provide necessary information, determinations may be made on the basis of the facts available. Relying on the plain meaning of the term, the Panel stated:

[59] *Ibid.*, para. 7.341.   [60] Appellate Body Report, *US – Softwood Lumber IV*, para. 91.
[61] Appellate Body Report, *US – Anti-Dumping and Countervailing Duties (China)*, footnote 197.

Regarding Viet Nam's argument that the Article 6.8 facts available mechanism does not apply in respect of non-selected respondents, we note that the first sentence of Article 6.8 envisages the use of facts available in cases of non-cooperation by 'any' interested party. The reference to non-cooperation by 'any' interested party suggests that Article 6.8 is of broad application. There is nothing in the text of Article 6.8 to suggest that the facts available mechanism only applies in respect of non-cooperation by a limited category of interested parties. In particular, there is no indication in the text to suggest that, in cases of limited examination (under Article 6.10), Article 6.8 only allows the use of facts available in respect of those interested parties that were selected for individual examination, as alleged by Viet Nam.[62]

16.7.2 'And' versus 'or'

In *US – Line Pipe*, the Appellate Body examined the meaning of the term 'or' in the context of Article 2.1 of the Agreement on Safeguards, which refers to imports that 'cause or threaten to cause' serious injury to the domestic industry. At issue was whether an investigating authority may make a finding that both forms of injury exist at the same time: **16.66**

> Our view is that the phrase 'cause or threaten to cause' can be read either way. As we read it, the dictionary definition of 'or' supports either conclusion. *The New Shorter Oxford English Dictionary* provides several definitions of the word 'or'. The dictionary definitions accommodate both usages. *The New Shorter Oxford English Dictionary* recognizes that the word 'or' can have an inclusive meaning as well as an exclusive meaning.
>
> Thus, 'or' can be exclusive, and 'or' can also be inclusive. The text of Article 2.1 does not provide decisive interpretative guidance in this respect. This is not to say that we believe that 'serious injury' and 'threat of serious injury' are the same thing, or that competent authorities may make a finding that both exist at the same time. Rather, we believe that the text of Article 2.1 lends itself to either interpretation.
>
> As with every word of the Agreement, we must identify a proper meaning for this word. Having found that the text of Article 2.1 is not determinative of the meaning of the word 'or', we must look to the context of this treaty provision for guidance in interpreting it. In doing so, we must consider the provisions of the *Agreement on Safeguards* as a whole.[63]

In *EC – Salmon (Norway)*, the Panel examined a claim under Article 6.10 of the Anti-Dumping Agreement, which provides in relevant part that the authorities shall, as a rule, determine an individual margin of dumping 'for each known exporter or producer concerned of the product under investigation'. The Panel observed that, '[b]ecause of the nature of the functions of the word "or", its meaning in different provisions of the AD Agreement will very much depend **16.67**

---

[62] Panel Report, *US – Shrimp (Viet Nam)*, para. 7.263.
[63] Appellate Body Report, *US – Line Pipe*, paras. 163–5.

upon the obligations at issue and the specific context in which it appears'.[64] As regards the use of the term 'or' in the specific context of Article 6.10, the Panel stated:

> The word 'or' has multiple grammatical functions, the most common being the introduction of two or more alternatives into a phrase or sentence. This suggests that the obligation set out in the first sentence of Article 6.10 to 'determine an individual margin of dumping' could be understood as leaving open the possibility to determine an individual margin of dumping for only 'each known exporter' or, alternatively, only 'each known … producer' … A second usage of the word 'or' is to connect two words denoting the same thing. Thus, the obligation to determine an individual margin of dumping for each known exporter or producer may also be understood as an obligation to determine an individual margin of dumping for one and the same entity, a result that would obtain whenever a known exporter was also a producer.
>
> … [W]e find it particularly telling that the drafters of the AD Agreement chose to use the word 'or' and not the word 'and' in agreeing on the text of this provision. This choice of language suggests the drafters intended that Members be left with discretion to choose the focus of their investigations …
>
> Thus, the ordinary meaning of the text in Article 6.10 suggests that Members may choose to focus their investigations on either all known exporters, all known producers, or all known exporters and producers.[65]

16.7.3 'Affecting', 'based on', 'governing', 'relating to'

16.68 As regards the word 'affecting', in *EC – Bananas III* the Appellate Body examined Article III:4 of the GATT, which requires that imported products be accorded non-discriminatory treatment in respect of measures 'affecting their internal sale, offering for sale, purchase, transportation, or use'. The Appellate Body stated:

> In our view, the use of the word 'affecting' reflects the intent of the drafters to give a broad reach to the GATS. The ordinary meaning of the word 'affecting' implies a measure that has 'an effect on', which indicates a broad scope of application. This interpretation is further reinforced by the conclusions of previous panels that the term 'affecting' in the context of Article III of the GATT is wider in scope than such terms as 'regulating' or 'governing'.[66]

16.69 In *US – Upland Cotton*, the Appellate Body addressed whether a Member can challenge measures that are no longer in existence at the time that the panel is established. In that context, the Appellate Body referred to Article 4.2 of the DSU, which refers to 'measures affecting the operation of any covered agreement'. The Appellate Body stated:

[64] Panel Report, *EC – Salmon (Norway)*, para. 7.171.
[65] *Ibid.*, paras. 7.165–7.167 (citing the *New Shorter Oxford English Dictionary*).
[66] Appellate Body Report, *EC – Bananas III*, para. 220.

We agree with the Panel that the word 'affecting' refers primarily to 'the way in which [measures] relate to a covered agreement'. As the Appellate Body stated in *EC – Bananas III*, '[t]he ordinary meaning of the word "affecting" implies a measure that has "an effect on"' something else. At the same time, we also concur with the United States that the ordinary meaning of the word 'affecting' suggests a temporal connotation. As the United States submits, the present tense of the phrase 'affecting the operation of any covered agreement' denotes that the effects of such measures must relate to the present impact of those measures on the operation of a covered agreement. It is not sufficient that a Member alleges that challenged measures affected the operation of a covered agreement in the past; the representations of the Member requesting consultations must indicate that the effects are occurring in the present.[67]

16.70 In *China – Publications and Audiovisual Products*, the Panel found that the various measures at issue were measures 'affecting trade in services' within the meaning of Article I:1 of the GATS. The Panel noted that it was not in dispute that the measures at issue 'regulate or govern' certain matters, and stated that '[s]ince the term "affecting" is wider in scope than "regulating" or "governing", we therefore consider that these measures are "affecting" the supply of [services]'.[68]

16.71 As regards the words 'based on', in *EC – Hormones* the Appellate Body examined a claim under Article 5.1 of the SPS Agreement, which requires that SPS measures be 'based on' a risk assessment. The Appellate Body stated:

[T]he ordinary meaning of 'based on' is quite different from the plain or natural import of 'conform to'. A thing is commonly said to be 'based on' another thing when the former 'stands' or is 'founded' or 'built' upon or 'is supported by' the latter. In contrast, much more is required before one thing may be regarded as 'conform[ing] to' another. the former must 'comply with', 'yield or show compliance' with the latter. The reference of 'conform to' is to 'correspondence in form or manner', to 'compliance with' or 'acquiescence', to 'follow[ing] in form or nature'. A measure that 'conforms to' and incorporates a Codex standard is, of course, 'based on' that standard. A measure, however, based on the same standard might not conform to that standard, as where only some, not all, of the elements of the standard are incorporated into the measure.

. . .

We believe that Article 5.1, when contextually read as it should be, in conjunction with and as informed by Article 2.2 of the *SPS Agreement*, requires that *the results of the risk assessment must sufficiently warrant – that is to say, reasonably support – the SPS measure at stake*. The requirement that an SPS measure be 'based on' a risk assessment is a substantive requirement that there be *a rational relationship between the measure and the risk assessment*.[69]

---

[67] Appellate Body Report, *US – Upland Cotton*, para. 261 (citing Appellate Body Report, *EC – Bananas III*, para. 220).
[68] Panel Report, *China – Publications and Audiovisual Products*, para. 7.971.
[69] Appellate Body Report, *EC – Hormones*, paras. 163, 193.

16.72 As regards the term 'governing', in *EC – Selected Customs Matters* the Panel examined the requirement, in Article X:3(b) of the GATT, that decisions of national courts 'govern the practice' of the agencies entrusted with the administration of customs matters. In that context, the Panel stated:

> Regarding the ordinary meaning of the term 'govern', the Panel notes that it is defined as 'control, influence, regulate, or determine (a person, another's action, the course or issue of events)'. When considered in the light of this definition, it would appear that the term 'govern' in Article X:3(b) of the GATT 1994 means that the decisions of judicial, arbitral or administrative tribunals and procedures, established for the review of administrative action relating to customs matters, must have binding effect.
>
> The Panel recalls its conclusion in paragraph 7.528 that, under Article X:3(b) of the GATT 1994, the decisions of judicial, arbitral or administrative tribunals and procedures for the prompt review and correction of administrative action must govern the practice of the agency whose action was the subject of review by a tribunal or procedure in a particular case. Accordingly, when considered in the light of the ordinary meaning of the term 'govern', the Panel understands that the decisions of tribunals or procedures for the review and correction of administrative action relating to customs matters must bind the administrative agency whose action is the subject of review pursuant to Article X:3(b) of the GATT 1994.[70]

16.73 In *Canada – Renewable Energy / Feed-In Tariff Program*, the Appellate Body examined Article III:8(a) of the GATT, which provides that the non-discrimination obligation in Article III does not apply to laws, regulations, or requirements 'governing' the procurement by governmental agencies of products purchased for certain purposes. The Appellate Body stated:

> We note that the word 'governing' links the words 'laws, regulations or requirements' to the word 'procurement' and the remainder of the paragraph. In the context of Article III:8(a), the word 'governing', along with the word 'procurement' and the other parts of the paragraph, define the subject-matter of the 'laws, regulations or requirements'. The word 'governing' is defined as 'constitut [ing] a law or rule for'. Article III:8(a) thus requires an articulated connection between the laws, regulations, or requirements and the procurement, in the sense that the act of procurement is undertaken within a binding structure of laws, regulations, or requirements.[71]

16.74 As regards the words 'relating to', in *US – Shrimp* the Appellate Body found that the measure at issue was one 'relating to the conservation of exhaustible natural resources' within the meaning of Article XX(g) of the GATT. The Appellate Body stated:

---

[70] Panel Report, *EC – Selected Customs Matters*, paras. 7.529–7.530 (citing the *New Shorter Oxford English Dictionary*).

[71] Appellate Body Report, *Canada – Renewable Energy/Feed-In Tariff Program*, para. 5.58 (citing the *Oxford English Dictionary* (online edition)).

In its general design and structure, therefore, Section 609 is not a simple, blanket prohibition of the importation of shrimp imposed without regard to the consequences (or lack thereof) of the mode of harvesting employed upon the incidental capture and mortality of sea turtles. Focusing on the design of the measure here at stake, it appears to us that Section 609, *cum* implementing guidelines, is not disproportionately wide in its scope and reach in relation to the policy objective of protection and conservation of sea turtle species. The means are, in principle, reasonably related to the ends. The means and ends relationship between Section 609 and the legitimate policy of conserving an exhaustible, and, in fact, endangered species, is observably a close and real one.[72]

In *US – Softwood Lumber IV*, the Appellate Body examined Article 14(d) of **16.75** the SCM Agreement. This provision establishes certain guidelines that must be followed to determine the existence and amount of a subsidy. In the case where a government provides goods or services, the test is whether there was 'adequate remuneration' which, in turn, shall be determined 'in relation to prevailing market conditions for the good or service in question in the country of provision'. The Appellate Body considered the meaning of the phrase 'in relation to' in this context, and stated:

> We now examine the meaning of the phrase 'in relation to' in Article 14(d). We are of the view that the Panel failed to give proper meaning and effect to the phrase 'in relation to' as it is used in Article 14(d). The Panel reasoned that the phrase 'in relation to' in the context of Article 14(d) means 'in comparison with'. Hence, the Panel concluded that the determination of the adequacy of remuneration has to be made 'in comparison with' prevailing market conditions for the goods in the country of provision, and thus no other comparison will do when private market prices exist. We do not agree.
>
> As we see it, the phrase 'in relation to' implies a comparative exercise, but its meaning is not limited to 'in comparison with'.[107] The phrase 'in relation to' has a meaning similar to the phrases 'as regards' and 'with respect to'. These phrases do not denote the rigid comparison suggested by the Panel, but may imply a broader sense of 'relation, connection, reference'. Thus, the use of the phrase 'in relation to' in Article 14(d) suggests that, contrary to the Panel's understanding, the drafters did not intend to exclude any possibility of using as a benchmark something other than private prices in the market of the country of provision. This is not to say, however, that private prices in the market of provision may be disregarded. Rather, it must be demonstrated that, based on the facts of the case, the benchmark chosen relates or refers to, or is connected with, the conditions prevailing in the market of the country of provision.

---

[107] We observe that the phrase 'in relation to' is used in other provisions of the *SCM Agreement* in a manner that does not connote 'in comparison with'. For instance, Article 15.6 of the *SCM Agreement* states that '[t]he effect of the subsidized imports shall be assessed in relation to the domestic production of

---

[72] Appellate Body Report, *US – Shrimp*, para. 141.

the like product'. Article 15.6 cannot properly be read as requiring a comparison between '[t]he effect of the subsidized imports' and 'the domestic production of the like product'. Similarly, Article 15.3 of that Agreement provides that, in order to assess cumulatively the effects of imports of a product from more than one country that are simultaneously subject to countervailing duty investigations, investigating authorities must determine that, *inter alia*, 'the amount of subsidization established in relation to the imports from each country is more than *de minimis*'. In this provision, the phrase 'in relation to' is not used in the sense of 'in comparison with' but rather in the sense of 'in proportion to'. Therefore, the precise meaning of the phrase 'in relation to' will vary depending on the specific context in which it is used.[73]

16.76 In *US – Upland Cotton*, the Appellate Body examined paragraph 6(b) of Annex 2 to the Agreement on Agriculture, which contains a condition to which domestic support measures must conform in order to be exempted from the reduction commitments contained in the Agreement. The condition is that certain payments 'shall not be related to, or based on, the type or volume of production (including livestock units) undertaken by the producer in any year after the base period'. As regards the words 'related to' and 'based on', the Appellate Body stated:

> The ordinary meaning of the term 'related to' in paragraph 6(b) of Annex 2 denotes some degree of *relationship* or *connection* between two things, here the amount of payment, on the one hand, and the type or volume of production, on the other. It covers a broader set of connections than 'based on', which term is also used to describe the relationship between two things covered by paragraph 6(b). Nothing in the ordinary meaning of the term 'related to' suggests that the connections covered by this expression may not encompass connections of either a 'positive' nature (including directions or requirements to do something) or a 'negative' nature (including prohibitions or requirements not to do something) or a combination of both. As the Panel indicated, the ordinary meaning of the term 'related to' conveys 'a very general notion'.[74]

In *US – Upland Cotton*, the Appellate Body also noted that:

> Like the expression 'related to', the expression 'based on' also requires a connection between two or more things. However, even though 'based on' does not require a strict relationship between two things (see, e.g. Appellate Body Report, EC – Hormones, paras. 165–166 and 171), the meaning of 'based on' indicates a relatively close connection between the things being linked. By contrast, the meaning of 'related to' can apply to connections more general in nature than situations in which one thing is 'based on' another (see, e.g. Appellate Body Report, US – Softwood Lumber IV, para. 89, where the Appellate Body interpreted broadly the phrase 'in relation to' in Article 14(d) of the SCM

---

[73] Appellate Body Report, *US – Softwood Lumber IV*, paras. 88–9.
[74] Appellate Body Report, *US – Upland Cotton*, para. 324 (citing the *Shorter Oxford English Dictionary*).

Agreement). Accordingly, the meaning of the term 'related to' cannot be entirely subsumed into the meaning of 'based on'.[75]

16.7.4 'Including', 'such as', 'i.e.'

The Panel in *China – Publications and Audiovisual Products* explained that 'the **16.77** word "including" in ordinary usage indicates that what follows is not an exhaustive, but a partial, list of all covered items'.[76] Statements to the same effect may be found in numerous other cases, including the Appellate Body reports in *Korea – Dairy*,[77] *Chile – Price Band System*,[78] and *EC – Chicken Cuts*,[79] and many panel reports. The Panel in *China – Electronic Payment Services* stated:

> The Panel first observes that the phrase 'including credit, charge and debit cards, travellers cheques and bankers drafts' refers to payment and money transmission instruments, not to services. In our view, this phrase sets out various types of instruments that require payment and money transmission services for them to work effectively. We also note that the instruments listed are preceded by the word 'including'. As explained by the panel in *China – Publications and Audiovisual Products*, 'the word "including" in ordinary usage indicates that what follows is not an exhaustive, but a partial, list of all covered items'. In a similar vein, we consider that the phrase 'including credit, charge and debit cards, travellers cheques and bankers drafts' in subsector (d) provides a non-exhaustive list of instruments used in connection with payment and money transmission services. In the Panel's view, the explicit reference to 'credit, charge and debit cards' in subsector (d) of China's Schedule sheds light on the type of services covered by the phrase 'all payment and money transmission services' as it appears in China's Schedule. It notably suggests that the phrase covers payment and money transmission services that are essential for the use of the enumerated instruments.[80]

In *Thailand – H-Beams*, the Panel contrasted the meaning of the word 'includ- **16.78** ing' with the meaning of the words 'such as'. The Panel was examining a claim under Article 3.4 of the Anti-Dumping Agreement, which provides that, in an anti-dumping investigation, in particular the examination of the impact of dumped imports on the domestic industry, must include an evaluation of all relevant economic factors and indices having a bearing on the state of the industry, 'including' actual and potential decline in sales, and a number of other indicators and indices specified in the text of Article 3.4. In the precursor to the WTO Anti-Dumping Agreement, i.e. the Tokyo Round Subsidies Code, the list

---

[75] *Ibid.*, footnote 315.
[76] Panel Report, *China – Publications and Audiovisual Products*, para. 7.294.
[77] Appellate Body Report, *Korea – Dairy*, para. 110.
[78] Appellate Body Report, *Chile – Price Band System*, para. 209.
[79] Appellate Body Report, *EC – Chicken Cuts*, para. 283.
[80] Panel Report, *China – Electronic Payment Services*, para. 7.109 (citing Panel Report, *China – Publications and Audiovisual Products*, para. 7.294).

of indicators and indices was preceded by the words 'such as'. The Panel explained the difference in meaning:

> The term 'such as' is defined as '[o]f the kind, degree, category being or about to be specified' . . . 'for example'. By contrast, the verb 'include' is defined to mean 'enclose'; 'contain as part of a whole or as a subordinate element; contain by implication, involve'; or 'place in a class or category; treat or regard as part of a whole'. We thus read the Article 3.4 phrase 'shall include an evaluation of all relevant factors and indices having a bearing on the state of the industry, including . . .' as introducing a mandatory list of relevant factors which must be evaluated in every case. We are of the view that the change that occurred in the wording of the relevant provision during the Uruguay Round (from 'such as' to 'including') was made for a reason and that it supports an interpretation of the current text of Article 3.4 as setting forth a list that is not merely indicative or illustrative, but, rather, mandatory.[81]

16.79 In *US – Large Civil Aircraft (2nd complaint)*, the Panel considered the meaning of 'i.e.' in the context of Article 1 of the SCM Agreement. This provision states that a subsidy exists where there is a financial contribution by a government, and a benefit is thereby conferred. With respect to the first of those two elements, a financial contribution, Article 1.1(a)(1)(i) through(iv) list four forms of financial contributions, preceded by the expression 'i.e.'. The Panel observed that 'Article 1.1(a)(1) is a definitional provision that sets forth an exhaustive, closed list ("... i.e. where ...") of the types of transactions that constitute financial contributions under the SCM Agreement'.[82]

16.80 In *US – FSC (Article 22.6 – US)*, the Arbitrator considered the meaning of 'i.e.' in the context of Article 5 of the SCM Agreement. The Arbitrator recalled that Article 5 of the SCM Agreement provides that no Member should cause 'adverse effects' through the use of any specific subsidy, 'i.e.' (a) injury to the domestic industry of another Member; (b) nullification or impairment of benefits accruing to other Members under the GATT; or (c) serious prejudice to the interests of another Member. As regards the use of 'i.e.', the Arbitrator stated:

> It should be emphasized that a positive finding of nullification and impairment is, by definition, also a finding of 'adverse effects' (this ultimately deriving from the use of i.e. in Article 5 which makes it plain that nullification and impairment is one category of the overarching concept of 'adverse effects' under the *SCM Agreement*).[83]

---

[81] Panel Report, *Thailand – H-Beams*, para. 7.225 (citing the *New Shorter Oxford English Dictionary*).
[82] Panel Report, *US – Large Civil Aircraft (2nd complaint)*, para. 7.955.
[83] Decision by the Arbitrator, *US – FSC (Article 22.6 – US)*, footnote 61.

INDEX